CONVEYANCING PRACTICE IN SCOTLAND

Dedications

Ann Stewart:

For my children, Rhu and Mirren, whose enthusiasm for life, energy, intellect, determination, humour, and sense of fun (all, I suspect, despite, rather than because of, my parenting skills) give me daily joy. I am incandescent with pride and love for these two remarkable human beings.

Euan Sinclair:

To Fleur, Martha and Henry – my little Canadians:

"I went to the woods because I wished to live deliberately, to front only the essential facts of life, and to see if I could not learn what it had to teach, and not, when I came to die, discover that I had not lived."

– Henry David Thoreau

And also to Marie Ramsay: you are a constant inspiration to me.

CONVEYANCING PRACTICE IN SCOTLAND

Seventh Edition

Ann Eileen Atkinson Stewart WS, LLB, Signet Accredited (Commercial Property)

Senior Associate and Professional Support Lawyer at Shepherd+Wedderburn

Writer to the Signet, Solicitor in Scotland

Founding member of the Property Standardisation Group

Euan Fraser Fitzpatrick Sinclair LLB, MBA, LLM

Writer to the Signet, Solicitor in Scotland

Former member of the Conveyancing Committee of the Law Society of Scotland

Bloomsbury Professional

Bloomsbury Professional Limited, Maxwelton House, 41–43 Boltro Road, Haywards Heath, West Sussex, RH16 1BJ

© Bloomsbury Professional Limited 2016
Reprinted 2017

Bloomsbury Professional is an imprint of Bloomsbury Publishing Plc

A CIP Catalogue record for this book is available from the British Library.

ISBN: 978 1 78043 866 5

Typeset by Phoenix Photosetting, Chatham, Kent

Printed and bound in Great Britain by CPI Group (UK) Ltd, Croydon, CR0 4YY

Introduction

When the manuscript of the last edition in 2011 was passed to the publisher, we breathed a big sigh of relief. It had been a massive undertaking to completely revise the old *Conveyancing Handbook*. The 6th Edition wasn't just a standard revision, however. It was a major review, and much new content was added. The final manuscript was almost twice the size of the previous edition.

However, we were not to rest. The conveyancing landscape has changed yet again. Many of the recent changes to property law and conveyancing practice have been driven by the Scottish Parliament. Quite rightly, the Scottish Parliament has focused on the relationship between the Scottish people and our beautiful land, often in the context of public policy – equality and social justice; micro-economic development; subsidiarity; and sustainability. This has led to a number of significant legislative initiatives in the past 16 years, with more on the way.

While many of the changes to property law have been welcome and beneficial – the statutory recasting of the law of the tenement and feudal abolition, for example – the profession has appeared to suffer from a lack of confidence in how to proceed in this legislation-heavy environment. In the years before the Scottish Parliament, the conveyancing part of the profession was necessarily quite resilient. It was able to adapt its custom and practice to make transactions run smoothly. The relentless tide of change in property law, together with the rejection by the courts of established practices (as the cases of PMP Plus and Park, Petitioner demonstrate) have undermined previous confidence. While striving to adapt practice to new legislative provisions, many in the profession feel that they are walking on quicksand. The familiar ideologies are gone; the application of new rules is uncertain.

And yet, resilience persists. The latest innovations introduced by the Land Registration etc (Scotland) Act 2012 have resulted in a fundamental shift in approach to many time honoured practices but, quicksand or not, the profession is already adapting. The 2012 Act is the reason for this latest edition as, while that Act purported merely to 'pour concrete into the foundations' of the existing practice, the reality is that the effect on conveyancing practice has been, and continues to be, immense.

While conveyancing practice may currently appear 'unsettled', it is more settled than people might think. We call on all solicitors involved in conveyancing to lift their heads above the parapet to engage more with legislators and policy makers, in the interests of their clients and the commercial well-being of Scotland. Equally, Parliament and the Registers need to take more account of the profession's experienced and informed views of the reality of buying and selling property, and generally 'doing business' in Scotland. The effect that LBTT has had on the residential property market is a prime example.

There continues to be a key role for the property lawyer, even if it is a changing one. We hope that this 7th edition will be a helpful bridge between the past, and our current brave new world. It is accepted that the policy makers at the Registers of Scotland have a huge task on their hands to align their practices with the 2012 Act provisions and the law of property in Scotland. The end of bijuralism is a fiction, if registration practice perpetuates 'registration law' and we offer our help and support in making the alignment of laws a reality.

Although we have tried to retain the practical tone of the previous editions, there are some changes to style in this edition, namely:

In place of 'conveyancer', we have substituted 'solicitor', to be more consistent in our references (we previously used 'solicitor', 'conveyancer' and 'practitioner' interchangeably).

- We have removed the alphabet soup of acronyms when referring to legislation. LREtc(S)A was just plain ugly. Solicitors commonly refer to 'the 2012 Act' anyway.

- For the first time, we have introduced footnotes. Professor Sinclair was not keen on footnotes – he believed that they overcomplicated the narrative. While perhaps that was true for a conveyancing handbook in the pre-internet age, we found that the references to legislation, paragraphs and websites, often in the same sentence, looked cluttered.

- Finally, we have dropped the sample purchase transaction file and the checklists – at least for now. A sample transaction was consistently threaded through the first five editions, which helped bring the text to life. The sample file was consolidated as an appendix in the last edition. For this edition, we have concentrated on commenting and opining on the changes to practice. What a typical file will look like now is still a matter for conjecture.

As ever, there are numerous contributions to acknowledge and be grateful for. Thanks to John King and the Registers of Scotland for permission to use the plan on the cover. Thanks also to Ross Mackay of the Law Society's Property Law Committee for permission to use the Scottish Standard Clauses. Although Ann is a founder and current member of the Property Standardisation Group, thanks to the PSG for allowing us to reproduce their styles.

Euan would like to add personal thanks to Scott Peterkin for sense checking his contributions to this edition and to Debbie Stoddard and Alison Smith for secretarial support.

Ann would like to add personal thanks to her PSG co-members: the legendary Iain Macniven, who retired from private practice in 2015, his able and enthusiastic replacement, Paul Haniford, and the steadfast Rachel Oliphant and Douglas Hunter. The PSG has been, and continues to be, a hugely successful and satisfying collaboration.

Ann would also like to express her huge debt of gratitude to the network of property PSLs in Scotland. As a forum in which to share knowledge and formulate practice in the face of new legal developments, the PSL Group has, since its formation several years ago, been a great source of support and cooperation for all concerned. It has proved to be invaluable in the run up to, and implementation of, the 2012 Act, and we have shared the pain together: Rachel Oliphant, Mandy Soppitt, Fiona Alexander, Catherine Reilly, Elaine Piggott, Sally Alexander, Heather Nisbet, Mark Davenport, Louise Harkness, Sharon Drysdale and Andy Duncan, and newcomers Lisa Cruickshank and Sarah Peock – quite honestly, I couldn't have done it without you.

Ann Stewart and Euan Sinclair
January 2016

Contents

Chapter 1 – The Legal Profession

Chapter 2 – The Framework

Chapter 3 – New Clients and New Instructions

Chapter 4 – The Seller's Preparations

Chapter 7 – Searches and Enquiries

Chapter 8 – Examination of and Reporting on Title

Chapter 11 – Settlement and the Final Steps

Table of Statutes

Table of Orders, Rules and Regulations

Table of European Legislation

[All references are to paragraph number]

Table of Cases

W

Chapter 1

The Legal Profession

CONVEYANCERS

1.1 First of all, let's establish the correct terminology for people engaged in conveyancing.

A **solicitor** is a person who is qualified and licensed to practise as such by having obtained a law degree (or passing equivalent examinations assessed by the Law Society), a Diploma in Legal Practice, and then having served a two-year traineeship in a solicitor's office, which incorporates trainee specific seminars, and from 2011 onwards, has also focused on achieving professional skills outcomes. This rigorous basic training occupies at the very least six years, which is the equivalent of the basic medical training. The aspiring Scottish solicitor must also be shown to be a fit and proper person to be admitted as a solicitor.

Solicitors have long enjoyed being considered as 'men of business', that is to say people who dealt with a wide variety of affairs—they used to be town clerks of small local government units, banking agents, land and estate agents, company secretaries and a variety of other engagements, as well as looking after what we now think of as legal business. Increased specialisation has closed many opportunities for solicitors, but equally it has opened other doors: employment law, pensions law, corporate finance law and many others, not mention the variety of 'in-house' legal jobs. Despite a requirement for increased commercialism, however, there remains a place for the key skills of the 'trusted adviser' in all aspects of the provision of legal services.

The Law Society of Scotland regulates the solicitors' branch of the legal profession in Scotland. In this book we will refer to the Law Society of Scotland simply as the '**Law Society**'.

Solicitors are also often involved in the marketing of residential property, offering a co-ordinated selling service for the client. Local Solicitors' Property Centres, eg the ESPC in Edinburgh and GSPC in Glasgow have given even the smallest firm of solicitors a shop window for estate agency services, but there remains healthy competition among solicitors and estate agents.

A **surveyor** is the professional who will report on the condition of property offered for sale in the Home Report. Surveyors are regulated by the Royal Institute of Chartered Surveyors (**RICS**).

An **estate agent** may be engaged by the seller to market the property. Unlike the practice in other countries, estate agents typically act for the seller only. They will often organise the bidding process and pass the offers to the seller's solicitor for evaluation and to complete the conveyancing. Many solicitors' firms in Scotland offer an integrated estate agency service and it is common for surveyors' firms also to market property.

Estate agents are not regulated by a professional body, but reputable agents will be members of voluntary bodies such as the National Association of Estate Agents (**NAE**), or The Property Operations Scheme (**TPOS**).

A **lawyer** is anyone who practises law, which includes solicitors and also advocates and judges. Advocates are specialists in pleading before the supreme courts and are rarely conveyancers. Paralegals do not practise law in a technical sense and are not lawyers.

A **conveyancer** is a solicitor or the employee of a solicitor, who deals in practice mainly with the purchase and sale of heritable property. Conveyancers include paralegals.

A **paralegal** is a skilled employee of a solicitor or legal firm who carries out specific and less complex conveyancing. The first course in paralegal conveyancing was held in the University of Strathclyde in the 1980s and soon was extended to other cities, other methods (by distance learning) and in other subjects (executry, court work etc).

The paralegal, in conveyancing, executry, court work, debt collection etc is now a highly valued part of the legal team, and the Scottish Paralegal Association (**SPA**)[1] is recognised by the Law Society. The SPA categorises paralegals according to three grades, qualifications and experience and recommends salary scales accordingly. The paralegal's immense supporting role has now been recognised by the Law Society's Registered Paralegal Scheme[2].

1   See www.scottish-paralegal.org.uk.
2   See www.lawscot.org.uk/members/paralegals.

However attractive delegation seems in terms of the business model, it should not be forgotten that the oversight of the conveyancing transaction is the responsibility of the solicitor. It is the solicitor who will have to account to the client, the Law Society and his or her partners for any shortcomings in the service provided and consequent complaint.

THE SOLICITORS' CONVEYANCING MONOPOLY

1.2 Having outlined how difficult it is to become a solicitor, and perhaps having indicated how expensive this is all going to be for the aspiring solicitor, it is now appropriate to consider the benefits of being a solicitor. Quite apart from the intangible benefits of the profession, which are many and depend on the perception of each individual, one of the most important privileges has been the so-called 'solicitors' monopoly' of conveyancing matters. This is contained in the Solicitors (Scotland) Act 1980[3], which states:

> 'any unqualified person, including a body corporate who draws or prepares ... any writ relating to heritable or moveable estate ... shall be guilty of an offence'.

The definition of a 'writ' excludes: '(a) a will or other testamentary writing; (b) a document *in re mercatoria* (in business matters), missive or mandate; (c) a letter or power of attorney; and (d) a transfer of stock containing no trust or limitation thereof[4].'

Thus, of the four major steps of a property transaction: marketing, concluding the contract of purchase and sale (completing missives), completing title and drafting the deed, and settling up, it is only the third part that is protected by the conveyancing monopoly. A person who is not legally qualified, or employed by a solicitor, may market heritable property, and even complete missives on behalf of a purchaser or seller. When, however, it comes to drawing up the formal deeds to transfer the title this work must be done by a solicitor (advocates are included in the conveyancing monopoly as well, but as a matter of tradition they do not handle conveyancing, except perhaps on a personal basis).

---

3 Section 32.
4 Section 32(3).

3

It tends to be the case that other peoples' monopolies are seen as oppressive, while one's own is of course 'in the public interest'. Statutory monopolies, like other kinds of anti-competitive arrangements, are not popular, and are gradually being dismantled. The Law Reform (Miscellaneous Provisions) (Scotland) Act 1990, created the solicitor-advocate to break the advocates' monopoly of appearing before the supreme courts. A solicitor-advocate is a solicitor with coveted rights of audience in the upper courts (solicitors already have rights of audience in Sheriff Courts and other lower courts and tribunals). The concept has worked well, and solicitor-advocates regularly appear in the supreme courts, and some have also been recognised with the dignity of QC.

The categories of person entitled to participate in the 'solicitors' monopoly' has expanded over the years through successive enactments. As well as conveyancing practitioners, it now includes registered foreign lawyers and may soon include 'licensed legal services providers' under the Legal Services (Scotland) Act 2010. The concept of the solicitors' monopoly is becoming increasingly illusory.

Nothing said above, however, limits the right of non-qualified parties selling or buying property, to act on their own behalf in the matter. As a rough analogy, if you have a sore tooth, you may pull it out yourself with a doorknob and string, but do not even ask a non-dentally qualified person to do the job for you, as that will be an offence. Thus, if the Smiths sell a house there is no reason why they should not do all the work themselves—sell the property on the internet or otherwise, complete missives and check the disposition, prepare a discharge of any security over the property, and present it for registration. A solicitor need not be employed. But a non-solicitor must not be employed, at a fee, to draw up a writ covered by the monopoly, *unless* that person is prepared to act gratuitously. The only snag from the Smiths' point of view is that if a bank were involved, they would also have to pay the bank's solicitors, negating any saving as their solicitor could act for the bank for around the same fee[5].

---

5 The issue of enforcing separate representation for borrowers and lenders in a house purchase transaction was vigorously debated, and ultimately defeated, at the Law Society AGM in 2013. For an excellent discussion of the issues, see "Time to draw a line" by Peter Nicholson in the March 2013 Journal.

PROFESSIONAL RESPONSIBILITIES

1.3 The solicitors' profession was the last of the non-specialising professions. A solicitor is still qualified to advise on a great number of matters, although, inevitably, with the greater complexity of matters, a degree of specialisation is becoming more prevalent and desirable. Thus we are seeing an increase in 'boutique' firms who handle only (for example) commercial conveyancing, employment law, corporate finance law etc. It is very difficult for the individual to combine 'chamber' work with litigation, as attendance at court can take up so much of the working day. At the other end of the scale, large firms are split into discrete practice areas, where specialised expertise is developed. Most solicitors these days will focus their practice on one or only a few areas of proficiency.

The solicitor, like other agents, is bound by duties of agent to client imposed by the common law of agency which, although often woven into modern statutory duties, remain as clear duties and should not be forgotten:

- (a) the agent must carry out the principal's instructions;
- (b) the agent is in a personal relationship with the principal, and must not delegate the duties of the principal to another, without the principal's instructions;
- (c) the agent must keep the money and property of the principal separate from the agent's own money and property, and keep accounts of dealings with it;
- (d) the agent must give the principal the full benefit of contracts made with third parties, and any secret commission must not be gained without the principal's consent.

In return for these duties, the agent is entitled to receive a reasonable remuneration, reimbursement of expenses, to be relieved of all liabilities incurred in the performance of the agency, and to the agent's lien over the property of the principal in the agent's hands in the course of the agency, until remuneration has been received.

To the law of agency there must now be added various regulatory controls, principally under the Law Society Regulations, and under Financial Services and Markets Act 2000 (generally known as **FSMA** and pronounced 'fisma'), and various other statutes. These regulatory controls are designed to protect the general public from unscrupulous individuals, and are a feature of twenty-first century life.

The financial services provisions are particularly important. They are designed to protect investors from obtaining incompetent or dishonest advice from incompetent and dishonest advisers and dealers, who are, regrettably, more prevalent in our society than any of us would wish. The Acts are framed on the basis that investors must accept responsibility for the risk involved in every investment to be made. Although investors are not protected from the consequence of their own folly, they are nevertheless entitled to the benefit of sound and impartial advice from someone who is skilled at giving such advice. This is known technically as 'best advice' and the concept is not greatly different from that laid down by the law of agency.

Best advice is therefore precisely what every competent solicitor, registered as a financial adviser under the Act, would, or should, have offered anyway. The Act is aimed at rather more 'colourful' figures on the financial spectrum. Nevertheless solicitors who give financial advice are inevitably brought into the regulatory net and, again, this involves the Law Society under the umbrella of the **Financial Conduct Authority (FCA)**.

The solicitor who gives any form of financial advice must now be registered in one of three ways:

(a)   FCA authorisation.

(b)   An Incidental Financial Business (IFB) Licence from the Law Society.

(c)   Acting as an introducer to an independent financial adviser – this option can be undertaken in connection with either of the first two options[6].

The provision of financial advice, without registration, is a criminal offence, punishable by up to two years in prison. Sales of heritable property are not covered by FSMA, but sometimes the solicitor will be asked for financial advice by clients as part of a sale or purchase. The solicitor who is not registered should avoid even discussing certain stocks or shares, as a criminal offence might be committed.

---

6   For more detail, see Rule C2 of the Law Society of Scotland Practice Rules 2011 in the Rules and Guidance section of the Law Society's website: www.lawscot.org.uk/rules-and-guidance/.

Under Rule C2 of the Law Society of Scotland Practice Rules 2011, solicitors who give financial advice must comply with these rules, and submit to regular inspection to ensure compliance.

Consequently, solicitors must be able to show that they have given 'best advice' taking into account the clients' means and needs, and that the product recommended is best suited to these circumstances, taking into account other products offered on the market. The clients' instructions must also be shown to have been followed through on the best basis— the 'best execution' rule. Records must be kept to prove compliance with the best advice and best execution rules, and these records are frequently inspected by the Law Society.

The FSMA and FCA requirements are expensive and compliance is time consuming. Solicitors who do not do much financial business are therefore well advised to seek an IFB licence (and will need one if they are arranging title indemnity insurance), act as an introducer or simply avoid offering any form of financial advice.

Other duties incumbent on the solicitor are:

1. To effect through the Law Society's nominated broker and its Master Policy, professional indemnity insurance covering the solicitor's clients against any loss caused by the solicitor's negligence[7]. As a guideline, the maximum payment from the policy is £2 million per claim, unless an additional premium is paid, which may be justified for a large firm or for a small firm with an exceptionally large transaction. The premium is calculated having regard to the number of partners; the ratio of partner to staff; the fee income of the firm as a proportion of the whole profession; and the firm's claim experience in the last five years. Many solicitors may feel that they could reach a better bargain using their own broker, but this is doubtful, bearing in mind the Law Society's negotiating experience and formidable market presence. In fact, they have been able to negotiate reductions in the annual premiums in certain years.

2. To contribute to the Solicitors' Guarantee Fund. This reimburses persons who have been defrauded by their solicitors[8]. The

---

7   Rule B7 of the Practice Rules.
8   Rule B6 of the Practice Rules.

amount payable by each solicitor depends on the amounts paid out by the Fund in the previous period.

3.   To observe the Advertising and Promotion Practice Rules 2006[9]. Advertising was formerly strictly forbidden by the Law Society, but is now allowed in the interests of informing the general public of the contact details and specialities of the solicitors' advertising. Such advertising is useful, but not, by and large, particularly entertaining. The former prohibition on claims of superiority and comparison of fees was removed in 2006, although the prohibition on inaccurate and misleading advertising, unsurprisingly, remains.

4.   To observe the Accounts Rules[10]. The general reminder is merely given that each partner of a firm will be responsible for ensuring compliance by the firm with the provisions of these Rules. While the operation of this rule is slightly relaxed for junior partners who are not given responsibility in accounting matters (*Sharp v Council of the Law Society of Scotland*[11], solicitors cannot wash their hands of accounting matters, and knowledge of, and compliance with the Accounts Rules applies to solicitors of all levels.

Reliance on staff, or on computer programmes, without understanding them, is a theme of Discipline Tribunal cases. There was a particularly distressing case a few years ago of a solicitor who fell victim to one of the first e-mail scams. Unfortunately, he committed his firm's clients' account to a withdrawal of almost $3 million for a scheme which promised untold riches, but was just too good to be true. Needless to say this was done without the knowledge of the other partners of the firm, who nevertheless were all declared bankrupt.

Some larger practices now employ accountants as their partnership accountants or secretaries, and they may employ other professional people, such as chartered surveyors, to deal with specialist functions within the firm. The names of such

9   Rule B3 of the Practice Rules.
10 Rule B6 of the Practice Rules.
11 [1984] SLT 313 at 316.

persons may be printed on the firm's stationery, provided that the public are not misled as to the status of the individual within the firm or to think that they are solicitors[12]. This will no doubt change with the advent of Alternative Business Structures (see below). A smaller practice probably could not justify having a chartered accountant in the practice, but might consider having access to the services of a competent bookkeeper, who will probably be trained by the excellent Society of Law Accountants in Scotland (**SOLAS**).

5. To accept unlimited liability for the debts of the partnership, and even, in extreme cases, of the other partners. The financial obligations of this requirement are, however, to some extent mitigated by:

   (a) The possibility of forming a limited liability partnership (LLP) under the provisions of the Limited Liability Partnerships Act 2000 or a limited company in terms of the Companies Acts. An LLP is a corporate body, not a partnership, and limits the liability of the partners (styled 'members' in the Act). In return for limited liability, annual accounts have to be lodged with Companies House for public inspection, showing the income of the highest paid member of an LLP. Many firms of solicitors have taken advantage of these arrangements and are now incorporated as LLPs.

   (b) The cover against defaulting partners offered by the compulsory professional indemnity policy (see Point 1 above).

6. Not to act in the same matter for two parties who might have conflicting interests[13]. Many years ago a solicitor might have acted, and sometimes did, for both seller and purchaser in a house transaction. Where there was no substantial conflict of interest, the result was usually, somehow, satisfactory to both parties. However, you only need to consider how different the

---

12 Rule D2.3 of the Practice Rules.
13 Rule B2 of the Practice Rules.

position would be in a court case, where one solicitor acts for both parties, to realise how unrealistic it is to expect one person to represent both sides fairly. There is basically a conflict of interest where one person is buying and another selling – even when parties are married *Smith v Bank of Scotland*[14]. The general principle against acting for clients when there is a conflict of interest was codified in 1986 and has been developed over the years in successive Practice Rules.

7.   To observe the code of conduct contained in Standards of Conduct Practice Rules[15]. These have the following principles at their core:

- Competence;
- Diligence;
- Communication; and
- Respect.

8.   To observe the Anti-Money Laundering legislation. Briefly, these Regulations are intended to prevent the placing of 'dirty' money acquired through drug dealing, terrorism or crime generally into a 'clean' investment, such as a bank account, bonds or house purchase. The investment is then realised and the proceeds emerge as 'clean' or 'laundered' money. See Chapter 3 for a more detailed consideration of Anti-money laundering requirements. There are five money laundering offences: assistance, concealment, acquisition, failure to disclose and tipping off.

9.   It should be noted that, in 2002, a solicitor was jailed for six months, for receiving a sum of money from a client to account of expenses, and then refunding it in a laundered condition, when the sums came to be reimbursed when the transaction did not proceed.

10.   To maintain complete confidentiality and silence as to a client's affairs, (except making a Suspicious Activity Report in terms of the Money Laundering Regulations). Solicitors should not reveal details, even the names, of their clients, especially where complete secrecy is required. A major difficulty can arise where

14 [1977] SC(HL) 111.
15 Rule B1 of the Practice Rules.

solicitors are asked to act against a former client. The rule is that the knowledge they have gained of the former client's affairs should not be used in any way against their interests. That is a vague enough proposition; often the only solution is for the solicitor to decline to act for the new client against the former client because suspicions of double dealing are bound to arise. The leading case in this respect – *Prince Jefri Bolkiah v KPMG*[16] – concerns an accountancy firm.

11.   The solicitor will also be subjected to occasional visits from the Law Society, as the profession's regulator, and tax or VAT inspectors, none of which are, even remotely, social in character. Regular and random inspections of this type are designed to help to ensure compliance and maintain standards throughout the profession. This is of benefit to all concerned, and should be prepared for and embraced in a spirit of full co-operation. Some firms even use retired or former regulators to do a 'dummy run' before the visit, which is undoubtedly useful, as the former regulators may spot something that might cause embarrassment.

12.   It goes without saying, that a group of solicitors, like any other group, must resist the temptation to get together and fix agreed fees. This is anti-competitive behaviour and is prohibited by the Competition Act 1998. The Law Society itself had to abandon its former table of fees and the rate for a unit of ten minutes in 2005, following worries that its practices might be breaking competition law, after the European Commission found the Belgian Architects' Association, another professional body, guilty of price fixing for adopting recommended minimum fees.

REGULATION AND COMPLIANCE

1.4 The solicitor is governed by the Solicitors (Scotland) Acts 1980 and 1988, which supersede the Legal Aid and Solicitors (Scotland) Act 1949, the foundation Act which set up the Law Society as the governing body for the profession. The 1980 Act continues to empower the Council of the Law Society to make regulations, with the concurrence of the Lord

16 [1999] 1 All ER 517. See also *Koch Shipping Inc* v *Richards Butler* [2002] All ER (Comm) 957.

President of the Court of Session. Under the provisions of the Legal Services (Scotland) Act 2010, the regulatory functions of the Law Society require to be exercised on their behalf by a regulatory committee, so that those functions are exercised independently and properly (for the purposes of achieving public confidence). The Practice Rules are available online in the Rules and Guidance section of the Law Society's website[17]. The Council is now permitted to delegate functions to committees, sub-committees or individuals in terms of the Council of the Law Society of Scotland Act 2003.

To practise as a solicitor, the solicitor must hold a practising certificate under section 4 of the 1980 Act, and is automatically a member of the Law Society (unlike English solicitors in England who need not be a member of their Law Society: they are regulated by the Solicitors' Regulatory Authority, which is a separate body.)

The Law Society, as part of the first object of its duty under the 1980 Act, is responsible, among other things, for the training and admission of solicitors, continuing professional development, legal education, practice development, maintaining links with other societies, publications, giving advice on numerous professional topics through a network of specialist committees and the secretariat, scrutinising proposed legislation and making representations as necessary, ensuring that accounting rules and the regulations under FSMA are observed, liaising with the Scottish Government and the Scottish Law Commission, corporate public relations and advertising, and negotiating professional indemnity insurance through the Law Society's block policy.

COMPLAINTS

'An error does not become a mistake until you refuse to correct it.'

(John F Kennedy)

1.5 The dread of every solicitor is a complaint. Even the threat of a complaint can make the solicitor feel vulnerable. But this threat can be neutralised by the firm having proper systems in place.

---

17 They are also printed in full in Green's *Parliament House Book* (Edinburgh: W Green, looseleaf), or in the offprint known as Green's *Solicitors Compendium* (Edinburgh: W Green).

First, a firm should have an office risk or quality management policy, so that the solicitor can be sure that best practice was followed. Second, a firm should have a robust complaints procedure so that a complaint can be escalated to the firm's Client Relations Partner and hopefully 'nipped in the bud' and resolved at that level. Defending a claim is time-consuming and expensive business, therefore it is far preferable to put resources into ensuring client satisfaction. A badly handled complaint can also spin out of control very quickly, so that the firm's reputation can be damaged as well. Spreading news of bad service was bad enough with old fashioned word-of-mouth, but with the advent of social media, a complaint can 'go viral' within days, if not hours and is always recorded on the internet.

With a robust complaints procedure, the solicitor should be confident that the firm will support him or her in the defence or settlement of the claim. If there is a mistake by the solicitor (they do happen) then the firm should use this as a learning opportunity to ensure that it does not happen again.

There should not be a 'blame culture' or any recriminations. Such a culture is counter productive, because lawyers will be afraid to ventilate any problems at any early stage and may instead try to put things right themselves, which often compounds the problem.

Failing resolution within the firm (and some claims are irresolvable at the firm level), then the client can make a formal complaint to the Scottish Legal Complaints Commission (**SLCC**).

The SLCC was created by the Legal Profession and Legal Aid (Scotland) Act 2007 and started work in October 2008. This entailed the redeployment of some 40 Law Society complaints staff. The initial costs of establishment were borne by the Scottish Government, but the ongoing revenue costs are borne by the legal profession and collected by the Law Society. The creation of the SLCC sought to address concerns and the public's perception of the Law Society's system of self-regulation. The SLCC acts as a gateway for complaints. Service complaints are dealt with by the SLCC whilst conduct complaints continue to be referred to the Law Society for resolution.

Of course, not all complaints are justified and many are dismissed, sometimes causing great ill-will against the profession, because justice has not been perceived to have been done.

Solicitors in private practice have to pay an annual levy[18] to fund the SLCC.

In serious cases of professional misconduct arising from complaints received, or from the investigations of the Law Society under the Practice Rules, the Law Society may make a complaint to the Solicitors Discipline Tribunal[19]. The Discipline Tribunal operates under the Scottish Discipline Tribunal Procedures Rules 2008 and its members are appointed by the Lord President of the Court of Session. The members are made up from lay people and lawyers who must not be members of the Law Society Council, lest the Law Society is seen to be both judge and prosecutor.

The tribunal has the power to order a solicitor's name to be struck off the roll of practising solicitors, or to suspend or restrict their practising certificates quite independently of any criminal prosecution there may be. A right of appeal exists against the decisions of the Discipline Tribunal to the Court of Session.

Although one might form a contrary conclusion, a very small proportion of the many transactions that must be carried out by solicitors every year in Scotland actually result in a complaint to the SLCC, the Law Society, or the Discipline Tribunal. It is a matter of pride that this is so, and the standard should be maintained and improved in the interests of the profession. The Law Society requires each firm to have a designated partner to handle all complaints. Many can be sorted out quite easily—often by a statement of regret[20], or a modification of the fees charged. It should be remembered that there is a requirement for a high degree of regulation in the profession, and that the disciplinary functions of the Law Society, the SLCC and the Discipline Tribunal are in the interests of the whole profession, however irksome they may seem, to ensure the preservation of the highest levels of integrity, honesty and ethical behaviour.

REPRESENTATION

1.6 The Law Society, as regulator of the profession, has to maintain an impartial role in resolving or adjudicating disputes. In terms of the 1980 Act[21], the objects of the Law Society include the promotion of:

18 £312 for 2015. Although there has been much congratulation on a decrease from the previous year, we noted in the previous edition (2011) that the levy was £209.
19 Constituted under the 1980 Act.
20 Or an apology, if the Apologies (Scotland) Bill is enacted.
21 Section 1(2).

(a)   the interests of the solicitors' profession in Scotland; and

(b)   the interests of the public in relation to that profession.

It seeks to support and represent the interests of solicitors at every stage of their careers, through provision of:

- Education: focusing on the education and training of solicitors in Scotland from the foundation (university) stage, through PEAT1[22] (diploma) and PEAT2 (traineeship) and into all levels of post qualifying practice;

- Continuing professional development (CPD); through Update, which organises post-qualification CPD events and training programmes for solicitors and other legal providers;

- A professional practice advice service: through its Professional Practice Department, which provides training, business information and other support, for example for solicitors wishing to become an accredited specialist or a solicitor-advocate;

- Law reform: by working to improve the law in Scotland and the legal system for the benefit of the profession and the public, and representing the views of solicitors and their clients in response to legislative proposals; and

- Regulation liaison: by offering help, training and support on client complaints handling, including advice on how to avoid complaints.

If a solicitor finds himself in trouble, as well as approaching the Law Society for help, he can turn to various other bodies for assistance such as the Legal Defence Union **(LDU).** The LDU is analogous to the well-established Medical and Dental Defence Union **(MDDU),** which represents the interests of doctors and dentists who are in trouble, and meets their costs.

The Society of Writers to Her Majesty's Signet **(WS Society)** is an independent association for lawyers and one of the oldest professional bodies in the world with over 500 years of history. It supports Scottish

22 Professional Education and Training.

lawyers and legal businesses, with professional support lawyer and research services, highly regarded training seminars and programmes, an accreditation system, and networking and social events, as well as offering the facilities of a first class law library, located in the iconic Signet Library in Edinburgh.

Similarly, the Royal Faculty of Procurators in Glasgow (**RFPG**) was incorporated some time before 1668 and continues to support the legal profession in Glasgow and the West Coast of Scotland. The RFPG occupies an historic building in the classical Venetian style in the centre of Glasgow. It has a large law library in its building, an excellent CPD programme, and an independent auditor. Its iconic building is also used for a wide variety of events.

The Scottish Law Agents Society (**SLAS**) was incorporated by Royal Charter in 1884 and membership is open to all Scottish solicitors and trainees. SLAS is concerned with all legal and practical matters affecting its members and endeavours to represent and promote their interests and standards. SLAS recently led high-profile campaigns against Alternative Business Structures (see para 1.8), and in favour of 'Sep Rep'.

Additionally, local faculties, professional societies and bar associations can provide much advice and support for the solicitor.

CLIENT SERVICE DELIVERY

> 'There is only one boss. The customer. And he can fire everyone in the company from the chairman on down simply by spending his money elsewhere.'
>
> *(Sam Walton, founder of Wal-Mart Asda Supermarkets)*

1.7 As a conveyancer starting out, it is important to remember who is the boss. The original author of this handbook, John Sinclair, used to have a banner at his desk that said 'clients make pay day happen'. While the banner has long since been lost, the maxim should not be forgotten.

Some lawyers are uncomfortable with the idea that clients are also customers. As a profession we pride our integrity and independence and these virtues are valued by clients. That said, law firms are businesses, and need new and repeat business to survive. So there is a line to be drawn between offering robust advice that will save clients from themselves, and executing clients' instructions mechanically. Above all, one aim of working with clients is to form the relationship of trusted adviser, being someone who knows and understands their business and requirements, and can add value to the client through experience and wisdom.

During the recession of 2009 (and beyond), the economic outlook for law firms worsened considerably, leading to many redundancies and a wave of mergers and consolidations. This has had an impact on clients, so that client loyalty has become a scarcer commodity. Legal services are often now procured like any other service. To the extent that they cannot be taken for granted, solicitors need to nurture relationships and one of the best ways to do this is to ensure excellence in the delivery of your service.

Consider how best you can communicate with your clients. Do they know and understand the various stages that they will have to go through and what is expected of them? Are you bombarding them with letters or emails when they would prefer one summary email? Are you following a checklist so that every stage is completed in the right order and in good time? Would the client like to see a flow chart, with all the steps mapped out? How do you collect and evaluate the client's feedback at the end of the transaction?

There are some minimum expectations, however. Accept no interruptions to meetings with clients, even 'very important' telephone calls. The client will think you have other things on your mind, and you should never give that impression. Do not constantly look at your mobile phone. Give your clients the impression that they are the only people that matter, for they are, and they think that as well. Telephone messages should be carefully recorded and returned that day. Letters and emails should be speedily and helpfully answered.

Above all lawyers should remember that they are engaged to help people and businesses through some of the biggest financial events of their lives. They should give them a service that smoothes out the bumps and, as one client once put it, gives them 'a warm feeling inside' and leads to further recommendations. If you have done a good job and the client is delighted you should capitalise on that. Don't be afraid to ask them to recommend you to their friends or colleagues by word of mouth, or even on LinkedIn or Twitter.

ALTERNATIVE BUSINESS STRUCTURES

'Legal advice will be "just like buying a tin of beans".'

(Headline in *Daily Telegraph*, 18 October 2005, after the
Lord Chancellor announced reforms to legal regulation
in England and Wales)

1.8 The fifth edition of this book broke with tradition in the introduction. Instead of the 'welcome to the profession(?)' title in the previous four editions, the title was changed to 'welcome to Tesco law(?)' as a reflection of the despondency at that time about the introduction of Alternative Business Structures. It was clear then that the Scottish Government's preferred position was that solicitors' firms should be able to be owned 100% by non-solicitors, which would change the face of the legal profession in an unknown way forever.

The ability for Scottish legal firms to establish as, or convert into, an 'alternative business structure' was introduced by the Legal Services (Scotland) Act 2010. What this means in practice is that solicitors' firms no longer have to be owned exclusively by practising solicitors.

After a long-running debate within the profession, which was consulted by the Scottish Parliament on the proposed reforms, a compromise between the 'Tesco law' position of allowing any external investors to own 100% of a solicitors' firm, and the trenchant position against any dilution of the *status quo* was reached and accepted by the Scottish Parliament. The 2010 Act provides that a Scottish solicitors' firm need only be 51% owned by Scottish solicitors and other regulated professionals, still to be defined by regulations.

The new structures will be known as Licensed Legal Services Providers. They will hold a licence and be regulated by a regulator to be appointed by the Scottish Ministers, possibly the Law Society. The non-professional owners of the remaining 49% of the firm will be subject to a 'fitness for involvement' test by the regulator. If the non-solicitor owner is subsequently found to be unfit for involvement, he or she may be disqualified from being involved in solicitors' firms in future.

This legislation represents a radical break from the past for the legal profession and, depending on the experience, the 51% rule may not rest as the final position. Although it remains to be seen how these structures will be used in practice, as a relatively commoditised service, domestic conveyancing is likely to become an active area for investment by companies involved in associated services. The day may yet come when conveyancing is indeed like buying a tin of beans, in one way or another.

At the time of writing this edition, we still await the Scottish Government's detailed regulations on the proposed ABS Scheme.

Chapter 2

The Framework

1617 AND ALL THAT

2.1 Registration of title is a key driver of economic growth: one of the fundamentals of any developing economy is to have certainty in property rights for investment potential and granting security, and for ease of transacting for liquidity of investment. Such a system encourages banks and other lenders to lend in security of property and so the virtuous cycle of a flourishing market economy begins. That we have had such a system in Scotland for almost four hundred years should be a source of immense pride, as it has enabled the Scottish economy to grow out of relative poverty to the prosperous, mercantile country that we are today.

In 1617, the General Register of Sasines was created, overseen by the 'Keeper'. The office of Keeper is a personal commission from the sovereign, distinct from government appointments, and endures to this day. The Keeper of the Registers of Scotland of course has a multitude of staff these days who assist her to maintain 17 different registers and over half a million registration transactions every year. The Keeper's office is called the Registers of Scotland Executive Agency (it is a self financing agency of the Scottish Government), but is still referred to by conveyancers colloquially and, often formally, as the Keeper, as in the dread phrase 'the Keeper bounced my deed'.

The Register of Sasines and the Land Register that is succeeding it, are public registers. Therefore, rights in property are there for everyone to see. Once a right to land is published in either Register, it gives the holder a 'real right' in the property, which is to say it is defensible against anyone on the basis of being preferred, as it was registered first. This contrasts with a personal right under a private contract, which could be challengeable by another party who has a competing right.

In essence the Register of Sasines is beautifully simple. In 1617, the majority of Scotland's landmass was owned by surprisingly few owners[1]. Each property or estate was given a search sheet with a chronological number, which was categorised by (now historic) counties. Any subdivision is given a search sheet and new number but also recorded as a 'break-off' from the original estate it is recorded against. As a register of deeds rather than property, this entry only contains abstract details of the type of dealing eg disposition, servitude etc and the parties, consideration (price), date of execution, date of recording and the folio and fiche number. Each party will also have an index search sheet for each county recording their transactions, so that it is possible to search against individuals, not just properties.

So for example, the sale of an acre of land from the Inverlour estate by the estate owner Sir Murray Plaice to Harriet Roe would be recorded as a break off from the Inverlour Estate search sheet, numbered 238 in the county of Moray. This transaction would then trigger the creation of a new search sheet Moray 4536 for the new holding of land that Harriet Roe has acquired. If Harriet Roe sold 0.23 hectare (measurements must now be metric) of her land for development to Hammerhead Properties Ltd a number of years later, this would be noted against the search sheet for the one acre, Moray 4536, and also trigger the creation of a further new search sheet Moray 73537. The land is then developed and once the roads have been adopted by the Local Authority they are given official names.

This was a crucial limitation. As noted above, the searcher could either search against the property or the person. However, because Hammerhead Properties Ltd had not developed its land into housing at the time of sale, it remained categorised as 0.23 hectare in the Parish of Inverlour. The new address of Bream Avenue would not appear anywhere in the records until the road had been adopted and Hammerhead Properties started to sell their new homes with new addresses. A searcher could use some intuition to find out if this is the correct property. She could cross-refer the names index, but it was not uncommon for several deeds by the same parties to be recorded on the same day.

---

1   Although precise statistics are elusive, it is estimated that, in 1996, half of Scotland was owned by just 500 people. See *Who Owns Scotland Now?* Alistair Cramb (Mainstream, 1996) and *Who Owns Scotland?* Andy Wightman (Canongate, 1996). Both books owe a debt of gratitude to John McEwen's ground-breaking *Who Owns Scotland?* (BUSPB, 1977).

Further, because only abstract details are noted in the search sheets, you may know that Harriet Roe has sold 0.23 hectare but the only way to see where the boundaries are was to order a 'quick copy' (as opposed to the more expensive, but no slower, Official Extract of the same deed, which can be used for evidential purposes) of the disposition by Sir Murray Plaice from the National Archives and await its arrival several days' later. Although it was customary to annex a plan to a Sasine deed, as a register of deeds all that was required was that property was sufficiently described, so there may not even have been a plan. Even if you were 'lucky' and a plan had been annexed, many plans presented to the Sasine Register were badly prepared and inaccurate. They followed no consistent pattern of scales, or even north points, and matching plans of adjoining lands is difficult. It is not unusual to have a 'floating rectangle' plan, which is a plan showing a rectangular area of land but, the utility of which is seriously limited without reference points to tie it into features on a map.

An even more terrible prospect is to try to establish the extent of the Inverlour Estate at any point in time. There is likely to be an 'estate search' which was started many decades ago and was 'brought down' (updated) every time there was a break off. It may be the size of a book and will almost certainly be kept in a tin box within a trunk full of old titles (and maybe a few moths…).

On the first page, in copperplate handwriting, will be the original description of the estate 'ALL and WHOLE the lands and estate of Inverlour, in the Parish of Inverlour extending to one thousand two hundred and sixty acres or thereby as more particularly described in Conveyance by the Testamentary Trustees of George Square to Sir Carlton Plaice recorded in the General Register of Sasines for the County of Moray on tenth November 1874'. Then the succeeding pages will list all the break off dispositions, any servitudes, statutory wayleaves and so on.

It can actually be an almost impossible job to decipher. While many landed estates have an understanding of what they own, that is often more through good estate management than any official record keeping.

Carrying out a Sasine purchase and sale transaction was time consuming and repetitive, and potentially involved several people doing exactly the same work in a short space of time. Thus for example, solicitors would note title for their client Harriet Roe (if they hadn't already for her purchase) before she sells the land to ensure that she has good title. When missives are concluded and Harriet Roe is committed to sell to

Hammerhead Developments Ltd, their solicitors then had to note title, and their bank's solicitors, too and so on, all down the ownership chain. This all added to the overall expense

Another limitation of the Sasines system was that once the sellers' solicitors handed over the title deeds at settlement in a Sasine transaction, the sellers' responsibility for the validity of the title ceased, unless a successful claim for warrandice (the sellers' warranty against ejection from the property, granted in the disposition – see para 9.18) was established. The Sasine Register is a register of deeds. Titles on that Register do not benefit from any state guarantee.

LAND REGISTRATION: A BETTER WAY

2.2 From the late nineteenth century and throughout the twentieth century a different way of recording titles to land emerged in other Commonwealth jurisdictions, such as the 'Torrens' system, named after a Robert Richard Torrens, the Registrar premier of the State of South Australia who introduced it to the then colony in 1858. The Torrens system is based on the method of insuring ships used by Lloyds of London, using a single register for each land holding and recording all details and interests affecting the land. It is similar to the Sasine system in that each new grant is given a unique folio number but, crucially, this number relates to a universally accepted map. The greatest advantage of Torrens title is that it is a single document guaranteed by the government.

These systems of registration of title offer three significant advantages over the Sasines:

(i) **The 'mirror' principle** – the register reflects accurately and completely the current state of the title;

(ii) **The 'curtain' principle** – it is not necessary to go behind the registered title, as it contains all the necessary information on the title; and

(iii) **The 'insurance' principle** – the validity of the title is guaranteed by the state registrar. In the event of any error, the injured party can claim compensation for any loss from the registrar. This principle ensures that registered titles can be relied on[2].

2 Under the Land Registration (Scotland) Act 1979 this guarantee is known as 'Keeper's indemnity', and under the Land Registration etc (Scotland) Act 2012, as 'Keeper's warranty'.

These systems of registration of title (or interests) rather than deeds caught the imagination in Scotland. Even as far back as 1903, Professor Wood wrote in his lectures on conveyancing: 'I am unable to see any real difficulty in the way of introducing registration of title into Scotland'[3].

In 1959 the Secretary of State for Scotland set up a committee under Lord Reid to investigate the introduction of registration of title into Scotland. This committee reported favourably[4] and recommended that another committee be set up to devise a scheme. This committee under Professor Henry reported in 1969[5] with a workable scheme, which after a trial, was introduced by the Land Registration (Scotland) Act 1979.

To set things in context, in 1959 there existed only a few huge mainframe computers and the electric typewriter was the latest luxury. There was no thought of personal computers, with the same, or greater, power than the mainframe computer. The fact that the Reid Committee produced a scheme that fitted personal computers so perfectly was fortuitous, and it is hard to see how the concept of registration of title could work so well without the personal computer.

The scheme is based on the Ordnance Survey of Scotland using the scale 1:1250 for urban areas where modern house plots are small, 1:2,500 in villages and small towns where plots are rather larger, and 1:10,000 for farms and mountain and moorland areas. Ordnance Survey maps are extremely accurate, and are consistently updated. It should be noted, however, that they reflect boundaries as they actually exist on the ground, and not necessarily as they exist in title plans registered in the Property Register. This difficulty is met by requesting a Plans Report (see para 7.7) which among other things (if a Level 2 or Level 3 Report is obtained) will compare the title plan with the Ordnance Survey map.

The Land Register is based, like the General Register of Sasines, on the old Scottish county system, which was phased out for local government purposes in 1974. Thus regions and districts, introduced by the Local Government (Scotland) Act 1973 have no significance in land registration, and have in any event been superseded by Councils and City Councils,

3   As the reader will discover, there are real difficulties in completing registration of title in Scotland, however!
4   Scottish Home and Health Department, Registration of Title to Land in Scotland: 1963, Cmnd 2032.
5   Scottish Home and Health Department, Scheme for the Introduction and Operation of Registration of Title to Land in Scotland: 1969, Cmnd 4137.

introduced by the Local Government etc. (Scotland) Act 1994 in 1996. However, as a system of categorisation, the old county system was left untouched so far as the Land and Sasine Registers were concerned.

The original intention was to make all Scotland operational in nine years, starting year one on 6 April 1981 with the County of Renfrew; then in year two – The City of Glasgow; year three – Lanark; year four – Midlothian; year five – Rest of Central Belt; year six – Angus, Kincardine, Aberdeen; year seven – Ayr, Dumfries and Galloway; year eight – Southern Rural Areas; year nine – Northern Rural Areas.

This programme however, proved wildly over-optimistic, and by 1990 only four counties were operational: Renfrew, Dumbarton, Lanark and Glasgow. It appeared at that time that the scheme was irretrievably stalled, for the Register was under-staffed, and could not keep pace with the applications pouring in, let alone the arrears that were building up. Long delays were commonplace. The Keeper acknowledged this problem in his 1988 report, and explained that the backlogs on his shelves would generate a fee income of £9m, if only he could process them.

The property boom of the late eighties coupled with the success of the 'right to buy' legislation led to a soaring demand for the services of the Registers of Scotland at a time when the department was subject to both staffing and accommodation constraints. The situation was steadily deteriorating and invidious comparisons were being drawn with the English system, which had only covered 50–52% of the country after 63 years. Fortunately, the position in both countries has since been rectified.

The Registers of Scotland was created Scotland's first (and only) executive agency in 1990 and the consequent removal of constraints enabled the agency to tackle its problems. In particular the land registration process picked up momentum, as shown by the extension of land registration to the counties of Clackmannan (1 October 1992); Stirling (1 April 1993); West Lothian (1 October 1993); Fife (1 April 1995); Aberdeen and Kincardine (1 April 1996); Ayr and Dumfries, Kirkcudbright and Wigtown (1 April 1997); Angus, Perth and Kinross (1 April 1999); Berwick, East Lothian, Peebles, Roxburgh and Selkirk (1 October 1999); Argyll and Bute (1 April 2000); Inverness and Nairn (1 April 2002); Banff, Caithness, Moray, Orkney and Zetland, Ross and Cromarty, and Sutherland (1 April 2003). Thus, the whole of Scotland is now on the land registration system.

The Register of Sasines still operates in parallel with the Land Register, and will continue to do so until it is finally phased out (see para 2.5). The Keeper reports that there are currently some 1.6 million titles on the Land Register, representing 26.58% of the landmass of Scotland and around 58.37% of titles[6]. The remainder, estimated by the Registers at around 1.5 million titles and amounting to just over 73% of landmass, is predominantly the subject of Sasine recorded titles (although title to some property (for example some of the lands owned by Universities) pre-date the Sasine register).

ONE SYSTEM, TWO REGISTERS, THREE REGIMES

2.3 When we talk about titles in the Sasine Register, we refer to them being 'recorded' in that Register. Titles in the Land Register are referred to as being 'registered'. Now, all transfers of property, whether for valuable consideration or not (ie including gifts of property) must be registered in the Land Register. It would have been nice to be able to tell twenty-first century conveyancers that there is no need for them to know about the Sasine Register, however, it remains in operation for deeds affecting Sasine titles, unless the deed is a disposition, a lease or an assignation of a lease. From 1 April 2016, it will no longer be competent to record a standard security over a Sasine title in the Sasine Register;the underlying title will have to move to the Land Register if a standard security is to be granted.

With much of the land mass of Scotland and many titles to it still on the Sasine Register, Sasine title examination skills are going to be needed for some years to come. Without further reform, some land may never be registered (eg parks, landed estates remaining in the family and large tracts of land owned by public bodies such as the Forestry Commission), unless the owners apply to register the title voluntarily. Over the past few years, there has been increasing pressure to accelerate the transfer of titles from the Sasine Register to the Land Register (now commonly referred to as 'Completion of the Register').

Accordingly, in 2001, Registers of Scotland asked the Scottish Law Commission to review the system. The Commission published three discussion papers in 2004 and 2005 and the review culminated in the

---

6   As at December 2014.

Commission's 'Report on Land Registration' in 2010, with a draft Bill annexed[7]. A Bill in modified form was introduced to Parliament on 1 December 2011; this resulted in the Land Registration etc (Scotland) Act 2012. The 2012 Act repealed most (but not all) of the 1979 Act, and came fully into force on 8 December 2014 – the 'designated day'. It contains provisions that are intended to speed up the transfer of titles onto the Land Register, resulting in the eventual closure of the Sasine Register.

In presentations to stakeholders and interested parties, during the passage of the Bill, many of the changes were characterised as 'pumping concrete into the foundations' – an allusion to the fact that the 1979 Act was very short on detail and much of registration practice had been developed, semi-informally, by the staff at the Registers of Scotland, who had found practical ways to deal with many registration issues. So, the 2012 Act would provide legislative authority for what was already going on. Reference was also made to 'under the bonnet' changes, meaning that, actually, we wouldn't really notice too much difference.

The reality is that there are many changes – some of them quite significant. Even though some things feel similar, land registration procedures under the 2012 Act are quite different to 1979 Act procedures. Many of the underlying concepts are also quite different. Time, therefore, to brush up on your basic car mechanics.

THE PRINCIPAL DIFFERENCES BETWEEN THE 1979 ACT AND THE 2012 ACT

2.4 The basic concept of what land registration is all about essentially stays the same – a map-based system of registration of title to land, benefiting from a state guarantee. If there is an error on the Register, then it is possible, in certain circumstances, to rectify it; a person who suffers loss as a result of such rectification is entitled to claim compensation from the Keeper for that loss. At this highest level of consideration, therefore, it is possible to derive some comfort from the fact that Scotland still has a Land Register on which reliance can be placed, backed by a state guarantee. Let's investigate further.

---

7 'Report on Land Registration', Scottish Law Commission 222, 2010. Available at: www.scotlawcom.gov.uk/law-reform-projects/completed-projects/land-registration/.

2.4.1 The End of Bijuralism

Many conveyancers may have thought on many occasions over the past decades that certain things that happened under the land registration regime simply could not have taken place in the Sasine Register. Some things just seemed 'wrong' in the context of property law, but the Keeper had wide discretion. It is now clear that such things were 'wrong' under property law, but were being implemented under 'registration law'. There were many instances where the tension between property law and registration law stretched this difference almost to breaking point.

A classic example of this tension was the Keeper's so-called 'Midas touch' by which the act of registration itself resulted in validity[8]. In some cases, this had the effect of creating a valid title where none could exist under the rules of property law. The 2012 Act abolishes the Midas touch (other than in certain exceptional circumstances – see para 2.6.2(i)): the validity of a title now relies on property law alone.

Under the 2012 Act, instead of describing the Land Register as a register of *interests* in land, it refers to a public register of *rights* in land. The property section of the Title Sheet now describes the nature of the proprietor's right in the plot of land (eg ownership) reflecting that what is registered is the land itself, not someone's 'interest'.

2.4.2 Structure of the Register

The Land Register is now officially made up of four parts, again in some respects reflecting what happened informally under the 1979 Act.

2.4.2(i) The Title Sheet record

This consists of a record of all the Title Sheets of registered plots and registered leases; each Title Sheet has a title number, so there is really no significant difference compared to a 1979 Act Title Sheet. The Title Sheet itself will contain the same four sections, although the charges section has been renamed the securities section, but most of the content of the various parts of the Title Sheet will be the same with the same layout.

---

8   Section 3 of the 1979 Act.

2.4.2(ii) The cadastral map

A cadastre is well established concept. It is a register or inventory of land parcels, with details as to ownership, extent, location and other information. A cadastral map is a pictorial representation of all of these land parcels shown in one place.

The cadastral map replaces the title plan. Under the 2012 Act, all registered property is to be depicted on the cadastral map, as cadastral units. However, individual title plans will only show the extent of that particular title. So, title plans under both regimes are the same. Tenements continue to be shown as a single cadastral unit under the 'steading' method of mapping. Now, however, a title plan is an excerpt from the cadastral map.

In fact, it appears that the Registers had already been keeping a cadastral record for some time, although it only exists electronically.

A key requirement under the 2012 Act is that there can be no overlaps on the cadastral map. If you apply to register a property that includes part of an already registered title, it will be rejected.

The base map from which the cadastral map is drawn is the Ordnance Survey, although other systems of mapping could be used. The Keeper is able to go beyond the Ordnance Survey Map, so that, for example, areas of seabed which are acquired by title transfer or by lease can also be shown on the cadastral map.

2.4.2(iii) The archive record

Officially, this is a 'new' part of the register, but it formalises what has been going on informally for some time. We knew that the Keeper kept copies of all documents submitted to the Registers, but it used to be sort of a secret; and until comparatively recently, you couldn't access materials from this archive. It is now formally recognised and you are now entitled to obtain an extract from the Registers of any document in the archive record. This will be a useful resource, since there are times when it is difficult to work things out from information on the Title Sheet, and sight of the underlying deeds can sometimes be the only way to satisfactorily interpret the title.

2.4.2(iv) The application record

This is a formalised record of all applications received. It is also the part of the Register where current or extant advance notices are going to be held. Due to their transitory nature, it was felt that they shouldn't go onto the Title Sheet, but simply sit in the application record until they lapse and are either removed or discharged.

2.4.3 Land Certificates and Title Sheets

The practice of issuing a Land Certificate has ceased under the 2012 Act. A Land Certificate is an official record of the contents of a 1979 Act Title Sheet. You will still see these for some considerable time to come, when you are acting in the purchase of a registered title for the first time under the 2012 Act.

Under the 2012 Act, there is no equivalent of the Land Certificate once the title is registered. Instead, what you get is a PDF version of the Title Sheet which is correct as at the date of registration and will be issued on completion of registration. It does not have evidential status and is not covered by the Keeper's warranty. To have something with evidential status you need to obtain an extract. This is available for all or part of the Title Sheet and any part of the cadastral map.

You can also obtain an extract of any document in the archive record, and certified copies of any application, advance notice or any other document that is at the application stage. Extracts and certifies copies have evidential status[9].

An extract or certified copy costs £30. The registers also provide a 'plain copy' – equivalent to a quick copy of the Title Sheet, for £16.

2.4.4 Registrable Deeds

There were no particular limitations on the type of deed that could be registered under the 1979 Act. In contrast, the 2012 Act provides that only such documents as are 'authorised by an enactment' can be registered in the Land Register. The Keeper has produced a comprehensive list of registrable deeds[10].

It is interesting to observe that if the 2012 Act itself hadn't authorised dispositions, then it seems they might not have been regarded as registrable deeds. Other deeds that are rescued from a registration wilderness by

---

9 Section 104 of the 2012 Act.
10 See www.ros.gov.uk/about-us/2012-act/general-guidance/registrable-deeds.

the 2012 Act include renunciations, variations and assignations of long leases, and ranking agreements. The statutory authority may be express or implied, which probably saves servitudes, which it seems are nowhere expressly authorised by statute. However, the Title Conditions (Scotland) Act 2003 contains provisions about dual registration of servitudes[11] that must impliedly authorise actual registration of this type of deed. Several enactments are specifically mentioned in the Act[12].

2.4.5 Advance Notices

One of the most significant changes under the 2012 Act, for property lawyers and their clients is the introduction of the system of advance notices, one effect of which is to remove the requirement, where an advance notice can be obtained, for a letter of obligation. The advance notice concept is similar to, but not exactly the same as, the priority period which exists for registration of documents in the Land Registry of England and Wales. In England and Wales it is tied in with a register search.

An advance notice is applied for, in respect of the deed that it is intended to be granted, for a fee of £10, and once it is registered it provides a period of protection of 35 days (beginning with the day after the advance notice is registered) for the deed in question, against competing deeds, inhibitions, or another advance notice. See para 11.5 for full details of the effect of advance notices and the procedures to follow.

2.4.6 Overriding Interests and Encumbrances

Under the 1979 Act, a property could be affected by other interests in land that were not shown on the Title Sheet. One always has to be alive to the fact that there could be an interest in land which, while not registered in the Land Register or recorded in the Sasine Register, could nonetheless be a real right. These 'overriding interests' were defined in section 28(1) of the 1979 Act and included: a right or interest over land of a lessee under a lease which is not a long lease who has acquired a real right by virtue

---

11 Section 75(1) of the 2003 Act.
12 The Registration of Leases (Scotland) Act 1857, the Conveyancing (Scotland) Act 1924, the Conveyancing and Feudal Reform (Scotland) Act 1970 and the Law Reform (Miscellaneous Provisions) (Scotland) Act 1985.

of possession; a crofter or cottar; the proprietor of the dominant tenement in a servitude; the Crown or other authority under an enactment which does not require the recording of a deed in the register to complete the right; the rights of a non-entitled spouse or civil partner, the holder of a floating charge, whether crystallised or not; a member of the public in respect of a public right of way; *regalia majora* (property in right of the Crown); or any person having a right which has been made real other than by registration. The inside front cover of every Land Certificate lists overriding interests in full.

Section 28 is repealed by the 2012 Act. That is not to say that such rights have ceased to exist, but the emphasis, for land registration purposes, has shifted. Instead, we must consider whether a property is affected by any 'encumbrance' defined in section 9 of the 2012 Act. Encumbrances include title conditions (ie burdens and servitudes), long leases (or if the title relates to a long lease, long sub leases), public rights of way, core paths, and any other encumbrance 'the inclusion of which in the register is permitted or required, expressly or impliedly, by an enactment'[13]. A heritable security is not an encumbrance for these purposes. The Keeper must now incorporate reference to such encumbrances in the burdens section of the Title Sheet. The submitting solicitor now has to investigate the existence of such things as public rights of way, and provide details of them with an application for registration.

2.4.7 Shared Plots

Any land that is owned in common by two or more people is now entitled to be a 'shared plot', with its own title number and Title Sheet. Not all mutual areas need to be shared plots, but where a shared plot is created after the designated day, the *quantum* of the share (eg a third, a fiftieth) in the shared plot owned by each proprietor of a sharing plot must be specified, so the woolly 'together with a right of common property along with the other proprietors in the development'-type of wording will no longer suffice. For sharing plots generally see paras 8.28.4(v) and 9.9.10.

---

13 Section 9(10(f) of the 2012 Act.

2.4.8 Prescriptive Claimants

Getting *a non domino* disposition registered was never an easy task. The 2012 Act sets out detailed requirements for registering such deed, involving notification procedures and, most importantly, the requirement for a period of one year's possession immediately prior to the date of application. For prescriptive claimants and *a non domino* dispositions see para 8.10.

2.4.9 Caveats

Part 6 of the 2012 Act introduces a new concept of registrable caveats affecting property. These will be a warning that, because of court proceedings that have been raised, changes may be made to the Register. Caveats can be applied for in civil proceedings relating to reduction of registered deeds, or for a determination that the register is inaccurate, or where an order for rectification of the Register is being sought. While any of these proceedings are in dependence, any party to the proceedings may apply to the court for warrant to place a caveat on the Title Sheet of a plot of land to which the proceedings relate.

Certain conditions must apply before a caveat can be obtained. The court has to be satisfied that there is a *prima facie* case on the merits; that there is a real and substantial risk that if the caveat were not granted that enforcement of any decree would be defeated or prejudiced because the other party was likely to deal with the plot of land; and that it is reasonable to grant the caveat.

So a caveat is something that we might see from time to time appearing on a Title Sheet, and a search will disclose its existence. A caveat will remain on the Title Sheet for 12 months after which it will expire unless renewed or it has been recalled or discharged before expiry. A caveat can be renewed more than once provided the conditions are satisfied.

The Keeper will obviously have regard to any relevant caveat placed on a Title Sheet when she is granting warranty and deciding on the appropriate level of warranty.

Anyone transacting with a property which shows a caveat on the Title Sheet will be taken to be aware of this, and if there were to be title problems in the future, the likelihood of any potential compensation would be diminished.

2.4.10 General Application Conditions and Particular Conditions of Registration

Under section 22 of the 2012 Act, all applications for registration must comply with the General Application Conditions. The 2012 Act also refers to particular Conditions of Registration that additionally apply to an application, depending on whether it is a registered or unregistered[14] title and for automatic plot registration and voluntary registration. If the conditions are not met, then the application must be rejected. It is up to the submitting solicitor to confirm (in the declaration given in the application form (see para 14.11.3) that the conditions are met.

2.4.10(i) General Application Conditions

All applications have to meet the General Application Conditions. These conditions are not easily discernible from the 2012 Act – you have to dig around to find out what they are. Section 22, which defines the 'general application conditions' is somewhat circuitous. In essence, the application must be such that it enables the Keeper to comply with the duties she has under Part 1 of the Act.

So what are the Keeper's duties under Part 1? She must make up and maintain a Title Sheet for each registered plot of land, or for a registered lease by entering:

(a) a description of the plot of land (by reference to the cadastral map) in the property section of the Title Sheet, and the nature of the proprietor's right in the plot of land; if the plot is a separate tenement, the nature of the tenement, particulars of any pertinents, and details of any burdened property, so far as known;

(b) the name and designation of the proprietor, and for land owned in common, the respective shares of the proprietors, in the proprietorship section of the Title Sheet;

(c) particulars of any heritable security, including the name and designation of the creditor in the security, in the securities section of the Title Sheet; and

---

14 'Unregistered' in the language of the 2012 Act will generally mean a Sasine title (which is recorded, not registered).

(d)   the terms of any title condition, a description of any benefited property (so far as known to the Keeper), the existence of any long lease or long sub-lease, particulars of any path order and any other encumbrance, in the burdens section.

In addition, the property must not be a souvenir plot[15]; the deed must be properly executed (or digitally signed if an electronic deed); the application must be in the form prescribed by Land Register rules; and the registration fee is paid or is to be paid under arrangements satisfactory to the Keeper ie by direct debit).

2.4.10(ii) Particular Conditions of Registration

Depending on the type of application, there are additional Conditions of Registration that must apply. These will depend on whether the title is registered or unregistered, or triggers 'automatic plot registration' (APR) or is a voluntary registration (VR) application. Broadly, these conditions are the same for each application type.

(1)   The principal condition is that the deed is valid. A deed is 'valid' for the purposes of the 2012 Act if, by registering it, a right would be acquired, varied or extinguished. So it must be granted by the correct person, be properly executed and witnessed, correctly describe the plot of land, be in any particular format that is required, use appropriate operative words, such as 'dispone', 'impose' or 'grant' and so on. Under the 1979 Act, the act of registration created validity. Now, it's up to us.

(2)   The description must be sufficient to enable the Keeper to delineate the boundaries on the cadastral map, although flats in tenements will continue to be dealt with as they are now, and the steading or tenement block is what will be shown on the map, not each individual flat.

(3)   If the land to be registered is affected by a burden or other encumbrance which affects only part of the plot, then a plan showing the extent of that lesser area must be included in, or

---

15 Ie a plot of land which is of inconsiderable size and of no practical utility (and not already registered).

submitted with the application, or a description is submitted that will allow the Keeper to delineate the lesser area on the cadastral map. Generally, this requirement relates to unregistered plots (which includes APR and VR applications).

(4)   If there is a right of way within the plot, so far as the applicant is aware, then the application has to include a description of it.

2.4.11 Searches and Reports

The new style Legal Reports replace Forms 10, 11, 12 and 13 that were available under the 1979 Act, but do, essentially, the same job. Plans Reports have become essential for all types of application and the former P16 Report, while still a component of Level 2 and Level 3 Plans Reports, is of lesser significance than whether or not the extent of the proposed application will conflict with the extent of a title that is already registered on the cadastal map. Of course, the 2012 Act itself says nothing about Legal Reports or Plans Reports – these are practical tools that have been developed to provide information and confirmations required during the course of a transaction.

2.4.12 Application Forms

One of the most common reasons for rejection of an application under the 1979 Act was that the wrong application form had been used. Under the 2012 Act, Forms 1, 2, 3 and 4 are replaced by a single all-purpose application form[16] (see para 14.11 for details). The questions in the 2012 Act application form are quite different from the questions in the Forms 1, 2 and 3. As the applicant and their solicitor certify the title, there is no longer any requirement to tell the Keeper about status of companies, compliance by heritable creditors acting under a power of sale, matrimonial homes etc, as checking these things is up to the solicitor. She must be able to confirm that the deed is valid and meets the General Application Conditions and Conditions of Registration in each case. This is further expansion of the 'tell me, don't show me' approach developed by the Keeper under the 1979 Act regime.

16 Land Register Rules etc (Scotland) Regulations 2014.

2.4.13 No Examination of Title by the Registers

Procedurally, one of the more significant consequences of the new regime is that the staff at the Registers no longer carry out an examination of the title deeds submitted with the application for registration. Although they carry out a series of checks for basic validity of the deed submitted – that it has been correctly executed and witnessed, for example – the Keeper will now rely on the declaration given by the applicant's solicitor in the application form instead (see para 14.11.3).

2.4.14 Notification

New notification procedures involve e-mail acknowledgments, which include the same information as that previously provided: the type of deed to be registered, the names of the parties, the date of application, the application number, the title number or provisional title number, and the particulars of the plot of land or subjects of lease. The e-mail address of the granter (usually the granter's solicitor) can also be given, meaning that they will also get notification of receipt.

Once the application is accepted onto the Land Register an e-mail notification is sent, providing access to a pdf of the updated or newly created Title Sheet. This provides a link to access a web page – a 'landing page' from which the pdf version of the Title Sheet can be accessed. It will be visible on the landing page for 50 days from the date of the notification e-mail, but can be saved locally to your matter file. The link to the landing page can be forwarded, so that, if you want to, you can send it to your client.

The pdf will also include the relevant excerpt from the cadastral map.

2.4.15 Requisitions and the 'One-shot' Rule

Under 1979 Act procedures, if there was further information, documentation or clarification required in respect of an application, the Keeper did not necessarily reject the application, but could put it in 'stand-over' and requisition further information from the applicant. This would, hopefully, resolve the matter, and allow the application to proceed. This was quite a common practice, and the advantage, of course, to the applicant was that the original date of registration was preserved.

Probably the most radical consequence, for solicitors, under the 2012 Act is the withdrawal of the requisition procedure, and the requirement for the application to be right first time[17].

If any of the statutory conditions for an application is not met, then the Keeper must reject that application[18]. Importantly, the conditions must be met at the date of the application, so, it is no longer possible to amend a deed or substitute a corrected deed for one that is defective in some way, as was frequently permitted under a 1979 Act application. This is characterised as the 'one-shot' rule[19], and it is based on the premise, with which it is difficult to argue, that it is up to applicants to submit valid deeds and make sure that they meet any other legal and practical requirements.

An amendment or substitution is only permitted in very limited circumstances (see para 14.6.5).

2.4.16 The Keeper's Indemnity and the Keeper's Warranty

A title registered under the 1979 Act benefited from the Keeper's Indemnity, unless the Land Certificate clearly disclosed that indemnity was excluded for some reason. Given that indemnity was underpinned by the Keeper's 'Midas touch', this was of considerable comfort. The Midas touch ceases under the 2012 Act, and the state guarantee that is now provided is the Keeper's Warranty, which guarantees to the applicant that what is contained in the Title Sheet is accurate in reflecting all acquisitions, variations and discharges in favour of the applicant, and that any encumbrance that is not shown is permitted to be excluded from the Title Sheet. The benefit of warranty extends only to someone to whom the benefit of warrandice by the granter of a deed would extend. The Keeper may decide to limit or exclude warranty in certain circumstances. For further commentary on the differences between Keeper's indemnity and Keeper's warranty see para 2.6). A breach of warranty could still, in certain circumstances, lead to rectification and then compensation.

---

17 Ideally any application for registration should get things right. The reality, of course, is that this is not always possible.

18 Section 21(3).

19 Registers' guidance is available at: www.ros.gov.uk/__data/assets/pdf_file/0017/11375/General-Guidance-One-Shot-Rule.pdf.

2.4.17 The Duty to the Keeper

The introduction of a statutory duty to the Keeper was probably the most controversial provision of the 2012 Act and generated much concern and debate during the passage of the Bill through Parliament. Whereas previously, the staff at the Registers would carry out their own checks and examination of the title, to ensure that the indemnity provided by the Keeper could be justified, now, the Keeper will rely on the information given and certification made by the applicants and submitting solicitors.

2.4.17(i)   The duty of care

Section 111 of the 2012 Act imposes a duty on granters of deeds, applicants and their solicitors to take reasonable care to ensure that the Keeper does not inadvertently make the Register inaccurate as a result of a deed that is granted and presented for registration.

    Arguably, a solicitor should be taking that reasonable care anyway, so on one view there should be nothing to fear from this new statutory duty. However, a breach of that duty will result in the Keeper being entitled to claim compensation. The effect of this is, therefore, that in the event of an inaccuracy on the Register, resulting in a successful claim against the Keeper's warranty, the Keeper has the option to offset such a claim, against the solicitor's duty of care.

2.4.17(ii)   The offence of recklessly misleading the Keeper

There is a separate offence created by the 2012 Act under section 112 – that of recklessly misleading the Keeper, or failing to disclose material information in an application. The inclusion of this provision in the 2012 Act was, it is understood, sought by the Serious Fraud Office, whose concern is principally centred around mortgage fraud.

    The offence is clearly a far more serious matter, and would involve a person making a materially false or misleading statement in relation to an application for registration knowing that or being reckless as to whether, the statement is false or misleading, or intentionally failing to disclose material information in relation to such an application or being reckless as to whether all material information is disclosed. This is a criminal offence which would be subject to prosecution. It will be a defence that the person relied on information supplied by someone else.

2.4.18 New Triggers for Registration

As the number of registrations in the 30-plus years since the introduction of land registration had still only achieved transfer to the Land Register of a small proportion of the land mass of Scotland (see para 2.2) the 2012 Act contains provisions to help to accelerate this transfer. There are new triggers for registration. Certain deeds will no longer be capable of being recorded in the Sasine Register, but must instead be registered in the Land Register. Where the title is Sasine, the effect of this will be to induce a first registration of that title in the Land Register. Voluntary registration, which was always available under the 1979 Act, is to be positively encouraged. A new trigger, of Keeper-induced registration permits the Keeper to register a title, without any application having been made, and without requiring the consent of the owner. See para 2.5 for details of the triggers, and proposals for Completion of the Register.

2.4.19 The Seabed

As the Keeper is no longer restricted by having to plot titles onto the Ordnance Survey map[20] – although that is currently the base map for the cadastral map, it is now possible to map titles to areas of seabed. A new county – SEA – has been created. Areas of of seabed (particularly useful for renewables projects such as long leases of pipelines, and sites for off-shore platforms) can now be registered and shown on the cadastral map. See paras 9.9.7 and 14.5.9 for requirements for description and plotting coordinates for areas of seabed.

COMPLETION OF THE LAND REGISTER

2.5 One of the main policy drivers for the 2012 Act is the Completion of the Land Register. To provide greater certainty, there is a desire and need to get land and property onto the Land Register and out of the Sasine

---

20 Section 11(6) of the 2012 Act.

Register, more quickly that was happening under the 1979 Act (see para 2.3). Eventually (and now sooner rather than later), the Sasine Register will be closed, although it will be preserved as an historical record.

Shortly after the designated day, it was announced that Scottish Ministers had asked the Keeper, and she had agreed, to complete the Land Register within 10 years (ie by 2024). That is undoubtedly a tall order, but the 2012 Act contains a number of provisions in the Act that will accelerate that process.

2.5.1 New Triggers for Registration

Whereas, under the 1979 Act, only dispositions for valuable consideration would induce a first registration, from and after the designated day, all dispositions whether for valuable consideration or not now induce a first registration if the property is not yet in the Land Register. All registrable leases, sub-leases and assignations of long leases must also be registered in the Land Register. From 1 April 2016, any standard security must be registered in the Land Register. If it is granted over a property where title is still in the Sasine Register, the security will trigger a requirement for voluntary registration of the underlying Sasine title at the same time. In due course, regulations will prescribe other types of deeds that must only be registered, and eventually the Sasine Register will close to all new deeds.

So, where the title to the property to be transferred (or let, or in the case of a registrable lease, that lease is to be assigned) is in the Sasine Register, that title must be transferred to the Land Register ie first registration is induced in all cases. We are already familiar with this where the property is being transferred for valuable consideration. Where a lease is recorded or registrable, an assignation of that lease will require a new lease Title Sheet to be made up for the lease. If the landlord's title is registered, no action is required in relation to that title, but if it is still a Sasine title, it too must be moved to the Land Register, under automatic plot registration provisions (see para 2.5.2).

2.5.2 Automatic Plot Registration

A consequence of leases and sub-leases, or assignations of long leases still in the Sasine Register inducing a first registration, is to trigger the requirement for the underlying title to the affected land, if it is still in the Sasine Register, also to be registered. Other applications relating to subordinate real rights, such as the granting of a standard security over a lease, and notices of title over subordinate real rights, are also affected (although, from Registers' Guidance, it seems that an applicant for such notices of title or standard securities can choose to record in the Sasine Register in the meantime). This is referred to as 'automatic plot registration' (APR).

Where APR applies, it is the responsibility of the applicant, eg the tenant who is applying to register the lease, also to register the landlord's underlying title to that leasehold interest. Accordingly, the application does two things and will result in two Title Sheets: one for the lease and one for the landlord's title. Tenant's solicitors, therefore, need to liaise closely with the landlord's solicitors on the title, and ensure that they are provided with all the title information they require to be able to certify that title as well as the validity of the lease itself. In these cases, it is, obviously, as much in the interests of the landlord to ensure that the Title Sheet for its heritable title is correct, as it is for the tenant to be sure that the lease Title Sheet is accurate[21]. APR only applies to the title to the extent of the leased property, so if the landlord has title to a larger area, only part of its title will be registered. It is open to the landlord to choose to register all of its title simultaneously, but the remainder of the title would need to be the subject of a voluntary registration application.

2.5.3 Voluntary Registration

Voluntary registration (VR) by an owner of a Sasine title has always been possible under land registration, although under the 1979 Act the Keeper had discretion as to whether or not to accept such an application, and did not always do so. That discretion was continued under the 2012 Act, but is to be removed in April 2016.

VR is one of the principal ways in which the target to complete the Land Register can be achieved. Local authorities and other public bodies have been asked by the Keeper to register their land holdings within five years of the designated day. This poses a significant challenge to many

---

21 Wording to cover this situation is available from the PSG Letter of Consent to Assignation at
http://www.psglegal.co.uk/documents/lease_management/LetterOfConsentToAssignation_
V7.doc.

authorities whose land holdings are often held on old, obscure titles. Other owners, such as heritage bodies, eg the National Trust for Scotland and major land holders such as the Forestry Commission face similar challenges, although whether such holdings will make it to the Register under VR applications, or by way of Keeper-induced registration (see para 2.5.4) is currently a moot point.

Many owners of large estates are being encouraged to apply for VR of their land, and the Registers are building a specialist team of staff whose job it will be to assist such applications. There is currently a 25% discount on registration fees for VR applications. It is clear that incentives are required to encourage land owners to take this step, particularly since the nature of many such titles is that they are old and vague, so defining the precise extent of land held, with sufficient accuracy for mapping purposes, is difficult. Many estates will have sold off parcels of land over the years; identifying the extent of split offs is a key element in identifying what is comprised in the application. Such applications can, therefore, be complex and time consuming and the costs in terms of legal fees can be off-putting for many owners. The alternative, of doing nothing and waiting for Keeper-induced registration to deal with these holdings is, however, unlikely to be a viable or an attractive alternative.

2.5.4 Keeper-induced Registration

The 2012 Act introduces an entirely new concept, of Keeper-induced registration (KIR). KIR gives the Keeper the right to register an unregistered plot of land without any application having being made and without the consent of the owner or any other person. This might be regarded as the ultimate power for the Keeper, but the reality of the challenges of KIR, not least for the Registers' staff, is likely to mean that it is not the big stick it might appear to be.

At the time of writing, the Registers are consulting on how they will go about this process of KIR[22].

2.5.4(i) KIR pilot

In the months preceding the publication of the KIR consultation, the Registers conducted a number of pilots to test the processes that would

22 See www.ros.gov.uk/consultations/keeper-induced-registration.

need to apply in KIR. The consultation reports on the findings of these KIR pilots, concentrated on a mix of three property types:

- Registers of Scotland 'research areas' (areas of land that have been, or are likely to be, split up into several units of property sharing common burdens, such as residential developments);

- Heritage assets, for example properties owned by the National Trust for Scotland, where the Registers worked with the organisations concerned; and

- Other property types (not in research areas) including residential and commercial property, farms and rural estates, and land relevant to other Scottish Government initiatives, but without any involvement of the property owner or their advisers.

No actual registrations were effected, other than a small number of heritage assets, including the island of St Kilda. The purpose of the pilot was to identify how easy or difficult it would be to register the different categories of property type, without reference to owners or their advisers, and the local information that they have, that is not evident from the title deeds alone.

2.5.4(ii) Pilot conclusions

The Registers conclude that research areas are likely to be the most fruitful and successful source of property for KIR. With an estimated 700,000 unregistered properties located in research areas, this will make a significant dent in the approximately 1.5 million unregistered properties that will need to be transferred from the Sasine Register to the Land Register. The Keeper already has a lot of information about these properties, their likely extent and the burdens and rights that will affect them, as most of these are private and public sector residential developments, which will typically have common prior titles.

While some heritage assets were successfully transferred to the Land Register under KIR during the pilot, this was achieved with the collaboration of the organisations themselves. One purpose of this part of the pilot was to evaluate how KIR could operate in partnership with the land owner. Prioritising such collaborations can be problematic, without the commercial imperative of a transactional deadline, and the Registers concluded that such partnerships are overly resource intensive, making this an unviable option from their perspective.

A selection of property types in the third category was investigated: residential and commercial, urban and rural. Without the involvement of the property owner, or solicitors, it is likely that, for many properties in this category, it will be difficult to produce a clear and accurate land register title. As solicitors are well aware, and as many property owners know, what is in the title deeds is only part of the story. Sometimes those titles are vague or obscure, with outdated descriptions and poor-quality plans, meaning that without the benefit of the owner's local knowledge, the resulting Land Register title under KIR is likely to be incomplete.

Many key aspects of a title arise 'off-register'. A right of access may be established through exercise alone, ownership may be transferred by way of an unregistered event, eg the death of a spouse holding joint title equally and to the survivor of them, or by way of docquet of nomination in favour of a beneficiary. Tenants' interests will not be apparent, unless the lease is one of over 20 years' duration (and consequently registered, too). The actual occupational extent of many properties can be in conflict with the title plan, or the Ordnance Survey map, or in the absence of a plan, a key determinant of extent. None of this information will be available or apparent to the Registers in a KIR situation.

2.5.4(iii) Research areas

For these reasons, the Registers propose to focus KIR principally on those properties which are located in research areas, predominantly urban, where the occupational features are more easily determined and a direct comparison with the title description is easier to achieve. This is more likely to result in a Land Register title that the Keeper can warrant, without any limitation or exclusion, although it is recognised that there may still be off-register information that will only come to light after registration, when the owner is informed. The consultation recognises that, at that point, owners may wish to have the title corrected to reflect the effect of such additional information, and it is proposed that a normal rectification application would be the route to make such changes. It is inevitable that discrepancies and errors will arise in such an exercise, although the Keeper expects that these will be in the minority. It will be essential that a swift and accommodating reception is given to owners' requests for changes and corrections.

The Keeper intends to approach KIR on an area-by-area basis. This may mean that properties which are not in a research area, but which are nonetheless capable of clear identification from the title, and able to be mapped satisfactorily onto the land register map, will be included.

THE KEEPER'S INDEMNITY AND THE KEEPER'S WARRANTY

2.6 A key feature of most systems of land registration is the concept of some form of state guarantee. Under the 1979 Act, this was known as Keeper's Indemnity. Under the 2012 Act, Indemnity is replaced with Keeper's Warranty for titles registered after 8 December 2014.

2.6.1 Keeper's Indemnity under the 1979 Act

Under a 1979 Act title, indemnity from the Keeper was available where a person had suffered loss because of rectification of an inaccuracy on the Register. or a refusal by the Keeper to rectify. Indemnity was also available where the Keeper had lost documents, or they had been destroyed while in her custody, or an error or omission had been made in the Land Certificate[23]. This indemnity is set in the context of the Keeper's 'Midas touch', by which the act of registration could make a 'bad' title good. The key protection was that the Keeper must refuse to rectify in favour of the 'true' owner, if the owner with a registered title was a 'proprietor in possession'. So, even if the person seeking rectification was, in fact the true owner, (ie with a clear Sasine title to the land), if the registered proprietor was in possession of the land covered by the registered title, the Keeper could not rectify. The Keeper would have to pay compensation to the true owner instead. From the point of view of 'reliance on the register', a 1979 Act title is unimpeachable in this respect.

Other qualifications to the right to claim compensation were set out in section 12(3) of the 1979 Act, which contained a long and miscellaneous list of exclusions where indemnity was not available. These included loss

---

23 Section 12(1) of the 1979 Act.

due to the existence of a prescriptive title acquired through an *a non domino* disposition, reduction of deeds under the Bankruptcy (Scotland) Act 1985 and certain other statutes; loss because the person was presumed dead; minor inaccuracies in boundaries due to the limitations of the Ordnance Survey map; loss arising due to an inability to enforce real burdens or in relation to an interest in mines and minerals where the Title Sheet did not expressly state that the minerals were included in the title; loss from any omission to mention any overriding interests (such as an unregistered servitude created by passage of time, or 'prescription'), or where the loss had been caused by the fraud or carelessness on the part of the claimant. None of these exclusions will be noted on the 1979 Act Title Sheet of a property.

The Keeper could expressly exclude indemnity, either against the whole title or in respect of particular aspects where it was thought likely that a claim may be made, such as where there was an obvious defect in the title, or there was apparent adverse possession. Any such exclusion will be stated on the face of the Land Certificate.

In any of these situations, there is no recourse against the Keeper's Indemnity for defects in title.

2.6.2 Keeper's Warranty under the 2012 Act

Keeper's warranty under a 2012 Act title is slightly different. In the first place, there is no 'Midas touch', so if a deed presented for registration is flawed, registration does not make that deed good. For the purposes of being able to rely on the Register, it could be said that Keeper's Warranty replaces the Midas touch. However, under the 2012 Act, there is no protection against rectification just because the registered owner is in possession. Instead there are good faith protections, but certain conditions have to be met, and the application of the protection may be postponed (see para 2.6.2(i)).

The Keeper's warranty is simple: a Title Sheet is accurate to the extent that it records the effect of a deed that has been presented. So, if a deed is submitted and accepted, that shows an acquisition, variation or discharge in favour of the applicant (or in the case of an application for first registration, shows the applicant to be the proprietor or proprietor in common), then the Keeper warrants that acquisition, variation or discharge. In doing so, of course, the Keeper is relying on the certification given by the submitting solicitor. The benefit of warranty extends to persons to whom the benefit of warrandice by the granter of a deed would extend.

This shifts the emphasis of warranty/indemnity. Indemnity flows from the Midas touch. Warranty is based on the accuracy of the documentation. On one view, you might think that the reliability of a 2012 Act title is only as good as the expertise of the person examining the title and the certification given by them on that basis. But therein lies the path to madness. It cannot be the intention of Parliament, nor should it be the practical approach taken by solicitors, to question a 'warranted' title under the 2012 Act by thinking – 'unless you know that the solicitor who certified the title knew what they were doing, then you can't rely on the title and must conduct your own title investigation (including underlying titles) to be sure'. You are entitled to rely on a 2012 Act title with Keeper's warranty. This is still a fundamental element of the 2012 Act, and should not be belittled. A breach of Keeper's warranty will entitle someone who suffers loss to claim compensation (see para 2.7.4).

Remember that there can be inaccuracies in a 1979 Act title, just as there can be inaccuracies in a 2012 Act title. An inaccuracy in a 2012 Act title must be manifest, in other words, obvious, or plain to the eye. The context in which to put this is: most titles are good and have no need of Keeper's warranty or indemnity (or prescription) to make them so. It is only if they are bad, that statutory protection and indemnity or warranty (or prescription) kicks in. So in the 2012 Regime, if a title is 'bad' eg if the wrong person is shown on the Title Sheet as owner, that means that the Register is inaccurate. Under the 2012 Act, the Keeper can rectify an inaccuracy, but only if it is 'manifest', and that what is required to rectify it is also manifest. 'Manifest' in this context is not defined, but it must be said that if an inaccuracy on the Title Sheet is 'clear, or obvious to the eye or mind' as per the dictionary definition, then it should be apparent to anyone looking at the Title Sheet that something is wrong, and in that case the remedy is also plain eg allow rectification to show the correct owner.

2.6.2(i) 'Realignment of rights'

But what if the Title Sheet looks fine, but there is a problem that is not 'manifest'? What if someone other than the 'true owner' has fraudulently granted a deed but there was nothing to indicate that they were anything other than the true owner and the registered owner is in possession, so all appears to be in order? You will never be able to tell if that apparently good title was in fact, bad. In those (very rare) cases, the 2012 Act provides protection in the form of 'Midas touch light' under section 86.

It works like this: say Icabod Innocent acquires the property from Dermot Dodgy Title who is shown on the (2012 Act) Title Sheet as the registered owner and is in possession. However, Dermot is not, in fact, the true owner (because maybe he acquired title from Francis Fraudster, or because the title included, or was of, land that the granter to Dermot did not own, but was conveyed in error). Icabod will nonetheless obtain a good title protected from challenge, if he acquires in good faith, and either Dermot had possessed the property (openly, peaceably and without judicial interruption) for a continuous period of at least one year, or the property is possessed by Icabod and Dermot for periods which together consist of a continuous period of at least one year. In this way, the protection from challenge might be postponed: if Dermot only registered his title nine months before he sold the property to Icabod, then Icabod will have to possess the property for another three months, before the protection applies.

Dermot could be oblivious as to the fraud or error in his title, or he could himself have granted the fraudulent deed on which his title is based. Either way, Dermot does not benefit from the protection – it only applies to Icabod, provided he acquires in good faith. Dermot would only be able to get a good title by openly possessing since the date of registration for a period of ten years. For Icabod to benefit from this protection, being in good faith and possession for a continuous period of one year (since registration of Dermot's title) are the key elements, but other conditions must apply:

- the Keeper must not have been aware of any inaccuracy (ie because either Dermot or Icabod was not the 'true owner') at any time during that one-year period;
- the disposition is otherwise valid, so that it would have conferred ownership on Icabod had Dermot been proprietor when the land was disponed;
- there must be no caveat on the Title Sheet relevant to the acquisition by Icabod at any time during the one-year period;

- there must be no statement on the Title Sheet (under section 30(5) of the 2012 Act, where the Keeper cannot determine the name and designation to be entered on the Title Sheet) that the name and designation of the proprietor are not known or not known with reasonable certainty to the Keeper; and
- the Keeper warrants (or is to be taken to warrant) Dermot's title.

Provided all of the conditions are met, Icabod obtains a good title after the one-year period has run. The 'true owner', should he appear at a later stage, cannot retrieve the title, but is entitled to compensation. In this way, section 86 'realigns' the rights of the respective parties, by making Icabod's title good, despite the position of the true owner. In this respect, the 2012 Act applies 'registration law' despite what property law says.

At first glance, section 86 appears to be quite scary, but it should be borne in mind that the vast majority of titles are good and have no need of statutory protection. Section 86 provides protection for titles that are bad, but instead of making them immediately good in the way the Midas touch did, on registration, the 2012 Act protection depends on the running of the one-year period, so there might in some circumstances be a delay in the protection, if it is needed, applying.

Since it will never be apparent from the Title Sheet whether or not Dermot's title is 'bad', in practice one should always check, as a matter of course, that a seller with a 2012 Act title has possessed for at least one year. If you ask this question on every occasion, there is no compromise to the purchaser's good faith position. If the seller (with a 2012 Act title) has not yet possessed for a period of one year, the protection (in the rare cases that it is needed) will only apply once the purchaser's possession has run to complete the one-year period (with whatever period the seller has possessed counting towards the total). It is for this reason that the PSG offers to sell include a standard clause in which the seller is required to confirm that he is currently in possession of the property and had been in possession of it openly, peaceably and without judicial interruption for a continuous period of at least one year.

All is not lost if a true owner appears before the one-year period has run, since the purchaser will have a title with Keeper's warranty, and will be entitled to claim compensation if the Title Sheet is rectified against them.

2.6.2(ii) Exclusions from warranty

There are, of course, exceptions from the warranty:

- There is no guarantee that there is no public right of way or core paths affecting the property, that are not shown on the Title Sheet or title plan.

- The Keeper does not warrant that a right appearing on the Title Sheet as a pertinent is of a kind capable of being a valid pertinent, nor that a pertinent which is extinguishable or variable without registration (eg a servitude acquired by prescription) has not been extinguished or varied as the Keeper cannot be aware of these types of 'off-register' events.

- A right to mines or minerals (where the Title Sheet is silent) is not warranted. (This was also the case under 1979 Act.)

- The Keeper does not warrant that a registered lease has not been varied or terminated without the variation or termination having been registered. Again, an off-register event could have varied or terminated the lease.

- Where a plot of land is bounded by a river or other water, warranty does not extend to changes to such a boundary caused by alluvion.

- Warranty does not cover any case where, due to an administrative error by the Keeper, the completed registration is more favourable to the applicant, such as including more land than is in the underlying Sasine title. This is a prime example of the end of the Keeper's Midas touch. Registration will not now give you good title to land that was not in the Sasine title (as covered by the deed inducing registration) regardless of possession, and there would be no compensation if it is taken away through rectification.

The Keeper can grant a more limited warranty, or exclude warranty altogether, if she is not satisfied as to the validity of the acquisition, variation or discharge in question, or that the applicant is the proprietor. The Keeper has power, in limited circumstances, to vary the warranty.

The Keeper can grant more extensive warranty than that originally given, if she is satisfied that it is appropriate to do so. This would apply, for example, in situations where the original warranty was excluded or limited, and the reason for such exclusion or limitation had been resolved. An applicant can request an 'upgrade' to full warranty in those circumstances.

No warranty will be given in relation to a prescriptive claimant acquiring title by *a non domino* disposition, but warranty may be given later, if the title is subsequently perfected by prescription.

RECTIFICATION OF THE REGISTER

2.7 Most titles in the Land Register are accurate and can be relied on. But errors can occur and a Title Sheet may be inaccurate for a number of reasons, and steps can be taken to rectify it. An inaccuracy may be a small one, or one that need not be overly concerning: many Title Sheets are inaccurate because they show a feudal burden that has, in fact, been extinguished by feudal abolition, for example. Such burdens can be removed in the course of an application for registration (see para 14.11.2(ix)). But the Title Sheet might be inaccurate for more serious reasons, where someone other than the registered owner has a 'better' title to the land or part of it. That person can apply for rectification of the position. But if rectification is successful, someone loses out. The person with a registered title who is rectified against loses the property. In those circumstances, they have a claim against the Keeper's indemnity, or for a breach of Keeper's warranty, and are entitled to compensation. Compensation is the other side of the equation. In the words of the Scottish Law Commission, you get either the 'mud' or the 'money'.

2.7.1 Rectification under the 1979 Act

Generally, the main effect of the 1979 Act is to protect the proprietor with the registered title (if that proprietor is in possession) even against someone who may have had a better claim to the title to the property and to compensate that other party by way of a monetary payment under the indemnity scheme.

Rectification is about remedying an inaccuracy in the Register, such as an entry on the register that gives a registered title to someone who is not the true owner of the land in question. The term 'inaccuracy' is not defined in the 1979 Act and its meaning has been less than clear.

The Keeper could, either on request or otherwise, or by order of the court or the Lands Tribunal, rectify any inaccuracy in the Register, except that, if rectification would prejudice a proprietor in possession, then the Keeper could not rectify unless:

- the purpose of the rectification was to note an overriding interest or to correct any information in the Register relating to an overriding interest;
- all persons whose interests in land were likely to be affected by the rectification had been advised by the Keeper of her intention to rectify and had consented in writing;
- the inaccuracy had been caused wholly or substantially by the fraud or carelessness of the proprietor in possession; or
- the rectification related to a matter in respect of which indemnity had been excluded.

The court could order rectification where a deed or document had been rectified by the court under provisions relating to defectively expressed documents (section 8 of the Law Reform (Miscellaneous Provisions) (Scotland) Act 1985).

The Keeper could also rectify the Land Register without consent, if the rectification was to take account of anything done as a consequence of feudal abolition. So the Keeper could cancel any Title Sheets relating to superiorities. In these cases, a feudal superior is not deemed to be a proprietor in possession for the purposes of rectification, nor is any compensation payable as a result of the rectification.

2.7.2 Compensation under the 1979 Act

The Keeper's Indemnity means that a person who suffers loss is entitled to indemnity from the Keeper. Indemnity in these circumstances takes the form of compensation. Compensation arises when rectification takes place, or when the Keeper refuses or omits to rectify.

2.7.3 Rectification under the 2012 Act

Under the 2012 Act, rectification is possible if there is a 'manifest inaccuracy' in either the Title Sheet or in the cadastral map. Where there is an inaccuracy in the Register, the Keeper must rectify it, provided that it is a manifest inaccuracy, and that what is needed to rectify it is also manifest, even if that means rectifying against a proprietor in possession (subject to the good faith exemption (see para 2.6.2(i)). Effectively, this is the reverse of the position under the 1979 Act.

Rectification does not need the consent of the registered proprietor.

The 2012 Act does contain a definition of 'inaccuracy' which is that a Title Sheet is inaccurate if it:

- misstates what the position is in law or in fact;
- omits anything that legislation requires to be included in it or
- includes anything, the inclusion of which is not expressly or impliedly permitted under an enactment.

The cadastral map is inaccurate if it:

- wrongly depicts or shows what the position is in law or in fact;
- omits anything required, under an enactment, to be depicted or shown on it; or
- depicts or shows anything the depiction or showing of which is not expressly or impliedly permitted by or under an enactment.

The key thing to remember is that an inaccuracy has to be 'manifest' for rectification under the 2012 Act to be possible. This ought to give us some comfort, as although there is no definition of manifest in the 2012 Act, the ordinary meaning of it is 'clearly revealed to the eye, mind or judgement; obvious; open to view or comprehension', meaning that it should be easy to spot a rectifiable inaccuracy on a Title Sheet. Early indications are that the Keeper is taking a strictly literal approach to this, although policy is still developing. It seems likely that the standard required for rectification will be high, due to the 'double manifest' requirement. In most extreme cases, you would expect that the remedy will be obvious; if someone has a registered title to land which obviously belongs to someone else, then the remedy is clearly that the land should be returned to the true owner.

However, both parts of the 'double manifest' test must be met: even if the Keeper accepts that there is a manifest inaccuracy, she may not consider that there is a manifest remedy. In that situation, instead of rectifying, she can insert a note on the Title Sheet, or on the cadastral map, with details of the inaccuracy. That would make it plain for any future purchaser to see, which would of course affect any claim by a future purchaser in respect of the Keeper's Warranty regarding that inaccuracy.

Registers' Guidance suggests, by way of illustration, that a manifest inaccuracy would exist where:

- effect is given to a void deed;
- the Keeper has incorrectly delineated a plot on the cadastral map;
- rights or burdens have been omitted; or
- the existence of an inaccuracy has been judicially determined.

Some examples given of where a perceived inaccuracy may not be considered manifest would include:

- the existence or extinction of prescriptive rights;
- habile competing titles with disputed claims of possession; or
- anomalies between a description and plan within a deed.

The Keeper applied a high standard under the 1979 Act and it is likely that she will continue to do so under the 2012 Act.

2.7.4 Compensation under the 2012 Act

The Keeper must pay compensation for loss incurred as a result of a breach of the Keeper's warranty, if the inaccuracy giving rise to the claim for compensation is rectified. Compensation only arises if, and when, the inaccuracy is rectified. So, it is not the inaccuracy itself that triggers the claim for compensation – it is the rectification of that inaccuracy that triggers entitlement. However, this liability to pay compensation is subject to a number of exceptions.

The Keeper has no liability to pay compensation:

- if there is an inaccuracy because of an error in the cadastral map, which the Keeper made because she relied on the base map. The base map is the Ordnance Survey Map at the moment. Any error in the OS map will not be a breach of the Keeper's warranty, if she relies on it.
- if the existence of the inaccuracy was, or ought to have been, known to the applicant, or any person acting as solicitor or other legal adviser to the applicant, at the time of registration;

- where the inaccuracy is due to a failure of the applicant or any person acting as solicitor or legal adviser to him to comply with their duty of care to the Keeper[24]. The Keeper will be entitled to rely on what the applicant and its solicitor certify in the application form.

- if the claimant's loss could have been avoided by the applicant, owner or claimant taking certain measures which it would have been reasonable for him to take. What these measures could be is unclear, but failing to ensure that all necessary conveyancing steps have been taken, or all usual reports instructed and examined could fall into this category.

- if the connection between the claimant's loss and the inaccuracy is too remote, or if the loss is non-patrimonial (ie does not relate to the land). So compensation for emotional distress will not be covered.

These last two points clearly give the Keeper considerable discretion, and it is likely that all of these elements would be considered before compensation was agreed to be paid.

Compensation will include reimbursement for reasonable extra-judicial expenses and other consequential loss. Quantification of the amount of compensation will be as at the date on which the inaccuracy giving rise to the claim is rectified, not the date on which the inaccuracy is discovered. Interest is payable on the amount of compensation.

Payment of compensation by the Keeper does not extinguish any rights which the claimant may have against another person in respect of the loss compensated. It will however be a condition of any payment that the claimant assigns any such rights to the Keeper. This could apply to a situation where the applicant has taken out title indemnity insurance in respect of the matter.

There is clearly a shift in emphasis from the 1979 Act approach, which was to look at actual losses which could be quantified and fully vouched. Now it appears that a more subjective approach will apply. There is no benchmark as yet, of course. However, the state of knowledge of the applicant and its solicitor, the duty of care of both, and what those ought

---

24 The duty is to take reasonable care to ensure that the Keeper does not inadvertently make the Register inaccurate.

or ought not to have resulted in, is likely to mean that meeting the tests for payment of compensation to be made could be a lot less straightforward.

2.7.5 Transitional Arrangements

It is still possible for a person to make an indemnity claim under the 1979 Act after 8 December 2014. Transitional provisions in Schedule 4 to the 2012 Act make provision for post-designated day claims under 1979 Act indemnity. If a person has an entitlement to claim indemnity immediately before the designated day – in other words, the inaccuracy exists before 8 December – then they will still be entitled, after 8 December 2014, to claim against the Keeper's indemnity. That entitlement applies even if no claim has actually been made, or, where a claim had been made, but was not yet determined[25].

There are other transitional provisions in the 2012 Act that are intended to deal with inaccuracies in the Register that come about because of the property law - registration law conflict under the 1979 Act:

(a)   if an inaccuracy that existed on the Register immediately before the designated day (ie in the era of the 1979 Act), was one that the Keeper would not have been able to rectify under 1979 Act rules[26] – usually because there was a proprietor in possession – that inaccuracy will be disregarded for the future, and the Register will be regarded as accurate[27]. This seems to be a sensible blanket approach: rectification wouldn't have been possible anyway, so it is no longer an option;

(b)   conversely, if the pre-existing inaccuracy was one that the Keeper would have had power to rectify, then it remains an inaccuracy after the designated day. So it will continue to be possible for someone having rights in these circumstances, such as the 'true owner' to apply for rectification[28].

Determining possession for the purposes of the 'proprietor-in-possession' exception under the 1979 Act is however, for the purposes of the

---

25 Paragraph 15 of Schedule 4 to the 2012 Act.
26 Section 9 of the 1979 Act (now repealed).
27 Paragraph 22 of Schedule 4 to the 2012 Act.
28 Paragraph 17 of Schedule 4 to the 2012 Act.

application of these provisions, to be based on the state of possession on the day immediately before the designated day, 7 December 2014. There is also a presumption that the person registered as the proprietor of the land was in possession on that date, unless evidence to the contrary can be demonstrated. As time passes, it will be increasingly difficult to demonstrate possession by someone who was not the registered proprietor on that date, so it seems that rectification of a 1979 Act title will become more and more unlikely. Compensation may however be paid to someone who loses a right under these provisions.

E-REGISTRATION

2.8 The Scottish e-registration system is called ARTL – Automated Registration of Title to Land, (and is referred to by its abbreviation, pronounced 'ar-til'). It has been operating since August 2007. The system works well enough, with the right kind of deed and with a fair wind. Some difficulties and frustrations in using ARTL have been reported for whole conveyancing transactions that have completed using the system, but practitioners report that it works well for discharges of a security, which are in a standard form.

At the moment however, the use of ARTL is limited to transactions that involve 'dealings of whole', by which is meant a disposition and/or standard security that transfers or secures the whole of a registered title. Discharges of securities over a registered title can, as already mentioned, be dealt with in this way, as well as some other simple conveyancing documents. Another current limitation is the fact that processing transactions involving limited companies through ARTL are problematic, as, while it is perfectly possible for a discharge or a disposition by or in favour of a company to be processed, standard securities granted by companies cannot, because the charge created by the security also requires to be registered in the Register of Charges, and electronic communication between ARTL and Companies House is not, at present, possible. That has meant that there has not as yet been any significant take-up of ARTL for commercial property transactions.

The ARTL system effectively allows the solicitor to go online to submit deeds and populate Land Registration forms in real time on the Register. While it has long been the practice that solicitors conclude missives on behalf of clients, ARTL requires solicitors to sign deeds electronically on their behalf. The solicitor must have a mandate from clients to allow him or her to sign deeds in this way. The signature is adhibited by means of a secure e-signature using a chip and PIN card. The registration fees and Land and Buildings Transaction Tax are collected by Registers of Scotland from the solicitor's account at the point of registration. The use of ARTL in practice is considered further at para 14.12.

BENEFITS OF E-CONVEYANCING

2.9 Contracts for the sale and purchase of heritable property in Scotland must be in written form, and are usually constituted by missives, consisting of a series of formal letters entered into either by or on behalf of a purchaser and a seller dealing with the conditions that are to apply to the purchase and sale. It can, of course, be effected by a sale and purchase agreement between the parties themselves. One of the perceived advantages of missives is that they can be concluded more quickly because they are signed on behalf of seller and purchaser by their respective solicitors.

However, while that may have been true a few decades ago, technological advances, starting with fax, then e-mail, then the ease of creating and sending PDFs of documents, coupled with greater demands for speed, tighter deadlines, and greater complexity have meant that, often, the traditional approach has shortcomings that sit awkwardly with the commercial realities of contracting in the digital age.

Traditionally, the missives take the form of an offer to purchase by the purchaser, (especially in residential transactions) which is accepted by either an outright acceptance from the seller, or may be met with a qualified acceptance if there are any elements of the purchaser's offer that the seller does not wish to accept, or wants to suggest an alternative. Offers to sell are often used in commercial property transactions, but the principle is the same, although more usually the offer will be adjusted between the parties' solicitors in draft, and the 'formal offer and series of acceptance letters' model is becoming somewhat old fashioned, with the increasing use of standardised offers in both residential and commercial transactions.

But simply agreeing what the contract will say is only part of the story.

To be effective there must be delivery. Under Scots law, actual physical delivery is required. As a general legal principle, delivery is necessary because as long as a writing remains in the granter's own custody, he is free to change his mind and to destroy it or at least not to deliver it.

But what is 'delivery' in the modern technological world? It is now commonplace to send pdf versions of signed missives letters via e-mail (or by fax) to the other party's solicitors during the course of the transaction. Although the principals of the letters are then sent by post, DX or Legal Post, the parties had come to regard the missies as 'concluded' on the date on which they were signed and faxed or e-mailed. Where conclusion of the missives and completion were simultaneous or occurred close together, it would not be unusual for completion to take place and funds be transferred on the strength of faxed or e-mailed missives, particularly, apparently, in residential transactions.

This practice came into sharp relief, of course, following on the decision in the case of *Thomas Park and Another, Petitioners*[29], which concerned a petition for partial recall of an inhibition, to release from the ambit of the inhibition the petitioners' leasehold interest in the Grapevine Restaurant in Bothwell. The basis for the recall was that, before the inhibition was effective, missives had been concluded for the sale of the business and property.

It was agreed that the effective date of the inhibition was midnight on 31 August 2007, but earlier on that day, in response to an offer to purchase the lease of the property that had been made in early August, the petitioners' solicitors had sent a fax with a signed qualified acceptance to the purchaser's solicitors, who faxed back a full acceptance, that same day. Both formal letters were then put in the post.

The point at issue was whether missives had effectively been concluded on 31 August. In support of their contention that they had, the petitioners sought to rely on the postal acceptance rule, and also on some case law that indicated that communication by fax would be sufficient to constitute a contract. The postal acceptance rule provides that, while an offer is effective only when it is received, an acceptance is effective from the date of posting (*Thomson v James*[30]). This, however, assumes

---

29 [2009] CSOH 122.
30 [1855] 18 D 1.

that the acceptance is a clear and complete acceptance of the offer, not a qualified acceptance setting out new terms. In *Park*, the judge decided that the inhibition did attach to the property, as actual delivery is necessary for offers and qualified acceptances: although the letter concluding the contract was posted on 31 August, the qualified acceptance, or counter offer to which it referred, had not been delivered, and so the contract could not be regarded as concluded until that acceptance actually arrived.

The decision in *Park* caused considerable tremors in conveyancing practice. *Obiter* references in the case to the possibility of 'constructive delivery' set off the practice of giving undertakings not to withdraw a formal letter delivered electronically (by fax or e-mail) and irrevocably undertaking to put it in the post.

There are, however, doubts that 'constructive delivery' of missives letters is possible. Given that the remarks made in *Park* were *obiter* and did not form part of the *ratio* or actual decision of the judge, it seems that while the undertakings that are given by solicitors in these cases, although forming a binding obligation on the solicitor to do what is stated in the undertaking, do not necessarily have the effect of rendering the missives letters themselves binding and enforceable. The timing of delivery issue may not be crucial, in the way that it was in *Park*, but there could be circumstances (eg a need to conclude a contract before the end of the financial year to benefit from a tax break) when the certainty of actual delivery is vital and the prudent course of action is to ensure physical delivery of the letters.

Is that really good enough in the context of twenty-first century dealings? There are few, if any, who would say it is. Two legislative arrangements have now transformed the law in this area.

2.9.1 E-conveyancing

Part 10 of the Land Registration etc. (Scotland) Act 2012 amended the Requirements of Writing (Scotland) Act 1995 to permit electronic documents (ie documents which are not written on paper, parchment or some other tangible surface, but are instead created in electronic form) to be executed electronically; provided the method of electronic execution complies with new validity and authentication requirements in the 1995 Act, it will be valid and binding. Word and Adobe documents in their electronic, as opposed to hard copy form, are types of electronic document.

Electronic execution of an electronic document requires a digital (or electronic) signature. To a certain extent these terms are interchangeable (or at least in ordinary language, we tend to mean the same thing), although the Law Society distinguishes between the two terms in its guidance on the use of Smartcards (which are being supplied to Scottish solicitors during 2015).

The 2012 Act introduces a new Part 3 – Electronic Documents section to the 1995 Act. New sections 9B and 9C are concerned with validity, and presumption of authentication of electronically signed documents. For a detailed consideration of electronic execution of documents see para 11.2.

2.9.2 E-delivery

If using electronic signatures makes you nervous, then another option is now available. Section 4 of the Legal Writings (Counterparts and Delivery) Act 2015 provides that contracts consisting of traditional paper documents and signed with a 'wet signature' (ie using ink) can be effectively delivered by sending the document electronically, eg a PDF of it by e-mail. This remarkable little section has transformed previous hopeful, and possibly blissfully ignorant, practice into something that now has real legal effect (you're welcome).

Delivery is achieved by sending electronically a copy of the document, or a part of such a copy. The need to only send a part of the document electronically for effective delivery is quite ground-breaking. It is essential that the part must be sufficient in all the circumstances to show that it is part of the document in question, and be, or include, the page on which the subscriber has signed the document.

Delivery in this way will invariably be by way of e-mail or fax, although it can be by other electronic means, and in a form which the recipient has agreed to accept. If no accepted method has been agreed, or if there is uncertainty about the accepted method, or the accepted method is impracticable in some way, then delivery may be by such means (and in such form) as is reasonable in all the circumstances.

Although electronic delivery will constitute effective delivery of a traditional document, what is received by that means is not to be treated as being the traditional document itself. That is also an important point to remember. So if it is necessary to register the deed following delivery, for example, then the original signed deed will be required. In reality, solicitors will want the principal of a deed to be delivered at settlement, so that they can immediately submit it for registration, rather than wait for the original to arrive, possibly some days later in the post. It is not, therefore, recommended that electronic delivery of deeds that require to be registered should be regarded as a substitute for the real thing at settlement.

What this provision does mean is that missives, or parts of them (particularly offers and qualified acceptances) will be effectively delivered and be binding on electronic delivery. The 2015 Act does not consider whether the point of delivery is the sending of the document by the sender, or the receipt by the recipient of the document in their system. Might analogies with what constitutes effective delivery of a traditional document provide some help? It is clear that 'a writing, while it is in the granter's own custody, is not obligatory; for as long as it is in his own power, he cannot be said to have come to a final resolution of obliging himself by it'[31].

Consequently, there must be sufficient 'delivery' of the writing to the grantee to put the document beyond the granter's control. Arguably, pressing the 'send' button on an e-mail to which the document is attached could be said to be such an act, although e-mail does provide a facility to recall an e-mail that has been 'sent'. What the effect of such recall would be on electronic delivery, when the e-mail had already reached the system of the recipient is somewhat unclear.

However, the essential requirement for delivery to have taken place is whether or not the granter of the document has deliberately put the document beyond his further control with the intention of becoming bound by it. So, where a document is physically transferred from one party to another without the intention to deliver to that party, there is no delivery. 'Holding as undelivered' depends on this, of course.

Perhaps the European Draft Common Frame of Reference (DCFR), which the Scottish Law Commission describes as 'in general the yardstick against which we are measuring the Scots law of contract...' provides

---

31 Erskine Institute III,ii, 43.

some clarification? The DCFR describes an obligatory document as a 'juridical act', ie a statement intended to have legal effect as such, which is communicated as a notice to the other party and 'becomes effective' when it 'reaches' that party. 'Reaching' is constituted by delivery to the other party in person, or to that party's place of business or habitual residence. If we can, therefore, extrapolate from that, that electronic delivery is achieved when it reaches the recipient, then arrival in the inbox or other system of the recipient would be the equivalent. This hypothesis is tentatively presented, as of course there is not yet any case law to support it. In practical terms, a receiving solicitor will wait for the e-mail or fax to arrive anyway, before advising a client that 'the bargain has been concluded'.

What is to happen to the original traditional document is up to the parties to decide between or among themselves. It should be held by the sender in accordance with whatever arrangements have been made by the sender and the recipient (or recipients as a group). For best evidence purposes, delivery of the principal missives should follow electronic delivery.

In making electronic delivery of traditional contractual and other documents legally binding, the 2015 Act is really an innovative and ground-breaking provision which will, at a stroke, both dispense with an antiquated procedure, not to mention uncertainty, and modernise and make more effective Scottish practice. Both commercial and residential conveyancing practice, in particular, will see enormous benefits. Not only is this new enablement consistent with the Scottish Government's digital strategy, it will also provide greater clarity and certainty for parties transacting in Scotland.

It fills the gap in procedure that was not addressed by Part 10 of the 2012 Act, which enables electronic delivery of electronic documents, but not of traditional ones. The vast majority of legal documents are still created in traditional format, and executed traditionally. The 2015 Act brings these types of document on a par with their electronic equivalents, and provides significant efficiencies and cost savings to current commercial and domestic legal practice in Scotland.

Chapter 3

New Clients and New Instructions

NEW CLIENTS AND ANTI-MONEY LAUNDERING

3.1 However tempting it may be to start work on a new client matter immediately to show your (prospective) new client how efficient you are, that temptation must be resisted. There are important prospective client due diligence procedural hurdles that have to be cleared first.

An established solicitors' office will already have robust procedures for client clearance and you should always follow these to the letter. Of these procedures by far and away the most significant is the anti-money laundering check for a client. Nothing should be done and no money accepted until this is completed.

This is a super-important legal requirement that, once explained to the client, they should understand. Sophisticated clients will be used to this kind of due diligence, which is also required for banking and financial services. Do not allow yourself to be persuaded by the prospective client. In fact, be extra suspicious of those prospective clients who do try to persuade you to act for them before you are ready. Conveyancing is deemed to be high risk by the **Serious Organised Crimes Agency (SOCA)** so you must always be on your guard.

On no account should you disclose any of the firm's bank account details in advance of clearance, in case the prospective client deposits 'dirty' money in your firm's account without your knowledge. If this should happen and then has to be returned to the client before you have completed your checks, this money is 'clean' because it has been 'laundered' by your firm and the full weight of the criminal law will bear down on you.

THE ANTI-MONEY LAUNDERING REGIME

3.2 The Money Laundering Regulations 2007 are the main instruments of the anti-money laundering regime. There are four key requirements under the Regulations, namely to:

- Verify the identity of the prospective client on the basis of documents, data or information obtained from an independent, credible source before carrying out any occasional transactions or establishing a business relationship;

- Understand the ownership and control structure of a legal person, trust or similar arrangement. Where there is a 'beneficial' owner under a trust or other arrangement, you should be satisfied as to the beneficial owner's identity as well as any trustees;

- Know your clients' business and obtain information on the nature and purpose of the intended business relationship; and

- Maintain vigilance through monitoring of the client and the transaction, being alert to any changes in behaviour during the course of the transaction.

3.2.1 Verification

There are many types of independently issued documentation that can verify the prospective client's identity, and the prospective client will normally provide evidence such as original passports, driving licences etc. For companies and other legal persons, you can also check details electronically or obtain information from other bodies such as Companies House.

For a private individual, the 2007 Regulations require at least two of the following original documents, one from each section, as proof of identity of an individual:

Section 1	*Section 2*
Full national passport	Gas, electricity or telephone bill, dated within the last three months
Full national driving licence with photograph	Mortgage statement, dated within last three months
Armed Forces ID card	Council Tax bill, dated within last three months
National ID card	Bank/Building Society/Credit Card statement
Signed photographic ID card of reputable employer	Copy of telephone entry from online directory enquiries

Section 1	Section 2
Reference from a partner of the firm stating that they have known the prospective client in a non-business context for at least five years	Visit to prospective client's home address

Two hard copies (preferably in colour for photographs) of the evidence should made in all cases: one for the firm's **Money Laundering Reporting Officer (MLRO)** and one to be retained in your file.

If a client cannot satisfy you as to the nature of the business and their identity, you should decline to act. You are not obliged to take on any particular client or piece of business. If in doubt, err on the side of caution.

You should complete a checklist for your file – usually completion of such a checklist will be a prerequisite of opening a new file for the prospective client.

VERIFICATION OF CLIENT IDENTITY CHECKLIST

FOR CLIENT

Name:_____

    A.   **Evidence not obtained – reasons:**

        1.   Client previously identified in Month…............. Year......

        2.   Client identified personally by – Name _____

                                                Position _____

        3.   Other – state reason fully_____

        _____

    B.   **Evidence obtained to verify name and address**

        Full National Passport   –

        Full National Driving Licence   –

        Pension Book   –

        Armed Forces ID Card   –

        Signed ID Card of employer known to you   –

        Young person NI card (under 18 only)   –

        Pensioner's travel pass   –

        Building Society passbook   –

        Credit Reference agency search   –

National ID Card   –
Copy Company Certificate of Incorporation   –
Gas, electricity, telephone bill   –
Mortgage statement   –
Council tax demand   –
Bank/Building Society/credit card statement   –
Young persons medical card (under 18 only)   –
Home visit to applicants address*   –
Check of telephone directory*   –
Check voters roll*   –
Suitable for proof of address only

C. **Evidence for unquoted company or partnership**
Certificate of Incorporation or equivalent   –
Certificate of Trade or equivalent   –
Latest report and audited accounts   –
Principal shareholder/partner   –
Principal director   –

I confirm that:

(a) I have seen the originals of the documents indicated above and have identified the above Customer(s), or

(b) In accordance with the Regulations, evidence is not required for the reasons stated.

Signed_____**Date**_____

Solicitors' firms are permitted to take a risk based approach to anti-money laundering. This means that firms will carry out enhanced due diligence where the prospective client has a higher risk profile, and reduced due diligence where the risk profile is lower than normal, such as acting for a clearing bank or local authority.

As the first line of defence, it falls to the individual conveyancers to determine whether the prospective client is in a higher or lower risk category. You need to be satisfied, therefore, that the documentary evidence provided by the prospective client is satisfactory for the purposes of identification. If there is a trust or other structure, you have to be sure that you understand the nature of the structure and can identify the beneficial owner. It's an important responsibility and you can't rely on others in the firm or the MLRO to carry out all the diligence for you. You are the one in direct contact with the prospective client and you need to be vigilant and alert to any aspects of the instructions which could affect the risk profile.

3.2.2 The 'Smell Test'

As the eyes and ears of the firm, you should have a feeling about a prospective client and whether they are being honest or evasive. The following 'smell test' provided by HM Treasury illustrates some of the questions you might ask yourself about the behaviour of the prospective client:

- Has there been any reluctance on behalf of the client to provide adequate ID?

    A common theme amongst money laundering problems is endless promises to provide ID, which is then produced at the last minute and given little or no scrutiny.

- Why has the client advised at a late stage that a third party will become involved in the transaction/provide the funds?

    Both of these should be a concern.

- Does the client appear to have a deep understanding of the money laundering regulations?

    This is beginning to appear as a concern, on the simple principle that some criminals are very good at being criminals.

- Is the client proposing a transaction that is unnecessarily complicated?

    The stock explanation for complexity is that it is for 'tax reasons'. Ask to see the tax advice upon which the whole proposal is based.

- Why have I been chosen for instructions on this particular matter?

    Another common thread with money laundering problem cases is a solicitor being engaged to do work outwith their normal sphere of expertise. Do not be flattered but consider the money laundering implications and also issues of general risk management.

- Why is a client so disinterested in the proposed level of fee?

    If a significant sum of money is being laundered, criminals tend to regard fees as irrelevant.

3.2.3 Suspicion of money laundering

Section 328 of the Proceeds of Crime Act 2002 (**POCA**) creates the offence. It says that 'a person commits an offence if he enters into or becomes concerned in an arrangement which he knows or suspects facilitates (by whatever means) the acquisition, retention, use or control of criminal property by or on behalf another person'. This is clearly dangerous for a law firm which could unwittingly become concerned in such an arrangement by holding 'dirty' funds.

The question of what suspicion means in this context has occurred in a number of cases. In the case of *Shah v HSBC Private Bank (UK) Ltd*[1], a bank customer (Mr Shah) suffered considerable penalties because the bank delayed remitting his funds due to the suspicion of illegal activity. Mr Shah sought substantial damages from the bank. (Letters of engagement are considered below, but you should be aware that the Law Society 'strongly' recommends the use of robust clauses in letters of engagement to limit compensation payable in the case of disruption or delay caused by anti money laundering procedures.)

The court confirmed the test of suspicion as set out in the cases of *R v Da Silva*[2] and *K Ltd v National Westminster Bank plc*[3]. For the purposes of section 328 of POCA, a suspicion does not have to be firmly grounded and targeted on specific facts or on reasonable grounds, it just has to be 'more than fanciful'.

The key point to remember, however, is that the suspicion must be that *the person is engaging in money laundering*. It is not sufficient simply to suspect that the client is 'dodgy', poses a reputational risk to the firm, or that the transaction seems somehow 'fishy'.

3.2.4 What to do if you are suspicious

If you realise something is not right during the course of the transaction, you should raise your concern in writing (including e-mail) with your firm's MLRO. This effectively passes responsibility for reporting to your MLRO and it is now their responsibility to make a decision on whether

1   [2009] EWHC 79 (QB).
2   [2006] EWCA Crim 1654.
3   [2006] EWCA Civ 1039.

to make a Suspicious Activity Report (SAR) to SOCA and to inform you how to proceed.

Section 328(2) of POCA provides protection for solicitors in relation to money laundering offences. It says that an offence is not committed if the person makes a SAR, or intended to make a SAR but has reasonable excuse for not doing so, or if the act is done in carrying out enforcement of POCA or any other similar Act.

The case of *R v Anwoir*[4], shows that there are two ways you may form a suspicion of existing criminal property:

- If you know or suspect that a specific type of criminal conduct, such as fraud, tax evasion, drug trafficking, is occurring and you suspect such conduct has generated property.

- If there are such a cluster of warning signs which cannot be satisfactorily explained so that the manner in which you are asked to handle the funds gives rise to an irresistible inference that the funds must be criminal in origin.

If the problem arises at the last possible moment, remember that professional money launderers often engineer this situation to put you under pressure. However, you must think rationally, and do not put yourself or your firm in jeopardy out of misplaced loyalty to the client. If you have good grounds for suspicion, alert the MLRO as early as possible. If a transaction fails to settle on schedule despite heavy contractual penalties, it is likely to be due to failure on the client's part to comply with the Money Laundering Regulations. It may even lead to a complaint or claim but if you have good grounds for suspicion of money laundering the firm will support you. In any event, a complaint is preferable to an accusation of criminal conduct.

3.2.5 'Tipping off'

If you do have reasonable grounds to suspect that your prospective client is engaged in money laundering and you have reported it to the MLRO, generally speaking, you cannot 'tip off' the client or any other third party. In terms of section 333A of POCA it would be an offence to disclose

---

4   [2008] EWCA Crim 1354.

to a third party that a SAR has been made or that an investigation is contemplated or being carried out, if that disclosure is likely to prejudice the investigation. This offence can only be committed after the SAR has been made, but it is good practice that the 'shutters should come down' on the transaction as soon as the MLRO is alerted.

Although this will potentially result in awkwardness in dealing with your client, it is better to dodge calls and risk a complaint than prejudice the investigation. Sections 333B and C permit disclosures from a lawyer to another lawyer within the same firm or in a different (European) firm and this would avoid the frustration and confusion that the other side would experience when the otherwise smooth transaction suddenly stalls for no apparent reason.

TAKING INSTRUCTIONS

3.3 Whether you are taking instructions over the telephone or in person, be very meticulous in noting all the details. Although overly 'defensive lawyering' is not generally good practice, remember you may be called to produce evidence to support your actions or omissions some years later. There have been a number of professional negligence cases in the Court of Session where a file note has saved the day for the lawyer.

It is good practice to prepare for the initial meeting or call, so that you have all the bases covered. The Property Law Committee of the Law Society avoid pronouncements of best practice, which could rebound on solicitors, so how you record these instructions is up to you or your firm's practice. You may use a pro forma instruction form with a checklist, a file note or make your own notes. Marsh, the Law Society's Master Policy insurer suggests that it is good practice to use a checklist.

It is not uncommon these days to communicate with clients by e-mail. This is an excellent medium for recording instructions, since there will be evidence of the e-mail having been sent to the client and generally speaking, even if the e-mail has been accidentally deleted from the solicitor's own computer, it should have been backed up on a server and can therefore be recovered relatively easily by those who know about these things.

Instructions will change according to circumstances. If you are talking to your client on the telephone or in person, at the end of the conversation, you should sum up your understanding of the position, the action points arising and any new instructions. Then confirm these points by sending the client a letter or an e-mail to recap the discussion and the instructions. E-mail may be preferable, simply because it is more immediate.

In the initial conference, you should glean some basic information from the purchasers. You clearly need to know all about your clients. You should note their full names, contact details, dates of birth and marital status. If a company, you need to understand who is authorised to give you instructions, the ownership of the company and where the company fits into any group structure.

If your clients are married, consider whether they will own the property jointly and also whether they require a survivorship destination. A survivorship destination is a clause in the title that will vest the survivor of the couple in the half share of the property belonging to the deceased automatically, without needing a will or executors. Many law firms advise against survivorship destinations in the strongest terms because of the difficulty in getting out of (or 'evacuating') them (but see para 9.5 for a detailed consideration of this issue).

If the purchasers are not married, you may also want to advise on the pitfalls of a joint purchase. It would certainly be in the purchasers' interests to set out the ground rules of their cohabitation in a minute of agreement to avoid or settle disputes at a later stage. If the purchasers are buying other than equal shares, you should make a careful note of the proportions to be reflected in the title at a later stage in the process.

You need to discuss the price, date of entry and any suspensive conditions (sometimes called 'conditions precedent') that need to be fulfilled before the deal will be binding.

Avoid being drawn into areas that are not within your expertise, such as how much the purchaser should offer. By all means provide some market data to help inform the purchaser but do not cross the line between advising and taking instructions (which is encouraged) and taking decisions (which oversteps the mark).

Use your expertise to guide the purchaser. If the address is, for example, 'Artillery Lane', you might want to flag up the possibility of a former use that could cause potential contamination and advise that the property be referred for further investigation as part of the initial due diligence.

CONFLICTS OF INTEREST

3.4 The principle of conflict of interests is laid out in Rule B2 of the Practice Rules (the **'Conflict of Interest Rules'**). The Conflict of Interest Rules state simply enough that a solicitor must not act for two or more parties whose interests conflict. As usual, the devil is in the detail. What is meant by a conflict? The Law Society's guidance note suggests (somewhat unhelpfully for newer solicitors) that it is hard to define but that 'you know it when you see it'. Or perhaps not – the guidance note also refers to the concern expressed by the Discipline Tribunal in their Annual Reports about continuing failure of solicitors to recognise conflicts of interest.

The Law Society advises that there will be a conflict of interest if you find yourself agreeing with any of the three following statements:

(1)   You would give different advice to different clients about the same matter;

(2)   Your actings on behalf of one client would have an adverse impact on a matter you are dealing with for another client, even when the matters are unrelated.

(3)   You are unable to disclose relevant information to one client because of a duty of confidentiality to another client.

The term 'solicitor' is broadly defined in the Conflict of Interest Rules so as to apply to firms of solicitors rather than just individuals.

The Conflict of Interest Rules set out some broad exceptions from the general principle:

- Associated Companies (in the same group) or public bodies;
- Connected Bodies within the meaning of section 839 of the Income and Corporations Taxes Act 1988;
- Parties related by blood, adoption or marriage;
- Established client – a client for whom a solicitor or his firm has acted on at least one previous occasion; and
- Where there is no other solicitor in the vicinity who the client could reasonably be expected to consult.

The Conflict of Interest Rules also deal with the same solicitor acting for borrower and lender. It is permitted to act for both the borrower and the lender (in residential transactions, and for commercial loans of under

£250,000), but the terms of the loan must have been agreed between the parties before the solicitor has been instructed by the lender and the granting of the security must only be to give effect to such agreement. You must always remember that, in these circumstances, the lender is also a client.

LETTER OF ENGAGEMENT AND FEES

3.5 Following the initial contact with the client, a terms of business letter and/or letter of engagement outlining the terms of the professional relationship should be sent to the client as soon as possible. The Letter of Engagement is usually a customised letter to the client, which outlines the details of the work undertaken, the day-to-day contact and the responsible partner and details of the proposed fee. This is usually a summary of the initial discussion where these matters are discussed. It can include the detailed terms of business but it is common for firms to have a separate Terms of Business Letter as a standard letter containing the 'small print'. It extends to around five or six pages (depending on the size of the print).

It is not usual to expect a reply or acknowledgement of the Letter of Engagement and the Terms of Business Letter – silence implies consent.

Style of a basic Letter of Engagement approved by the Law Society, as reported in the Journal (November 2003)

Dear [Name]

We refer to your recent meeting with [Name]

We are pleased to confirm that [the Firm] will be acting on your behalf in connection with [work to be carried out].

The solicitor who will be dealing with your work on a day to day basis is [Name].

We will advise you at regular intervals regarding the progress of your work and keep you informed of all significant developments. If you are uncertain about what is happening at any time, please ask.

We enclose an Estimate of our Fees and Outlays for this transaction. If the work turns out to be more complex than normal, we may require to increase our estimate to take account of this. We will inform you as soon as possible about any such increase.

The Money Laundering Regulations require us to be satisfied as to the identity of our clients and as to the source of any funds passing through our hands. In order to comply with these Regulations, we may need to ask you for proof of identity and other information in relation to these matters. We reserve the right to withdraw from acting for you if you fail to provide us with the information requested of you and required in connection with our Anti-Money Laundering Procedures.

Finally, our aim is to provide a service which is satisfactory in every respect. However, if you have any concerns about the manner in which work is being carried out on your behalf, please contact our Client Relations Partner [Name] who will be happy to discuss your concerns.

Yours faithfully,

[Name]

This letter should clearly outline the following:

1   The source of authorisation of the solicitor – the Law Society of Scotland.

2   The work to be carried out by the solicitor.

3   Method by which instructions should be given and received and any other aspects of communication, such as setting out the firm's normal office hours.

4   The requirement to identify for Anti-Money Laundering purposes the client's identity and that of directors, partners, trustees, controllers of companies or firms and all of the connected shareholders. You should also notify the client that in some circumstances otherwise confidential information is required to be shared with authorities by law without their permission and that the firm will cease acting until clearance is received from those authorities.

5   Authority of the client to instruct (eg who is the authorised person if the client is a company or a partnership, husband/wife or other multiple clients.)

6   The fees and outgoings to be charged or the basis on which they are to be charged (including VAT).

7   Supervision of client business (ie name and status of person responsible for day-to-day conduct of matter and principal responsible for overall supervision if different).

8   Conflict of interest policy.

9   Requirement of confidentiality.

10   Procedures for resolving problems, including the identity of the person to whom the client should refer in the event of there being any dissatisfaction in relation to the work.

The following matters would normally be included in addition to those listed above:

1   Holding client money in a separate clients' account and the notification of rates of interest and where the rate will be displayed.

2   Timing of payment of fees and outlays, late payment provisions and the ability to pay fees and outlays from funds held on the client's behalf.

3   Timescale of the proposed transaction in general.

4   Provisions for the termination of the engagement.

5   Governing law – law of Scotland.

6   Any areas of advice that are specifically excluded. It cannot be assumed that it is implicitly understood by the client that although you are acting in a conveyancing matter, you will not be advising on, for example, taxation or environmental aspects – you should expressly exclude these in your letter of engagement.

In addition, it is good practice for the following matters also to be included:

1   Indemnity/liability for loss.

2   Client's right to taxation (independent audit of fee).

3   Document retention policy and any charges for storing deeds and documents.

4   Lien (claim in security) over titles and papers.

5   Level of service to be provided.

Chapter 4

The Seller's Preparations

READINESS FOR SALE

4.1 The key to a smooth conveyancing transaction from the seller's point of view, and that of his solicitor, is preparation. Most residential sale and purchase transactions start with the property owner deciding to put their property up for sale, although it is not unknown for the purchaser to initiate the process. The seller will usually market the property through estate agents, their solicitors or other agents. There are many firms of solicitors, particularly in the central belt, who carry out a large volume of residential property marketing, largely due to the success of solicitors' property centres (SPCs). It should be made quite clear, however, that property marketing has become a separate skill; if a solicitor is to market property it must be done professionally and properly. As we have seen (para 1.2) the marketing process is not part of the solicitors' monopoly, and may be done by anyone. The choice between a solicitor and an estate agent is for the property owner to make. To a large extent the decision will depend on the services offered, and the part of the country in which the property is situated.

Conversely, solicitors are unlikely to be involved in the marketing of commercial property, unless it is to check some aspect of the draft sales particulars, such as the terms of a right of access or confirming that the plan conforms to the title extent. Marketing will usually be conducted through commercial estate agents or firms of Chartered Surveyors, who will have considerable expertise in marketing the types of property being offered for sale. Some solicitors' firms with a large estate agency practice might also market the odd small commercial property, such as a shop, from time to time.

Where the seller's solicitor can assist the process is to assemble all of the necessary due diligence items, or to identify items that will need to be ordered when a purchaser emerges. This means that the title examination element of the transaction and the inspection of reports and certificates can be conducted speedily and comprehensively, avoiding a back and forth exchange of communications seeking further items of information that the purchaser's solicitors need to complete their investigations.

The seller should be encouraged to contact their solicitor at the earliest opportunity, so that preparations can be made in good time. Obviously there is nothing the solicitor can do to be organised in advance if the first intimation she receives of a sale is when an offer hits her desk, or arrives in her inbox, requiring urgent attention. Clients who sell property regularly can be encouraged to alert their solicitor in good time. Usually estate agents or surveyors will ask who the seller's solicitor is and then contact them directly; they will want to put the relevant details of the seller's solicitor onto the sales particulars.

THE HOME REPORT

4.2 Until recently, it would be fair to say that the practice of conveyancing in Scotland has evolved gradually and does not normally seek (or respond well to) radical change. From time to time, however, significant changes have taken place. The early part of this century has been such a time. Since the re-establishment of the Scottish Parliament, property land tenure and land registration has received what may seem to be more than a fair share of transformational legislation in the form of the Abolition of Feudal Tenure etc (Scotland) Act 2000, the Title Conditions (Scotland) Act 2004, the Tenements (Scotland) Act 2004 and now the Land Registration etc. (Scotland) Act 2012.

Of course, that list is far from exhaustive. The Housing (Scotland) Act 2006 introduced a revolutionary new arrangement for residential properties in the form of the Home Report. Following on the heels of, and similar in a number of respects to its ill-starred English cousin, the Home Information Pack (HIP), the Home Report became compulsory in Scotland from 1 December 2008. It must be said the Home Report was introduced in the teeth of fierce opposition from the legal profession. The requirement for a Home Report fundamentally changed the way that a purchaser of residential property receives information on the condition of a residential property. Since that date, the vast majority of homes for sale have to be marketed with a Home Report (the narrow band of exceptions is described below). Ironically, the HIP has been abandoned, described as expensive and unnecessary. The Home Report prevails and, at the time of writing, there are no plans to scrap it.

The Home Report is the collective name for documentary information to help prospective purchasers make an informed decision about a property. It includes:

(i)   a Single Survey Report by the seller's choice of surveyor detailing the condition of the property, accessibility for disabled people and a valuation;

(ii)   an Energy Report, which consists of an Energy Performance Certificate (EPC), also compiled by the surveyor, detailing the house's grade of energy efficiency, including recommendations for improvement. The EPC is not a home-grown initiative, but implements a European Union Directive on energy efficiency; and

(iii) a Property Questionnaire, in which the seller discloses some (quite a lot. actually, if properly completed) information about the property in very general terms, such as their knowledge of services, septic tanks, common parts, replacement windows, the existence of any guarantees or notices, and the council tax banding for the property etc. This should be completed as fully as possible, but there may be gaps if the seller does not have knowledge of the information sought, for example if they have not lived at the property for very long or if the sale is being instructed by an executor, who has never lived at the property.

A Home Report is required even if the property is being marketed privately by the seller himself, or if the house is being sold at auction. A Home Report is not required for a private deal off the market (although an EPC will still be required), new build houses being sold for the first time, or for newly converted homes. A secure tenant purchasing his home under 'right to buy' legislation is not entitled to a Home Report. Also exempt from the requirement are mixed sales where a house is sold along with, or forms a part of, a non-residential property. Seasonal and holiday accommodation (but not holiday homes) do not require a Home Report. Sales of a portfolio of residential properties are considered to be commercial transactions and, as such, are exempt. Homes that are to be demolished, or are in such a state of disrepair that they are unfit for habitation, do not need a Home

Report (clearly there would be little point in obtaining either a survey or an energy report in such circumstances).

The penalty for not having a Home Report, once a property is put on the market, is £500[1]. This is a heavy penalty, so clearly the obtaining of a Home Report is a priority matter.

The Home Report should be instructed as soon as instructions are received to put the property on the market. The timing is important however, as a property must not be put on the market with a Home Report that is more than 12 weeks old, although it is possible to take the property off the market for up to four weeks without having to obtain a new Home Report. A survey commissioned at the outset of the marketing campaign will obviously date in a slow market. There is no need for a seller to refresh a Home Report after 12 weeks, if the property has not been sold.

The purchaser's lender may require the survey to be refreshed before it will accept it. This means that the surveyor is asked to confirm that the original terms of the survey, in particular the valuation, are still good (or not – and if not, an amended valuation given). It is a matter for negotiation who pays for that refresh (which will normally be significantly less than the cost of the original survey). In a buyers' market, it is likely that the seller will be expected to meet the cost.

From a practical point of view, the estate agent, surveyor, or solicitor will normally organise the single survey and EPC inspection to coincide with the visit to measure up the property and take details (and photographs) for the sales brochure. Most SPCs offer a service through which the solicitor can commission a Home Report online, although they can also be – and often are – instructed in a more traditional way.

At the same time, the seller should be asked to fill out the Property Questionnaire, giving as much information as possible. In some cases, the seller will simply be asked to complete this as far as possible and return it to the agent. Some solicitors or agents will help clients to complete the form, while others prefer, for a number of reasons, to leave it to the seller. It can be a time-consuming process, which places an additional burden on the solicitor or agent. If they are involved, they must also be concerned about being liable for any mistakes or misleading information that it contains. That said, the more detailed and accurate the information in the Property

1 Housing (Scotland) Act (Amount of Penalty Charge) Regulations 2007.

Questionnaire, the less time the solicitor may need to spend dealing with queries and requests for information from prospective purchasers or their solicitors during the marketing or the sale transaction.

Once the property has been put on the market, the seller or his agents must provide a copy of the Home Report to a prospective purchaser within nine days of receiving a request; they may make a reasonable charge to cover the costs of copying and postage, although in practice this does not usually happen. Most properties for sale will appear on the website of their selling agents, the relevant SPC or on another website such as RightMove or Zoopla. The Home Report will usually be available through the particulars on the websites, as well as by request by phone or e-mail. It is a good idea to make the Home Report readily available (ie not expect to charge for it), subject, perhaps, to taking some contact details for the person enquiring. It is good property marketing practice to keep a log of people expressing some interest in the property so that it can be followed up later (eg if a closing date is fixed) or to obtain feedback on what they thought about the property, which can be useful for the seller to know. This is best done by requiring people to provide an e-mail address to access the Home Report.

MARKETING A RESIDENTIAL PROPERTY

4.3 If your clients are going to employ an estate agent, they should carefully consider the wording of the contract. They may consult their solicitor about this, although the seller will usually have already engaged an estate agent by the time they get in touch with their solicitor. The estate agents will seek sole selling rights, that is: they are entitled to commission if the property is sold during the agreed period, whoever finds the buyer—even if it is the clients themselves. As to commission, the law is quite clear on the subject: if the estate agent is instrumental in the sale of the house, the agent is entitled to claim commission at the standard rate (*Walker Fraser & Steele v Fraser's Trustees*[2]). In practice, these days, terms and conditions are set out in detail in the terms of engagement.

In particular, the clients should not be panicked into employing two agencies. The dangers of this arrangement were highlighted in an

---

2 [1910] SC 222.

unreported case in Paisley Sheriff Court: Mr and Mrs A decided to sell their house, and asked estate agents F to handle the sale. F duly advertised the sale, and several parties, including a Mr Q, inspected the property. No sale resulted. Mr and Mrs A then saw a property advertised by estate agents Z; while negotiating with Z, they decided to entrust the sale of their own house to Z. They signed Z's standard sale contract, which required a commission to be paid on sale, whether or not they were instrumental in effecting a sale.

In the meantime, Mr Q returned from abroad, looked again at Mr and Mrs A's house, and bought it. Agents F claimed a commission as they had introduced Mr Q to the sellers. Agents Z also claimed a commission in terms of their contract, which granted them a sole selling agency. It was held that Mr and Mrs A had to pay both agents. (See also *Lordsgate Properties v Balcombe*[3]).

Marketing a property requires particular skills; many of the firms who undertake significant volumes of property marketing employ staff to perform this role exclusively. Presentation is all important, so good quality photographs and brochures and clear appealing descriptions are essential. Particulars of the property now appear on the internet, and most prospective purchasers will pre-view the property by accessing those details. Armed with as much knowledge as possible, the solicitors who are marketing the property through their own firm will prepare property details and instruct advertising.

The solicitor who engages in selling houses will adopt a procedure broadly similar to that outlined here, although practice will obviously vary from firm to firm.

4.3.1 Visit the house in question, and take measurements and details

Take photographs of the exterior and several interior shots. The dimensions of rooms are taken, so that prospective purchasers can have an indication of the size of the property. Measurements should be accurately given in metres. A lot of people, however, still think in imperial measurement, and subsidiary measurements in feet and inches, are often provided. The

3   [1985] 1 EGLR 20, (1985) 274 EG 493.

conversion should, however, be made accurately, as they can sometimes be relied on for ordering carpets and working out areas. Viewing arrangements should be discussed – the easiest arrangement is to have the owners show the property at times that suit them. If the house is empty, the solicitor can arrange to show it, but the amount of remuneration sought for this service may be more. Some firms retain the services of retired persons who will conduct viewings on their behalf. It is advisable that, wherever possible, two people conduct the viewings; no representative of your firm should be alone in an empty house. Keep careful control of keys.

4.3.2 Basic rules to make the property more attractive to buyers

The seller should try to make the house and garden appear attractive from the street; attend to essential repairs; don't spend money on expensive redecoration which may not be to potential buyers' tastes, but a fresh coat of paint in a neutral colour can assist with the all-important first impression; keep the house clean and tidy and as attractive as possible from the outside – so-called 'kerb appeal'; avoid cooking and other smells – even freshly ground coffee, which, contrary to popular belief, some viewers may not like; make sure that there is a parking space for buyers' cars if at all possible; be ready to show the house at short notice. While furnishing, decor and personal items are usually insignificant compared to structure and location, clearing clutter will make a good first impression on potential buyers.

4.3.3 Evaluation and asking price

The single survey that forms part of the Home Report will provide a market valuation of the property. Solicitors who market properties regularly will have knowledge of the current market and be able to advise sellers on a suitable asking price for the property, although if it does not sell quickly this can be revised at any time. The SPC will provide details of recently achieved sale prices from their proprietary database, or this information can be found on Registers Direct. The SPC information is more up to date, as solicitors provide data once an offer has been accepted. Data provided by the Keeper is based on registration. The Keeper offers a service that provides a free house price search[4]. Also, many other websites conduct property price comparisons which can be checked.

Selling techniques have to be adjusted to suit market conditions, and in a slow market 'fixed price' asking prices are more popular than 'offers over' an upset price, usually pegged below the Home Report valuation.

The idea of a fixed-price offer is that the first offer of the price fixed by the seller is usually accepted. However, the Law Society guidance on fixed-price offers is that a property advertised at a fixed price is an invitation to submit an offer at that price, but does not imply any obligation on the part of the solicitor that the first offer at that price will be accepted (see *Pharmaceutical Society of Great Britain v Boots Cash Chemists (Southern) Ltd*[5] – the advertisement is only an offer to treat, the bargain must be concluded by written offer and acceptance, as is the rule with heritable property generally). A fixed price offer that is stated to be subject to the purchaser's own property being sold for example would probably be unacceptable to a seller, and it is recommended that sales particulars should make it clear whether or not suspensive conditions (see for example para 6.9 Clause (Third)) of this type will be entertained.

4.3.4 Prepare a schedule of particulars

These are made available via websites and through the SPC, as well as being available at the property, to be handed out to reasonably interested enquirers. They serve as a preview to prospective purchasers to encourage them to come and view the property, and as a useful reminder once they have visited and may compare the advantages of various properties they have seen. The details in the sales particulars should give truthful and accurate details of the house, with photographs and floor plans and a location plan (if available). Moveable items included in the sale should be clearly specified. The Consumer Protection from Unfair Trading Regulations[6] makes it a criminal offence for an agent to engage in a commercial practice, which is misleading or is a misleading omission[7].

---

4   See www.housepricescotland.co.uk.
5   [1953] EWCA Civ 6, [1953] 1 QB 401, CA.
6   SI 2008/1277.
7   Articles 9 and 10.

4.3.5 'For Sale' board, SPC registration and advertising

Placing details of the property in the local SPC will give the property good exposure on the market by providing a high street display facility for all properties, and will publish an advertisement in its regular property list. Successful SPCs are often the first port of call for the purchaser, who will regularly check online or the listings that are produced each week for newly added properties. SPCs generally charge a single registration fee, and will hold the property on their books until is sold. If the property has not sold after a certain period (eg six months) then a re-insertion fee is usually required. The solicitor will supply the SPC with details of the property and a supply of property schedules. The SPC will put the details on its website, along with 'virtual tours' if required and access to the Home Report. It will display the property in its centre, publish details in its weekly newspaper and will also make available to prospective purchasers copies of the property brochure or particulars supplied by the solicitors.

Discuss advertising and an advertising budget with the seller and plan a suitable marketing campaign. Newspaper advertising is generally more expensive than online advertising but it is useful to highlight the availability of the property. Descriptions and advertisements should be concise and truthful, giving a summary description and a telephone number for further details and viewing arrangements. Over-elaborate advertisements are unnecessary. The solicitors will supply the For Sale board, which incidentally advertises their own services as estate agents too. The SPC's weekly lists of properties also raise the profile of the solicitors who are active in marketing property.

4.3.6 Have main details available; record enquiries and interest

Every firm that is engaged in marketing property will have a system for keeping track of interest in each property. The seller will want to know how the marketing of the property is going, and useful feedback can be obtained from parties who view the property, even if they decide not to proceed further. They may point out some feature of the property that is off-putting, and steps can be taken to change or minimise that effect. Keep a list of all serious enquiries for future reference. In particular, all formal notifications of interest must be carefully and scrupulously recorded, so that in the event of a closing date, all relevant parties are given an opportunity to make an offer. There may be a fair amount of 'hand-holding' required, with the residential client, particularly if the marketing period is protracted, so that regular updates and a sympathetic ear are appreciated by a seller, for whom this can be a particularly stressful time.

CLOSING DATES

4.4 If several parties have indicated their interest in a property, then a closing date can be fixed. A 'closing date' is a date and time selected by the seller's agents by which any interested parties must submit their best offer. A good agent should have a feel of when there is sufficient serious interest to merit a closing date. Sometimes closing dates are fixed to try to galvanise potential purchasers into action, but a closing date at which no offers are received can be a demoralising experience for a seller.

You should collect all the offers, and arrange to discuss these with the seller. The seller will generally accept the most attractive offer. You should call to advise the purchaser's solicitor that their offer is acceptable in principle and then advise the solicitors to all the unsuccessful offerors that the seller is pursuing another offer. There are clear guidelines issued by the Law Society about conduct before, during and after a closing date; these are available to view on the Law Society website[8]. It is important to let your clients know what they can and cannot do, and that once they have instructed you to accept an offer, and you have done so, they should not seek to renege on that instruction. If they do so, you will have to stop acting for them.

It is also important to act scrupulously fairly and openly, to ensure that aggrieved unsuccessful purchasers can have no complaint as to the conduct of the closing date. In particular, the terms of one party's offer should never, under any circumstances, be made known to another.

If there is a delay due to, for example, a client being abroad, or the terms of acceptance being subject to committee or board approval, then it is courteous, when setting the closing date, to let all offering solicitors know that there will be a delay, and suggest a timeframe for a decision.

Over the years, attempts have sometimes been made to circumvent the closing date system, but offers that constitute either referential or

---

8   See www.lawscot.org.uk/rules-and-guidance/section-f-guidance-relating-to-particular-types-of-work/division-c-conveyancing/guidance/gazumping,-gazundering-and-closing-dates/.

progressive bids should not be entertained. A referential bid is where a purchaser submits an offer of, say, '£100 more than the highest offer received by you'. This would be a dangerous strategy for a purchaser in any event, as he has no way of knowing precisely what the highest offer will be (see *Harvela Investments Ltd v Canada Royal Trust Co Ltd*[9], where a referential bid for a company's shares was briefly approved by the court, but the decision was reversed by the House of Lords). A progressive bid would be where a bidder frames a number of offers that are identical except that the price in each is progressively higher than the last. They are then put in numbered envelopes, and the sellers are told to open them in sequence, until a satisfactory price is reached. The snag, from the bidder's point of view, is that the sellers must be tempted to open only the envelope last in the sequence. In practice, offers of these types are rarely seen, and purchasers' solicitors will know to discourage this type of suggestion.

A seller is not obliged to accept the highest offer received, or any offer at all. A slightly lower offer may actually be preferable to a higher offer, if there is a significant difference in the dates of entry and the lower offeror is offering a date of entry suitable to the seller, while the higher offeror is not. There have doubtless been many occasions on which a lower offer has been accepted for reasons that have nothing to do with price (eg 'they were such a nice young couple') although it is much more common for sellers to accept the most financially advantageous offer.

This pleasure of accepting a lower offer from someone you like is not, however, open to persons acting in a fiduciary or representative capacity, such as trustees, heritable creditors, administrators etc

When missives are concluded, the SPC should be informed, any other advertisements cancelled and the 'For Sale' board removed.

OTHER TYPES OF SALE METHOD – AUCTION

4.5 Heritable property can be sold at auction, or to use the old Scots word, 'roup'. There is a fairly brisk market in auctions of unusual properties, such as railway and telecoms property, although sale by auction, being

---

9   [1985] 2 All ER 966, [1985] 1 All ER 261.

open and fair, and producing a fair market price, can be an attractive alternative for a seller. It is not much used in Scotland by the private seller, since the property is sold at the drop of the auctioneer's hammer. However, a reserve price can be set, meaning that if a minimum amount is not reached, the property remains unsold.

The process of a sale by auction is:

(i)   the Auctioneer will have advertised the properties for sale and usually publishes general auction conditions which will apply to all of the properties being sold. Key among these conditions is that the property is to be accepted by the purchaser *tantum et tale*. This means that the purchaser must take the property and its title 'as it stands', with all or any defects and problems. For a solicitor acting for a prospective purchaser, this means that unless specifically instructed not to by your client, you must examine the title before the auction takes place. This can be a time consuming process and of course you will not know until the day whether your client's bid will be the preferred one. You must obviously advise your client of the risks in not checking the title, and should also consider the need to instruct searches and obtain other reports such as a Property Enquiry Certificate in advance of the auction;

(ii)   the seller's solicitor prepares Articles of Roup, which is effectively an open offer to sell. If there are any special conditions attaching to the property, these need to be advertised by the Auctioneer, and should be contained in the Articles of Roup;

(iii) the auction takes place, and when the hammer falls, the highest bidder is preferred;

(iv)   the successful bidder and the auctioneer then sign a Minute of Enactment and Preference, which is usually contained in the Articles of Roup, and has the effect of an acceptance of the offer, producing a binding contract, similar in effect to missives;

(v)   a deposit is usually taken from the purchaser on the day of the auction. This will be applied toward the price at settlement.

INTERNET SALES

4.6 Sales of heritable property by online auction appear from time to time on the internet. Details of the property are given on the seller's website, and bids are requested. The size of bids is publicised on the website, and interested parties are given a certain time to raise the bid. If this is not done, the highest bid received is the successful one. One difficulty here is that a signature to the documents must be given, which although possible electronically, is not widespread. The necessary framework for electronic signatures is contained in the Electronic Communications Act 2000 and the Electronic Signatures Regulations 2002[10].

Heritable property crops up from time to time on eBay. Originally conceived as an electronic noticeboard for pedlars of junk in the San Francisco Bay Area, it has grown to become part of modern life. Although intended for unwanted items and collectibles, it also has a section for residential property. eBay works like any other auction – the highest bid at the close secures – but for heritable property, e-Bay and similar online sites are generally used as a form of advertising

ENERGY PERFORMANCE CERTIFICATES

4.7 An Energy Performance Certificate (EPC) is required whenever an existing building (or building unit (ie part of a larger building)) is sold or let. For residential properties, the EPC forms part of the Home Report, but for commercial buildings, the EPC is a standalone document that the seller must obtain, to be available to exhibit to prospective purchasers, in accordance with The Energy Performance of Buildings (Scotland) Regulations 2008, as amended (EPB Regulations). The requirement also applies to landlords and prospective tenants, but landlord/tenant issues are outside the scope of this current work.

For new buildings, an EPC is required as part of the building warrant procedure for construction of the building, where the application for a building warrant was made on or after 1 May 2007, before the Certificate of Completion can be issued. For building warrants applied for after 9

---

10 SI 2002/318.

January 2013, the EPC must be produced by an Approved Organisation[11], from data submitted to the Scottish EPC Register.

The idea behind the requirement, which emanates originally from the EU Energy Performance of Buildings Directive, is that a certificate giving information about the energy performance and efficiency of a building will help a prospective purchaser to decide whether to buy the building. An EPC gives an energy performance indicator (ie A to G, with A being the most efficient) for the property.

It used to be the case that it was not that uncommon for the seller to wait until there was actually a purchaser in prospect before organising an EPC. However, amendments made to the EPC regime in 2012 mean that from 9 January 2013, it became a requirement that the energy performance rating of a building had to be included in any marketing materials. This includes sales brochures as well as online website advertising.

Clearly, the considerations for an Energy Performance Certificate of a large commercial building are somewhat different to those of a residential property, be it a house or flat. Accordingly, the costs of obtaining EPCs for commercial properties can be considerably more than those for residential properties – one of the reasons why commercial sellers would try to hold off incurring that expense until they absolutely had to.

Residential EPCs had their own register for some time. However, since January 2013, all EPC data has to be registered and this is done through the Scottish EPC Register hosted by the Energy Saving Trust.

There are also to be changes made to the Energy Performance of Buildings regime that will have an impact on larger commercial buildings. Section 63 of the Climate Change (Scotland) Act 2009 introduces a new scheme for commercial properties called 'Action on Carbon and Energy Performance' (ACEP), which will become a part of the EPC regime in Scotland. At the time of writing, the final form of the regulations is still awaited. However, according to the Scottish Government timetable, ACEP is due to come into force mid-2016. Once obtained, an EPC lasts for ten years.

---

11 See www.scotland.gov.uk/Topics/Built-Environment/Building/Buildingstandards/enerperfor/
    epcorgprg.

4.7.1 When is an EPC required?

The EPB Regulations provide that the 'triggers' for the EPC requirement are when a prospective purchaser (or prospective tenant) requests information about the building from the owner or makes a request to view the building, or makes an offer, whether oral or written, to buy (or lease) the building. Then the EPC has to be produced, free of charge to any prospective purchaser or tenant.

The EPC should be affixed to a building, but it doesn't need to be displayed in the building unless it is a public building (new build or existing) (ie a building with a floor area of more than 250 square metres (reduced from the previous threshold of 500 square metres from July 2015. It was originally 1,000 square metres)) which is occupied by a public authority or by an institution providing public services and which can be visited by the public. A public building must display an EPC. Any building which is frequently visited by the public, including shops, cinemas, health centres etc must display an EPC if they have one. The EPC must be displayed in a prominent place, visible to visiting members of the public.

For multi-occupancy buildings, (eg an office block that is let to several separate tenants) an EPC can be obtained for the whole building, or individual EPCs can be obtained for individual lettings within the building. In the case of a mixed use building of both residential and commercial properties however, separate EPCs are required for each type of use. An EPC would only be required for the common parts of the building alone if they are heated or conditioned. An EPC for the whole building will probably include the common parts unless the common parts were not heated or cooled mechanically, in which case the EPC would not be required to cover them. For multi-occupancy developments however, where each unit is standalone or separated from other units in such a way that each unit would need to be separately rated, then separate EPCs are needed for each unit. A surveyor qualified in producing EPCs should be able to advise appropriately.

4.7.2 When is an EPC not required?

EPCs are not required for:

- temporary buildings with a planned time of use of two years or less, workshops and non-residential agricultural buildings with low energy demand;

- small standalone buildings with a total useful floor area of less than 50 square metres which are not dwellings (a standalone building may be detached, or attached, but thermally separated from a main building);

- public buildings with a floor area of less than 1,000 square metres;

- buildings which do not use fuel or power for controlling the temperature of the internal environment;

- conversions, alterations and extensions to buildings other than alterations and extensions to stand-alone buildings having an area less than 50 square metres that would increase the area to 50 square metres or more, or alterations to buildings involving the fit-out of the shell which is the subject of a 'continuing requirement' under standard 6.1 or 6.9 of building regulations; and

- buildings that are subject to Schedule 1 of the Building (Scotland) Regulations 2004, as amended, such as certain agricultural buildings or those not frequented by people or governed by other legislation such as nuclear or explosives legislation[12].

4.7.3 Penalties for failure to obtain or exhibit an EPC

There are penalties for failing to produce an EPC, although there are some limited defences for not having an EPC at the point at which a prospective purchaser or tenant is entitled to see one. Local authorities are responsible for enforcing the EPB Regulations and can require an owner (in this case, the seller) to comply with its obligation to make an EPC available to a prospective purchaser or tenant, at any time up to six months from the date when it appears to the local authority that the EPC should have been produced. The owner has nine days to comply, unless he has a 'reasonable excuse' defence for not complying, such as: that she had commissioned an EPC at least 14 days before the relevant time (ie when the prospective purchaser requested information, or asked to view, or made an offer) and despite all reasonable efforts and enquiries by the owner, she did not have possession or control of a valid EPC at the relevant time.

---

12 For a full list see: www.legislation.gov.uk/ssi/2004/406/schedule/1/made.

Where the local authority believes an owner to be in breach, it can give a Penalty Charge Notice to the owner. The amount of the penalty charge is (currently) £500 for dwellings and £1,000 in other cases.

It should be noted that there are separate EPC regulations that apply to property in England and Wales, which although similar contain some differences of detail.

GREEN DEAL

4.8 Part 1, Chapter 1 of the Energy Act 2011 introduced the Green Deal and Green Deal Plans. The Green Deal is an initiative from the UK Government which is intended to help energy efficiency measures to be carried out in households and businesses without the owners (or occupiers) having to meet any upfront capital costs of those measures.

Broadly, the proposals provide a framework within which homeowners and businesses can carry out energy improvements to their property, by having them carried out by participating energy companies, and other accredited organisations. Instead of charging for the work at the time it is completed, the participating organisation recovers the cost of the works over time, and in instalments, by payments added to and recovered through the consumer's energy bills.

There is a catch, of course: the measures have to pay for themselves over their own lifetime. This is known as the 'golden rule'. It means that the additional costs of the plan, which are recovered through the electricity bill, must not be more than the cost savings achieved by the reduction in energy consumption from the energy efficiency measures. The repayment of the cost of improvements can take place over many years – as much as 25 years, and the repayments themselves will include interest.

The kinds of energy efficiency measures envisaged include cavity wall insulation, loft insulation, solid wall insulation, condensing boilers, double glazing, floor insulation, solar panels, photovoltaic PV panels, ground source heat pumps, electric storage heaters or wind turbines installed in the property. All the eligible measures are set out in Regulations[13].

There has been, overall, little take-up of the Green Deal, (and the UK Government's decision in July 2012 to stop funding the Green Deal

---

13 The Green Deal (Qualifying Energy Improvements) Order 2012 (SI 2012/2105) and The Green Deal (Qualifying Energy Improvements) (Amendment) Order 2014.

Finance Company makes take up even less likely). There may, however, be odd occasions when you actually come across a property for sale that has the 'benefit' of a Green Deal, and there are requirements that must be met when a Green Deal property changes hands.

4.8.1 Selling a Green Deal Property

It is important to understand that the Green Deal finance debt is attached to the property's electricity bill, not to the person taking out the Green Deal plan (nor actually to the property, so in that sense it is not like a security or a charge).

This means that on the change of owner or other occupier who is the bill payer, the repayments for the Green Deal finance will be continue to be recovered, by instalments, from a charge on the new occupier's electricity bill.

Green deal regulations set out two requirements in particular that must be done on sale or letting: disclosure on sale or letting, and acknowledgement on sale, lease or licence.

When a Green Deal Property is being sold or let, information about the Green Deal Plan must be disclosed.

A seller, prospective landlord or licensor is required to disclose information about a Green Deal Plan by providing 'the document' produced or updated. Section 8(4) and section 12 of the 2011 Act set out the particulars that must be produced to a prospective buyer, tenant or licensee of a Green Deal Property at a specified time. The Regulations provide a whole variety of trigger points depending on circumstances. The simple answer is to provide disclosure straight away. An obvious place to make initial disclosure is in the sales (or letting) particulars, indicating that a Green Deal affects the property. Further details of what work was carried out and the cost will need to be provided to the purchaser or tenant.

4.8.2 Buying a Green Deal Property

The purchaser, tenant or licensee must produce a written acknowledgement, by which he accepts that, as the prospective bill payer, he is liable to make the payments due under the Green Deal Plan.

The form of acknowledgement must be signed by the purchaser, tenant or licensee and be in (or substantially in) the statutory form.

This acknowledgement must be incorporated into the contract. This gives Scottish solicitors a bit of a procedural dilemma – since our contracts for purchase are traditionally signed by the solicitors.

It seems from the terms of the statutory wording that the acknowledgement must actually be signed by the bill payer, so a clause in the missives won't suffice. A suggested way to achieve this could be to obtain a signed acknowledgement from the purchaser (in duplicate) before the principal offer to sell is issued. The duplicate acknowledgment can incorporated in the offer to sell as an attachment. On acceptance of the offer, the acknowledgement is thus clearly included in the contract. Signing the acknowledgement in duplicate means that the seller can retain the principal acknowledgement and, because the duplicate is attached to the offer to sell, that version will be retained by the purchaser's solicitors. For offers to purchase, the acknowledgement can be attached so that the seller receives a signed copy, and the purchaser's solicitor retains the duplicate for his own records.

GATHER INFORMATION EARLY

4.9 Under the 'readiness for sale' principle, it is good practice for the seller's solicitor to obtain as much information and documentation as you can, as soon as you can. This means that the seller's solicitor should start gathering together all the documents that the purchaser's solicitor is likely to want to see, as soon as she is told that the property is to be sold.

A word here about getting really ahead of yourself in this connection: take some time, at the end of a purchase transaction, to organise and catalogue all the relevant purchase documents. If you are instructed in the sale some months or years later, these good housekeeping steps will make a significant difference to the speed with which you are able to react to offers and progress a transaction. More frequently than most solicitors would probably like, instructions come in requiring them to complete a sale in a very short window of time. This is perhaps more common in commercial transactions, but it is not unheard of in residential ones.

If your client is selling a portfolio of properties, or a retail park with dozens of units and occupational leases, then there can be a vast amount of documentation to go through. Having this available, with all documents listed, and sensibly assembled in 'bibles' (bound or lever arch folders, or scanned copies loaded into a CD, of all the documents (or copies of them), that relate to a particular property or transaction) can give all parties a good, often essential, head start on the due diligence process which will help to keep the transaction on track.

If your client has used estate agents to sell his property, it might mean that you have little advance warning of an acceptable offer arriving with you for acceptance. If the title is unfamiliar to you, it is a wise move to make quick check before you conclude missives that there are no pre contract issues that need to be attended to, such as a right of pre-emption (see para 8.25.13).

4.9.1 Titles

If you acted for the clients when they purchased the property, then you will probably already have details of the whereabouts of the titles, and may, in fact, hold them on behalf of your client. If not, obtain the mortgage account details or other access information, and request the titles to be sent to you.

If the title is already registered, then the Land Certificate, Charge Certificate or a copy (preferably an Extract) of the Title Sheet, strictly speaking, is all that is required. If the prior Sasine titles are still available do not throw them away; often they can contain essential information or provide clarification that is not evident from the Title Sheet on the Land Register.

If the title is still in the Sasine Register, or if a Land Certificate or Title Sheet has not yet been produced, then check through the title to ensure that everything that will be required is there (see Chapter 8 on Examination of Title). If the Land Certificate, Title Sheet or the titles are missing, extracts, office copies or quick copies (where appropriate) may be obtained from the appropriate Register. Search organisations, such as Millar & Bryce, can do this for you.

Checking the terms of the title at this stage is important, so that you can ascertain if there are any unusual conditions of title, such as rights of pre-emption, unusual servitude rights, or an exclusion of indemnity. If there is a weakness or defect in the title, it is as well to know about it before entering into missives, and take a decision, in consultation with the seller, about how to deal to with it and whether to disclose it to the purchaser before missives are concluded. It may be better to reveal the difficulty before conclusion of missives, when it can be negotiated, than after conclusion, when the purchaser may prefer to use a breach of warranty as to good title as an excuse to resile from the bargain. It is, however, a matter of judgement, depending on the nature of the issue, how best to deal with it. There is a school of thought, on the *caveat emptor* principle, that the purchaser may not notice a title defect, and that unless or until they do, the seller should not necessarily volunteer that information. Provided that you do not tip into misrepresenting the position or misleading a fellow solicitor, it is hard to argue against this approach.

4.9.2 Certificates, Surveys, Records and Reports

It is also helpful at this stage to obtain a Property Enquiry Certificate from the relevant local authority or from specialist PEC providers, planning and building warrant histories, planning permission, building warrants, completion certificates, a coal mining report (if required), any guarantees for damp proofing, timber or dry rot treatments, or double glazing, any site investigation or environmental reports that might be relevant or which might be able to be made available to a purchaser (subject to the person who produced the report being prepared to update it and/or readdress it to the purchaser, for which they may request a fee). Bear in mind, however, the time limits on the transitional 'shelf life' of such things as PECs (three months for residential, 60 days for commercial) and coal authority reports (90 days). In residential transactions, the standard form missives provide that the PEC must be dated **after** the date of conclusion of missives.

You should also obtain copies or principals of any other records or surveys that will be relevant to the purchaser, such as (in relation to commercial property) any asbestos register or reports or correspondence in connection with the Control of Asbestos Regulations[14] and fire risk assessments in terms of the Fire (Scotland) Act 2005 and the Fire Safety (Scotland) Regulations 2006[15].

In the case of a first registration, it is also important to obtain a Legal Report – Unregistered Land (equivalent to a Sasine Register search), and

---

14 The Control of Asbestos at Work Regulations 2002, the Control of Asbestos Regulations 2006 and the Control of Asbestos Regulations 2012.
15 As amended by the Fire Safety (Scotland) Amendment Regulations 2010.

a Plans Report to check that the deed plan or any plan in the title being relied on for description is suitable for registration purposes and to ensure there is no conflict with another registered title in case there is any major discrepancy in the boundaries. For registered properties, a Legal Report – Registered Land and a Level 1 Plans Report[16] should be ordered. Amongst other things a Legal Report would disclose if any preservation notices had been registered in terms of Abolition of Feudal Tenure (Scotland) Act 2000 or Title Conditions (Scotland) Act 2003. For more detail on searches and reports see Chapter 7.

4.9.3 Plan

If the property is not yet registered in the Land Register, or if what is being sold is only part of the title (Sasine or Land Register) then an accurate taxative plan (ie an accurate plan that can be founded on) of the property to be sold should be obtained as soon as possible. A full bounding description will often still be required to establish actual physical features of the boundaries (see para 9.9.3), but a plan will be easier for everyone involved in the transaction, and for the Keeper to map the title onto the cadastral map in due course. Any plan that is to be submitted for registration must comply with the Registers Deed Plan Criteria.

Ideally, any sales particulars should contain a plan showing what is being offered for sale, (where appropriate) and it is also the opportunity for the seller's solicitor to compare that plan against the title to make sure that the seller (i) owns everything he plans to sell; or (ii) will sell all the property that he owns (if that is the intention).

4.9.4 Matrimonial Homes/Civil Partnership Documentation

When selling residential property on behalf of an owner who is an individual, it is necessary to have regard to the provisions of the Matrimonial Homes (Family Protection) (Scotland) Act 1981 and the Civil Partnership Act 2004. If the title to the home is in the joint names of both husband and wife or of both civil partners, then neither Act is relevant. Only when the title is in the name of one spouse or one civil

---

16 There is debate about whether a Plans Report is required for registered property. See para 7.7.1.

partner will the provisions of the relevant Act apply. As the name of the Matrimonial Homes (Family Protection) (Scotland) Act 1981 implies, the purpose of that legislation is to protect spouses and children from being excluded from the matrimonial home.

The legislation was originally brought into being principally to provide protection for victims of domestic abuse and violence (usually women), by giving them a statutory right not to be excluded from, and to occupy (or to enter and occupy) the matrimonial home[17], even if the home was owned only by the husband. In extreme cases, the 'non-entitled spouse' can apply to the courts to have the 'entitled spouse' excluded from the home by obtaining an 'exclusion order'[18]. These statutory occupancy rights also apply when the home is rented rather than owned.

Similar rights were created for civil partners by section 101 of the Civil Partnership Act 2004, in the context of which the property is termed a 'family home'[19]. Both Acts provide for other subsidiary rights, such as paying rent or the mortgage, or carrying out repairs. The protection also extends to any children of the family and, of course, the Matrimonial Homes Act equally applies to husbands, where the title to the home is in the wife's name, and also to non-entitled spouses in same-sex marriages under the Marriage and Civil Partnership (Scotland) Act 2014.

Such is the importance of these rights that they have precedence over the rights of third parties (including purchasers and lenders) in dealing with the entitled spouse or civil partner. The effect of this is that, without the agreement of the non-entitled spouse or civil partner, a third party would not be able to occupy the home even if they had otherwise validly contracted to do so with the entitled spouse or partner, paid the price and taken delivery of a disposition. In the case of a lender to the entitled spouse or partner, since one of its remedies on default is the right to sell the property (after due process) any rights of a non-entitled spouse or partner could potentially prevent that.

Accordingly, section 6 of the Matrimonial Homes (Family Protection) (Scotland) Act 1981 and section 106 of the Civil Partnership Act 2004 provide a procedure that will protect third parties in dealings with the

---

17 Defined in section 22 of Matrimonial Homes (Family Protection) (Scotland) Act 1981.
18 See section 3 of above.
19 Defined in section 135 of the Civil Partnership Act 2004 in similar terms to the definition of 'matrimonial home'.

entitled spouse or civil partner, while also protecting the non-entitled parties. The consent of the non-entitled party must be obtained to the dealing, or as an alternative, they can renounce their occupancy rights. If a non-entitled party is unreasonably refusing to consent to a dealing, or is incapable of consenting either because of physical, mental or legal disability or because their whereabouts are unknown, then application can be made to the court to dispense with their consent.[20]

You should establish the relationship status of the seller. If they have a spouse or civil partner, who is not included in the title, the consent of that spouse or civil partner will be required. Usually, the non-entitled party's agreement is denoted by obtaining their signed consent rather than by renunciation, but either is effective. The renunciation is a separate document that must be signed by the spouse or civil partner, and notarised by a notary public, but the consent can be either a standalone document or incorporated into the body of the disposition. It is prudent to establish at this early stage that the non-entitled party is ready and willing to consent, and if there is any doubt or any suggestion of coercion, then they must be advised to seek independent legal advice.

The terms of the documentation are the same for spouses and civil partners, and most firms will usually use a style that provides for both, and strike out the wording that does not apply in the circumstances.

The renunciation of occupancy rights is in the following style:

I, [   ], residing at [   ], [spouse][civil partner] of [   ] residing at [   ], HEREBY RENOUNCE THE Occupancy Rights to which I am or may become entitled in terms of the [Matrimonial Homes (Family Protection) (Scotland) Act 1981, as amended by Section 13 of the Law Reform (Miscellaneous Provisions) (Scotland) Act 1985] [Civil Partnership Act 2004], in the property known as [ ] being/intended to become a [Matrimonial][Family] Home as defined in the said Act [as amended]; And I hereby swear/affirm that this Renunciation is made by me freely and without coercion of any kind; And I declare that this renunciation is irrevocable.

Given under my hand at [   ] this [   ] day of [   ] Two Thousand and [   ] in the presence of [   ] Notary Public and in the presence of this witness:

20 See also section 7 of the Family Law (Scotland) Act 2006.

The renunciation must be signed in the presence of a notary public. If it is signed outside Scotland, this can be any person duly authorised by the law of that country to administer oaths or receive affirmation (eg a commissioner for oaths in England). It is recommended that if a renunciation is being obtained, the spouse should seek independent legal advice.

The form of consent as a separate document (which does not need to be signed before a notary public) is:

I, [   ], residing at [   ], [spouse][civil partner] of [   ], residing at [ ], CONSENT for the purposes of the [Matrimonial Homes (Family Protection) (Scotland) Act 1981][Civil Partnership Act 2004], to the undernoted dealing of the said [   ] relating to [   ].

Dealing referred to:

[insert details of dealing]

Signed by the said [   ] at [   ] on the [   ] day of [   ] 20[   ] in the presence of the following witness:

Where the consent is incorporated into the body of the disposition which is being granted by the entitled spouse or civil partner:

...with the consent of [   ] residing at [   ], the [spouse][civil partner] of the said [   ], for the purposes of the [Matrimonial Homes (Family Protection) (Scotland) Act 1981 as amended][Civil Partnership Act 2004] ...

But what of the single person? There is no spouse or civil partner to consent or renounce rights, but there is the need to 'prove the negative' (ie to confirm that they have no non-entitled spouse or civil partner. This is done by way of declaration, and the form of words varies according to whether the dealing referred to is a sale or a standard security:

I, [   ] proprietor of the subjects known as [   ] 'the subjects of sale' DECLARE as follows:

With reference to the sale of the Property (defined) to [   ] the Property is neither a matrimonial home in relation to which a spouse of mine has occupancy rights, the expressions 'matrimonial home' and 'occupancy rights' having the meanings respectively ascribed to them by the Matrimonial Homes (Family Protection) (Scotland) Act 1981, as amended, nor a family home in relation to which a civil partner of mine has occupancy rights under the Civil Partnership Act 2004.

Declared by the above named [   ] at [   ] on the [   ] day of [   ] 20[   ] in the presence of [   ];

or

I, [   ], residing at [   ] DECLARE as follows:

With reference to the grant by me of a Standard Security over [   ] (the 'security subjects') in favour of [   ] the security subjects are neither a matrimonial home in relation to which a spouse of mine has occupancy rights, the expressions 'matrimonial home' and 'occupancy rights' having the meanings respectively ascribed to them by the Matrimonial Homes (Family Protection) (Scotland) Act 1981, as amended, nor a family home in relation to which a civil partner of mine has occupancy rights under the Civil Partnership Act 2004.

Declared by the above named [   ] at [   ] on the [   ] day of [   ] 20[   ] in the presence of [   ]

Occupancy rights do not automatically apply in the case of co-habiting couples but a 'non-entitled co-habitee' may apply to the court for occupancy rights, which may be granted for a period or successive periods of six months.

An exception to the rule applies where the 'entitled' spouse occupies a matrimonial home which is jointly owned (or tenanted) along with another individual who is not the other spouse. That other spouse is not a non-entitled spouse, unless the other individual has waived his or her right of occupation in favour of the 'entitled' spouse. An example might be where a mother and son jointly own and occupy a property, and the son and his wife also live there. Unless the mother waives her right of occupation in favour of the son's wife, the wife cannot be a 'non-entitled spouse' and would not benefit from statutory occupancy rights.

4.9.5 Builders' Sale Packs

Selling plots for a builder requires a great deal of preliminary preparation. Gone, (or going) are the days when unruly piles of copy title deeds would be sent out to prospective purchasers' solicitors to examine, and it is becoming more the norm for title and other key documents such as Legal Report, possibly a Plans Report, or details of Development Plan Approval, Planning Consent and Building Warrants, Property Enquiry Certificates, the Deed of Conditions and title plans to be digitally scanned, copies of which are then sent or e-mailed to the purchaser's solicitor. This allows the purchaser's solicitor to access all of the relevant title documents on screen and save them to file if they want. This process must be done carefully and methodically, but once the master copy is created, making additional copies is a lot quicker, more economical and more environmentally friendly than producing many sets of photocopies.

Plans of individual plots, and NHBC (or other home warranty provider) documents must also be obtained from the builder, and style missives and dispositions and any other standard form documents, such as deeds of disburdenment of any standard security granted by the builder, should also be drafted and assembled well in advance of the first plot sales. It is also a good idea to organise some standard form letters or e-mails of routine correspondence that can be used during the conveyancing process. The procedures for the sales of plots or units by a builder or developer lend themselves well to systemisation.

4.9.6 Leasehold Documentation

The sale of an investment property can involve a large amount of documentation. It is particularly useful to organise and inventory all of the documents at the end of acting in the purchase of investment property, as these can often change hands every few years.

While the property is being marketed, the seller's solicitor should be taking the opportunity to assemble all of the titles, certificates and reports, and check for and assemble all letting documents, which will include the leases with coloured plans, and any back letters, guarantees, rent deposit agreements, licences for works, letters of consent, notices, subleases, rent review memoranda, assignations and any management regulations.

The seller and the selling agents (who may also be the managing agents for the property, or if not, the managing agents) should be asked about any transactions that may have taken place since the purchase of the property (although if your firm has acted in respect of new leases, or consent to assignations, then you should have copies, which should be placed with the principal documents for the property).

There may be some minor transactions that have taken place without your involvement, so you should always check, particularly to find out if there are any informal, undocumented arrangements in place, or applications for consents, or new lease negotiations that are ongoing. Information about rent collection, service charge and management issues should all be obtained from the managing agents. See also para 4.9.9.

Where you act for the landlord in connection with the lettings, then it is also a good idea to provide the purchaser's solicitor with copies of all the current management documentation, including the pro-forma lease, licences and any other documents used in connection with lettings of the property, so that there is continuity for the future lettings.

If the seller is a participant in the Carbon Reduction Commitment Energy Efficiency Scheme (CRC) then you may want to obtain some basic information, such as whether the tenants have been charged for the cost of CRC allowances or any other CRC costs and expenses (such as administrative charges) incurred by the seller in relation to the energy supplied to the property, and whether these have been charged directly or indirectly (under the lease, service charge accounts or any informal arrangements). Obtain copies of any correspondence between the seller or its agents and the tenant or their agents in this connection. CRC issues will only be relevant if the purchaser is also a CRC participant.

4.9.7 Construction and Alterations Documentation

When acting in the purchase of a new (ie less than 12 years old) commercial property, the purchaser's solicitor will require to inspect all of the original construction documentation, so this should also be carefully preserved and itemised with the other documentation relating to the property. This will also apply to any works that have been carried out to older properties, but which required Planning Consents and/or Building Warrants.

In the case of large developments, there can be massive amounts of documentation to exhibit, as well as the planning and building warrant permissions, including building/engineering contracts, appointment agreements, sub-contracts, collateral warranties, certificates of practical completion, snagging lists, 'as built' drawings for the buildings or the works, Health & Safety file, any service or maintenance contracts, tenant fit-out works, crane oversail agreements, evidence of contractors' and consultants' PI insurance etc. See also para 4.9.9.

Less documentation is required in the case of new or altered residential properties (eg you wouldn't normally expect to examine the contractor documentation). Again, you should find out from the seller whether they have carried out any alterations and obtain from them the Planning Permission, Building Warrant, Certificates of Completion, or Notice of Acceptance of Completion Certificate and stamped warrant drawings (ie the copies of the drawings that have been stamped by the local authority's building standards department in connection with the application for a Building Warrant). It is important to ask about and obtain this documentation as early in the transaction as possible, as the missives will contain a provision about these documents. It is surprising how frequently (particularly with residential property) either no permissions at all have been obtained, or the seller has been unaware of the requirement for, and has done nothing about obtaining, a Certificate of Completion or Notice of Acceptance of Completion Certificate. If that is the case then steps will need to be taken either to obtain a Letter of Comfort from the local authority, or even apply for a retrospective Building Warrant. This can take many weeks, so early identification of this issue is imperative.

4.9.8 VAT

Not an issue when buying or selling a dwelling house, but the VAT status of commercial property should always be ascertained. If the seller has opted to tax the land and VAT applies in the transaction, or if it is a TOGC (see para 6.14.4) then the seller will have to exhibit copies or certified copies of certain documents, which may include the seller's VAT Registration Certificate, documents evidencing an option to tax or real estate election given to HM Revenue & Customs, and any relevant notices and correspondence. See also para 4.9.9 below.

4.9.9 Using the Due Diligence Questionnaire

Although designed to be used by the solicitor for the commercial purchaser, as a list of their requirements to be able to conduct a full due diligence examination, the solicitor for the commercial seller will also find the Due Diligence Questionnaire (DDQ) a useful tool in helping to ensure that their pre sale preparations are thorough and effective, by using it as a checklist of items to identify, locate, order or ask the client or the selling agents about.

Produced by the Property Standardisation Group (PSG) and available to download from its website,[21] the DDQ provides a comprehensive list of the likely due diligence requirements of a purchaser and their solicitor, and is particularly appropriate to large transactions where there are a number of properties or units. The main body of the DDQ deals with fairly comprehensive commercial property enquiries relating to such matters as titles, property enquiries, fire certification, planning and building control matters, insurance and the like. The detail of more specialised areas which may not necessarily apply to all transactions, namely VAT treatment of the transaction, capital allowances, staff/TUPE matters, occupational leases and construction documentation, are dealt with in a detailed annexe on each of those topics. For the seller's solicitor therefore, acting in the sale of a two year old building, the annexe dealing with construction documents will be an essential checklist of items to assemble in readiness for the sale. The annexe on occupational leases, similarly will assist when preparing for the sale of a multi-let building or development.

SALES BY INSOLVENCY PRACTITIONERS

4.10 As we will see elsewhere (paras 6.19, 8.18.5 to 8.18.9 and 9.6.8), acting for an insolvency practitioner has its own specialities in conveyancing terms. You are required to exhibit the evidence of the IP's appointment or other entitlement to sell the property and convey the title, so copies of these should be obtained to exhibit along with the titles and other documents. See paras 8.18.5 to 8.18.9 for details of the documentation required for each insolvency situation.

Each insolvency procedure allows for appointment of the IP by various different routes and the various documents constituting the appointment should be exhibited to the purchaser.

Often any option to tax documents are not with the company records and as such, whether VAT can be charged on the sale of the property is

21 See www.psglegal.co.uk/due_diligence.php.

not known. In most cases the IP will try to obtain this information from HMRC prior to sale, or will seek an indemnity for any VAT that is found to be due on the sale price subsequently. An IP may also apply to opt to tax.

IPs are not automatically immune from the application of statutory liability and the terms of each statutory notice and statutory regime affecting the property should be checked. A defective building notice requiring rectification of defects is an example of this, as the notice may specify that liability on an owner of a building arises under the Building (Scotland) Act 2003. If the owner does not take the necessary rectification steps required by the notice, the legislation provides that the owner is guilty of a criminal offence and that the local authority may carry out the work, recovering any expenses reasonably incurred from the owner. A Trustee in Sequestration or Liquidator would become an owner if they registered title but they are specifically carved out as an exception to the regime. Similarly, any notice of liability registered under the Tenements (Scotland) Act 2004 will affect an owner, but a Trustee in Sequestration will only be affected where they have registered title to the property. In any event these notices would still require to be dealt with on sale.

Prior Ranking Securities: Inhibitions and standard securities are treated differently under the different regimes, and you may require to obtain a discharge of the inhibition or standard security where there is no ability to deal with the property with the security in place, eg a discharge of an inhibition will be required for a sale in Administration.

Searches and Property Enquiry Certificates may or may not be obtained by the IP, depending on their funding arrangements, and instructions should be taken. It would not be unusual to require the purchaser to obtain and pay for these.

SALES BY HERITABLE CREDITORS IN POSSESSION

4.11 When a heritable creditor calls up its security and exercises its power of sale (see para 10.7) there are certain steps that it must follow when marketing the property, to ensure that it obtains the best price that could reasonably be obtained (see para 8.18.3). You should obtain the service copy calling up notice(s) and extract of any decree (both are required for sale of residential property, but a decree is not compulsory for the sale of commercial property). You should also obtain certificates of advertising to comply with the advertising requirement. If newspaper advertising has been used, these are usually obtained from the newspaper's publisher. An SPC will be able to provide confirmation of exposure in their Lists and on their website. The purchaser's solicitor will need to see these.

A sale by a heritable creditor provides the purchaser of the security subjects with as good a title as the debtor had. The property is disburdened of the security in favour of the creditor and also all other heritable securities and diligences (eg inhibitions) that rank *pari passu* with, or postponed to that security.[22] A prior ranking security holder's rights are not affected, but the enforcing creditor has the same rights to redeem that security as the debtor had. In practice, the enforcing creditor will pay any prior security holder from the sale proceeds, to redeem the prior security (or securities if more than one) so that a clear title can be given to the purchaser, who will insist on one. There exists the possibility that the whole of the sale proceeds could be taken up by the indebtedness due to the prior security holder, meaning that the postponed enforcing creditor gets nothing. Clearly the amount of prior ranking indebtedness (where applicable) is a key piece of information for any postponed creditor considering this route. When the sale has completed, the sale proceeds require to be distributed as follows:

(i)   in payment of all expenses that the creditor properly incurred in connection with the sale; then

(ii)   payment of the whole amount due under any prior ranking standard security; followed by

(iii)   payment of the whole amount due under the standard security being enforced and, if there are any other standard securities that rank equally with it, equal payment of the whole sums due under those standard securities; then

(iv)   payment of any amounts due under any postponed standard securities, according to their ranking; and finally

(v)   any balance left over is paid to the debtor or the owner of the security subjects (as appropriate).

22 Section 26 of the Conveyancing and Feudal Reform (Scotland) Act 1970.

THE 'SELLER'S DRAFTS'

4.12 Traditionally, the solicitor on each side of the transaction is responsible for preparing drafts of certain of the conveyancing documents, and providing then to the other side for checking, revisal or approval. Once the missives are complete (see Chapter 6) the seller's solicitor sends to the purchaser's solicitor the following (at the same time as sending the titles and other documents for examination):

(a) the Legal Report (unless the seller's solicitor intends to leave obtaining this until closer to settlement);

(b) a draft discharge or deed of restriction/deed of disburdenment of any security (see paras 10.3.5 and 10.3.6; and

(c) a draft Advance Notice application.

Chapter 5

The Purchaser's Overture

FINANCING THE RESIDENTIAL PURCHASE AND DEALING WITH LENDERS

5.1 It is absolutely imperative that you discuss with your purchasing clients their arrangements for financing their purchase and ensure that they will have access to the full amount of money required to complete the purchase (including significant outlays like Land and Buildings Transaction Tax). It is very useful for this purpose to produce for them a statement showing how much money will be required. Many purchasers underestimate the total costs, once all the outlays and taxes are added on. It may also have a material bearing on how much they will be prepared to offer for the property.

If the purchase requires to be financed with a loan, you need to know how much has been offered to the purchaser. With any luck, the purchaser will have organised funding ahead of consulting you, and will already have a written offer of loan or mortgage 'promise'. If so, he can tell his lender that you are acting for him in the purchase transaction and, in the majority of cases (in residential purchase transactions), the lender will want you to act for them as well. The lender will send you an instruction pack, with a pro-forma report on title form for you to complete, and a copy of the offer of loan with any conditions. You should also check if the lender is a member of the Council of Mortgage Lenders (CML), and if so, (most are) check that lender's requirements in the CML Handbook[1]. For other third party lenders, or where the loan has not yet been agreed with the lender, consider the Conflict of Interest Rules carefully before thinking about acting[2].

Few (if any) lenders these days will offer 100% loans; they require purchasers to contribute some equity to the purchase price. You should find

1 See http://www.cml.org.uk/lenders-handbook/
2 This rule is codified in rule B2.1.2 which simply states that 'You shall not act for two or more parties whose interests conflict.'

out from your clients where those other funds will come from (eg if not from the sale of their current property). It is important that the purchaser understands that these funds have to be liquid (ie readily accessible) so that they can be applied to the purchase in good time.

If it becomes clear that the purchasers may not have access to liquid funds (for example, it may transpire that they have to give many months' notice to uplift funds, or have to sell a property before they have all the funds they need) then you have to advise them that it is not prudent to pursue the particular property until the funding is in place. It is possible to offer without the finance being in place, but this needs to be made clear in the offer. That said, the seller would be entitled to treat an offer 'subject to satisfactory finance' or 'subject to the sale of the purchaser's property' as pretty worthless and would be well advised to continue to market the property in the hope of achieving a more concrete result.

Similar considerations apply to the purchase of commercial property, although a lender's loan is summarised in a term sheet and detailed in a facility letter. As commercial properties are generally higher in value, and therefore represent greater risk to the bank, invariably, the lender will instruct another firm of solicitors to protect its interest and ensure that sufficient security is in place. For commercial loans of £250,000 or more, solicitors are not permitted to act for both borrower and lender under the Conflict of Interest rules (see paras 10.6.1 and 10.6.2).

ESTATE AGENTS AND SURVEYORS

5.2 Once you have advised your client and taken instructions, you will have to deal with other property professionals, including estate agents. The estate agent's job is to market the property effectively in order to achieve the best price for the seller in the shortest time.

If you are acting for a purchaser, you will probably contact an estate agent for the first time after the initial meeting with your client, to ask them for a copy of the marketing materials – generally known as the property particulars or the 'schedule' (see para 4.3.4) and the Home Report (see paras 4.2 and 5.3). This is also the opportunity to ask any questions about the property or the seller's position or matters arising from the Home Report. You may also 'note' your client's interest (see below) or intimate that an offer will be forthcoming, depending on your instructions from the purchaser.

As noted in Chapter 1, an estate agent could also encompass a solicitors' or surveyors' firm.

THE HOME REPORT

5.3 One of the principal problems perceived with Home Reports is that the seller can choose the surveyor who provides the Single Survey and valuation. It is common practice for the upset price of the property to be set significantly lower than the valuation contained in the Home Report. This technique is often a marketing tool. In times of financial fragility, the valuation might be quite a bit higher than the price achieved in the market.

The traditional method that the Home Report replaced was itself far from perfect. In that system, the purchaser would make an offer based on his survey which he would commission from a chartered surveyor. Where there were multiple notes of interest, sometimes the purchaser's solicitor would ask the seller's solicitor whether any surveyors had already surveyed the property. Armed with this information, the purchaser's solicitor could then contact the surveyors direct for a copy of the survey, but addressed to the purchaser, so that a duty of care existed. There were also cases of multiple surveys from different surveyors being commissioned for the same property, leading to wasted expenditure for the purchasers collectively (and hence the term 'Single Survey' in the Home Report)

Under the old system, when the property market began to overheat, some offers were solely based on an assessment of the market but made 'subject to survey'. Once the offer was found acceptable, the seller would then commission a survey and deduct the cost of remedying any defects highlighted by the survey. The problem with this practice was that the amount of money offered was not necessarily directly related to the value of the house, because without a survey, the price was driven by emotion and market forces. In this respect, the Home Report can be a useful tool for the purchaser, who can get a good idea of any likely issues that affect the property. If the conditions list shows a sufficient amount of category 1 and only a few category 2 comments[3], then most purchasers will be happy enough. Lots of category 3 comments means the dilapidated condition of the property should be reflected in the valuation.

---

3   The Single Survey has three repair categories: 1 – no immediate repair required; 2 – repair or replacement requiring future attention; and 3 – urgent repair or replacement required.

RESIDENTIAL SURVEYS

5.4 For residential purchasers wishing to commission their own survey there are three grades of survey:

- a brief valuation for mortgage purposes;
- a full conditional survey, which investigates most of the accessible 'nooks and crannies'; and
- a structural survey.

The third of these surveys is rare in residential property, as it is usually only appropriate if there is some concern over the structural integrity of the building. Most residential purchasers – or, if not, their lenders – will be put off by an earlier survey that indicates structural problems. The conditional survey would normally recommend a specialist opinion, whether from a structural engineer or an infestation specialist.

The Home Report Survey contains a valuation and some comments on the condition, so is something of a hybrid.

COMMERCIAL SURVEYS

5.5 For commercial property, the traditional system endures, namely the purchaser commissions their own survey of the property. The commercial survey will give a detailed report on the condition of the property as well as the situation, location and any other relevant considerations, such as planning and environmental considerations, as well as a valuation.

COMMERCIAL PROPERTY – HEADS OF TERMS

5.6 In commercial property, clients are generally advised by surveyors, also sometimes called agents. It would be usual for the seller's and purchaser's respective surveyors to agree a document that reflects the broad terms of the consensus that they have reached. This is normally set out in one or two page document called the heads of terms. Although it reflects the consensus *ad idem*, it is stated that the parties' intention is that this document does not constitute a contract, because the actual terms of the contract will be agreed by the solicitors in the missives. The heads of terms will cover the main points such as parties, price, date of entry, the property, suspensive conditions, legal costs and any other conditions, such as option to purchase additional subjects.

Once agreed, the heads of terms are passed to both sets of solicitors to progress the contract and the conveyancing in accordance with the agreed terms.

FIXED PRICE

5.7 In a cooling market, marketing a property at a fixed price can be a useful way to entice offers. Even in a good market, fixed prices can be used to secure a quick sale or to differentiate your property from others.

It is a simple system. The first purchaser to make a satisfactory offer at the correct price secures the deal. However, it can be difficult to manage when multiple offers are received. The Law Society considers that marketing at a fixed price is an invitation to prospective purchasers, not an offer in itself. There is therefore no obligation on the seller to accept the first or any other offer.

Advice from the Law Society is that, if marketing a property at a fixed price, you must make clear at the outset if there are any material conditions that will need to apply to the offer. It is also useful to set out whether any suspensive conditions will be entertained, such as being subject to finance or subject to the sale of the seller's own property. There is clearly no need to note interest in these circumstances.

NOTING INTEREST

5.8 It is customary for the purchaser's solicitor to 'note' their client's interest with the seller's agent. A note of interest is sometimes intimated by a letter identifying the client and containing all your contact details as the prospective purchaser's solicitor, so that you will be informed should a closing date be set. It is an indication to the selling agent that your client is serious enough to speak to a solicitor about making an offer.

These days, it is more usual for interest to be noted by telephone, or e-mail. A telephone call should be followed up with an e-mail to be safe. Very often, this telephone conversation is an opportunity to gauge the interest received by asking about the number of other notes of interest. However, it's worth being cautious here. Although it is courteous to withdraw a note of interest if the purchaser's interest wanes, this is not always done in practice. It's not especially in the seller's interest to follow up on older notes of interest that might lead to withdrawal, as a higher number makes the property look more sought-after to prospective purchasers - although the agent may have a feel for their true weight.

Estate agents, and sometimes surveyors, can also treat an expression of interest by the prospective purchaser direct (such as requesting particulars) as a note of interest. There can often be doubt, therefore, as to what exactly is a 'note of interest'. Notes of interest have been developed by custom and practice and are governed only by professional bodies. There is no statutory footing for notes of interest, so they can mean different things to different professions.

Once a critical mass of good quality, recent notes of interest have been received, the seller should have a good indication of the number of seriously interested parties who would be likely (but are not committed to) offer. Once satisfied, the seller will normally set a closing date, but this is again custom and practice, rather than a legal requirement. Clients interested in purchasing should therefore be advised that noting interest will not guarantee an opportunity to submit an offer. There is no obligation incumbent on the seller's solicitor to set a closing date, and the seller is at liberty to accept any offer from any party up until the point a closing date is set. This state of affairs may not be fully appreciated by prospective purchasers, who may be under the impression that noting interest 'guarantees' them an opportunity to make an offer. The reality is however, that where there several notes of interest, a seller will want to go to a closing date, as this is likely to elicit a prospective purchaser's best price.

CLOSING DATES

5.9 A closing date is a date and time set by the seller's solicitor or estate agent for the receipt of offers (akin to best and final offers or sealed bid procedure in England).

It can be a tricky balancing act between forcing prospective purchasers' hands too early and leaving it too late, by which time serious parties have drifted off and found somewhere else. It's the seller's call. Once the seller's solicitor or estate agent receives instructions to proceed, they will notify everyone who noted interest that a closing date has been set. Any new prospective purchasers enquiring about the property can be made aware of the position and any marketing materials updated (eg a 'Closing Date set' banner may appear in the last advertisements for the property) (See also para 4.4).

If acting for a purchaser, make sure that you have received full instructions in plenty of time. Draft your offer in advance, and check the details with the client if you are in any doubt about your instructions. It is good practice to confirm, or ask for confirmation, in writing (usually these days by email) before submitting the offer. Make sure that you have inserted any special conditions that the purchaser instructed. Closing dates are drop-dead deadlines – if your offer is late it should not be considered. It is, therefore, of utmost importance that the date and time is recorded in a system. Most offices have a double diary system or linked computer calendars. Technology is fine, but it needs humans to act on the information.

Mistakes can happen. See *Watts v Bell & Scott WS*[4] for a really simple mistake where the offer was accidentally faxed to the client (who was away on holiday) rather than the chartered surveyors to whom it ought to have been transmitted. The result was that what would have been the highest offer was never received and the client successfully sued the firm for damages.

There are occasions when clients instruct an offer but then try to renegotiate the price once the closing date has been 'won'. This practice has been largely halted by the introduction of Home Reports, since information on the condition of the property is now available upfront and offers are now less likely to be submitted 'subject to survey' for valuation purposes. However, in instances where it is clear that the purchaser has got cold feet and wishes to reduce the price for no good reason, you must consider the client/solicitor relationship as at an end and cease acting for that client.

Unsuccessful offerors' solicitors should be notified as soon as possible by the seller's solicitor. Purchasers' solicitors should try to gather some feedback for their clients as to how many offers were received, the highest price and where their offer was ranked. It can provide some solace but also will help to form a view as to the current state of the market for next time.

4   [2007] CSOH 108.

DUE DILIGENCE QUESTIONNAIRE

5.10 The PSG Due Diligence Questionnaire (DDQ)[5] is specifically designed to help purchasers and their solicitors at the start of a commercial property transaction (although elements of it will be helpful to the residential purchaser's solicitor too, by way of checklist).

The original concept of the DDQ is that it is sent to the seller's solicitor as a way of finding out and obtaining all the information that a commercial purchaser might need to conduct its due diligence processes. It is similar in some ways to the English Commercial Property Standard Enquiries (CPSEs) that are in common use, but is not intended to form part of any contract. Instead, it is supposed to elicit a full disclosure of all relevant information. If the document is actually marked up by the parties, it can form a record of what information has been exchanged, and act as a road map for the transaction. It is used as a robust checklist of requirements that a purchaser's solicitor will seek to examine. It includes information similar to that contained in the Property Questionnaire part of the Home Report, as well as listing all title, searches, certificates and reports that the purchaser's solicitor requires to see, and information about tax matters, employees, tenants and construction documentation for new or recently constructed buildings (see also para 4.9.9).

---

5   See www.psglegal.co.uk/due_diligence.php.

Chapter 6

The Contract

'A verbal contract isn't worth the paper it's written on.'
(Samuel Goldwyn)

MODERN PRACTICE

6.1 In modern conveyancing practice, much more emphasis is placed on the preparation and content of the missives than used to be the case. Several decades ago, an offer consisted of only the bare essential clauses: property, price, date of entry and a requirement for a valid marketable title, for example, but now many of the matters formerly dealt with at the examination of title stage are dealt with in the contract, which can run to many pages, particularly in commercial purchases.

It also seems that there are many more regulatory and legal issues to take into account than ever before, and so it is important for a solicitor to know their way round all the clauses and conditions in a modern offer for the purchase or sale of heritable property, their purpose and effect, and how they interact with the rest of the conveyancing process: the due diligence procedures of examination of title, searches, reports and other documents; the transfer of the property; the payment and settlement/ completion arrangements and the perfecting of the purchaser's real right in the property through the registration stages.

WHAT ARE MISSIVES?

6.2 'Missives' is the name we give to the contract for the sale and purchase of heritable property in Scotland that is constituted by a series of formal letters entered into by or on behalf of a purchaser and a seller dealing with the conditions that are to apply to the purchase and sale. A contract for the purchase or sale of land must be in written form, and while that usually takes the form of missives, it can equally be effected by a Sale and Purchase Agreement between the parties themselves, although one of the advantages of the missives (which are signed by the respective solicitors on behalf of seller or purchaser) is that they can be concluded with more speed, particularly if the parties themselves are in different countries, or if execution formalities are subject to an approval process, which is not uncommon in a number of organisations. For the purposes of this chapter we shall refer to missives only, although the terms apply equally to a Sale and Purchase Agreement, as the content is very similar, it is the format that is different. Incidentally, there might sometimes be a perception of some disadvantage from the client's point of view re loss of control. English clients buying property without a loan are often surprised that they don't actually need to sign any document or deed.

Traditionally, the missives take the form of an Offer to buy from the purchaser, which is accepted by either a *de plano* (without argument) outright acceptance from the seller, or may be met with a qualified acceptance if there are any elements of the purchaser's offer that the seller does not wish to accept, or wants to suggest an alternative. This can be something as simple as a change to the date of entry, or deleting a time limit for acceptance that has not been met, to more significant changes in relation to undertakings or warranties that the seller is being asked to give, or shifting the onus back to the purchaser, such as where the purchaser will be expected to 'satisfy himself' as to the position in relation to matters such as titles and condition of the property. The process is referred to as 'adjusting the missives'. Once all matters are agreed between the parties, which may involve the back and forth exchange of a number of letters, the final letter of acceptance with no new conditions, 'concludes the bargain'.

While missives can be entered into directly between the contracting parties, invariably the missive letters are prepared by the solicitors on behalf of their respective clients and are signed by the solicitors. The missives need not necessarily be witnessed, but it is common practice for this to be done. It means then that they are self proving and can be registered in the Books of Council and Session if required and thus provide for faster diligence, if it comes to that. By the missives the sellers bind themselves to sell, and the purchasers bind themselves to buy the property in question. The conclusion of missives represents *consensus ad idem* and the formation of a binding contract.

It is becoming increasingly common in commercial property transactions, for an offer to sell to be issued by the seller's solicitors, once the essential terms of the deal have been agreed by the parties or their agents in Heads of Terms, which consist of a document setting out the principal points agreed by the parties eg price, entry, suspensive conditions. It is also common for offers to sell to be issued in transactions involving insolvency, as these circumstances generate specific requirement of the parties (see para 6.19).

The contract will describe the property, the price being paid, the date that the price is to be paid and all other conditions affecting the transaction. For both residential and commercial property, the missives will also contain a wide variety of additional conditions according to circumstances relating to such matters as: condition of the property and the systems in it, tax, title and title conditions, planning and building control and other construction matters, roads and services, and details regarding any occupational leases affecting the property. Some types of property, such as farms or licensed premises, have their own specialist clauses.

Strictly speaking, there is no legal requirement for missives to be entered into. Parties can, and occasionally do, go straight to completion of the transaction without any prior contract at all, the documentation consisting only of the disposition to transfer the title, which will be delivered to the purchasers in return for payment of the price. This would be most unusual – not to mention risky – in an arms-length transaction, but might take place if the property is being transferred between members of the same family, for example. However, missives not only bind the parties into the transaction, they also deal (as we shall see) with many other matters not normally dealt with in the disposition, but which are equally important to the purchaser of the property.

ADJUSTING MISSIVES

6.3 The 'formal offer and series of acceptance letters' model is becoming somewhat old fashioned, however, with the increasing use, either of standardised offers (see paras 6.9, 6.10 and 6.14), or of treating the offer that has been submitted as a draft document, which the parties then adjust, as a single document, until its terms are agreed between the parties. It is rare these days that solicitors need a set of coloured pens for this purpose: it is usual for changes to be marked up electronically.

The days of having to craft complicated sentences in the missives to express small changes in a previous letter are rapidly becoming a thing of the past. It is so much easier, not to mention less risky, to make a manuscript or on-screen change of words, replacing the previous words with your alternative provision, than having to produce tortuous sentences along the lines of: 'The words 'within three months' where they appear in lines four and five of clause ten of your qualified acceptance will be deleted and there will be substituted the words 'by not later than 31 August 2015', both in terms of drafting, and, later on, when reading and understanding the final basis of the agreement between the parties. It is not necessary to flip backwards and forwards between letters to work out what the final version actually says – it is set out in the final agreed version of the single document.

If you do have to exchange formal letters in this way for any reason, it is vital to ensure that your revisals are accurate, and to check that the new provision that results says what it is supposed to say. It is too easy to delete reference to a string of words, and substitute them with an alternative that no longer makes grammatical (or legal) sense within the sentence. Each qualified acceptance is in effect a counter offer, and if a complex offer is followed by a complex acceptance, there is still no *consensus ad idem*, and the purchaser's solicitors will have to write again formally, accepting the qualifications made by the seller before a binding contract can exist. Theoretically this process could go on indefinitely. The more letters that are exchanged, the more complex the contract becomes, and the longer the missives remain unconcluded, the greater the uncertainty, and the possibility of the whole deal collapsing. The dire consequences of having too many letters can be seen in the case of *Rutterford Ltd v Allied Breweries Ltd*[1], in which, after a series of qualified acceptances, Rutterford's solicitors acting in their client's purchase of the property, purported to withdraw the qualifications in their previous qualified acceptance to Allied Breweries' solicitors, and to hold the bargain as concluded. Unfortunately the effect of the earlier acceptance had been to cancel out the offer represented by the previous qualified acceptance, so that the final letter in the chain was not sufficient to conclude the contract, but should properly be regarded as a proposal that a contract be concluded on the basis of the earlier exchange of letters.

1   [1990] SLT 249.

Clearly the practice of adjusting the draft single document is preferable.

The offer can stay in draft format for some time, particularly if there are complex issues to deal with, or some essential pieces of information are outstanding. It may be useful to insert drafting notes, either in bold type, or italics or square-bracketed, into the document to remind you to return to these points and resolve them before the final version is produced for signing. During the adjustment period, there may be a number of iterations of the draft offer that are passed between the solicitors. You must check the terms of each version you receive against the previous version produced by you. Sometimes the other solicitors will have used revision indicators (like 'Track changes' in Word) to show the changes they have made, and while this is an easy way to see only the changes that have been made, without having to re-read the whole document again, it is not entirely without risk. Some changes may have been made inadvertently without having the revision indicator function 'switched on', and so the best way to be sure that you are seeing all of the changes is to use a document comparison tool, like Workshare™. Some solicitors will send you a comparison document to accompany their new version of the document but you may prefer to produce your own comparison. It is very easy to get out of sync with multiple versions of a document, and so careful version control procedures are required.

At all times of course it is important to be alive to the effect that changes to one clause may have on another clause elsewhere in the document.

If the process of adjusting the offer is becoming protracted, (and even if it is not, for speed), often the best course of action is to have a meeting, or lengthy phone call with the other solicitors, to thrash out the differences, although often nowadays the negotiation takes place through exchange of emails.

CONCLUDING THE CONTRACT

6.4 A regrettable feature of modern conveyancing is (or has been) the long delay in conclusion of missives, sometimes until the date of settlement. While occasionally necessary due to protracted negotiations as to the terms of the missives, simply delaying the conclusion of the contract until the last minute is poor practice and it equates to the English system of the contract only being complete when contracts are exchanged, and runs the risk of the English features of gazumping, gazundering and contract chains to enter Scottish conveyancing. Sometimes the reason is that the lending institutions, which are taking longer and longer to issue loan papers means that the purchaser's solicitor does not want to run the risk of concluding the contract only to have his client unable to settle, if an offer of loan is not forthcoming. Sometimes, it is simply pressure of work that is to blame. It may be that some solicitors, faced by increasingly complex contracts, are quite happy not to conclude them. While solicitors must have regard to the interests of their clients and take their clients' instructions, they must also act professionally and not mislead other professionals. Law Society Guidance[2] which refers to residential transactions states that solicitors acting on behalf of both purchasers and sellers have a professional duty to conclude contracts without undue delay, to inform their clients of the requirement to do so, and advising of action that they should take if instructed by their client to delay concluding the bargain pending resolution of some other matter such as selling their own house or waiting for confirmation of funding, which may include withdrawing from acting for that client.

DELIVERY

6.5 There have been differing views concerning the requirement for delivery of missives. Some commentators describe missives as a bilateral contract, which is effective as soon as it has been executed. Others considered that, to be effective, the writing must physically be delivered to the other party, because (*Erskine Institutes* at 3.2.43) as long as a writing remains in the granter's own custody, he is free to change his mind and to destroy it, or at least not to deliver it. The issue has now effectively gone away with the ability to conclude a binding contract by way of electronic delivery of a signed traditional document under the Legal Writings (Counterparts and Delivery) (Scotland) Act 2015[3].

It has been commonplace for some time to send pdf versions of signed missives letters via email to the other party's solicitors during the course

---

2   LSS Rules and Guidance, Division C: Conveyancing – Avoidance of Delay in Concluding Missives. See www.lawscot.org.uk/rules-and-guidance/section-f-guidance-relating-to-particular-types-of-work/division-c-conveyancing/guidance/avoidance-of-delay-in-concluding-missives/.
3   Section 4 of the Legal Writings (Counterparts & Delivery) Act 2015.

of the transaction. Solicitors who do not have the capability to create pdf documents can, and do, resort to sending facsimile versions of the letters via fax machine. Although the principals of the letters are then sent by post or DX or Legal Post, the parties had come to regard the missies as 'concluded' on the date on which they were signed and faxed or emailed. Where conclusion of the missives and completion were simultaneous or occurred close together, it would not be unusual for completion to take place and funds be transferred on the strength of faxed or emailed missives, particularly, apparently, in residential transactions.

This practice came into sharp relief following on the decision in the case of *Thomas Park and Another, Petitioners*[4], which concerned a petition for partial recall of an inhibition, to release from the ambit of the inhibition the petitioners' leasehold interest in The Grapevine Restaurant in Bothwell. The basis for the recall was that, before the inhibition was effective, missives had been concluded for the sale of the business and property.

It was agreed that the effective date of the inhibition was midnight on 31 August 2007, but earlier on that day, after an offer to purchase the lease of the property had been made in early August, the petitioners' solicitors had sent a fax with a signed qualified acceptance to the purchaser's solicitors, who faxed back a full acceptance, that same day. Both formal letters were then put in the post.

The point at issue was whether missives had effectively been concluded on 31 August. In support of their contention that they had, the petitioners sought to rely on the 'postal acceptance rule', and also on case law that indicated that communication by fax would be sufficient to constitute a contract. The postal acceptance rule provides that, while an offer is effective only when it is received, an acceptance is effective from the date of posting (*Thomson v James*[5]). This, however, assumes that the acceptance is a clear and complete acceptance of the offer and not a qualified acceptance setting out new terms. In *Park*, the judge decided that the inhibition **did** attach to the property, as actual delivery was necessary for offers and *qualified* acceptances. Although the letter concluding the contract was posted on 31 August, the qualified acceptance, or counter

4 [2009] CSOH 122.
5 [1855] 18 D 1.

129

offer to which it referred had not been delivered, and so the contract could not be regarded as concluded until that acceptance actually arrived.

The decision in *Park* threw something of a judicial cat among the conveyancing pigeons at the time. *Obiter* references in the case to the possibility of 'constructive delivery' set off the practice of giving undertakings not to withdraw a formal letter delivered electronically (by fax or email) and irrevocably undertaking to put it in the post.

There were, however, considerable doubts that 'constructive delivery' of missives letters was possible, given that the remarks made in *Park* were *obiter* and did not form part of the *ratio* or actual decision of the judge. It seems that while the undertakings that were given by solicitors in these cases, although forming a binding obligation on the solicitor to do what is stated in the undertaking, did not necessarily have the effect of rendering the missives letters binding and enforceable.

Law Society guidance on electronic communications is that there is a duty on a solicitor to follow up a fax or email of a contractual document with the original as soon as possible[6]. If the solicitor is instructed by the client not to send the hard copy, that fact must be communicated to the other solicitor immediately; the solicitor must withdraw from acting if the client cannot be persuaded to withdraw those instructions. This is somewhat out-of-date now (at the time of writing), due to the effect of Legal Writings Act. It is, however, important to note that although a binding contract has been created, the electronic version is not to be treated as being the traditional document itself[7], so it remains important for the actual physical document to be delivered, for retention by the recipient.

OPTIONS

6.6 There are occasions when parties agree that property, or land, may be sold by the owner to a prospective purchaser, but not right now, or only if certain circumstances apply. For example, a party might want to obtain detailed planning permission for a proposed development of the property, conclude a contract with a third party to take a lease of the site

---

6   Law Society Rules and Guidance, Division C: Conveyancing – Delivery of Missives See www.lawscot.org.uk/rules-and-guidance/section-f-guidance-relating-to-particular-types-of-work/division-c-conveyancing/guidance/delivery-of-missives.
7   Section 4(6) of the Legal Writings (Counterparts & Delivery) Act 2015.

(conditional on the purchase being completed), enter into a contract to purchase some adjoining land (again conditional on the purchase being completed), and so on. Missives can be entered into on a conditional basis (see para 6.15), but another alternative is for the parties to enter into an option agreement, giving the prospective purchaser an exclusive option to buy the property in question at some future date. A well-drafted option will contain details of the terms and conditions on which the purchase, if it goes ahead, will proceed, very similar to adjusted missives. Separate missives are not, strictly speaking, necessary, but it may sometimes be preferable to adjust missives at the time the option is exercised. One essential difference with an option is that, unless its terms provide otherwise, the party need not ever purchase the site and cannot be made to do so by the owner. An option can, however, contain a provision that the owner of the land can call on the party to purchase the land at some point (known as a 'call option').

The option will ordinarily only be enforceable for a certain period of time, after which one or other of the parties will be entitled to bring the contract to an end. Obviously, the owner of the land does not want to be tied into a contract for an unlimited period of time where there is no possibility of the sale ever taking place. The period of time for which the option is in place will depend on the circumstances of the transaction. It could be months, or even years. In many instances the potential purchaser will pay a fee for the option, which will be retained by the seller even if the option is never exercised. Options are typical in situations where a developer might want to acquire an unzoned piece of land and then try to get a planning consent. Usually he will want an option with as long a duration as possible since obtaining the right planning consent can be a very long drawn out process.

It is common for the option holder's rights also to be protected by having the landowner grant a standard security over the land in favour of the option holder. That way, any attempted sale to a third party would be prevented, as the standard security would appear as a marker on the title, and of course would need to be discharged (by the option holder) for the landowner to be able to produce a clear title to a purchaser. This device is used in preference to imposing a condition in the title, which would not be enforceable in any event as a real burden, because if it attempted to prevent the landowner from selling, it would be repugnant with ownership.

Remember that a badly drafted suspensive condition can also amount to an option, in effect (see para 6.15.1).

EXCLUSIVITY ARRANGEMENTS ('LOCK-OUT' OR 'LOCK-IN' AGREEMENTS)

6.7 From time to time in commercial transactions, the parties may agree that for a, usually short, period of time, a prospective purchaser may be given complete exclusivity to carry out due diligence and agree the terms of the contract with the seller, to the exclusion of any other parties. This arrangement should be distinguished from the process of 'noting interest' where, once parties have intimated their interest with a selling agent, they are entitled to an opportunity to offer for the property along with other interested parties (see para 5.8). Exclusivity agreements are not generally known in residential transactions, although they can happen – perhaps with a large estate, where a purchaser, having a clear run at offering for the property, wants to have the freedom to negotiate the terms of the purchase without other potential purchasers appearing on the scene, which would prompt the seller to set a closing date.

Exclusivity agreements, which are also sometimes called lock-out or lock-in agreements, will tie the parties into an arrangement in advance of entering into a legally binding contract and provide time to carry out all the investigations a purchaser needs to conduct. The seller cannot sell, or attempt to sell, the property to a third party for the duration of the agreement. In other words, the parties have 'locked-out' third parties and 'locked-in' themselves. However, the arrangements within the exclusivity agreement do not need to be too prescriptive, for example neither party need necessarily be committed to proceed with a transaction.

The purchaser benefits from the comfort that the seller will not dispose of the property for a certain period of time, during which the buyer can carry out surveys, arrange funding, set up a tenant, discuss commercial terms with the seller in greater detail, and examine the title and any leases. In many agreements, the buyer will be under a positive obligation to take those steps which it needs to progress the transaction during the period the agreement is in force.

Often a seller may seek payment of a premium or fee, to compensate for the fact that it is unable to dispose of the property for a fixed period.

The amount of premium will depend on the circumstances, however, it is sometimes paid on the basis that if the sale does take place, then the price paid on completion will have that premium deducted from it.

STANDARDISED OFFERS – RESIDENTIAL STANDARD CLAUSES

6.8 As offers became progressively longer and more complex, each firm of solicitors developed its own style of offer (sometimes different solicitors in the same firm had their own individual preferred style of offer). This meant that the terms of the offer had to be carefully studied in each transaction, and a bespoke qualified acceptance prepared. Considerable time could be spent negotiating all the terms of the contract.

The Law Society tried to introduce a standard Scottish contract a number of years ago, but at that time, it was never really adopted by the profession at large, due to the lack of flexibility. More recently, however, local faculties and associations of solicitors produced a series of standard clauses for residential missives, couched in terms that ought to be acceptable for many transactions. There were a number of regional variations to cater for, and standard clauses for Aberdeen, Ayr, Borders, Dumfries and Galloway, Dundee/Tayside, Highland, Inverclyde, Moray, Paisley and Combined Standard Clauses for Edinburgh and Glasgow appeared. Standardisation does not work so well if there are so many variations that the benefits of standardisation are diluted or even lost, but the production of the Combined Standard Clauses proved to be an important step towards greater standardisation among the various regional options, resulting in the Scottish Standard Clauses for residential missives, in December 2014[8]. There has been widespread adoption of the Scottish Standard Clauses, effectively making them National Conditions of Sale for residential property.

The idea with the residential offers to purchase is that they are designed to be accepted unconditionally, with the terms that they contain regarded as a reasonably fair representation between the interests and requirements of the seller and purchaser. They consist of a single page (or short) letter

---

8   Available on the Law Society website. See www.lawscot.org.uk/rules-and-guidance/section-f-guidance-relating-to-particular-types-of-work/division-c-conveyancing/advice-and-information/scottish-standard-clauses/.

which refers to a set of standard offer clauses that have been registered in the Books of Council and Session, and by reference are incorporated into the offer.

Most residential conveyancers will be familiar with the terms and conditions of the standard clauses and so will know, in any particular set of circumstances, whether or not there are conditions that they would not be able to accept from the point of view of their seller client or, in the case of the purchaser's solicitors, whether there are additional conditions that they would want to impose.

In practice, it seems most solicitors will have their own favourite qualifications to make to standard form offers both as solicitor submitting for the purchaser, and as solicitor accepting for the seller.

The concept of the standard offer has proved to be successful and enjoys widespread use, although it is not mandatory to use it.

STANDARDISED OFFERS – THE RESIDENTIAL OFFER

6.9 The one page offer will look something like this, which is the version included with the Scottish Standard Clauses (2014 Edition 1):

Dear Sirs

Seller

Purchaser

Property address

For the purposes of this offer and the Scottish Standard Clauses (Edition 1) aftermentioned:

The Purchaser means [   ] residing at [   ]

The Property means [   ] together with any garden, carport, garage, parking space and/or outbuildings pertaining thereto and all other parts and pertinents.

The Price is [   ] POUNDS (£[   ]) STERLING, and

The Date of Entry shall be [   ] or such other date as may be mutually agreed in writing.

The Purchaser hereby offers to purchase from your client (hereinafter referred to as 'the Seller') the Property at the Price and upon the conditions contained in the Scottish Standard Clauses (Edition 1) specified in the Deed of Declaration by Ross Alexander MacKay dated 2 December and registered in the Books of Council and Session for preservation on – December both 2014, and upon the following further conditions:-

Note: The Scottish Standard Clauses are imported into each offer with this wording. If for any reason it is necessary to depart from any provision in these Clauses (which is, naturally, discouraged, but may in some circumstances, be unavoidable) then such variations should be clearly set out in this offer letter.

(First)   The Price will include the following additional items (if any):
    [   ]

Note: When the purchasers of a house buy furniture and furnishings with that house, the purchasers' solicitors should ask the sellers to confirm that they own these effects, and that there are no outstanding hire purchase, credit sale, leasing or other debts, which would mean that the sellers do not own the moveables they have sold. A warranty to this effect is included at Clause 1.3 of the Scottish Standard Clauses.

(Second)   This offer unless earlier withdrawn is open for verbal acceptance by -pm (insert time and date) with written acceptance reaching us no later than – on the – (insert time and day) working day following the date of this offer and if not so accepted shall be deemed to be withdrawn.

(Third)   This offer and any contract to follow hereon are entirely conditional upon (a) a satisfactory survey report and (b) a satisfactory valuation report being obtained by the Purchaser in respect of the Property. The Purchaser and his lenders shall be the sole judges as to what constitutes satisfactory reports.

Note: The offer may also include a clause making the offer conditional on the purchaser obtaining a loan, or selling his own property. In the first case, the seller's response will probably be to delete this clause in any acceptance, and the purchaser should get on with getting the loan arrangements in place as soon as possible. The second case is of course more problematic, and is tantamount to no offer at all. If the purchaser has difficulty in selling, the seller could find himself tied into a contract indefinitely, and so at the very least, if this condition is to be accepted, a long stop date **must** be included in the acceptance, after which, if the purchaser has not sold, the seller is free to find another purchaser. It all depends on the circumstances, eg the purchaser may be waiting for interested parties to offer for her property, at a closing date in a few days' time. The seller's solicitor should find out as much about the purchaser's circumstances to be able to advise the seller if this type of condition can be entertained.

While there might be a few qualifications to this offer because of specific circumstances of the transaction, the hope and expectation is that the seller's solicitors will be able to issue a *de plano* acceptance (see para 6.21).

STANDARDISED OFFERS – THE SCOTTISH STANDARD CLAUSES

6.10 The following clause by clause consideration is of the current version (2014 (Edition 1) of the Scottish Standard Clauses. It is expected that the Scottish Standard Clauses will be regularly reviewed, probably annually, and so you should always make sure that you are using the most up-to-date edition.

6.10.1 Interpretation

In these Clauses:

'Date of Settlement' or 'settlement' means the date on which settlement is actually effected whether that is the Date of Entry or not;

'the Missives' means the contract of purchase and sale concluded between the Purchaser and the Seller of which the Offer incorporating reference to these Clauses forms part;

The terms 'the Purchaser', 'the Seller', 'the Property', 'the Price' and 'the Date of Entry' have the meanings set out in the Offer or other document incorporating reference to these Clauses;

'the 2012 Act' means the Land Registration etc (Scotland) Act 2012;

'working day' means any day on which clearing banks in Edinburgh, Glasgow and London are open for normal business;

'the Building' means, where applicable, the larger building or tenement of which the Property forms part.

The masculine includes the feminine and words in the singular include the plural and vice versa.

Any intimation shall be in writing (which shall include, for avoidance of doubt, faxes or emails).

Where any intimation must be given within a specified period, time will be of the essence.

Note: Some basic definitions and interpretation provisions are included at the start of the Scottish Standard Clauses, although it should be noted that there are other defined terms peppered throughout the Clauses. Interpretation provisions of this type are intended to clarify the terms of the document as well as cutting down unnecessary wording, such as having to specify the plural of things as well as the singular and so on, throughout the document, which could make for extremely tortuous provisions. It also provides some definitions of the meaning of certain expressions and applies an approach that should be taken for certain activities – such as time being of the essence, without the need to state it every time the relevant situation applies throughout the document. As a matter of general practice you should always read the interpretation provisions of a document carefully, and not just assume that it is the usual boilerplate, as some specific interpretative provisions may have a significant effect on the terms of the clauses that appear elsewhere in the document, and it is important to be aware of the fact that the words in the clause itself may not give the whole picture.

6.10.2 Clause 1: Fixtures, fittings & contents

1.1 The Property is sold with:

1.1.1 all heritable fittings and fixtures;

1.1.2 all items of whatever nature fixed or fitted to the Property the removal of which would materially damage the fabric or decoration of the Property;

1.1.3   all items stated to be included in the sales particulars or advertisements made available to the Purchaser; and

1.1.4   the following insofar as any were in the Property when viewed by the Purchaser: garden shed or hut, greenhouse, summerhouse; all growing plants, shrubs, trees (except those in plant pots); all types of blinds, pelmets, curtain rails and runners, curtain poles and rings thereon; a carpets and floor coverings (but excluding loose rugs), stair carpet fixings; fitted bedroom furniture; all bathroom and cloakroom mirrors, bathroom and toilet fittings; kitchen units; all cookers, hobs, ovens, washing machines, dishwashers, fridges and freezers if integral' to or encased within matching units; extractor hoods, extractor fans, electric storage heaters, electric fires, electric light fittings (including all fluorescent lighting, external lighting, wall lights, dimmer switches and bulbs and bulb holders but not shades); television aerials and associated cables and sockets, satellite dishes; solar panels; loft ladders; rotary clothes driers; burglar alarm, other security systems and associated equipment; secondary glazing; shelving, fireplace surround units, fire grates, fenders and associated ironmongery; and

1.1.5   oil in any storage tank and gas in any gas cylinders or tank remaining at the Date of Settlement.

1.2   Where a wheeled bin or other receptacle for the collection of refuse is provided free of charge by the Local Authority or other body responsible for the collection of refuse, the Seller shall ensure that the wheeled bin or other receptacle is left at the Property for the Purchaser failing which the Seller shall meet the cost of replacing same.

1.3   The Seller warrants that at the Date of Settlement all items included in the Price are owned by the Seller, are or will be free of all debt, and are not the subject of any litigation.

1.4   The Seller undertakes to remove all moveables from the Property not otherwise included in the Price as at the Date of Settlement.

Note: The rule is all property that is heritable is included in the sale, and that moveable property is excluded. More and more the distinction between the two becomes blurred, and it is not unknown for sellers to strip the house, especially of bulbs—both light bulbs, which are moveable, and garden bulbs, which are heritable. This clause sets out that all heritable property is included in the purchase, but also items which might be either heritable or moveable, to avoid tiresome disputes. Any moveable items which are to be included in the sale should be specifically mentioned in the main offer. Conversely, other moveable items should be removed from the property, as the purchaser does not want to be faced with having to clear out the property of unwanted items.

6.10.3 Clause 2: Awareness of circumstances affecting the property

2.1   So far as the Seller is aware (but declaring that the Seller has made no enquiry or investigation into such matters) the Property (including in respect of Clauses 2.1.3 and 2.1.4 the Building, if appropriate) is not affected by:

2.1.1   any Notice of Potential Liability for Costs registered in terms of the Tenements (Scotland) Act 2004 or the Title Conditions (Scotland) Act 2003;

2.1.2   any Notices of Payment of Improvement/Repairs Grants;

2.1.3   flooding from any river or watercourse which has taken place within the last 5 years;

2.1.4   other than as disclosed in the Home Report for the Property any structural defects; wet rot; dry rot; rising damp; woodworm; or other infestation.

Note: Several general warranties are set out in Clause 2 about the seller's state of awareness on matters that could affect the property. Some of these, such as notices of potential liability for costs or repairs notices should be disclosed by searches or property enquiry certificates. However, incorporation of a warranty about these important matters at the offer stage, ought to elicit a disclosure, at an early stage, of any of them that affect the property, which may alter the purchaser's attitude to the property, or require further provision to be made in the missives.

6.10.4 Clause 3: Specialist reports

3.1   Any guarantees in force at the Date of Entry in respect of (i) treatments which have been carried out to the Property (or to the Building, if appropriate) for the eradication of timber infestation, dry rot, wet rot, rising damp or other such defects, and/or (ii) insulation and double glazing, together with all supporting estimates, survey reports and other papers relating thereto ('the Guarantees') will be exhibited on conclusion of the Missives and delivered at settlement.

3.2   The Seller confirms that he is not aware of anything having been done or omitted to be done which might invalidate the Guarantees.

3.3   If requested, and insofar as necessary and competent, the Guarantees will be assigned to the Purchaser at the Purchaser's expense.

Note: If there have been any specialist treatments carried out to the property, these are normally accompanied by a guarantee – sometimes covering a period of many years – against failure of the treatment, so the purchaser will want to have the benefit of those guarantees if they are still valid and enforceable. The existence of any such guarantees should have been flagged up in the Questionnaire section of the Home Report. The guarantees should be examined, in case of recurrence of the problem, and should be checked to identify the areas affected, and the status of the guarantor. If the company that originally gave the guarantee is no longer in existence and there is no insurance or industry back-up for the guarantee, then it is unfortunately worthless. Many of these guarantees do not require a formal assignation to the purchaser, and transfer automatically, but you should check the terms of the documentation to be certain.

6.10.5 Clause 4: Central heating, Systems and Appliances

4.1   The Seller undertakes that any systems or appliances of a working nature (including central heating, water, drainage, electric and gas) forming part of the Property or included in the Price will be in working order commensurate with age as at the Date of Settlement.

4.2   The Seller will make good any defect which prevents any system or appliance being in such order provided said defect is intimated in writing within 5 working days of settlement. Failing such intimation, the Purchaser will be deemed to be satisfied as to the position.

4.3   The Seller will only be responsible for carrying out any necessary repairs to put any system or appliance into such order and shall have no liability for any element of upgrading (except to the extent such upgrading is required to put any such system or appliance into such order).

4.4   The lack of any regular service or maintenance of any system or appliance or the fact that it may no longer comply with current installation regulations shall not, of itself, be deemed to be a defect.

4.5   The Purchaser shall be entitled to execute any necessary repairs at the expense of the Seller without reference to the Seller or the Seller's tradesmen (i) in the event of an emergency; (ii) in the event that the Seller's tradesmen do not inspect the alleged defects within 5 working days of intimation; or (iii) in the event that any necessary repairs are not carried out within 5 working days of inspection.

4.6   The Seller confirms that he has received no notice or intimation from any third party that any system (or any part thereof) is in an unsafe or dangerous condition.

Note: The purchaser will have had the property valued on the basis that the systems and appliances included in the property are in good working order. Obviously if the central heating system was installed 12 years ago, then the property is clearly being sold with a 12-year old system and the purchaser is not entitled to seek works that would upgrade it to a current state of the art system, hence the reference to 'commensurate with age'. However, if any of these systems or appliances are found not to function on taking entry, then it is entirely appropriate that the purchaser should seek recompense from the seller, always subject to the *de minimis* level of £300 in Clause 26: Limitation of Claims. Clause 4 provides for the purchaser to check immediately that all systems and appliances are working, and to formally (ie in writing) intimate any problems with them within a tight timescale of 5 days. Note: The purchaser should get these systems checked by a qualified person at the date of entry, and submit any claim timeously. The seller does not want to be kept hanging on for a long time with the possibility of a claim by the purchaser, so when acting for the purchaser, you should be sure to remind him to check all the systems thoroughly as soon as he moves in.

From the point of view of the seller, if they have had the central heating system regularly serviced, for example, then they should be less concerned about this type of clause. Details of any maintenance contracts will show up in the Home Report. It makes sense of course, if there are any problems with any of the systems or appliances, that these are disclosed during the contract stage so that liability can be excluded or limited, or repair work carried out before settlement.

If repairs are necessary then it is up to the seller to have them done as soon as possible. A five-working-day period is allowed, except in the case of emergency. Clearly the seller would prefer to be in control of instructing the work, as he is the one meeting the cost. You may find yourself involved in some of these arrangements immediately post settlement.

6.10.6 Clause 5: Development

5.1   The Seller warrants that he has not served or been served with nor received any neighbour notification notice issued in terms of planning legislation in respect of any development. This warranty shall not apply (i) in respect of a development which has been completed, (ii) where any planning permission has lapsed, or (iii) where an application for planning consent has been refused or withdrawn. In the event of any such notice being served on or received by the Seller prior to the Date of Settlement, the Seller will forward such notice to the Purchaser within 5 working days of receipt of such notice.

5.2   Without prejudice to the foregoing, the Seller warrants that he has no knowledge of any proposal which could be reasonably deemed to materially affect the value or amenity of the Property.

Note: The position regarding planning notices actually issued and affecting the property can be verified either by the planning department of the local council or by a Property Enquiry Certificate that specifically deals with planning matters. This clause only deals with matters that should be within the knowledge of the seller, and should have already been disclosed in the Home Report, although of course they might have been served after the questionnaire was completed. The seller's solicitor should already have checked whether the seller has received any notices and is therefore able to give this warranty. The clause also makes it clear that the seller's warranty doesn't extend to completed works or lapsed, refused or withdrawn permissions. The clause also seeks a general warranty from the seller about proposals that might affect the property. This would extend to such things as future intended works, perhaps new roads, tramways, or other infrastructure proposals, which while not yet the subject of any planning agreement, are being consulted on or discussed locally.

6.10.7 Clause 6: Statutory notices

6.1   Any Local Authority (or other public body) notices or orders calling for repairs or other works to the Property dated prior to or on the date of conclusion of the Missives (or any other work affecting the Property agreed to or authorised by the Seller outstanding at the Date of Entry) will be the responsibility of the Seller. Liability under this condition will subsist until met and will not be avoided by the issue of a replacement notice or order.

Note: This covers notices or orders issued prior to the date of conclusion of the missives, not the date of entry. This distinction used to be the subject of an east-west divide, with the west holding out for the date of entry when liability passed. It had long been felt in the alternative that if a statutory notice, for example, for repairs to the roof of a tenement in which a flat that was the subject of the purchase was located, was issued just after conclusion of missives, but before settlement, then it was unfair to expect the seller to have to be liable for that cost, particularly when the purchaser would have offered for the property on the basis of it in its unrepaired state, and presumably also at a valuation that reflected that state of repair. The existence of any such notices prior to the sale will be stated in the Home Report, and the PEC will disclose any that have been issued.

6.2   The Seller warrants that he has not received written notification of, approved, entered into or authorised any scheme of common repairs or improvement affecting the Building. Where the Seller approves, enters into or authorises any such scheme or where any such scheme is instructed, the Seller shall remain liable for his share of the cost of such works. Details of any such scheme will be disclosed to the Purchaser prior to settlement. The Seller undertakes not to enter into, approve or otherwise authorise any such scheme prior to settlement without the consent of the Purchaser.

Note: This provision relates principally to tenements.

6.3   When any work in terms of clauses 6.1 or 6.2 above is incomplete or unpaid for at the Date of Settlement the Purchaser will be entitled to retain from the Price a sum equivalent to the estimated cost of the Seller's share of such works (which estimate shall be augmented by

25%). Such retention shall be held in an interest bearing account by the Purchaser's solicitor pending settlement of the Seller's liability. The retention shall not be released or intromitted with without the written authority of the solicitors for the Purchaser and the Seller. Any shortfall will remain the liability of the Seller.

Note: Common repairs in tenements can be fraught with issues. The costs of major schemes can be huge, and the disruption significant. If there are common repairs ongoing in a tenement building, then full details need to be obtained and decisions made about respective liabilities of the seller and purchaser. This will usually mean that estimates of the remaining cost of repairs will have to be provided so that the purchaser can determine what sum to retain from the price until the repairs are finished (this is the usual arrangement, but other provision can be made if the parties want). The usual position is that the seller will bear the whole costs (which need to be vouched or verified) and an appropriate sum is retained from the price – not handed over to the seller, but reserved in some account until the works are finished. Usually, the purchaser's solicitors will arrange for consignation of the funds and will hold these until the works are finished and paid for .

    6.4   On issue of invoices for such works in terms of clauses 6.1 and/or 6.2 above by the Local Authority or other authorised party the retention shall be released to make payment of such invoices as soon as reasonably practical.

Note: If the purchaser has retained funds, then payment should be met from these.

    6.5   Notwithstanding any other term within the Missives, this condition will remain in full force and effect without limit of time and may be founded upon until implemented.

    6.6   Without prejudice to the above, the Purchaser may retain from the Price such sum as is reasonably required to meet any costs for which he may be contingently liable under s 10(2) of the Title Conditions (Scotland) Act 2003 or s 12(2) of the Tenements (Scotland) Act 2004 as amended. Such retention shall be held in an interest bearing account by the Purchaser's solicitor pending settlement of that liability. The retention shall not be released or intromitted with without the written authority of the solicitors for the Seller and the Purchaser. Any shortfall will remain the liability of the Seller.

6.7 Prior to the Date of Entry the Seller will provide full details of any common repairs in respect of which a Notice of Potential Liability for costs has been or is to be registered.

Note: the arrangements under section 12 of the Title Conditions (Scotland) Act 2003 and section 10 of the Tenements (Scotland) Act 2004 provide for a notice to be registered against the title to a property where there is an obligation to pay a share of costs relating to maintenance or other work (but not local authority work) carried out before the property is sold. The notice must be registered at least 14 days before the purchaser's 'acquisition date' for the new owner to be liable for these costs. What this means in practice is that a purchaser is given notification that costs are due, so that arrangements can be made for a suitable retention from the price. This clause provides an equitable agreed mechanism for retention of a sum to deal with notices served on the property, a situation which in the past has provided many problems through the default of sellers.

6.10.8 Clause 7: Property management and factors

7.1 Where the Property is part of any larger subjects (the Building or otherwise) or a development, it is a condition that:

7.1.1 common charges will be apportioned between the Seller and the Purchaser as at the Date of Entry on the basis that the Seller will be responsible for all common repairs and improvements carried out, instructed or authorised on or prior to the Date of Entry;

7.1.2 there are no major repairs or improvements proposed, instructed, authorised or completed but not yet paid for in respect of the Property or the larger subjects or the Building or development of which it forms part;

7.1.3 the Seller shall provide the Purchaser with full details of any factoring and block insurance arrangements affecting the Property; and

7.1.4	all other outgoings and charges payable in respect of the Property will be apportioned as at the Date of Entry.

Note: This applies an equitable scheme of division between seller and purchaser of accounts for maintenance and repair of parts of a building which is in multiple ownership. If there is a factor or property manager, he will carry out an apportionment between the parties, and should be asked to do this by the seller's solicitor. It is up to the seller's solicitor, and obviously desirable, to inform the factor of the change in ownership so that the seller's responsibility for such accounts will cease as at the date of entry. The seller will remain liable for repairs authorised or instructed, or work undertaken but not yet completed, or completed but not yet paid for prior to the date of entry.

6.10.9 Clause 8: Alterations

Where there have been additions or alterations (including change of use) completed to the Property within 20 years of the Date of Entry, or if the Property has been erected within that period then the Seller shall exhibit before and deliver at the Date of Entry:

8.1.1 all necessary Listed Building Consents and either:

8.1.1.1 all necessary Building Warrants (including stamped warrant drawings where available) and Certificates of Completion (or, if applicable, Notices of Acceptance of Completion Certificate); or

8.1.1.2 an unqualified Property Inspection Report, Letter of Comfort, or equivalent provided by the relevant Local Authority or other mutually agreed supplier.

Note: The importance of this provision cannot be overstated. Any building work, with only very minor exceptions, carried out to the property after its construction requires building regulation consents (building warrant) from the local authority, to ensure that it is carried out safely and correctly. Although one could seek confirmation that *any* such works have been done with the appropriate authorisation from the local authority, in practice a cut-off period of 20 years has been agreed. Often information and assistance will be required from the surveyor to (a) point out in the first place if any works have been carried out and (b) when these works are likely to have been done. Equally as important is the completion certificate (pre Building (Scotland) Act 2003), or notice of acceptance of completion certificate (post 2003 Act (date of commencement 1 May 2005)) – when the work is complete the building will be inspected, to ensure that the approved plans have been faithfully followed; and if so, a certificate will be issued. Prior to May 2005, this inspection was carried out by the local authority inspector who produced the certificate. Now the certificate is produced by a certifier, such as an architect, and sent to the local authority, which issues the notice of acceptance (following an inspection) to complete the documentation.

Listed building consent is only required for alterations to buildings that are listed as being of architectural or historic importance. The consent is obtained from the planning authority, and is strictly monitored.

Failure to obtain or comply with, planning or building consents can, at worst, entitle the local council to require that the property be restored to its original condition, even if this involves demolition. It is vital that the purchaser is satisfied of these consents, and form part of the purchaser's marketable title, and any lender will insist on these being available or obtained.

If work has been carried out without obtaining the necessary building warrant then it may be possible to apply to the local authority for a retrospective consent. Depending on when the work was carried out, and the type of work entailed, this may involve either an application for a completion certificate with no prior warrant being obtained, or the local authority may be prepared to carry out a property inspection (when the work pre-dates the Building (Scotland) Act 2003) and, if it complies with the necessary buildings standards, issue a unqualified report or a 'letter of comfort' confirming that the local authority will take no enforcement action regarding the unauthorised works. Note, however, that it is more difficult to obtain a letter of comfort for missing Listed Buildings Consent, as the local authority does not have the same opportunity for discretion, and a retrospective application may be required, with the prospect of remedial work being required if the alterations fail to comply. Not all types of alterations will be eligible for this service and it does not apply to commercial property.

8.2 All Planning Permissions or other Local Authority consents necessary for additions or alterations (including change of use) completed to the Property (or if the Property has been erected) within 10 years of the Date of Entry shall be exhibited before and delivered at the Date of Entry.

Note: Any additions to or alterations to the external parts of a property must have planning permission from the local authority that certifies that it meets the requirements of planning legislation. Planning permission is also required for original construction. This applies not only to the dwellinghouse itself but also to some outbuildings such as garages. Again, the surveyor should confirm in his report, whether there are any works that required planning permission, in his report. There are some exceptions for minor additions or alterations in terms of the Town and Country Planning (General Permitted Development) (Scotland) Order 1992[9], as amended eg by the Town and Country Planning (General Permitted Development) (Scotland) Amendment Order 2011[10] unless this has been suspended by an Article 4 Direction (in terms of the 1992 Order, as amended) for Conservation areas.

8.3 The Seller warrants (i) that any building work carried out to the Property has been in a state of substantial completion for a period of not less than 12 weeks prior to the date of conclusion of the Missives; and (ii) that no valid objection to the work was made at any time by a person with title and interest to do so under a valid real burden.

Note: This is to take account of the acquiescence provisions in section 16 of the Title Conditions (Scotland) Act 2003. They provide that where a burden is breached (eg erecting an extension in contravention of a prohibition against alterations) and there has been material expenditure, which would be substantially lost if the burden were to be enforced, then if no objection to the work is made within a period of 12 weeks after the work is substantially complete, the burden is extinguished to the extent of the breach. The persons entitled to enforce the burden must have either consented, or have had actual or constructive knowledge of the breach and did not object.

9   SI 1992/223.
10 SSI 2011/357.

8.4   There are no planning conditions of a continuing nature which restrict or prohibit the current use of the Property.

Note: The Property may be subject to continuing planning conditions under a previous consent, but the use of the property might have changed in contravention of these. Although not arising very often, this Clause acts as a sweep-up to cover such situations.

6.10.10 Clause 9: Disputes/Litigation

9.1   The Seller warrants that neither the Property nor the Seller's title are affected by or are under consideration in any court proceedings or other litigation or are the subject of any dispute.

Note: The Family Law (Scotland) Act 1985[11] enables either party in an action of divorce, or dissolution of a civil partnership, to apply to the court for an order transferring property to him or her by the other party to the marriage or civil partnership. Such an order has to be registered but the purchaser's solicitor should be satisfied that no such order has been granted and not yet registered.

9.2   There are no current disputes with neighbouring proprietors or occupiers or any other parties relating to access, title or common property.

Note: Clearly any serious disputes as to eg disputed ownership of part of the property or the right to use a road or way for access to the property must be fully disclosed by the seller. Any dispute that relates to the property or title should properly be disclosed. Neighbour disputes can often be very bitter, insoluble, expensive, and regrettably, sometimes often very petty. In fact, sometimes, disputes can go away when one of the protagonists leaves, as a clash of personalities can add fuel to the flames of minor grievances.

6.10.11 Clause 10: Access

10.1   The Seller will after conclusion of the Missives and upon receipt of reasonable notice by the Purchaser give access to the Purchaser or his agents to the Property at reasonable times for the purposes of

11 Section 8(1)(aa).

inspection, measurement or the provision of quotations. This right of access however shall not be exercised on more than 2 occasions without the consent of the Seller.

Note: It is only human nature, in a state of some excitement, to want to visit the property again, once the contract for purchase has been concluded. They may want to take measurements for carpets and curtains, arrange for estimates of work they plan to carry out, and generally just have another look around their prospective new home. Mostly, the seller is happy to permit this, but only after a binding contract is in place – just in case the purchaser has second thoughts. However, no-one wants to be constantly pestered by repeated visits, and so such access is contractually limited to two visits, although the parties are, of course, free to agree to more if they want.

6.10.12 Clause 11: Utilities and services

11.1 Unless the services have been terminated (which termination shall be intimated to the Purchaser) prior to conclusion of the Missives, the Seller will co-operate in the transfer of gas, electricity, telephone and other service supplies to the Purchaser but the Seller will not be responsible for any re-connection charges incurred. The Seller may retain the existing telephone number.

11.2 Roads

11.2.1 The Seller warrants that:

EITHER

All roadways, footpaths and kerbs ex adverse the Property have been made up and paid for and are maintained by the Local Authority

OR

There is a private access road to and from the Property from a roadway maintained by the Local Authority.

11.3 Water

11.3.1 The Seller warrants that:

EITHER

The Property is connected to the mains water supply

OR

The Property is connected to a private water supply system and the water supply is of sufficient quality to comply with the bacteriological and chemical parameters laid down in the Private Water Supply (Scotland) Regulations 2006 as amended. So far as the Seller is aware the supply is adequate in quantity at all times for all normal domestic purposes and for the present use of the Property. The Seller will deliver prior to the Date of Entry a report dated not earlier than 6 months prior to the Date of Entry from the Local Authority or where applicable, the Public Analyst evidencing that the said supply meets the said Regulations.

11.4   Drainage

11.4.1 The Seller warrants that:

EITHER

The Property is connected to the public sewer and drainage system

OR

The Property is connected to a private drainage system comprising a septic tank, treatment plant, or reed bed with relative outfall pipe and/or soakaway and all relative pipes, drains and connections ('the Drainage System'). There will be exhibited prior to and delivered at the Date of Entry evidence that the Drainage System relating to the Property is either registered or licensed with the Scottish Environment Protection Agency or any other appropriate authority under the Water Environment (Controlled Activities) (Scotland) Regulations 2005. The Seller warrants that he has done nothing nor has any event occurred to contravene or prejudice the terms of the registration or licence.

Note: Most, if not all of this information will be contained in the Home Report, and the usual Property Enquiry Certificates (PECs) will confirm the position regarding mains services and the status of the road giving access to the property. For rural properties, where access, water and drainage may be private, there are specific regulations that must be complied with (see also para 6.18 for other rural considerations).

6.10.13 Clause 12: Breach of contract by seller

12.1 If at the Date of Entry the Seller does not give vacant possession or otherwise fails to implement any material obligations due by the Seller in terms of the Missives, then the Purchaser will be entitled (provided the Purchaser is in a position to settle the transaction on the Date of Entry) to claim damages for any reasonable loss incurred by the Purchaser arising from such failure.

12.2 In the event that the Seller's breach of contract continues for 14 days after the Date of Entry the Purchaser will be entitled to treat that breach as repudiation and to rescind the Missives on giving the Seller notice to that effect.

12.3 This condition (i) shall apply without prejudice to any other rights or remedies available to the Purchaser, and (ii) shall not apply in the event of the Seller's failure to settle being attributable to the fault of the Purchaser.

Note: Thankfully, most missives are successfully implemented, but it is more common for the purchaser to fail to honour the contract, through financial or personal difficulties, than the seller. However, it does occasionally happen that the seller has a change of mind and refuses to fulfil the contract. The remedy of the purchasers lies in the case of *Mackay v Campbell*[12].

The purchaser can ask the court: (1) for declarator that the seller has failed to implement missives; (2) for decree ordaining the seller to implement the missives and deliver a valid title in exchange for the price; and (3) failing such implement for the payment of a sum in damages.

This clause in missives entitles the purchaser merely to accept the seller's repudiation and rescind the contract and claim damages for loss thus caused ie cost of alternative accommodation, storage of furniture, etc.

If the seller refuses, or is unable, to sign a valid disposition the court may order the Deputy Principal Clerk of Session or the sheriff clerk to sign a disposition on the seller's behalf (see *Pennell's Trustee*[13]).

12 [1967] SC (HL) 53.
13 [1928] SC 605.

6.10.14 Clause 13: Breach of contract by purchaser

13.1   The Price will be paid in full on the due date.

13.2   The Seller will not be obliged to give vacant possession of the Property except as against payment of the Price and any interest or losses due as aftermentioned.

13.3   If the Price is paid after the due date, whether in whole or in part, the Seller will be entitled to payment from the Purchaser, at the Seller's option, of one (but not both) of:

13.3.1   ordinary damages in respect of all proper and reasonable losses arising out of the late payment of the Price (which includes but is not limited to Wasted Expenditure); or

13.3.2   interest on the amount of the Price outstanding at the Prescribed Rate from the due date until the date when payment is made.

13.4   If the Price remains unpaid in whole or in part at any time more than 14 days after the due date, the Seller will be entitled to rescind the Missives, and to payment from the Purchaser, at the Seller's option, of one (but not both) of:

13.4.1   ordinary damages in respect of all proper and reasonable losses arising out of the non payment of the Price and failure of the Missives (which includes but is not limited to Wasted Expenditure); or

13.4.2   liquidated damages, payable on the end date, calculated as the amount of interest which would have run on the amount of the Price outstanding at the Prescribed Rate from the due date until the end date (under deduction of any amount by which the Price obtained by the Seller on a re-sale of the Property exceeds the Price).

13.5   In this clause:

13.5.1   The 'due date' means whichever is the later of:

(i)   the Date of Entry; or

(ii)   the date on which payment of the Price was due having regard to the circumstances of the case including any entitlement to withhold payment owing to non-performance by the Seller.

13.5.2   The 'end date' means whichever is the earlier of:

    (i)   the date falling 12 months after the due date; or

    (ii)   where the Property is re-sold following rescission, the date of entry under the contract of re-sale.

13.5.3   'Wasted Expenditure' means the aggregate of:

    (i)   any capital loss sustained by the Seller on the resale of the Property being the difference between the Price under the Missives and the resale price under any such resale;

    (ii)   any estate agency, marketing and other advertising expenses properly incurred in connection with the resale;

    (iii)   any legal expenses properly incurred in connection with the resale;

    (iv)   any expenses in connection with the cancellation of removal of furniture, storage of furniture and transfer or retransfer of furniture properly incurred as a result of the Purchaser's breach of contract; and

    (v)   any bridging loan costs incurred by the' Seller in respect of any purchase transaction which they require to complete under concluded Missives.

13.5.4   'Prescribed Rate' means the rate of 4% above The Royal Bank of Scotland plc base rate from time to time in force.

Note: This clause deals with the usual provision in missives that if the purchaser delays or fails to pay the price on the due date, the seller is entitled to extract some compensation for that delay or failure. Following on the decisions in 2006 in the cases of *Black v McGregor*[14] and *Wipfel Ltd v Auchlochan Developments Ltd*[15], the previous approach to 'penalty' clauses, by which a seller would make provision for entitlement both to interest on the price **and** all loss and damages that he may have incurred in the event of the purchaser's failure, is no longer followed. The approach now taken is that the seller is entitled to **either** interest or damages, but not both. This is also the approach taken by the PSG in the Offers to Sell (see commentary on Clause 2.4 of that offer in para 6.14.3).

14 [2006] CSIH 45, [2007] SC 69.
15 [2006] CSIH 183.

Note, however, that if the seller opts for damages, in the Scottish Standard Clauses, he has two choices: either ordinary damages based on his actual loss or a 'liquidated damages' sum, based on the amount of interest that would have run on the amount of the price unpaid until the date of resale. There is, however, a longstop date of 12 months imposed on the second of these options, as it is generally considered that a liquidated damages amount based on a longer period might be regarded as more of a penalty, and potentially unenforceable, so the provision of an 'end date' in this option is intended to remove that risk.

For an explanation of liquidated damages clause see para 12.4.4).

Rate of Interest: Interest runs at the rate of 4% over bank base rate. This rate is now universally accepted for these purposes in both commercial and residential transactions. It is intended to compensate for the overdraft interest that the sellers might have to incur, or for the costs of their other borrowings or expenses.

These provisions are standard boilerplate in modern missives and are rarely, if ever, qualified. In the majority of transactions of course, there is never any need for these clauses to be applied.

6.10.15 Clause 14: New home warranty schemes

14.1 If the Property was constructed or converted within 10 years prior to the Date of Entry, there shall be delivered at settlement either:

14.1.1 appropriate NHBC documentation or such equivalent new home warranty documentation as provided by any alternative warranty provider as approved by and acceptable to the Purchaser's Lenders, in which event, the Seller warrants that no claims have been made or reported or are pending under the relevant warranty scheme; or

14.1.2 a Professional Consultant's Certificate with other necessary information all in compliance with the current edition of the CML Lenders' Handbook for Solicitors (Scotland).

Note: A house is treated as being 'new' for ten years from the date of its construction, in that it is covered for most defects for two years, and for major defects for up to ten years. The cover is a form of insurance provided either by the National House Builders Council (NHBC) or by some other company providing similar warranties, approved by the Council of Mortgage Lenders (CML), the organisation representing most mortgage lenders.

Not all builders are covered by these schemes, in which case they will require to produce a Professional Consultant's Certificate (PCC) certifying that a qualified person has supervised the building and that they certify that the work is satisfactory (see para 6.12.3(xiii)). The granter of the PCC should, of course, have professional indemnity insurance, and you should ask to see evidence of this. You must also check if the lender will accept a PCC and if so whether the lender has any other specific requirements of a provider of a PCC. For example some lenders will only accept PCC instead of NHBC or similar provided there are no more than 15 properties on the development.

6.10.16 Clause 15: Title conditions

15.1   Any part of the Property which is common or mutual with any adjoining property (including the roof and roof systems; rhones and downpipes; drains and boundary walls; fences or divisions) falls to be maintained, renewed and upheld by respective proprietors, on an equitable basis.

Note: the provisions of the Tenements (Scotland) Act 2003 should mean that even if the titles are silent, incomplete or inconsistent, the position with regard to maintenance etc of common parts of tenement buildings ought to be equitable (see para 8.27). The titles will need to be checked for arrangements applicable to such features as mutual walls and fences between houses, communal lanes and so on.

15.2   Any reservation of minerals will be subject to conditions as to adequate compensation and will not include any right to enter the Property or lower its surface. The minerals are included in the Property so far as the Seller has right to same.

Note: This refers to the situation where the original sellers of the property (often a former feudal superior), or some previous owner reserved the minerals in their own ownership when the property was sold. This is quite common, and the mineral owner will also reserve certain rights to work the minerals. There should also be provisions for payment of compensation to the owner (see para 8.25.12). Failure to mention the exclusion of the minerals from the sale can mean that there is not a proper contract, as there is no *consensus ad idem*. See *Campbell v McCutcheon*[16] in which, in missives the owner of a house undertook to give the purchaser vacant possession of the house together with a valid marketable title. There was no mention of the minerals in the missives, and it transpired that they were in fact reserved to the superior. The purchaser resiled from the contract and when the seller sued, the court held that the purchaser was entitled to resile from the contract because, as the missives made no reference to reservation of the minerals, that meant in effect that the seller had contracted that the purchaser would be entitled to the whole property, including the minerals.

15.3   The existing use of the Property is in conformity with the title to same. There are no unusual, unduly onerous or restrictive burdens, conditions or servitudes affecting the Property.

Note: Burdens, conditions, and servitudes can limit the use of property. The impact of some burdens has been somewhat lessened by the terms of the Abolition of Feudal Tenure (Scotland) Act 2000 and the Title Conditions (Scotland) Act 2003, but many still exist (see para 8.25). Arguably. the 2003 Act creates as many issues as it solves. Normal burdens are acceptable, but if they are unduly onerous and restrictive, the purchaser may withdraw from the purchase (see para 8.3). This is part of the task of examining title, and satisfying the purchaser that the title is valid and marketable (ie readily resaleable). Although it doesn't happen all that often, if you act for a purchaser who has special requirements which would make normal burdens unacceptable to them (eg for cultural or religious reasons) then this would need to be taken into account – for example, provisions relating to common ownership.

15.4   There is no outstanding liability for any part of the cost of constructing walls, fences, roadways, footpaths or sewers adjoining or serving the Property.

16 [1963] SLT 290.

Note: This paragraph is largely self-explanatory, but some mention must be made of roadways, footpaths and sewers. As a general rule (for properties in urban areas, at any rate) these are taken over and maintained by the council, and this can be confirmed by the terms of the PEC. But, particularly in rural areas or certain urban areas where the roads have never been made up to council standards, the ownership remains in the adjoining proprietors and they maintain the roadway at their own expense in accordance with their respective frontages, or as otherwise provided in the titles. There are certain advantages in having the roadway private, in that access and third party parking can be restricted. Nevertheless, most homeowners opt for public ownership of these features and an ongoing liability for maintenance of roads is often perceived as unacceptable for a residential purchaser, due to the potential costs. It is obviously important to find out the status of any roads, footpaths and sewers, and to be sure that there is no inherited debt from the previous owner.

15.5　The Property has the benefit of all such servitudes and wayleaves as are required for its proper and existing use (including but not limited to vehicular access, any private water supply or the Drainage System).

Note: This is to ensure that the owner has all rights of access and egress to and from the property that are required for people and vehicles, and other servicing etc rights. In urban areas it is often the case that the road immediately opposite the property will be publicly adopted, meaning that access can be exercised over it without any specific rights being in the title. Likewise, water and drainage will come from a public supply. However, when that is not the case, adequate servitude or other rights will be needed, and this must always be carefully investigated (see paras 8.19 and 8.21).

15.6　If the title to the Property discloses a position other than as stated in this Clause 15, the Purchaser (regardless of his previous state of knowledge) will be entitled to resile from the Missives without penalty to either party but only provided (i) the Purchaser intimates his intention to exercise this right within 10 working days of receipt of the Seller's title; and (ii) such matters intimated as prejudicial are not rectified or clarified to the Purchaser's satisfaction (acting reasonably) by the Date of Entry or within 6 weeks from the date of such intimation whichever is earlier. The Purchaser's right to resile

shall be his sole option in terms of the Missives. Failing the exercise
of such right to resile, (i) the Purchaser shall be deemed satisfied as to
the position, and (ii) the Seller shall be deemed not to be in breach.

Note: The built-in time limit in this clause and clauses similar to it is
essential to assist the rapid conclusion of missives. If something
unacceptable is found in the title exhibited, the purchaser must intimate
that fact within ten working days. It is vital to look at the titles as soon as
they arrive, if you have concluded missives on this basis, as, if the deadline
is missed, the purchaser will have lost the right to get out of the contract
if something adverse is found in the title after that time. Obviously you
must receive all of the titles before this clock starts to run. The Seller is to
be given six weeks to sort the problem if he can, before the purchaser can
withdraw completely – another good reason for preparedness (see para
4.1).

The final sentence of this Clause is important to bear in mind in this
connection. A difficulty could arise because, even if the purchaser has not
intimated anything unacceptable and therefore lost the right to resile, if
there was some major flaw in the title, the sellers would be in breach of
their obligation to deliver a good and marketable title in terms of Clause
18. This additional wording at (ii) resolves this conflict.

6.10.17 Clause 16: Awareness of Encumbrances

16.1   The Seller is not aware of any encumbrances as defined in Section 9
of the 2012 Act affecting the Property which are not disclosed in the
title to the Property.

Note: 'Encumbrance' is an old concept with a new definition[17]. As well
as title conditions such as real burdens and servitudes, it includes long
leases and long sub-leases, any public rights of way, core path orders, and
generally any other encumbrance which could be included in the Land
Register under an enactment[18]. In some respects, therefore, this provision
replaces the concept of 'overriding interests'[19].

---

17 Section 9 of the 2012 Act.
18 Note, however, that heritable securities are not 'encumbrances' for the purposes of this particular
definition.
19 'Overriding interests' were defined in section 28(1) of the 1979 Act, now repealed.

This clause should elicit a disclosure from the seller of any matters of which he is aware, especially if there are any servitudes being exercised which have been acquired through prescription. The seller's solicitor should check this point with the seller.

6.10.18 Clause 17: Advance Notices

17.1   An 'Advance Notice' for the purposes of the Missives means an advance notice as defined in Section 56 of the 2012 Act.

17.2   The Seller will apply to the Keeper for an Advance Notice for the Disposition, in the form adjusted with the Purchaser, to be entered on the application record for the Property no earlier than 10 working days prior to the Date of Entry. The cost of the Advance Notice for the Disposition will be met by the Seller.

17.3   The Seller consents to the Purchaser applying to the Keeper for Advance Notices for any deeds which the Purchaser intends to grant in relation to the Property. The cost of any Advance Notices which the Purchaser applies for will be met by the Purchaser.

17.4   If the Seller rescinds the Missives in the circumstances set out in Clause 13 above the Purchaser consents to the discharge of the Advance Notice for the Disposition and the Purchaser confirms that it will immediately discharge at his own cost any Advance Notice submitted by him if requested to do so by the Seller,

17.5   If settlement is likely to occur after the Date of Entry, the Seller, if requested to do so by the Purchaser, will apply for a further Advance Notice for the Disposition, in the form adjusted with the Purchaser, and the cost of any additional Advance Notices will be met:

     17.5.1   by the Seller, if the delay in settlement is due to any failure or breach by or on behalf of the Seller to implement its obligations under the Missives on time; or

     17.5.2   by the Purchaser, if the delay in settlement is due to any failure or breach by or on behalf of the Purchaser to implement its obligation under the Missives on time.

17.6   The Seller's Solicitors will not provide any letter of obligation undertaking to clear the records of any deed, decree or diligence. However, the Seller shall procure that his Solicitors will grant a

Letter of Undertaking obliging them to deliver within 28 days of the Date of Settlement to the Purchaser's Solicitors a Discharge of any outstanding Standard Security granted by the Seller over the Property together with relative Land Registration Application Form ('the Letter of Undertaking').

Note: Advance notices were introduced to Scottish conveyancing practice by Part 4 of the Land Registration etc (Scotland) Act 2012[20]. The PSG provided suitable wording for offers (see paras 6.14.14 and 11.5) to cater for the appropriate conveyancing procedures, and this wording has been adopted, with some minor variations, in the Scottish Standard Clauses.

To comply with the legislation, the Seller must apply for the advance notice (see para 11.5). In residential transactions, it is recommended that the application be made no earlier than 10 working days before settlement (compared with five working days before completion suggested in the PSG commercial offers). The seller is responsible for the cost (a mere £10) and the consents required under the 2012 Act, (to allow the Purchaser to apply for advance notices for any deeds it intends to grant and, if required, to allow the seller to apply for a discharge of an advance notice that has been recorded or registered, during its currency) are incorporated. Provision is also made for a further advance notice to be obtained if the date of entry is delayed, meaning the first advance notice expires, or is about to run out at or just after settlement.

Although it is generally understood that the existence of advance notice protection means that a letter of obligation is no longer required, this is specifically spelt out. However, the Scottish Standard Clauses make specific provision for the usual undertaking (in residential transactions) to be given to deliver the executed discharge of the seller's standard security within 28 days, since, invariably, these are not available at settlement. The discharge is to be accompanied by an application form for registration.

6.10.19 Clause 18 Settlement/Registration of title

18.1   The Price will be payable on the Date of Entry in exchange for (i) a good and marketable title; (ii) a validly executed Disposition in

20 Sections 56 to 64.

favour of the Purchaser or his nominee(s); (iii) vacant possession of the Property; and (iv) if applicable, the Letter of Undertaking and (v) all keys held by the Seller for the Property as also any code for any operational alarm system; together with:

18.1.1 If the provisions of the 2012 Act relating to a first registration apply:-

    18.1.1.1 a Legal Report (obtained at the cost of the Seller) brought down to a date not more than 3 working days prior to the Date of Entry (which Report will show (a) no entries adverse to the Seller's interest in the Property; (b) any Advance Notice for the Disposition; and (c) no other Advance Notices other than those submitted by the Purchaser); and

    18.1.1.2 such documents and evidence, including a plan, as the Keeper may require to enable the Keeper to create the Title Sheet of the Property without exclusion or limitation of warranty in terms of Section 75 of the 2012 Act.

    Such documents will include (unless the Property comprises only part of a tenement or flatted building and does not include an area of ground specifically included in the title to that part) a plan or bounding description sufficient to enable the whole Property to be identified on the cadastral map and evidence (such as a Plans Report Level 3 or equivalent) that (i) the description of the whole Property as contained in the title deeds is habile to include the whole of the occupied extent and (ii) there is no conflict between the extent of the Property and registered cadastral units.

18.1.2 If the title to the Property is already registered in terms of the 2012 Act or in terms of the Land Registration (Scotland) Act 1979 ("the 1979 Act"), there will be exhibited in exchange for the Price a copy of the Title Sheet of the Property containing no exclusion or limitation of warranty in terms of Section 75 of the

2012 Act or exclusion of indemnity in terms of Section 12(2) of the 1979 Act with all necessary links in title evidencing the Seller's exclusive ownership of the Property together with:

18.1.2.1   a Legal Report (and Plans Report Level 1 if requested) obtained at the cost of the Seller brought down to a date not more than 3 working days prior to the Date of Entry (which Reports will show (a) no entries adverse to the Seller's interest in the Property; (b) any Advance Notice for the Disposition; and (c) no other Advance Notices other than those submitted by the Purchaser); and

18.1.2.2   such documents and evidence as the Keeper may require to enable the Keeper to update the Title Sheet of the Property to disclose the Purchaser as the registered proprietor of the Property without exclusion or limitation of warranty under Section 75 of the 2012 Act.

18.1.3   Where Clauses 18.1.1 or 18.1.2 apply the updated or newly created Title Sheet of the Property will contain no exclusion or limitation of warranty in terms of Section 75 of the 2012 Act and will disclose no entry, deed or diligence (including any Notice of Potential Liability for costs under the Tenements (Scotland) Act 2004 or the Title Conditions (Scotland) Act 2003)) prejudicial to the Purchaser's interest other than such as have been created by or against the Purchaser or have been disclosed to and accepted in writing by the Purchaser prior to the Date of Settlement.

18.1.4   If an Application for First Registration of the title to the Property is still being processed by the Keeper, the Seller warrants (i) that no requisitions have been made by the Keeper but not implemented, and (ii) the Keeper has not indicated any concern with the Application such as might result in any exclusion or limitation of warranty under the 2012 Act or exclusion of indemnity in terms of the 1979 Act, refusal to register, or rejection of the said application.

18.1.5   Without prejudice to the above, the Seller warrants that
the Property is not affected by any entry in the Register of
Community Interests in Land.

18.1.6   Notwithstanding any other term with in the Missives, this
Clause shall remain in full force and effect without limit of
time and may be founded upon until implemented.

Note: This clause sets out the obligations of the seller which are: (i) to
provide a good and marketable title; (ii) to deliver a valid disposition (iii)
to give vacant possession (iv) to provide a letter of obligation, but only if
it is appropriate to do so under the circumstances of the transaction (see
the note at para 6.10.18 to Clause 17 above and para 11.6) and (v) to hand
over the keys of, and/or any entry key-code to the property.

If it is a first registration the seller will show the purchaser a clear Legal
Report which should disclose the advance notice, so that the purchaser can
be confident that it is settling within the protected period provided.. It is
thought that to leave obtaining the initial Legal Report until just before
settlement is extremely risky, as it would allow no time to sort out any
unexpected matters that might show up in the Legal Report, such as an
inhibition against the seller. So it is recommended practice to obtain
the Legal Report as soon as possible, and then follow it up with a Legal
Continuation Report just before settlement. However, as noted in para
7.5.1 it is more usual in residential transactions to only obtain the initial
report and, in terms of this Clause, the seller is only contractually obliged
to obtain a Legal Report, not a Legal Continuation Report as well.

Similarly, the seller should obtain and exhibit to the purchaser a Level
3 Plans Report (for unregistered property) see para 7.7) in good time so
as to allow for any corrective action that might be required, if the Plans
Report discloses any conflict with another title on the cadastral map, or
any discrepancy between the legal extent and the occupational extent of
the property.

In a sale of land that is already registered, provision is made for the
seller to obtain a Level 1 Plans Report, if requested (see Chapter 7 for
searches and reports generally, and for issues concerning potential
overlaps in registered titles specifically).

Transitional provisions are also set out in cases where the title to
the property is still undergoing registration under the 1979 Act. These

provisions should become redundant, once the Registers confirm that all outstanding 1979 Act applications have been completed.

6.10.20 Clause 19: Incorporated bodies

19.1 If the Seller is a limited company, or Limited Liability Partnership, then prior to the Date of Entry the Seller will exhibit searches in the Register of Charges and company file of the Seller brought down to a date not more than 3 working days prior to the Date of Entry which searches will confirm (a) that there is no notice regarding the appointment of a receiver, administrator or liquidator, winding up, striking off or change of name affecting the Seller and (b) the full names of the present directors and secretary of the Seller.

19.2 In the event of such searches disclosing any floating charge affecting the Property at the Date of Entry, there will be delivered a certificate of non-crystallisation of such floating charge granted by the chargeholder, dated not more than 3 working days prior to the Date of Entry, confirming that no steps have been taken to crystallise such floating charge and releasing the Property from the floating charge.

19.3 Within 3 months after the date of settlement such searches against the Seller will be delivered or exhibited brought down to a date 22 days after the date of registration of the Disposition in favour of the Purchaser or his nominees or 36 days after the Date of Entry whichever is the earlier disclosing no entries prejudicial to the registration of the said Disposition.

19.4 The Seller will exhibit or deliver clear searches in the Register of Charges and company files of all companies disclosed as owner or former owner of the Property, in any Land Certificate, copy Title Sheet, or Legal Reports, brought down in each case to a date 22 days after registration in the Land Register of the deed divesting the relevant company of its interest, disclosing no entries prejudicial to the registration of the said deed. The Seller's solicitors will not provide a letter of obligation in respect of such searches.

Note: This clause deals with the possibility that the seller is a limited company, or a limited liability partnership, and the additional searches that should be made in the Register of Charges and in the company's file. For more detail on companies searches see para 7.4. Where there is a floating charge, it will be necessary to ensure that the floating charge holder has not taken any steps to crystallise it (see para 10.6.5).

This clause also reflects the change in procedure adopted by the PSG offers, for solicitors to cease giving an undertaking on behalf of their client, to deliver or exhibit updated company searches. Clause 19.4 imposes this obligation on the seller, and so it is unnecessary for an additional solicitor's obligation to be given. Seller's solicitors should, however, remember to continue the company searches after settlement and exhibit or deliver them to the purchaser's solicitors.

6.10.21 Clause 20: Risk

20.1   The Seller will maintain the Property in its present condition, fair wear and tear excepted, until the time at which settlement takes place.

20.2   The risk of damage to or destruction of the Property howsoever caused will remain with the Seller until the time at which settlement takes place.

Note: Paradoxical as it may seem, at common law the risk of destruction of, or damage to, the property passes on the completion of missives according to the case of *Sloan's Dairies Ltd v Glasgow Corporation*[21]. In most areas of the country, it has long been standard practice to amend the common law position and provide that risk will not pass until the date of entry, or settlement if that is a different date. The reference to 'the time at which settlement takes place' is to avoid the possibility that risk passes immediately after midnight.

20.3   In the event of the Property being destroyed or materially damaged prior to the time at which settlement takes place, either the Purchaser or the Seller shall have the right to rescind the Missives without penalty to the other.

Note: Although the eventuality of damage or destruction will presumably be covered by insurance – the seller should ensure that he maintains cover and does not cancel it until after settlement – clearly, if the property is substantially damaged or destroyed before the date of entry, the purchaser

21 [1979] SLT 17.

is unlikely to want to proceed with the purchase if the property is a burnt-out shell, and so will want the right to withdraw. Equally, the seller will probably not want the trouble that would be involved in restoring the property to its original condition for the benefit of the purchaser, and so this arrangement normally suits both parties.

6.10.22 Clause 21: Property enquiry certificate

21.1   A Property Enquiry Certificate ('PEC') dated after the date of conclusion of the Missives but not earlier than 3 months prior to the Date of Entry will be exhibited at least 5 working days prior to the Date of Entry. The PEC shall require to report on all matters required for the Purchaser's solicitors to comply with the current edition of the CML Lenders' Handbook for Solicitors (Scotland).

21.2   If the PEC discloses any matter which is materially prejudicial to the Purchaser or the Property, the Purchaser shall be entitled to resile from the Missives and that without penalty to either party but only provided that (i) the Purchaser intimates his intention to exercise this right within 10 working days of receipt of the PEC; and (ii) such matters intimated as being prejudicial are not rectified or clarified to the Purchaser's satisfaction (acting reasonably) by the Date of Entry or within 6 weeks from the date of such intimation whichever is earlier. The Purchaser's right to resile shall be his sole option in terms of the Missives. Failing the exercise of such right to resile, (i) the Purchaser shall be deemed satisfied as to the position, and (ii) the Seller shall be deemed not to be in breach.

21.3   For the avoidance of doubt, should the Property be sited within a Conservation Area; form part of or be a Listed Building; be subject to the Local Authority Windows Policy or an Article 4 Direction; or be affected by a Tree Preservation Order, this shall not be deemed to be a prejudicial ground entitling the Purchaser to so resile.

Note: PECs can be obtained from the local authority or from specialist agencies, on payment of a fee. (See para 7.2). A PEC should be obtained as early as possible by the seller, in case it discloses any matter that might present a difficulty, but it should be borne in mind that the information contained can become out of date, hence the requirement for a PEC not more than 3 months old. The Scottish Standard Clauses require that the PEC should be dated after the conclusion of missives, so that it discloses the position regarding statutory notices at the date of conclusion of missives, when the respective responsibilities change (see Clause 6). The seller should know if there are any notices etc affecting the property, but it is always possible that a PEC might show up something of which the seller is unaware. The PEC should therefore be ordered straight away on conclusion of missives, so that the position can be established with certainty at the earliest opportunity.

The PEC gives details of any notices served on the property owners, such as a repairs notice, and so careful attention should be paid to the matters it discloses, as further action may be required. Rather more benevolent notices, such as a notice that the property lies within a conservation area, although disclosed, are not generally regarded as problematic, but all of the details should be notified to the purchaser immediately on receipt of the PEC, as there may be circumstances where a notice gives the purchaser cause for concern.

As with clause 15, there is a built-in time limit for intimating any issues of ten working days.

6.10.23 Clause 22: Coal Authority Report

22.1 If the Coal Authority or similar statutory body recommends that a Coal Mining Report is obtained for the Property, then such report shall be exhibited prior to settlement. In the event that such report discloses a position materially prejudicial to the Property or the Purchaser's proposed use of same, then the Purchaser shall be entitled to resile from the Missives and that without penalty to either party only provided (i) the Purchaser intimates his intention to exercise this right in writing within 10 working days of receipt of the said report; and (ii) such matters intimated as being prejudicial are not rectified or clarified to the Purchaser's satisfaction (acting reasonably) by the Date of Entry or within 6 weeks from the date of such intimation whichever is earlier. The Purchaser's right to resile shall be his sole option in terms of the Missives. Failing the exercise of such rights to resile, (i) the Purchaser shall be deemed satisfied as to the position, and (ii) the Seller shall be deemed not to be in breach.

Note: Many parts of Scotland have been affected at some time by coal mining and there is a comprehensive list available of cities, towns and villages where, if you are purchasing a property in that location, you must also examine a coal authority report (see para 7.3). The position must be 'materially prejudicial' to the purchaser, and not something that is quite minor. If you are in any doubt about what is disclosed in the report then it may be necessary to make further investigation, which may include referring the terms of the report to the surveyor for comment.

6.10.24 Clause 23: Occupancy rights

23.1   At the Date of Entry the Property will not be affected by any occupancy rights as defined in the Matrimonial Homes (Family Protection) (Scotland) Act 1981 as amended or the Civil Partnership Act 2004.

Note: Any rights of non entitled spouses or civil partners under either of these two Acts must be dealt with in the course of the sale to ensure that there is no need to qualify the certificate in the registration application form which might result in a limitation or exclusion of warranty on the purchaser's Title Sheet. No action is required if the title is held in the joint names of spouses or civil partners, or by legal persons other than individuals, but if not then you will need to see consent or a renunciation or a suitable declaration (see paras 4.9.4 and 8.33).

6.10.25 Clause 24: Supersession of missives

24.1   The Missives shall cease to be enforceable after a period of 2 years from the Date of Settlement except insofar as (i) they are founded upon in any court proceedings which have commenced within the said period; or (ii) this provision is excluded in terms of any other condition of the Missives.

Note: The rule at common law was that the delivery of the disposition superseded the terms of the preceding contract (*Winston v Patrick*[22]). Following on that case 'non supersession' clauses appeared in missives

22 [1981] SLT 41.

to counteract the effect. The Contract (Scotland) Act 1997 brought relief by making it the law that a prior contract (ie missives) would not be superseded by a subsequent deed (ie disposition) but allowed parties to agree a date when the prior contract would no longer be enforceable. In this case the time agreed is two years, (which is the usual period specified) unless the dispute arises under clause 6.5 or 18.1.6. In the latter cases, the missives never go out of force (until of course, they prescribe (after 20 years)) (see also para 9.13).

6.10.26 Clause 25: Address details

25.1   The Seller and the Purchaser irrevocably authorise their respective solicitors to release their current address on demand.

Note: A previous version of this clause in the Combined Standard Missives stated that the seller's new address could be disclosed to the purchaser's solicitors after settlement if it was needed in the event of any claim arising after settlement – obviously to make it quicker to raise an action against the seller if it was required. This version is obviously intended to be less inflammatory and more practical, as it applies before as well as after settlement.

6.10.27 Clause 26: Limitation of claims

26.1   No claim will be available or competent to the Purchaser in respect of (i) matters disclosed to and accepted by the Purchaser prior to the Date of Entry or (ii) any items or claims amounting in aggregate value to less than £300.

Note: Section 3 of the Contract (Scotland) Act 1997 provided that the rule of Scots law, that the purchaser could not claim damages for defective performance of a contract, but must reject the property and rescind the contract, would no longer be applicable. Prior to the 1997 Act, missives had started to incorporate a clause that permitted the *actio quanti minoris* – a remedy available under the Sale of Goods legislation, and developed from the Roman Law, which would allow an action for damages to be raised to claim in respect of the amount by which the value of the property was diminished by some defect, for example.

This is infinitely preferable to both parties, compared to the sledgehammer of rescission, when the problem may have been comparatively minor. However, the seller will usually want to set some *de minimis* level so that very minor claims are not permitted. This clause sets the threshold at £300.

6.10.28 Clause 27: Entire agreement

27.1   The Missives will constitute the entire agreement and understanding between the Purchaser and the Seller with respect to all matters to which they refer and supersede and invalidate all other undertakings, representations, and warranties relating to the subject matter thereof which may have been made by the Seller or the Purchaser either orally or in writing prior to the date of conclusion of the Missives.

Note: An entire agreement provision is common in modern contracts, to prevent either of the parties disputing the terms of the basis of agreement between them, by reference to prior communings and claiming that pre-contractual statements made during negotiations but not included in the final contract are part of the arrangement. It is likely, however, that a clause of this type would not enable a party to escape liability for a misrepresentation that leads to the formation of the contract.

6.10.29 Clause 28: Minimum period of ownership/possession

28.1   The Seller warrants that he has owned the Property for at least 6 months prior to the date of the Offer. This provision shall not apply where the Seller is a personal representative of the proprietor; or is an institutional heritable creditor exercising its power of sale; or is a receiver, trustee in sequestration or liquidator.

Note: This clause deals with the '6-month rule' introduced by the Council of Mortgage Lenders. Clause 5.1 in part 1 of the CML Handbook (see para 10.5.2) which is entitled 'Surrounding circumstances' requires the lender's solicitors to report to them if the owner of the property (seller) has owned it for less than six months, unless the seller is acting in any of the three capacities mentioned in the clause above (personal representative; institutional heritable creditor; receiver, trustee in sequestration or liquidator). Clause

5.1 of the CML Handbook also excepts a sale by a developer or builder selling a property acquired under a part exchange scheme.

Lenders introduced this requirement to prevent potential price rigging and mortgage fraud, and counteract the practice that was 'prevalent' (presumably in England) of properties being bought at below market value, for example on a distressed sale basis, financed through bridging and then immediately mortgaged on a market value basis at a higher valuation.

> 28.2 The Seller warrants that the Property has been possessed openly, peaceably and without judicial interruption by the Seller since the Seller's acquisition of same.

Note: This clause addresses the issue of the period of the seller's possession for the purposes of the new rules in the 2012 Act[23] for 'realignment of rights' which require good faith and possession for a continuous period of one year, See para 2.6.2(i).

Since possession for at least one year is a key component, this clause provides on all occasions for confirmation of possession to be required. In this way the purchaser will always check the possession requirement, so that, in the unlikely event of a challenge, it can be demonstrated that the requirement for possession has been confirmed, without jeopardising the good faith requirement.

The Scottish Standard Clauses do not specify any minimum period (compare this with the one year minimum specified in Clause 8.4 of the PSG Offer (see para 6.14.12). If it appears from the title that the seller has owned the property for less than a year, then the purchaser would need to own the property for the remaining period to make up a total of one year before this protection (if it were to be needed) would apply.

6.10.30 Clause 29: Green Deal etc

> 29.1 The Property is not subject to a green deal plan as defined in Section 1 of the Energy Act 2011.

Note: The Green Deal is an initiative from the UK Government[24] intended to help energy efficiency measures to be carried out in households and

---

23 Section 86.
24 Introduced by Part 1, Chapter 1 of the Energy Act 2011.

businesses without the owners (or occupiers) having to meet any upfront capital costs of those measures.

It provides a framework within which homeowners and businesses can carry out energy improvements to their property, by having them carried out by participating energy companies, and other accredited organisations, who, instead of charging for the work at the time it is completed, recover the cost of the works over time, and in instalments, by payments added to and recovered through the consumer's energy bills. The liability remains with the property, not the person who took out the original Green Deal, and so, on a sale, steps have to be taken to ensure that the new owner is signed up for the repayment liability, through their energy bills.

The reality is that there has been little actual take up of Green Deals – anecdotally only a handful apply in Scotland. In July 2012, it was announced that the UK Government had decided to stop funding the Green Deal Finance Company (set up to lend money to Green Deal providers). As it is going to be only very rarely that a solicitor will come across a Green Deal in a purchase transaction, this Clause simply acts as a flag, to elicit disclosure from the seller. In the unlikely event that you come across a property with a green deal in place during a transaction see para 4.8 for the contractual and conveyancing requirements. Note, in particular, that an acknowledgement signed by the purchaser must be incorporated into the missives.

> 29.2 The Seller shall deliver at or prior to settlement an Energy Performance Certificate in compliance with The Energy Performance of Buildings (Scotland) Regulations 2008, as amended.

Note: All properties that are being sold, with only a few exceptions, require an Energy Performance Certificate. The EPC forms an integral part of the Home Report (see para 4.2). Properties cannot be marketed without providing the energy performance indicator (shown on the EPC), so there should usually be no difficulty in complying with this Clause. However, it makes provision of an EPC a contractual obligation on the seller to the purchaser.

6.10.31 Clause 30: Crofting

> 30.1 The provisions of the Crofters (Scotland) Act 1993, as amended, or the Crofting Reform (Scotland) Act 2010 do not apply to the Property.

30.2   Any Decrofting Direction or Resumption Order under the said
Crofting Acts relating to the Property shall be exhibited prior to and
delivered at Settlement.

Note: The crofting legislation only applies to certain counties in Scotland[25].
Where the property being sold is a croft, it will be affected by crofting
legislation, unless de-crofted. This provision again acts as a flag, to elicit
disclosure from the seller, although it is expected that where a croft is
being sold, it will be clear from the marketing etc. that this is the case, and
other appropriate procedures need to be followed (see para 6.17).

BUYING A NEW HOUSE FROM A BUILDER

6.11 So far, we have been looking at the procedures when acting in
the purchase of a 'secondhand' residential property. When acting in the
purchase of a new house, while much of the procedure is similar, there are
some very important differences; especially at the missives stage. When
purchasing a new property from a builder the accepted practice is, not to
submit an offer to purchase, but for the builder either to produce an offer
to sell, or provide standard missives for the purchaser to sign.

The terms of the builders' missives are usually stated to be not open
for negotiation, and have come in for much criticism over the years.
Helen Eadie MSP went as far as proposing a Missives for New-Build
Houses (Scotland) Bill in 2007, but the proposal fell at dissolution of that
particular parliament. More recently, however, a Working Party, set up
by the Edinburgh Conveyancers Forum and the Glasgow Conveyancers
Forum, decided to look at producing a style of New Build offer[26] that
would represent a reasonable balance between the requirements of the
builder and the purchaser, in effect representing what often becomes the
'settled for' position that is reached in traditional builders' missives, when
the purchaser is allowed to make some qualifications. Most major builders

---

25 The traditional crofting counties are: Argyll, Inverness, Ross and Cromarty, Sutherland,
Caithness and Orkney and Shetland. In February 2010, additional areas of Arran, Bute, Greater
and Little Cumbrae, Moray and parts of Highland not already within the traditional counties were
added.
26 The Scottish New Build Standard Clauses are available from the Law Society of Scotland
website at: www.lawscot.org.uk/rules-and-guidance/section-f-guidance-relating-to-particular-
types-of-work/division-c-conveyancing/advice-and-information/scottish-new-build-standard-
clauses/

have their own preferred form of missives, and so in the short term at least, it is expected that the users of the New Build offer are likely to be smaller developers.

TRADITIONAL BUILDERS' MISSIVES

6.12 There are normally tight time limits for conclusion of missives and builders' missives are one of the few occasions in Scotland where a deposit is routinely taken from the purchaser of heritable property.

Nowadays, and despite the assertion that the missives are not to be amended, it may still be worth asking for some adjustments that might be necessary or desirable from the purchaser's point of view, and if your qualifications are reasonable, some builders might be prepared to accommodate them. Although only recently introduced, it may be that if the Scottish New Build Standard Clauses meet with market acceptance, attitudes will start to change. The purchaser generally enjoys more bargaining power in a weaker market. From the point of view of the purchaser's solicitor, it is no less important to ensure that you take clear instructions from your client, and check that the terms of the missives are acceptable from a legal standpoint.

6.12.1 Environmental issues

Before entering into an agreement, one preliminary point that should be considered is a check that the houses are not built on an environmentally unsound site. While this may sound rather dramatic, there have been a number of instances over the years of housing developments being built on sites which have some degree of contamination. The development of brownfield land is encouraged from a town planning perspective, and not just for residential purposes. A 'brownfield' site is not necessarily one that is contaminated, nor is it necessarily a site that is located in an urban area, but it will have been developed previously. Some sites can be contaminated by substances such as asbestos, petroleum, arsenic, explosives, creosote and radioactive substances, or have been subjected to mining or quarrying, or waste tipping. It is estimated, by Landmark Information Group[27], who

27 See www.landmark.co.uk.

provide information about contaminated sites, that 'approximately 40% of homes in Scotland are built on or near former industrial land which could potentially be contaminated'. Naturally, some more industrialised parts of the country will be more prone to this issue, than others.

Reputable builders acquiring sites will conduct extensive site investigations with a view to assessing the risks involved and determining the potential costs of development, which will include site remediation costs where this is necessary, and may even include abnormal development costs which will need to be factored in to the overall cost of the development and will affect the price the builder can pay to acquire the site. Environmental consultants will be employed to provide reports and warranties will be sought from them. Environmental issues will also be considered by the local planning authority at the planning stage.

Even when the site appears to be an attractive 'greenfield' site, it should be remembered that it may have been used for some other purpose in the past, particularly in wartime. The history of 'brownfield' sites – that is sites that have been previously occupied – should always be carefully checked. The builders should be able to provide sufficient evidence of the prior uses of the land, or treatment that has been done to the site, but if they do not, certain information as to past uses can be obtained from the local library, online, or from asking a specialist surveyor or environmental consultant to investigate the history of the land. It may also be possible to shed some light on past uses from the title deeds, but an ironic aspect of land registration is that the Title Sheet does not provide the history of the title[28]. Therefore, if you wish to find out who owned the site in previous years, investigations would have to be made in the old Sasine title.

It is possible to obtain comparatively inexpensive 'desktop' reports from a variety of providers, disclosing former uses, details of coal-mining and subsidence risks, as well as flood and other risks.

The current Law Society guidance on giving advice on contaminated land and environmental reports for both residential and commercial property is that due to the complexity of this area of law, if a solicitor does not feel qualified to comment on these issues, either in general terms or

---

28 Access to land use and other information may soon become a lot easier under the ScotLIS proposals which will be a map-based information system, drawing on a variety of sources including environmental information. Currently, a launch date of October 2017 is proposed.

with particular reference to contaminated land matters, then, that solicitor may seek to exclude liability for environmental law and/or contaminated land matters in respect of a transaction. That exclusion must be made quite clear to the client in the solicitor's letter of engagement and terms of business. A lawyer should not 'dabble' in areas of law in which he is inexperienced (certainly not without proper supervision and support) and this area is clearly one of them. Equally clearly, however, if contaminated land could be an issue, then this should be flagged to the client and possibly other specialist advice sought. This is an aspect of conveyancing that needs to be dealt with extremely carefully (see para 7.10). It should also be borne in mind that it might be a requirement of a lender, in terms of its loan instructions or the CML Handbook that an environmental report be obtained.

6.12.2 'Off plan'

The average new house is often bought 'off plan', that is to say, before it is built, or only partially built. The surveyor's job is therefore somewhat different at this early stage, but a valuation will still need to be obtained for mortgage purposes, and a final inspection is normally required before funds will be released, as well as helping with matters of 'snagging'. The key thing here, is to make absolutely sure that your clients know exactly what they are buying, and that they have as much detailed information as possible about the site location and orientation, how close it will be to other properties, build specification and layout, quality standards and materials, and internal finishings and fittings.

6.12.3 The builders' missives

The builder has to show a good marketable title, just as for any normal transaction and the missives will contain some familiar clauses of that nature, including the provision that the purchaser should be able to register his title without exclusion of warranty, and that the Title Sheet to be issued in favour of the purchaser will disclose no adverse matters other than those that have been disclosed to and accepted by the purchaser prior to settlement. However, there are a number of issues that are particular to the contracts for the purchase of new houses.

6.12.3(i) Price

New properties are usually offered for sale by the builder at fixed prices, and so the process of noting interest, 'offers over' and closing dates would not apply. These days there are likely to be a variety of discounts and incentives available as well. The usual procedure will be for the purchaser to 'reserve' a 'plot' (which may be a house and garden, a flat, or some other unit in the builder's development) and pay a reservation fee (which should, in terms of the Consumer Code (see para 6.12.3(v) below), be returnable under deduction of any expenses incurred by the builder). The prospective purchaser may be given missives at that time and should be advised to take them to a solicitor to obtain proper advice on the purchase. There will normally be a deadline by which the missives must be returned to the builder's solicitors, usually something like 14 days, failing which the reservation will fall. That 14-day period will allow time for the surveyor to produce a valuation, and for the lender to be lined up. If this timescale is too tight, it may be possible to negotiate a short extension.

There is also usually provision for a deposit to be paid by the purchaser on conclusion of the missives. Both the deposit and the reservation fee will count toward the purchase price of the plot. Once missives have been concluded, the deposit (and the reservation fee) will often be non-returnable unless there are circumstances where the purchaser may be permitted to cancel the contract. The deposit should be protected under the terms of the Home Warranty scheme against the insolvency of the seller.

6.12.3(ii) The plot

The property will usually be described in the builders' missive in general terms, probably by reference to a plot number, and there should be a plan showing the location of that plot attached to the missives, so that the parties are clear where in the development the property is situated. The site plan needs to be as accurate as possible and in particular, the boundaries of the property should be clearly delineated. Difficulties have been caused to the Keeper by properties not being laid out as they were stated to be, in cases where estate plans have been submitted to the Keeper prior to sales. For this reason, issuing of Title Sheets for new houses can take some time, if the layout of the development is not finalised or does not yet appear on the Ordnance Survey map. Note that any illustrative estate plans are unlikely to be sufficient for attaching to the Disposition. These identification and registration issues can be resolved if the builder applies for Development Plan Approval[29] from the Registers of Scotland prior to selling any plots (see para 6.12.3(iii)) The more information the purchaser can obtain from the builder about the property such as house type, ground and other pertinents like parking spaces or a garage, for the purposes of clear identification in the missives, the better.

6.12.3(iii) Development Plan Approval

Development Plan Approval (DPA) is a free service offered by the Registers of Scotland, the purpose of which is to ensure that any title extent issues for a development are identified and addressed prior to the submission of applications for individual plots. DPA will look at a plan (submitted digitally) for the development and compare the development extent against the registered title, to ensure that there are no areas in the proposed development lying outside the title extent (a problem that has been encountered on numerous occasions).

There are two types of DPA application: (1) checking the external boundaries – usually at the land purchase stage. The external boundaries of the site will be checked and confirmed against the land registered title; or (2) confirming the internal layout, either in the course of a planning application, or after planning consent has been obtained for the development, when the internal layout of the development, such as the extent of plots, roads, common driveways, and open spaces can be approved, all of which can assist with the terms of deed of conditions, and greatly facilitate advance notice applications for each plot, as well as the applications for registration of them.

DPA applies to both residential and commercial developments.

The benefits of DPA are that any external boundary extent issues are identified before any building takes place, providing greater certainty for developers, purchasers, and their solicitors and lenders. It eliminates the risk of paper deed plans being rejected, and once approved, means that

---

29 See www.ros.gov.uk/services/dpa.

there is no need to submit paper deed plans for advance notices of part or, indeed to attach plans to the dispositions of plots for registration. Instead, the DPA reference number and the plot number are given, and these will sufficiently identify the plot in question for the Registers' purposes, including mapping onto the cadastral map.

DPA only applies to developments where the title is land registered, or there is a pending land register application. Where the title is in the Sasine Register, it can be voluntarily registered prior to applying for DPA. Development of the site must be imminent.

Data for the site is supplied digitally and must be geo-referenced to the British National Grid (OSGB 1936) and a pdf of the layout should also be submitted for the Registers to use as a visual representation. Digital data can be submitted in a number of formats (most commonly by AutoCAD .dwg files). Presenting the digital drawings in a structured/layered manner allows the Registers to extract the relevant information – plot extents, roads etc. directly onto their system.

6.12.3(iv) Date of Entry

This can be a problematic provision for both parties. From the purchasers' point of view, they would like as much certainty as possible, particularly if they are selling another house, and are due to move out of that on a particular date. On the other hand, the builder, while clearly wanting to get to the point of sale as quickly as possible, has to build the house first, and that can be subject to all sorts of variables, such as weather, availability of building materials, the contractor's building programme, labour issues and more. So there will be no fixed date of entry in a builders' missive (unless the house being purchased has already been completed), and instead, settlement will be conditional on the house being completed and passed as fit for habitation by the local authority. The builders may give a probable completion date, but they will not warrant this, nor pay any sort of damages if this date is not met. Thus a default or so-called 'penalty' clause and a *force majeure* clause, of the type seen in commercial development contracts, are not appropriate, which would force the builders to pay damages if the house is not ready by a certain date (default clause), but exempting the builders for any failure caused by certain events such as war or strikes (*force majeure* clause).

In many ways the problem is insoluble, since it is not economically viable for a builder to build all the houses speculatively, and the building programme will inevitably be dictated by sales and prospective sales. Attempts have been made, however, to provide purchasers with as much information as possible and with realistic estimates of when completion will be achieved.

6.12.3(v) Consumer Code for Home Builders

Since April 2010, any builder registered with the major home warranty providers – the National House-Building Council (NHBC), Premier Guarantee and LABC New Home Warranty – must comply with the Consumer Code for Home Builders[30]. Some builders who are registered with other home warranty providers nonetheless voluntarily comply with the Code.

The aim of the Code is to ensure that purchasers of new homes are treated fairly and know what levels of service to expect. They should get reliable information from the builder, before they purchase, to enable them to make appropriate decisions in connection with their purchase, including a written reservation agreement, explanation of the Home Warranty cover available, details of any management services and costs and reliable information about what the house will look like and the specification to which it will be built. The purchasers must also know how to get access to speedy, low-cost dispute resolution arrangements if they are dissatisfied.

The Code is a voluntary industry code but it takes account of OFT code criteria. However, for builders who are registered with NHBC, or Premier Guarantee and LABC, failure to comply with the Code could mean that they are struck off that home warranty providers' register – which would be fairly disastrous for that builder. Among the obligations on the builder is the requirement to provide reliable and realistic information about when construction of the house may be finished, when settlement will take place and the date for handover. Although not mandatory, it is suggested that the builder provides estimates of completion dates at various stages during the construction, since the nearer the property is to completion the more able the builder should be to provide a definite date. For example, before

---

30 See www.consumercodeforhomebuilders.com.

completing the foundations and floor, the builder should indicate in which calendar quarter the house is likely to be ready; then when the roof is completed and the building is weatherproof, provide the month in which the house is likely to be ready, and when the house has been decorated and connected to the main services indicate what week the house is likely to be ready.

Purchasers should also be given clear termination rights to end the missives if there is an unreasonable delay in finishing the construction of the house. The New Build offer makes provision for stating an 'anticipated date of entry', and sets out provisions for when either party may resile where there are delays in completion of the property, based on the stage of construction at the time of the offer eg if the roof of the property was completed before the date of the offer the period of delay after which either party can resile is two months for a house or four months for a flat. If the roof wasn't completed at the time of the offer, these periods are extended to six months and 12 months respectively.

6.12.3(vi) Snagging

Inevitably with any builder's work, there are bound to be items that need to be tidied up or rectified after completion; the missives should contain provisions obliging the builder to attend to any such 'snagging' items. The builder will normally want to have their own surveyor or buildings inspector certify what needs to be done, but the purchaser will have the opportunity to look round the property, (probably with the builder's surveyor) and agree a list of works that need to be put right (the 'snagging list'). The purchaser is not usually entitled to delay settlement until the snagging is done. The purchaser may want to get their own surveyor to look at the property before they settle, to check that it has been completed, and advise on items of snagging that need to be done (although this is not routinely done if there is a properly organised inspection arranged with the builder). It is possible, however, that the lender might need a re-inspection to be conducted by the purchaser's surveyor, before releasing funds. The requirement should be checked and may be specified in the loan instructions from the lender, or in the CML handbook. It is also a good idea for the purchasers to check round the property themselves, once they get the keys, and make a note of any further items of this nature that they think should be fixed by the builder, and pass on that information. A useful snagging checklist is provided by the NHBC[31]. Obviously the purchaser needs to be prepared to permit access to the builder's workmen to allow the snagging to be carried out. It is unlikely that the builder will entertain any retention from the price pending completion of the snagging work.

6.12.3(vii) Title conditions

In most instances the builder will have arranged for his solicitor to prepare a Deed of Conditions for the whole development, containing arrangements for preservation of the amenity of the properties and for maintenance of common parts of the development (see para 9.11.6). This may contain arrangements for an annual maintenance charge to be paid by the owners in the development, and the missives may contain provisions for an initial maintenance deposit to be paid by the purchaser at the date of entry. If there is a manager or factor appointed for the development, additionally there might be a requirement to sign a management agreement or some other form of appointment. Purchasers will also be expected to join any residents association that is in existence (and will automatically be a member of any Owners' Association set up by the application of the Development Management Scheme to the development (see para 9.11.7).

6.12.3(viii) Roads and services

The cost of constructing the roads and other services will be included in the price of the plot. The builder must have a roads construction consent and obtain a road bond in respect of completion of the roads to an adoptable standard (see para 8.20) and should exhibit copies of these, but will not therefore normally contemplate any retention from the price pending completion of the roads.

A feature of new housing developments is the creation of service strips which, if they are formed, are usually located between the road or pavement, and the garden of the houses affected, although in some cases, they can be located within the curtilage of a plot. This is a dedicated

---

31 See www.snaggingchecklist.co.uk/new-homes-articles/58-nhbc.

strip of land into which service cables, pipes and other conduits are laid and to which statutory undertakers and other providers of services can have access. The strip will sometimes be included in the title to the plot, but cannot be built on, although planting is sometimes permitted. The local authority may adopt the service strips, although this will not be warranted.

6.12.3(ix) *Planning and building consents*

The builders will have applied for and obtained planning permission for the development and building warrant for construction of the houses. These days, the title pack that is produced for purchaser's solicitor to examine will usually include a copy of these consents. The missives should contain an obligation on the builder to deliver a completion certificate (or notice of acceptance of completion where applicable) from the local authority, but settlement should not take place until the property has been inspected and passed as fit for habitation by the local authority, as it is not permitted to occupy a property until it has been certified. In some cases the plot may be passed as fit for habitation on a temporary basis, then the certificate will be granted for a limited period. In these circumstances the missives should contain an obligation the builder to update the temporary certificates as and when required until the final completion certificate is granted. It should also have been inspected and passed by NHBC or other home warranty provider, or the provider of the Professional Consultant Certificate if appropriate. Often, the practice is to advise the purchaser's solicitors by email or phone when the property has been passed, and it is recommended that the purchaser's solicitor should obtain the name of the relevant inspector and contact him or her to confirm, as it is usually a few days before the certificate itself is issued, and in the meantime, steps will need to be taken to have the property inspected by the purchaser's surveyor, and requisition the mortgage and other funds, and the missives will normally provide for a tight window of time between intimation that the property has been passed, and settlement. Note that the system of 'verbal habitation' was judicially criticised in *FM Finneston v Ross*[32].

---

32 [2009] CSOH 48.

6.12.3(x) Variation of materials

The purchaser is entitled to have the property built more or less in accordance with what he expected and has contracted for, but the builder will usually reserve the right to make alterations and in particular to substitute materials, although these should be of an equivalent or better quality than those originally specified. The Consumer Code for Home Builders also provides that the purchaser should be entitled to terminate the contract where there is a substantial and significant change to the house.

6.12.3(xi) Deeds and searches

The prior titles or parent Land Certificate or Title Sheet that relate to the development will not be delivered, as of course they relate to the larger area that comprises the development, but will be exhibited for examination. If the title to the development is in the Sasine Register, often the builder may decide to do a voluntary registration of the title, so that examination of title is a lot more straightforward for purchaser's solicitor, although if the Land Certificate or Title Sheet has not yet been issued or updated, then the purchaser's solicitor may still need to see the Sasine title deeds. Well prepared builder's solicitors will have lending sets of the titles, or copies of the Land Certificate or Title Sheet available for purchasers to examine.

However, while the builder's solicitor may have obtained a Legal Report for the development, it is usual practice that they will not update searches or deliver reports, and it is therefore up to the purchaser's solicitor to instruct their own searches. Builders are usually limited companies and again, the missives will generally provide that no Companies searches will be exhibited. Reports such as PECs or Coal Authority reports are not usually provided, either. Most builders will instruct an advance notice for the plot, although usually the cost of obtaining this is to be met by the purchaser.

A disposition will of course be delivered in exchange for payment of the balance of the price (see *Gibson v Hunter Home Designs Ltd*[33] for a case when it was not, and the terrible consequences for the purchaser that flowed from this failure, who lost both the house and the money).

---

33 [1976] SC 23.

6.12.3(xii) Discounts and incentives

As part of the marketing of new homes, builders have, over the years, used more and more inventive ways of encouraging prospective purchasers to buy one of their homes, and these can range from the financial, including discounts, cashbacks, mortgage subsidies, payment of LBTT, removal costs and legal and survey fees, to the non-financial such as appliances and equipment or even holidays or cars. Incentives can also be used by builders to encourage purchasers to settle on time. Such is the extent of these incentives and the effect that they have on the price, and price to value ratio, that lenders now require any incentives given to be fully disclosed. The CML require the builder to complete a Disclosure of Incentives form[34] for all newly built property, prior to occupation for the first time, and for existing property that has been renovated or converted, prior to occupation in its current form, in all cases where mortgage finance is being made available. The form provides full details of any incentives or incentive schemes applicable, and must be provided to the lender's solicitor/conveyancer as a standard part of the process, and to the valuer when requested. The seller or the seller's solicitor should complete it and give it to the purchaser's solicitor (or the lender's solicitor, if for any reason that is a different solicitor). Note that the lender will need to see a Disclosure of Incentives form even if there are no incentives being given. The purchaser/lender's solicitor should pass a copy of the form to the valuer so that the incentives will be reflected in the valuation.

6.12.3(xiii) NHBC or other Home Warranty provider

Most builders are members of the National House-Building Council, or one of the other Home Warranty providers, and as such offer a certificate (the NHBC certificate is branded as their 'Buildmark' Certificate) to cover the house against major defects arising over a ten-year period[35]. The certificate is transferable to subsequent purchasers of the house, and so missives of 'secondhand' houses will include a provision to this effect (see para 6.10.15).

---

34 The Disclosure of Incentives Form and guidance notes for completion can downloaded at: www.cml.org.uk/lenders-handbook/disclosure-of-incentives-form/.

35 For details of Buildmark cover, see: www.nhbc.co.uk/Warrantiesandcover/Homeowners/WhatdoesBuildmarkcover/.

In the first two years of the certificate the builder is bound to make good any defect arising from a breach of NHBC requirements. This does not include, however, fair wear and tear caused by neglect or failure to maintain, damage caused by shrinkage of plasterwork, cement and wood, provided it was not caused by a defect, or for anything caused by carrying out alterations. After two years and up to ten years, NHBC will make good any major defects in the structure or weather proofing caused by the builder's failure to comply with NHBC requirements.

The seller's solicitor will usually have the Buildmark documentation for all the plots in the development, and following conclusion of missives will send the documents for the plot in question to the purchaser's solicitors. The documents include an Acceptance Form which should be completed by or on behalf of the purchaser and returned to NHBC to ensure that the plot will benefit from the cover available. There is limited cover from conclusion of missives to settlement, but on completion of the house, the NHBC will inspect it and, provided they are satisfied, issue their cover note, which is handed to the builder, and transferred to the purchaser's solicitor. Most lenders will not release funds until this cover note has been issued, and so timing of the inspection and transfer of documents is crucial. The final piece of paper is the Buildmark Insurance Certificate, which NHBC recommends be sent to the purchaser, although some solicitors might prefer, with their clients' permission, to retain it on their behalf, in case it gets lost.

A small builder may not be a registered with NHBC or one of the other Home Warranty providers, in which case a certificate of inspection will need to be produced from the independent architect who supervised the development, stating that the development is complete in accordance with the plans. The architect should possess full professional indemnity insurance cover, in the event that a mistake is made. In these cases, the lender will require a Professional Consultant Certificate[36], which will provide confirmation to the lender that a professional consultant has checked the progress of construction of the property and that it conforms with approved building regulations drawings, and with drawings and instructions issued under the building contract. The professional consultant will remain liable to the first purchasers and their lender, and

---

36 Details of the Professional Consultant Certificate are at www.cml.org.uk/lenders-handbook/pcc/.

187

to subsequent purchasers and lenders for 6 years from the date of the certificate. The certificate also provides confirmation of the consultant's level of experience in the design and/or monitoring of the construction and conversion of residential buildings, and requires the consultant to maintain an appropriate level of professional indemnity insurance to cover his liabilities under the certificate.

Note that not all lenders will accept a Professional Consultant Certificate, so it is important to check at the very earliest opportunity, as soon as you know that the builder is not registered with an acceptable Home Warranty provider. This should be apparent from the missives.

BUYING COMMERCIAL PROPERTY

6.13 Commercial conveyancing is similar to domestic conveyancing in many ways, in that the same sort of basic sequence of events applies. There are the same four main stages: (1) negotiation; (2) missives; (3) examination of title and other materials (also referred to as 'due diligence'); and (4) settlement (referred to as 'completion'). There are some significant differences in the details, such as the types of parties involved and structures of transactions, different forms of documentation that are found exclusively in one discipline and not the other. Both types of conveyancing have their specialities. Within both types (if there can be said to be only two) are further specialities: eg dealing with the acquisition of a major shopping centre is quite different from the purchase of a small high street retail unit, just as buying a city centre tenement flat is quite different from the purchase of a large country estate. Often, of course, commercial transactions can involve extremely large amounts of money and therefore carry significant responsibility, but the basic building blocks of conveyancing are equally applicable to 'both' types of transaction.

It is at the missive stage where many of the specialities emerge, and the considerations when acting in the purchase of a commercial property for owner occupation are quite different from some of the key considerations that apply when negotiating the contract for the purchase of an investment property with occupational leases, and different again when dealing with the purchase of land for development.

Some of these issues are considered in the following paragraphs, which look at a commercial offer to sell an investment property, (ie one that is occupied by tenants, and is therefore being purchased, not for the purchaser's own occupation, but as an 'investment', with income from the property being generated from the rents payable under the leases).

Note that commercial offers to *purchase* will contain more clauses, similar to the residential offer to purchase, although many of the clauses are likely to be heavily qualified on a 'satisfy yourself' basis by the seller. However, although not referred to in the offer to sell, offers to purchase will often contain references to many of the 'due diligence' items that are referred to in the PSG Due Diligence Questionnaire[37], such as compliance with fire regulations, control of asbestos regulations, disability discrimination requirements under the Equality Act 2010, construction documentation in respect of original construction or extensions and alterations, Health and safety file and so on and on.

STANDARDISED OFFERS – THE PSG OFFERS TO SELL INVESTMENT PROPERTY

6.14 Although commercial offers to purchase are often used, the use of the offer to sell, drafted by the seller's solicitors using the seller's existing knowledge of the property, as opposed to the offer to purchase which is often drafted in a state of ignorance about the property, is becoming more prevalent. It can be more targeted and specific – for example, the seller knows what his VAT status is and that of the property, and so can provide the factual position in the initial offer, rather than the fishing expedition that an offer to purchase can often be. The traditional route of the offer to purchase is that the purchaser's solicitor sends out the offer often without knowing very much about the details of the property, and then gets the titles and all of the other materials he needs to find out what the offer should have said in the first place.

The PSG Offers to Sell[38] are designed to be used for a variety of commercial property types and deal with commercial property being purchased with vacant possession, and a separate form for properties that are tenanted. There are different considerations for the purchaser in these

---

37 The PSG due diligence questionnaire and accompanying guidance notes can be downloaded at: www.psglegal.co.uk/due_diligence.php.
38 The PSG Offers to sell and accompanying guidance notes can be downloaded at: www.psglegal. co.uk/offer_to_sell.php.

two types of purchase – in many ways the terms of the leases are of more importance to the investor purchaser, as that is where the value in his investment lies.

The approach taken in the PSG Offers to Sell presupposes that (a) the seller accepts that it needs to provide a full package of titles and other due diligence information, and that some warranties or confirmations will need to be given by the seller to the purchaser and (b) the purchaser accepts that it will be expected to do full due diligence and satisfy itself as to title, planning etc from the documentation supplied to it by the seller. The content of the offers represents a reasonably balanced document, close to a negotiated end product, that purchasers and sellers alike will find reasonably acceptable to enable the parties to conclude missives more quickly and with less argument. It should be noted that some styles of offers to sell may not take such a balanced approach and instead seek to pass all of the requirements onto the purchaser, but with none of the confirmations that the seller gives in this more balanced approach. In practice, however, most reasonable sellers will not have too many difficulties with the balanced approach. Whereas the Scottish Standard Clauses for residential purchases are intended to be adopted wholesale without amendment, there is no such constraint on the PSG Offers to Sell, although in practice there have been many commercial transactions where only minimal adjustments have been required. The PSG Offers to Sell are to be regarded as a balanced starting point, to help the parties to concentrate on the key commercial elements of the contract negotiation, although it is felt that most issues are addressed, and so the solicitors using the Offers should not feel under an obligation to make changes for change's sake. The PSG Offers are free for the parties to adapt as they see fit, but they should not then hold it out as being the PSG version of the offer.

The parties and their solicitors can, if they wish, use the PSG Due Diligence Questionnaire when conducting the transaction, either as a running record of information requested and received, or, as many users prefer to use it, as a list of requirements to check against and as an aide memoire for the various due diligence requirements of the transaction. Not everything in the DDQ will be relevant for every transaction; in fact there will be few transactions where all of the elements appear. However, the Annexes to the DDQ can be useful when gathering information about tax, employees or construction documentation, or when obtaining tenancy information from the managing agents of the property.

Everything that is exhibited to the purchaser by the seller, which the purchaser examines and satisfies itself on, then becomes 'Disclosed Documents' on which the purchaser is deemed satisfied, and which are listed in the Schedule to the Offer.

It should be noted also that there are a number of optional clauses available in a separate document in the Offers section of the PSG website. These provide drafting relating to other matters which need to be referred to in offers from time to time, but which are not necessarily always incorporated in every offer. These include provisions for payment of a deposit; a guarantee of the purchaser's obligations; imposition of burdens and servitudes; service contracts; construction documents; and also provision for company searches when the title to the property is still in the Register of Sasines.

The structure of the Offer includes a Schedule of several parts at the end which incorporates lists of the Title Deeds and the Disclosed Documents and other information and style documentation. The Schedule can run to many pages and is a convenient way of assembling a number of pieces of information that are referred to in the Offer, and includes agreed form documents. For example, it is typical in commercial offers to agree the draft of the Disposition and other key documents at the missives stage and attach them to the offer. In the body of the offer these will be referred to as eg: 'the disposition of the Property in favour of the purchaser in terms of the draft set out in Part 8 of the Schedule'. For the purposes of the following consideration of the Offer to Sell, the Schedule has been omitted.

The Offer to Sell – Investment Property deals not only with the transfer of the property itself to the purchaser, but also the various issues that apply to the leases that are in place for the actual occupation of the property, including such matters as tenants' compliance with the provisions of the leases, apportionment of rent and service charges, how the parties will deal with any arrears of rent and notification of the change of ownership to the tenants. It should also be pointed out that with the sale of the property and the change of ownership, the new owner becomes the landlord under the leases, by virtue of his registered title, without any form of documentation being required in respect of the leases themselves ie no transfer or assignation of the lease is required for the landlord's part to vest in the new owner. This can be contrasted with the requirements when there is a change of tenant under a lease. In those circumstances an assignation by the outgoing tenant to the new tenant is required, and to be effective there must be intimation to the landlord, whose consent to the assignation is probably also required in terms of the lease.

Offer to Sell Investment Property (Version 16)

Dear Sirs

[Seller's Name]

[Purchaser's Name]

[Postal Address of Property]

On behalf of and as instructed by the Seller, we offer to sell the Property to the Purchaser on the following conditions:

6.14.1 Clause 1 Definitions

1.1   In the Missives:

'**2012 Act**' means the Land Registration etc (Scotland) Act 2012;

'**Advance Notice**' means an advance notice as defined in Section 56 of the 2012 Act;

'[**Back Letters**' means the back letter(s) in terms of the draft(s) set out in Part [5] of the Schedule;]

'**Completion**' means the Date of Entry or, if later, the date when the Completion Payment is paid and the purchase of the Property is completed in terms of the Missives;

'**Completion Payment**' means the Price subject to all adjustments provided for in the Missives (including all rent and other apportionments);

'**Conclusion Date**' means the date of conclusion of the Missives;

['**Current Service Charge Year**' means the service charge year in which Completion falls;]

'**Date of Entry**' means [[ ] 20[ ]] [the first Working Day occurring [ ] [days] [weeks] after the Conclusion Date] or such other date as the Purchaser and the Seller may agree in writing with specific reference to the Missives;

'**Disclosed Documents**' means the documents listed in Part 1 of the Schedule;

'**Disposition**' means the disposition of the Property in favour of the Purchaser [(or its nominees)] [in terms of the draft set out in Part [8] of the Schedule];

'**Encumbrances**' are encumbrances as set out in Section 9 of the 2012 Act;

'**HMRC**' means HM Revenue & Customs;

'**Interest**' means interest on the sum in question at 4% per annum above the base rate from time to time of [ ] from the date that such sum is due for payment or, if there is no such date specified, the date of demand for such sum until such sum is paid;

'**Landlords**' means the landlords under the Leases;

'**Leases**' means the lease(s) and other documentation listed in Part 3[A] of the Schedule;

'**Missives**' means the contract constituted by this offer and all duly executed letters following on it;

'**Moveables**' means the moveable items set out in Part [12] of the Schedule;

'**Plan**' means the [demonstrative] plan contained in Part [9] of the Schedule;

'**Price**' means [ ] POUNDS (£[ ]) Sterling exclusive of any VAT;

'**Property**' means **ALL** and **WHOLE** [ ] [shown edged red on the Plan]: Together with (i) the whole buildings and erections on it known as and forming [ ], (ii) the whole Landlords' fixtures and fittings in and on it, (iii) the whole rights, parts, privileges and pertinents, and (iv) the Landlords' interest in and under the Leases [and together also with [ ]], being the property [more particularly described in [the Disposition] [and disponed by [ ]] [registered in the Land Register of Scotland under Title Number [ ]];

'**Purchaser**' means [ ], incorporated under the Companies Acts (Registered Number [ ]) and having its Registered Office at [ ];

'**Purchaser's Bank**' means (a) the client account of the Purchaser's Solicitors and/or (b) the client account of the solicitors acting for the Purchaser's heritable creditor and/or (c) if it is a bank which is a shareholder in CHAPS Clearing Co Ltd, and the funds in question are loan funds from the bank for the purpose of acquiring the Property, the Purchaser's heritable creditor;

'**Purchaser's Solicitors**' means [ ] (Ref: [ ]) or such other solicitors as the Purchaser may appoint in their place from time to time and who have been notified in writing to the Seller's Solicitors;

'**Schedule**' means the schedule annexed to this offer;

'**Seller**' means [ ], incorporated under the Companies Acts (Registered Number [ ]) and having its Registered Office at [ ];

'**Seller's Bank Account**' means [Bank: [ ], Sort Code: [ ], Account Number: [ ], Account Name: [ ] or] such [other] UK clearing bank account as the Seller's Solicitors nominate by written notice to that effect at least 3 Working Days prior to the Date of Entry;

'**Seller's Solicitors**' means [ ] (Ref: [ ]) or such other solicitors as the Seller may appoint in their place from time to time and who have been notified in writing to the Purchaser's Solicitors;

['**Service Contracts**' means the service, maintenance and other contracts entered into by or on behalf of the Seller (or its predecessors in title) in connection with the maintenance and management of the Property, brief details of which are set out in Part [14] of the Schedule;]

['**Subleases**' means the sublease(s) and other documentation listed in Part [3B] of the Schedule;]

'**Tenants**' means the current tenants (both collectively and individually) under the Leases;

'**Title Deeds**' means the title deeds of the Property [listed in Part 2 of the Schedule];

'**TOGC**' means a transfer of [part of] a business as a going concern for the purposes of section 49(1) of the VAT Act and Article 5 of the Value Added Tax (Special Provisions) Order 1995;

'**VAT**' means value added tax as provided for in the VAT Act and any tax similar or equivalent to value added tax or performing a similar fiscal function;

'**VAT Act**' means the Value Added Tax Act 1994;

'**VAT Group**' means two or more bodies corporate registered as a group for VAT purposes under s 43 of the VAT Act;

'**Working Day**' means any day on which clearing banks in [Edinburgh, Glasgow and London] are open for normal business.

Note: Using defined terms in appropriate circumstances helps to streamline the text of the clauses in the Offer. Ideally any terms which are defined should appear in the Definitions section rather than within the body of the deed or document. There are two exceptions to this approach in the Offers to Sell, in the case of the environmental and employment law definitions, which are specific to those clauses only and which would otherwise considerably clutter up the Definitions section at the start.

Additional definitions can be incorporated to suit particular circumstances, and equally, unnecessary definitions can be removed, along with their corresponding clauses, if, for example, there are no service contracts.

6.14.2 Interpretation

1.2   In the Missives, unless otherwise specified or the context otherwise requires:

    1.2.1   any reference to one gender includes all other genders;

    1.2.2   words in the singular only include the plural and *vice versa*;

    1.2.3   any reference to the whole is to be treated as including reference to any part of the whole;

    1.2.4   any reference to a person includes a natural person, corporate or unincorporated body (whether or not having separate legal personality) and words importing individuals include corporations and *vice versa*;

    1.2.5   any reference to a Clause, Schedule or Part of the Schedule is to the relevant Clause, Schedule or Part of the Schedule of or to this offer and reference, in any part of the Schedule, to a numbered paragraph is a reference to the relevant numbered paragraph in that Part of the Schedule;

1.2.6   any reference to a statute or statutory provision includes any subordinate legislation which is in force from time to time under that statute or statutory provision;

1.2.7   any reference to any statute, statutory provision or subordinate legislation is a reference to it as it is in force from time to time taking account of any amendment or re-enactment;

1.2.8   any phrase introduced by the words 'including', 'include', 'in particular' or any similar expression is to be construed as illustrative only and is not to be construed as limiting the generality of any preceding words;

1.2.9   a document will be duly executed only if it is executed in such manner as meets the requirements of s 3 or section 9B and 9C of the Requirements of Writing (Scotland) Act 1995;

1.2.10   where at any one time there are two or more persons included in the expression 'Purchaser' or 'Seller' obligations contained in the Missives which are expressed to be made by the Purchaser and/or the Seller are binding jointly and severally on them and their respective executors and representatives whomsoever without the necessity of discussing them in their order;

1.2.11   any reference to funds being cleared means that the funds are immediately available for withdrawal from the holder's bank account;

1.2.12   any reference to 'reasonable consent' means the prior written consent of the party in question, such consent not to be unreasonably withheld or delayed; and

1.2.13   where a Clause provides that Interest is payable and that the sum must be paid within a specified period, no Interest will accrue on the sum provided it is paid within that period.

1.3   The headings in the Missives are included for convenience only and are to be ignored in construing the Missives.

1.4   The Schedule forms part of the Missives.

Note: Much of this clause is standard interpretation boilerplate. Note, however, the terms of the two additional general interpretation provisions have been added in clauses 1.2.12 and 1.2.13 providing a definition of 'reasonable consent' and clarifying that interest (on late payment) does not run if the principal sum to which it relates is paid within the specified period of grace. As with the interpretation provisions in the standard residential clauses, these provisions qualify some provisions that appear throughout the offer, and avoid constant repetitions.

6.14.3 Clause 2: Price

2.1 Payment

2.1.1 The Completion Payment will be paid by the Purchaser on the Date of Entry by instantaneous bank transfer of cleared funds from the Purchaser's Bank to the Seller's Bank Account in exchange for the Disposition and other items to be delivered by the Seller referred to in Clause [10].

2.1.2 A payment not made in accordance with Clause 2.1.1 may be refused.

Note: The Offer provides for the price to be paid by telegraphic transfer of funds. While this is the usual method for commercial property transactions, any alternative method of settlement that the parties decide on would need to be provided for. Clause 2.5 (below) makes it clear that the funds are cleared and must be in the relevant bank account and available for use by the seller on the day of completion.

There is always concern, from an anti-money laundering point of view, when funds are sent to the seller's solicitor's Bank Account direct from a purchaser. If this is unexpected, then delays can result, while the seller's solicitors run anti-money laundering checks, and there are often recriminations as a result. Property transactions are seen as a fertile source of money laundering activity. To address the practical issue, without adding further AML complications, it is made a contractual provision that funds must come either from a firm of solicitors, or direct from a lender who is a shareholder in CHAPS (the Clearing House Automated Payment System, or 'telegraphic transfer'), provided that the funds in question are loan funds for purchase of the property in question (see the definition of

'Purchaser's Bank' above). Thus the purchaser and his solicitor are on notice to route the funds in the appropriate way and the seller's solicitors can legitimately decline to accept funds that do not come from the correct source.

2.2 [Apportionment

The Price will be apportioned as follows:

Property – £[ ]

Fixed Plant – £[ ]

Moveables – £[ ]].

2.3 Interest

If the Completion Payment (and any VAT which the Purchaser has agreed in terms of Clause 3 to pay to the Seller on the Date of Entry) or any part of it is not paid to the Seller on the Date of Entry then, notwithstanding consignation or that the Purchaser has not taken entry, the Purchaser will pay to the Seller Interest on the outstanding money.

2.4 Cancellation of Sale

If the Purchaser fails to pay the Completion Payment (and any VAT which the Purchaser has agreed in terms of Clause 3 to pay to the Seller on the Date of Entry) with Interest as set out in Clause 2.3 within [10] Working Days after the Date of Entry the Seller is entitled to rescind the Missives, to re-sell the Property to any third party and to claim damages from the Purchaser which may include:

2.4.1 all costs and expenses incurred in relation to the re-marketing of the Property and the re-sale of it;

2.4.2 any shortfall between:

(i) the sale price received by the Seller on any such re-sale; and

(ii) the Price; and

2.4.3 financial losses including increased funding costs which the Seller would not have incurred had the Price been paid on the Date of Entry and interest which the Seller could have earned on the Price had it been paid on the Date of Entry.

If the Seller rescinds the Missives, no Interest will be due by the Purchaser in terms of Clause 2.3.

2.5   Receipt of Money
For the purposes of this Clause 2, money will not be deemed paid to the Seller until such time as same day credit on it is available to the holder of the Seller's Bank Account in accordance with normal banking procedure.

2.6   Suspension
The provisions of Clauses 2.3 and 2.4 will not apply and the Seller will not be entitled to the rents under the Leases in terms of Clause 4.2 for any period of time during which the delay in payment by the Purchaser is due to any failure or breach by or on behalf of the Seller to implement its obligations or duties under the Missives on time.

Note: The Interest and Cancellation of Sale provisions reflect the change in approach to penalty interest provisions following on the decisions in 2006 in the cases of *Black v McGregor*[39] and *Wipfel Ltd v Auchlochan Developments Ltd*[40].

The offer provides in the traditional way for interest (at the normally agreed rate of 4% over base rate) to be payable on the price, if the purchaser does not pay on the date of entry.

If, however, the seller decides that it wants to rescind the missives and re-sell the property, on account of default by the purchaser, it would no longer be entitled to any interest on the price. Instead, it would seek to recover costs and losses actually incurred, which it is entitled to do at common law. Several heads of loss are identified: re-marketing costs; any shortfall in the price, and generally other financial losses that are actually incurred because of the purchaser's failure to pay on the date of entry. The list is not, of course, exhaustive, and there is a degree of flexibility at common law. This is the approach also taken in the standard residential clauses, which additionally provide for an alternative option to common law damages, namely 'liquidated damages', but with a longstop date in that case, of 12 months. See para 6.10.14 for commentary on liquidated damages provisions).

In addition to interest, as the rents under the leases are apportioned at completion (whether or not that is also the date of entry), the seller will be entitled to the rents for any delayed completion (unless of course it is the

39 [2006] CSIH 45, [2007] SC 69.
40 [2006] CSIH 183.

seller that is responsible for such a delay). This represents a fair balance of the seller's and the purchaser's respective interests.

6.14.4 Clause 3: VAT

3.1   [OPTION 1 – VAT Exempt

3.1   [OPTION 2 – TOGC relief applies and supply of Property would otherwise be exempt

3.1   [OPTION 3 – TOGC Non-exempt – option to tax made by the Seller and TOGC relief applies

3.1   [OPTION 4 – Non-exempt – supply of Property standard-rated within para (a) of the VAT Act Sch 9, Group 1, Item 1 and TOGC relief applies

3.1   [OPTION 5 – TOGC relief does not apply and VAT is payable

Note: The PSG offer to sell contains wording for five VAT options, which runs for several pages; for the purposes of this commentary we have not replicated all of the wording. In fact, once you know which set of circumstances apply to the seller and the property it is really a question of selecting the relevant option and deleting the rest. The wording sets out the statutory basis for whichever option applies and the parties' requirements of each other in relation to registration, opting to tax the property and so on. In addition the Guidance notes that accompany the PSG Offer to Sell on the website contain a detailed commentary on the purpose and effect of each option.

What is a TOGC? Whether the transfer of a property constitutes a 'transfer of a going concern' ('TOGC') is of importance in relation to the VAT treatment of the transfer of that property. Whether the transfer of a commercial property constitutes a TOGC is a question of both fact and degree. However, if the circumstances of the transfer meet the criteria for a TOGC, then the transfer has to be treated in that way. The effect of treating a transfer as a TOGC is to make what would have otherwise been a transfer that was liable to VAT fall outside the scope of VAT, meaning no VAT is payable on the transfer price.

The main element for the transfer to be a TOGC is that the transfer must be of a business. A property might be transferred as a business where, for example, it is leased and is held as an investment (a property rental business) or is being developed (a property development business). It is also essential that the same business being transferred (whether property rental or development or some other business) must be continued by the purchaser for a sufficient period of time after the transfer.

Before the transfer takes place, both the seller and the purchaser must be registered for VAT (or, in the case of the purchaser, be liable to become registered as a result of the transfer) and have opted to tax the property being transferred.

The five options of VAT clause are:

Option 1 – VAT Exempt: Where no option to tax or real estate election has been made which affects the property, and the sale of the property does not otherwise fall outside the exempt category of supply, and TOGC relief does **not** apply (eg the purchaser is not going to carry on the same kind of business as the seller), no VAT should be payable on the part of the price apportioned to the property and fixed plant; or

Option 2 – TOGC relief applies and supply of property would otherwise be exempt: Where no option to tax or real estate election has been made which affects the property and the sale of the property does not otherwise fall outside the exempt category of supply, if the purchaser is going to carry on the same type of business as the seller, the sale of the property should constitute a TOGC and no VAT should be payable; or

Option 3 – TOGC Non-exempt – option to tax made by the seller and TOGC relief applies where the seller has opted to tax the property or made a real estate election which affects the property and, in either case, the purchaser is going to carry on the same type of business as the seller, the purchaser should be able to obtain relief under the TOGC provisions from VAT which would otherwise have been payable; or

Option 4 – Non-exempt – supply of property standard-rated within para (a) of the VAT Act Schedule 9, Group 1, Item 1 and TOGC relief applies: Where the property is a standard-rated supply within para (a) of the VAT Act 1994 Schedule 9, Group 1, Item 1 (ie new commercial buildings) and the purchaser is going to carry on the same type of business as the seller, the purchaser should be able to obtain relief under the TOGC provisions from VAT which would otherwise have been payable; or

Option 5 – TOGC relief does not apply and VAT is payable: Where the seller has opted to tax the property or made a real estate election which affects the property or where the property falls outside the exempt category (eg new commercial buildings) and TOGC relief does **not** apply (eg the business to be carried out by the purchaser is different from that carried out by the seller), VAT will be payable.

> 3.2 [Capital Goods Scheme
>
> The Seller confirms to the Purchaser that none of the assets to be transferred to the Purchaser in terms of the Missives is a capital item to which the Capital Goods Scheme (per Regulation 112 to 116 of the Value Added Tax Regulations 1995 as amended) applies or will apply in the period up to Completion other than those assets specified in Part [11] of the Schedule.]

Note: This clause should only be included where the sale of the property constitutes a TOGC.

It broadly applies where VAT is incurred by an owner on capital property expenditure of £250,000 or more and provides a mechanism for adjusting input tax over a period of years to reflect any changes in the taxable use of a capital item. Where a property is disposed of as a TOGC, the purchaser will take over responsibility for operating the Capital Goods Scheme in respect of any of the remaining intervals in the adjustment period and will therefore need details of the Capital Goods Scheme history of the property.

In relation to the capital goods scheme, the seller confirms that the Capital Goods Scheme does not apply to any assets included in the transaction other than those listed in the specified part of the Schedule. The CGS rules are complex and specialist VAT advice should always be sought.

6.14.5 Clause 4: Entry and Apportionments

> 4.1 Entry
>
> Entry to the Property subject only to and with the benefit of the Leases [and the Subleases] will be given on the Date of Entry.

Entry: Entry is granted by the Seller subject to (and with the benefit of) the Leases and any Subleases. Note therefore that the usual requirement for vacant possession is inappropriate.

4.2 Rent Apportionment

    4.2.1 The rents payable under the Leases will, subject to Clause 2.6, be apportioned (net of VAT) at Completion on the basis that the Purchaser will receive a 1/365th part of the rent for each day from (and including) Completion to (but not including) the next rent payment date(s) under the Leases.

    4.2.2 The rents will be apportioned on the assumption that the Seller has received payment of all sums due prior to Completion, whether or not that is in fact the case.

    4.2.3 In the case of any rent review under a Lease where the date of such review occurs prior to Completion but the reviewed rent has not been determined by Completion the rent will be apportioned on the basis of the passing rent.

4.3 Other apportionments

    4.3.1 All other payments under the Leases and all other outgoings for the Property (other than rates [and], insurance [and service charge]) will be apportioned as at Completion on an equitable basis.

    4.3.2 Within 5 Working Days after Completion, the Seller or the Seller's Solicitors will advise the local authority of the change of ownership of the Property so that any apportionment of rates can be carried out by the local authority.

Note: All apportionments of rent and other sums due under the lease are calculated with effect from completion, whether or not that is also the date of entry.

The standard approach to apportionment of rents is on a daily basis over a year (365 days). This irons out any imbalance which could result if the apportionments were carried out on a monthly or quarterly basis, where the periods may not be equal in number of days. This is particularly the case where the old Scottish quarter days (Whitsunday, Lammas, Martinmas and Candlemas) are referred to in the leases. In accordance with HMRC guidelines, any VAT on the rent is not apportioned. For an example of a Completion Statement showing an apportionment of rents see para 11.7.1.

It is also assumed that all rent has been paid up to date whether or not that is actually the case, so that the purchaser will receive from the seller the proportion of the rents due under the leases, counting from the date of completion to the next rent payment date under each of the leases. This means that if the Tenants have not paid the current quarter's rent or if there are any other arrears under the leases, they remain the seller's responsibility to recover. Clause 5.1 of the Offer (see para 6.14.6) deals with steps that the seller can take to recover these sums.

Naturally, the purchaser is only entitled to receive the rents under the leases for the actual date of completion, on condition that the seller receives the price on that day.

It is possible that there may be ongoing rent review negotiations when a let property is being sold. If there is an outstanding rent review under any of the leases, then an apportionment of the passing rent payable under that lease is calculated as at completion. Once the new rent is determined any uplift that applies to the period both before and after completion can be apportioned between the parties. Clause 5.4 of the Offer deals with the mechanism for this.

Other apportionments are dealt with in clause 5.2 (service charge), and clause 12 (insurance). Apportionment of rates is done by the local authority to whom notification of change of ownership is sent.

All other payments under the leases and any outgoings for the property which require apportionment are to be dealt with on an equitable basis.

6.14.6 Clause 5: Other Payments

5.1   Arrears

       5.1.1   If any rents or other payments under the Leases are in arrears at Completion the Purchaser will use all reasonable endeavours to procure payment from the Tenants as soon as practicable after Completion provided that the Seller keeps the Purchaser free of expense.

       5.1.2   The Purchaser will pay to the Seller all sums relating to such arrears (together with any interest paid by the Tenants in terms of the relevant Lease) within 5 Working Days of cleared funds being received from the relevant Tenant.

       5.1.3   If the Seller or its agents receive any payments from the Tenants after Completion which do not relate to arrears due to the Seller it will pay them to the Purchaser within 5 Working

Days of cleared funds being received from the relevant Tenant.

5.1.4   If requested by the other, the Seller and the Purchaser will each assign to the other such rights as are reasonably necessary to enable them to recover from the Tenants any sums due under the Leases to which they are entitled in terms of the Missives [The Seller will may not take any steps to sequestrate any Tenant or appoint a receiver or liquidator to any Tenant except with the reasonable consent of the Purchaser.]

Note: Since the seller retains responsibility for all arrears under any of the leases (see Clause 4 of the Offer), it is entitled to pursue the tenants for these arrears in the same way as any other debt. However, the purchaser will not want the seller to do anything which might adversely affect the solvency of what will now be the purchaser's tenants, and so, in recovering any arrears, the seller is not to be allowed to go to the extent of sequestrating or appointing a receiver/liquidator to the tenants, unless the purchaser agrees.

The purchaser should co-operate with the seller's attempts to recover any arrears.

6.14.7 Clause 5.2: Service Charge

5.2.1   The Seller will take, and will ensure that its managing agents take, such action as the Purchaser may reasonably request in writing from time to time in relation to the transfer to the Purchaser on Completion of all service charge funds for the Property in accordance with the Missives.

5.2.2   The Seller will be responsible for all service charge expenditure properly incurred and invoiced prior to Completion, and will be entitled to apply any advance service charge monies received from the Tenants prior to Completion in respect of such expenditure.

5.2.3   The Seller will as soon as practicable and in any event within [10] Working Days after the Conclusion Date deliver to the Purchaser the service charge budget for the Property for the Current Service Charge Year and an interim service charge reconciliation showing, for the Current Service Charge Year:

(i) the advance service charge payments invoiced to and paid by the Tenants and the sums attributable to unlet space;

(ii) the Landlords' service charge expenditure which has been properly incurred under the Leases and paid by the Seller; and

(iii) the service charge expenditure which it is anticipated will be incurred in the period up to the Date of Entry.

5.2.4 Except with the reasonable consent of the Purchaser the Seller will not after the Conclusion Date enter into any new contracts or commitments relative to the matters covered by service charge under the Leases unless they have already been taken into account in either the budget or interim reconciliation.

5.2.5 At Completion the Seller will deliver to the Purchaser an update of the interim service charge reconciliation disclosing the position as at Completion and containing (with copy invoices) details of all further service charge expenditure which has been properly incurred and invoiced but not paid at that time.

5.2.6 If the advance service charge payments shown in the update (including the sums attributable to unlet space) exceed the aggregate of the Landlords' service charge expenditure shown as having been paid and the further service charge expenditure, the Seller will pay or make over the excess to the Purchaser at Completion. For the avoidance of doubt, the Seller will, as soon as practicable [but in any event within [ ] Working Days] after Completion, pay all further service charge expenditure not paid at that time, but the Purchaser will be responsible for settling any service charge invoices received following Completion.

5.2.7 If the aggregate shown in the update exceeds the advance service charge payments, the Purchaser, who will be entitled to all service charge arrears, will pay and make over the excess once it has received the necessary funds to do so from the Tenants under the Leases.

5.2.8 The Seller confirms to the Purchaser that:

(i) the Seller's expenditure on the Property for the Current Service Charge Year has been fully, properly and accurately kept and recorded in its accounts and records and will be reflected in the interim reconciliations which will not contain any material discrepancies or inaccuracies of any kind;

(ii)   no repayment or credit is outstanding to any Tenant in respect of any overpayment by the Tenant arising from an excess of contributions towards estimated service expenditure over service expenditure actually incurred, in relation to any prior service charge year;

(iii)   all sums received by the Seller from the Tenants by way of contribution towards insurance premiums have been duly applied to meet such premiums;

(iv)   there are no outstanding claims from any current or former Tenant for reimbursement in relation to service expenditure in relation to any prior service charge year;

(v)   no part of any common parts to which the service charge relates is currently rated.

5.2.9   The Seller will pay to the Purchaser any sum recovered at any time from any third party (whether by way of insurance proceeds, compensation or otherwise) to the extent that such sum ought properly to be taken into account in the calculation of the level of actual service expenditure for any service charge year.

5.2.10 Within [3] months after the end of the Current Service Charge Year, the Purchaser will prepare service charge accounts and deliver a copy of them to the Seller. The Seller's contribution to the service charge for the Current Service Charge Year in relation to unlet space will be re-calculated at that stage and any over or under-payment repaid within [10] Working Days of such recalculation and any Interest. The Seller will also bear the cost of any item incurred prior to Completion and attributed to the service charge which is not recoverable under the Leases.

5.2.11 The Seller will be liable for the service charge attributable to unlet space for the period up to Completion. The Seller's liability to contribute to the service charge for the Current Service Charge Year in relation to unlet space will be assessed on an equitable basis consistent with the provisions of the Leases for the Current Service Charge Year by being multiplied by the number of days between the expiry of the last service charge year and Completion and divided by 365 and, in the event of there being any dispute as to the amount of such contribution, the matter will be referred to the decision of an independent surveyor, who will act as an expert, appointed jointly or failing agreement, by the Chairman of the RICS in Scotland on the application of either party. The independent surveyor's decision will be binding on the parties. If the independent surveyor dies, delays or becomes unwilling or incapable of acting then either the Seller or the Purchaser may apply to the Chairman to discharge that independent surveyor and appoint a replacement. The fees and expenses of the independent surveyor and the cost of appointment are payable by the Seller and the Purchaser in the proportions which the independent surveyor directs and if no direction is made, equally.

5.2.12 [There is no sinking or similar fund held by or to the order of the Seller (or its agents) as Landlords]

[At Completion the Seller will:

(i)   pay to the Purchaser all sinking and similar funds held by the Seller (or its agents) as Landlords together with all interest earned on them;

(ii)   deliver to the Purchaser certified accounts detailing all intromissions with and all interest earned on such sinking funds.]

5.2.13 The Seller will, with effect from the Conclusion Date, allow the Purchaser and its authorised representatives to inspect, by prior arrangement, the Seller's accounts and other records relating to the service charge, rent collection and all matters relating to the management of the Property. Following Completion, the Seller and the Purchaser shall procure that their respective managing agents co-operate with each other in relation to the handover of all documentation and information in relation to service charge and management matters generally.

5.2.14 The Seller will provide details of any managing agents employed in respect of the Property together with a copy of their terms of appointment, immediately following the Conclusion Date. The Purchaser will have no obligations or liabilities in respect of the continuing employment of such agents except to the extent expressly undertaken by the Purchaser in the Missives.]

Note: Where the property is subject to a number of leases and contains common parts, which each of the tenants is entitled to use, such as in a retail park, there are usually provisions in the leases for maintenance of these parts to be dealt with by the landlord. The landlord will then recover the costs through a service charge which the tenants are required to pay. The arrangements for dealing with service charge before and after the sale are set out at length in the Offer. The provisions reflect typical, well established procedure for ensuring that equitable arrangements are made, but these details should be discussed with the seller and purchaser to make sure that both parties (and their respective managing agents) are satisfied that it reflects the arrangements which they wish to apply, and also, to the extent necessary to comply with the RICS Code of Practice for Service Charges in Commercial Property (2014, 3rd edition).

The procedure will be for the seller to produce an interim reconciliation of the service charge for the current year, which is then updated at completion, and shows the service charge payments received from the tenants, and the service charge expenditure actually, or anticipated to be, incurred before the date of entry. Broadly speaking, if the payments received are more than the expenditure, then the difference between the two is the amount which should be handed over to the purchaser at completion. The purchaser needs to be satisfied the expenditure is properly incurred and thus recoverable from the tenants. The seller is responsible, prior to completion, for the amount of the service charge that applies to any unlet space in the property.

As a matter of practice, the purchaser should obtain, prior to completion, a copy of the service charge accounts for the last three years.

6.14.8 Clause 5.3: Rent Deposits

[There are no rent deposits paid by the Tenants and held by or to the order of the Seller (or their agents) as Landlords.]

5.3.1 [At Completion the Seller will:

(i)   pay to the Purchaser all rent deposits paid by the Tenants and held by or to the order of the Seller (or its agents) as Landlords together with all interest earned on them;

(ii)   deliver to the Purchaser certified accounts detailing all intromissions with and all interest earned on the rent deposits.

5.3.2 The Seller will indemnify the Purchaser against all liability to the Tenants in relation to the rent deposits in respect of the period up to Completion and the Purchaser will indemnify the Seller in respect of the period from (and including) Completion.

5.3.3 In so far as the Seller can validly do so, the rent deposits will be assigned to the Purchaser in terms of the draft assignation of rent deposits forming Part [16] of the Schedule.

5.3.4 The Purchaser will:

(i) within 15 Working Days after Completion duly execute the assignation of rent deposits delivered to the Purchaser at Completion; and

(ii) within 20 Working Days after Completion, intimate the assignation of rent deposits to the appropriate parties and deliver a copy of the intimation to the Seller.]

Note: Where the seller is holding any rent deposit sums from any of the tenants, provision should be made for the transfer of these sums to the purchaser at completion, along with any relevant financial details. The purchaser will then need to set up a deposit account to reflect the terms of the rent deposit agreement.

The rent deposit agreements themselves will also need to be assigned to the purchaser, and there is a style of assignation attached as part of the Schedule in the actual Offer. To be effective the assignation will need to be intimated to the tenant.

6.14.9 Clause 5.4: Outstanding Rent Reviews

In the case of any rent review under a Lease where the date of such review occurs prior to Completion but the reviewed rent has not been agreed or determined by Completion:

5.4.1 subject to Clause 2.6, the reviewed rent will be apportioned (net of VAT) on the basis that the Seller will receive a 1/365th part of any increase in the rent for each day from (and including) the rent review date to (but not including) Completion assuming:

(i) that any increase in rent which is agreed or determined is payable by the Tenants under the Leases from the rent review date in each case in equal instalments without any undue weighting being afforded to any one period of time over another period of time; and

(ii)   that, if the Purchaser has traded off any proposed or actual extension, variation or relaxation of enforcement of any terms of the Leases against any reduction in any uplift in rent otherwise achievable, that the rent to be apportioned is the rent so achievable as if there had been no such reduction;

5.4.2   the Purchaser will use all reasonable endeavours, at its own expense, to procure that any balancing payments due following settlement of any outstanding review are paid by the relevant Tenants as soon as practicable; and

5.4.3   the Purchaser will pay to the Seller the sums properly referable to the period prior to Completion together with any interest paid by the Tenants in terms of the relevant Lease up to Completion within 5 Working Days of cleared funds being received from the relevant Tenant.]

Note: When there are any outstanding rent reviews under any of the leases, the rent is apportioned on an interim basis at the passing rent, and there will be a further accounting of any uplift in the rent (assuming that the rent review provisions provide for upwards only review) once it has been determined. If the review is not upwards only, then drafting will be needed to take account of the possibility that a shortfall may have to be paid, if the reviewed rent turns out to be less than the passing rent.

6.14.10 Clause 6: Disclosed Documents

6.1   Subject to Clause[s 7 and [10]] the Purchaser is deemed to have examined the Disclosed Documents and accepts that it is purchasing the Property on the basis that it has satisfied itself on all matters disclosed in them and on the validity and marketability of the Seller's title to the Property.

6.2   Clause 6.1 will override any other provision of the Missives apparently to the contrary and any confirmation given by the Seller in the Missives is given subject to the Disclosed Documents whether or not that is expressly stated.

Note: The structure of the Offer and its interaction with the due diligence process is that, once documents, such as titles etc have been examined by the purchaser, they become 'disclosed documents'. The effect of this is that the purchaser is deemed to have accepted the content of all the disclosed documents and accepts that it is purchasing the property having satisfied itself on all matters disclosed in them. The disclosed documents (whatever they might be) are to be listed in the first part of the Schedule. In this way there is a clear record of what the purchaser has examined in case of any dispute at a later stage.

The purchaser has an agreed period in which to examine all the titles, leases and other documents that are exhibited, and if not satisfied, can raise queries or requisitions with the seller. Once the time limit has expired without any objections having been raised, the purchaser is deemed to be satisfied with the terms of the documents.

6.14.11 Clause 7: Documents to be Disclosed

7.1   To the extent it has not already done so, the Seller will exhibit to the Purchaser as soon as reasonably practicable after the Conclusion Date:

7.1.1   [the Title Deeds;]

7.1.2   [the Leases][and the Subleases];

7.1.3   [property enquiry certificate in respect of the Property which is dated not more than [sixty] days prior to the date of this offer;] and

7.1.4   [coal mining search from the Coal Authority in respect of the Property which is dated not more than ninety days prior to the date of this offer.]

7.2   The Purchaser will have [15] Working Days from receipt of each of the respective items referred to in Clause 7.1 to satisfy itself on their terms.

7.3   If any of the items referred to at Clauses 7.1.1, 7.1.3 or 7.1.4 disclose any matters materially prejudicial to the interest of the Purchaser or the Purchaser (at its sole discretion) is not satisfied with the terms of the Leases [or Subleases] the Purchaser will be entitled to resile from the Missives without penalty on delivery of written notice to that effect to the Seller's Solicitors within the [15] Working Days period, time being of the essence. Failing such notice, the Purchaser is deemed to be satisfied as to the terms of the items referred to in Clause 7.1 and each of such items will become a Disclosed Document for the purposes of the Missives.]

Note: A list of the documents that are typically disclosed is provided in the Offer, and can be added to or altered according to circumstances. They include the usual documents such as titles, leases, searches and property enquiry certificates (which are to be listed in full in the Schedule). These are exhibited to the purchaser as soon as possible after missives have been concluded.

The 90-day time limit for coal authority reports is based on Law Society guidance. There is no equivalent guidance for PECs, but a 60-day expiry limit for PECs is a reasonable balance, since there are different risks associated with the information contained in PECs and coal authority reports. In all cases it will depend on the circumstances whether either expiry limit is appropriate, depending upon the nature of the property, the terms of the information contained in the report and the purchaser's plans for the property, and the parties should be prepared to be flexible. Contrast this with the three-month period specified for PECs in the residential offer (see para 6.10.22) which is a requirement of the Council of Mortgage Lenders.

A reasonable number of working days from receipt of each of the items should be provided for the purchaser to satisfy itself, depending on the nature and complexity of the property and its title. For example, if the title is not yet registered in the Land Register then more time will be needed in which to examine and report on title, particularly if it is complex.

Again there is a deemed provision that means that the purchaser is taken to be satisfied with what has been disclosed, unless objections are raised with in the specified period.

6.14.12 Clause 8: Title

8.1 Encumbrances

8.1.1 So far as the Seller is aware there are no Encumbrances affecting the Property other than as referred to in the Disclosed Documents.

213

8.1.2 The Property is sold with and under the Encumbrances affecting the Property whether specified or referred to in the Title Deeds or not.

Note: 'encumbrances' is the new term that we can apply to title conditions, including real burdens and servitudes and other matters affecting the property, such as long leases, public rights of way, core paths and other encumbrances authorised by statute.

8.2 Minerals
The minerals are included in the sale to the extent to which the Seller has any right to them.

8.3 Outstanding Disputes
During the period of the Seller's ownership of the Property, there have been no disputes which remain outstanding with neighbouring proprietors or third parties about items common to the Property and adjacent premises, access to or from the Property, the title to the Property or similar matters.

8.4 Possession
The Seller confirms that it is currently in possession of the Property and has been in possession of the Property openly, peaceably and without judicial interruption for a continuous period of at least one year.

Note: Clause 8.4 addresses the issue of the period of the seller's possession for the purposes of the new rules in the 2012 Act[41] for 'realignment of rights' which require good faith and possession for a continuous period of one year (see para 2.6.2(i)).

Since possession for at least one year is a key component, this clause provides on all occasions for confirmation of possession to be required. In this way the purchaser will always check the possession requirement, so that, in the unlikely event of a challenge, it can be demonstrated that the requirement for possession has been confirmed, without jeopardising the good faith requirement.

The Scottish Standard Clauses do not specify any minimum period (see para 6.10.29). If the seller cannot confirm that it has owned and possessed the property for at least a year, or if it appears from the title that the seller

41 Section 86 of the 2012 Act.

has owned the property for less than a year, then the purchaser would need to own the property for the remaining period to make up a total of one year before this protection (if it were to be needed) would apply.

8.5 [Community Interests
The Seller has not received any notices in terms of s 37 of the Land Reform (Scotland) Act 2003 in respect of the Property.]

Note: The provisions in the commercial property offer concerning title, disputes and similar matters are similar to the equivalent provisions in residential missives. The seller is required to confirm that it is not aware of any encumbrances affecting the property which are not disclosed in the titles. It may not be possible to identify such rights from an inspection of the property either, but the seller ought to be able to confirm the position from its own knowledge. Notices under the the Land Reform (Scotland) Act 2003 relate to registration of community interests in land.

6.14.13 Clause 8.6: Occupancy Rights

The Seller warrants that no part of the Property is (or has within the prescriptive period been) used as a private residence and consequently that the provisions of none of the Matrimonial Homes (Family Protection) (Scotland) Act 1981 as amended, or the Family Law (Scotland) Act 1985, or the Civil Partnership Act 2004 apply to the Property or any part of it, or to the Seller's interest in the Property.]

Note: The provision confirming that none of the 'family law' legislation (ie Matrimonial Homes (Scotland) Act 1981; Family Law (Scotland) Act 1985 and Civil Partnership Act 2004) affects the property has been included[42] as there may be occasions where the property incorporates some residential element such as a caretaker's flat. In this case the following alternative wording can be substituted:

8.6 The Seller warrants that:

8.6.1 the Property is not and will not be affected by any Transfer of Property Order made in terms of the Family Law (Scotland) Act 1985 at Completion;

42 Note that this should also apply to same-sex marriages under the Marriage and Civil Partnership (Scotland) Act 2014 by virtue of section 4 of that Act.

8.6.2   the Seller is not a party to any action in which any such Order is being or has been sought; and

8.6.3   at Completion the Property will not be affected by any occupancy rights as defined in the Matrimonial Homes (Family Protection) (Scotland) Act 1981 as amended or the Civil Partnership Act 2004.

6.14.14 Clause 8.7: Advance Notices

8.7.1   The Seller will apply to the Keeper for an Advance Notice for the Disposition, in the form adjusted with the Purchaser, to be either (i) entered on the application record for the Property or (ii) recorded in the Register of Sasines, no earlier than [5] Working Days prior to the Date of Entry. The cost of the Advance Notice for the Disposition will be met by the Seller.

8.7.2   The Seller consents to the Purchaser applying to the Keeper for Advance Notices for any deeds which the Purchaser intends to grant in relation to the Property. The cost of any Advance Notices which the Purchaser applies for will be met by the Purchaser.

8.7.3   If the Seller rescinds the Missives in the circumstances set out in Clause 2.4 (Cancellation of Sale) the Purchaser consents to the discharge of the Advance Notice for the Disposition and the Purchaser confirms that it will immediately discharge at its own cost any Advance Notice submitted by it if requested to do so by the Seller.

8.7.4   If Completion is likely to occur after the Date of Entry, the Seller, if requested to do so by the Purchaser, will apply for a further Advance Notice for the Disposition, in the form adjusted with the Purchaser, and the cost of any additional Advance Notices will be met:

(i)   by the Seller, if the delay in settlement is due to any failure or breach by or on behalf of the Seller to implement its obligations under the Missives on time; or

(ii)   by the Purchaser, if the delay in settlement is due to any failure or breach by or on behalf of the Purchaser to implement its obligations under the Missives on time.

8.7.5   The Seller's Solicitors will not provide any letter of obligation which undertakes to clear the records of any deed, decree or diligence.

Note: An advance notice is a notice in the Registers of Scotland that protects an intended deed between two or more parties for a 35-day period (see para 11.5.2).

The advance notice for the disposition must be in terms that have been adjusted with, and approved by the purchaser's solicitor. This is because the purchaser's solicitor will want to ensure that the purchaser is correctly designed in the application for the advance notice and that the property it is purchasing is correctly identified. If the purchaser's name is incorrect, for example, the disposition in favour of that purchaser will not be protected by the advance notice. Particular care will be required if title is to be taken in the name of a nominee to ensure that the disposition in favour of the nominee is protected by the Advance Notice.

The PSG offer suggests that the advance notice is entered on the application record no earlier than 5 working days prior to the date of entry. This will provide the purchaser with around 30 days of protection after completion in case there is any delay in the disposition being registered. Requisitions will be very rare under the 2012 Act. The Keeper must reject any application which does not meet any of the general application conditions[43] or conditions of registration[44] as at the date of application. This is known as the 'one-shot rule' (see para 14.5). The Purchaser will need to have sufficient protection under the advance notice, in case the application is initially rejected.

See also para 6.10.18 for commentary on the advance notice clause in standard residential missives.

6.14.15 Clause 8.8: Land Register Requirements

8.8.1 Subject to Clause 8.8.2, the Seller will deliver to the Purchaser, on demand from time to time and at the Seller's expense, such documents and evidence as the Keeper may require to enable the Keeper to update or create (as the case may be) the Title Sheet of the Property to disclose the Purchaser [(or its nominees)] as the registered proprietor of the whole of the Property. Such documents will include (unless the Property comprises part only of a building):

---

43 Section 22 of the 2012 Act.
44 Set out in ss 23–28 of the 2012 Act.

217

(i) a plan or bounding description sufficient to enable the Property to be identified on the cadastral map; and

(ii) evidence (such as a plans report) that (i) the description of the Property in the Title Deeds is habile to include the whole of the occupied extent and (ii) there is no conflict between the extent of the Property and any registered cadastral units.

8.8.2 After Completion, the Seller will deliver such documents and evidence as are specified in Clause 8.8.1 only if the Disposition is presented for registration not later than 14 days after Completion.

Note: As the Keeper will not deliver a physical Land Certificate, this clause provides for the updating or creation of the Title Sheet in the Land Register. Invalid applications for registration will be rejected by the Keeper under the 'one shot rule'. Clause 8.8.1 is therefore aimed at ensuring that all documents and evidence which may be required to support the application for registration will be delivered by the Seller. By definition, these should be delivered on or before completion, to enable the purchaser's solicitors to complete their application for registration and sign the declaration on the application form. However, Clause 8.8.2.makes it clear that the seller will only be required to deliver such items after Completion if the Disposition has been presented for registration within the standard period of 14 days.

It is incumbent on the purchaser (through his solicitor) to present his title for registration as soon as possible after completion in any event. The thinking behind this time limit is that, without it, the seller could be expected to produce further documents and evidence, without any limit of time., This may include things over which he has no control, due to the passage of time, or which would not have occurred had the purchaser registered his title expeditiously. Provided that the application for registration was originally presented for registration within fourteen days of completion, then even if it is subsequently rejected, the intention is that the seller would continue tobe bound under this clause.

6.14.16 Clause 9: Leases

9.1 Confirmations

The Seller confirms that, except as disclosed in Part [4] of the Schedule:

9.1.1   The Leases accurately set out the whole terms of the letting or occupation of the Property [and the Subleases accurately set out the whole terms of the subletting or occupation of the Property].

9.1.2   The Leases [and the Subleases] have not been amended or varied in a manner which is binding on the Purchaser and they will not be so amended or varied, prior to Completion, except with the prior written consent of the Purchaser.

9.1.3   The information disclosed in the rent and service charge payment history (forming part of the Disclosed Documents) is complete and accurate in all respects.

9.1.4   The Seller is not aware of any material breach by the Tenants of any of their obligations under the Leases which would not be reasonably ascertainable from an inspection of the Property.

9.1.5   The Seller has not received written notification from any of the Tenants of claims or disputes under the Leases against the Landlords which are outstanding.

9.1.6   There are no notices issued by the Seller to any of the Tenants, or by any of the Tenants to the Seller, under the Leases which remain to be implemented.

9.1.7   No notices by or on behalf of any of the Tenants exercising any option to break or terminate any of the Leases have been served on the Seller or vice versa.

9.1.8   The Seller has not received written notification of the insolvency, liquidation, administration or receivership of any of the Tenants.

9.1.9   The Seller has not received written notification of the creation of any fixed or floating charges over the interest of any of the Tenants under the Leases.

Note: The leases are the key element in any investment purchase. An investment purchaser wants a property that will more or less pay for itself, in that as much of the repair, maintenance and insurance liabilities for the property (hence FRI – full repairing and insuring) or the obligation to pay for them, have been passed on to the tenants. Examination of the leases and other leasehold documentation, including assignations, rent review documents, licences for works, back letters and so on, is a major part of the due diligence process for the purchaser's solicitors, but there are some key pieces of information that a purchaser needs, that are not readily ascertainable from the documentation or otherwise verifiable by the purchaser, but ought to be in the knowledge of the seller, or its advisers.

Some careful consultation with the seller is needed before this provision can be finalised to ensure that the statements are accurate. Rather than start to alter and dilute the wording of the confirmations, the approach is to leave them as they are drafted, but, to the extent that the seller does not have the knowledge or information to make these statements, or to the extent that the position is, in any individual circumstances, different from these confirmations, then these matters are disclosed in the relevant part of the Schedule. So if, for example, there is an ongoing dispute about the amount of the service charge payment with one of the tenants, instead of deleting Clause 9.1.5, the details of that dispute are disclosed in the Schedule. This gives a much clearer indication of the actual situation, on which the purchaser is able to make a judgement or seek further details. The use of the expression 'so far as aware' is avoided as much as possible, because of the difficulty of establishing awareness, particularly where the seller is a corporate entity.

Traditionally, these statements would be couched in an offer to purchase as 'lease warranties'. Many offers still use this terminology, but it is often a sticking point with sellers, whose preferred approach is to sell the property with the minimum of liability, and the requirement to 'warrant' something is often perceived as unattractive to an investment seller, particularly when it is probably not directly involved in the day-to-day running of the property. However, while it appears that there is a distinction in English law between terms in a contract that are conditions or warranties, and thus the remedies that an aggrieved person is entitled to in the event of a breach of either, there does not appear to be any such distinction in Scots law. To quote McBryde[45]: 'Scots law looks at the nature of the breach, and its concept of material breach does not depend on a classification of the term of the contract. There is no distinction in Scots law between a condition, a term and a warranty.'

45 William McBryde *Law of Contract in Scotland*, 3rd edn (W Green).

So, the materiality of the term can be determined according to its construction in the circumstances of each individual case, rather than on how the term itself is classified. The classification of these statements as 'confirmations' is conceptually more palatable to a seller, while still offering a suitable level of accountability to a purchaser, and should be pressed for, rather than reverting to the former 'warranty' method of dealing with such matters. Always remember that the object of the exercise is to streamline, simplify and accelerate the negotiations between the parties, so it would be counter-productive for the solicitors to rack up hours of time arguing about semantics, tempting though that may be to some lawyers.

9.2 Period to Completion

The Seller will take all necessary steps which a prudent landlord (acting reasonably) would take in the interests of good estate management to ensure that the confirmations given in Clause 9.1 apply at Completion.

Note: The confirmations are given at the date on which the offer is issued. From that date until completion, the seller is only required to disclose to the purchaser any changes to the confirmations which arise during that period – it is not required to take any further action, other than any required in the interests of good estate management, which one would expect a conscientious landlord to take anyway.

9.3 Interim Management

9.3.1 In the period from the date of this offer until Completion, the Seller will:

(i) implement its obligations under the Leases;

(ii) continue to manage the Property and the Leases as a responsible landlord and in accordance with the principles of good estate management; and

(iii) disclose in writing any changes to the confirmations given in Clause 9.1.

9.3.2 The Seller will not:

(i) terminate or accept a renunciation of any Lease; or

(ii) grant any new lease; or

(iii)   vary any Lease; or

(iv)   settle any rent review under the Leases, propose or agree any reference to a third party for determination of any rent review or make or agree any proposal for a reviewed rent; or

(v)   serve any notice under the Leases; or

(vi)   carry out any alterations to the Property except with the prior written consent of the Purchaser.

9.3.3   [The Seller may complete the current management transactions set out in Part [6] of the Schedule.]

9.3.4   If any application to the Seller for its consent under the Leases is still outstanding, or if any such application is made prior to Completion, the Seller will not grant consent without the prior written approval of the Purchaser. In relation to each such application, the Purchaser will timeously comply with the obligations of the Seller, as Landlords, failing which the Purchaser will indemnify the Seller fully in respect of all liability incurred by the Seller to the Tenants in relation to the relevant applications.

Note: The seller has continuing obligations for the management of the property between conclusion of missives and completion. While it is important that the position does not change significantly from that disclosed in the missives, the seller needs a reasonable degree of flexibility in the ongoing management of the property until it is handed over to the purchaser, but should continue to manage the property in accordance with the provisions of the leases and in accordance with the principles of good estate management. This is a standard catch-all phrase, although there is no published definition that can be pointed to, but guidance can be gleaned from codes such as the RICS Service Charge Code and the Code for Leasing Business Premises in England and Wales.

Consultation with the purchaser, who now has a vested interest in what happens at the property, is required before the seller takes any action such as termination of a lease, or settlement of a rent review that could affect the value of the investment.

The seller should not, however, be able easily to irritate or terminate any lease since this is a critical component of the investment. Rent history reports of the tenants should be given to the purchaser, to assist him in assessing the financial covenant of the tenants.

However, matters cannot grind to a halt during the interim period, so if the seller is approached by any tenant for consent for works for example, or even with a request to assign the tenant's interest under one of the leases, while the purchaser's agreement must be sought, it has to act as if it were the landlord under the relevant lease. In other words, it should consider precisely the same issues as the seller has to, when looking at the request, and also be bound by any requirements in the lease, such as having to act reasonably and not unduly delay a decision.

9.4   Rent Reviews

[There are no outstanding rent reviews under any of the Leases.]

[In the case of any rent review under a Lease where the date of such review occurs prior to Completion but the reviewed rent has not been agreed or determined by Completion:

9.4.1   the Seller confirms that:

(i)   it has and will in the period up to Completion take all necessary action to preserve and safeguard the Landlords' rights to effect the outstanding reviews;

(ii)   no agreement has been reached in relation to the reviewed rent in any of the outstanding reviews and none of the outstanding reviews has been either waived or referred to a third party for determination.

9.4.2   The Seller will, immediately after the Conclusion Date (in so far as not already done) provide the Purchaser with a copy of all written material in its possession relative to the outstanding reviews.

9.4.3   In the period from the date of this offer until Completion, the Seller will, immediately after receipt, advise the Purchaser in writing of all written communications from the relevant Tenants or their advisers in connection with the outstanding reviews and will not take any action except as instructed in writing by the Purchaser (who will act reasonably in the matter and timeously comply with the obligations of the Seller, as Landlords, failing which the Purchaser will indemnify the Seller in respect of all liability incurred by the Seller to the Tenants in relation to the outstanding reviews).

9.4.4 The Purchaser will take over the conduct of the outstanding reviews with effect from Completion and the Purchaser will have freedom at its discretion as to the manner in and level at which each of the outstanding reviews is settled.

9.4.5 For the avoidance of doubt, the Purchaser will have no liability or responsibility for the fees and costs of any agents or advisers appointed by the Seller in regard to the outstanding reviews.]

Note: There may be no outstanding rent reviews under any of the leases, but if there are, then the seller must conduct any discussions or negotiations in the best interests of the landlord of the building, which is, of course, soon to be the purchaser. In other words, the seller cannot take the view that the outcome of rent review negotiations no longer matters, just because it is soon to relinquish any interest in the property. Accordingly, the purchaser really runs the show through the seller, until the property changes hands, when it will pick up the negotiations direct with the tenant (usually through respective agents). Any portion of the increased rent due to the seller will be dealt with in accordance with Clause 5.4 of the offer.

6.14.17 Clause 10: Completion

10.1 At Completion, the Purchaser will:

10.1.1 pay the Completion Payment (and any VAT on the Price) to the Seller in terms of Clause 2.1.[; and

10.1.2 [deliver to the Seller, duly executed by the Purchaser, the Back Letters.]

10.2 In exchange for the items referred to in Clause 10.1, at Completion the Seller will deliver to the Purchaser:

10.2.1 Disposition

the Disposition duly executed by the Seller.

10.2.2 Title Deeds

(i) the Title Deeds[; and

(ii)   all necessary links in title evidencing the Seller's exclusive ownership of the Property];

10.2.3 Leases

the Leases [and the Subleases].

10.2.4 Disclosed Documents

the remaining Disclosed Documents.

10.2.5 Legal Reports

(a)   a legal report brought down to a date as near as practicable to Completion which report will show:

    (i)   no entries adverse to the Seller's interest in the Property;

    (ii)   the Advance Notice for the Disposition; and

    (iii) no other Advance Notices other than those submitted by the Purchaser;

(b)   [a search in the Register of Community Interests in Land brought down as near as practicable to Completion showing nothing prejudicial to the ability of the Seller validly to transfer title to the Property to the Purchaser [or its nominees]].

10.2.6 Charges Searches

Searches in the Register of Charges and Company File of the Seller [(including a Search to identify the directors and the secretary of the Seller as at the date of signing the Disposition)] from the date of its incorporation or the date of inception of the Register (whichever is the later) brought down:

(i)   as near as practicable to Completion; and

(ii)   within 3 months following Completion, to a date at least 36 days after Completion

in both cases disclosing no entry prejudicial to the Purchaser's [or its nominees] interest.

10.2.7 [VAT Invoice

a valid VAT invoice addressed to the Purchaser.]

10.2.8 [Discharge/Deed of Restriction

a discharge/deed of restriction duly executed by the heritable creditor in any standard security affecting the Property together with completed and signed application forms for recording/registration and payment for the correct amount of recording/ registration dues.]

10.2.9 [Letter of Consent and Non-crystallisation

a letter of consent and non-crystallisation in the holder's usual form (releasing the Property from charge or otherwise in terms that confer a valid title on the Purchaser [or its nominees] subject to compliance with any time limit for registration of the Purchaser's title) in respect of the transaction envisaged by the Missives from each holder of a floating charge granted by the Seller.]

10.2.10 [Retrocession of Assignation of Rents]

a retrocession of assignation of rents duly executed by the creditor in terms of the draft forming Part [17] of the Schedule]

10.2.11 Change of Landlord

a notice of change of landlord in terms of the draft notice forming Part [7] of the Schedule addressed to each of the Tenants and signed by the Seller's Solicitors.

10.2.12 [Assignation of Guarantees

the assignation of guarantees in terms of the draft forming Part [13] of the Schedule duly executed by the Seller.]

10.2.13 [Assignation of Service Contracts

the assignation of service contracts in terms of the draft forming Part [15] of the Schedule duly executed by the Seller and, if required, by the Service Providers (as defined in it).]

10.2.14 [Assignation of Rent Deposits

the assignation of rent deposits in terms of the draft forming Part [16] of the Schedule duly executed by the Seller.]

10.2.16 Other Documents

any other deeds and documents to be delivered to the Purchaser on or before Completion in terms of the Missives.

Note: This clause lists all of the items which the seller and the purchaser are required to deliver to each other, and provides a useful checklist for both parties of the items that they are expected to deliver or receive. It is also recommended that the parties use a Completion Checklist (see Chapter 11) which not only helps to keep track of items and issues with which the parties have to deal by completion, but also identifies who is responsible for obtaining, completing or delivering each item. Last minute disasters because each party thought the other was dealing with some item are to be avoided at all costs.

The purchaser will need to see a Legal Report or Legal Continuation Report brought down as close as possible to completion disclosing the advance notice for the disposition and otherwise clear of any entry adverse to the seller's interest in the property. It is not clear if an advance notice is an entry adverse to the seller's interest in the Property so this clause specifically provides that there will be no other advance notice other than those submitted by the purchaser. If, in fact, another advance notice is disclosed, the purchaser's solicitors will be able to check its terms and decide if it is for a deed that it is prepared to accept, or already knows about in the context of the transaction and has accepted. Obviously, an advance notice for eg a competing disposition would not be acceptable.

Where the title to the property is still in the Sasine Register (meaning the transaction will induce a first registration) or where the property is still undergoing first registration and either a Land Certificate has not yet been issued[46], or the Title Sheet has not yet been created, it would be appropriate for the purchaser's due diligence to include a check against any other corporate owners of the Property during the prescriptive period. Appropriate alternative wording in this situation is:

> 'Searches in the Register of Charges and Company File of every limited company having an interest in the Property in the prescriptive period (including, where appropriate, a search to identify the directors and secretary of the granter as at the date of signing of the disposition or other deed divesting such company of its interest in the Property) in each case from the date of their incorporation or the date of inception of the Register (whichever is the later) brought down to the date twenty-two days after the date of recording of the disposition or other

46 Only applicable to applications for registration made prior to 4 December 2014.

deed divesting such company of its interest in the Property in each case disclosing no entry prejudicial to the Purchaser's interest.'

6.14.18 Clause 11: Post Completion

Provided that the Disposition is presented for registration prior to the earlier of 14 days after Completion and the date of expiry of the last Advance Notice registered in relation to the Disposition in terms of Clause 8.7, the updated or newly created Title Sheet of the Property will contain no exclusion or limitation of warranty in terms of Section 75 of the 2012 Act and disclose no entry, deed or diligence (including any charging order under the Buildings (Recovery of Expenses) (Scotland) Act 2014 or any notice of potential liability for costs registered under the Tenements (Scotland) Act 2004 or the Title Conditions (Scotland) Act 2003) prejudicial to the interest of the Purchaser [or its nominees] other than such as are created by or against the Purchaser [or its nominees] or have been disclosed to, and accepted in writing by, the Purchaser [or its nominees] prior to Completion.

Note: This Clause provides that if the Disposition has been presented for registration timeously, the purchaser's title will not be subject to any exclusion or limitation of warranty and will contain no prejudicial entries other than those created by or against the purchaser or previously accepted by them prior to completion. It reflects the similar provision in pre-2012 Act missives, obliging the Seller to be contractually bound that the purchaser's title would be clear, other than in respect of entries that it already knew about before completion, and had accepted, or entries created by or affecting the purchaser.

6.14.19 Clause 12: Insurance

12.1   From the Conclusion Date until Completion, the Seller will keep the Property insured in accordance with the Landlords' obligations under the Leases. As soon as reasonably practicable after the Conclusion Date, the Seller will make available to the Purchaser written details of such insurances, if it has not already provided this information.

12.2   Immediately following the Conclusion Date, the Seller will use its reasonable endeavours to have the Purchaser's interest in the Property (as Purchaser, price unpaid) endorsed or noted on or otherwise (either specifically or generically) covered by its policies of insurance and will exhibit evidence to the Purchaser that it has done so.

12.3   The Seller will:

12.3.1   within 5 Working Days after Completion cancel such insurances (under reservation of all prior claims), and

12.3.2   provided that the insurance premiums have been paid in full by the Tenants in question, within 5 Working Days after receipt, refund to the relevant Tenants all repayments of premium due to them and exhibit evidence to the Purchaser of having done so.

Note: This provides what is fairly standard procedure in handover of commercial let property. Usually under an FRI lease, although the tenants pay for the cost of insurance, it is the landlord that actually arranges it (through the managing agents if there are any) and there will be obligations to do so in terms of the leases. Insurance companies will not always note a purchaser's interest on the policy, but this is usually a matter for the managing agents to deal with, and the solicitors do not normally get involved. There will be an adjustment to be done with the tenants once the property changes hands, as they are likely to have paid the insurance premium in advance. On cancellation of the policy, there is likely to be some repayment of premium due, and the purchaser will need to set up his own insurance arrangements. Again, this is usually a matter for the managing agents.

6.14.20   Clause 13: Damage or Destruction

13.1   Risk of damage to or destruction of the Property will not pass to the Purchaser until Completion.

13.2   If prior to Completion the Property sustains damage (whether insured or otherwise) which at common law would entitle a hypothetical tenant under a hypothetical lease of the Property to an abatement of rent of an amount exceeding [20%] of the rent, either party will be entitled to resile from the Missives without penalty on delivery of written notice to that effect to the other's solicitors no later than midday on the date on which Completion is due to take place, time being of the essence.

13.3   If there is any dispute as to whether the Property has suffered such damage, the matter will be referred to the decision of an independent surveyor, who will act as an expert, appointed, failing agreement, by the Chairman of the RICS in Scotland on application by either party. The independent surveyor's decision will be binding on the parties. If the independent surveyor dies, delays or becomes unwilling or incapable of acting then either the Seller or the Purchaser may apply to the Chairman to discharge that independent surveyor and appoint a replacement. The fees and expenses of the independent surveyor and the cost of appointment are payable by the Seller and the Purchaser in the proportions which the independent surveyor directs and if no direction is made, equally.

13.4   Subject to Clause 13.2 if the Property is damaged or destroyed by an insured risk prior to Completion, the Seller's responsibility to the Purchaser, at Completion, will be:

    13.4.1   to pay to the Purchaser the insurance proceeds received by the Seller to the extent that they have not been spent on reinstatement; and

    13.4.2   to assign its rights in respect of the insurance proceeds specified in Clause 13.4.1 to the Purchaser.

Note: As with missives for residential properties, the common law rule (that the risk of damage or destruction of property passes to a purchaser on conclusion of missives) is also generally displaced in commercial property transactions. The seller will retain the risk until completion and maintain insurance until that time. The provisions about what is to happen if there is damage or destruction are a little bit more complicated, as the commercial property might be quite a large building, and even serious damage might not render it totally incapable of use. The rule of thumb concerning abatement (suspension) of rent is intended to be a reasonably objective test as to how much damage constitutes sufficient damage to entitle either party to resile. Even then the parties might not agree, particularly if the extent of the damage is borderline, so reference to an independent third party expert is provided. If the purchaser decides to go ahead with the purchase anyway, then provision is made about transferring, or assigning rights to, the insurance proceeds to the purchaser.

It is also worth considering whether, even if the property were to be destroyed or seriously damaged, the purchaser might want to proceed anyway (eg where the Leases are about to expire and the Property is being purchased for re-development) in which case the purchaser would not necessarily want the seller to have a right to resile. The right of either party to resile is the standard starting off point, but in these circumstances the reference to 'either party' should then be amended.

6.14.21 Clause 14: Statutory Matters

14.1 Statute

[Subject to Clause 7,] the Purchaser is deemed to have satisfied itself on the application of all statute and statutory regulations and rules in so far as affecting or relating to the Property and, except as expressly provided for in the Missives, the Seller gives no warranties or assurances on such matters.

14.2 Statutory Repairs Notices

Any local authority statutory repairs notices (other than any notice or requirement of any Environmental Authority made pursuant to any Environmental Law (as such terms are defined in Clause [15])) affecting the Property which are issued prior to Completion will as between the Purchaser and the Seller be the responsibility of the Seller except to the extent that (i) they are instigated by or with the authority of the Purchaser or (ii) they are the responsibility of any of the Tenants in accordance with the Leases. Liability under this Clause will subsist until met and will not be avoided by the issue of a fresh notice.

14.3 Energy Performance Certificate

The Seller confirms that a valid current energy performance certificate (in terms of the Energy Performance of Buildings (Scotland) Regulations 2008) has been obtained for, and affixed to, the Property.

14.4 Green Deal

The Property is not subject to a green deal plan as defined in section 1 of the Energy Act 2011.

Note: The Seller will exhibit the usual PECs from which the purchaser will be deemed to have satisfied itself as to all statutory matters.

If the property is affected by any statutory repairs, this Offer provides that liability will remain with the seller. In the past, practice varied in different parts of the country as to whether liability for statutory notices passes to the purchaser on conclusion of missives or at completion. It seems to be more or less settled now that conclusion of missives is the appropriate cut-off point and this is now the more-or-less settled position for both residential and commercial offers. However, the provision is qualified with reference to repairs notices instigated by the purchaser or which are the responsibility of the tenants under the leases.

Reference is made here to the requirement for an EPC for the property. For multi-occupancy buildings, there may either be several EPCs relating to different parts of the Property and the common parts, or a single EPC for the whole building.

The UK Government's Green Deal has not really taken off in the way the government had hoped. Much of the commentary in relation to commercial property was that the 'golden rule' – that the energy efficiency measures have to pay for themselves over their own lifetime – was going to be extremely difficult to achieve. In light of this, the PSG Offer to Sell sets a default position that there is no green deal plan affecting the property. It is expected that this will be the situation in the majority of cases for commercial properties.

In the unlikely event that you come across a property with a green deal in place during a transaction, see para 4.8 for the contractual and conveyancing requirements. Note, in particular, that an acknowledgement signed by the purchaser must be incorporated into the missives.

6.14.22 Clause 15: Environmental

15.1 Definitions

In Clauses 14.2 and 15:

'**Environment**' means any and all organisms (including humans), ecosystems, natural or man-made buildings or structures, and the following media:

(i) air (including air within buildings or structures, whether above or below ground)

(ii) water (including surface and ground water and water in wells, boreholes, pipes, sewers and drains); and

(iii) land (including surface land and sub-surface strata and any land under seabeds or rivers, wetlands or flood plains);

'**Environmental Authority**' means any person or legal entity (whether statutory or non-statutory or governmental or non-governmental) having regulatory authority under Environmental Law and/or any court of law or tribunal or any other judicial or quasi-judicial body;

'**Environmental Law**' means all laws, regulations, directives, statutes, subordinate legislation, rules of common law and generally all international, EU, national and local laws and all judgments, orders, instructions, decisions, guidance awards, codes of practice and other lawful statements of any Environmental Authority applying from time to time in relation to the Property in respect of pollution of or protection of the Environment or the production, processing, treatment, storage, transport or disposal of Hazardous Substances, in each case insofar as having the force of law;

'**Hazardous Substances**' means any natural or artificial substance (whether in solid or liquid form or in the form of a gas or vapour and whether alone or in combination with any other substance) capable of causing harm to the Environment and/or harm to the health of living organisms or other interference with the ecological systems of which they form part and/or harm to property and/or in the case of humans, offence caused to any sense;

15.2   Agreement as to Environmental Liabilities

The Seller and the Purchaser agree that:

15.2.1   if any notice or requirement of any Environmental Authority made pursuant to Environmental Law is served on or made of either of them in respect of the Property or any Hazardous Substances attributable to the Property, then, as between the Seller and the Purchaser, the sole responsibility for complying with such notice or requirement is to rest with the Purchaser to the exclusion of the Seller; and

15.2.2   if any Environmental Authority wishes to recover costs incurred by it in carrying out any investigation, assessment, monitoring, removal, remedial or risk mitigation works under Environmental Law in respect of the Property or any Hazardous Substances attributable to the Property from either or both of the Seller and the Purchaser then, as between the Seller and the Purchaser, the sole responsibility for the

233

payment of such costs is to rest with the Purchaser to the exclusion of the Seller.

The agreements outlined under Clauses 15.2.1 and 15.2.2 are made with the intention that any Environmental Authority serving any notice or seeking to recover any costs should give effect to the agreements pursuant to the statutory guidance issued under Part IIA of the Environmental Protection Act 1990.

The Seller and the Purchaser agree that the appropriate Environmental Authority may be notified in writing of the provisions of Clause 15 if required to give effect to the agreements outlined under Clauses 15.2.1 and 15.2.2.

15.3   Sold with Information

15.3.1   The Purchaser acknowledges to the Seller that:

(i)   [it has been provided with the following reports, surveys and other environmental information prior to the date of this offer:

[   ];]

(ii)   [it has carried out its own investigations of the Property for the purposes of ascertaining whether, and if so the extent to which, Hazardous Substances are present in, on, under or over the Property;]

(iii)   such information [gathered through those investigations] is sufficient to make the Purchaser aware of the presence in, on, under or over the Property of any Hazardous Substances referred to in the reports;

(iv)   it relies at its own risk on the contents of any report, plan and other written material and information either disclosed to it or orally communicated to it by or on behalf of the Seller both as to the condition of the Property and as to the nature and effect of any remedial works which may have been carried out [(including but not limited to the Report by [ ] dated [ ])] and no warranty is given or representation made by or on behalf of the Seller in this respect; and

        (v)   it has satisfied itself as to the condition of the Property.

15.3.2 Both parties agree that:

        (i)   [both the Purchaser and the Seller are [large commercial organisations] [public bodies]] [the Purchaser is a large commercial organisation and the Seller is a large public body] [the Seller is a large commercial organisation and the Purchaser is a large public body];

        (ii)   the Purchaser has been given permission and adequate opportunity to carry out its own investigations of the Property for the purpose of ascertaining whether, and if so the extent to which, Hazardous Substances are present in, on, under or over the Property;

        (iii)   the transfer of the Property pursuant to the Missives is an open market arm's length transaction; and

        (iv)   the Seller will not retain any interest in the Property or any rights to occupy or use the Property following Completion.

15.3.3 The acknowledgements in this Clause 15.3 are made in order to exclude the Seller from liability under Part IIA of the Environmental Protection Act 1990 so that the Seller is not an appropriate person, as defined therein.

15.4 Environmental Indemnity

The Purchaser will indemnify the Seller in respect of all and any actions, losses, damages, liabilities, charges, claims, costs and expenses which may be paid, incurred, suffered or sustained by the Seller arising (directly or indirectly) out of or in connection with the presence of any Hazardous Substances in, on or under the Property or migrating to or from the Property.

Note: This standardised clause is very much in favour of the seller, and assumes that if there are any environmental issues in respect of the property, there has already been agreement in principle between the parties, and that there will be a 'clean break' at completion, with liability transferring from the seller to the purchaser at that date. This approach is suitable for example when there are no environmental issues, but it is up to the purchaser to have conducted any necessary investigations and surveys to satisfy itself about the extent, if any, of environmental issues affecting the property.

Be aware, however, that in each transaction, the environmental provisions should be carefully considered to ensure that they reflect the parties' intentions, and if there are likely to be any issues, advice should be sought from environmental specialists, and alternative wording to reflect, for example, the 'polluter pays' principle may then have to be negotiated. It is beyond the scope of this work to consider such issues, however.

If environmental reports relating to the property have been previously obtained, the parties should consider whether these can be readdressed to the purchaser, to allow it to rely on the benefit of such reports.

6.14.23 Clause 16: Moveables

The Moveables comprise all the moveable items owned by the Seller in connection with and located at the Property and will be included in the sale without further payment or other consideration. They will be handed over to the Purchaser at Completion in their then current condition free from any hire purchase, lease or credit agreements, licences, reservations, retention of title or other encumbrances whatsoever.]

Note: It will be a question of fact whether there are any moveables belonging to the seller that are included in the sale, and these should be listed in the Schedule. Such moveable items as are listed are included in the Price.

6.14.24 Clause 17: No Employees

17.1   As at the Conclusion Date and Completion, the Seller confirms that there are no persons to whom the provisions of the Transfer of Undertakings (Protection of Employment) Regulations 2006 (**'Employment Regulations'**) will apply in relation to:

17.1.1   the sale of the Property and

17.1.2   the creation or cessation of any contractual relationship consequent to such sale with the effect of such person's employment (or liability for it and its termination) being deemed to transfer to the Purchaser [or any contractor of the Purchaser] at Completion.

17.2 If it is asserted or found by a court or tribunal that the Employment Regulations apply in relation to any person (**'Employee'**), the Purchaser [or any of its contractors] may terminate the employment of the Employee within 10 Working Days, where it has not already terminated, and if the Purchaser complies with its obligations under this Clause 16 (where applicable), the Seller undertakes to keep the Purchaser [and/or its contractors] indemnified, on demand, against all costs, claims, liabilities and expenses (including reasonable legal expenses) of any nature arising out of the employment of the Employee prior to Completion or the termination of it (whether it is terminated by the Purchaser or any other person and whether before, on or after Completion).

17.3 [The Seller acknowledges and agrees that the Purchaser will grant an indemnity in favour of each and any of its contractors to the same extent that the Seller is undertaking to indemnify the Purchaser in terms of Clause 16 and agrees that in the event of a claim on any indemnity in terms of Clause 17 for loss incurred by the Purchaser, that loss will include the amount, if any, which the Purchaser has paid or is required to pay to any of its contractors by virtue of any indemnity granted by the Purchaser in accordance with the provisions of Clause 17.]

Note: This is another area where specialist advice may be necessary. If there are employment issues, then potentially the Transfer of Undertakings (Protection of Employment) Regulations 2006 as amended (TUPE) could apply. A solicitor experienced in employment law should be consulted.

For the purposes of the Offer, it is assumed that there are no employees who are transferring from the seller to the purchaser and that therefore no TUPE issues arise. However, if there are employees and there are actual or potential TUPE issues, then advice should be taken from employment specialists, and specific provisions to cater for the actual circumstances will need to be drafted.

6.14.25 Clause 18: Guarantees

18.1 In so far as the Seller can validly do so, the guarantees will be assigned to the Purchaser in terms of the draft assignation of guarantees forming Part [13] of the Schedule.

18.2   The Purchaser will:

   18.2.1   within 15 Working Days after Completion duly execute the assignation of guarantees delivered to the Purchaser at Completion; and

   18.2.2   within 20 Working Days after Completion, intimate the assignation of guarantees to the appropriate parties and deliver a copy of the intimation to the Seller.]

Note: It is quite common, particularly if the tenant is a subsidiary company in a larger group of companies, or is newly formed and so does not yet have a track record to show that it is a reliable (known as a tenant's 'covenant'), that the landlord will have sought a guarantee, usually from a parent company, which will provide that if the tenant defaults in any of its obligations under the lease, the parent company will step in and meet the obligations. Where such guarantees have been given, they need to be assigned to the purchaser, and you need to check whether the original guarantee is capable of being assigned. Note that the guarantee may appear in the body of the lease or in a separate document.

   Although it is unlikely that the consent of the guarantor will be required to assignation of the guarantee, this should be checked. A style of Assignation of Guarantees is attached to the principle style Offer (part 13 of the Schedule).

6.14.26 Clause 19: Service Contracts

19.1   Liability

   With effect from Completion, the Purchaser will accept and take over liability for the Service Contracts and accordingly the Purchaser will, in respect of the period following Completion, keep the Seller indemnified from all liability arising under the Service Contracts.

19.2   Assignation

   19.2.1   In so far as the Seller can validly do so, the Service Contracts will be assigned to the Purchaser in terms of the draft assignation of service contracts forming Part [15] of the Schedule.

   19.2.2   The Purchaser will:

> (i)   within 15 Working Days after Completion duly execute the assignation of service contracts delivered to the Purchaser at Completion; and
>
> (ii)   within 20 Working Days after Completion, intimate the assignation of service contracts to the appropriate parties and deliver a copy of the intimation to the Seller.

19.3   Termination

The Purchaser will have no responsibility for any [other] service, maintenance, management or similar contracts relating to the Property entered into by the Seller (or its predecessors in title) prior to Completion and [(subject to Clause 19.1)] the Seller will, in respect of the period following Completion, indemnify the Purchaser from all liability arising under such contracts. The cancellation costs of any such contracts will be met by the Seller out of its own funds and will not, as between the Seller and the Purchaser, qualify as allowable expenditure for the purposes of any service charge calculations.]

Note: This clause contains practical arrangements for transferring any service, maintenance or management contracts to the purchaser, assuming they are transferable and/or assignable. The seller will be responsible for dealing with any existing service, management and/or maintenance contracts which the purchaser is not taking over, and for any termination costs that might be applied (which would not be allowable expenditure under the service charge provisions). Again a style of Assignation is attached in the Schedule to the principal style offer.

6.14.27 Clause 20: Capital Allowances

The provisions of Part 18 of the Schedule will apply.

Note: Capital allowances are tax reliefs on expenditure on plant and machinery and need to be considered in the sale of property containing plant and machinery. The capital allowance rules which govern how capital allowances can potentially transfer from the seller to the buyer changed in April 2014.

Whether you are acting for the seller or the purchaser, capital allowances must be considered at the outset of the transaction (ideally at the heads of terms stage).

Guidance on capital allowances is outside the remit of this book, and of the PSG. However, the PSG has, working in collaboration with tax colleagues at their respective firms, identified four commonly occurring scenarios for capital allowances, and drafting, provided as a starting point for each of these scenarios, is set out in Part 18 of the Schedule to the offer, but this must be tailored for each specific transaction. Accordingly, capital allowances advice should always be sought from a specialist capital allowances adviser.

The seller has a number of options when preparing the draft Offer :

Option 1:   The seller has claimed capital allowances and the seller and the purchaser have agreed to enter into a section 198 election to determine the value of the capital allowances to be transferred to the purchaser – Part 10 of the Schedule contains a form of election notice for the parties to complete and sign.

Where the seller has claimed capital allowances and, although the purchaser cannot claim them (eg because it is tax exempt), it still wants to safeguard the capital allowances for any onward sale, the suggested wording for Option 1 should also be used and amended as appropriate. The seller and the purchaser will need to agree the tax written down value for the transfer of capital allowances which will then be recorded in a section 198 election.

Option 2:   The seller has not claimed capital allowances because it was not entitled to do so and the seller and the purchaser have agreed that any unclaimed capital allowances are to be transferred to the purchaser – If the seller has not claimed capital allowances because it is not entitled to do so (eg because it is a charity or it is a property trader) the purchaser can benefit from the unclaimed capital allowances provided that, at the time it acquired the property, the seller (i) obtained the necessary information about capital allowances but (ii) did not enter into a section 198 election for £1.

Option 3:   The seller has not claimed capital allowances but could have done so and the seller and the purchaser have agreed that any unclaimed capital allowances (where amount of qualifying expenditure is not known) are to be transferred to the purchaser – An expert in the field of capital allowances is appointed to determine a reasonable amount of qualifying expenditure incurred by the Seller on the General Pool Available Fixtures and the Special Rate Available Fixtures which are to be pooled and, once determined, recorded in a s 198 election.

Option 4: The seller is not the past owner of the property and entered into a £1 section 198 election at the time it acquired the property – If the seller either:

- was not entitled to claim capital allowances and did not obtain any information about capital allowances at the time it acquired the property (and cannot now obtain that information) and entered into a section 198 election at £1; or

- would have been entitled to claim capital allowances but entered into a section 198 election at £1

then (unless the seller has itself incurred any further expenditure on fixtures during the time it owned the property) no capital allowances are available to the purchaser. Accordingly, no provisions dealing with capital allowances s need to be included in the Offer and Clause 20 and Parts 10 and 18 of the Schedule can be deleted.

6.14.28 Clause 21: Access

Subject to the terms of the Leases access to the Property prior to the Date of Entry will be given to the Purchaser, its surveyors and other professional advisers [with machinery, plant and equipment] for all reasonable purposes (including examining the Property), provided that the Purchaser will ensure that in doing so they:

(i) comply with the Seller's reasonable requirements,

(ii) comply with the access restrictions imposed on the Landlords under the Leases; and

(iii) exercise reasonable restraint and make good all loss, injury and damage caused to the Property.

Note: Provision is made in the Offer for reasonable access to the property to be given to the purchaser prior to the Date of Entry, subject to any access restrictions contained in the Leases.

6.14.29 Clause 22: Confidentiality

22.1 Pre-Completion

The Purchaser and the Seller will not disclose details of the Missives or the acquisition of the Property by the Purchaser to the press or otherwise prior to Completion except:

22.1.1 with the [prior written consent] [reasonable consent] of the other party;

221.2 to the Purchaser and the Seller's respective agents and professional advisers in connection with the acquisition/sale of the Property;

22.1.3 to the Purchaser's bankers or other providers of finance (and their professional advisers) in connection with the acquisition of the Property;

22.1.4 where required by law; and

22.1.5 where required to comply with the requirements of the Stock Exchange or any other regulatory or government authority.

22.2 [Post-Completion

Any press release after Completion relating to the acquisition/sale of the Property is to be agreed in writing between the Purchaser and the Seller prior to its publication (both parties acting reasonably).]

22.3 Agents

The Purchaser and the Seller will ensure that their respective agents and professional advisers comply with the undertakings in this Clause 22.

Note: There may be many reasons why the parties to a commercial transaction wish to keep the terms of the deal, or even the existence of the deal itself, confidential. Usually, the parties will want to keep the transaction and other details confidential prior to completion and, if there is to be any press release, to control both its content and timing. Where confidentiality is required this should extend to agents and professional advisers as well, and they should be informed of this.

6.14.30 Clause 23: Formal Documentation

23.1 Formal Documentation Required

Neither the Seller nor the Purchaser will be bound by any acceptance of this offer or any other letter purporting to form part of the Missives or any amendment or variation of the Missives unless it is duly executed.

23.2 Complete Agreement

The Missives (including the annexations) will represent and express the full and complete agreement between the Seller and the Purchaser relating to the sale of the Property at the Conclusion Date and will supersede any previous agreements between the Seller and the Purchaser relating to it. Neither the Seller nor the Purchaser has been induced to enter into the Missives on account of any prior warranties or representations.

Note: This provision ensures that the missives are to be properly executed to be effective, and that the Missives record the complete agreement between the parties in relation to the purchase and sale of the Property. This clause serves the same purpose as the Entire Agreement clause in the Scottish Standard Clauses in the Residential offer (see para 6.10.28).

6.14.31 Clause 24: Supersession

The provisions of the Missives (other than Clauses [2.4, 8.8, 11,15,17 and 20] which will remain in full force and effect until implemented) in so far as not implemented by the granting and delivery of the Disposition and others, will remain in full force and effect until:

24.1 in the case of the lease confirmations given in Clause [9] [six] years after the Date of Entry; and

24.2 in the case of all other provisions the earlier of:

24.2.1 the date when such provisions have been implemented; and

24.2.2 [two years] after the Date of Entry except in so far as they are founded on in any court proceedings which have commenced within such [two year] period.

Note: As with the Scottish Standard Clauses for residential offers, the commercial missives also provide for the contract to continue only for a period of two years (see commentary at para 6.10.25), other than the clauses specified, and of course there is no reason why the supersession provisions cannot be tailored to suit the particulars of the transaction and a shorter or longer period specified.

However, specific provision has been made for the lease confirmations provided in clause 9 to remain in force for a period of six years. The reason for this significantly longer period is that, if any of the confirmations are incorrect, the time when that would be most likely to come to light would be when the next rent review negotiations with the tenants take place. A period of 6 years assumes a 5-year review cycle (which is typical) and an extra year to cover any delays in carrying out a review, so a shorter or longer period would be appropriate if the rent review cycle is different.

6.14.32 Clause 25: Exclusion of Personal Liability

25.1 No personal liability will attach to the Purchaser's Solicitors by virtue of their entering into the Missives in their capacity as agents for the Purchaser.

25.2 No personal liability will attach to the Seller's Solicitors by virtue of their entering into the Missives in their capacity as agents for the Seller.

25.3 The Seller and the Purchaser will be solely liable to each other for compliance with, and fulfilment of, their respective obligations under the Missives.

Note: These provisions are to make it clear that both the purchaser's solicitors and the seller's solicitors are acting as agents only for their respective clients. It is principally relevant where either or both solicitors act for foreign parties such as offshore and foreign registered companies and nominees.

6.14.33 Clause 26: Assignation

The Purchaser may not (whether at common law or otherwise):

26.1 assign, transfer, grant any fixed security over, hold on trust or deal in any other manner with the benefit of the whole or any part of its interest in the Missives;

26.2 sub-contract any or all of its obligations under the Missives; nor

26.3 purport to do any of the foregoing.]

Note: This is a default position, but can be changed if, in the particular circumstances of a transaction, there is no objection to assignation, although the parties would have to consider what requirements would be necessary in the event of assignation (eg consent of the other party). The seller cannot be constrained in the same way in respect of any possible dealings on his part, provided he does nothing to put him in breach of the conditions of the missives.

27 **Proper Law and Prorogation**
The Missives and the rights and obligations of the Seller and the Purchaser will be governed by and construed in accordance with the law of Scotland and the Seller and the Purchaser will be deemed to have agreed to submit to the non-exclusive jurisdiction of the Scottish courts.

28 **Time Limit**
This offer, if not previously withdrawn, will fall unless a binding written acceptance has been received by us by 5 pm on [ ] 20[ ].

Yours faithfully

6.14.34 The Schedule

The style offer contains a Schedule of 18 parts, which include style documents, or spaces for transactional documents to be inserted, once drafted and agreed. Accordingly, once it has been tailored to suit the transaction, the Offer to Sell and all the parts of the Schedule (to which of course more parts can be added, and those parts that are not applicable, removed) provides a comprehensive document for the transaction and recording the agreement between the parties, and also what the parties need to do at completion.

Part 1 of the Schedule is replicated below, showing the typical documents that will form the 'Disclosed Documents' for the purposes of the transaction (see Clauses 6, 7 and 10 of the Offer).

Part 1 – Disclosed Documents

1 **Title Deeds**
2 **Leases**

3   **[Subleases]**

4   **Property enquiry certificate(s) dated [ ]**

5   **[Note: complete to include**

- coal mining searches
- planning and building warrant documents
- VAT documents
- construction documents (appointments, building contract, collateral warranties, Health & Safety File etc)
- if either of the last two rent reviews under any of the Leases have been referred to third party for determination, all submissions, counter submissions and determinations in connection with such reviews
- rent payment schedule
- service charge records for last [3] years (including payment history, estimates, reconciliations etc)
- details of any servitudes, rights of way or similar rights other than as disclosed in the Title Deeds
- Energy Performance Certificate
- Asbestos Report
- other searches or documents]

Part 2 – Title Deeds

An inventory identifying the title deeds (together with a description of whether they are principals, Extracts, or quick/photo copies) relating to the Property should be listed in this Part of the Schedule.

Part 3 – Leases/Subleases

An inventory identifying the leases and subleases (together with a description of whether they are principals, Extracts or quick/photo copies) and any relevant documents to the letting of any part of the Property (eg outstanding applications for consent) should be listed in Parts 3A and 3B respectively of the Schedule.

Part 4 – Disclosures against Lease Confirmations

Full details of any disclosures which the Seller needs to make to any of the confirmations about the Leases should be provided in this part of the Schedule. If there are none, that should be stated.

Part 5 – Back Letters

The drafts of all of the current Back Letters which are to be granted by the Purchaser to the Tenants at Completion should be incorporated here.

Part 6 – Current Management Transactions

Full details of all management transactions (ie applications by tenants for consent to assign, carry out alterations, rent review discussions etc) which the Seller is entitled to complete should be provided here.

Part 7 – Notice of Change of Landlord

A Notice of Change of Landlord will need to be completed for each of the Tenants. Although not essential, you may want to consider sending it by a tracked delivery method as proof of postage. If there is no Retrocession of an Assignation of Rents then the third paragraph incorporating the intimation of it needs to be deleted. See also Chapter 11 for matters to be dealt with at and after completion.

Part 8 – Disposition

It is suggested that a copy of the proposed Disposition be attached to the Missives in this Part of the Schedule.

Part 9 – Plan

A clear plan of the Property should be included here, where required, and if it is to be attached to the Disposition (or otherwise to be registered in the Land Register of Scotland), then it must satisfy the cadastral mapping Deed Plan Requirements of the Land Register of Scotland[47].

---

47 See www.ros.gov.uk/services/registration/land-register/faqs/cadastral-mapping-deed-plan-requirements.

Part 10 – Capital Allowances Election

On the disposal of a property which contains fixtures on which the seller has claimed capital allowances, the seller is required to apportion part of the sale price to those fixtures. This apportionment will affect the amount of allowances available to the seller and, in certain circumstances, could result in a tax charge.

The purpose of an election under section 198 of the Capital Allowances Act 2001 is to fix the apportionment to the fixtures. If the parties are unable to agree on the apportionment, they may apply to the First Tier Tax Tribunal within two years of the transaction to have the apportionment fixed. If no election is made and no application made to the tribunal to fix an apportionment, the purchaser will be treated as having acquired the fixtures for nil consideration and be unable to claim allowances. An election once made is irrevocable and cannot be challenged by HMRC. A style of Election is contained in Part 10 of the Schedule.

Subject to two restrictions the parties can decide the part of the price that they wish to apportion to the fixtures. The restrictions are that the election cannot be for an amount greater than was originally spent on the fixtures by the seller or greater than the sale price of the property. Usually the election will be made for an amount that will allow the purchaser to benefit from any remaining capital allowances in respect of the fixtures, while allowing the seller to retain the benefit of the allowances it has already claimed. However, an election does not have to be made for such a figure and ultimately the decision will be a commercial one.

The part of the purchase price apportioned to fixtures must then be further apportioned on the section 198 election between fixtures which are integral features and those which are not integral features. Integral features are a special class of plant and machinery introduced into the legislation in March 2008. The definition of integral features can be found at section 33A of the Capital Allowances Act 2001 and means:

- an electrical system (including a lighting system);
- a cold water system;
- a space or water heating system, a powered system of ventilation, air cooling or air purification and any floor or ceiling comprised in such system;

- a lift, an escalator or a moving walkway; or
- external solar shading.

The reason the apportionment in the section 198 election is necessary is that integral features attract a writing-down allowance of 8% per annum whereas other plant and machinery fixtures will attract a writing-down allowance of 18% per annum. If the apportionment is not made in the election this could lead to a distortion of the tax treatment of the fixtures.

Part 11 – Capital Goods Scheme

The assets to be transferred to the purchaser to which the Capital Goods Scheme applies should be listed in this part of the Schedule.

Part 12 – Moveables

Any moveable items included in the sale and included in the Price are to be listed here.

Part 13 – Assignation of Guarantees

This part of the Schedule contains a style Assignation of Guarantees, which, if it applies, should be completed incorporating details of the guarantees and any leases which incorporate guarantees.

Part 14 – Service Contracts

The existing service, maintenance and/or management contracts which the purchaser is taking over should be listed here.

Part 15 – Assignation of Service Contracts

If there are service contracts to assign, this style document should be used.

Part 16 – Assignation of Rent Deposits

Likewise, where there are Rent Deposits to be assigned to the purchaser this style Assignation of Rent Deposits should be completed incorporating details of the existing rent deposits which are being taken over by the purchaser.

Part 17 – Retrocession of Assignation of Rents

The draft of the retrocession of assignation of rents referred to in clause 10.2.11 of the Offer should be inserted here, if applicable.

SUSPENSIVE CONDITIONS

6.15 Properly completed missives which represent consensus ad idem ('complete agreement to the same thing') between the parties constitute a legally binding contract. It is, however, possible to conclude missives that are nonetheless conditional on some event or events happening, and which, if they do not happen, or do not happen in the way specified in the contract, will entitle one or both parties to withdraw from the contract. These are called conditional missives and they contain suspensive conditions, that is, conditions that suspend the final binding effect of the missives until the terms of the condition are met.

6.15.1 Conditionality

In fact, most missives for the purchase of property, both residential and commercial, contain some element of conditionality. There is a distinction to be made between suspensive conditions and resolutive conditions, and it is not always clear where the distinction lies[48]. Sometimes, in fact, the terminology is conflated, and the contract will say that it is subject to 'the following suspensive and resolutive conditions'. From a practical point of view, the distinction may not matter to the parties. If the suspensive condition is not purified or if the resolutive condition does not come to pass, either the contract automatically falls or the parties can terminate it. Either way, the matter does not proceed and the parties walk away from the arrangement.

6.15.2 Subject to survey

The simplest and most common suspensive condition is the 'subject to survey' clause often found in both residential and commercial offers. The

---

48 See K Reid and GL Gretton *Conveyancing* (4th edn) para 3–19.

offer is submitted with price, date of entry and all the other conditions, but is declared to be suspensively conditional on a satisfactory survey being obtained. The effect of this is that even if the seller were to issue a *de plano* acceptance, the purchaser would not be bound to the contract until the survey clause had been satisfied (or 'purified', in the language of suspensive conditions).

The intention behind making an offer conditional on obtaining a satisfactory survey, is to find out first of all if the price and other conditions are acceptable to the seller, before spending money on getting the property surveyed. Although the availability of the single survey in the Home Report should mean that a purchaser of residential property has a clear idea of value and basic condition, there could be a number of reasons why the purchaser wants to have her own survey carried out: for example, it may not be clear if her lender will accept the single survey report, or the Home Report may have disclosed matters that require a more specialised survey to be conducted, and the purchaser wants to obtain more detail as to condition before definitely committing to the price or indeed the purchase. A typical survey clause in a residential offer will say:

> This offer and any contract to follow on it are entirely conditional on (a) a satisfactory survey report and (b) a satisfactory valuation report being obtained by the Purchaser in respect of the Property. The Purchaser and his lenders will be the sole judges as to what constitutes satisfactory reports.

Sometimes a time limit by which the satisfactory reports must be obtained will be stated, but more often than not, there will be none, and the usual procedure is for the seller's solicitors to indicate acceptance either by phone or informally by email, or if formally in writing, deleting the survey condition. The purchaser then needs to organise the survey as soon as possible and, if all is well, confirms that the position is satisfactory and accepts deletion of the survey clause. Strictly speaking the condition is not purified – it is removed from the contract. It would be unusual, but not entirely unheard of, for residential missives to be concluded with a subject to survey clause still to be purified, since price and condition are such fundamental elements of whether the purchaser proceeds or not, the seller will prefer to know that these essentials are agreed before putting time and effort into tying the property into a contract, and equally the purchaser will not want time and effort to be put into other aspects of the purchase (the missives will also contain other time limits about satisfaction with title and searches), until it is clear that the property itself is acceptable.

For commercial purchasers, there is no equivalent to the seller's Single Survey, and so all surveys as to value and condition have to be instructed by the prospective purchaser. Depending on the type of property, this may involve considerable cost which the purchaser will not want to incur until he knows that his offer is otherwise acceptable. The nature of the property might require types of survey that are extensive and involve, not just a valuation, but any of a full measured survey; structural reports; an environmental audit; ground condition and mineral stability assessments; geotechnical reports, site and soil condition examinations or even the requirement to make trial bores and sink pits to ascertain if the land is suitable for the development proposed, eg:

> It will be an essential and suspensive condition of the Missives that the Purchaser obtains reports in terms wholly satisfactory to it (as to which it will be the sole judge) on a full measured survey and structural survey in respect of the Property. The Seller will co-operate with the Purchaser and its surveyors and other agents in arranging such surveys and in securing unrestricted access to the Property. Such surveys will be carried out within [five] working days of the date of conclusion of the Missives [or as soon as reasonably practicable after that date].

Again, the seller may prefer simply to allow the purchaser to get on with conducting its surveys before progressing the terms of the contract, but if the suspensive condition is accepted, then it would be usual for a reasonably (but realistically) short time limit to be imposed, with the provision that if the purchaser has not indicated by the expiry of the time limit that the survey is unsatisfactory and has withdrawn, it is deemed to be satisfied and the condition purified. The costs of carrying out site investigations can be considerable, and so the purchaser may not want to incur these costs until he has the protection of a signed contract. Bear in mind, however, that if site and soil surveys are required, purification can sometimes take three or four months.

6.15.3 Subject to Planning Permission

The purchase of a property or land that is to be developed will invariably be made 'subject to planning'. The offer will contain a suspensive condition, often in considerable detail, that a satisfactory grant of planning permission (and other consents) must be obtained. At the very least, the type of planning permission should be specified – eg 'in principle' or detailed planning permission. Note that it is usual for the definitions section of the offer to contain definitions of a number of the terms that are used throughout the clauses:

1.1   It will be an essential and suspensive condition of the Missives that the Purchaser obtains in terms wholly satisfactory to it (as to which it will be the sole judge):

         (i)   Planning Permission in principle/detailed Planning Permission for the Development and including any consent to change of use of the Property required for the Development;

         (ii)   [any other consents required for Development will usually be specified as well, including building warrant, listed building consent etc];

1.2   The Purchaser will submit the Planning Application to the relevant Planning Authority seeking planning permission for the Development within [specify period] after conclusion of the Missives. In the event of such permission being refused or granted subject to conditions which are unacceptable to the Purchaser, the Purchaser will be entitled (but not bound) either (i) to terminate the Missives (without penalty) by written notice to the Seller to that effect or (ii) to appeal against such decision, including, if the Purchaser considers it desirable, by application to the Court of Session.

1.3   The Seller will not object to the Planning Application(s) or concur with or assist any other person in objecting to the Purchaser's Planning Application(s) or any other application for consents, warrants or authorisations made by the Purchaser in respect of the Property;

Note: – (i) See below at paras 6.15.5 and 6.15.6 for further wording for this clause dealing with the essential time limits and long stops; (ii) an essential condition is one that would give rise to material breach.

Often the developer will have a particular type of consent in mind, on which he has based his costings and projections for the viability and profitability of the development, and the price that he is prepared to offer for the land is dependent on the terms of the planning permission that is granted, being in terms that will support the development proposal. This may involve density of units for example. The developer may have calculated the price offered on the basis of obtaining permission for one hundred dwellinghouses, so if planning permission is granted for only seventy five, this will make a considerable difference to the developer's profit and may make the proposal unviable. In these circumstances the offer may provide for the price to be reduced by £X per unit under the developer's optimum number of units, for which consent is actually given. Conversely of course the seller might want the price to be increased by £X per unit above the number of units specified, if consent is actually granted for a higher number.

The seller has an interest in the terms of the consent that is granted, as the price offered is usually dependent on the type of use to which the purchaser intends to put the property. If the seller agrees a price based on construction of a single house, but permission is obtained for ten houses, this considerably increases the value of the land to the purchaser. The seller will want to have clarity over what is to be obtained by way of planning, and the resultant price. However, the developer should be careful about being tied into requirements that are too prescriptive eg providing that planning must be obtained for an office building with a floor area of 3,000 square metres. Unless consent in these precise terms is obtained, the condition will be frustrated, whereas the parties might be equally as happy with a consent for 2,500 square metres of offices. Accordingly, consideration should be given to providing sufficient flexibility, so that the respective parties' interests are considered, but the proposal is not frustrated by overly rigid requirements.

Other statutory and other consents may be required for the development and should be specified. This may include roads construction consent, demolition warrants, or consents from SEPA or Scottish Water. Note also that as part of the planning consent, particularly for large-scale developments, the local authority may require the developer to undertake certain planning obligations under section 75 of the Town and Country Planning (Scotland) Act 1997, which may include requirements regarding construction of roads, roundabouts or other infrastructure, for example, or restrictions on types of uses to which the development can be put. Planning obligations that are imposed by virtue of section 75 of the 1997 Act are an integral part of the planning permission and are usually embodied in a separate document known as a 'Section 75 Agreement', which is registered against the title of the development and the terms of which are effectively burdens on the title to the property. The Section 75 Agreement invariably needs to be in place before the planning consent is granted.

The Section 75 Agreement can only be granted by the landowner, and since planning permission will not be issued until the Agreement has been signed and registered, it is essential that the Missives bind the seller to sign such an agreement so that the consent can actually be issued. However, in the case of *Cala Management Ltd v Messrs A & E Sorrie*[49] an obligation on the landowner to enter into a Section 75 Agreement at the reasonable request of the prospective purchaser created a requirement for the terms of the Section 75 Agreement itself to be reasonable, rather than simply meaning that the request must be reasonable.

There are, of course, timing issues for the seller in signing a binding agreement affecting what can be done with the land while he still owns it, and the purchaser has not purified the conditions in the contract. The seller may, as a *quid pro quo*, look for confirmation that if the Agreement is signed, the developer will be deemed to be satisfied with the terms of the planning permission, or look for an indemnity against any costs or losses until the title transfer takes place.

The parties may also decide to specify what is to happen if planning permission is refused ie whether the purchaser is to appeal. Once the planning consent is granted, the developer will also want to be assured that it is valid and unchallengeable, and that the planning suspensive condition is not purified until this is established. When planning permission has been granted by the planning authority it may be open to a legal challenge by way of a judicial review. Until recently, there were no fixed timescales for when a judicial review could be lodged in Scotland. Section 89 of the Courts Reform (Scotland) Act 2014 introduced a time limit for bringing a judicial review challenge. A challenge must now be brought within three

---

49 [2009] CSOH 79.

months[50] from the date on which the grounds for bringing the action arose (ie the date of the planning authority's decision to issue the consent)[51].

Section 89 also introduces a new 'permission' stage of the judicial review process, as a preliminary to consideration of the application. At this initial stage, the Court will either grant or refuse permission to proceed with the judicial review. To make that decision, the Court will consider two things: first, whether the applicant has 'sufficient interest' in the subject matter of the application; and second, whether the application for judicial review has a 'real prospect of success'. If permission to proceed is refused, or only granted on certain conditions, the applicant can request a review of that decision at an oral hearing, but must do so within seven days of the decision.

6.15.4 Other conditions

In putting together a site for development, there might be a requirement to acquire other land, and if this is essential for the viability of the development, eg where it is needed to provide access perhaps, then the missives should be made suspensively conditional on acquiring that other land.

It should also be borne in mind that there might be consents or requirements that will be needed once the development has been built out such as an off sales licence for a new supermarket. Again the requirement for such essential components of the overall scheme should be incorporated where appropriate into the purchase contract.

6.15.5 The benefit of the condition

Most suspensive clauses are drawn to allow the purchaser absolute discretion, to avoid arguments, and to allow the purchaser to withdraw a suspensive condition even though the condition has not yet been met. In *Manheath v H & J Banks Ltd*[52] the contract was subject to a suspensive condition relating to the obtaining of planning permission which had not

---

50 In England and Wales there is a statutory time limit for bringing a judicial review of 12 weeks, and in practice, prior to the change, Scottish courts would broadly follow this timescale

51 Section 89 allows the court to make an exception to the three-month time limit in certain cases, and extend the period for raising a judicial review if it would be 'equitable' to do so, having regard to the circumstances of that particular case.

52 [1966] SLT 42.

been obtained by the deadline stated in the condition. When the sellers sought to terminate the contract on that basis, the purchasers said that, as they had written to the sellers stating that the condition was purified, the contract had been concluded. However, whether a condition was for the sole benefit of a party seeking to waive it, was a question to be decided on the terms of the contract, and it was clear from the contract that both parties had an interest in the obtaining of planning permission, so that the purchasers' right to waive the condition was excluded.

In *Imry Property Holdings Ltd v Glasgow Young Men's Christian Association*[53], the purchasers intimated that they were satisfied with the permissions and consents which had been obtained for the proposed development and accordingly held the relevant suspensive condition to be purified, whereas at the date of their intimation the necessary permissions and consents had not been obtained. The purported purification of the condition by the purchaser was incompetent because the condition required all the necessary permissions to have been actually obtained.

Accordingly, suspensive conditions will normally contain wording specifying that the condition is for the benefit of the purchaser only and allowing them to waive the condition should they choose to do so, which will have the same effect as if the condition had in fact been purified:

> 'This clause will be construed solely for the benefit of the Purchaser and it will be in the sole option of the Purchaser at any time to intimate to the Seller in writing that any or all of the suspensive conditions contained in Clause [ ] is/are waived, in which case the Missives will be deemed purified to that extent.'

A condition that a condition is met 'to the purchaser's complete satisfaction' will be construed as excluding capriciousness and arbitrary actings and will imply a condition of reasonableness (*Gordon District Council v Wimpey Homes Holdings Ltd*[54]).

6.15.6 Time limits

A prudent seller will want to put a time limit on the operation of the condition, so that the parties are not tied into the obligation indefinitely, and

53 [1979] SLT 261.
54 [1989] SLT 141.

prevent giving the purchaser, in effect, a free option. Usually, a longstop date will be specified, by which time, if the condition has not been waived or purified, either or both parties will be entitled to terminate the contract. There might be several longstop dates for different conditions, or one date for all of them:

> In the event that all of the suspensive conditions contained in Clause [ ] have not been purified or waived by the Purchaser by **[insert here long-stop date]** (or by such later date as the parties may agree in writing) either party will be entitled (but not bound) at any time after that date, provided this Clause remains unpurified, to resile from the Missives by written notice to that effect served on the other party, and that without penalty except in respect of any antecedent breach.

It is important to allow for a realistic timescale within which to purify conditions, although it is always open to the parties to try to negotiate an extension of time, but there may be reasons why one party is unwilling to extend the longstop period, or may only be prepared to do so in exchange for changes to the other terms of the contract, which may not be so attractive to the party seeking the extension. Depending on the complexity of the offer, there may be a series of long-stop provisions for various milestones in the process.

PURCHASING PROPERTY FOR A BUSINESS

6.16 A business is simply a collection of assets, bound together by the goodwill of the business, and the sale of the business is really only a transfer of the various assets, with certain safeguards built in for the purchasers.

The assets of a business are generally regarded as: heritable property (whether owned or leased), stock-in-trade, trade fittings and fixtures, work-in-progress (although not particularly with retail businesses), money owing, vehicles, trade name, trade marks, copyrights, patents etc, domain name, website, knowhow, and any licences or franchises owned by the business. All of these assets are also wrapped up in the intangible goodwill of the business, which encompasses reputation and customer loyalty.

The liabilities of the business, which are deducted from the valuation of the assets, are basically money owing to suppliers, employees, pension fund, the taxman, and so on. The people of the business, are probably an asset in a good business, and a liability in a bad business, but not always so.

The missives for the purchase of a business need to deal with the various issues that apply to these assets and liabilities. The sale agreement should, where necessary, call on the sellers or their accountants to grant warranties that the situation is as they have stated. The purchasers will also conduct a thorough inspection of company records and other information provided by the sellers. Warranties need to be backed up by indemnities to cover them. For this reason agreements for the sale of large companies are very lengthy and complex, but that is outwith the scope of this work.

6.16.1 Heritable property

The property of the business is valued by a surveyor, and the offer should make the usual stipulations for the purchase of heritage, that is: date of entry, clauses dealing with heritable and moveable property, clauses dealing with title, property enquiry certificates and outstanding notices, and so on. It should be remembered that there are certain statutory requirements for commercial property, particularly the Health and Safety at Work legislation, and the offer should stipulate that all requirements under this legislation have been met, along with compliance with fire regulations. When the missives are proceeding by way of an offer to sell, the purchaser's solicitor should use a tool such as the Due Diligence Questionnaire to make sure that all such requirements are checked

Where the property is leasehold, the lease will be valued taking a number of considerations into account, including: (a) the remaining duration of the lease; (b) the rent being charged; (c) the frequency of rent reviews and the terms of the rent review clause; (d) the use permitted by the lease; (e) the authorised planning use of the property; (f) restrictions on assigning, charging and subletting (alienation); (g) general fairness of the lease to the tenant; and (h) location and trading prospects of the site.

Transfer of a leasehold interest will take place by way of assignation by the outgoing tenant (the seller). Precaution should be taken that there are no outstanding liabilities to the landlord for, eg rent and dilapidations of the property (the cost of restoring the property to the condition it was in when it was first let), and if there are, the basis on which the purchaser takes over the property should take these into account, given the usual full repairing and insuring obligations that apply to tenants under most commercial leases.

As well as receiving permission from the landlord for the assignation of the lease or sublet, confirmation should also be sought from the landlord that there are no outstanding liabilities, and that the proposed use of the property by the purchaser is approved.

Check whether the purchaser has opted to tax the property for VAT purposes with HM Revenue and Customs (see para 6.14.4), and ensure that the correct VAT provisions are included in the missives. How the VAT position affects your client's financial circumstances will usually be a matter for them to consult on with their accountant or finance director.

6.16.2 Stock-in-trade

An ongoing business will need stock to continue to trade, and so generally stock remaining at the date the business changes hands is valued on (or as near as possible to) that date either by agreement between the parties, or by an independent valuer specialising in stocktaking. This is known as SAV, or Stock at Valuation. Depending on the nature of the business, or the purchaser's intentions for it, (for example they may plan to obtain different stock from a different supplier) it might be appropriate for the purchaser to provide that the seller must run down the stocks so that the amount of stock at handover is as low as possible. The valuer's fee will often be divided equally between the parties. A typical condition would be:

> 'The purchaser will take over the [non-perishable] stock of the business so far as of a usable and saleable nature commensurate with good business practice, as at the date of entry and transfer, at a price [NB consider inserting provision regarding cost basis (eg wholesale price) according to customary practice for the type of business] to be agreed between the parties, and payment for such stock together with VAT on it (if any) will be made within [14] days of the value being agreed or determined in accordance with this clause.

> Failing agreement, the valuation of the stock will be referred to a single valuer to be mutually appointed by the parties, or in the absence

of agreement as to appointment, by a single valuer appointed by the [Chairman of the Scottish Branch of the Incorporated Society of Valuers and Auctioneers] on the application of either party. The valuer's decision on the valuation of the stock and his determination on liability for the costs of his appointment will be final and binding on both parties. Failing a determination by the valuer, the costs of his appointment will be met equally by the seller and the purchaser.'

6.16.3 Trade fittings and fixtures

These include counters, shelving, cash registers etc. Some of these items are expensive to buy and may be on hire purchase or other credit arrangement. This should be clarified in the offer to buy, and if the item is owned by a finance company, arrangements for the transfer of the item should be made subject to the amounts still payable under the contract. Again the applicability of VAT on such items should be ascertained and provided for, including the requirement to obtain a VAT receipt from the Seller for any VAT paid on items (including the property itself).

The purchasers of a business relying largely on internet or telephone orders, will also want to acquire the website and telephone number(s), and to make sure that the telephone company has not withdrawn the number.

The offer should contain a fairly tight condition about the working order of any central heating, refrigeration, air-conditioning or other mechanical plant, and the liability of the sellers to pay for any repairs. The purchasers should inspect the mechanical equipment concerned, and arrange for the sellers to pay for any necessary repairs, before parting with any money. The contractual position should, however, also be preserved. See the provisions of Clause 4 of the Residential Scottish Standard Clauses for suitable wording (para 6.10.5).

To describe the business, the various component parts should be specified eg

'The "Business" means

the shop premises at 44 Angus Avenue, Inverness together with all the heritable fittings and fixtures (the 'Property');

the goodwill of the business of Fishmonger and Poulterer carried on in the shop premises by the seller under the name "Seafresh";

the Fittings and Equipment; and

the non-perishable stock-in-trade;'

Fittings and equipment should be set out clearly and provision made regarding outright ownership:

> "Fittings and Equipment" means the whole trade fixtures and fittings, trade utensils and equipment including counters, refrigerators, cash registers and scales.

> The Seller warrants that there are no hire-purchase or credit sale agreements, diligences, liens or charges of any kind affecting any of Fittings and Equipment, and that the title of the seller to them cannot be reduced or affected at the instance of third parties.

6.16.4 Work-in-progress

This refers particularly to business people like solicitors or builders who do work and get paid at the end of that work. If the business is transferred while the work is continuing, a valuation needs to be made of the work done but not yet paid for, and that forms an asset of the business.

6.16.5 Money owing to the business

The debts owing to the business are generally retained in the ownership of the sellers, who collect them as and when they can. If the sellers are emigrating or retiring, however, this may not be appropriate, and the purchasers may take these over. The purchasers should then pay the sellers for this asset, and it should be remembered that the debts should be assigned to the purchasers, and the assignation intimated to each debtor, both to satisfy the requirement that the right of a creditor in a debt is fully transferred by an assignation followed by an intimation, and to let the debtor know who the creditors are. The intimation can simply be printed on the account when it is rendered. A simple statement requesting the debtor to pay the account to the assignee should suffice.

Similarly, the purchasers of a business, who take over the collection of the debts, can have the benefit (or liability) of any court actions in which their predecessors were engaged, or the benefit of any court decrees that they hold. The valuation of the debts of the business should reflect the likely outcome of the cases they have started.

6.16.6 Vehicles

Vehicles being taken over are valued at date of sale, by reference to suitable trade values. Again, care must be taken to ensure that there is no outstanding debt on these vehicles, or alternatively that the debt is allowed for in the price.

6.16.7 Trade name

Some trade names form a very valuable part of the business; others may be of no or doubtful value, and may be changed on takeover. Requirements about company names and their disclosure and display are now contained in the Companies Act 2006.

6.16.8 Intellectual property

A small retail business is unlikely to own any patents, designs, trade marks or copyrights, but a small electronics business, for example, might own all four, and be completely dependent on their existence. It is important, therefore, to check: (a) that the sellers own the right to the particular intellectual property; (b) that the rights are validly registered; (c) any dates of renewal or re-registration required; and (d) that they are properly assigned and intimated, in the case of trade marks and patents, to the appropriate registrar. The specialist advice of a chartered patent agent should probably be sought, unless the firm has expertise in this area. Intellectual property rights in overseas countries should be protected as well.

6.16.9 Licences and franchises

Many businesses depend almost entirely on a licence or franchise for their existence. There is little point in buying the business unless you can be sure the licence or franchise can be transferred to the purchaser. The purchasers should include a suspensive condition making the purchase dependent on getting a transfer of the licence or franchise. The most common example of the former is a hotel or shop licensed to sell alcohol, and of the latter, a business which owns a franchise outlet of one of the franchise companies like McDonalds or Your Move estate agencies.

Liquor licensing is now dealt with under the Licensing (Scotland) Act 2005. A property where the sale of alcohol takes place needs a premises licence, applications for which must be accompanied by an operating plan, layout plan and certificates from Building Control, Environmental Health and Planning departments of the local authority in question. Once it is granted a premises licence remains in force for an indefinite period, subject to payment of an annual fee. The premises must be operated in accordance with the operating plan, and any changes require a variation of the operating plan. All premises are subject to mandatory conditions that are set out in the 2005 Act. The Licensing Board for an area can add local conditions. Every premises must have a premises manager ie the person named on the operating plan, who must hold a Personal Licence. An applicant for a personal licence must hold a licensing qualification. Premises Licences can be transferred at any time by application to the relevant Licensing Board. A number of changes have been made to the 2005 Act licensing regime by the Air Weapons & Licensing (Scotland) Act 2015, but at the time of writing these are not yet in force. The principal change will be that in future an application to transfer and existing licence must be made by the incoming buyer, but must be accompanied by a consent statement from the existing licence holder.

The purchase of a business which depends on a franchise will depend on the consent of the franchisers, who will want to be satisfied as to the suitability of the purchasers to run the business, and ability to pay for the supplies. The reputation of the brand is an important element of franchises, and so it should not be assumed that it will be a foregone conclusion that the purchaser will be acceptable to the franchiser. Franchises are licences privately granted authorising the licensee to use the business style of the licensor.

Many other activities require a licence, eg road haulage, post offices, bookmakers, the operation of taxis and private hire-cars, second-hand dealing, boat hire, street trading, private markets, operation of places of entertainment, late-hours catering, window cleaning and many more. Requirements vary widely and enquiries should be made of the appropriate council when acting in the acquisition of property involved in these and similar areas.

6.16.10 Goodwill

Goodwill has been defined as 'the probability that the old customers will revert to the old place' (*Crutwell v Lye*[55]). But perhaps it is something more prosaic as suggested by Dr Samuel Johnson remarking on the sale of Thrale's Brewery in 1781: 'We are not here to sell a parcel of boilers and vats, but the potentiality of growing rich beyond the dreams of avarice.'

Goodwill is an asset that cannot be precisely valued, and its valuation will vary widely from case to case. To some extent it will also vary with the purchaser's opinion as to whether it is a good business that can be extended, or it is a poor business that will require an investment of time and money to bring it round. You must always be careful, especially in small businesses, of highly personal goodwill that will simply disappear when the sellers leave. Customers or clients of a business cannot be counted on not to take their business elsewhere. Advice on the appropriate basis of valuation of the goodwill of a business should be taken from the purchaser's accountant.

6.16.11 People

A good business which is being sold will probably have high calibre employees whom the purchasers will wish to retain. A bad business may have been significantly affected by its employees, and the purchaser is unlikely to feel a great compulsion to inherit these liabilities.

Good employees may be hard to retain. They may feel upset at the business being sold over their heads, and the owner disappearing with a large sum, representing their unrewarded hard work. They may even decide that they could do the same thing better, and will leave to start up their own businesses. This is more of a personnel management exercise, than a legal one, in many respects.

The position of employees of a business that is changing hands is governed by the Transfer of Undertakings (Protection of Employment) Regulations 2006 (as amended) (TUPE) which protects the employees' terms and conditions of employment on transfer to a new owner. It is not competent to provide in the sale agreement that the sellers are to dismiss

---

55 [1810] 17 Ves 335 at 346 per Lord Eldon.

employees before the business changes hands, if the sole reason is the transfer of the business. The matter was finally settled by the House of Lords in *Litster v Forth Dry Dock and Engineering Co Ltd*[56], where it was ruled that employees, dismissed by the receivers of the company one hour before the receivership took effect, had continuity of employment, and, therefore, a claim for redundancy.

The complexities of employment law are such that specialist advice should be sought as soon as it is identified that employees are an element of any transaction. The PSG Offer to Sell provides wording that caters for the position where there are no employees (see para 6.14.24). Where there are employees of a business, then TUPE compliant provisions will need to be drafted, and full details of each employee, and their terms and conditions of employment, including position, salary and benefits, hours of employment and holiday entitlement, as well as length of service, pension arrangements and other relevant information should be obtained from the sellers.

6.16.12 Restrictive covenant

What of the departing sellers? Hopefully they will have made enough to enjoy a well-earned retirement, but whether they have or not, the attempt is sometimes made to impose a restrictive covenant (or non-competition clause) on them to prevent them from returning to business to compete with the purchasers. It should be borne in mind, however, that competition law is another area which has become increasingly complicated and prevalent, and especially with the Competition Act 1998 now applying to all land agreements by virtue of the Competition Act 1998 (Land Agreements Exclusion Revocation) Order 2010, great care should be exercised when drafting such clauses. The covenant should be neither too loose to prevent the sellers from competing unfairly, nor too tight to be declared unenforceable by the courts and fall foul of competition law. Any protection provided by a restrictive covenant must be limited both in time and area to what is necessary for a purchaser to take over the market position of the business to the same extent enjoyed by it when the seller was in control.

---

56 [1989] SLT 540.

'The seller will not in any way carry on directly or indirectly (unless with the written consent of the purchaser) within [one year] after the date of transfer and within [one mile] of 44 Angus Avenue either on his own account or as a partner with, or in the name of, or as a servant or agent to any person or persons, firm or company, the business of Fishmonger or Poulterer.'

6.16.13 Accounts and records

The books of account and financial, customer and other records relating to the business should be transferred to the purchaser on the date of transfer, but a period of time (eg six months) after transfer will need to be allowed for reasonable access for inspection by the seller or his agents for completing tax returns and the like.

SELLING PART OF A PROPERTY

6.17 When the property being sold is an area that is being split off from a larger title, there are several specific issues to bear in mind.

6.17.1 Title conditions

The principal title of the larger area (or building of which the property being sold forms part) may be subject to a number of real burdens and servitudes. It may be necessary to specify in the missives whether, and the extent to which, existing burdens will affect the property and the extent to which it will (or can) benefit from existing servitudes (see para 9.10.3).

If new burdens or servitudes are required, then the missives should provide as clearly as possible what the terms of those are to be, and should also make provision regarding forms and payment of registration fees in respect of the dual registration requirement. When using the following suggested wording, a definition of 'Retained Property' will need to be added to the Definitions clause in the offer. Alternatively the burdens and servitudes can be added to the draft Disposition that is attached to the missives, in which case only clause 1.5 below suitably amended would be required

1.1   In the Disposition the following servitude rights will be imposed on the Property in favour of the Retained Property:

[Here list all new servitude rights in favour of the Retained Property]

267

1.2   In the Disposition the following servitude rights will be imposed on the Retained Property in favour of the Property:

[Here list all new servitude rights in favour of the Property]

1.3   In the Disposition the following real burdens will be imposed on the Property for the benefit of the Retained Property:

[Here list all new real burdens in favour of the Retained Property]

1.4   In the Disposition the following real burdens will be imposed on the Retained Property for the benefit of the Property

[Here list all new real burdens in favour of the Property]

1.5   [If the Disposition creates real burdens or servitudes or both affecting the Property, (whether as the burdened property or the benefited property), and dual registration is required, the cost of registering any new real burdens or servitudes against the Seller's property will be paid by the Seller. In addition:

    1.5.1   If the Seller's property is in the Register of Sasines:

        (i)   the Seller will deliver a completed and signed SAF, in respect of registration of the real burdens or servitudes (or both) against the Seller's property;

        (ii)   the Purchaser will submit the SAF contemporaneously with the Purchaser's application for registration of the Disposition.

    1.5.2   If the Seller's property is registered in the Land Register of Scotland, the Purchaser will include the title number for the Seller's property and the Seller's Solicitors' [two] email address[es] on the application form for registration of the Disposition.]

Particular attention should be given to ensuring that all necessary rights of access are obtained, and rights to services, in, over or through common parts of a larger building and rights of access over adjoining land or properties for repairs, cleaning and other essential purposes are granted.

6.17.2 Plan

Clear accurate plans are important in many aspects of conveyancing, and when identifying a piece of property for the first time, it is particularly important to have a plan that shows the precise extent, and this should be confirmed by the purchaser. The plan must be taxative (such as an Ordnance Survey plan), suitable for annexing to the disposition of the Property and be sufficient to allow the Keeper to plot the property onto the cadastral map (see para 9.9.7 for the Keeper's requirements).

6.17.3 Reservations

The seller needs to make certain to reserve to himself any rights required to continue to use the remainder of the property retained by him. There have been instances where areas become landlocked or otherwise deprived of essential rights though a failure to make adequate reservations. While there may be essential servitudes implied by law, the practicalities of the configuration of the land might make these difficult to use, and so full consideration needs to be given not just to the property being sold, but the one being retained.

RURAL PROPERTY

6.18 When offering for property in the countryside, there are some specific issues that need to be borne in mind. Agricultural property and crofting have their own specialisations, and it is not the intention of this text to consider those, rather the more general matters that should be taken into account for rural property. If agricultural holdings or crofting issues apply, specialist advice should be sought.

6.18.1 The property

When describing the property in the offer, especially if it comprises or includes land, the description should include rights to woodlands, sporting rights and minerals, as these can be subject to leases or in some cases owned outright.

Salmon fishings are capable of being owned separately from the land in which the river or loch is situated, and the chances are if the property being purchased forms part of a larger estate, then the estate owner will reserve the salmon fishing rights, unless, of course, part of the benefit of the property being sold is that the salmon fishings are included. The purchaser of rural property that includes salmon fishings should be made aware that salmon beats, by their nature, are often discontiguous from the rest of the property. Vigilence is required to ensure that sufficient rights of access to the river bank, and possibly for parking exist, or are granted.

Sporting rights, which include freshwater fishing and shooting of game, are not generally held as a separate tenement in land except for such rights which had been held by a former feudal superior and which were capable of being preserved as a separate title by procedures under section 65A of the Abolition of Feudal Tenure (Scotland) Act 2000 prior to feudal abolition. However, leases of sporting rights are common; the existence of such rights need to be identified and the terms on which they are held and exercised should be checked.

Accordingly, in addition to the property, which should be described as fully as possible (perhaps by reference to the schedule of sales particulars, and identified on a plan, the offer should also include:

(i)   all buildings and steadings, all heritable fixtures and fittings and all fixed equipment in and on the Property including without prejudice to the foregoing generality all fences, hedges, dykes, pens, troughs, gates and gateposts

(ii)   the whole shooting and other sporting rights, including the salmon and trout fishing in all rivers, lochs and streams lying within or *ex adverso* the Property so far as the seller has right to them;

(ii)   all plantations and all timber, standing, cut and fallen within the Property at the date of the offer;

(iii)   the whole mines, metals and minerals located in the Property including stone, sand and gravel (except coal and mines of coal) so far as the seller has right to them;

(iv)   the solum of all roads intersecting and bounding the Property;

(v)   heritable and irredeemable servitude rights to use the water, drainage and sewerage systems serving all or any part of the Property and situated outwith the boundaries of the Property including all springs, connections, wells, tanks, drains, pipes, sewers and the like at present so used together with all necessary servitude rights of way and wayleave for the same and all necessary rights of access to any part or parts of them on all necessary occasions for the purposes of inspecting, cleaning, maintaining, repairing and renewing them and altering their levels;

(vi) all necessary heritable and irredeemable servitude rights of access to and egress from all parts of the Property for both vehicular and pedestrian traffic for any purpose whatsoever over all existing roads and tracks (and where appropriate show these delineated on a plan)..

Other issues, such as grants, basic payment entitlements, crops (both growing and harvested), fuel in fuel tanks etc need to be considered in the context of agricultural land, and provision made in the contract for a valuation of them at settlement.

The foreshore and seabed are traditionally Crown property. Therefore, if your client is proposing to purchase a coastal property bear in mind that rights to moorings, jetties or using the seabed (eg for oyster farming) are likely to need to be separately negotiated with the Crown Estate. It should also be borne in mind that, as it is now competent to register title to the seabed (see paras 2.4.19 and 14.5.9) that such areas need to be accurately identified for the purposes of mapping onto the cadastral map: the area in question must be described using OSGB36 coordinates, and a location plan showing the plot of land in relation to the coast of Scotland is also required.

In addition it should be specified that the Property is not subject to an agricultural tenancy or any other form of lease or tenancy agreement, nor affected by crofting tenure. Crofts may exist in the original crofting counties of Argyll, Caithness, Inverness, Orkney, Ross & Cromarty, Sutherland and Zetland and in the extended areas (since February 2010) of Arran, Bute, Greater and Little Cumbrae, Moray and parts of Highland that are not already covered within the traditional crofting counties. Where appropriate, you should require a search in the Register of Crofts, maintained by the Crofting Commission[57]. The Registers of Scotland also maintain a Crofting Register[58], although this Register is comparatively new and not all croft properties are on this Register.

---

57 See www.crofting.scotland.gov.uk.
58 See www.crofts.ros.gov.uk/register/home.

Where the property is subject to agricultural holdings tenancies or crofting tenancies, be aware that these may give rise to a tenant's right to buy, and expert advice should be sought. Grazing leases of less than a year's length should not pose a problem, as a grazing tenant has no security of tenure, so long as the let has been properly terminated at the ish (end date).

6.18.2 Roads and access

All property needs to be served by adequate access according to the nature of the property. In rural areas, often access roads and others are not publicly maintained and accordingly provision should be made in the Missives for adequate servitude rights to be available. For example:

> The title to the Property contains a heritable and irredeemable servitude right of access for pedestrian and vehicular traffic, from the public road to the Property for all purposes [over the route(s) shown on the Plan]. Maintenance of the access route(s) is shared on an equitable basis, according to user. There are no outstanding maintenance, repair or renewal obligations in respect of the route(s).

In addition, depending on the use of the property, it might be necessary to check for the existence of local roads authority consents for uses such as agricultural and forestry purposes in relation to access off public roads. Confirmation should be sought that there are no road widening or road construction proposals which could adversely affect the Property or any part of it, and that there are no height, width or weight restrictions affecting roads, bridges, footpaths and verges providing access to the Property.

6.18.3 Water and drainage

6.18.3(i) Drainage

Very often, drainage systems for rural properties will be private, rather than connected to the mains drainage system. This raises issues of access to systems, if they or parts of them are located in other land, and regulatory and environmental issues, if any part of the system discharges into a watercourse. Private drainage will be to a septic tank which may incorporate a soakaway, outfall, and other pipes and connections. Other types of septic tank act as stores and require to be emptied from time to time and this is dealt with by the local authority. Since April 2006, septic tanks which discharge to land via a soakaway need to register under the Controlled Activities Regulations (CAR), the current version of which is the Water Environment (Controlled Activities) (Scotland) Regulations 2011, unless they were already registered under the Control of Pollution Act 1974. These regulations principally affect residential properties, but there may also be implications for developers if their activities involve water abstraction, engineering works or impoundment (see para 8.21.3).

A suggested clause for missives is

> If the drainage of the property is private, evidence will be produced to show that the septic tank, soakaway, tail pipe and other pipes and connections are in good working order, condition and repair and comply in all respects with the local authority and water authority standards and other relevant regulations, and in particular the Water Environment (Controlled Activities)(Scotland) Regulations 2011. Either (i) an existing valid authorisation from the Scottish Environmental Protection Agency, under the Control of Pollution Act 1974 or (ii) a Discharge Registration Certificate from SEPA under the Water Environment (Controlled Activities) (Scotland) Regulations 2011 will be exhibited prior to and delivered at the date of entry.

That wording will deal with the compliance aspects. If the septic tank has not been registered and needs to be, information on what to do can be obtained from SEPA[59]. If the septic tank or any part of the system it uses is, or might be located outwith the land being purchased, then adequate servitude rights must be available:

> If, to any extent the septic tank, soakaway, tail pipe and other pipes and connections are located outwith the Property, [there exists][the Purchaser will be granted] an unrestricted heritable and irredeemable servitude right to use, inspect, maintain, empty, repair and when necessary renew the same, with rights of access on all necessary occasions subject only to an obligation to make good all surface damage occasioned by the exercise of such rights. The location of the septic tank, soakaway and tail pipe will be indicated to the Purchaser on a plan accompanying your acceptance of this offer.

---

59 See www.sepa.org.uk.

Provision should also be made in the missives if water supplies, drainage and sewerage are mutual:

> The liability to maintain any private water supplies, drainage and sewerage and other services which are mutual to the Property and any other subjects is shared on some equitable basis.

6.18.3(ii) Water supply

Private water supplies are less common than private drainage systems, but more remote parts of the country may not have access to mains water, and require to take their supply of water from private reservoirs or water courses. It is estimated that over 150,000 people in Scotland rely on a private water supply, and many others, such as visitors and tourists, will use them occasionally each year. Private water supplies are currently regulated by the Private Water Supplies (Scotland) Regulations 2006[60], which enable local authorities to monitor them to check they meet wholesomeness standards. The 2006 Regulations also implement EU requirements in relation to drinking water quality to ensure the provision of clean and wholesome drinking water. Where the Property is served by a private water supply the Missives should provide:

> The Property is served by a private water supply. Evidence will be produced to show that the water supply is constant and sufficient in quality and quantity for the domestic and the other requirements of the Property and complies with The Private Water Supplies (Scotland) Regulations 2006 (as amended), and all other regulations and requirements of the relevant Local Authority, the European Union and other relevant bodies. If, to any extent, the water supply or supplies and any tanks, pipes, connections and others relating to the supply lie outwith the Property, [there exists][the Purchaser will be granted] an unrestricted heritable and irredeemable servitude right to use, inspect, maintain, repair and when necessary renew the same, with rights of access on all necessary occasions subject only to an obligation to make good all surface damage occasioned by the exercise of such rights. The location of the source of the supply and all tanks, pipes, connections

---

60 As prospectively amended by the Private and Public Water Supplies (Miscellaneous Amendments) (Scotland) Regulations 2015.

and others will be indicated to the Purchaser on a plan accompanying your acceptance of this offer.

It is also possible that the source of the water supply is in the Property being purchased by your client and so you should add:

'There are no water supplies emanating from within the Property and serving adjoining properties'.

If there are such water supplies, then this will elicit a response that should provide more information including particulars of the properties that benefit from this supply, and whether there are any requirements to guarantee quantity or quality of the water supplied.

6.18.3(iii) Reservoirs

Proximity of a property to a large raised reservoir (ie with a capacity of more than 25,000 cubic metres of water above the natural level of the adjoining land) raises issues of risk of flooding, and therefore if there is a large raised reservoir in the vicinity the risks attendant with that will need to be assessed by the purchasers and their surveyor.

No part of the Property is, or is affected by, or situated *ex adverso* a raised reservoir or a large raised reservoir within the meaning of the Reservoirs Act 1975 or comprises a controlled reservoir as defined for the purposes of the Reservoirs (Scotland) Act 2011, nor is it within any water catchment area in relation to any public water supply.

6.18.4 Walls and fences

Maintenance of boundary walls and fences can be a significant liability in large rural areas, and where they separate the Property from other subjects, the liability to maintain and repair should be borne equally:

'All boundary fences which separate the Property from adjoining subjects (other than those adjoining public roads which may belong solely to the Seller) are mutual between the seller and the adjoining proprietors, and the obligation to maintain, repair and renew them to a stockproof standard is shared equally.

There are properly constituted servitude rights of access in favour of the Property over adjoining or neighbouring properties for the purpose of inspecting, maintaining, repairing and renewing such boundary walls or other common or mutual items or buildings on the Property.

There are no outstanding obligations in respect of the boundary fences, and in particular, no obligation to erect or maintain deer-proof or rabbit-proof fences.'

6.18.5 Rights of way and access rights

6.18.5(i) Rights of way

There are many rights of way across Scotland, some of which are well known. However, a right of way can be established through use by the public for the prescriptive period of 20 years, for the purposes of getting from one public place to another, and not all rights of way are signposted, or marked as such. The Scottish Rights of Way and Access Society (SRWAS)[61] maintains a record of all known rights of way in the National Catalogue of Rights of Way (CROW) and other routes. Sometimes the route of a right of way will be shown on plans of the property, or on the Ordnance Survey map, but you can also obtain information from CROW by contacting SRWAS, although it should be borne in mind that not all rights of way are logged with them, as many are only known about locally. Nor does it mean, if nothing is shown on a plan, that no rights exist. Only a small percentage of rights of way have been formally identified as such, or 'vindicated', and the vast majority of rights of way are in the category known as 'claimed' in which the basic requirements for establishment of a right of way appear to have been met, but no formal process has taken place. In the middle, are rights which have been 'asserted', where the local authority is interested in protecting them, or where the landowner affected has accepted the use of the route by the public.

SRWAS deals with hundreds of enquiries every year about problems with particular rights of way and other access matters, and can be asked to provide details of any rights of way or other routes affecting the property being purchased. The offer should provide that:

61 See www.scotways.com.

'there are no servitudes, rights of way, wayleaves, any provision or proposal in relation to core paths (in terms of the Land Reform (Scotland) Act 2003) or similar rights affecting the Property other than those disclosed in the titles. Written evidence of the position regarding rights of way will be exhibited prior to settlement, both by way of the titles and by way of letters from the Scottish Rights of Way and Access Society and the Local Authority Access/Rights of Way Department.'

If the Property is affected by a right of way, and this is something that the purchaser is willing to accept, a plan showing routes of any rights of way should be obtained, as this will need to be provided to the Registers for plotting on to the cadastral map.

6.18.5(ii) Access rights (the right to roam)

The general public have enjoyed rights of access of one sort or another over our beautiful countryside for a variety of recreational purposes, and for passage, for many years and these have been expanded over the years by local government and town and country planning legislation, and by the Countryside (Scotland) Act 1967 and the Countryside (Scotland) Act 1981. However, public rights of access were transformed significantly by Part 1 of the Land Reform (Scotland) Act 2003, which extended statutory access rights to 'everyone' to encompass: (i) the right to be on land (which includes inland waters, canals and the foreshore) for (a) recreational purposes, (b) carrying on a relevant educational activity or (c) carrying on a commercial activity, provided it is an activity that is capable of being carried on uncommercially; and (ii) the right to cross land.

These access rights are exercisable above, below and on all land, other than land over which rights cannot be exercised defined in s 6 of the 2003 Act and including land with buildings or other structures on it or forms the curtilage of a building or land used for the purposes of a school, etc. There is power to exclude or restrict land from the exercise of access rights for the purposes of defence or national security. Included within the exemption is 'sufficient adjacent land' next to a house so that the occupants of the house can have a reasonable amount of privacy. This will normally mean the garden around the house.

There have been several quite high-profile cases in the courts since the introduction of access rights, the first of which was *Gloag v Perth*

& Kinross Council[62] a well-publicised case due to the celebrity of the applicant, business woman Ann Gloag. Mrs Gloag successfully applied for a declaration that certain land adjacent to her house at Kinfauns Castle was not land in respect of which access rights were exercisable, arguing that an area of approximately 11 acres fell within the 'privacy exemption' in section 6 of the 2003 Act, which allows an owner 'sufficient adjacent land to enable persons living there to have reasonable measures of privacy in that house…and to ensure that their enjoyment of that house…is not unreasonably disturbed'. This was an unpopular decision not only with the Ramblers' Association, but also in the Scottish Parliament where Sarah Boyack, a Labour MSP, obtained a parliamentary debate on a motion which was strongly critical of the decision, stating that it was contrary to the intention of the Act and 'undermined the clear will of Parliament, which legislated for the widest possible access to the countryside'. See also *Snowie v Stirling Council*[63].

Access rights must be exercised responsibly, and for the most part they are. Landowners must use and manage their land and otherwise conduct their ownership of it in a responsible way, and for the most part they do. As directed by section 10 of the 2003 Act, Scottish Natural Heritage produced the Scottish Outdoor Access Code[64], which gives detailed guidance to both access takers and land managers about enjoying and facilitating the access rights.

Local authorities have the duty to provide a plan for a system of core paths for giving access rights to the public throughout their area. Part of the idea here is that, if there are designated paths for ramblers and other access takers to use, they will use those paths, rather than randomly wandering across land. For this purpose, local authorities can enter into core path agreements with landowners. Such agreements do not need to be recorded in the Sasine Register or registered in the Land Register, (although their predecessors under the Countryside (Scotland) Act 1967 did). If a core path agreement cannot be obtained, the local authority has compulsory powers to delineate paths in land by way of core path order. If the land being purchased is affected by a core path, the existence of the core path must be disclosed in the application for registration, and a copy of the path

---

62 [2007] SCLR 530.
63 [2008] SLT (Sh Ct) 61.
64 See www.outdooraccess-scotland.com.

order (which will include a map showing the route of the path) must be submitted to allow the Keeper to note the particulars of the core path in the burdens section of the Title Sheet, and delineate it on the cadastral map.

The wording concerning rights of way and similar rights suggested in para 6.18.5(i) includes reference to rights exercisable over core paths and subject to a core path agreement or core path order. Any such arrangements should be disclosed in any letter obtained from Local Authority Access/ Rights of Way Department. Additional wording to cover the matter specifically could be included:

'If the property is affected by the exercise of rights of access exercisable by the public in terms of Part 1 of the Land Reform (Scotland) Act 2003, whether routinely or infrequently, then full details of the routes of such access and the quantity and frequency of such exercise will be provided with your acceptance of this offer, along with copies of any path agreements or path orders affecting the Property.'

6.18.6 Community right to buy

Part 2 of the Land Reform (Scotland) Act 2003 created a new concept of the Community Right to Buy, by which communities are allowed to register their interest in land within their neighbourhood, and have a right of first refusal to buy the land if it comes on the market for sale. Accordingly it is a pre-emptive right, ie it is only triggered by the proposed sale of land over which an interest has been registered. If the landowner never puts the land on the market or takes steps to transfer it, the right to buy will never by triggered. A registered interest will lapse after 5 years, but the community body can apply to re-register it for another 5 years. The community's interest (through a community body which must be set up specifically for the purpose) must be registered in the Register of Community Interests in Land (see para 7.9), and Scottish Ministers must have given written confirmation that they are satisfied that the main purpose of the community body is consistent with furthering the achievement of sustainable development.

The type of land over which the Community Right to Buy may be exercised is predominantly rural at the time of writing (but this is soon to change – see below). Land over which the right to buy cannot at present be exercised is defined as 'excluded land', details of which are contained in the Community Right to Buy (Definition of Excluded Land) Order 2009. The order specifies 'settlements' which are excluded from the right to buy, because of their population size, and includes cities and major towns in Scotland. Plans showing the extent of these excluded areas are accessible on the Scottish Government website[65]. Once a community interest has been registered against land, and for five years from the date of its registration (or longer if renewed), the owner of that land (or heritable creditor with a right to sell the land) is prohibited from transferring the land, or taking any action with a view to transferring the land, except in certain exempt cases (for example if missives have already been concluded for the sale of the land)[66] and any transfer in breach of this prohibition will be of no effect.

Since the existence of a Community Right to Buy will effectively prevent a sale of the land affected (unless, of course, the community decides to decline to purchase) then any offer for land that is not excluded land should contain the following clause:

'Where the Property or any part of it is registrable land for the purposes of Part 2 of the Land Reform (Scotland) Act 2003, the Seller confirms that there is no interest of a community body either registered against the Property or any part of it, or any larger area of which the Property forms part, nor is an application for registration of such an interest pending, and the Seller knows of no proposals either for formation of a community body or for making an application for registration of an interest. If the Search in the Register of Community Interests in Land referred to in Clause [see below] of this offer contains a registered interest or application the Purchaser will be entitled to rescind the Missives without any penalty.'

and the following additional section should be added to the searches clause in the offer:

'Where the Property or any part of it is registrable land for the purposes of Part 2 of the Land Reform (Scotland) Act 2003, the Seller will deliver prior to the date of settlement a Search in the Register of Community Interests in Land, from the date of commencement of the Register, or (if later) from the date occurring 5 years prior to the date

---

65 See www.gov.scot/Topics/farmingrural/Rural/rural-land/right-to-buy/MappingTool.
66 See section 40 of the 2003 Act.

of conclusion of the Missives, which Search will disclose no entry in the Register as at the date of conclusion of the Missives which would prohibit the Seller from transferring the Property to the Purchaser.'

For wording that must be incorporated into a Disposition in case of a registered interest in land, see para 9.15.

Part 4 of the Community Empowerment (Scotland) Act 2015 extends the community right to buy to 'all of Scotland' and makes a number of administrative and procedural amendments to the right to buy provisions in the 2003 Act. Most of the 2015 Act, including the extension of the right to buy provisions, will come into force on 15 April 2016. From that date, therefore, the community right to buy will no longer be just a 'rural' issue.

In addition, proposals under the Land Reform (Scotland) Bill, introduced to the Scottish Parliament on 22 June 2015, include provisions for a non pre-emptive (in other words, it can be exercised at any time, without having to wait for the property in question to come onto the market) community right to buy, entitling certain community bodies (yet to be defined) to have land transferred to them if they can demonstrate that this would further the achievement of sustainable development in relation to the land, if the transfer would result in significant benefit to the community, and not granting consent to the transfer would result in significant harm to the community.

A Crofting Community Right to Buy under Part 3 of the 2003 Act does not depend on the landowner putting the land up for sale, and can be exercised by eligible crofters at any time.

6.18.7 Grants, Schemes, Agreements and Zoning

Many rural areas are affected by a variety of grants, schemes, or agreements, or may be zoned or specially designated in some way. It is as much a matter of finding out what sorts of arrangements affect the property, some of which will of course be beneficial, but in some cases, there might be a repayment or apportionment required, or certain conditions applied to the land which must be complied with, eg as to use of the land. Note that the names of and availability of various schemes and grants change over the years and it is prudent to check which types of schemes and other arrangements are likely to affect the type of property being purchased when drafting the offer. Currently, these include the Countryside Premium

Scheme, Rural Stewardship Scheme and Land Management Contract Menu Scheme. However, some grant and other schemes which have been discontinued may continue to apply for some time to properties already subject to them:

> 'No part of the Property is affected by (i) any [list current rural schemes and agreements including provisions or orders that are relevant under the Common Agricultural Policy] Section 75 Agreement, actual or proposed Conservation areas, Tree Preservation Order, or any other schemes, designations or restrictions or (ii) any sites of Special Scientific, Historic or Archaeological Interest. The Property is not situated in a National Scenic Area.'

Grants and other payments, if satisfactory to the purchaser, will usually be transferred, if appropriate. The Scottish Government Rural Payments and Inspectorate Division (SGRPID) is usually the responsible body for making these payments. It should be remembered that, in exchange for receiving grant monies, the landowner will invariably have to assume certain obligations and responsibilities. When the land is transferred, transferring the right to the grant monies and assuming the obligations and responsibilities have to be dealt with.

The seller will expect the purchaser to take over responsibility for all ongoing schemes, which will usually involve a considerable amount of form filling.

When a purchaser is taking over any grant schemes, they will want to be satisfied as to the whole terms and conditions that apply, whether there are any works still to be carried out and how much funds they will receive, so full particulars of the scheme and the conditions affecting the Property should be requested, and the purchaser should be given time to inspect these and make a decision. The purchaser will also want to have confirmation that there are no breaches of the schemes which could potentially lead to an obligation to repay grant monies at a later date. A letter from SGRPID should be sought to confirm that all obligations have been implemented to date and there are no circumstances under which remaining grant monies could be withheld (provided any further works required are carried out) or previous grant payments retrieved. If the position is not satisfactory to the purchaser, the right to resile should be available, or alternatively the parties may agree that the purchaser can deduct an appropriate amount from the price to reflect the amount of the remaining grants that the purchaser would have otherwise received.

6.18.8 Woodland and timber

If the Property contains any woodland areas, particularly if these are being worked or have economic value, then in addition to checking for schemes, grants and other arrangements in terms of para 6.18.7 above, provision should be made for protection of and preservation of the resources that exist as at the date of the offer, and the offer should specify that all forestry records are delivered at settlement:

(i)   There are no timber harvesting contracts which remain uncompleted and no timber on the Property will be cut or removed between the date of this offer and the date of entry;

(ii)   Until the date of entry the seller will maintain and manage the Property and, in particular, the whole timber on the Property in accordance with the rules of good husbandry and prevailing principles of silvicultural practice, and will not do anything to obstruct or limit the harvesting potential of the existing timber planted on the Property;

(iii)   the Seller will maintain adequate insurance cover in respect of all timber against damage by fire, storm, windblown trees and public liability and such other risks as the Purchaser, acting reasonably, may require.

If the Property is subject to an existing Forestry Dedication Agreement (in terms of section 5 of the Forestry Act 1967) then further information will be required and specific provision made in the missives depending on circumstances. Forestry Dedication Agreements could be recorded in the Sasine Register or registered in the Land Register. While the use of Forestry Dedication Agreements discontinued some years ago, there may still be exiting agreements in effect, and when they exist, they provide that the land must not be used for any use other that the growing of timber or other forestry products. The Forestry Commission Scotland maintains registers of legacy grant schemes and Forest Design Plans; felling licence and Forestry Grant Scheme applications; and relevant Environmental Impact Assessments[67].

---

67 See http://scotland.forestry.gov.uk/supporting/grants-and-regulations/public-registers.

SALES BY INSOLVENT PARTIES

6.19 Missives for the purchase of property from a trustee in sequestration, administrator, receiver or liquidator (known generally as Insolvency Practitioners or IPs) are likely to be somewhat shorter than the usual form of offer, due to the limited knowledge of the IP, both in respect of the insolvent owner, and the property itself. The IP is unlikely to have anything other than the most basic knowledge of the property, and in corporate insolvencies in particular, he may have incomplete or even chaotic records from the company. Accordingly he is usually unable to provide much information or assurance on matters affecting the property. The requirement to exclude any personal liability on the part of the IP also means that there are few if any warranties or confirmations given, and the purchaser will have to satisfy himself on most aspects of the purchase from his own investigations, observations and reports, and accept the property and any moveables in their current condition.

The IP may not be able to ascertain the VAT status of the property from the company's records, and so it may be some time before it can be established for example whether the sale of the property will qualify as a TOGC. Even if that status can be established, the IP may not be in a position to produce other VAT documentation or make any warranty as to the tax status of the company

Often IPs will arrange for their own solicitor to produce an offer to sell, which will contain the various protections that IPs seek, as well as omitting much of the seller's warranties that traditional offers contain. In addition, the offer will contain: (i) a clause that deals with the exclusion of any personal liability on the part of the IP (and this will be repeated in the Disposition (see para 9.6.8); and (ii) a clause that extracts acknowledgements from the purchaser that it is not relying on any representations or warranties from the IP or the insolvent seller. These clauses are belt and braces affairs and now follow a fairly standardised format. A typical example appears below (para 6.19.2).

In sales of commercial premises by insolvent owners, there are often issues relating to moveable items that may be left in the property. If they do not belong to the insolvent owner, for example office equipment like printers and photocopiers, or vending machines, refrigerated cabinets and the like, that are the subject of hire purchase or leasing arrangements, they are frequently affected by a 'retention of title' clause in the hire agreement, which means that the supplier of the item has a prior claim to the item in preference to any of the creditors. Where such clauses validly (apply) to any of the moveables, the items will need to be restored to the supplier, and so the purchaser should be careful to identify any items which might fall into this category and at the very least not take their value into account when purchasing, as it will be very difficult to recover any costs from the IP, or argue that the price should be reduced accordingly.

6.19.1 Limitation of conveyancing procedures

In an insolvency sale, generally the IP will not grant any warrandice and the usual procedure is also now that no warrandice will be granted by or on behalf of the insolvent seller (see para 9.11.15). This is normally specified in the missives, so the purchaser is in no doubt.

In the days of letters of obligation, no letter of obligation would be granted by the solicitors acting for an IP. The good news is that, particularly since the obtaining of an advance notice does not commit the IP to anything, or incur any liability on his part, there is no reason why the purchaser cannot benefit from advance notice protection in an insolvency sale, and some IPs will be prepared to obtain one, although may expect the purchaser to pay the cost.

Usually the missives will provide that the purchaser must satisfy himself as to matters of title, statutory compliance, searches and that no representations or warranties as to condition or fitness for purpose of the property will be made or implied. Accordingly the purchaser will have to carry out his own surveys, which would in any event be usual, satisfy himself as to title which again, his solicitors would expect to do, and also obtain his own PECs, searches and any other reports required, and which are usually provided by the seller but which, invariably, the IP will not provide.

6.19.2 Exclusion of personal liability

This is, arguably, the most important clause in insolvency missives (from the viewpoint of the seller, at any rate) as it is essential to the IP that they have no personal liability in respect of either the property or the transaction. It states the exclusion from any liability and underlines that the purchaser will have no claim against the IP in respect of any aspect of the transaction. For good measure it excludes any personal liability that might be imposed on the IP by the provisions of the Insolvency Act 1986 as well:

(i)   The [IP] contracts solely as agent of the seller and will incur no personal liability of any nature (whether directly or indirectly, express or implied) including without prejudice to the foregoing generality, personal liability in respect of any action or actions in pursuance of the seller's rights and/or obligations under the missives and whether formulated in contract and/or delict, or by reference to any other remedy or right, and regardless of the jurisdiction or forum in which it is raised;

(ii)   No claim which may be or become competent to the Purchaser arising directly or indirectly from the missives or [any deed or document executed in connection with the missives or under any arrangement collateral to the missives][68] will lie against the [IP] personally and the [IP] will be entitled at any time to have any such deeds or documents amended to include an exclusion of personal liability in terms of this clause; and

(iii)   Any personal liability of the [IP] which would arise in terms of the Insolvency Act 1986, but for the provisions of this clause, is expressly excluded.

6.19.3 Exclusion of Representations and Warranties

The purpose of this clause is to ensure that the purchaser is relying entirely on its own investigations and advice received from its own advisers, and that nothing that may have been said or implied by the seller or the IP or any information or paperwork provided in the course of the marketing of the property or the transaction should be relied on. The following example clause sets out the main exclusions normally provided, but some offers on behalf of IPs will contain additional specific provisions along similar lines. Note also that if there are any moveable items included in the sale the exclusions should apply to them as well:

---

68 In some offers, such deeds and documents may be described and defined as eg 'Transactional Documents'.

(i)   The Purchaser agrees that in effecting the purchase of the property it is not relying on any information, warranty, statement, undertaking, representation or silence on the part of the seller or the [IP] or any of their solicitors, advisers, valuers, employees, agents, or representatives, or anyone acting for them or on their behalf, or all or any of them, whether or not made within any document prepared by or on behalf of the [IP] (whether acting as agents of the seller or otherwise) and that the Purchaser is not relying on any other written or oral representation made to it or to its representatives or agents by the [IP] or their representatives or agents.

(ii)   All representations, warranties and conditions, express or implied, arising under statute, at common law or otherwise (including representations, warranties and conditions as to the right, title or interest of the seller or the [IP] to the Property [and the Moveables] and as to the existence of the Property [and the Moveables] or any part of [it][them]) in respect of the Property [and the Moveables] or any part of [it][them] are expressly excluded.

(iii)   The Purchaser agrees that the Seller and/or the [IP] having not given any warranty, guarantee or other assurance will have no responsibility or liability arising from the nature, condition, quality, state, description, fitness for purpose or use or any other aspect of the Property [and the Moveables], or any matters concerning or incidental to [it][them].

(iv)   The Purchaser agrees that the provisions of the missives are fair and reasonable in the circumstances of the insolvency of the Seller, and are in accordance with normal practice, on [bankruptcy] [administration] [receivership] [liquidation] sales, where it is usual that no representations, warranties and conditions express or implied, statutory or otherwise, are given by or on behalf of the Seller or the [IP] (or either of them). This is the case in particular in the light of the fact that:

    (a)   the Purchaser has had every opportunity it may wish to inspect and investigate the Property [and the Moveables]

    (b)   the Purchaser is aware of the need to rely on that opportunity, by reason of the absence of representations, warranties and conditions;

(c)   the Seller is insolvent and consequently faces the constraints on selling necessarily imposed on it in that circumstance;

(d)   the knowledge of the property available to the [IP] and their partners, staff and advisers, including but not limited to solicitors and valuers, is necessarily limited;

(v)   Nothing in the missives or any deed or document executed in terms of the missives will oblige the seller and/or the [IP] to discharge in whole or in part any liability or obligation of the seller, regardless of how it arises, outstanding at the time of the [IP's] appointment.

In addition there will usually be some form of specific statement about the purchaser being totally satisfied as to the quality, state and condition of the property (and any moveables included in the sale if applicable):

(vi)   The Seller and the [IP] have informed the Purchaser that the Purchaser must rely absolutely on the Purchaser's own opinion and/or professional advice concerning:

(a)   the Property [and the Moveables];

(b)   the quality, state and condition of the Property [and the Moveables];

(c)   [its][their] fitness and/or suitability for any purpose;

(d)   the possibility that the Property [and the Moveables] (or any part of [it][them]) may have defects not apparent on inspection and examination (which could even render it inappropriate that [it][they] should be described as [it is][they are] in fact described in the Missives or in any list referred to in the Missives); or

(e)   the reason that the Purchaser has or should have for purchasing the Property [and the Moveables] and the use that the Purchaser intends or should intend to put [it][them] to.

Various other disclaimers and caveats along similar lines may also appear.

SALES BY HERITABLE CREDITORS IN POSSESSION

6.20 Purchasing property from a heritable creditor in possession is also likely to mean that the seller has very little actual knowledge about the property, and that can affect the due diligence process. However, the missives do not usually limit the searches and reports available to the purchaser in the same way as they do in insolvency sales, although the purchaser will be expected to satisfy itself as to title, and the heritable creditor is unlikely to be interested in engaging in arrangements that might reduce the amount of the funds that it receives as sale proceeds.

The heritable creditor exercising its power of sale must obtain the best price that could reasonably be obtained (see para 8.18.3). Even though a heritable creditor's principal concern is to recover the amount that it lent to the borrower, the duty to obtain the best price means that if the borrower considers that the price obtained is not the best price that could have been obtained, which might for example mean the difference between the borrower receiving some of the sale proceeds, and not, then they can challenge the sale.

THE *DE PLANO* ACCEPTANCE

6.21 If the seller is able to accept all the condition in the offer without qualification then his solicitors can issue a letter concluding the missives in the following terms:

Dear Sirs

[ ] ('Seller')[ ] ('Purchaser')[ ] ('Property')

On behalf of the Seller, we accept your offer on behalf of the Purchaser dated [ ] and confirm that we are holding the Missives concluded on the basis of:

1. Your offer of [ ];and

2. This letter.

Yours faithfully

[solicitors]

(Signed by a partner and witnessed)

Quite often the original offer will contain a time limit for acceptance – see clause (Second) of the standard offer in para 6.9. If the seller's solicitor fails to comply with the time limit, then the usual practice is to issue a qualified acceptance with one qualification, namely the deletion of the time limit, which then needs to be accepted in writing by the purchaser's solicitors. Note, however, that the terms of clause (Second) state that if not accepted within the time limits specified, the offer is deemed to be withdrawn. Strictly speaking, therefore, if the seller's solicitors fail to issue the acceptance in time, there is no offer to accept, it having been withdrawn. The five-working-day period referred to in the clause is considered sufficient time within which even the most disorganised seller (or solicitor) ought to be able to respond. A time limit will of course not be relevant if the parties are both treating the offer as a draft.

CONCLUDED MISSIVES

6.22 Once missives are concluded, remember that unless the risk is shifted back to the sellers in missives, the risk passes to the purchasers on completion of the missives. It is, however, usual and normal for the sellers to accept the insurance risk until entry, but if for any reason this has not been agreed, then it will be necessary for the purchaser to arrange insurance cover immediately on completing missives. In this connection, remember that most general insurance contracts are regulated insurance contracts, which are regulated by the Financial Conduct Authority (FCA), and that solicitors may not arrange insurance for their clients without authorisation from the FCA, or licensed to conduct incidental financial business by the Law Society of Scotland.

The insurance cover, whether in name of the seller or the purchaser, should be for full reinstatement value and not for market value. In a modern property there may not be much difference between the two values but in an older building, built of traditional materials, the cost of repairing it to the same standard may well be considerably in excess of what the house cost to buy. Most commercial clients will expect to make their own insurance arrangements and would not expect their solicitor to be involved in this process.

Don't forget to inform your client that missives have been concluded and particularly for purchasers of residential property to remind them that they have entered into a formal binding contract. They should, of course, have been kept informed at all stages of formation of the contract.

Chapter 7

Searches and Enquiries

'Care and diligence bring luck' — *Thomas Fuller*

Part of the 'due diligence' process, the purchaser's searches and enquiries are of paramount importance in a system of *caveat emptor* (let the buyer beware). If there is any defect with the property, in the period before the purchaser settles, she should know about it and be able to decide how – or whether – to proceed.

If there are any mistakes in, or omissions from, this vital process, then the purchaser could end up buying a property that may be difficult to sell on for the right price, or at all, because of the failure in due diligence. Due diligence falls into one of two categories: 'private' due diligence, where enquiries are made of the seller as to the position of any matter; and 'public' due diligence, where public registers are interrogated to disclose the position of any relevant matter. This chapter will consider the latter, while the following chapter on examining title will consider the private due diligence aspects.

Precisely what public due diligence enquiries will be made will be dictated by the missives, as we have seen in the previous chapter.

The good news is that although the due diligence must be thorough, it need not be exhaustive. There are standard searches and enquiries that solicitors should make, and any expert searches or determinations should be carved out of the scope of services in the initial letter of engagement[1].

THE SELLER'S KNOWLEDGE

7.1 We have already seen in Chapter 5 that the seller's knowledge of the property can be a considerable resource for the purchaser, whether contained in the Property Questionnaire of the Home Report or the

---

1 For example environmental matters. See LSS guidance at: www.lawscot.org.uk/rules-and-guidance/section-f-guidance-relating-to-particular-types-of-work/division-c-conveyancing/guidance/contaminated-land-and-environmental-reports/

Disclosed Documents section of the PSG Offer. The analysis of that knowledge can inform the nature and extent of the public due diligence package. The generally available public searches are as follows.

PROPERTY ENQUIRY CERTIFICATES (PECS)

7.2 Also variably called 'Property Clearance Letters' or 'Property Clearance Certificates' in some areas of Scotland, PECs can be obtained from the local council or from specialist searching agencies, on payment of a fee. The PEC should be obtained as early as possible by the seller, in case it presents any difficulty, but it should be borne in mind that the information contained is already out of date, and that the Scottish Standard Clauses require a PEC to be dated after conclusion of missives (see para 6.10.22) but not earlier than three months prior to the date of entry. To be satisfactory to a client lender, the PEC must comply with the current edition of the Council of Mortgage Lenders' (CML) Handbook (or the bank's loan instructions); the standard position in the Scottish Standard Clauses is consistent with the CML Handbook. Check, however, that your client lender accepts PECs from private firms. Most do, but it is always better to check. The seller's solicitor should ask the purchaser's solicitor for an updated PEC (or parts of it) before settlement if no warranty from the seller can be obtained.

There is no standard form of PEC. Each of the 32 Councils and each private searching firm take a similar but different approach. Broadly speaking, the PEC encompasses searches of the following statutory registers:

7.2.1 Planning

This search will disclose any planning applications and consents (or refusals). Any planning information will, of course, just be in abstract form: you will need to ask the purchaser's solicitor for any drawings or plans that you need to see. Make sure that the versions you see are certified copies or originals, with the planning authority's approval stamped on its face.

As with building warrants etc, the purchaser's solicitor should match up known alterations to the approved documentation and refer to the surveyor or architect in cases of any doubt. Whether the property is a listed building, whether it is in a conservation area, whether it is affected by an Article 4 Direction (where some developments might have had deemed consent in general law, this Article disapplies the deemed consent) or whether it is subject to any enforcement action.

The listing of a building may make an enormous difference to the purchaser as to the desirability of a property. Some purchasers may be antiquarians, art historians or the like and actively welcome a listing. For most purchasers it means that there will be significant restrictions on what they can do with the property (or the site, since demolition is seldom an option).

There are three grades of legal protection for listed buildings: A, B and C, with A being the greatest protection for national treasures. Any alterations to listed buildings will need listed building consent, which will involve the consultation and approval of Historic Scotland[2]. Alterations to listed buildings will therefore require patience and deep pockets. See the Scottish Government guidance on conservation areas and Article 4 directions[3].

7.2.2 Building Control

This will disclose if there are any building warrants that have been applied for in respect of alterations to the property. Crucially, it will also show whether the corresponding completion certificate confirmation has been issued by the council approving the works. The importance of this information will be considered in more detail in the following chapter. The purchaser's solicitor should analyse the information that the council holds about the building warrants and completion certificates to ensure that all works have been properly documented and that the necessary documentation is in place. Almost as important, is to consider the information in the register in light of the single survey (and perhaps even the Schedule of Sales Particulars) to ensure that any work revealed to have been carried out has been properly authorised. If not, then the solicitor should insist getting confirmation from the council that it will not take

---

2   See www.historic-scotland.gov.uk/listing.
3   See www.scotland.gov.uk/publications/2005/03/29141519/15200.

any enforcement action in relation to unauthorised work. This may take the form of a letter of comfort (only available (if the council is prepared to give one) for works completed prior to 1 May 2005) or, for works completed after that date, some form of confirmation from the council, such as 'confirmation of completion' or a property inspection report[4].

7.2.3 Roads

The council is the roads authority. Roads authorities have the power (and duty) to adopt roads as public roads, to be maintained at public expense. Your client will need to know whether the road is adopted *ex adverso* (to the boundary) of the property. If the road is so adopted, then you need not make further enquiry, since you can assume that a public right of passage exists over the road, which provides rights for any type of traffic to use the road at any time, subject only to the roads authority's regulations and road traffic law generally. The purchaser's solicitor will require to ensure that the property enjoys adequate rights to and from the adopted road. If the road is not adopted, then further investigation of the ownership and maintenance of the private road will be required (see para 8.19 for further information). This section of the PEC will also disclose whether the property is affected by any transportation proposals, such as a proposal for a bypass or road widening scheme.

7.2.4 Statutory Notices

This part of the PEC will disclose whether the council has served any statutory notices under a variety of statutes, including requiring the owners to deal with defects or disrepair to their building. If a statutory repairs notice has been served on a building, the responsibility for this will usually remain with the seller. The purchaser's solicitor would normally retain an adequate amount from the purchase price delivered at settlement to cover the liability, which would arise after settlement.

The PEC will also disclose whether the council has served any notices under housing, environmental protection, and health & safety legislation.

---

4 Each council has its own procedures and names for these services, so it is advisable to check the website of the relevant council for the property to check their requirements.

7.2.5 Water and sewerage

For a separate charge, Scottish Water will produce a report stating whether the property is connected to the water and sewerage mains, and will usually produce a helpful OS plan with the route of the mains. Most urban properties will be connected and, if this is the case, there should be no need for further enquiry. That said, as with roads, the purchaser's solicitor should ensure that the property enjoys adequate rights for the pipes to and from the mains. Do not assume that Scottish Water has statutory powers to compel owners of other properties to allow your client to connect to the mains – its powers are limited to the route of the main itself. In the same way as access can be 'ransomed' by a ransom strip, so can services for a property.

PECs produced by specialist searching agencies will usually include this information as well.

If the water supply and sewerage outflow is not connected to the mains, then the purchaser's solicitor will need to consider the adequacy of any private arrangements. See para 6.18.3.

7.2.6 Contaminated land

Most councils will disclose only whether the property is actually contaminated, by virtue of being on the contaminated land register kept under Part IIA of the Environmental Protection Act 1990, which is the extent of their statutory duty. There are few properties on the register. Councils would rather money was spent on remediating properties through giving grant assistance and imposing planning conditions rather than effectively 'blighting' land by declaring it to be actually contaminated.,

COAL MINING REPORT

7.3 As a rapidly industrialising country in the nineteenth and twentieth centuries, Scotland needed masses of coal to power the great manufacturing industries. Coal was mined across Scotland. However, in the post-war period, demand slumped due to clean air initiatives and cheaper imports of coal and coke. The majority of coal mines have been closed down. However, in place of heavy industry, property development flourished. The result is that some houses may have been unwittingly built over old, disused coal mines and may now be liable to movement or worse, subsidence or collapse.

Therefore, it is important to ensure that a search is requested from the Coal Authority, which holds records of where mines were constructed. There are some areas where there has never been any history of coal mining; the Law Society allows solicitors to dispense with the requirement in these areas. You can check lists on the Coal Authority website[5] to find out whether the property your client is selling (or buying) is in an area where a coal mining search is necessary.

COMPANIES SEARCH

7.4 If the seller is a company, the purchaser's solicitor requires to be satisfied as to the continued good standing of the company. A company is a 'legal person' with the legal personality to transact property in its own name, but as a legal person, it can be killed off more easily than a natural person. Therefore, a specialist company searcher is engaged to search the records held by Companies House (the companies registrar, named after the building). All being well, the companies search will disclose that there are no proposals to strike off or wind up the company.

In addition the purchaser's solicitors will need to check if there are any outstanding charges granted by the company as these either need to be dealt with or discharged prior to completion. Accordingly, the searchers should be asked to provide a search in the company's Register of Charges. You should also ask to see a search disclosing the details of the current directors and the secretary so that you can check these details against the signatories to the disposition or other deeds.

PROPERTY REGISTER SEARCH (LEGAL REPORT)

7.5 One of the main concerns of the purchaser is to obtain a good and marketable title to the property. As we will see in the next chapter, the purchaser's solicitor will satisfy themselves on the sufficiency of the title either by examining the title deeds that have been recorded in the General Register of Sasines or by examining the title sheet registered in the Land

---

5   See www.coal.decc.gov.uk.

Register. Those titles clearly show an historical position. The purchaser's solicitor must therefore ensure that he has seen recent evidence of the continuing good and marketable title position and check that there is nothing prejudicial to granter's title (such as a lease when the purchaser is expecting vacant possession, or a sale to someone else, any outstanding securities, or inhibitions against the seller).

A search report, obtained from firms of professional searchers, such as Millar & Bryce, First Scottish, or direct from the Registers of Scotland will report on the searcher's findings regarding deeds, documents or other entries that appear in the relevant property register. The search will typically include a search for records for a particular property - and the Register of Inhibitions (the Personal Register) (see para 7.6) - in relation to any records appearing against particular individuals or other legal persons - and provide you with a report on any deeds documents or other entries that appear in the relevant register.

In addition to confirming things that you may already know about the property from your examination of the title, a search report will also disclose whether there are any other titles that you need to examine that are not included in the pack you have been given.

Searches can also be used to confirm that the person from whom your client is buying or renting is the owner of the property, or as a way of identifying who is the current owner of a property.

The principal types of search that you will come across are:

- legal reports (property and personal searches);
- company/charges search;
- register of insolvencies; and
- register of community interests in land.

Obtaining a traditional Sasine search is now a very rare (or possibly non-existent) occurrence. However, when examining Sasine titles, you may come across a document entitled 'Search for Incumbrances'. This is the precursor to Form 10 under the 1979 Act, and the Legal Report under the 2012 Act and contains a list of all of the recorded writs affecting the property (sometimes split off writs as well) and relevant personal searches. As such, it can be a useful historical record which might assist the title examination.

Search reports are now known as Legal Reports; the type you require will depend on the registration status of the property.

7.5.1 Legal Report over Unregistered Land

Invariably, instead of a traditional Sasine search, a Legal Report over Unregistered Land will be instructed, when you are dealing with a property to which title is still in the Sasine Register. The 'Legal Report – Unregistered Land' is equivalent to a Form 10 under the 1979 Act and is the Report to obtain in first registration transactions. As well as providing the same information as the old Form 10, this Report will also disclose any advance notices that have been recorded in the Sasine Register. If, as is usual practice, (at least in commercial property transactions) the Report is obtained early in the transaction, then it is likely to pre-date the advance notice application for the transaction. However, a Legal Continuation Report (the equivalent of a 1979 Act Form 11 or Form 13) can be obtained (at no additional cost if ordered from the Registers, provided it is requested within six months from the date of the original report. Searching firms may charge for continuation reports). A Continuation Report obtained immediately before settlement will disclose the advance notice, meaning the purchaser knows he can proceed to complete the transaction, safe within the shelter of the advance notice protection.

Here, practice tends to differ between residential and commercial practitioners. In commercial transactions it is more common for a Legal Report to be obtained reasonably early on in the transaction. Perhaps this is because it is more likely in a commercial deal that something out of the ordinary or unexpected could be disclosed, and time is needed to deal with it. In residential transactions, this is less likely to happen, so it is more usual for the Legal Report to be ordered just before settlement, with no continuation report being instructed. This approach, while understandable, is not without its risks. If the Legal Report discloses an inhibition, or an unexpected 'double glazing' standard security, there is very little time to resolve the issue before the settlement date, which may result in a delay to settlement. It is, of course, a matter for each firm to determine, but for a relatively modest additional cost (if using private searchers) or no additional cost (if using the Registers' service (provided the continuation is ordered within six months)), obtaining a Legal Report early in the transaction, and following it up with a Legal Continuation Report just before settlement, when the advance notice will be disclosed, means there should be no last-minute settlement surprises.

7.5.1(i) Identification of subjects

When drafting a request for a Legal Report over Unregistered Land (usually when acting for the seller (or borrower)) or when inspecting a report (when acting for a purchaser) you should ensure that the search covers the all of the property you are interested in.

Usually the property will be identified by reference to a descriptive writ or writs, and you should check that all of the property is included. Sometimes you may be shown an earlier Report which covers a larger area.

7.5.1(ii) What do you need to see in the report?

When you receive a Legal Report over Unregistered Land, you should check it for the following:

- The foundation writ (the first writ conveying the property that was recorded more than ten years ago).

- A prescriptive progress (all writs from the foundation writ to writ in favour of current granter).

- Any undischarged securities (these will probably be discharged as part of the transaction, or a deed of restriction will be granted if the security covers a larger area than just the property you are interested in).

- Any split offs (so that you can tell what parts of the land are no longer owned by the current granter).

- Miscellaneous deeds (minutes of waiver (of real burdens etc)/ servitudes etc.).

Not every search will disclose all of the above. If the search is silent on eg undischarged securities, then you are entitled to rely on this fact, that there are none.

299

7.5.1(iii) Length of search

The period covered by the search should be ten years or more for the prescriptive progress, starting with the foundation writ, and 40 years to show any undischarged securities (as if any older, they have probably been extinguished by payment, or long negative prescription) or other miscellaneous writs.

7.5.2 Legal Report over Registered Land

This Legal Report is the equivalent of the Form 12 under the 1979 Act and replaces that Form. The Title Sheet or Land Certificate of the registered title will contain a date to which it is current. The Legal Report should be instructed from that date to the latest date available. If an advance notice is to be obtained, then a Legal Continuation Report can be instructed, shortly before completion, to disclose it.

PERSONAL SEARCHES

7.6 A personal search is usually included with the Property Search and included in the standard fee. In this case, the seller's solicitor enters the full name and address details of each party to the transaction that will grant a deed. In the request to bring down the search just before settlement, the names and addresses of all the parties are added. The search is in the Register of Inhibitions (the personal register) and will look for any impediment against the parties. It's not like a credit search or a County Court Judgement search. The most usual impediment that would be disclosed would be an inhibition, which is an interim or final court order preventing a party from selling the property. The case of *Park, Petitioners* (see paras 2.9 and 6.5) is an excellent example of how an inhibition can prevent the sale of property.

PLANS REPORTS

7.7 Plans reports did not really play a major part in land registration under the 1979 Act. The P16 Report, which compared a plan or bounding description with the Ordnance Survey map, while extremely useful, was too often inadequate or inconclusive and had no particular impact on what was ultimately entered on to the Land Register. The title extent could easily conflict with the features shown on the OS map, without that being a problem. An owner might have decided to place their boundary walls inside their title extent for perfectly good reasons – perhaps to improve visibility at an entrance way from a tricky road junction, for example. Some title boundaries may not be apparent as features on the OS map.

An essential part of the 2012 Act regime, however, is the requirement for the Keeper to be able to plot the property being conveyed onto the cadastral map. There can be no overlapping titles on the cadastral map, and any application for registration which includes land that is already plotted will be rejected. So, obtaining detailed plan and mapping information has become an even more crucial part of the due diligence process. Plans Reports have been developed to provide the information that solicitors need, to ensure that their application will not compete with any other registered titles; and that the property in question can be accurately plotted onto the cadastral map.

There are five separate components to Plans Reports; three levels of report are available: Level 1, Level 2 or Level 3. The level of report you request will determine the detail of plans information you receive. Invariably, either a Level 1 or a Level 3 Report will be appropriate.

The different components of Plans Reports are:

- Part 1 – Suitability of submitted plan and/or bounding description for Registration.

- Part 2 – Comparison with the Ordnance Survey Map.

- Part 3 – Existing exclusive registered areas which conflict with the property.

- Part 4 – Existing shared registered areas which affect the property.

- Part 5 – Additional registered interests affecting the property.

In addition to a Plans Report, a Plans Continuation Report is also available. All three levels of Plans Report will answer Part 1 and clarify whether the plan meets basic registration requirements.

7.7.1 Plans Report Level 1

This Plans Report provides a basic comparison with the cadastral map, and will identify any conflicts with existing cadastral units prior to submission of an application for first registration. This information may appear in Part 3, 4 or 5, but it will not provide any extracts or other details of the actual conflict. Having information about any conflicts at the earliest opportunity will allow corrective or remedial action to be taken, and will reduce the risk of rejection of the application.

There is some debate about whether you need to obtain a Plans Report over subjects that are already registered. Strictly speaking you do not need an answer to Part 1 of the Report, of course. Where you are dealing with the whole of a registered plot, you will not normally need a new plan, and therefore you don't need to ask if a plan is suitable for registration and mapping purposes. The plot is already registered, and usually, all that the Keeper will do, for a straightforward transfer of whole, is update the title sheet with the name of the new owner, consideration, and date of entry.

7.7.1(i) But what about any conflicts?

Guidance from the Keeper[6] advises that where there was an overlap between two registered titles under 1979 Act registration that came to the Keeper's attention, although both titles would be registered, if appropriate to do so, an exclusion of indemnity would be noted, or a qualifying note entered, on the title sheets in respect of the area concerned, if appropriate.

Although there can be no conflicts on the cadastral map under the 2012 Act, there is no requirement on the Keeper to correct any pre-existing overlaps as at the designated day. Under transitional arrangements (paragraph 3 of Schedule 4 to the 2012 Act) any amendment required to existing title sheets can be made 'at such later date as the Keeper considers appropriate'.

What this means is that, for some considerable time to come, there will be overlaps between registered titles. The number of instances is unknown, but many will contain a qualifying note or exclusion of indemnity. There is anecdotal and experiential evidence of competing title extents on the Land Register, which are **not** flagged by a qualifying note or excluded from indemnity; mapping errors cannot be ruled out.

---

6 See www.ros.gov.uk/__data/assets/pdf_file/0020/11387/General_Guidance_Competing_Titles.
   pdf.

In reality, many solicitors (and also professional searchers) have experience of situations where an overlap is identified, but nothing on the title sheets indicates its existence. It may be as small a thing as the same boundary wall appearing in both adjacent titles. In these circumstances, it would only be at the stage where the conveyance is presented for registration that the overlap would appear. Without having previously checked, by way of a Plans Report, the first indication of it for the submitting solicitor would be when the application was rejected. Given the thousands of registered titles that already exist the risk is, admittedly, quite small. But it is a 'known unknown'. Far better, therefore, to obtain a Plans Report so that any overlap – which may be minor, but significant – can be identified, and steps taken, before money has changed hands, to resolve it.

Much of this material is anecdotal, but errors can occur that are not picked up. This is not a criticism – it is a fact of life. Many (particularly commercial property) firms have therefore taken the policy decision to routinely obtain or request a Level 1 report for registered properties, to ensure there are no problems, rather than run the risk of having to tackle remedial conveyancing. Worse yet would be to discover a ransom area post-completion, or indeed, to have to explain to a client why, when a procedure was available that would have identified the problem, it wasn't applied.

Our recommendation, therefore, is that this is the appropriate Plans Report to obtain for a registered plot.

When acquiring part of a registered title, a Plans Report will be able to confirm that there is no conflict with any other part of the larger title that has been conveyed (although note that if the larger area is a development that has the benefit of Development Plan Approval, then there should be no boundary conflicts between plots in that development).

7.7.2 Plans Report Level 2

A Level 2 Report will provide the information in a Level 1 report and at Part 2 provide a comparison with the OS map (i.e. a service akin to the primary function of the P16). It will also identify whether there are any conflicts, but not provide additional details of what these conflicts are (i.e. extract titles). For this reason, the Level 2 Report is rarely requested.

If there are conflicts, then of course you want to know precisely what they are. Far better to obtain the Level 3 Report which will give you this information.

7.7.3 Plans Report Level 3

A Level 3 Report will provide all of the information in each of the five sections, and provide extracts defining the extent of any potential conflicting cadastral units, and other information from the cadastral map that affects the land such as minerals titles, servitudes etc. A Level 3 Report should accordingly be obtained for all first registrations and transfers of part.

7.7.4 When will you need a Plans Report?

All three levels of Plans Report are suitable for applications for first registration. Which level you opt for will depend to some extent on the complexity of the title, and the type of property. The difference in cost between Level 1 and Level 2 is only around £10, but, other than the OS map comparison, neither will provide you with an illustration showing where any conflicts lie. Only a Level 3 Report will provide that information, so for higher value or complicated titles, the modest additional cost is justified.

REGISTER OF INSOLVENCIES

7.8 The Register of Insolvencies is a statutory register which provides information about the insolvency of individuals, businesses and companies in Scotland. It is updated on a daily basis during the working week. It provides information about:

- Sequestrations (bankruptcies) of individuals awarded in Scotland together with protected trust deeds for the benefit of creditors;
- Trust Deeds – public notices for the benefit of creditors; and
- Details of limited companies which are in receivership or liquidation.

Information regarding sequestrations is available from the Register of Insolvencies for two years following the discharge of the trustee.

Information concerning protected trust deeds is available from the Register for one year following the date of the trustee's discharge. Information regarding advertised notices of trust deeds is available on the Register of Insolvencies for five weeks from the date of advertisement. If the trust deed gets protected status, then the notice is removed; the protected trust deed is then shown on the register.

Information about corporate insolvencies is available from the Register of Insolvencies for one year following the discharge of the liquidator or receiver.

REGISTER OF COMMUNITY INTERESTS IN LAND (RCIL)

7.9 The RCIL was set up following on the introduction of the Community Right to Buy in Part 2 of the Land Reform (Scotland) Act 2003. Before a community body can exercise the Community Right to Buy, it must register its interest in the RCIL, which is maintained by the Registers of Scotland.

It is accessible online[7] and contains information relating to each community interest registered in it, including the name and address of the registered office of the company which constitutes the community body which has registered the interest; and a description of the land, including maps, plans or other drawings. Particulars of agricultural tenants' interests are also available at this Register.

Instructions to search in the RCIL should be included when instructing searches against land that could potentially be affected, although the seller should know whether such an interest has been registered against land that they own, as notification has to be given to landowners affected. The online facility is kept up to date, so it is easy to run an informal check. When offering to purchase land that could potentially be affected by a registered interest, confirmation should be sought from the seller that the land is not, and will not at the date of conclusion of missives be, affected by any registered interest by a community body. See also para 6.18.6.

Under the Community Empowerment (Scotland) Act 2015, the Community Right to Buy will extend to all of Scotland from April 2016, so it will become routine to search this Register in all transactions.

---

7   See http://rcil.ros.gov.uk.

ENVIRONMENTAL SEARCH

7.10 The issue of contaminated land is considered in para 7.2.6. We also look at this issue in the context of new houses in para 6.12.1. The position is that an environmental search is not a standard requirement as part of the Scottish conveyancing process. They are routinely excluded by solicitors because the Law Society and the CML do not require solicitors to obtain them (although note that some lenders may have requirements in this connection, so you should always check the relevant Part 2 of the CML Handbook (see para 10.5.2). There is perhaps a danger that once the client has become aware of the potential contamination but does nothing about it, they can become a 'knowing permitter' in terms of the Environmental Protection Act 1990 – *see Circular Facilities (London) Ltd v Sevenoaks District Council*[8]. The current advice from the Law Society[9] is as follows:

'The Society's Professional Practice and Property Law Committee's view is that if a solicitor does not feel qualified to comment on environmental matters whether in general and/or in particular in regard to contaminated land matters, then, whatever the nature of the property in the transaction (including both residential and commercial property), that solicitor is entitled to seek to exclude liability for environmental law matters and/or contaminated land matters provided that exclusion of indemnity is made clear in the initial terms of business issued to the client with respect to the transaction in question.'

In reality, few solicitors will feel qualified to comment on environmental matters other than in the abstract and will, therefore, exclude liability automatically in the letter of engagement. However, an environmental search contains potentially interesting pieces of information that a residential purchaser (or commercial one for that matter) might really care about – and that may sway their purchasing decision. It seems illogical that there is so much information provided upfront in the Home Report, without any environmental or contamination information being made available. The reports generally include information about the site history, standard environmental enquiries, past uses that are potentially

8 [2005] Env LR 35, [2005] JPL 1624.
9 See www.lawscot.org.uk/rules-and-guidance/section-f-guidance-relating-to-particular-types-of-work/division-c-conveyancing/guidance/contaminated-land-and-environmental-reports/.

contaminative, and mining and stability history. Almost as important, these days, is the flood risk information where flooding data is matched to the property's location.

A typical residential environmental report is comparatively easy to interpret. It has two outcomes, summarised as PASSED or REFERRED. If a report is referred, then a specialist will consider the nature of the potential contamination and whether any further investigation will be required. The reports are based on historical use, mainly based on old OS maps. Such maps are not always helpful, eg if a property is within 500m of a railway line, it may be deemed to be potentially contaminated. The purchaser has to take a view: should further investigation be considered necessary, it will invariably involve drilling for soil samples that are then analysed by scientists for evidence of contamination. This is expensive for the seller (usually a few thousand pounds) and hugely disruptive to the conveyancing process. If remediation is required, then the seller may have a horrible liability to face up to.

It is, however, interesting to reflect that contaminated land is one area where the seller of land cannot ordinarily walk away from liability, despite the *caveat emptor* principle. The liability will remain, whether or not the seller is aware of it. In terms of the Environmental Protection Act 1990, the principle of the legislation is that the 'polluter pays'. To effect that principle, the Act creates a chain of liability all the way up the ownership chain to the original polluter. The seller can, however, end his or her liability by 'selling with information'. This means that the purchaser is provided with environmental reports and has enough information to make a decision.

It is interesting to note that the lenders do not routinely require environmental reports in residential transactions. According to the CML this is because:

- They are not detailed enough to inform on current or future risk;

- There are no details of actual contamination or risks from contamination, what remediation would be required, or any effect on valuation; and

- There are a small number of properties affected by actual contamination, possibly less than 5%.

The practical position is that the jury is out. It is not common practice in Scotland to obtain these reports routinely for residential purchases. As a seller, there may be little advantage in offering an environmental report, as it would seem to open a Pandora's Box. On the other hand, some clients may want to be reassured that there will be no continuing liability. For 5% of purchasers (one in every 20) a report that costs (approximately) £150 may be worth every penny if it saves them from the nightmare of discovering that their new property is built on contaminated land or prone to flood. At some point they will have to sell on, when the sentiment may be different! Although we reiterate the advice from the Law Society that this is not a requirement for a solicitor in terms of exercising a duty of care, you will be doing a good job in protecting your client's interests by insisting on a report from the seller with an option to resile if anything materially prejudicial is discovered. The report is relatively modestly priced, so many clients might not object to paying for it. Either way, it is best to discuss the options with clients and keep a file note of the discussion.

The position with commercial clients is different in that, generally speaking, sophisticated property developers are well aware of the position and the risks and will have their own procedures for dealing with them. Equally, the financial risk may be higher, so again it is prudent to flag the issue with clients. However you should not give advice unless you have the appropriate expertise, so refer the matter to someone who does.

OTHER SEARCHES

7.11 Other searches that may be carried out will vary according to the nature of the property. In most cases the 'searches' in this section will be ones you conduct yourself online. So they are more about information gathering, and can provide you with information that may be of significance to your client.

7.11.1 Historic Buildings

7.11.1(i) Pastmap

Pastmap[10] is a search of the online records of Historic Scotland and the Royal Commission on the Ancient and Historical Monuments of Scotland

---

10 See http://pastmap.org.uk/.

(RCAHMS) to disclose if there are any scheduled monuments, listed buildings or other entries affecting the property. These can restrict what clients can do on the property and must be reported. For example, no work can be carried out on or in the vicinity of a scheduled monument. This report can be useful for rural properties in particular.

7.11.2 Rural Property

Rural land has a number of specialities. There are additional searches that will be of assistance in obtaining a clearer picture.

7.11.2(i) Past map

See 7.11.1(i) above. The information available from this source is often particularly relevant in the rural context.

7.11.2(ii) SNH Sitelink[11]

This is a search of SNH's online records to disclose if any SSSIs or other designations affect the property. These can restrict what clients can do on the property and must be reported.

7.11.2(iii) Scotways

Scotways[12] maintains the National Catalogue of Rights of Way and records all the rights of way in Scotland (that are known to it). It maintains a website of records detailing the history of paths, routes and trails across Scotland, including Roman roads, drove roads and military roads turnpike roads, and is a rich source of information about the network of paths, old roads and rights of way across Scotland.

This organisation should be the first port of call when dealing with a rural property title. Under the 2012 Act, if a property is affected by a right of way, the applicant is under a duty to provide information about the route.

---

11 See https://gateway.snh.gov.uk/sitelink/.
12 See www.scotways.com/.

7.11.2(iv) Forestry Commission

It will be of interest to know whether the Forestry Commission has any schemes or dedication agreements over the land. The Forestry Commission provide a useful, interactive map[13].

7.11.2(v) Sites of Special Scientific Interest

The Registers of Scotland operates a Register of Sites of Special Scientific Interest[14], which it is also prudent to check in rural or semi rural areas, particularly if development is proposed. It can be searched free of charge.

13 See http://maps.forestry.gov.uk/imf/imf.jsp?site=fcscotland_ext.
14 See www.ros.gov.uk/services/registration/sssi.

Chapter 8

Examination of and Reporting on Title

INTRODUCTION

8.1 When land registration was introduced to Scotland in 1981[1], many experienced practitioners at the time forecast the demise of the art of the conveyancer. Title would be reduced to a few lines on a title sheet. No skill would be required to decipher the provisions that applied to the property.

Reflecting on that view more than 30 years later, the reality has been quite different. Feudal abolition, changes to title conditions and tenement law and the transformation of registration practice, have all added layers of complexity. The practicalities of title examination have become increasingly complicated.

The similarities between various aspects of the conveyancing process for residential and commercial properties are most apparent when examining title. Precisely the same legal fundamentals come into consideration, although the implications of what the title examination discloses may be quite different. A use restriction limiting the use of the property for residential purposes matters not at all when purchasing a dwellinghouse for residential occupation. It would, however, represent a major obstacle if the purpose of the purchase is to build a retail park.

WHY IS IT NECESSARY TO EXAMINE TITLE?

8.2 An essential element of the conveyancing process is to ensure that the purchaser obtains a good and marketable title to the property. In the third edition of *Conveyancing*[2], Professors Reid and Gretton defined a marketable title as one:

    (a)   which makes the buyer the owner of the property; and

---

1   The appointed day for commencement of land registration, for the first county to become operational – Renfrew – was 6 April 1981.
2   3rd edition (2004) W Green, p. 111. The 4th edition is now available.

(b)   after acquiring ownership, will not be subject to any third party rights, other than title conditions of an ordinary nature and with the possible exception of title leases.

Examination of title is a process: a voyage of discovery with an identified destination in mind. We embark on it to discover:

(i)   who is the current owner of the property (it should be the seller);

(ii)   what is the extent of the property and its boundary features;

(iii)   what rights and pertinents benefit the property;

(iv)   whether there are any restrictions on the use of the property;

(v)   what obligations fall on the owner of the property;

(vi)   whether any third parties have rights in relation to the property; and

(vii) whether the title is valid and marketable.

It is for the seller to show that they have a valid marketable title, and for the purchaser to be satisfied that this is so. It will usually be the preference of the seller that missives are concluded before the titles are passed to the purchaser's solicitors for examination. The Scottish Standard Clauses (see para 6.10) will invariably result in a swift conclusion of missives. Solicitors who use the PSG Offers to Sell (see para 6.14) often find that an agreed contract can be achieved more quickly than when starting from the polarised position of a first offer heavily weighted in favour of one of the parties.

In both residential and commercial conveyancing, it would be preferable to achieve conclusion of missives before sending the titles to the purchaser's solicitor for examination. Experience shows that once the purchaser's solicitor has received the titles he starts looking at them and incorporating requirements that arise as a result of title examination into the missives.

The Scottish Standard Clauses Guidance advises not to send the titles until missives are concluded (unless one or more of the titles need to be exhibited to clarify a particular issue that has arisen during the missives adjustment period). The advice in those situations is to send only the relevant documents, which may be a Land Certificate or PDF copy or extract of the Title Sheet.

This is not always possible in commercial transactions. There might be compelling reasons to submit the titles (or some parts of them) to the purchaser's solicitors to resolve some point at issue, which will help to facilitate the progress of the transaction. Sensible judgement should be exercised in those cases. Refusing to show the titles might well be considered obstructive.

In the disposition, the seller will (usually) grant absolute warrandice (see para 9.18). That is to say, the seller undertakes to indemnify the purchaser against any title defect. When a title was registered in the Land Register under the 1979 Act, the Keeper would (usually) issue a Land Certificate with a guarantee of indemnity. Some people might be forgiven for thinking that there was, therefore, no need for the purchaser's solicitor to examine the title in such detail. Could they not just assume, or expect that previous solicitors will have checked that the title is marketable and rely on that?

The short answer is no. Title is examined for a number of reasons, and has to be checked on each transfer to ensure that it is marketable and that no new dealings affect the property. The purchaser is owed no duty of care by solicitors who have previously investigated the title, and generally there will be a degree of *caveat emptor*. The precise terms of the title may be unacceptable to your client depending on what she plans to do with the property. If the property is a commercial property, your title examination will be needed to establish that there are no impediments to what is proposed. The 'safety net' previously available from the Keeper[3] has been discontinued. Since the 2012 Act came into force, the Keeper's staff have stopped carrying out any examination of title, as a result.

As many experienced conveyancers know, errors and mistakes can exist in titles that have been passed along several times. It is, therefore, the role of the purchaser's solicitor to conduct a proper investigation of title as part of what is known as the 'due diligence' process of examining all elements that affect the property being purchased. It may be the case that the solicitor is required to certify the title to the purchaser's lender. In some cases (usually commercial transactions) the seller's solicitor can be asked to certify title to the purchaser. Those parties will be entitled to rely on the certificate as though the solicitor giving the certificate were acting

---

3   Under the 'Midas touch' of section 3 of the 1979 Act.

for them. Often in such cases, the beneficiary of the certificate of title will have their own solicitors, who will often be expected to advise their client on the terms of the certificate being given (see para 8.38).

Warrandice is not a particularly effective remedy, in practice. It depends on 'eviction' having taken place. The innocent party has to go through the process of losing his property before he can claim warrandice (see *Welsh v Russell*[4]). 'Eviction' in this case means any interference with the property right, rather than merely being put out of the property. Even if there is a valid remedy under warrandice, it might prove impossible to trace the granters of warrandice or, if appropriate, their predecessors in title.

THE STUFF OF CONVEYANCING

8.3 Title examination is truly the stuff of traditional conveyancing.

It is a usual stipulation of missives that the title will contain 'no unduly onerous conditions or restrictions'. The meaning of this expression can be quite subjective, and depends very much on the circumstances of each case. This is an unsatisfactory state of affairs. If the seller gives this assurance in the missives, the purchaser can claim at a later date that there is, in their opinion, an onerous condition or restriction in the title. The matter will have to be argued and compromised. At worst, the purchasers may withdraw. Often a stipulation of this type in a purchaser's offer will be qualified by the seller to the effect that the purchaser must satisfy herself as to the adequacy of the title. It will usually impose a time limit within which the purchaser will be deemed to have done so.

Lord Young commented on the phrase in *Whyte v Lee*[5] as follows:

'If a man simply buys a house he must be taken to buy it as the seller has it, on a good title of course, but subject to such restrictions as may exist if of an ordinary character, and such as the buyer may reasonably be supposed to have contemplated as at least not improbable.'

The leading case is the House of Lords' decision in *Armia Ltd v Daejan Developments Ltd*[6]. In this case, a property in Kirkcaldy High Street had

4   [1894] 21 R 769.
5   [1879] 6 R 699 at 701.
6   [1979] UKHL 8, (1979) SC (HL) 56.

314

been bought for redevelopment. It was found to be subject to a servitude right of access along a 10-foot-wide passage through the property from front to rear, coupled with a prohibition on building on the passage. The width of the passage was just slightly over a sixth of the length of the entire frontage of the property. This prohibition effectively sterilised the redevelopment. It was held that this was a sufficiently unusual condition to allow the purchaser to resile.

In the case of *Morris v Ritchie*[7], a piece of ground being sold for commercial development turned out to be burdened by a servitude right of access, which would have reduced the number of car parking spaces by seven out of 18. This reduction would, therefore, have a bad effect on the pursuer's proposed business turnover and consequently, the market value of the property. This only became known to the pursuer after missives had been concluded and a deposit paid. The pursuer was allowed to withdraw from the purchase because of the diminution in value of the ground. On a practical note, sellers who know of restrictions of this nature would do well to disclose them to the purchasers before missives are concluded.

In *Snowie v Museum Hall LLP*[8], six sets of missives were concluded to buy six flats in the same development, all subject to a requirement that the title to the development should 'contain no unduly onerous or unusual conditions'. The purchasers sought to resile, in reliance on this provision, when they learned that the Deed of Conditions affecting the development contained a prohibition against using a residential apartment for any trade, business or profession, even in an ancillary capacity. This is a typical burden in residential deeds of conditions, and indeed, features in a style Deed of Conditions to be found in Greens Practice Styles. Lord Glennie was clear that restrictions of this type were not unusual, and the fact that they were not uncommon showed that neither were they unduly onerous.

TITLE EXAMINATION

8.4 Examination of title needs to be methodical and thorough. While principally it involves checking the provisions of the title deeds, it will

7   [1992] GWD 33–1950.
8   [2010] CSOH 107, 2010 SLT 971.

315

also involve looking at the terms of other documentation that affects the property. Depending on the type of property, the examination will or may include Property Enquiry Certificates, Planning and Building Warrant documents, Leases and other leasehold documents, construction documents and contracts, VAT and other taxation matters, Coal Authority Reports, Searches in the Property, Personal and Companies registers, energy performance certificates and so on[9].

A comprehensive list of items that you might need to examine in the course of your investigations is contained in the 'Due Diligence Questionnaire' available on the PSG website. The purpose of the Due Diligence Questionnaire is to provide the seller and the seller's solicitor with a comprehensive list of the purchaser's and the purchaser's solicitor's due diligence requirements at an early stage of the transaction. The Questionnaire is an information gathering exercise and is not a substitute for the normal conveyancing procedures. Often solicitors will use the Questionnaire as an *aide-memoire* of items they might need to examine during the course of a transaction. Bear in mind of course that not all items in the Questionnaire will be relevant for every transaction. See also paras 4.9.9 and 5.10.

GETTING STARTED

8.5 You will need to make a record of what you find during your examination of the titles and other ancillary papers, and the best way to do this is to write down 'Notes on Title' with all the salient details from the titles and other papers. While senior solicitors might find that they are able to dictate their Notes, experience shows that it is much more effective to hand write or type these notes, particularly for the more junior practitioner. However, in these days of digital dictation and on-screen working, the handwritten Notes on Title may be becoming something of a lost art.

Your notes should be sufficiently comprehensive so that if need be you (or a colleague) would be able to check an aspect of the title from them, without having to ask to get the title deeds back from the seller's solicitor. For some titles, particularly where the text is dense (and this can include

---

9 See Chapter 7: Searches and Enquiries.

some sections of Land Certificates and Title Sheets) it can help to use coloured highlighters on the photocopies you have taken, to emphasise particular parts of the title, perhaps adding handwritten annotations in the margin, but this should be supplementary to your main notes.

While you may find it helpful to take photocopies of certain title deeds or sections of the Land Certificate or Title Sheet, you should resist the temptation to substitute copying for making notes. There is no doubt that, particularly with old archaic titles, it is very easy to miss or misinterpret provisions if you do not subject the documents to careful and thorough scrutiny. You may need copies of certain writs for the purposes of reporting on the title to your client or, in some cases, certifying the title, and you will definitely need to take photocopies of any plans included in the title.

There will be issues that arise out of the titles as you progress through them, on which you may need further information, or that may give cause for concern or require some clarification. Ideally, you should make a note of these as they occur, rather than once you have finished your examination, so that you can be sure that none are missed. Make a separate list, or dictate a running note of these, by all means. You will find that some of your queries or observations are answered when you look at other parts of the titles, but there are inevitably going to be matters that you will need to raise with the seller's solicitor (see para 8.34).

EXAMINING A SASINE TITLE

8.6 The requirement to examine a title in the Sasine Register should diminish over time, as more titles move from the Sasine Register to the Land Register. In practice, however, it is still the case that title to the majority of Scotland by land mass is still recorded in the Sasine Register (see para 2.2). The skills and knowledge required to examine a Sasine title will continue to be essential to the solicitor until at least 2024, when the Keeper has undertaken that the Land Register will be complete (see para 2.5). However, even with the completed Land Register, it will continue to be necessary sometimes to examine the underlying writs. Well-developed title examination skills will, therefore, continue to be relevant into the foreseeable future.

In most cases, your examination of a Sasine title will be in the course of a transaction which will induce a first registration in the Land

Register. All transfers of a Sasine title will trigger first registration. But there are still occasions when first registration will not be triggered, for example, examining title for purposes of taking security over property that is already owned by a borrower (until 1 April 2016, when the Sasine Register will no longer accept standard securities). The approach to title examination is no different, although the follow-on processes may be.

8.7 In a first registration, or in a Sasine transaction, the first thing to do is to check the title deeds against the Inventory of Writs, which should accompany the titles (whether these consist of a bundle or a couple of boxes). This is your first opportunity to get a feel for what is involved in the title and possibly also identify if titles are missing. It is usual and courteous to acknowledge receipt of the titles and some solicitors ask you to mark a copy of the Inventory and return it to them. If there is a 'Search for Incumbrances' with the titles, this will help you put the title deeds into order and make sure that all the deeds mentioned in the Legal Report have been sent to you. You will start to form a rough history of the property in your mind. In particular, you can spot any split-offs or acquisitions as well as the writs referred to for burdens. Some fairly basic organisational techniques will help you at this stage. Sort the titles into categories: the prescriptive or foundation writ (see para 8.9) and writs within the prescriptive progress; the descriptive writ; writs referred to for burdens; undischarged securities and so on. Identifying writs with garish sticky notes is a good way of seeing at a glance what role that writ plays in the overall title picture.

8.8 Some of the deeds that have been sent to you need not concern you. Solicitors never seem to throw anything out and even when a Land Certificate has been issued, or a Title Sheet created, the prior underlying titles may still accompany the Land Certificate or the PDF copy or extract of the Title Sheet. In fact, these can be quite helpful, as we shall see. Some deeds can be ignored, such as writs that are well outwith the prescriptive period and old, discharged securities. It can be quite satisfying to make a bundle of these at the start, and then concentrate on what you need to look at.

POSITIVE PRESCRIPTION

8.9 Where a person has possessed land openly, peaceably and without interruption for ten years, on the basis of a sufficient recorded or registered title, the title will be unchallengeable[10]. This process is known as positive prescription. Prescription does not operate however, where the title was not valid *ex facie* (on its face), or if it turns out to have been forged.

It is not thought that many pieces of land are acquired in this way. Yet, for another reason, this is a vital provision for the solicitor. It has often been said that good titles have no need of prescription (see for example *Duke of Buccleuch v Cunynghame*[11]). Prescription is only required to cure bad titles. What it means from the point of view of title examination is that prior titles that fall outside the prescriptive period need not be checked. The effect of prescription is to give an absolute presumption that the title deed is good. So, if you take the first recorded transfer of the land that you are buying, which is more than ten years old (the prescriptive or foundation writ) and find that it is free from an intrinsic objection, then that is a valid foundation for a prescriptive title and you need look back no further. You may set aside all older transfers of the land, unless these contain valid title conditions to which you must refer. You must, however, check this foundation writ for any intrinsic objection, and check everything after it to make sure that it correctly flows down to the present seller (see para 8.13).

An intrinsic objection is one which can be observed from the terms of the deed itself and does not require proof from outside sources. An example of this is given in *Cooper Scott v Gill Scott*[12], where a destination detailed in the narrative clause of the disposition did not correspond with a further narration of the same destination in the dispositive clause. A majority of the seven judges, however, held that this deed was not intrinsically null and was therefore a good foundation for prescription (see also *Simpson v Marshall*[13]).

An extrinsic objection, that is to say an objection which can only be proved from outside evidence, or an intrinsic objection that can be proved only by extrinsic evidence, does not affect the use of the disposition as a foundation of title.

---

10 Section 1 of the Prescription and Limitation (Scotland) Act 1973.
11 [1826] 5S 53.
12 [1924] SC 309.
13 [1900] 2 F 447.

A NON DOMINO DISPOSITION/PRESCRIPTIVE CLAIMANTS

8.10 As a demonstration of the power of prescription consider the disposition *a non domino* (a disposition granted by someone who is not the owner). If a piece of land lies vacant, and the owner cannot be traced, it is possible for someone who does not own that land to obtain a disposition, granted by anyone in her favour. Note, however, that a disposition granted by the granter in favour of himself (from A to A, rather than from A to B) is *ex facie* invalid and will not be a foundation writ for prescription. This reflects the principle that a man cannot contract with himself. As Lord Clyde said in *Kildrummy (Jersey) Ltd v Inland Revenue Commissioners*[14]:

> '...where the same person is both debtor and creditor in the same matter there can be no obligation created. It is in my view ineffective to enter into a contract with continuing mutual rights and obligations with oneself, and it is whimsical to grant a lease of one's own property to oneself.'

The principle of A to A *a non domino* dispositions was clearly rejected in *The Board of Management of Aberdeen College v Stewart Watt Youngerson and Anor*[15].

Only simple warrandice is given, for the granter has no claim to the land at all. The disposition is then recorded to make it public and the disponee occupies the land 'openly and peaceably', as if it were owned, so that anyone who has a better title may see the occupation and object. If no objection is made by anyone having a better title within ten years, the *a non domino* disponee then becomes the unchallengeable owner of the land. If prescription can perfect a title in such circumstances, it will be seen that it can also cure much more minor defects in a deed.

It should not be thought however that the *a non domino* disposition is an easy way to acquire odd bits of land. Under the 1979 Act, the Keeper's policy was very strict on allowing *a non domino* deeds to be registered, and applications for registration of such deeds would be carefully scrutinised to prevent unscrupulous acquisition of land and were sometimes rejected.

---

14 [1990] STC 657, [1992] SLT 787.
15 [2005] CSOH 31.

The Keeper required the applicant to show that no-one else had a better title. The applicant could conduct searches over neighbouring titles to fulfil this requirement. The evidence was kept by the Keeper in case of a challenge. At the end of the prescriptive period, the applicant could apply to have the exclusion from indemnity removed.

The concern about *a non domino* dispositions being used in bad faith has translated itself into statutory provisions[16] setting out the steps that must now be followed if an *a non domino* disposition is to be accepted by the Registers.

8.10.1 The Case for *a non domino*

On the one hand, the provisions in the 2012 Act are bad news for *a non domino* deeds. There is an obvious tension between the notification provisions in the Act, and the invariable requirement by solicitors for supporting title indemnity insurance. For insurance cover to be provided, the underwriters require that there be no contact with anyone who could have an interest in the property.

On the other hand, while it is fair to say that using this approach is never going to be easy, at least we now have a statutory statement of what is required for the Keeper to register an *a non domino* disposition and the Keeper has issued Guidance[17]. This Guidance should be read carefully before embarking on an *a non domino* procedure. All of the steps must be followed, and evidenced, for the application to be successful. It seems, however, that currently applications for registration of *a non domino* dispositions are being rigorously scrutinised at the Register. The majority of (admittedly a small number of) applications received in the first few months following the designated day were rejected, largely due to failure to comply with the notification procedures.

So the *a non domino* route is not for the faint-hearted. But most solicitors will tell you that the *a non domino* disposition is an extremely useful tool. It can fill in little gaps in all sorts of situations, when making up a development title, or tidying up the title to the bottom of a garden maybe. It is rarely some ruthless land-grab. And we now have certainty over what a 'prescriptive claimant', as an applicant in these cases is to

16 Sections 43 to 45 of the 2012 Act.
17 See www.ros.gov.uk/about-us/2012-act/general-guidance/prescriptive-claimants.

be known[18], has to do. In reality, the procedure is very similar to what was done before the 2012 Act came into force, except previously, the notification procedures would rarely, if ever, be followed. That is one essential difference.

8.10.2 The One-year Rule

The other essential condition for a successful prescriptive claimant application is the additional requirement for possession of the land in question for a continuous period of at least one year.

A prescriptive claimant must satisfy the Keeper that the land has been possessed openly, peaceably, and without judicial interruption for a continuous period of at least one year immediately prior to the date of the application. Without this requirement the Keeper will not accept the application.

It will be very unusual for a purchaser of land that includes an area like this to have possessed it at all, but the 2012 Act provides that the possession may be either by the disponer, or by the applicant, or by a combination of both[19]. Note that the ten-year prescriptive period that must run before a good title can be acquired is unchanged. The one year possession is merely a requirement for an application to register an *a non domino* disposition to be considered at all – it does not count towards prescription.

8.10.3 Evidence Required for Possession

The evidence that the Keeper will need to be satisfied there has been sufficient possession will certainly include affidavits. However, it will not be sufficient to produce something that merely attests that the land has been possessed 'openly, peaceably and without judicial interruption'[20]. Affidavits from the applicant or the person granting the *a non domino* disposition (eg the seller) should contain clear wording as to the scope and character of possession.

Typically, proof of possession will include:

---

18 *A non domino* title can become good, if the disponee then possesses the property openly, peaceably and without judicial interruption for the prescriptive period – hence the term 'prescriptive claimant' in the 2012 Act.
19 Section 43(3) of the 2012 Act.
20 The authors doubt whether such a bare statement would be satisfactory for any type of affidavit as to possession.

- a plan showing the extent of the area possessed;
- affidavits from owners of neighbouring land;
- information from utility providers and local authority records; and
- photographic evidence.

Clearly the more evidence that can be obtained the better, if the Keeper is to be assured that the possession criteria have been met.

The Keeper's Guidance[21] sets out the following key information that should be set out in an affidavit[22]:

- A sworn statement[23] by the relevant party that the land has been possessed openly, peaceably and without judicial interruption;
- The duration of the applicant's and/or disponer's possession. Where possession extends back further than the required one year period, and an accurate duration cannot be given, an approximate start date may be acceptable provided the required one year period is covered;
- Details of the type of land it is, eg garden ground, parking place, grazing land, overgrown space, etc;
- A detailed statement as to the specific nature of the possession, ie not a bald statement. For instance, that the land has been used as garden ground for a house, and that a shed has been constructed on it;
- A plan that clearly identifies the extent of the land possessed, unless relating to the whole of a registered title;
- Confirmation of who has access to the land, who uses the land, and who maintains the land; and
- Confirmation of the apparent age and nature of the boundary features surrounding the ground, eg stone walls, wire fencing etc, and details of any maintenance provisions in place for these boundaries.

---

21 See www.ros.gov.uk/__data/assets/pdf_file/0020/11369/General-Guidance-Prescriptive-Claimants.pdf.
22 Reproduced under Crown Copyright.
23 Any affidavit must be sworn before a notary public (Rule 9 of the Land Register Rules etc. (Scotland) Regulations 2014). Note that Rule 9 does not allow for any substitute to a notary public such as a Commissioner for oaths.

A style of affidavit for possession that can be used as a useful starting point is available in the Residential styles section of the PSG website[24].

8.10.4 Procedure – Search and Notify

Trying to trace the owner to property being conveyed by way of *a non domino* disposition can be frustrating. Usually, after extensive searching, no owner can be traced.

If an owner is found, the prescriptive claimant rules state that they must be notified of the proposed deed. This may seem a bit strange to solicitors. Experience suggests that if you can find the owner, you get in touch with them and start negotiations, rather than just take title to the land anyway. However, there might be some other person, an executor perhaps, who could take steps to complete title. If so, they will have to be contacted instead.

The notification must be in the statutory form[25]. The notification needs to be sent using a recorded delivery postal service to the last known address of the party identified as the owner. That notification is required to take place at least 60 days before the application for registration is submitted to allow the owner to check their title and take legal advice etc. The applicant will have to submit evidence of this notification with their application.

If you cannot locate an owner or someone who could complete title, then you must notify the Crown. In most cases this will mean the Queen's and Lord Treasurer's Remembrancer (QLTR) (see para 8.10.5). If the land in question forms part of the foreshore or seabed (or other *regalia*) then the Crown Estate Commissioners must be notified.

In addition to the requirement for the applicant to notify these potential owners, or the QLTR, the Keeper must also notify them, if she considers it reasonably practicable to do so[26]. Any such notification will have to be made, before the Keeper accepts the application, and there is another period of 60 days within which any person so notified can object to the application.

---

24 See www.psglegal.co.uk/residential.php.
25 See Regulation 18 of and Schedule 2 to the Land Register Rules etc. (Scotland) Regulations 2014.
26 Section 45 of the 2012 Act.

8.10.5 QLTR, *Bona vacantia* and *Ultimus haeres*

8.10.5(i) Ownerless land

Sometimes, land becomes 'ownerless'. Probably the most common situations where you will come across this in examination of title is where the last recorded or registered owner was a company (or a limited liability partnership) that has since been dissolved. Where this happens, any assets (including heritable property) of the dissolved company vest in the Crown[27] and are known as *bona vacantia*[28]. The assets of missing persons and lost or abandoned property also fall into this category. The QLTR[29], as Crown representative in Scotland, deals with such assets.

In cases where the last recorded or registered owner has died, without leaving a will, and has no surviving spouse or civil partner, or any other blood relative (or none who can be traced), that person's estate (including heritable property) can be claimed for the Crown by the QLTR as *ultimus haeres*[30].

In cases of *ultimus haeres*, the QLTR can claim and administer the deceased's estate and can sell any heritable property on the open market.

8.10.5(ii) Buying bona vacantia land

Where the land is *bona vacantia*, the QLTR can be approached with a request to buy the land from her, unless she has, or is going to, disclaim the land. More often than not, the first the QLTR will know about *bona vacantia* property, is when she is approached in this way.

If there is a value in the land, it is most likely that the QLTR will want to dispose of it, and not disclaim. It should be borne in mind that there is no requirement on the QLTR to deal with any property, in any particular way, or to dispose of a property to any particular person at any particular time or for any particular price, or at all'[31].

The land must be valued by the District Valuer to determine the price to be paid for it. The QLTR's fees and any other professional fees and outlays, including the District Valuer's fee must be met by the purchaser.

---

27 Section 1012 of the Companies Act 2006 (or statutory predecessors).
28 'Ownerless goods'.
29 See www.qltr.gov.uk.
30 'Last heir.' For the Latin scholars among us, it is the principle of '*quod nullius est fit domini regis*' that applies – that which belongs to nobody becomes the King's (or Queen's).
31 See the QLTR policies on dealing with *bona vacantia* at www.qltr.gov.uk/content/policies#overlay-context=

8.10.5(iii) Disclaimer by the QLTR

The QLTR can choose to disclaim any asset which falls to her as *bona vacantia*, either at common law or under section 1013 of the Companies Act 2006. In the latter case, the QLTR has three years from the date on which she was told of the Crown's ownership of the property (or, if later, from the time the Crown's ownership was established), in which to disclaim.

It is entirely at the discretion of the QLTR, whether or not to disclaim, but this is more likely to happen in cases where the property has no value, or is a liability, or where the QLTR considers that the property has only become *bona vacantia* due to a genuine error.

8.10.5(iv) The QLTR and prescriptive claimants

It is not difficult to work out that if the QLTR has to be notified of a proposed prescriptive claimant application (because it has not been possible to locate the owner, or the owner no longer exists or is missing) then, if there is value in the land, it is more likely that, if it is to be acquired, this will be through the QLTR, for a payment, and not by way of *a non domino* disposition. The QLTR can object to the proposed prescriptive claimant application, following notification.

Accordingly, if it seems likely that the property has vest in the Crown, it would be prudent to contact the QLTR to explore options, before settling on the *a non domino* route. The QLTR prefers solicitors to get in touch[32], rather than simply serving the prescriptive claimant notice. She will want to see the titles and consider all the circumstances. With the notification procedures and her entitlement to object, it seems sensible to communicate and explore this option. The alternative might be to spend time and effort in gathering all the prescriptive claimant evidence, sending notifications etc, only to have the application rejected because the QLTR has objected to it[33].

There may be circumstances where the reason why the land has fallen to the Crown is because of error. Perhaps 'title' to a property has been 'transferred' from one group company to another, but the conveyancing

---

32 Contact details are on the website at: www.qltr.gov.uk.
33 See section 45(5) of the 2012 Act.

formalities have not been completed, and in the intervening period the 'transferring' company has dissolved. In such circumstances the QLTR might decide that it is not appropriate to profit from such a genuine error. There are of course other options open to the parties in such circumstances. A company can be restored to the Companies Register up to six years after it has been dissolved[34]; such options should be considered before making an approach to the QLTR.

8.10.6 Provisional Title Sheet

If you actually manage to navigate your way through all of these obstacles, and the Keeper accepts the *a non domino* application, she will make a 'provisional' entry on the title sheet. The rights will remain provisional until the prescriptive period has run. Once the ten-year period has elapsed, it is not, however, the case that the provisional entry will automatically be removed. It will be necessary to apply to the Keeper for removal and, at that stage, to provide evidence of the ten years' possession.

8.10.7 Title Indemnity Insurance

One important consideration here is the question of title indemnity insurance. It is common to obtain indemnity insurance in *a non domino* situations, but it is invariably a condition of such insurance that you must not contact anyone who might have a potential claim. The prescriptive claimant requirements accordingly make this aspect of *a non domino* arrangements far more difficult, because often they only go ahead with the backing of title indemnity insurance. In some respects, this could be considered to be an irreconcilable conflict. However, Title Indemnity Insurers continue to be willing to look at *a non domino* situations on a case by case basis, and assess the risks in light of the particular circumstances. One option, albeit a fairly limited one, may be not to register title at all, and instead insure against dispossession[35]. Discussing the prospects of availability of cover with the insurers at an early stage is recommended.

---

34 Section 1030(4) of the Companies Act 2006.
35 See www.firsttitle.eu/media/4526/What-Now-for-a-Non-Domino-Dispositions_Scotland.pdf.

8.10.8 Transitional Arrangements for *a non domino* Title in the Sasine Register

There are situations where there is already an *a non domino* title still in the Sasine Register. If prescription operated to put the title of the current proprietor beyond challenge then a disposition granted by them will be valid and can be registered in the usual way.

However, if the prescriptive period is still running, then the recorded disposition will still be *a non domino*. This means that on a first registration of the title being transferred during the prescriptive period, the Keeper will require the applicant to go through the same prescriptive claimant provisions under the 2012 Act as are required for a first time *a non domino* disposition.

Transfer from the Register of Sasines into the Land Register will not interrupt the running of prescription. The period of possession of the granter can be combined with the period of possession of the grantee. Although certain checks will have been carried out by the Keeper before accepting the *a non domino* disposition into the Sasine Register, the Keeper's position is that, on submission of an application for a transfer, she will require the new notification procedures to be followed. This could cause difficulties with title indemnity cover, as many of these titles will already have title indemnity insurance in place on 'non-notification' terms.

One way to get around this issue, according to the Keeper's Guidance, would be to voluntarily register the Sasine title before the transfer takes place. The Keeper will create a title sheet, marked as provisional, and the subsequent transfer will simply be treated as a standard transfer of a registered plot, although the title will continue to be marked as provisional until the prescriptive period has run.

NEGATIVE PRESCRIPTION

8.11 Taken together, sections 6, 7 and 8 of the Prescription and Limitation (Scotland) Act 1973 provide that, where an obligation has subsisted unacknowledged or a right has not been enforced or exercised for the continuous period specified, then that obligation or right will be extinguished. This is known as negative prescription. Sections 7 and 8 relate to the long negative prescriptive period of 20 years. These provisions can be of benefit to the solicitor where, for example, the titles include an old bond or a security that is over 20 years old, but no payments have been made in that time, and it has not been enforced by the creditor, it can be said to have prescribed. Servitudes which have not been exercised for a period of 20 years can be extinguished by prescription as well. The snag of course can be getting sufficient evidence of absence of payment or non-use.

Section 6 provides for a five-year period of prescription for obligations to pay sums of money and obligations to pay compensation that fall within certain categories[36].

The well-equipped solicitor should be thoroughly familiar with the rules relating to prescription. An excellent commentary on the 1973 Act is contained in an annotated edition of the Prescription and Limitation (Scotland) Act 1973 by David M Walker *Law of Prescription and Limitation of Actions in Scotland*[37]. See also *Prescription and Limitation* by David Johnston[38].

GOOD FAITH

8.12 Some conveyancing defects can be cured by *bona fides* or good faith. Section 17 of the Succession (Scotland) Act 1964 provides that where a person for good faith and for value acquires title to land from an executor, or from somebody who has derived title directly from an executor, the title will not be challengeable on the ground that the Confirmation of the executor was reducible or had, in fact, been reduced or even that the title should not have been transferred by the executor to the person who is offering the title.

For example, say you are buying from sellers David and Jeffrey who do not have a recorded or registered title to the property in question. Instead they produce: (a) a Confirmation in the estate of their Aunt Nicola, which appoints George as executor; and (b) a docquet of nomination in terms of section 15 of the Succession (Scotland) Act 1964, signed by George, transferring that property to David and Jeffrey, describing them as the persons entitled to take the property under Nicola's will. Provided your client is buying in good faith and for value, it need not concern you: (i)

---

36 Schedule 1 to the Prescription and Limitation (Scotland) Act 1973.
37 6th edn (2002) W Green & Son.
38 2nd edn (2012) W Green & Son.

if someone produces a later-dated will appointing Alex as executor and nominating Harriet as the legatee entitled to the property; or (ii) someone alleges that the will is a forgery. You need look no further than the Confirmation itself.

There is an analogous provision in section 2 of the Trusts (Scotland) Act 1961, which provides that titles acquired from trustees or executors are also protected from being challenged on the ground that the transaction was at variance with the terms or purpose of the trust.

When checking discharges of previous standard securities, section 41 of the Conveyancing and Feudal Reform (Scotland) Act 1970 provides that, where a discharge of a security bears to be granted by a person entitled to do so (eg the creditor), subsequent acquirers of land *bona fide* and for value will not have their title to the land challenged after the expiry of a five-year period from the recording or registration of the discharge, merely by reason of the discharge being reduced. This means that if a discharge is more than five years old, and appears to have been granted by the creditor of the security that is discharged, you need not examine the origins of that discharge any further.

Statutory protection also exists for parties dealing in good faith with companies. Section 40 of the Companies Act 2006 safeguards such parties, by providing that the power of the directors to bind the company, or authorise others to do so, is deemed not to be limited by the company's constitution. Accordingly, a third party dealing with a company in good faith does not need to concern himself about whether a company is acting within its constitution. Note also that section 40 does not apply to companies that are charities. Nevertheless, third parties acquiring property for full consideration from a charity or directors exceeding their powers, still receive good title if they do not know that the company is a charity or that the act is *ultra vires*[39].

There is also protection afforded to a third party who acquires any right or interest in good faith and for value from or through the recipient from a bankrupt in a gratuitous alienation.[40] In practice, given the importance of enquiry concerning gratuitous alienations and unfair preferences (see para 8.32) good faith is likely to be difficult to demonstrate.

---

39 See section 42 of the Companies Act 2006 and section 112 of the Companies Act 1989.
40 See section 34(4) of the Bankruptcy (Scotland) Act 1985.

Section 17 of the Bankruptcy and Diligence (Scotland) Act 2007 provides protection for a good faith purchaser from a post-sequestration dealing by the debtor. This is an exception to the rule that such a dealing is void, unless consented to by the trustee. If a person who has been sequestrated grants a disposition (or other deed) to a good faith grantee, who has paid (or is willing to pay) adequate consideration for the property to which the deed relates, the sequestration does not invalidate that deed, provided that it is delivered not later than seven days after the sequestration has been registered in the Register of Inhibitions.

THE PRESCRIPTIVE PROGRESS

8.13 Start your title examination by looking at the disposition (or dispositions) in favour of the seller, and noting down its (their) terms. This will tell you what it is the seller owns and has to sell. It will either be all that the purchaser is acquiring, or may be a larger property of which your client is purchasing only a part. Compare the description of the title and any plan on this deed with whatever information you have, eg a survey report or Heads of Terms about what your client is purchasing. This disposition will also contain references to other rights and pertinents of title benefiting the seller, such as servitudes. These may be expressly mentioned or referred to in other parts of the titles for more details. This disposition will also contain details of, or references to, burdens and title conditions that burden the property. Such burdens may be set out in full in much older titles, which will need to be examined in detail (see para 8.25).

Now you should identify the foundation writ (see para 8.9) and examine it for intrinsic defects.

Next you have to examine all the writs that follow the foundation writ, until you get to the seller's title, ensuring that each one links with and follows on from every other one correctly.

LINKS IN TITLE

8.14 If the grantee (disponee) of one deed is not the granter (disponer) of the next deed, then you need to identify what the 'link in title', or midcouple, is between the two. Only certain deeds, (dispositions of land, or assignations, discharges or restrictions of heritable security), may be granted by uninfeft proprietors[41]. Strictly speaking, following the abolition of the feudal system, the words 'infeft' and 'uninfeft' no longer have current meaning, but in the absence of a post feudal equivalent, they remain a convenient expression for many to distinguish between being a proprietor of property with a recorded/registered title (infeft), and being a proprietor of property without a recorded or registered title (uninfeft). Formerly, heritable securities could not be granted by persons without a recorded title, but standard securities and their transmissions may now be granted by uninfeft proprietors[42].

A link in title can be a variety of things, and in some cases there may be more than one unrecorded link. Confirmation in favour of an executor and a docquet of nomination (see para 8.18.2) is one example. Often, residential properties will be held in the joint names of a husband and wife, and there may be a survivorship destination in the disposition in their favour. This means that the title will transfer automatically to the survivor on the death of the first of the owners[43], so the death certificate of that person would be the link. Generally, any statute, conveyance, deed, instrument, decree or other writing, by which a right to land or to any real right in land is vested in or transmitted to any person, is competent, and includes a minute of a meeting at which any person is appointed to any place or office, if such appointment involves such rights to land.

It is no longer necessary for the relevant links to be narrated in a disposition that is being granted, by incorporating a clause of deduction of title. Under the 1979 Act[44] once title to a property was registered in the Land Register no deduction of title clause was required. The 2012 Act extends that rule to all deeds, including dispositions inducing first registration[45]. However, deeds recorded in the Sasine Register will still need such clauses (where appropriate), so it is necessary when checking recorded deeds in the prescriptive progress to ensure that any links in title have been properly referred to. If a deed destined for the Sasine Register is being granted now by someone uninfeft (such as a standard security until 1 April 2016), a deduction of title clause must be incorporated.

---

41 Section 3 of the Conveyancing (Scotland) Act 1924.
42 Section 12 of the Conveyancing and Feudal Reform (Scotland) Act.
43 Provided it has not been extinguished on divorce or annulment (see section 8(1)(aa) of the Family Law (Scotland) Act 1985).
44 Section 15(3).
45 Section 101 of the 2012 Act.

You will always still require to examine and be satisfied with links in title where it is appropriate to establish that the disposition being granted to your client will be validly granted even though no deduction of title clause is required. You must certify that this is the case in the application for registration, but the links themselves do not need to be submitted to the Keeper (see para 14.11.2(vi)). However, some dyed-in-the-wool solicitors still like to include a deduction of title in their dispositions, and although it is not necessary for registration, it is not incompetent.[46] There may even be some merit in continuing to do so, if only to act as a proper double check that all of the necessary links have been identified and examined.

A style of deduction of title clause is provided in Conveyancing (Scotland) Act 1924[47]:

> 'Which lands and others (or subjects) were last vested [or are part of the lands and others (or subjects) last vested] in A.B. (designation of person last infeft), whose title thereto is recorded in (specify Register of Sasines and date of recording, or if the last infeftment has already been mentioned say in the said A.B. as aforesaid), and from whom I acquired right by (here specify shortly the writ or series of writs by which right was so acquired).'

It is important to note that this statutory style requires a designation of the person last infeft (usually their address and if the last vested person is deceased it is usual to say 'who resided latterly at …') and is ineffective otherwise.

If the difference between the last grantee and the next granter is merely a change of name, then no deduction of title clause is (or was) necessary, but the fact of the change of name should be narrated in the narrative clause. For people this is simply a question of stating their current name and previous name eg Mrs Joan McMillan (design), formerly Miss Joan Spencer (design). For changes of company name, the narrative should set out the current and previous name or names and refer to the Certificates of Incorporation on Change of Name by which the name changes were formalised.

It will be necessary to check the links themselves to ensure that they exist and are valid and correctly referred to in the deduction of title.

46 Section 101 of the 2012 Act is permissive, not mandatory.
47 Schedule A, Form 1.

Obviously the links must be sufficient to connect the previous title with the subsequent one.

THE DESCRIPTIVE WRIT

8.15 The first time a property or piece of land is fully described may be many years earlier than the foundation writ. When a property or piece of land is conveyed for the first time it needs to be sufficiently identified. This may be by way of a particular or bounding description in which the piece of land is identified by reference to its boundary features. This can range from a broad reference: 'bounded on the south by the road leading from Kinlochalmond to Kelvinforth' to a more detailed description: 'bounded on the north by the centre line of a stone wall separating the subjects from land now or formerly belonging to Richard Byron Childs and forming part of the lands and estate of Kinlochalmond and Dunvorlich, along which it extends 306 feet or thereby'. In older titles, however, the description of the property, particularly of land, might be expressed in a more generalised way, where the physical boundaries of the lands are not specified, but instead the land may be described in general terms such as 'ALL and WHOLE the lands and estate of Marchmain in the County of Sutherland'. The extent of these lands is generally established over time through prescriptive possession, but this means of course that it can be difficult if not impossible to be certain of the exact extent of the land in question. Often it is necessary to decide whether or not the description is habile to include the property or area concerned (in other words that the general description is sufficient to competently include the area concerned, and with nothing to indicate to the contrary). The plan annexed to an 1837 Feu contract which delineated the high water mark meant that the description in the deed was not habile to include the foreshore (*Luss Estates Co v BP Oil Grangemouth Refinery Ltd*[48].

This first description frequently arises when an area of land is split off from a larger area. It is customary to refer in the description to this larger area of which the property forms a part. Known as the 'part and portion' clause, this will refer to the larger area, usually by referring to the descriptive writ of that larger area, although it might also refer to a more general description of the larger land.

48 [1987] SLT 201.

Check carefully the first description of the land, either with your own observations or with a survey plan of the property. This first full description does not however need to be repeated each time the property is conveyed. The property can be referred to in subsequent conveyances with a description by reference to that earlier descriptive writ[49]. Make sure that the first full description has been validly referred to throughout the progress of titles in conformity with these provisions.

You should also take note of all additions to the land, and disposals of any part of the land, where this is relevant, to ensure that no part of the property you are acquiring has already been conveyed by the seller to another party. This is particularly relevant in titles of large estates, where parcels of land have been conveyed off over a long period of time. There might be photocopies of dispositions and other conveyances of these parcels with the titles deeds that have been sent to you, but it might be that these split-offs are only apparent from a Search, or are disclosed by the Legal Report, and you will need to ask for copies of the actual conveyances or Title Sheets to check their terms.

It can sometimes be difficult to identify the areas conveyed in previous split off writs, however, particularly if the conveyances contain no plan. Again, this is more common in older titles as more modern conveyances tend, where at all possible, to include a plan of some sort for easier identification.

BOUNDARIES

8.16 Where a particular description is used, there are a number of rules that determine what is the precise nature of a physical boundary, depending on the words used in the deed to describe it, although the position may not be capable of determination without recourse to other evidence. Generally, if land is described as being bounded 'by' something, such as a lane, then that thing will be excluded.

Land described as being bounded by a road will usually exclude that road. However if it is a public road, or a private road situated between two properties, then the mid-line (or *medium filum*) of the road will be presumed to be the boundary.

---

49 See section 61 of the Conveyancing (Scotland) Act 1874, and section 8 of and Schedule D to the Conveyancing (Scotland) Act 1924.

As a general rule, fences, walls and gables that lie between the properties are owned to the centre line by each proprietor, with each proprietor having an interest in the other half. It is possible, however, that the wall is owned jointly, in which case the boundary of each property is the nearest outside face of the wall, and the wall is jointly owned and maintained. Obviously, this must be closely checked from the deeds to establish the exact nature of the ownership of the fences or walls.

When there is no adjoining proprietor, the wall, fence or gable is usually owned and maintained solely by the landowner. Some titles provide, however, that at a future date when someone builds on the adjoining property and uses that fence, wall or gable then that person should refund one-half of the cost of building to the person who paid for it, and become partly responsible for its maintenance. You should check that there are no outstanding charges for formation or maintenance of mutual fences, walls or gables.

Where a property is bounded by a non-tidal river, and there is no specification of the boundary, this is taken to be the middle line of the river. This includes the fishing rights, but not salmon fishing, which must be specifically transferred to the purchasers (see *McKendrick v Wilson*[50]). The same applies to non-tidal lochs. Care should be taken when purchasing a riparian property (ie one situated on a river bank or lochside) that the landowner has not retained a narrow strip of land between the property purchased and the loch or river. If this is the case, the purchaser is not a riparian proprietor and has no rights in the loch or river. This last point is something that would be well to be addressed in the missives as a condition of purchase, if the purchaser expects to have rights in the river or loch.

Using Google Earth and Google Streetview to view the actual physical features of the boundaries can be a useful way of clarifying the terms of a title description, if a site visit is not practicable.

VALIDITY OF EACH DEED

8.17 Check that all parties granting deeds had the capacity to do so. For capacity generally see para 8.18.

Check also that the parties have been correctly named. This is particularly important in relation to limited companies, where even

---

50 [1970] SLT (Sh Ct) 39.

a minor error in the name of the company can be fatal to the deed (see below). This is because the legal personality of the company resides in the company of that name only. Check the name of the company against a copy of the certificate of incorporation or an online search at Companies House. It has always been good practice when designing a company to refer to its company number, as this is a unique identifier for UK registered companies. It is now essential to do so[51], as otherwise the deed will be rejected, by the Keeper.

Opinions have been expressed that even the omission of an apostrophe or brackets in the company name is a sufficient flaw. See *The Conveyancing Opinions of J. M. Halliday*[52]. While this might be considered an extreme example, the prudent approach should be a 'zero tolerance' one.

Ensure that the form of all deeds is correct, that they are properly executed and witnessed and that the testing clause is correctly completed, that all deletions, interlineations, additions and erasures have been properly acknowledged and referred to in the testing clause.

When the deed has been granted by a limited company, the requirements for valid execution by companies since 1995 are contained in Schedule 2 to the Requirements of Writing (Scotland) Act 1995. If you are checking a deed granted by a company dated prior to 1 August 1995 then different execution provisions apply. For example, deeds executed by companies prior to 31 July 1990 usually required to have the common seal impressed on them, accompanied by the signature of two directors or a director and the company secretary. In 1990, several methods of company execution applied, depending on the month in which the document was signed. This happened because new provisions that were introduced into the companies legislation that year were quickly discovered to be defective and had to be amended by further legislation. Gretton and Reid provide a chart, beloved of solicitors, in *Conveyancing*[53]. This provides the relevant dates and method of execution competent for companies since time immemorial until the coming into force of the 1995 Act.

---

51 Section 113(1) of the 2012 Act – the definition of 'designation' includes, where the person being designed is not a natural person, the number allocated to that person under section 1066 of the Companies Act 2006.
52 (1992) W Green, p. 265.
53 3rd edn (2004) W Green, para 14.07.

Check that each deed, if completed prior to 1 December 2003, has been correctly stamped with an impressed stamp reflecting the amount of stamp duty paid on the deed. A list of historical rates of stamp duty from 1 March 1958 used to be available online, but currently only rates of stamp duty between March 2000 and 1 December 2003 (when SDLT was introduced) are available[54]. That should be all that you need in most cases, as it covers a period of more than the ten-year prescriptive period. It will only be if your prescriptive writ is prior to March 2000 that this will be a challenge, as information about the older rates is no longer available online. You may have to resort to old publications or directories. Back issues of the now discontinued 'Blue Book', or the supplement to the 'White Book' directory, where the rates were set out will be available from law libraries, such as the Signet Library.

Finally, check that each deed has actually been recorded in the appropriate Division of the General Register of Sasines. This is denoted by an ink stamp impressed on the first page of the deed in one of the margins. In very old deeds it is handwritten. It will give the county in which the deed is recorded, the Book and Folio number (latterly the Fiche and Frame numbers once the Registers started storing copies of deed on microfiche) and the date of recording.

CAPACITY OF THE PARTIES

8.18 Where a sale is made by a person or persons on behalf of someone else, or in default of someone else, care must be taken to ensure that the power of sale is competent, and that it was properly exercised.

8.18.1 Trustees

Trustees have wide powers to sell, lease and grant securities over heritage[55]. The term 'trustee' includes trustees *ex officiis* (namely trustees who are appointed by virtue of an office they hold, say a president and secretary of a golf club, and who cease to be trustees when they demit office, giving way to the next incumbents automatically), executors-

---

54 See http://webarchive.nationalarchives.gov.uk/20140109143644/http://hmrc.gov.uk/sdlt/intro/
    rates-thresholds.htm
55 Section 4 of the Trusts (Scotland) Act 1921.

nominate and judicial factors[56]. Executors-dative also have this power of sale[57].

8.18.2 Executors

An executor on the estate of a deceased person can either be nominated in the will (executor nominate) or under the rules of intestacy, if there is no will or the nomination fails (executor dative). Although it is possible for an executor to deduce title through the will, this is not regarded as entirely safe, due to the fact that the good faith purchaser protection available under section 17 of the Succession (Scotland) Act 1964 (see para 8.14 above) is not available. In practice, the executor obtains Confirmation in the estate of the deceased, which will include heritable property, and the executor can sell the property by virtue of the Confirmation in his favour. A beneficiary or legatee under the will of the deceased can have the property transferred to him by way of a docquet of nomination which is endorsed onto a certificate of Confirmation that gives details of the property[58]. The docquet is signed by the executor, and that effectively passes the property out of the executor's control. Actual title is not transferred but the docquet endorsed on the certificate of Confirmation is an effective link in title for that person either to convey the property to a third party, or to complete their own title.

8.18.3 Creditors Selling Under a Standard Security

The power of sale may be exercised among other remedies when the debtor is in default. Following on the Supreme Court decision in *Royal Bank of Scotland v Wilson*[59], heritable creditors must serve a calling up notice as an essential part of the repossession of the subjects.

The Home Owner and Debtor Protection (Scotland) Act 2010 made changes to procedures for enforcement of standard securities over residential properties, and provided for new forms of calling up notice and notice of default for both residential and commercial properties. For residential repossessions, unless the debtor voluntarily surrenders the property, calling up notices must be followed by an action for

---

56 Section 2, *ibid*.
57 Section 20 of the Succession (Scotland) Act 1964.
58 Section 15 of the Succession (Scotland) Act.
59 [2010] UKSC 50.

possession[60]. The 2010 Act also imposes new obligations on heritable creditors in respect of securities over residential properties to carry out certain pre-action procedures with a debtor before they can raise an action.

In the case of *Westfoot Investments Ltd v European Property Holdings Inc*[61], a company that owned several residential properties objected to the calling up of the securities it had granted, on the grounds (it claimed) that the creditor had not complied with the pre-action requirements under the 2010 Act. The Sheriff concluded that, taking the provisions of the 2010 Act and the Conveyancing and Feudal Reform (Scotland) Act 1970 together, it is clear, that 'as the title to [that] Act suggests' it is designed to cover homeowners, not companies who own residential property. Accordingly, for the pre-action requirements to apply to the property, it must be used as a home by a homeowner; occupier or other entitled resident. The Sheriff stated that the legislation is designed for situations where a person's home may be imperilled, so it therefore does not include corporate borrowers granting security over residential property within their ownership.

In addition, section 11 of the Homelessness etc. (Scotland) Act 2003 requires notice of any calling up, or the fact that proceedings for re-possession have been commenced in respect of a dwelling house or 'land used to any extent for residential purposes' to be given to the relevant local authority in the form required by Regulations. This provision affects residential landlords (but not local authorities) who seek to recover possession of property which they have let, and heritable creditors who take steps to call up any security where all or part of the security subjects is used for residential purposes.

Section 25 of the Conveyancing and Feudal Reform (Scotland) Act 1970 entitles a selling creditor to sell the property either by private bargain (a sale normally concluded as outlined in previous chapters) or by exposure to sale (sale by public auction). It imposes a duty on the selling creditor to advertise the sale and to take all reasonable steps to ensure that the price at which the property is sold is the best that can reasonably be obtained. There are now no defined rules for advertising, but the approach previously set out for advertising of a sale under a bond in the Conveyancing (Scotland) Act 1924 is generally still used as a rule of thumb.

---

60 Section 24 of the Conveyancing and Feudal Reform (Scotland) Act 1970.
61 [2015] SCEDIN 58.

Those rules provided that advertisements had to be placed:

(i)   if the property is in Midlothian in a daily paper published in Edinburgh;

(ii)   if the property is in Lanarkshire in a daily paper published in Glasgow; and

(iii)   if the property is elsewhere in Scotland in a daily newspaper published in Scotland circulating in the district where the property is situated and in one newspaper (ie a local paper that may be weekly or twice weekly) circulating in the district and published in the county where the property is situated (or in an adjacent county).

The frequency of advertisement required was: where the sale is by public roup, one advertisement a week for three consecutive weeks and where the sale is by private bargain, one advertisement a week for two consecutive weeks.

If your client is purchasing a residential property from a heritable creditor in possession (and note that this applies to commercial properties where a part is residential), then, in addition to the certified copy calling up notice, (ie a copy of it, on which the creditor's solicitors have written a certification that it is a true copy of the original) you will also need to see:

- the section 24 decree;
- if the property has been voluntarily surrendered, copies of the relevant statements and any supporting evidence necessary to give the purchaser comfort this has been properly documented; and
- a copy of the notice served under section 11 of the Homelessness etc (Scotland) Act 2003.

For commercial properties, calling up on its own will be sufficient to entitle the creditor to take possession and sell the property.

When acting for a purchaser buying from a heritable creditor in possession acting under the power of sale, you should ask to see copies of the advertisements certified as to date of publication by the newspaper publisher (where this has been done). Advertisement in the property lists of the local SPC is generally regarded a sufficient to comply with the advertisement requirement. The relevant SPC will be asked to certify that the property was so advertised.

Provided the requisite procedures have been followed, sale by a heritable creditor will result in the standard security and all other heritable securities and diligences ranking *pari passu* (equally) with, or postponed to, that security being disburdened on registration of the disposition in favour of the purchaser. Where the property is affected by a prior security, the registration of a disposition will not affect the rights of the creditor in that security, but the creditor who has effected the sale will have the same right as the debtor to redeem that prior security. In practice, a postponed ranking creditor is unlikely to bother with calling up his security and selling the property unless there is a prospect of some repayment of the debt owed to him, which will mean having to satisfy the sums due to the prior ranking security holder first. In that event the creditor will be entitled to a discharge from the prior security holder to clear the title. Section 27 of the Conveyancing and Feudal Reform (Scotland) Act 1970 sets out the priority in which the proceeds are to be applied (see para 4.11).

8.18.4 Sellers under a Bond and Disposition in Security

It would now be extremely rare for an old-style bond and disposition in security to be the current document securing a property to a heritable creditor, since no new bonds of this type will have been capable of being created after 29 November 1970. Prior to the Conveyancing and Feudal Reform (Scotland) Act 1970, the rules of sale under a bond and disposition in security were strict, in that the sale had to be by public auction, and certain rules of advertisement had to be strictly followed. Section 69 of the Abolition of Feudal Tenure etc (Scotland) Act 2000 now applies the rules relating to assignation, variation, discharge and calling up of standard securities contained in sections 14 to 30 of the 1970 Act to any heritable security granted before 29 November 1970 (except securities constituted by way of *ex facie* absolute disposition[62]) (see also para 8.22.2).

8.18.5 Trustees in Sequestration (Bankruptcy)

Sequestrations of individuals are governed by a statutory code set out principally in the Bankruptcy (Scotland) Act 1985 as amended by various

---

62 From time to time you might still come across a security that was constituted by way of *ex facie* absolute disposition. Such securities can either be discharged under section 40 and Schedule 9 of the Conveyancing and Feudal Reform (Scotland) Act 1970 or by way of reconveyance.

enactments, and in particular Part 1 of the Bankruptcy and Diligence etc. (Scotland) Act 2007 (BAD Act 2007) and the Bankruptcy and Debt Advice (Scotland) Act 2014. Different arrangements apply depending on whether the bankruptcy commenced before 1 April 2008, between 1 April 2008 and 31 March 2015, or from 1 April 2015. There are detailed Notes for Guidance by the Accountant in Bankruptcy[63] in each case, which should be closely read by anyone practising in this field.

The legislation relating to bankruptcy in Scotland is quite a tangle. The good news is that the legislation is to be consolidated. The Bankruptcy (Scotland) Bill was introduced on 2 November 2015. Once enacted, it will consolidate the Bankruptcy (Scotland) Act 1985, the Bankruptcy (Scotland) Act 1993, Part 1 of the Bankruptcy and Diligence etc. (Scotland) Act 2007, Part 2 of the Home Owner and Debtor Protection (Scotland) Act 2010, the Bankruptcy and Debt Advice (Scotland) Act 2014, the Protected Trust Deeds (Scotland) Regulations 2013 and other related enactments.

The procedure, in summary, is that a trustee in sequestration will be appointed by the Sheriff, on application by a creditor or a trustee acting under a trust deed, or by the Accountant in Bankruptcy on application by the debtor. Prior to 1 April 2008, an interim trustee would be appointed and that appointment would be followed by the appointment of a permanent trustee. Since invariably, the interim and permanent trustee was the same person, and that person was usually the Accountant in Bankruptcy, the two-tier appointment was dispensed with under the BAD Act 2007. An interim trustee may still be appointed before the sequestration is awarded by the Sheriff, to protect the assets of the debtor, provided either the debtor agrees or the petitioner can show cause why an interim trustee should be appointed. A trustee must be a qualified insolvency practitioner and must have given a written undertaking that they will act as interim trustee in the sequestration.

The date of sequestration is either (i) the date on which sequestration is awarded, where the application for sequestration has been made by the debtor or (ii) where sequestration is being sought by a creditor or a trustee acting under a trust deed, the date (or if more than one, the first date) on which the Sheriff grants warrant to cite the debtor.

63 See www.aib.gov.uk/guidance/notes-guidance.

The Sheriff Clerk must send a copy of the court order making the award of sequestration to the Register of Inhibitions 'forthwith'[64], so that this will be disclosed in any search in the Personal Register. Where the Accountant in Bankruptcy awards the sequestration, he must send a copy of that determination for registration in the Register of Inhibitions.

Accordingly, the trustee's appointment consists of the court order (known as the act and warrant), or the determination of the Accountant in Bankruptcy. By virtue of the appointment, the whole of the debtor's property vests in the trustee on behalf of the creditors, as at the date of sequestration. You should ask to see a copy of the appointment. The name of the trustee in the disposition in favour of the purchaser must be the same as the name of the trustee in the order.

However, there is a 28-day moratorium[65], starting with the date on which the order or the determination is registered in the Register of Inhibitions, during which neither the trustee, nor any one deriving title from him or her can complete title to any of the debtor's heritable property. This takes much of the haste out of the 'race to the register' that might have ensued if the debtor had sold the property just before sequestration, but the purchaser had not managed to register his title until after the trustee's appointment. Formerly the trustee could, immediately on appointment, register his title to the property, by submitting the act and warrant to the Keeper if the property is registered in the Land Register, or by way of notice of title in the Sasine Register, as happened in the celebrated case of *Burnett's Trustee v Grainger*[66].

The appointment of the trustee will be confirmed at a statutory meeting of creditors, at which creditors also have the opportunity to select an alternative trustee. If there is no statutory meeting or no creditors attend, the original trustee will be the trustee.

The trustee cannot sell the property without the consent of the heritable creditors unless there are sufficient funds realised to pay off the heritable creditors. Further, the trustee cannot sell the property if a heritable creditor has already intimated an intention to sell[67]. Similarly, if the trustee intimates to the creditor his intention to sell the property first, the creditor is precluded from taking steps to enforce his security over that property.

---

64 Section 14 of the Bankruptcy (Scotland) Act 1985.
65 Section 17 of the Bankruptcy and Diligence (Scotland) Act 2007.
66 [2004] UKHL 8.
67 Section 39 of the Bankruptcy (Scotland) Act 1985.

In the case of a sale of a 'family home'[68], the consent of the bankrupt's spouse or civil partner, or of the debtor if he has no spouse or civil partner, is required. If consent is not given, the authority of the court will be required[69]. The court may, having regard to certain factors[70], grant or refuse consent or postpone granting consent for up to three years subject to conditions being met. 'Family home' in this context is defined in section 40(4)(a) of the 1985 Act.

On the expiry of three years from the date of sequestration the debtor's right or interest in the debtor's family home will cease to form part of the debtor's sequestrated estate and be reinvested in the debtor (without disposition, conveyance, assignation or other transfer)[71]. This period may be extended by the court on application by the trustee[72].

Title is deduced through the trustee's act and warrant.

8.18.6 A Trustee under a Trust Deed

A trust deed is a document signed by the bankrupt, under a voluntary arrangement with his creditors, without the necessity of a court order. The trust deed is, in effect, a conveyance by the debtor of all of the debtor's property to the trustee, for the benefit of the creditors. Trust deeds executed after 1 April 1986 are subject to Schedule 5 of Bankruptcy (Scotland) Act 1985. A 'protected trust deed' is one which has been given protected status under Act, ie it binds both acceding creditors (those that accede to the trust deed) and non-acceding creditors.

The trustee grants the disposition, deducing title through the trust deed, which will usually have been registered in the Books of Council and Session.

8.18.7 Liquidators of Limited Companies

The powers of a liquidator are detailed in Schedule 4 of the Insolvency Act 1986 and include the power to sell or otherwise dispose of property by public sale or private bargain. When a company is in liquidation, any

---

68 As defined in section 40(4) above.
69 See section 40, above.
70 Set out in section 40(2), above.
71 Section 39A, above.
72 Section 39A(7), above.

disposition of heritable property will normally be granted in the name of the company (in liquidation) and the liquidator, who will sign on behalf of the company. However, since 28 November 2004, a liquidator can deduce title to land belonging to the company under the provisions of section 3 of the Conveyancing (Scotland) Act 1924, or complete title by way of notice of title in terms of section 4, entitling the liquidator to grant the disposition in his own name. Notice of title would be required if the liquidator wished, for example, to grant a lease of property.

It is not usual for a liquidator to complete title to the property himself. It will be necessary to see and refer to the liquidator's appointment, by which he is empowered to intromit with the property of the company. The property remains vest in the company, unless the liquidator specifically asks for a court order for the company's assets to vest in him (although such a procedure is only exceptionally used). Title is deduced through the interlocutor ordering the winding up, if the liquidation is compulsory, and through the special resolution of the company, if it is voluntary. The interlocutor should have been registered in the Companies Register, and notified to the Accountant in Bankruptcy, as should the appointment of the liquidator.

In practice, the liquidation of a company is a matter of public knowledge, and is intimated in the *Gazette*[73] and in the public notice sections of newspapers, although in all cases of dealing with a limited company the searchers should be asked if there has been any liquidator, receiver or administrator appointed, or if the company has been struck off for failure to lodge documents (see para 7.4)

8.18.8 Receivers

A receiver (or administrative receiver) is an insolvency practitioner appointed by virtue of a floating charge, and his appointment will mean that the charge ceases to 'float' and becomes fixed on the assets of the company at the time of the appointment. Receiverships have become rare since they were effectively prohibited, except in a few quite specific circumstances by sections 72A to 72H of the Insolvency Act 1986. Receivers can only now be appointed under floating charges which were created before 15 September 2003, unless they fall into one of the restricted categories[74].

73 Available to search online at www.thegazette.co.uk/insolvency.
74 Set out in sections 72B–72H of the Insolvency Act 1986.

Where a receiver has been appointed, the floating charge should be carefully inspected to see that it has been properly executed and registered in the Companies Register within 21 days of the date of its execution. The floating charge and the appointment of the receiver, which should be registered in the Companies Register, and which should also be checked, are the receiver's authority to convey the property. Floating charges do not need to be registered in the Land Register or Sasine Register. The deed by the receiver runs in the name of the company (in receivership) and the receiver, but is signed by the receiver only.

8.18.9 Administrators

Holders of qualifying floating charges created after 15 September 2003 may appoint an administrator, but an administrator may also be appointed by a court order, or the directors of a company may pass a resolution to appoint an administrator. Anecdotally, it appears that administration is becoming the most popular method of corporate insolvency in cases of corporate distress. Whereas liquidation is a terminal process for a company, and receivership may or may not result in the survival of the company depending on what assets it has left after the floating charge holder has satisfied its crystallised claim, administration is more generally perceived as and can, indeed, often be used as, a corporate rescue process. In reality, administrations are used in a wide variety of circumstances, from cases where rescue is possible through to cases in which the company is to be effectively wound up.

As with receivership, the heritable property of the company does not vest in the administrator, and a disposition by an administrator runs in the name of the company (in administration) and the administrator, and is signed by the administrator. Title is linked through either the court interlocutor granting the administration order, the floating charge and the appointment by the charge holder of the administrator, or formal notice of appointment by the directors of the company, lodged in court. In each case the relevant link needs to be registered with the Registrar of Companies and the Register of Inhibitions. The administrator also needs to advertise his appointment in the (Edinburgh) *Gazette* and a relevant local newspaper.

Finally, it should be noted that a liquidator or administrator or receiver acts as an agent of the company.

8.18.10 Limited Companies

Most limited liability companies are reputable, especially public limited companies which have to submit to very rigorous scrutiny, although they can quite suddenly get into serious financial difficulties. Unfortunately, however, not all limited companies are sound. It should never be forgotten that the formation of a limited company is a way to escape unlimited personal liability in the event of liquidation. That said, the Insolvency Act 1986[75], may place personal liability for a company's debts upon directors of a limited company where, before the commencement of the winding up of that company, they knew or ought to have concluded that there was no reasonable prospect that the company would avoid going into insolvent liquidation.

A limited company is a legal person, separate from its owners, directors and shareholders, and therefore some specific checks are required when dealing with companies. The events of the recent recession have taught us, however, that no commercial organisation can be regarded as immune from financial difficulties. Much of the information you will need to know about the company will be available in the searches in the companies' registers (see para 7.4)

There are a number of aspects that you will need to check when purchasing, or taking security, from a limited company:

8.18.10(i) Incorporation and constitution

Has the company been properly incorporated and constituted? You do not want to buy property from a company that does not yet exist. This information will be evident from the search in the Companies Register. And as already stated, it is imperative to check that you have the exact name of the company absolutely correct.

8.18.10(ii) Foreign (overseas) companies

Is the company incorporated in the UK, which means it will be subject to the Companies Act 2006 and other company legislation and safeguards? Companies incorporated elsewhere are classified as foreign or overseas companies and this includes companies that are incorporated in the Isle of

---

75 See section 214.

Man and the Channel Islands, as well as the more obvious places such as the British Virgin Islands, the Cayman Islands and Gibraltar, for example.

When a foreign company is involved in a transaction, there is not necessarily the same type of protection available in relation to issues such as the capacity of the company to enter into the transaction. Normally, any judgement obtained against a foreign company will have to be enforced by action taken in the country of its domicile. If it transpires that the contract or transaction in question did not bind the company in the first place, remedies against the company might not be available.

To ensure that a foreign company has the relevant powers and capacity to transact, the usual procedure is to obtain an opinion letter from a lawyer qualified in the relevant jurisdiction. The content of such an opinion will vary, but the usual requirements are that it should confirm that the contract in question, when executed, will be legally valid and binding as an obligation on the company. Transactions where such an opinion letter would normally be sought are purchases/sales, security transactions, lease transactions (including assignations etc) and the grant of guarantees. Failure by solicitors to take steps to establish whether a document granted by a foreign company has been duly authorised within that country may amount to negligence[76].

Obtaining an opinion letter may take some time and there is usually a fee involved, so it is important to identify this requirement in good time and let the seller's solicitor know that you will require an opinion letter dated to coincide with conclusion of the transaction. The PSG has produced a style Foreign Opinion letter[77], accompanied by Guidance Notes explaining when it is required and what it should contain. Most firms of foreign lawyers routinely providing foreign company opinions will probably have their own preferred style of letter, in which case the PSG style can be used as a basis for checking that the basic component assurances are available.

8.18.10(iii) Dissolved companies

Is the company properly registered, and is it still registered, and not dissolved by the Register of Companies, without formal liquidation, in

---

76 See, for example, *Roker House Investments Ltd v Saunders & Another* [1997] EGCS137.
77 See www.psglegal.co.uk/foreign_opinion.php. This style is a 'kilted' version of the foreign opinion letter produced by the City of London Law Society.

terms of section 1000 of the Companies Act 2006. If you buy property from a dissolved company the disposition is invalid, and your only remedy would be to petition the court for a restoration of the company to the Register. That is not always possible or straightforward. Where a company has been dissolved any property or rights vested in it prior to its dissolution falls to the Crown as *bona vacantia* (see para 8.10.5). The Companies Search (see para 7.4) will identify that the company has been continuously registered, and that it is still in existence.

8.18.10(iv) Intra vires

It used to be necessary to check the memorandum and articles of association of the company, to examine what the objects and powers of the company were, to ensure that the transaction was *intra vires* (within the powers) of the company. Parties dealing with a company were presumed to be aware, or required to make themselves aware, of the purpose for which the company was set up. If a transaction was outside the company's objects (ie *ultra vires*), then the transaction was null and void. This issue has however eroded through successive legislation. Section 35 of the repealed Companies Act 1985 provided that where a person dealt with a company in good faith, a transaction entered into by the directors would be deemed to be within the capacity of the company. The Companies Act 2006 now permits companies to have unrestricted objects. Companies incorporated before 1 October 2009 can amend their articles of association to remove the objects clause, which would have the effect that nothing the company does will be *ultra vires*.

8.18.10(v) Floating charges

If the company has granted a floating charge, this will show up in a search in the Charges Register. For so long as it 'floats' over the property and undertaking of the company it will not concern a party transacting with that company, but if it 'crystallises' and 'attaches' to the company's property then it is in effect converted into a fixed charge over such property as is then owned by the company (see para 10.6.5). This happens when the holder of a floating charge appoints a receiver, but note that as a consequence of section 250 of the Enterprise Act 2002, the holder of a floating charge created on or after 15 September 2003 may not appoint or apply to the court for the appointment of an administrative receiver of property of the company. This provision has meant that the use of receivership has diminished over time. Receivers may still be appointed in floating charges created prior to that date. In practice where a floating charge exists, you should seek a Letter of Non Crystallisation (see paras 10.6.5 and 11.7.9). The seller's solicitor should obtain a letter from the holder of the floating charge confirming that it has taken no steps and does not intend to take steps to crystallise the charge. Ideally, the letter should also incorporate a specific consent to the sale of the property in question.

8.18.10(vi) Directors' warranties

There exists the possibility that a deed has been recorded adversely, affecting the company's property or that the company is no longer solvent. If these events have occurred recently, they have not been included in the search or advertised[78]. It is a practical problem, and one solution that used to be popular was requesting a personal warranty by the company's directors. In reality, such a warranty is rarely given and the practice of seeking such a warranty has died out somewhat over recent years. It is questionable what the value of such an undertaking would have been in any event, if the directors themselves were of limited means or became insolvent. No particular alternative practice has replaced the director's warranty but given the comparatively rare use of such warranties we have decided not to reproduce the style in recent editions[79].

In extreme cases, the parties might agree to consign the price until the title is registered without any adverse entries and then release the funds to the seller when a clear company search becomes available, but this is by no means routine. Company searches should be as up to date as possible at completion and deeds should be presented for registration immediately.

8.18.11 Partnerships

A partnership can be a separate legal entity in Scotland, as distinct from the partners of the firm[80]. While this was always the position, until 28 November 2004 it was not thought that a partnership could own land on its own account. Section 70 of the Abolition of Feudal Tenure

---

78 See *Gibson v Hunter Home Designs Ltd* [1976] SC 23.
79 A style of the form of warranty appears in the 5th edn, para 8.32.
80 Section 4(2) of the Partnership Act 1890.

(Scotland) Act 2000 provides that a firm may own land, if it has separate legal personality. How much this option is used in practice is unknown. Normally, the partners of the firm will hold title to the property as trustees for the firm. Under section 5 of Partnership Act, every partner is an agent of the firm and the other partners for the purposes of the business of the partnership. As such, they may bind the firm and the partners, unless they have no authority to do so. Of course, the actings of a partner is excess of his authority can be later ratified by the other partners. Section 6 of the Partnership Act provides that the firm and all the partners are bound by an act or instrument relating to the business of the firm and done or executed in the firm name or in any other manner showing an intention to bind the firm, by any authorised person. If a partner acts when he has no authority to do so, the firm and the other partners may still be bound, unless the third party dealing with the partner knew either that he had no authority for the act, or neither knew nor believed the partner to be a partner.

Note that there is no public register of firms, which will normally be constituted by a private partnership agreement (although there is no requirement that there has to be a written agreement). It would not be usual to be allowed to inspect the partnership agreement, which will invariably contain confidential information about the constitution of the firm. The law of partnership in both Scotland and England is the subject of a comprehensive joint review by the Law Commission and the Scottish Law Commission: *Report on Partnership Law*[81]. As with most publications by the Scottish Law Commission, this Report is a rich source of information on the current law.

8.18.12 Limited Partnerships

A limited partnership is a particular type of legal entity constituted under the Limited Partnerships Act 1907, and not to be confused with Limited Liability Partnerships (see para 8.18.13 below). Although governed by the Limited Partnerships Act, limited partnerships are also subject to the provisions of the Partnership Act so far as not inconsistent. Limited partnerships were quite often used in farming or agricultural tenancies until the law changed[82].

---

81 Scot Law Com 192.
82 See section 72 of the Agricultural Holdings (Scotland) Act 2003 and *Salvesen v Riddell* [2013] UKSC 22.

A limited partnership will have one or more 'general' partners and one or more 'limited' partners. Conceptually the idea behind a limited partnership was to allow investment in an entity without necessarily being subject to all the liabilities of that entity. So the general partner (or general partners) will have liability for all of the obligations including the debts of the partnership, while limited partners will not have liability beyond their initial stake. So, for example, in an agricultural tenancy, the general partner will be the farmer running the day-to-day operation and usually living on the farm, while the limited partner will be the owner of the land, but otherwise not involved in the farm business.

All limited partnerships have to be registered with the Registrar of Companies, and are issued with a certificate of registration which provides evidence of the existence of, and date of registration of, the limited partnership.

8.18.13 Limited Liability Partnerships

More akin to companies than partnerships, but benefiting from elements of both, limited liability partnerships established under the Limited Liability Partnerships Act 2000 are bodies corporate and, as such, have separate legal personality. On incorporation, particulars of the LLP must be registered with the Registrar of Companies, who will again issue a certificate of incorporation of the LLP confirming its name and allocating a registered number containing the date of incorporation. The name of the LLP must end with the words 'limited liability partnership' or 'LLP'. Many legal and other firms of professionals have taken advantage of the benefits of the limited liability of these entities and incorporated as LLPs since the introduction of the 2000 Act.

8.18.14 Power of Attorney

A power of attorney is a mandate granted by a person who, for any reason is either unable to, or chooses not to, deal with their affairs either temporarily or permanently, in favour of another person or persons known as the 'attorney'[83]. The power of attorney must contain an exact specification

---

83 Typical reasons include illness or absence abroad or, in the case of companies and commercial organisations such as banks, for convenience.

of the act or acts that the attorney is permitted to carry out. Unlike a will, no powers are vested in the attorney by law. Accordingly, if the power of attorney does not give the attorney power to sign a disposition of heritable property, for example, then no such power exists and the power of attorney is valueless for that purpose. Consequently, where a deed is granted by an attorney, the solicitor should ensure that the power of attorney authorises it.

A power of attorney may either in broad terms empower the attorney to do literally anything, or it may in particular terms, empower the attorney to perform only specific acts, such as to sell a property. An example of such a power is as follows:

'I, (name and designation), CONSIDERING that

(i) I am about to be absent from the United Kingdom and temporarily absent abroad and

(ii) to facilitate the management and sale of (specify property to be sold), owned by me (the "Property") it is convenient that I should grant a Power of Attorney.

THEREFORE I appoint (name and designation) as my Attorney with full power:

1 to enter into any agreement for the sale of the Property;

2 to sign all conveyances and other documents relating to the sale on my behalf,

3 from the proceeds of sale to discharge any standard security or other form of security in connection with the Property;

4 to sign any documents related to the Property;

5 from the net free proceeds of sale, to settle all expenses legally incurred in connection with the sale; and

6 generally to do whatever in his discretion my Attorney may think expedient for enforcing, carrying out and settling the said transaction;

And I further grant to my said Attorney power to employ the firm of (name and design) to attend to the legal matters arising from the sale of the Property;

And I further authorise my Attorney to institute on my behalf, pursue to finality, defend, compromise, all and any suits or actions, disputes or differences arising from the execution of these presents or otherwise affecting me or my property;

And I ratify and confirm and promise to ratify, allow and confirm all and whatever my Attorney lawfully does or causes to be done by virtue of this Power of Attorney without prejudice always to my right to demand just account and reckoning with me for the whole intromissions of my Attorney in terms of this Power of Attorney; And I declare that this Power of Attorney will subsist until it is recalled in writing; And I consent to registration of this Power of Attorney for preservation: IN WITNESS WHEREOF.'

Section 71 of the Law Reform Miscellaneous Provisions (Scotland) Act 1990 provided that powers of attorney granted on or after 1 January 1991 would continue, despite the supervening incapacity of the grantor. This provided a tremendous administrative advantage, as it no longer meant that a *curator bonis* had to be appointed in those circumstances. However, section 15 of the Adults with Incapacity (Scotland) Act 2000 repealed that provision, and provides that a continuing power of attorney executed after 2 April 2001 will be valid only if it contains a statement which clearly expresses the granter's intention that the power be a continuing power.

The Adults with Incapacity (Scotland) Act 2000 places all continuing powers of attorney under the supervision of the Public Guardian[84]. Regulations have been made to ensure that these continuing powers are signed and used properly[85].

When a deed is signed under a power of attorney, it is signed by the attorney. The narrative of that deed may either (a) run in the name of the attorney narrating the power and state in the testing clause that it is signed by the named attorney or (b) run in the name of the constituent without mentioning the power and state in the testing clause that it is signed by the attorney on behalf of the constituent by virtue of the power, which is then specified. Either method may be used (although (b) is more usual, and is

---

84 See www.publicguardian-scotland.gov.uk.
85 For example, the Adults with Incapacity (Certificates in Relation to Powers of Attorney) (Scotland) Regulations 2001.

recommended) but, in both cases, the power of attorney must be produced with the deed to authorise the signature of the attorney.

The attorney should sign their own name. Although there are instances of the attorney signing the name of the constituent, followed by the words 'per his attorney Jane McGregor', it is not thought that this is competent under the Requirements of Writing (Scotland) Act 1995. That Act provides that where a person is subscribing or signing under a power of attorney on behalf of the granter, references in the 1995 Act are to be construed as references to subscription by 'that person' (ie the attorney, not the granter) of the document[86].

ROADS AND ACCESS

8.19 It is essential to ensure that the property possesses suitable rights of access. This can be particularly relevant for rural property. Without proper rights of access, ownership of land is useless. Some years ago, it was reported in the press that a couple had bought a farmhouse (for £130,000) from a bank who had repossessed it. Unfortunately, however, the original owner still owned a small strip of land controlling access, and was not prepared to sell it. This is usually termed a 'ransom strip'. The owner of such a strip may be able to command a premium price for a comparatively small area of land.

In 2004, an area of land in West Lothian extending to nine square metres was sold for over £1 million as it was required by a developer to obtain access to its site. The retention of this strip was a deliberate 'clawback' strategy by the owner to share in the profits of the subsequent planning permission for a multi-million pound development on the site.

Depending on circumstances, the common law may imply a servitude right through necessity to prevent a property from being 'landlocked' or by implication, such as rights implied on severance of a property from adjoining property over which rights are necessary for the proper enjoyment of the property. Such rights can be extremely difficult to ascertain, and it is risky to rely on this as a satisfactory alternative to adequate and effective rights of access.

The problem is not so acute in the city and towns where, generally, but not universally, the streets have been adopted for maintenance by the local

86 Section 12(2).

authority. In that case anyone can use the road not only to exercise a public right of passage over it, but also to access private property that abuts it.

8.19.1 Adopted Roads

As part of your due diligence examination you should ask to see a Property Enquiry Certificate confirming the status of the roads *ex adverso* (on the other side of) the property (see para 7.2.3). If the road is not adopted for public maintenance, you need to check that the titles contain the necessary rights of access. In certain circumstances it may be relevant to ask for a roads adoption plan, which can be provided by the local authority or the PEC providers, on which is marked the precise extent of the adoption. This can be relevant to ensure there are no ransom strip issues, or gaps where part of the access route is not actually adopted. For residential property in urban areas, this is probably unnecessary, but you may need to exercise your judgement in circumstances where it may be appropriate to request a plan.

Where the road is a public road, the roads authority (either the local authority or Transport Scotland) maintains the road, and is responsible for any accident that occurs through lack of maintenance[87]. Provided access to the property is by an adopted (or public) road that abuts the property, you need make no further enquiry.

8.19.2 Private Roads

Where the road remains private, and this can be found even in towns and cities, there may be no-one with a specific obligation to maintain the road. Even though there is still a public right of passage, all that this imposes on the owner or owners is a requirement not to obstruct that right of passage.

In *Johnstone v Sweeney*[88], two individuals were injured on a towpath over which there was a public right of way, by falling into a gap on the towpath that had been covered over by a metal plate. An action was brought against the owner of the towpath, in which it was contended that the owner had a duty of care to pedestrians to ensure that the towpath was safe. The action was dismissed on the basis that the only duty to users of

---

87 See sections 1 and 2 of the Roads (Scotland) Act 1984.
88 [1985] SLT (Sh Ct) 2.

the public right of way was to take such care as in all the circumstances was reasonable, but there was no duty to make the public right of way safe for pedestrians.

It is important to distinguish between a public right of passage, which entitles the public in general to pass along the route[89], and a private right of access over the route in favour of the adjacent property.

In new developments, if a road is built to a standard that is sufficient for adoption by the roads authority for maintenance, the builders can, and invariably will, ask the roads authority to take over the maintenance of the road (see para 8.20). Owners of existing private roads seldom do this, usually because the cost of making the road up to an adoptable standard would be prohibitive and they lose control over who can use the road for access or parking.

8.19.3 Access to Rural Property

When buying rural property, it is more likely that some part of the access route to the property will be private road. The purchaser's solicitor must ensure that the purchaser will enjoy an unrestricted right to all necessary rights of access, and are not expected to pay a disproportionate amount of maintenance. Often, the road will be owned by someone else, such as the owner of a larger estate or the owner of surrounding agricultural land. In such cases, it would be usual to obtain a servitude right of access over the road. This right may be created by an express grant from the owner of the road, or might have been acquired by prescription. Prescription applies on the exercise of access over the road openly, peaceably and without judicial interruption for a period of 20 years[90].

It is sometimes overlooked by purchasing solicitors that prescription remains a perfectly valid way in which to acquire a right of access. It is as valid a right of access as one given by express grant, and, of course, it is now possible to add a prescriptive servitude to the Title Sheet of a property (see para 14.11.2(vii)). However, it should be remembered that a servitude acquired by prescription might be limited in its extent.

---

89 See definition of 'road' in section 151 of the Roads (Scotland) Act 1984.
90 See section 3 of the Prescription and Limitation (Scotland) Act 1973.

8.19.4 Increasing the Burden on a Servitude Right of Access

In addition, the owner of the benefited property[91] cannot 'increase the burden' on the burdened property[92], which often means that they cannot increase the use.

Generally, the 'rules' on not being able to increase the burden are more relevant when a servitude has been acquired by prescription, rather than by express grant. If the prescriptive use has been for access to a single dwellinghouse, then it is unlikely that the servitude will be good for using it to access a new industrial estate to be built at the end of the road, and new rights would need to be obtained or a different route found[93].

8.19.5 Express Grants of Servitudes of Access

Professor Halliday[94] suggests that when an express servitude of access is created, words such as the following should be used:

'The servitude has been granted with reference to the present state of the property and shall not be extended to apply to any substantially different condition thereof.'

Such words (perhaps in more modern language) would clarify that the parties intend to restrict the use. Alternatively, when acquiring land for development, the purchaser might want any servitude rights granted to acknowledge that the type and volume of use might increase over time.

Grants of servitudes should be drawn very carefully, and in the case of any ambiguity will be construed *contra proferentem* (against the party who seeks to rely on it). When examining the terms of a servitude, you should ensure that it is sufficient to provide the access your client requires to the property. A lesser right will not include the greater right, but the greater will usually include the lesser. In other words, a servitude right of access for pedestrian purposes will not permit the exercise of vehicular access but, conversely, the right to access using vehicles will normally permit access on foot as well.

---

91 Or the 'dominant tenement', in the traditional language of servitudes.
92 Traditionally, the 'servient tenement'.
93 On increasing the burden in a servitude, see the excellent work by Douglas Cusine and Roddy Paisley *Servitudes and Rights of Way* (1998) W Green & Son.
94 *Conveyancing Law and Practice in Scotland* (1996) 2nd edn, W Green, 1996 vol II, 20.11.

Servitudes are subject to servitude conditions which are for the benefit of the burdened property[95]. One of the principal legally implied servitude conditions is that a servitude should be exercised *civiliter* (so as to cause the least disturbance or inconvenience). Unless the provisions of the grant of servitude provide otherwise, the owner of the burdened property is not under any obligation to maintain the burdened property, he merely has to permit the servitude to be exercised, and he should not obstruct the way. In the absence of express provision, the benefited owner is not obliged to maintain the burdened property, or remedy defects which might affect the exercise of the servitude, but do not damage or put the property at risk. In practice, there will often be express provision about responsibility for the maintenance of a road, often, where the use of the road is shared, stated to be apportioned according to the extent of the respective uses. Maintenance 'according to user' is a common, if unhelpful, expression, as it would be rare for actual volume or frequency of use by several parties to be monitored in any detailed way[96].

ROADS IN NEW DEVELOPMENTS

8.20 The position with newly or recently constructed properties is rather different. Construction of the roads within a development, whether residential or commercial, takes place during the construction of the whole development. While access roads are formed early on in the development to allow access, some roads may not be finalised until later on in the development as, during the course of construction, heavy construction traffic may also be using these roads, and the finishing touches will usually only be added near the end, when the surface is not going to be damaged by heavy plant. This means that the purchaser of a new house or a commercial unit that is being constructed within a development could be buying property before the roads are completed and, certainly in that case, before the roads are maintained by the roads authority. In some commercial developments, although roads and other infrastructure is constructed by the developer, the decision is taken to keep the roads private and not to apply for public maintenance, but this is the exception rather than the rule. The usual practice in residential developments is for the builder to form

---

95 As to which, generally, see Cusine and Paisley *Servitudes and Rights of Way*, Chapters 13 and 14.
96 See Cusine and Paisley *Servitudes and Rights of Way*, para 14.68.

the road to the appropriate roads authority standard and, on completion, to apply to the roads authority to take over liability for future maintenance.

To be able to construct roads within a development, the developer must obtain a roads construction consent from the roads authority[97].

When acting for the purchaser of a newly or recently constructed property you must ask to see the roads construction consent to check that it: (a) exists and is current; (b) applies to the property your client is purchasing; and (c) does not contain any conditions that would impact directly on the property your client is purchasing. This will usually mean reviewing the plan relating to the consent (which may be large unwieldy item), showing the roads to which the consent relates.

Many years ago, it was common in cases where the road was incomplete at the time of purchase of a dwellinghouse in a development for the purchaser to make a retention from the purchase price to meet a proportion of the liability for completion of the roads, in case the developer failed to do so. This was particularly relevant since the cost of the house usually includes a provision for making up the roads to the necessary standard by the developer. Section 17 of the Roads (Scotland) Act 1984 instead requires a road bond to be provided by the developer to guarantee the cost of completion of the roads within a development of dwellinghouses. The road bond can either be the deposit with the roads authority of the requisite sum of money or a bond lodged with them. The amount of the deposit or the bond must be sufficient to meet the cost of constructing or completing the road to such satisfactory standard. So you should ask to see a copy of the road bond at the same time as requesting a copy of the construction consent, if these are not already with the title package that has been exhibited to you.

SERVICES

8.21 Just as a property needs to be adequately served by access rights, if there are buildings constructed on it, the property will require connection to services including supply of water, gas, electricity etc and drainage. The existence of these services, particularly water and drainage, should be checked as part of your investigations. In most cases of urban property,

---

97 See section 21 of the Roads (Scotland) Act 1984.

confirmation of connection to mains water and mains drainage will be disclosed in the Property Enquiry Certificate (see para 7.2.5). In rural or even semi-rural areas, the position might not be so straightforward and the titles may need to be consulted to ascertain the position (see para 6.18.3).

8.21.1 Water

Scottish Water is the entity responsible for ensuring supplies of water and provision for sewerage through the public water supply system and the public sewerage system respectively. Not all properties are directly connected to the public water supply. You might find that a property obtains its water supply from a private source such as a stream, reservoir or well, particularly in remote, rural areas. That stream, reservoir or well will often be located on land belonging to someone else, and transmitted to the property by private pipes. In these cases, the title needs to be checked to ensure that adequate servitude rights exist, both in relation to the water supply and the pipes, which might run through several lands in different ownership. Typically, what you might see is a split off title from a much larger estate, in which rights over the lands retained are granted in favour of the property being conveyed. Where pipelines cross the land of another property, make sure that there are clear servitude rights for running the pipe and a right of access to the pipe, should it require maintenance, repair or replacement.

Private water supplies are by their nature subject to the vicissitudes of the weather and quantity may not be guaranteed. Enquiries should be made of the seller as to availability of the water supply. You should also check that the terms of the grant include that the supply may not be interfered with.

It is also necessary to check on water quality and potability. Private water supplies are subject to environmental legislation and public health considerations. You need to ensure that the water supply is wholesome and drinkable, which may involve having water quality tests conducted.

8.21.2 Gas, Electricity and Telephone

The relevant utility companies should take care of the servitude rights (or wayleaves) for cables and pipes needed for transmission of these supplies, under statutory powers. These will not, therefore, normally be of concern in most transactions of existing urban properties. You should note the route and other details of wayleaves for cables and pipes leading to other properties, which must not be disturbed by digging, or obstructed in any way, for example, by building over the wayleave area.

8.21.3 Drainage

In many rural areas, drainage is not to a mains drain, but to a private septic tank and soakaway field. Any infrastructure would have to be surveyed to ensure that it is in order, and capable of treating the volume of waste generated by the property it serves. The main issue is to ascertain the exact location of the septic tank and any soakaway field. If they are located under other property than the subjects being purchased, then servitude rights will be required.

You should check that the requisite rights have been granted, both in relation to locating the septic tank and any soakaway field and for all pipes and connections that lead from them through adjoining property to the subjects being purchased. The responsibility for emptying septic tanks rests with Scottish Water to whom request can be made.

The discharge of effluent is controlled by the Scottish Environmental Protection Agency (SEPA). The Water Environment (Controlled Activities) (Scotland) Regulations 2011 (CAR) require all 'controlled activities' to be authorised either by general binding rule, registration or licence. Septic tanks with discharges to land via full soakaway are controlled activities and therefore require registration. General provision regarding private drainage arrangements should have been covered by the missives (see para 6.18.3). Accordingly if consent is required to be obtained retrospectively this should be identified at an early stage. If the septic tank discharges were authorised prior to 1 April 2006 by a Control of Pollution Act 1974 (CoPA) consent, that consent will have been transferred automatically into CAR and will be deemed as registered. However, many more septic tanks, that did not require registration under CoPA, require registration under CAR. Either way, you probably need to see a piece of paper.

The CAR regime is more likely to affect residential purchases, but there may also be implications for developers if their activities will result in abstraction or impoundment of water bodies or if, for example, they carry out works and need to re-divert or culvert a burn.

DISCHARGE OF SECURITIES

8.22 Bearing in mind the valuable protection afforded by section 41(1) of the Conveyancing and Feudal Reform (Scotland) Act 1970, it is important to check discharges which have been recorded within a five-year period. You should therefore check: (1) the details of the discharge – does it fully discharge the obligation that was created? (2) the form of the discharge; (3) the execution of the discharge; and (4) the recording of the discharge.

As to the form of the discharge, the required forms are:

8.22.1 Discharge of Standard Security

The form is provided in Schedule 4 (Form F) to the Conveyancing and Feudal Reform (Scotland) Act 1970. This is a simple form. Many lenders have their own 'style' of discharge, although most are a variation on the theme of this statutory style. Note, also, that with mergers, takeovers, changes of name, dissolutions and acquisitions of many former high street lenders, many discharges will probably need to incorporate some form of deduction of title[98] from the original creditor in whose favour the discharge was granted to the current entity, or narration of name changes. The Keeper maintains an index of these changes of name or status in the Common Links Index, which is maintained by the Land Register intake section. This can be a useful source of information when you are trying to work out the connection between the original creditor and the current one.

8.22.2 Bond and Disposition in Security

The requirement to discharge an old bond and disposition in security can still arise occasionally. Section 69 of the Abolition of Feudal Tenure etc (Scotland) Act 2000 now applies the rules relating to assignation, variation, discharge and calling up of standard securities contained in sections 14 to 30 of Conveyancing and Feudal Reform (Scotland) Act 1970 to any heritable security granted before 29 November 1970, but not to a security granted by way of *ex facie* absolute disposition.

---

98 Although see section 101 of the 2012 Act and para 8.14.

8.22.3 *Ex facie* Absolute Disposition in Security

Again, over time, the requirement to 'discharge' this type of security will diminish. It took the form of what looked, to all intents, like a disposition that transferred the property, and was granted by the owner of the property to the lender. That is the principal clue – that the disponee is a bank or building society. Usually, it would be accompanied by an unrecorded back letter narrating the circumstances of the lending. This covert security may be discharged in one of two ways:

8.22.3(i) The traditional method

A disposition back to the owner of the subjects, which takes the form of an ordinary disposition but which sets out in the narrative that the original disposition to the lenders was truly in security of a loan of £X which has now been repaid, and it is now 'right and proper' that the subjects be reconveyed. The lenders grant warrandice only from their own facts and deeds.

8.22.3(ii) The shorter statutory method

A short form of discharge, analogous to discharges (a) and (b)[99]. This has the effect (on being recorded) of disburdening the land and vesting the land in the person entitled to it.

Generally, it makes little difference which method is used. One school prefers to discharge securities in the manner in which they were created (*unumquodque eodem modo dissolvitur quo colligatur*); the other school prefers the shorter modern method. There is, however, a (very eminent) view[100] that unless it is the original 'debtor' in whose favour the discharge is being granted, the correct approach is by way of reconveyance.

8.22.4 Deed of Restriction or Disburdenment

A security may also be partially discharged on part payment, or restricted to any part of the land, freeing the remainder for sale. This is done by way of a Deed of Disburdenment or Deed of Restriction[101] (see para 10.3.5).

---

99 Section 40 of and Schedule 9 to the Conveyancing and Feudal Reform (Scotland) Act 1970.

100 Halliday *Conveyancing Law and Practice* 2nd Edn Volume 2 (W Green 1997), para 49–22.

101 For the appropriate forms, see Schedule 4 (Forms C and D) to the Conveyancing and Feudal Reform (Scotland) Act 1970.

EXAMINING A REGISTERED TITLE

8.23 Much of the previous commentary on examination of title (paras 8.6 to 8.22) applies to examination of Sasine titles (although not exclusively). Once the title to a property has been registered in the Land Register, a considerable amount of the steps referred to become redundant and, in theory at least, the process of title examination should become a lot easier. The reality of many land registered titles is, however, somewhat different. Perhaps not for the majority of urban, residential properties, but you should be in no doubt that there are skills to be acquired in examining and interpreting registered titles, too.

8.23.1 Land Certificates and Title Sheets

Although the procedure of examining title is very much the same (you are looking to identify owner, extent, rights and obligations etc), the recording of title deeds in the Sasine Register is replaced by registration of interests under the 1979 Act and rights under the 2012 Act in and to the property on the Title Sheet. The contents of the Title Sheet, which is permanently based at the Land Register, were formerly reproduced in a 'Land Certificate'[102] if the title was registered under the 1979 Act. The Keeper issued the Land Certificate following completion of the first registration of the property, and thereafter updated it on subsequent dealings that required the production of an updated Land Certificate.

Under the 2012 Act, Land Certificates are no longer produced. Instead, you will receive an e-mail that provides a link to a 'landing page' where you can view a PDF copy of the updated, or newly created, Title Sheet. In both cases, however, it is important to note that any Land Certificate or PDF copy of the Title Sheet is only a snapshot of what was in the Title Sheet at the time. To an extent, therefore, as soon as a Land Certificate was issued, or the PDF created, it will immediately become out of date. Any dealings subsequently added to the Title Sheet will not be apparent. It is important, therefore, to ensure that the Legal Report you receive is dated either from the date of any Land Certificate or of the PDF of the Title Sheet, and there is no gap.

---

102 Recognisable by its jaunty yellow covers.

8.23.2 The Title Sheet

The Title Sheet (and, where applicable, any corresponding Land Certificate) contains all the essential parts of the title, in four sections: a property section, a proprietorship section, a securities (formerly known as charges) section and a burdens section.

In theory, the fact that all redundant details from the prior Sasine titles are stripped out, and the remainder is clearly displayed, should make examining a registered title much easier. The reality often is that for any title that is less than straightforward, it can be unclear what the true position is. This is particularly so with tenement titles where the 'steading' method of registration (where the property is identified as 'lying within' an area shown outlined in red on a plan) can leave the title examiner in some doubt about what exactly is included in the title.

In *North Atlantic Salmon Conservation Organisation v Au Bar Pub Ltd*[103], a small area lying to the rear of the Au Bar pub in Edinburgh was used for alfresco dining and drinking. The right to do so was disputed by adjoining owners, but the title to the Au Bar pub was described as being within the land edged red on the title plan – which red outline included the disputed area. 'Within' does not mean 'comprises' of course. In this case there was no unequivocal evidence that either property was the clear owner, but the adjoining proprietor's entitlement was held to be more consistent with the original feuing plan[104].

Much of the checking as to validity required with Sasine titles is unnecessary with a registered title. Titles that are registered in the Land Register benefit from the 'curtain principle' which means that this examination should not be necessary. Nor would it be necessary to 'look behind' the Title Sheet to the underlying Sasine title where the title has been registered with full indemnity under the 1979 Act. Accordingly a purchaser is entitled to rely on the accuracy of a Title Sheet created under the 1979 Act, even when it is, in fact, inaccurate.

---

103 [2009] GWD 14-222.
104 As a matter of interest (especially for those of you interested in alfresco dining) for some time after the case, the area to the rear of Au Bar was 'off limits'. It is now being used again, so we assume that some 'accommodation' was subsequently arrived at by the parties.

The position has changed significantly under the 2012 Act. The Keeper's 'Midas touch'[105] no longer applies to titles registered after 8 December 2014. When a 1979 Act title is transferred after 8 December 2014, it will be subject to the Keeper's warranty (see para 2.6.2) rather than the Keeper's indemnity, although the fact that the title was formerly indemnified is relevant.

Titles that enter the Land Register for the first time under the 2012 Act, while no longer subject to the 'Midas touch', nonetheless benefit from the state guarantee of Keeper's warranty, that the title sheet is accurate. If that proves to be incorrect, meaning there is a breach of warranty, then a person who suffers loss as a result, may be entitled to compensation. The starting point for consideration of 2012 Act titles should therefore be no different – a state guarantee and reliance on the Register continue, albeit in an altered form (see para 2.6.2).

It is also possible that, during the transfer from the previous Sasine title onto the Title Sheet, errors or omissions can occur. While it ought not to be necessary to revert to the Sasine title for clarification, experience shows that sometimes this is the only way to ascertain the true position.

Subject to getting updated searches, the Title Sheet (or Land Certificate, where there is one) contains all information relevant to the title to the property (as at the relevant date) and it should therefore be a much simpler task to note the title. Where the copy Title Sheet (or Land Certificate, if there is one) is reasonably short, it is perfectly sensible to take a copy and highlight portions of it and add notes in the margins. With lengthier copy Title Sheets (or Land Certificates), it can be quite easy to misread the provisions, given that the details of writs are often presented in a continuous block of text. More recently, it seems that the Keeper is prepared to display detail in indented paragraphs and sub-paragraphs. Care should be taken to read through the details carefully and note the terms separately in the same way as you would for a set of Sasine titles (see *Willimse v French*[106] and para 8.5 *et seq.*).

---

105 Under section 3 of the 1979 Act, the Keeper possessed the power to guarantee ownership, irrespective of any defects in the underlying deeds.
106 [2011] CSOH 51.

8.23.3 Registers Direct

It is becoming more common for elements of the title examination of registered property (in particular) to be conducted using Registers Direct.

Registers Direct is the Keeper's internet-based service, which provides access to information from the Land Register, Sasine Register, Personal and other registers direct to your computer. It is primarily used by solicitors and other professionals, local authorities, Revenue Scotland and HMRC, the police, and fraud prevention authorities etc. Users must register to be given secure login details to access the records.

Solicitors frequently use Registers Direct for research and information gathering during examination of title, or to find out who owns a property or piece of land, or what title conditions affect a client's property etc. Access to information in the Land Register allows you to view any one of the four Title Sheet sections, (property, proprietor, burdens and securities), as well as being able to look at the Title Plan for any particular registered property.

It is also possible to check records of title to properties in the Register of Sasines. The Search Sheet shows transactions affecting a title in chronological order as well as the parties to the deeds, a description of the property, the price paid and the date of recording. The Presentment Book, which shows details of any pending deeds awaiting recording can also be viewed.

Using Registers Direct affords the advantage of ready access and speed. If your firm signed up to use Registers Direct, you can search the records in real time and see details of what is currently on the title sheet of any registered property. However, it is important to bear in mind that the information obtained from Registers Direct is not guaranteed by the Keeper. When you obtain information from Registers Direct it will state:

> 'This is a (Quick) Plain Copy which reflects the date the Title Sheet was last updated. [It does not have the evidential status of an (Office Copy) Extract]'[107].

While, latterly, information from Registers Direct was covered by Keeper's indemnity under the 1979 Act, the Keeper's warranty does not extend to Registers Direct under the 2012 Act. To be able to rely on the

---

107 More recently, the words in square brackets do not appear.

information from the Title Sheet, you must examine either an original Land Certificate or an Extract of the Title Sheet that can be obtained direct from the Registers.

Clearly, therefore, although obtaining information from Registers Direct can be useful and convenient, it should not be relied on for examining and certifying title. If no Land Certificate or Extract of the Title Sheet is available for inspection, you should ask the seller's solicitors to obtain an Extract for your examination. It is also good practice to print and retain a copy of what you have viewed on Registers Direct, in case of any discrepancy between what you have examined on Registers Direct and what is disclosed by the Land Certificate or an Extract[108] (and see para 8.23.4).

8.23.4 Extracts and Plain Copies

A few words need to be said about the status of what you are examining and the reliance you can place on it.

Titles recorded in the Sasine Register are not covered by state guarantee. When examining a Sasine title, you must use your own skill, knowledge and experience to work out whether the title is valid, marketable, and can be relied on. The original deeds, with a recording stamp impressed on them, are just that – the original deeds – and although quick copies can be obtained, the original deeds need to be examined for validity. Often, quick copies of burden writs are all that you will be able to inspect. Many of these will relate to a much larger area than the property your client is buying and the whereabouts of the original will be unknown. This is normal and acceptable practice, but they are just copies. If any original writs are untraceable, an extract can be obtained and may be relied on as though it was the original deed itself. Often, with older deeds, the plan may be missing or any plan that there is may be uncoloured or difficult to decipher. Such are the challenges of Sasine title examination.

Titles registered in the Land Register before 4 December 2014, are valid and can be relied on, simply by virtue of the act of registration[109]. Those titles benefit from the state guarantee of indemnity, unless, of course, there

---

108 Anecdotally, discrepancies have been known to occur.
109 Section 3 of the Land Registration (Scotland) Act 1979.

is an exclusion of indemnity noted on the Title Sheet. A Land Certificate is an extract of the Title Sheet for the property, and is the equivalent of the original. If the principal Land Certificate is lost, then an Office Copy can be obtained from the Keeper. This has the same evidential status as if it was the original, and can be relied on.

Issuing Land Certificates has been discontinued since the 2012 Act came into force. Instead, once the title is registered, you receive a PDF copy of the Title Sheet. This does not have evidential status. For that, you must obtain an extract of the Title Sheet, which will be accepted, for all purposes, as evidence of the contents of the original title sheet[110]. If you want a copy of anything that is in the application record (eg an advance notice) on which you can place the same level of reliance, then a certified copy can be obtained from the Registers.

So, best evidence of the title you are examining is either: original deeds or extracts, a Land Certificate or Office Copy of it, or an extract of the Title Sheet.

As mentioned above, a Registers Direct printout does not carry any evidential status. It will, however, be covered by the Keeper's liability in respect of extracts, information and lost documents etc. under section 106 of the 2012 Act. This entitles a person to compensation from the Keeper, for loss suffered due to information as to the contents of the Register issued by the Registers being incorrect.

This is not an absolute liability, however, and the Keeper is not liable for loss, if that could have been avoided by the person making the claim if they had taken certain reasonable measures, or if their loss is too remote, or non-patrimonial. It is, therefore, not clear whether any loss that arises because a person relied on a Registers Direct printout, which turned out to be incorrect, would definitely be covered by section 106 in all cases. It could be deemed that that person should have obtained an extract, or an Office copy, on which reliance could be placed, and that would have been reasonable for them to do, because it was known that a Registers Direct printout was not covered by Keeper's warranty. While this may be a slightly paranoid assessment, an extract can be obtained at a modest cost (£30) and puts the matter beyond doubt.

---

110 Section 105 of the Land Registration etc. (Scotland) Act 2012.

8.23.5 Keeper's Indemnity and Keeper's Warranty

A key element of the system of land registration in Scotland is that a person who suffers loss is entitled either to indemnity (for titles registered under the 1979 Act) or warranty (for titles registered under the 2012 Act) from the Keeper. For full details of what indemnity and warranty cover, see para 2.6.

Accordingly, one aspect of title examination of a registered interest, that does not apply to Sasine titles, is the possibility of qualifications to or exclusion of the Keeper's indemnity, or limitation of or exclusion of Keeper's indemnity, when some defect is apparent from the documents submitted for registration. An obvious example is a disposition *a non domino*, which, if accepted for registration under the 1979 Act, will be excluded from indemnity, the defect being that the granter has no title. There are few instances where such qualifications, exclusion, or limitation should be ignored. Even if you think you know the reason, you should raise it with the seller's solicitor. Where appropriate, you should ask their proposals for having it removed or dealt with in some other way. This is also a matter that needs to be reported to your client and, in some circumstances, will be a reason to withdraw from the purchase.

8.23.6 Charges and Securities

If a Land Certificate discloses any registered charges then there will also be a separate Charge Certificate which you should also obtain and examine. Often the original Standard Security will be attached to the Charge Certificate so that you will be able to check its terms, if appropriate. Under the 2012 Act, the charges section was renamed the securities section. Fixed securities affecting the property will be shown in this section, and there is no separate title sheet or Certificate.

ENCUMBRANCES

8.24 A new definition appears in section 9 of the 2012 Act – 'encumbrance' in the context of the burdens section of the title sheet. Encumbrance includes title conditions, such as real burdens and servitudes, long leases (and if the Title Sheet relates to a lease, long sub-leases), a public right of way, core paths and generally any other encumbrance that can be registered under the terms of an enactment, such as section 75 agreements. The concept of 'overriding interests' is absent from the 2012 Act. The Keeper must enter any encumbrances in the burdens section of the title sheet, which looks very similar to the burdens section of a 1979 Act title sheet.

REAL BURDENS

8.25 The title to an individual property may contain a number of conditions that operate to limit or restrict what can be done on the property, regulate the liability for maintenance of parts of the property, facilitate the use of, access to, or servicing of the property, or entitle others to use the property or parts of it for access or servicing. These real burdens and servitudes need to be checked carefully and, where appropriate, their terms reported to your client.

The subject of real burdens affecting property in Scotland has undergone a revolution in recent years. The abolition of the feudal system under the Abolition of Feudal Tenure etc. (Scotland) Act 2000 and the introduction of a new statutory regime of creation, enforcement, variation and discharge of real burdens under the Title Conditions (Scotland) Act 2003, coupled with the transformation of the law of the tenement by the replacement of the old common law rules with a new statutory regime under the Tenements (Scotland) Act 2004, has left even the most experienced practitioner struggling to come to terms with all of the implications and effects of the new legislative structure. Ten years on, there are still many aspects of this triumvirate of Acts that perplex, and frustrate, many practitioners. While you might expect that replacing the old complicated common law rules with a new statutory regime ought to simplify the position, the opposite appears to be most practitioners' experience. More than ten years into the post feudal world, there is still precious little case law on interpretation of this legislation. The Lands Tribunal, its powers significantly increased by section 90 of the Title Conditions (Scotland) Act 2003 have used the greater flexibility afforded to them by section 100 of the 2003 Act to apply the terms of some of the legislation in the course of applications for variation or discharge of title conditions. In a significant number of cases, this is largely a matter of balancing the different factors which they are entitled to take into account in terms of section 100, with reference to the particular facts and circumstances of the application before them.

The feudal system was abolished on 28 November 2004 which is the same day on which the majority of the provisions of the 2003 Act and the Tenements (Scotland) Act 2004 came into force; this date is referred to as the 'appointed day'. There was a perception in some quarters in the days immediately following feudal abolition, that all feudal burdens had been effectively wiped out, and the realisation that this was far from the truth came as a bitter disappointment to many solicitors. In fact, the realisation dawned that not only were many burdens, and feudal ones at that, still in force, but also that there appeared to be some new enforcement rights that we hadn't had to consider before[111]. Many solicitors were left yearning for the good old feudal days.

There are a number of ways in which feudal title conditions may have survived abolition. Therefore, when examining title, whether Sasine or land registered, it is necessary to consider each of the burdens in the title to identify whether or not they are still 'live', although surviving feudal abolition does not necessarily mean that the burden is valid and enforceable. Many burdens contained in titles are unenforceable for reasons other than feudal abolition, as we shall see. Not all burdens in titles will have been created in feudal deeds, of course, and those created in non-feudal deeds are unaffected by feudal abolition. So, there are a number of considerations to bear in mind when examining the burdens in the title, and in determining whether they are acceptable to the purchaser, or have the potential to have an adverse effect on what the purchaser plans to do with the property.

Not all burdens will fall to be treated in the same way and so there might be a different outcome for each burden in your title. In considering each burden it is very much a process of elimination that you must work though to determine whether the burden remains in force and who has rights to enforce it[112]. You should also check, of course, that the provision is a real burden and not some other condition such as a servitude or a servitude condition.

The key thing to remember about a burden imposed on a property is that it is only of concern if someone has the right to enforce it. In other words, for every burdened property there has to be a benefited property (unless the burden falls into one of the narrow post feudal categories of

111 Section 53 of the Title Conditions (Scotland) Act 2003.
112 For burdens created before the advent of dual registration.

'personal real burdens' (see para 8.25.4(ii)). In addition to the owner of the benefited property having title to enforce a burden, however, other interested persons also have such title, including a tenant or liferenter in the benefited property or a non-entitled spouse of an owner of the benefited property with occupancy rights in that property.

Rights of enforcement consist of two elements: title to enforce and interest to enforce. Both elements must exist for enforcement to be possible. The following paragraphs provide you with a guide to how to find out whether there are parties with title to enforce a burden, because they own (or have some other relevant right to) a benefited property. See para 8.25.8 for how interest to enforce affects the position, because, even if title to enforce can be determined, interest to enforce must also be established.

8.25.1 Is the Burden a Feudal Burden?

The first elimination criterion is whether the burden has, in fact, been extinguished by feudal abolition. Clearly the first check is to ascertain if the burden was created in a feudal writ (eg a Feu Disposition, Feu Contract or Feu Charter). If it was not, then there are other tests to apply, but extinction as a consequence of feudal abolition is not one of them. However, if the burden was created in a feudal writ, there are some specific points to check to determine if the burden has survived or been abolished.

8.25.2 Feudal Burdens that have already been Extinguished

It was not uncommon, prior to abolition, for a party wishing to remove a feudal burden from his title to approach the feudal superior for a discharge or waiver of the burden or burdens in question. Accordingly, if before the appointed day, the superior had granted a waiver of the burdens, and the superior was the only person entitled to enforce the burdens, then they will already be extinguished. The waiver will be disclosed in the titles or by a search. Unfortunately, what was often overlooked in these cases was that sometimes other parties – usually co-feuars – also had rights of enforcement. It was rarely the case that these co-feuars were also approached to waive the burdens and, as feudal abolition only extinguished the superior's right to enforce, if the third parties had **express** rights to enforce the burdens before the appointed day, these rights would survive feudal abolition. Such rights might have been expressed as a *ius quaesitum tertio* (third-party right) in favour of other feuars in the estate or development, or merely referred to rights to enforce burdens against the other feuars. All **implied** rights of enforcement were extinguished by section 49 of the Title Conditions (Scotland) Act 2003; although new implied enforcement rights are created for co-feuars and co-disponees by sections 52 to 56 of the 2003 Act, nothing in those sections will revive a right of enforcement waived or otherwise lost prior to the appointed day.

8.25.3 Feudal burdens which Automatically Survive Abolition

There are several categories of burden, which even if feudal, were not extinguished. As part of your title examination you will need to consider the provisions of the burden and identify if it falls into any of these categories:

8.25.3(i) Facility or service burdens

If a feudal burden is a 'facility burden' or a 'service burden' then it was automatically preserved on the appointed day[113]. A 'facility burden' is a real burden which regulates the maintenance, management, re-instatement or use of heritable property which constitutes a facility of benefit to other land. Examples of this are: a common part of a tenement; a common area for recreation; a private road; private sewerage; and a boundary wall[114]. A 'service burden' is a burden imposed on one property relating to the provision of services, water or electricity perhaps, to other land[115]. The party with rights to enforce these types of burdens will be the owner (or owners) of the land or properties that benefit from the facility, or that is provided with the services.

8.25.3(ii) Rights relating to minerals reservations

It should be remembered that the minerals in or under land, if reserved, constitute a separate tenement of ownership and consequently, any reservations of minerals in a feudal deed are not affected by feudal abolition. The former superior (or any person to whom the former superior

---

113 Section 56 of the Title Conditions (Scotland) Act 2003.
114 See sections 122(1) and (3), above.
115 See section 122(1), above.

may have conveyed the minerals) is the owner of the minerals, and any conditions which relate to the reservation which generally relate to the manner in which the reservation may be exercised, remain in force. A typical feudal minerals reservation clause would be:

> 'There is reserved to (a) the British Coal Corporation (now the Coal Authority, of course) the whole coal, mines of coal and other minerals, if any, in or under the Feu and interests therein now vested in the said British Coal Corporation and (b) the Superiors the whole minerals, metals and substances other than those vested in the said British Coal Corporation in so far as the Superiors have right thereto as also reserving to the Superiors full power to work, win and carry away the said other minerals but without entering on the surface of the Feu, on payment to the Feuars for all damage to the surface of the Feu or the buildings and other erections erected or to be erected thereon that may be occasioned by the Superiors' working, winning and carrying away of the said other minerals as such damage shall, failing agreement, be ascertained by two arbiters, one of whom to be named by the Superiors and the other by the Feuars or by an oversman to be named by the said arbiters in case of their differing in opinion.'

A distinction, however, needs to be made between these typical minerals reservation conditions, and any burdens imposed on the property title, which may be said to be for the benefit of the minerals title (usually restricting the use of property title to the surface of the land in some way, such as preventing building within a certain distance of actual mine workings). Burdens of this type in a feudal writ would have to have been preserved prior to the appointed day in the same way as other feudal burdens as described in para 8.25.4 below[116] by way of a notice registered against the title to the surface of the land[117].

8.25.3(iii) Rights relating to salmon fishings

Title to salmon fishings can also be held as a separate tenement, in a manner similar to title to minerals. Conditions integral to such title, and burdens on other land for the benefit of such title, fall to be dealt with in a

116 Section 18(7)(c)(i) of the Abolition of Feudal Tenure (Scotland) Act 2000.
117 For a detailed commentary on this point, see Robert Rennie: *Minerals and the Law in Scotland* (2001) EMIS Professional Publishing, para 1.10.

similar manner where the fishings have been reserved in a feudal title. So, while conditions that are an essential part to the right of salmon fishing – such as rights to use the shore – will be unaffected, burdens imposed on the other land, which is intended to benefit the fishings title, would have to have been preserved by registered notice[118].

8.25.3(iv) Sporting rights

The definition of real burden in Abolition of Feudal Tenure (Scotland) Act 2000 specifically excludes sporting rights, and accordingly excluded such rights from the immediate effects of feudal abolition. However, these rights, which include freshwater fishing and shooting of game (but exclude salmon fishings which are a separate tenement in land) had to be preserved before the appointed day in a different way. Instead of being preserved as a real burden, the former superior had to preserve the rights as a separate tenement in land by registering the appropriate form against the title to the land to preserve the sporting rights as a separate tenement[119]. If this was done, the right will be disclosed on the property title or in a search against it.

8.25.3(v) Manager burdens

A 'manager burden' is a condition in the title that permits a person to be, or appoint (and dismiss), a manager of related properties. Although such burdens existed before feudal abolition they are specifically defined in section 63 of the Title Conditions (Scotland) Act 2003. They often appear in some form or another in Deeds of Conditions relating to developments, and typically provide that the developer controls who is to be the manager in charge of coordinating maintenance and repairs. This type of burden – essentially personal in nature, could not be preserved by the preservation notice procedure described in para 8.25.4 below. Instead section 63 provides that this power will survive feudal abolition, but only for a limited period, which for the majority of property types is five years from the date of registration of the deed in which the burden was constituted (or three years in the case of manager burdens relating to sheltered or

---

118 Section 18(7)(c)(ii)) of the Abolition of Feudal Tenure (Scotland) Act 2000.
119 See section 65A, above.

retirement housing developments). That means that, in effect, feudal manager burdens have expired. The only exception in the case where the manager burden has been imposed in terms of section 61 of the Housing (Scotland) Act 1987, on the purchase by a council house tenant exercising his right to buy, where the power will endure for 30 years.

New manager burdens created after the appointed day are not feudal, of course, but are subject to the same time limits. In these cases, it should be noted that the burden is essentially a time limited monopoly to be or to appoint the manager, but is not the actual appointment of the manager.

8.25.3(vi) Maritime burdens

These are burdens in favour of the Crown, which relate to the seabed and foreshore, and where created in a feudal deed, were automatically preserved, to continue to be enforceable by the Crown following feudal abolition[120].

8.25.4 Feudal Burdens that have been Preserved

If the burden does not fall into one of the categories of automatic preservation referred to in para 8.25.3, the next step is to ascertain if the feudal burden has been preserved.

8.25.4(i) Nominating a new benefited property

The Abolition of Feudal Tenure (Scotland) Act 2000 (as amended) set out a series of preservation notices that a superior could complete and register, prior to the appointed day, against the title of the burdened property, and through which the superior could (usually) nominate other land which he owned to be the benefited property entitled to the benefit of enforcing the burden, in lieu of the superiority enforcement right. Over 3,000 such notices were registered, the vast majority of which were registered in terms of section 18 of the Abolition Feudal Tenure (Scotland) Act 2000, which provided for a number of qualifying criteria for preservation, the most common of which was that the superior could nominate as the benefited property, other land on which there was a permanent building used wholly

---

120 Section 60 of the Abolition of Feudal Tenure (Scotland) Act 2000.

or mainly for human habitation or resort, and located at some point within 100 metres of the burdened property.

8.25.4(ii) Personal real burdens

In addition to the ability to nominate a new benefited property, certain categories of feudal burden could be preserved as 'personal real burdens' which would nominate a person or body to be the person entitled to enforce the burden after the appointed day. These include conservation burdens, enforceable by conservation bodies or Scottish Ministers, economic development burdens, enforceable by Scottish Ministers or a local authority, and healthcare burdens, enforceable by an NHS Trust (until repealed) or Scottish Ministers. Feudal rights of pre-emption and redemption could be preserved either by nomination of a new benefited property or as a personal pre-emption or personal redemption burden, as the case may be. Maritime burdens, which were automatically preserved, (see para 8.25.3(vi) above) are also a form of personal real burden in favour of the Crown.

8.25.4(iii) Preservation notices

To be preserved, the notice had to be registered against the burdened property before the appointed day and so will be disclosed in the title or in a Legal Report. However, even though a preservation notice was registered prior to the appointed day and appears on the Register, this does not mean necessarily that the notice has been validly made. The Keeper was specifically excused from having to verify that the notices were correct, that the requisite procedure (eg as to service of the notice) had been followed, or that there was a building on the re-allotted property within 100 metres of the burdened property and so on. There might be an error in the description of the property, or in identification of the burden, or even in the way the notice is executed, which might render the notice invalid, and capable of challenge. How likely or prevalent errors or inaccuracies in the notices may be is impossible to quantify, and some errors may be such that they are not fatal to the validity of the notice. It might be possible, however, to challenge a notice and refer the matter to the Lands Tribunal who will look into the facts and circumstances surrounding the procedure and/or terms of the notice. Consequently, it will be important in some cases where a burden has been preserved by notice, to check the terms of the notice itself, in case there is an opportunity to challenge the preservation of a burden that your client would prefer did not apply to the title.

8.25.5 Feudal Burdens Enforceable in Terms of New Implied Enforcement Rights

Establishing whether or not a party had a right to enforce a burden arising by implication was often a complicated business under the feudal system. Clarity, at least, was provided by section 49(1) of the Title Conditions (Scotland) Act 2003, which abolishes all previously arising implied enforcement rights. However, due to the requirement to protect the property rights of individuals or provide for compensation to be made where such rights are affected[121], it was necessary to replace the abolished rights with new statutory equivalents. Therefore, new statutory implied rights of enforcement were created[122].

Feudal burdens which do not fall into any of the categories described in paras 8.25.2 to 8.25.4 might still be enforceable under one of the implied enforcement right rules. The provisions also applied[123] to non-feudal burdens created prior to 28 November 2004, where the benefited property or properties had not been expressly identified. All burdens created after that date, unless they are personal real burdens, require not only to identify the benefited property but also, the terms of the burden must be registered against the title to that benefited property as well (dual registration) or, in the case of burdens that apply to a number of units in a community, the extent of that community has to be identified[124]. See para 9.11.6 regarding creation of community burdens.

In addition to the enforcement rights that arise by implication in cases of facility and service burdens, (see para 8.25.3(i) above) these provisions of the Title Conditions (Scotland) Act 2003 applied to three other principal categories of burden, where the benefited property or properties had not been expressly identified:

---

121 Article 1 of the First Protocol to the European Convention on Human Rights and section 29(2) (d), the Scotland Act 1998.
122 Sections 49, 50, 52, 53, 54 and 56 of Title Conditions (Scotland) Act 2003.
123 Until 28 November 2014.
124 Section 4, above.

(a) 'neighbour' burdens, where burdens have been imposed when part of a property is split off from a larger area. These burden types are no longer enforceable, unless preserved – see para 8.25.5(i);

(b) common schemes, where two or more properties are affected by the same or similar burdens; and

(c) sheltered or retirement housing developments.

8.25.5(i) Implied enforcement rights arising on subdivision

Where a real burden was imposed on a property before 28 November 2004 by the person conveying that property, which forms part of land they own, but the benefited property was not expressly identified in the deed creating the real burden, the implication was that the retained property would be the benefited property. This is the rule expressed in *J A Mactaggart & Co v Harrower*[125] and applies to properties conveyed by disposition only, not in a feudal deed. A typical example of this is where a person sells off part of their large garden, for the purpose of building another house on it. In the disposition, a burden is imposed on the garden prohibiting the erection of more than one house, and specifying that the house to be built must not exceed a particular height. Such provisions are clearly designed to preserve the outlook and amenity of the rest of the seller's property, but often that is not expressly mentioned in the deed. Section 49 of the Title Conditions (Scotland) Act abolishes these implied rights. Where the right to enforce has been created by subdivision of a property in this way, transitional arrangements provided that the right would be preserved for a period of ten years from 28 November 2004, during which period the benefited proprietor had the opportunity to preserve the right permanently, by registering an appropriate notice[126], failing which the enforcement right would be lost. It is understood that a total of 159 preservation notices were registered prior to expiry of the 10-year period on 28 November 2014. This will be a tiny fraction of the number of burdens that would be affected, so it is likely that thousands of this type of burden on the registers are now

---

125 [1906] 8 F 1101, 14 SLT 277.
126 Schedule 7 to the Title Conditions (Scotland) Act 2003.

unenforceable. It will now be possible to discount burdens that fall into this category, if there is no Schedule 7 notice registered against the title.

8.25.5(ii) *Implied enforcement rights arising in common schemes*

In situations where two or more properties are affected by the same or similar real burdens created prior to 28 November 2004, enforcement rights may have arisen due to the existence of a 'common scheme'. Burdens that affect common schemes in this way are now known as 'community burdens' (see para 9.11.6) which has the effect that each burdened unit in the common scheme is also a benefited property, so that obligations and enforcement rights are reciprocal. However, note that the rules relating to implied enforcement rights under common schemes do not arise in relation to rights of pre-emption, redemption or reversion.

There is no definition of 'common scheme' in the Title Conditions (Scotland) Act 2003, but the Explanatory Notes to the Act indicate that the 'new' implied rights of enforcement are based on the previous common law rules and also specify that 'Common schemes exist where there are several burdened properties all subject to the same or similar burdens'[127]. Given that the requirement for community burdens is satisfied where there are two or more properties affected (see para 9.11.6), it seems likely that 'several' in this case will mean 'two or more', particularly as the definition for new community burdens can apply to burdens imposed on two or more properties[128]. The burdens imposed on each of the properties in the common scheme must be either identical, largely similar (*Botanic Gardens Picture House Ltd v Adamson*[129]) or at least in some way equivalent (*Lees v North East Fife District Council*[130]).

Another indicator of the existence of a common scheme would be where the burdens come from a common source, for example: they have been granted by the same person, although this is not essential, and there is nothing specifically to this effect in Title Conditions (Scotland) Act 2003. Indeed, the Explanatory Notes to the Act specifically state that 'it will no longer be necessary for title to have been obtained from

127 Explanatory Note 234.
128 Section 25(1) of TC(S)A 2003.
129 [1924] SC 549.
130 [1987] SLT 769.

a common granter' and to that extent it diverges from the rules in *Hislop v MacRitchie's Trustees*[131] (see below). In reality however, it is more likely to be the case that the burdens in a common scheme will have been granted by a common author or its successors. So, for example, Lightyear Development Company Limited may sell off the first 20 plots in a development all with the same burdens, and then sell the remainder of the land to Dunvorlich Homes Limited who continue to convey plots using the same style documentation with the same burdens.

There are two categories of implied enforcement rights in common schemes. These are set out in sections 52 and 53 of the Title Conditions (Scotland) Act 2003. Sections 52 and 53 have proved to be problematic to solicitors, as it is not always easy to recognise or be sure of when a common scheme exists, or the extent to which enforcement rights arise.

The main distinction between these two sections is that in section 53 common schemes, the properties must be 'related properties', whereas for section 52 to apply, there need be no such relationship. Section 53 is new law and the definition of what constitutes related properties, although some examples are given in the Act, is not altogether clear. The 2003 Act itself says that whether or not properties are related properties is to be inferred from all the circumstances. So, to that extent, there is still a lot of guesswork involved in working out whether or not section 52 or section 53 will apply.

The definition of 'related properties' does provide some examples, but the list is illustrative and not exhaustive, and there is still only scant case law to refer to, although section 53 has been cited in several Sheriff Court and Lands Tribunal cases – not always in particularly helpful terms. Properties might be considered to be 'related' where:

(a) it is convenient to manage the properties together because they share some common feature, or an obligation for common maintenance of some facility;

(b) there is shared ownership of common property;

(c) they are subject to the common scheme in terms of the same deed of conditions; or

(d) they are flats in the same tenement.

---

131 [1881] 8 R (HL) 95.

However, even if a case does not fall within the illustrative examples in the definition, it may still be possible for third party enforcement rights to exist.

Section 52 resembles a recognisable law, in that it is more or less a restatement of the old common law rules concerning third party rights of enforcement (or *ius quaesitum tertio*), formulated in *Hislop v MacRitchie's Trustees*. For common scheme enforcement rights to exist under Section 52 there must be:

- notice, express or implied, in the title that there is a common scheme of burdens; and also

- nothing in the title that negates the creation or existence of the third party enforcement rights, such as the reservation to the superior to vary the conditions.

So at least with section 52, we have a better idea of what we are looking for, even although sometimes it is still tricky to recognise. Notice of a common scheme may appear in different ways. It may be apparent by virtue of the fact that a Deed of Conditions imposes the burdens on a number of units, for example a block of flats. Alternatively, there might be a deed in the title that imposes burdens, but it transpires that those burdens were imposed on a larger area of which the property that you are considering forms a part. The other parts of that larger area, which may also have been conveyed off in parts, are similarly burdened since they stem from the same original title of the larger area. Or the landowner might have individually sold off a series of plots of land or units, using Feu Dispositions to impose the burdens on a plot by plot basis. So while there is no common document containing those burdens, each of the individual conveyances contains similar title conditions. This technique was commonly used by local authorities when selling off housing stock, and is also common in sales of parcels of land in large estates.

Section 53, on the other hand is far more wide-ranging than section 52. On the face of it, it ought to be more straightforward – the properties have to be related properties and that relationship clearly has to be factual. So, for example, the properties may all share a common access road or be subject to the same common scheme because they are all subject to the same Deed of Conditions. Those, however, are the simple section 53 situations, because section 53 differs from section 52 in that there is no requirement for the title to contain notice of the existence of a common scheme for section 53 to apply. So, even if there is nothing apparent from the title, a common scheme may still be in place. Neither does the requirement that there be nothing negating the existence of a common scheme apply. The only qualifying condition for section 53 is the 'related properties' requirement. This makes section 53 extremely flexible and gives rise to the possibility that enforcement rights which did not exist before the appointed day, arise after that date.

Russel Properties (Europe) Ltd v Dundas Heritable Ltd[132] is one of the first cases to look directly at the application of sections 52 and 53, although in the event the court's scrutiny of these sections was not particularly rigorous. The case primarily concerned an opposed application for interim interdict, which is possibly why the consideration of the statutory provisions was less detailed.

The owners of a pub in the Westwood neighbourhood centre in East Kilbride planned to let the ground floor for a Tesco Express convenience store. Russel Properties owned other properties in the centre, and they objected to the Tesco proposal, based partly on the provisions in the pub title not to use the property except as a licensed public house and/or public restaurant without the written consent of the superiors.

There was no deed of conditions for the units in this centre – the titles all came from individual feu dispositions by East Kilbride Development Corporation with burdens in each. The superior no longer had any rights, so this seemed a suitable candidate for sections 52 or 53 enforcement rights.

Section 52 was considered first, but rejected because the deeds contained provision for the superiors to waive it, thus precluding the creation of third party rights. That left section 53, with the requirement that the properties in the common scheme have to be 'related'.

The judge decided that there was no common scheme and consequently no enforcement rights, even though the other non-residential buildings in the centre contained similar conditions. The judge had also considered the titles to the car parks at the centre, which were in quite different terms: all building was prohibited, and a maintenance obligation was imposed which was declared to be enforceable by the other proprietors in the development

132 [2012] CSOH 175.

as well as by the general public. The judge decided that these differences were too great to indicate 'an underlying sense of equivalence' and so the required mutuality for reciprocal rights of enforcement to arise was absent.

It must be questioned whether this was the right outcome, and the judgement does not seem to have given a sufficiently detailed consideration of the circumstances in which a common scheme could arise, so as a contribution towards clarifying section 53, it disappoints.

It is worth bearing in mind that sections 52 and 53 are not complementary – they stand separately, so that even if a section 52 enforcement is out of the question because of some negatory wording in the title, section 53 may apply, since such wording will have no effect on those enforcement rights.

In *MacKay v McGowan*[133], a building restriction prohibiting the erection of new buildings or extensions without superior's consent was contained in Feu Dispositions of neighbouring properties on the island of Tiree, one: the former school building, that had been converted into a house and the other: the old school house, attached to the school building. Both titles, granted by the local authority to former tenants under the right to buy legislation, contained identical burdens.

The owner of the old school house objected to the proposal by the owner of the former school to build a house on ground included in the title. Section 52 rights were found not to apply in this case, due to the negating effect of the superior's ability to waive contained in the wording.

It was agreed that the neighbour had, however, acquired enforcement rights by virtue of section 53. Tantalisingly, the Tribunal does not expand on the grounds on which it was considered section 53 applied. It seems the parties accepted that section 53 applied without argument, although it appears likely that because the properties were conjoined – in effect semi-detached – that section 53(2)(b) 'there being shared ownership of common property' would apply.

One other key distinction between sections 52 and 53 is that, for section 52 to apply, the deed by which the burdens are imposed must have been registered before the appointed day. In section 53 common schemes, at least one of the deeds imposing the burdens in a common scheme must have been registered before the appointed day, but it will also apply to

133 [2015] SLT (Lands Tr) 6.

burdens imposed on properties within the common scheme, by deeds registered after the appointed day, and that even if the deed imposing the burden registered after the appointed day does not make any express nomination of the benefited properties. This exception to the requirement to identify the benefited property in any burden created after the appointed day is allowed by section 57(2) of the Title Conditions (Scotland) Act 2003.

8.25.5(iii) Examining and reporting on title affected by common scheme implied enforcement rights

Where the conditions in sections 52 or 53 are satisfied, the other properties in the 'common scheme' will have third party enforcement rights in respect of the burdens. Conversely, of course, the property your client is purchasing will have enforcement rights in relation to the burdens against the other properties. But how do you identify what those other properties are? The short answer in some cases is that you may never be able to say with absolute certainty precisely what other properties are involved. Often the only way to identify whether other properties have enforcement rights under a common scheme is to examine the title to those other properties, because unless there is a common deed in which the burdens were imposed, such as a Deed of Conditions, it is only by looking at the title of surrounding properties that you will be able to discover whether they contain the same or similar burdens.

But it is not always possible to be totally certain, even if you do conduct an examination of the titles of neighbouring properties, that you have identified **all** of the neighbouring properties that are similarly affected and therefore form part of the common scheme. In cases where the area affected by the burdens is a larger area identified in an earlier deed, when the title is in the Land Register, it will often not be possible to ascertain from the title sheet what area is affected, and you would need to obtain a copy, with a plan of the original deed itself, to be able to identify where the other properties are. If the copy plan is poor or unclear, the position may remain unascertainable.

Trying to identify all of the other properties in a common scheme can sometimes be a rather hit and miss affair. Clearly, the consequences for your client in terms of the time it takes to conduct investigation of other titles and the cost involved could be quite unacceptable. If you are working to a fixed fee for the transaction, it could be simply impractical to conduct these investigations, while, on the other hand, a purchaser will be unwilling to pay for additional researches only for the outcome to be inconclusive.

It is just as likely that the individual plots could have been sold off without the benefit of all burdens being located in a single Deed of Conditions. Each deed may have contained its own burdens and therefore, again, there may be many other titles which are similarly burdened, but it can be harder to spot given that there is no requirement for notice in the title. For example, there might be no common deed, but simply reference to maintaining areas along with others having right to them. That could mean different properties have enforcement rights against each other depending on the nature of the relationship. Another example would be where only some of the units might use a particular road, while another different combination of units might use a car parking area. The enforcement rights in those circumstances will be different.

Where the position is unclear it can help to consider the burdens in the context of the whole facts and circumstances surrounding the title and the property, including its location and physical features. Ideally, a site visit to the property should be conducted. Realistically, however, particularly if you are on a fixed fee, or the property is located in a remote area, the practicalities of conducting a site visit may be difficult. Do try to visit the site if you can though. If you can't, it is a good idea to see if you can locate the property on Google Earth and Google Streetview, which can give you a good idea of what the actual physical features on the ground look like. A restriction on building more than four storeys in height may not be considered too problematic if it becomes clear when you view the property that all the buildings round about it that are likely to be subject to the same title restriction are all ten storeys high.

It will be necessary, therefore, to find an appropriate balance for how far your investigations need to go. This will depend on: (a) the importance of the burden to your client and whether it might potentially prevent or inhibit them from doing what they want to do on the property eg a prohibition in the title against using the land for residential purposes, when your client is purchasing it with a view to converting the buildings into houses, would be a major consideration; and (b) the relevance of the burden: for example old burdens that are concerned with the construction of roads that are no longer applicable can be ignored, and obligations relating to maintenance of roads and drains etc that are now the responsibility of the local authority or Scottish Water are also no longer relevant.

It is often the case that the final position cannot be stated with complete accuracy, and reporting on title conditions may often have to be caveated to the extent that it is impossible to say with certainty who has rights to enforce and what measure of success they may have in securing those enforcement rights in the case of a breach.

For possible options to resolve these issues see para 8.35.

8.25.6 Negative Servitudes

The ten-year deadline referred to in para 8.25.5(i) (subdivided properties) also applies to the preservation of negative servitudes. These are (or more correctly, were) servitudes that prevent something from being done on the servient tenement, such as prohibiting building (*non aedificandi*) or building above a certain height (*altius non tollendi*) or building but so as not to obstruct light (*luminibus non officiendi*). On 28 November 2004, such servitudes were automatically converted to negative burdens[134] (and it is no longer competent to create any new negative servitudes[135]) and became 'converted servitudes'. Again, such rights (of the benefited owner) had to be preserved by notice (against the burdened property) within ten years, or again the right would be lost. It is not known how many negative servitudes might exist since they did not always have to be registered to exist. In modern times such restrictions were more likely to be created as negative burdens.

8.25.7 Compensation for Development Value Burdens

The Abolition of Feudal Tenure (Scotland) Act 2000 Act did not allow superiors to preserve feudal development value burdens, (essentially a clawback arrangement payable where land sold by the superior for a nil or nominal amount was subsequently developed in contravention of a burden restricting such development) but did permit them to register a

---

134 Section 80 of the Title Conditions (Scotland) Act 2003.
135 Section 79, above.

notice entitling the former superior to claim compensation in the event of a breach of the relevant title conditions[136]. However, one of the conditions for entitlement to such compensation is that there is or was a breach of the title condition either during the period of five years immediately before the appointed day, or during the period of 20 years after the appointed day. If the breach occurred before the appointed day, the claim for compensation had to have been made not more than three years after the appointed day (ie by 27 November 2007), so such breaches can now be disregarded. If the breach occurred after the appointed day, the claim for compensation must be made not more than three years after the date of the breach. Only about 50 of these notices were registered prior to feudal abolition, so in the unlikely event that you come across one, there will be a flag on the title about it.

8.25.8 Interest to Enforce

A key consideration in the enforceability of burdens however, even if you have established that they are still in existence, and who has title to enforce them, is whether or not those parties also have interest to enforce. The right to enforce consists of two elements: title to enforce and interest to enforce, and both must be present for the burden to be enforced. This might be the final stumbling block for enforceability of a burden, and should always be an element in your deliberations when looking at title conditions.

Interest to enforce is not a new concept. It existed prior to the appointed day but was often overlooked, largely because, prior to feudal abolition, the interest of a feudal superior to enforce a burden was implied, and it tended to be forgotten that others might have interest to enforce, too. The concept of interest to enforce is enshrined in section 8(3) of the Title Conditions (Scotland) Act 2003, which sets out two independent criteria for interest to enforce: a 'material detriment' test, and entitlement to payment in respect of some cost.

A person will have interest to enforce the burden if in the circumstances of any case, failure to comply with the real burden is resulting in, or will result in, material detriment to the value or enjoyment of the person's ownership of, or right in, the benefited property.

---

136 Section 33 of the Abolition of Feudal Tenure (Scotland) Act 2000.

Interest to enforce also exists in the specific case of burdens that relate to payment of some cost: where the real burden is an affirmative burden (ie an obligation to do something) that consists of an obligation to defray, or contribute towards, some cost, a person will have interest to enforce it, if that person seeks (and has grounds to seek) payment of, or in regard to, that cost.

So, after considering the terms of the burden and surrounding circumstances, you should apply the interest to enforce test. Would the persons who have, or who might have, title to enforce have interest to enforce? Even if you can be fairly sure that there is title to enforce, the nature of the burden and other circumstances might mean that those parties who have title to enforce have a harder time showing that they have interest to enforce. The case law shows us, from what was originally a fairly high threshold, it now seems settled that the bar for interest to enforce is set quite low.

The burden in question in the first two interest to enforce cases was the same – the requirement for dwellinghouses in a development to be used only as private dwellinghouses for occupation by one family only. But they had different outcomes. In the first case, *Barker v Lewis*[137] the property was being used as a bed and breakfast business, interst to enforce was not established. In *Kettlewell v Turning Point Scotland*[138], however, neighbours were able to establish interest to enforce against the proposed use of one of the houses as a residential care home for up to six unrelated individuals with social disabilities.

Since then, there have been several Lands Tribunal decisions, where it is increasingly clear that the threshold for interest to enforce is very low. In *Franklin v Lawson*[139], the Lands Tribunal set out their view on the standard for interest to enforce, which has become their current settled position: where there is an identifiable element of detriment which cannot be disregarded as just insignificant or of no consequence, then the test of materiality can be met. So, instead of being at opposite ends of the spectrum, 'material' just needs to be slightly more than 'immaterial'.

Accordingly, the cautious solicitor examining title and reporting to his client, should start from the point of view that the burden is enforceable

---

137 [2008] SLT (Sh Ct) 17.
138 [2011] SLT (Sh Ct) 143.
139 [2013] SLT (Sh Ct) 81.

and then try to establish through various tests and checks whether or not it actually is enforceable.

8.25.9 Construction of the Feudal Terms

Although many burdens were extinguished by feudal abolition, as we have seen, many feudal burdens survived. That poses another difficulty in interpreting what feudal terms and phrases in these burdens now mean. Section 73 of the Abolition of Feudal Tenure (Scotland) Act 2000 provides for substitution of certain feudal terms with their post-feudal equivalent, in other primary or secondary legislation passed before feudal abolition, in any document executed before the appointed day and in the Land Register issued before that day. So, for example, vassal becomes owner, *dominium utile* means the land or ownership of the land, references to feuing will be construed as disponing, and so on. References to a superior are replaced with references to the party who is now the owner of the benefited property, where the burden has been re-allotted onto land that is to be the new benefited property by way of preservation notice, and becomes a 'neighbour' burden[140] (see para 8.25.4) or, in the case of facility burdens and service burdens, by the owner of the land which benefits from that facility[141].

Not all references to superiors can be replaced in this way, however, and in the case of enforcement of community burdens, including those which arise under sections 52 and 53 the expression 'superior' will not convert to all of the owners in the community, and those acquiring enforcement rights under those sections are specifically excluded from the provision replacing references to superior.

In addition, there are circumstances where a reference to 'superior' in a community burden can actually be ignored. Any provision in a deed, the effect of which is that anyone other than the person entitled to enforce the burden may waive compliance with, or vary the burden, is to be disregarded (for example, a community burden that provides that additions to buildings may not be constructed without the consent of 'us and our successors as superiors')[142]. That requirement for consent does

---

140 Sections 18, 18A, 18B, 18C, 19, 20, 28, 28A or 60 of the Abolition of Feudal Tenure (Scotland) Act 2000.
141 Section 56 of the Title Conditions (Scotland) Act 2003.
142 See section 73(2A) of the Abolition of Feudal Tenure (Scotland) Act 2000.

not extend to all of the other parties in the community, and instead the wording is, in effect removed altogether because the superior no longer exists. The effect of this will often be to convert the burden into an outright prohibition, which would require a formal discharge rather than an informal consent. This provision does not only affect feudal superiors. In *Strathclyde Business Park (Management) Ltd v BAE Systems Pension Funds Trustees Ltd*[143], a deed of conditions contained a prohibition against putting up signs without the prior written consent of the 'Promoter' who was a management company: Strathclyde Business Park (Management) Ltd. This company did not own any part of the Park, and had no title to enforce on its own account as it wasn't an owner or tenant, nor was its mandate as manager clear, meaning that it was not a 'person entitled to enforce the burden' in terms of section 73(2A) of the 2000 Act.

8.25.10 Contractual Rights in Real Burdens

Not only could superiors enforce real burdens against the vassal for the time being, but feudal real burdens could also be enforced as a personal contractual provision as between the superior and the original vassal. There was some doubt as to whether it could also be enforced in this way against successive disponees, however.

While feudal abolition extinguishes real burdens, it does not extinguish these contractual rights, and therefore if the original vassal is still the owner of the land, then the conditions in the original feudal grant will remain enforceable as a matter of contract. This needs to be borne in mind when reporting on the survival of feudal burdens. Section 75 of the Abolition of Feudal Tenure (Scotland) Act 2000 confirms this, but excludes rights to feuduty and also confirms that contractual enforcement rights do not extend to successive disponees. Community burdens are also excluded from this contractual effect.

While these contractual enforcement rights are assignable, meaning a successor of the superior would be able to enforce against the original former vassal, the contractual liability ends when the original vassal ceases to own the land.

Contrast this with the effect on real burdens created after feudal abolition: the terms of section 61 of the Title Conditions (Scotland) Act

143 [2010] GWD 39-791, Sh Ct.

2003 mean that a real burden is enforceable either as a real burden or as a contractual provision between the original parties, but not both. If it is successfully created as a real burden, then on registration any contractual entitlement ceases. However, if it fails in some way as a real burden, it may still be enforceable contractually.

8.25.11 Use and Building Restrictions

Real burdens that contain use and/or building restrictions can be the most troubling for a prospective purchaser, if they limit or prevent what the purchaser wishes to do with the property. Many dwellinghouses are affected by conditions that prohibit certain uses: usually any trade or business or profession (although see *Snowie v Museum Hall LLP* para 8.3). An unreasonable restriction in the title might entitle your client to withdraw from the contract, but if the restriction is usual for the type of property then it should be expected and would not permit a purchaser to resile from the missives because of an unusual or unduly onerous burden (see *Snowie v Museum Hall LLP* again). A burden that is an unreasonable restraint of trade will be unenforceable, but not all restraints of trade are unreasonable (see para 8.25.16(i)).

It is important to identify at the outset what your client's plans are, so that appropriate provision has been made in the contract, and so that you will know what title conditions are likely to be problematic or unacceptable. Whatever the terms of any restriction, this should be noted and reported to your client, who may have other plans they haven't told you about.

Bear in mind that even the most 'usual' conditions can be unacceptable to a particular purchaser. The standard prohibition against keeping pets, for example, which appears in many modern deeds of conditions can be a source of much distress for your animal-loving client, so it is important that your client is aware of the conditions that apply to the property they are buying.

The most common applications to the Lands Tribunal for variation or discharge of title conditions relate to building or use restrictions. If the use restriction is unacceptable to your client who still wants to proceed with the purchase, then an application to the Lands Tribunal for a discharge of the condition is one option open to her. It would then be a matter of the seller making the application, as the owner of the burdened property at the time. Although it is a matter of negotiation in the circumstances of the transaction, ideally your client would want the issue to be resolved before the purchase takes place, rather than taking the risk of waiting until after he has acquired the property, to apply for a discharge.

8.25.12 Minerals

Minerals can be held as a separate tenement in land. This happens when the minerals are reserved in a conveyance, whether feudal or non-feudal. If no reservation has ever been made, the minerals are included in the title to land, based on the principle of ownership *a coelo usque ad centrum* (from the sky to the centre of the earth). More often than not, however, the minerals will have been reserved. Indeed, sometimes the title may contain several successive reservations of minerals, possibly caveated with the words 'so far as we have right thereto'. However, it is not always possible to be certain that there has not been a reservation of the minerals, because this may have been effected long ago, but the deed in which the reservation was made is no longer available. For these reasons, the treatment of ownership of minerals in the Land Register is subject to special provision. If there is no mention of the minerals in the title sheet, for 1979 Act titles, there is a statutory exclusion of indemnity in case of any loss arising in respect of an interest in mines and minerals, and the title sheet of the interest, which includes the surface, does not expressly provide that the interest in mines and minerals, is included. So there may be ownership of the minerals, but that ownership does not benefit from the Keeper's indemnity. This approach continues under the 2012 Act, so even if the Title Sheet does not contain any reservation of minerals the Keeper does not warrant that the owner has acquired a right to mines or minerals

However, if it can be established that the minerals are included in the title, the Keeper can be asked to extend warranty under section 75(1)(a) of the 2012 Act. To do so, she will require to see appropriate evidence of actual title, which will include a progress of deeds demonstrating good prescriptive legal title to the minerals, and evidence of possession in fortification of that title. Possession will usually mean actually working the minerals or leasing them to a third party. Alternatively, interdicting someone else from working the minerals may be regarded as possession. In rare cases, a court declarator of mineral ownership may be available.

Much of the time it will not matter to a purchaser whether the minerals are included in the title or not, although the position regarding minerals should always be reported to the client, particularly if they are reserved. Minerals reservations clauses have been known to cause problems unless adequate arrangements for compensation for any damage to the surface or buildings are expressed. Without this, the title is unmarketable, and particularly so if the reservation permits entering the surface and allows sinking bores and pits. In some parts of Scotland however, such as Lanarkshire (where historically there was a significant amount of mining) there are many titles that contain clauses of reservations of minerals that contain these onerous provisions. It is customary for the missives to contain provisions for any reservation of minerals to be in satisfactory terms and also a requirement to obtain a Coal Authority Report (see paras 6.10.23, 6.14.11 and para 7.3).

You should bear in mind, of course, that all coal is vest in the Coal Authority, and that there are statutory provisions providing for payment of compensation for subsidence caused by the working of coal, covering damage to land or buildings, structures or works in or over land caused by the withdrawal of support in relation to lawful coal mining operations. Reservations of titles to minerals will exclude coal and sometimes (unnecessarily) state so. It is, therefore, the existence of, and working of minerals other than coal that will be of concern, if the minerals reservation clause is onerous, and it is possible to conduct investigations, firstly by inspecting the terms of the Coal Authority report, and if further more detailed information is required, by requisitioning a report on the existence of minerals in the area from the British Geological Survey[144]. If ownership of the minerals can be identified, another possibility is to negotiate a purchase of them, which would effectively remove the problem of the reservation. This is not always a simple task given the difficulty with minerals titles referred to above, and in any event might be a disproportionate remedy. Clearly, of course, if there are viable minerals in the land suitable for working then the cost of acquiring them would probably be out of proportion to the value of the land – indeed the real value in the land may be the minerals themselves.

144 See www.bgs.ac.uk.

8.25.13 Pre-emption Rights

This is a particular class of burden which gives a person who has sold land or buildings an opportunity to repurchase them the first time they are resold. The right is usually expressed as an obligation on the owner of the land, if he decides to sell the property, to offer it back to the pre-emption holder at the amount of the highest offer received from other parties, and on the same terms and conditions. A classic style of a typical clause of pre-emption can be found in Halliday: *Conveyancing Law and Practice*[145]. For all pre-emptions created after 1 September 1974, the pre-emption holder has only one opportunity to exercise the right and if he declines the offer, then the pre-emption right is extinguished. It is important to note, however, that non-feudal pre-emption rights created before 1 September 1974 can be exercised more than once, so if an offer is refused the first time the property is sold, the right remains live and can be exercised on subsequent sales.

Former feudal rights of pre-emption could be preserved by the former superior by registration of a preservation notice (see para 8.25.4) prior to 28 November 2004, either by nominating land to be the benefited property, or as a personal real burden. Note also that even if the feudal superior has not preserved the right, and despite the elaborate scheme for preservation of feudal pre-emptions set out in Abolition of Feudal Tenure (Scotland) Act 2000, it seems clear in many cases that, even although the pre-emption has not been preserved under one of the preservation notices, it may still enforceable as a matter of contract by the original former superior where the original vassal is still in place. However, rights to enforce pre-emption rights do not arise by virtue of the common scheme provisions in sections 52 and 53 of the Title Conditions (Scotland) Act 2003.

The existence of a right of pre-emption should be disclosed to the purchaser at the missives stage, if not before. The contract should be made conditional on the pre-emption holder declining the offer. Otherwise, if missives are concluded and a pre-emption clause has been overlooked, the sellers cannot give a valid title without offering the property back to the person entitled to benefit from the pre-emption. If that person then accepts the offer, the seller will not be able to fulfil the missives to the purchaser and will be in breach of contract. Where a right of pre-emption has not been

---

145 (1997) 2nd edn, vol 2, para 32.80.

observed, the pre-emption holder is entitled to seek a court order to reduce the disposition granted in contravention of the pre-emption, and all other deeds flowing from it, but not to a right to purchase the property as well[146]. Note, however, that the negative prescription provisions in section 18 of the Title Conditions (Scotland) Act 2003 will apply after five years, so that if the pre-emption holder does not make any claim within that period then the pre-emption will be extinguished (although it seems that pre-1 September 1974 non-feudal pre-emptions will not extinguish completely).

From the seller's point of view, a valid clause of pre-emption is particularly irksome, as they may not know whether the pre-emption holder will exercise the right but still have to go through the process of a *bona fide* sale to establish the market value. The prospective purchasers are put to the trouble of submitting an offer, with all the hopes and dreams that can accompany that process. The dilemma is that if the seller warns prospective purchasers of the true position, they might not get as high an offer for the pre-emption holder to match. The practice, therefore, developed of approaching the pre-emption holder in advance of a sale to ascertain if they would be minded to exercise the right. If not, then often a letter would be provided by the pre-emption holder confirming that they did not wish to exercise the pre-emption, and the sale to a third party would proceed unencumbered. The difficulty with this approach is that, strictly speaking, the pre-emption has not been validly declined since it was never formally offered on the same terms as a third party offer.

Section 83 of the Title Conditions (Scotland) Act 2003 provides a solution to the problem, by providing for a statutory pre-sale undertaking that can be obtained from the pre-emption holder (the form of the undertaking is set out in Schedule 10 to the Act) that, subject to any conditions specified by the holder of the pre-emption right, they will not exercise the pre-emption right during the period specified in the undertaking. The sale to a third party of the land can proceed without triggering the pre-emption, provided any conditions specified in the undertaking are met, and on registration of the conveyance to the third party, the pre-emption right will be extinguished. However, if a sale does not take place within the specified period, then the pre-emption right will revive at the end of that period.

---

146 See *Roebuck v Edmunds* [1992] SLT 1055.

The existing method of dealing with a pre-emption right can also be used, ie offering the property to the pre-emption holder on the same terms and conditions as offered by a third party and the pre-emption holder has 21 days to accept (42 days in the case of a rural housing burden). Section 84 of the Title Conditions (Scotland) Act 2003 re-states the previous law, and also provides that the terms on which the property is offered to the pre-emption holder are either as set out in the pre-emption clause, or if no terms are stated, then it can be on such terms as are reasonable in the circumstances.

8.25.14 Right of Redemption

A right of redemption is a right of re-purchase granted to the holder of that right. It is similar in effect to the clause of pre-emption, but in this case the original owners may call for the land to be resold to them at any time they choose, and not just when a resale takes place. When that right can be exercised depends on what the deed creating it says: it may be at any time at the instance of the holder of the right, on the occurrence of a trigger event, or after the expiry of a pre-determined period of time.

It has not been possible to create new rights of redemption as real burdens since 28 November 2004[147] (although they can still be created as personal contractual rights). Rights of redemption created before then still exist if non feudal, but any granted after 1 September 1974 are only exercisable for a period of 20 years from the date of creation[148]. The reason for this provision was to prevent owners circumventing the restriction on creation of residential leases for more than 20 years, by selling property subject to a redemption clause, and then redeeming it some time after a period of 20 years had expired. Such clauses granted before September 1974 (many such clauses are contained in very old deeds) do not suffer from this 20-year restriction, so will need to be considered carefully. Potentially, it would have a damaging effect on marketability, so ideally you would want to require that it is discharged, or if it is sufficiently old, terminated.

Feudal rights of redemption were abolished on 28 November 2004 unless they were preserved by the former superior, either by nominating land to be the benefited property, or as a personal real burden (see para 8.25.4).

---

147 Section 3(5)(a) of the Title Conditions (Scotland) Act 2003.
148 Section 12 of the Land Tenure Reform (Scotland) Act 1974.

If there is a sale in breach of a right of redemption, the redemption right will be extinguished five years after the sale by virtue of negative prescription, provided there is no claim.

8.25.15 Reversions

Similar provisions apply to rights of reversion, which are very similar to rights of redemption, and it can sometimes be difficult to decide which type the burden is. As a general rule of thumb, a right of redemption entitles the holder to call for the land to be re-sold to them, whereas a right of reversion is usually triggered by some event occurring. Any reversion created after 1 September 1974 must be exercised within 20 years of its creation, and while reversions created prior to that date are still valid, feudal reversions will have been extinguished on feudal abolition unless preserved (see para 8.25.4). Nor is it competent to create rights of reversion after 28 November 2004[149].

Statutory reversions can be subject to special provisions, however. Section 86 of the Title Conditions (Scotland) Act 2003 provides for extinction of rights of reversion in respect of land originally conveyed for schools, playgrounds and schoolhouses, under the School Sites Act 1841, but provides compensation may be payable by the education authority. The Registers' *Update 7: School Sites Act 1841*[150] explains the approach the Keeper will take to reversions under the 1841 Act.

A right of reversion should not be confused with superior's irritancy rights, which were abolished on 9 June 2000[151]. Typically such clauses (also known as 'irritant and resolutive' clauses would provide that, in the event of any breach of a burden imposed in the deed, the property would revert to the superior (see para 8.26.4).

8.25.16 Burdens That Are or May Be Unenforceable

8.25.16(i) Restraint of trade

Some restrictions on the use of a property are more reasonable than others, but it is possible for some to go too far, and if they do, in extreme cases they

---

149 Section 3(5)(a) of the Title Conditions (Scotland) Act 2003.
150 See www.ros.gov.uk/__data/assets/pdf_file/0019/5905/update7.pdf.
151 Section 53 of the Abolition of Feudal Tenure etc. (Scotland) Act 2000.

will be unenforceable. There are rules about the content of real burdens (as to which generally see para 9.11.1(iii)). One of these is that a burden must not be an unreasonable restraint of trade. Simply because a burden appears in a deed or in the burdens section of a Title Sheet does not, of course, always mean that the burden is valid and enforceable. Non-feudal burdens may be unenforceable for a number of reasons, such as, for example, burdens that are intended to restrict a particular type of trade for competitive reasons, to confer commercial benefit (see *Aberdeen Varieties Ltd v James F Donald (Aberdeen Cinemas) Ltd*[152]). In commercial property titles, burdens that, in essence, constitute a restraint of trade are quite common. The seller may plan to set up a similar business half a mile down the road and does not want his buyer to operate in direct competition to him, so places a prohibition in the title of the property being sold against using the property for that particular type of business. While there may be some contractual nexus between the original parties to the deed, such provisions are, in many instances likely to be unenforceable as real burdens.

But just because a burden imposes some restriction on trade, does not mean that it is unenforceable in all cases.

Hill of Rubislaw (Q Seven) Ltd v Rubislaw Quarry Aberdeen Ltd[153] concerned a restriction contained in a Minute of Agreement preventing the owner of a new development, described as the Northern Quarry Subjects, from providing more than 2,025.29 square metres of office space in that development. Purchasers of the property argued that this burden was unenforceable as it was an unreasonable restraint of trade, but it is not the case that every condition which is in restraint of trade is unacceptable. In certain cases, the law recognises that limitations on future commercial activities may be legitimate, or even beneficial. The fundamental test to be applied in testing the validity of such real burdens should be that 'a contract which is in restraint of trade cannot be enforced unless it is reasonable as between the parties; [and] it is consistent with the interests of the public'[154].

So, in *Hill of Rubislaw*, while the maximum amount of lettable office space was limited, the condition did not prevent the use of the property

---

152 [1940] SC (HL) 52.
153 [2014] CSIH 105.
154 Lord Macmillan at 189 in *Vancouver Malt and Sake Brewing Co Ltd v Vancouver Breweries Ltd* [1934] AC 181.

to provide office space. The restriction was imposed as part of a wider commercial agreement that had the effect of enabling the development in the first place, by opening up access to it. Accordingly, in this context, the restriction was not unreasonable.

8.25.16(ii) Reference to external documents

Another common obstacle to validity is the fact that the burden has to be set out in 'the four corners' of the deed, so that references to external documents, or material like an Act of Parliament, for the purposes of establishing the precise content of the burden was not and still, except in some limited circumstances[155], is not a valid burden. A typical example of this is where a burden imposing a use restriction refers to the schedule to the Town and Country Planning (Use Classes) (Scotland) Order 1997 to define the use permitted.

Section 5(2) of the Title Conditions (Scotland) Act 2003 permits a real burden that relates to an obligation to pay, or contribute towards some cost, to refer to some other, public document (which includes an enactment, public register or some record or roll to which the public readily has access) for specifying the way in which the cost or the proportion or share of the cost can be arrived at. A typical example of this would be a reference to the valuation roll for determining the respective shares of the costs of repairing common parts to be borne by the flats in a building.

8.25.16(iii) Burdens for payment of money

Any attempt to secure payment of sums of money, such as for example, clawback payments, by way of imposing a real burden in the title, are definitely out of the question. However, it is perfectly legitimate to create burdens that are about paying or contributing towards the cost of something[156] – often maintenance of something like a fence, or common areas of a development or common parts of a tenement.

8.25.16(iv) Lack of praediality

To be valid a burden must be praedial, in other words, it must relate to the land: both the burdened property and the benefited property. It is a cardinal

---

155 Section 5(2) of the Title Conditions (Scotland) Act 2003. For a classic example of such an invalid burden see *Marriott v Greenbelt Group Ltd* LTS/TC/2014/27.
156 See section 2(1)(a), above.

rule that a burden should burden the burdened property for the benefit of the benefited property. This is something that is often missing from older burdens, particularly 'neighbour' burdens. The lack of praediality can manifest itself in a number of ways. It may be because the benefited property is simply too far away from the burdened property for there to be any genuine praedial connection, although it might also be simply because the burden is conveying a personal benefit to the owner of the benefited property, and not a praedial one.

The praedial rule was also considered in the *Hill of Rubislaw* case[157]. The burden in question placed a restraint on trade, in that it limited the amount of space the owner of the building could let, for the benefit of the owners of adjoining property. For a condition to be praedial there has to be a benefit to the property, not just to an owner of that property[158]. However, 'property is not recognised by the law of and for itself; it is recognised because of the benefits that it confers on proprietors, tenants and other occupiers'. Thus, the expression that a real burden must confer a benefit on a property is essentially shorthand for saying that it must confer a benefit on the owners, tenants or occupiers of the property from time to time, whoever they may be[159]. Of course, most obligations will benefit the owner, but the existence of substantial personal benefit does not mean that there is no praedial benefit.

Physical proximity is another important consideration: 'it can be said with some confidence that without physical proximity there can be no real burden'[160]. While many burdens reflect a requirement to protect amenity, it is not necessary that the validity of real burdens has to be confined to those that are purely physical in their effect. Anything that can be said to protect or enhance the value of the property itself will be sufficient. In the context of commercial properties, these are normally used to carry on some form of business and to generate profits, and this feature of commercial property should be recognised by the law. The beneficial effect of this burden for

157 See para 8.25.16(i).
158 'The starting point is that real burdens must concern land; that is their essential justification. Restrictions on land can be imposed by personal contract, but such restrictions would be entirely personal in nature and would not be binding on singular successors. A real burden is accorded the privilege of running with the land, but in exchange for that privilege it must concern the land; obligations unconnected with land cannot be real burdens, and that is the point of the praedial rule' (Lord Drummond Young at para 10).
159 Lord Drummond Young at para 14.
160 Ibid at para 13.

properties that are let is that it allows the commercial activity in that property to be carried on more effectively. By restricting the amount of property that could be let in the near vicinity, rent levels can be protected or enhanced, which in turn benefits the capital value of the property. So, 'protecting rental values in the neighbourhood of a commercial property is likely to result in a benefit that satisfies the praedial rule[161].

The court's analysis in this case is of great assistance in what has previously been an area of considerable uncertainty.

8.25.16(v) Burdens imposed on retained property

Another common blow to validity is where, prior to 28 November 2004, the burden is set up in a disposition of part of a property, but burdens the part of the property being retained. This is not effective, because prior to the coming into force of the Title Conditions (Scotland) Act 2003, it was a requirement that for a burden to be created it had to be done in a conveyance of the burdened property (or in a deed of conditions) whereas of course, there is no transfer of the restrained property. It is now possible to create real burdens in any kind of deed provided the deed is registered against both the benefited and the burdened properties (see para 9.11.1(vii)).

8.25.16(vi) Lack of a benefited (or burdened) property

Where burdens are created in a disposition which conveys the whole of the property owned by the granter (so that there would have been no implied right of enforcement arising as a result of the rule in *Mactaggart* (see para 8.25.5(i))) or where the burdened property has not been sufficiently clearly identified, no effective burden is created.

Real burdens created post-28 November 2004 ought, in theory, and for the most part in practice, to be more likely to be valid, because of the requirements of dual registration and because we have, in the Title Conditions (Scotland) Act 2003, a statutory code that tells us what we can and cannot do with burdens. It is still possible, however, that burdens which have been created since 28 November 2004 may fail some validity test, so don't assume that just because the burden has been created in the current climate of greater awareness, it automatically means that it is valid.

---

161 Lord Drummond Young at para 17.

8.25.17 Cleansing and Updating of the Registers

8.25.17(i) Feudal abolition

The Keeper is not required to remove a real burden extinguished by feudal abolition from a title sheet. Originally, section 46 of the Abolition of Feudal Tenure (Scotland) Act 2000 obliged the Keeper to remove extinguished feudal burdens from the Registers once ten years from the appointed day had elapsed. It would have been quite useful to have the Keeper tidy up titles in this way, and some Title Sheets were actually amended under this provision, and you may therefore sometimes see the following note on a Title Sheet:

> 'Where the Keeper considers that any real burdens which affected the subjects in this title were extinguished by virtue of s 17 of the Abolition of Feudal Tenure Etc (Scotland) Act 2000, these have been removed or omitted from the title sheet.'

However, section 46 was repealed by the 2012 Act[162], meaning there is now no obligation on the Keeper to remove extinguished or expired burdens from the Title Sheet for a property. Accordingly, many Title Sheets remain inaccurate. Burdens can be removed (or not added in the first place) to a Title Sheet when you apply for registration (see para 14.11.2(ix))

8.25.17(ii) Implied enforcement rights

A similar arrangement[163] applied to real burdens that subsisted by virtue of any of sections 52 to 56 of the Title Conditions (Scotland) Act 2003 or section 60 of the Abolition of Feudal Tenure (Scotland) Act 2000 (preserved right of Crown to maritime burdens). That provision, too, was repealed by the 2012 Act[164]. Prior to repeal, some of these enforcement rights were noted on Title Sheets, so you may sometimes come across a statement on the Title Sheet in the following terms:

> 'Note: In terms of section 58 of the Title Conditions (Scotland) Act 2003, the Keeper is satisfied that real burdens in the foregoing entry

---

162 Schedule 5 para 39(4).
163 Section 58 of Title Conditions (Scotland) Act 2003 (now repealed).
164 Schedule 5 para 43(4).

subsist by virtue of having been imposed as [eg facility burdens in terms of section 56,] of that Act.'

FEUDAL LEFTOVERS

8.26 As a consequence of feudal abolition, in addition to the effect this had on feudal real burdens, there are a number of other consequences that the conveyancer should bear in mind when examining title, particularly Sasine titles. Most of these are in the category of no longer having to trouble us.

8.26.1 Feuduty

Feuduties, whether cumulo, allocated or unallocated, ground annuals, and other payments that are like feuduty, such as teinds, skat, and standard charge, are all abolished and the period within which a former superior could claim compensation (two years after feudal abolition) has now long passed. These charges had to be extinguished if the recipient took the necessary steps to request repayment, but arrears no longer attach themselves to the property. Note, however, that while we do not have to be concerned with payment of feuduty, the amount of feuduty was often used as a basis on which to calculate the proportion or share of contribution towards common repair costs in tenements and this information may, therefore, still be relevant for that purpose.

8.26.2 Thirlage and Other Payments

Thirlage is the duty of the vassal to have corn ground at the local mill. This has long fallen into disuse, but had never been formally abolished. Other payments similar to feuduty, such as multures, standard charge, teinds and the like are no longer valid.

8.26.3 Superiority Title

Title relating to the superiority, including searches, minutes of consolidation, conveyances and the like can, for the most part, all be ignored following feudal abolition. You may come across a disposition of the superiority in pre-registration titles, and while it can be ignored, the trick is distinguishing between it and a normal disposition. The only guaranteed way is by looking at the warrandice clause – if it grants warrandice but excludes from the warrandice all feu rights in the land that have been granted, then it is a superiority disposition. Where superiorities titles can still be of relevance, however, is where the vassal relinquished his interest and returned it to the superior. This was done by way of disposition ad remanentiam perpetuam, colloquially shortened to 'ad rem'. Such a conveyance effectively extinguished the feudal relationship and restored the whole title – the dominium plenum to the superior – effectively making the superior an owner again.

8.26.4 Irritancy

The superior's remedy of irritancy was abolished by the Abolition of Feudal Tenure (Scotland) Act 2000 with effect from 9 June 2000 so irritancy, or 'irritant and resolutive' clauses in feudal deeds (which generally run along the lines of saying that in the event of a breach of any burdens imposed, the title will revert to the superior) can safely be ignored, and could not be preserved.

TENEMENTS

8.27 Historically, the common law of the tenement in Scotland was either unclear or unsatisfactory in many respects, and the Tenements (Scotland) Act 2004, which also came into force on 28 November 2004, has codified the previous common law in respect of boundaries and pertinents, regulated the rights and duties of owners of properties in a tenement, and also filled in some gaps in the law and clarified some areas of doubt.

8.27.1 Ownership and Maintenance

Although it has its complications, the introduction of the Tenements (Scotland) Act 2004 has simplified title examination of tenement properties in a number of respects, and rendered marketable some titles that would in the past have been considered unmarketable. For example, a top-floor flat in a tenement where the titles were silent as to liability for maintenance of the common parts, would be liable for the whole burden of maintenance of the roof of the tenement, and a failure to grant a right in common to the *solum* of the tenement also would have an adverse effect on the marketability of upper floors. The 2004 Act effectively restates the common law rules of ownership and applies both to existing tenements and new tenements, but it makes separate provision about maintenance of those parts (see para 8.27.1(i)). A top-floor flat will include the roof over the flat, and a ground-floor flat will include the *solum* beneath the flat.

The 2004 Act restates the common law in relation to the boundaries of the flats, which make default provisions in the event that the titles do not provide otherwise. In particular:

- each flat will own up to mid-point of the walls;
- a structure serving one flat only will belong to that flat (eg a bin store, or a single-storey extension);
- the ground-floor flat will own the *solum* and the top-floor flat will own the roof. A close (passage, stairs and landings) includes the *solum* and roof;
- the airspace above the tenement is owned by the owner(s) of the *solum*. In the titles this is very often expressed as common property, whereas in the statutory scheme, it will belong to the owner of the ground-floor flat; and
- where there is a pitched roof, the triangle of airspace between the extent of the actual slope of the roof and the imaginary horizontal and vertical lines from the highest and widest points of the building will belong to the owner of the top-floor flat. This allows owners of top-floor flats to install dormer windows, without encroaching on airspace owned by someone else.

In the same way, the 2004 Act makes default provisions for common property or pertinents of the tenement. A close or a lift will be owned only by the owners who would make use of them for access. Any land (other than the *solum* (surface of the ground), a path, outside stair or other access) will belong to the ground floor flat nearest to it. Any other pertinents (which includes such things as a path, outside stair, fire escape, rhone, pipe, flue, conduit, cable, tank or chimney stack) will be owned by the flat they serve or, if serving more than one, equally among them. The only exception to the latter rule is a chimney stack, where ownership in common will be determined according to the ratio which the number of flues in the stack serving a flat bears to the total number of flues in the stack. In other words, if one flat uses five flues, but five other flats only use one flue each, the first flat will own a one-half *pro indiviso* (common) share of the chimney stack whereas the other flats will each own one-tenth *pro indiviso* shares.

8.27.1(i) Scheme property

Where the Act changes the previous law, however, is in relation to maintenance. Ownership and maintenance no longer coincide. The Tenements (Scotland) Act 2004 provides a default Tenement Management Scheme (TMS) in Schedule 1, which will apply to all tenements, except to the extent that the titles provide otherwise. It provides principally for certain parts of a tenement, such as the roof, foundations, *solum* and external walls always to be common parts for the purposes of maintenance and repair, regardless of ownership of these parts. These parts are referred to as 'scheme property' (see Rule 1.2 of the TMS for the full definition). It may have the effect, in some instances, of imposing obligations on owners that they did not have in the past. But this provision removes the adverse effect on marketability that sole ownership of the roof previously had, where the title did not provide for shared maintenance.

8.27.1(ii) Application to all tenements

The key aspect of the 2004 Act that the solicitor should understand is that the Act applies to all tenements to the extent that the title deeds do not. So, even if the title deeds do contain provisions relating to maintenance of common parts, in other areas such as decision making, where the titles are silent, the TMS will apply. The practical significance of this is that now **all** existing tenement titles have to be read against the background of the TMS and the 2004 Act. So, when dealing with tenement properties, whether residential, commercial or a mixture of both, it is necessary to have a good grasp of the provisions of the 2004 Act.

8.27.2 Tenement Management Scheme

The Tenement Management Scheme (TMS) is a common scheme of management for tenement properties, which applies to both existing and new tenement buildings, except to the extent that the burdens in the title deeds already make provision. However, one of the problems often encountered, particularly with elderly tenement properties, is that the provisions in the titles of each flat are inconsistent with each other. The TMS will rectify gaps and inconsistencies in such titles.

8.27.2(i) Proportion of costs

Rule 4 of the TMS provides for how the costs of maintenance etc of scheme property ('scheme costs') are shared. Where the costs relate to scheme property which is owned in common by two or more of the owners in the tenement, in terms of the title, then the costs are shared among the owners in the proportions in which they share ownership of that common property. For the other types of scheme property, rule 4 states that the costs will be shared equally, except, where the floor area of the larger (or largest) flat or unit, is more than 1½ times that of the smaller (or smallest) unit, then each owner is liable to contribute in the proportion which the floor area of each owner's flat bears to the total floor area of both (or all) flats. The practicalities of this are not as easy as the provision might suggest. If floor areas have to be determined, then a surveyor would be required to measure and calculate these. This could prove difficult or impossible if access to some of the flats is not available (but see para 8.27.2(ii)).

8.27.2(ii) Inconsistencies in the title

The provisions of rule 4 of the TMS will apply in relation to scheme costs, unless there is a burden in the title which provides that the entire liability for those scheme costs is to be met by one or more of the owners (to the extent that that amount is not met by someone else).

What this means in practice is that rule 4 will apply in cases where the titles of all flats or units in the tenement, taken together, do not contain provisions which provide for the full amount (100%) of scheme costs to be paid[165]. There are titles where the shares of maintenance costs do not

---

165 Section 4(6) of the Tenements (Scotland) Act 2004.

add up, and 100% of the total liability is not fully accounted for. Often this can arise where, for example, the titles to seven out of the eight flats in a tenement contain provisions for liability for maintenance of common parts and the remaining title is silent. In these cases, Rule 4 will apply.

From the examination of title point of view, the requirement to examine the titles to all of the other flats in the tenement building becomes less imperative. It used to be necessary to see the titles of the other flats to check that they were all appropriately burdened, as otherwise there could be a gap in liability which the other properties in the tenement might have to absorb. Now, it does not matter if the titles of all the flats in the tenement do not provide for 100% liability as section 4(6) resolves the discrepancy.

8.27.3 Reporting on Tenement Titles

Many of the terms of 2004 Act provide for equitable arrangements in relation to ownership of a flat or floor in a tenement property, but because much of this is now contained in a statutory codified form, it will not be apparent to your client from the title. It will be necessary, therefore, to report to your client on some of the 'default' provisions in the 2004 Act that apply to their ownership.

8.27.3(i) Scheme decisions

Rule 2 of the TMS deals with what are referred to as 'scheme decisions' relating to maintenance, appointment of manager, common insurance, and other such matters. If the titles already provide for a method of making decisions, these will apply. Otherwise, rule 2 will apply. Decisions on the repair of scheme property can be made by a majority of owners.

8.27.3(ii) Access and installation of services

The owner of any flat in a tenement must give access to that flat to any other owner in the tenement, on reasonable notice being given, for the purposes of carrying out maintenance work or for inspection and for measuring the floor area where that is relevant for determining liability for costs.

An owner will be entitled to lead certain service pipes, cables or other equipment over other parts of the tenement, but not so as to lead anything through, or fix anything to any part of the tenement which is wholly within some other flat. Scottish Ministers have not yet specified either the types of services to which this part of Act will apply or the procedure that must be adopted when exercising this right, so that although the relevant provision[166] is in force, until regulations are made, the scope of this right is undetermined.

8.27.3(iii) Insurance

Each owner has an obligation to insure his flat and any part of the tenement attached to that flat as a pertinent against certain prescribed risks[167]. The duty to insure may be satisfied by way of a common insurance policy for the whole tenement.

The current prescribed risks are: (a) fire, smoke, lightning, explosion, earthquake; (b) storm or flood; (c) theft or attempted theft; (d) riot, civil commotion, labour or political disturbance; (e) malicious persons or vandals; (f) subsidence, heave or landslip; (g) escape of water from water tanks, pipes, apparatus and domestic appliances; (h) collision with the building caused by any moving object originating outside the building; (i) leakage of oil from fixed heating installations; and (j) accidental damage to underground services[168]. It is likely that most reputable insurance companies will cover these risks.

8.27.3(iv) Demolition and abandonment

Demolition of a tenement building will not affect ownership rights. Where flats have been owned exclusively, each former owner will own the slice of air space which that flat formerly occupied. However, it is extremely difficult to measure air space of a flat or of a building which no longer exists. The 2004 Act provides some solutions. Unless the title provides otherwise, the cost of demolition is to be shared equally except, as before, where the largest flat is more than 1½ times that of the smallest, in which case liability is based on floor area. The liability arises from the date the owners agree to demolish or, in any other case, from the date on which demolition is instructed. Partial demolition is also included.

---

166 Section 19, above.
167 Section 18, above.
168 Tenements (Scotland) Act 2004 (Prescribed Risks) Order 2007.

No owner may build on or otherwise develop the site unless all agree, or there is a rebuilding requirement in the title. If all of the owners do not agree, any one owner is entitled to require the entire site to be sold, by applying to the courts, and the net sale proceeds would be divided equally or in accordance with floor area. Similar provisions apply for tenements that have been abandoned due to their poor condition.

The Scottish Government published a useful guide entitled Management and Maintenance of Common Property[169], intended to help professional staff who are involved in advising owners of flats in tenements, including housing officers, solicitors, surveyors, architects and staff in advice bureaux. It is a useful practical guide to the effects of the Tenements (Scotland) Act 2004.

EXAMINING AND REPORTING ON DEEDS OF CONDITIONS

8.28 Many multi-occupancy sites, both residential and commercial, as well as mixed-use sites, are subject to burdens that are contained in a Deed of Conditions. These generally conform to a particular structure and also raise their own particular issues during the title examination process.

Many people regard Deeds of Conditions as something that is a bit scary and complicated. That perception is not helped by the often extremely dense drafting that can sometimes be used, particularly in Deeds of Conditions that relate to commercial developments, together with pages of Defined Terms, complicated Service Charge structures, convoluted meeting and voting structures, not to mention the slight anxiety that arises from concerns about ensuring that the document complies with all the legislative requirements of the Title Conditions (Scotland) Act 2003.

8.28.1 Amenity and Maintenance

Deeds of Conditions are generally used in developments or estates where there are several units or blocks or buildings of a similar kind, and where each of the owners or occupiers of these units will be expected to adhere to certain rules as to use, management, and maintenance of the units for the general benefit of the development as a whole.

169 See www.gov.scot/Resource/Doc/76169/0019425.pdf.

The sorts of conditions that are imposed are concerned primarily with the preservation of the amenity of the whole development, so you can expect to see conditions that relate to the use to which units can be put, or prohibitions against particular types of uses. In a residential development for example, you will often see restrictions against trade or prohibitions against certain activities, like carrying out car repairs, as well as prohibitions against erecting alterations, additional buildings or adding extensions.

Usually, there will be external areas in the development to deal with as well. Deeds of Conditions will concern the use and maintenance of these areas which will include roads and pavements, landscaped and recreational areas such as play parks, grassed areas and areas of planting, possibly parking as well as more exotic things like ponds and fountains, street lighting, directional signs, and so on. These provisions are about keeping the estate, office development, retail park or whatever it happens to be, nice and attractive for the people living, working or shopping there.

8.28.2 Community Burdens

The expression 'community burdens' was first used in Part 2 of the Title Conditions (Scotland) Act 2003, but the general idea is not new, and often the burdens set out in pre-abolition Deeds of Conditions will have been imposed on every unit in the development for the benefit of that community and may have provided for express rights of enforcement by each proprietor against the others. However, this element of reciprocity did not always exist in respect of units in a development, although there might be implied rights of enforcement created in terms of section 53 (see para 8.25.5(ii)).

Community burdens created in terms of the Title Conditions (Scotland) Act 2003 now mean something specific. By calling such burdens 'community burdens', they will automatically be enforceable by every unit in the community against any other unit in the community. Every burdened property is also a benefited property[170]. Some burdens created in Deeds of Conditions may be neighbour burdens – ie burdens imposed on one or more properties for the benefit of other different properties.

170 Section 27 of the Title Conditions (Scotland) Act 2003.

Strictly speaking, the Deed should make clear that they are not community burdens. The usual way would be to identify those conditions in the Deed which are community burdens, the others being identified merely as 'real burdens'.

8.28.3 Interest to Enforce

As outlined in para 8.25.8, title and interest to enforce are required to enforce compliance with a real burden. Most of the case law since 2004 concerns burdens imposed in Deeds of Conditions, including *Barker v Lewis; Kettlewell and Others v Turning Point Scotland;* and *Franklin v Lawson* (see para 8.25.8). It should be borne in mind that interest to enforce applies to community burdens as for other burdens and that, depending on the nature of the burden, not all proprietors in the development will have any interest to enforce even though it is clear that they will have title to enforce. For example, while a next-door neighbour might have interest to enforce a 'no extensions' provision against her neighbour who has erected a conservatory, another owner living five streets away, in the same development, might not.

8.28.4 Ownership of Common Parts

In any development on land, there will be parts of the development that are to be used in common by the owners of units in the development, whether they be roads, car parks, recreation or play areas and so on. There are several ways of dealing with title to these common areas, which will also need to be looked after, maintained and sometimes repaired and renewed.

8.28.4(i) Developer retains ownership of common parts

The first option is for the developer to retain ownership of these areas. This may be acceptable but invariably, once the developer has finished the development, he doesn't want any lingering involvement in it, particularly now that developers no longer have any continuing interest as feudal superior. Sometimes, in fact, the developer or owner of the land being developed may be a special purpose company set up for the duration of the development, and which it is intended to wind up once the development is complete, so continuing ownership simply isn't an option.

8.28.4(ii) Common parts are conveyed at the end of the development

An alternative is for the common areas to be conveyed at the end of the development to an owners' association, or to some third party, often a management company, which will look after the common parts and recover the cost of doing so from the owners of units. There have, over the years, been well-publicised problems with some of these arrangements, with bitter complaints from owners in developments about the standard of service, lack of service and heavy-handed tactics – allegedly – in recovering outstanding sums. This model was recently challenged, unsuccessfully, in the Lands Tribunal. In *Marriott v Greenbelt Group Limited*[171], the Lands Tribunal could find nothing in the Title Conditions (Scotland) Act 2003 to prohibit the 'land owning model' of maintenance of common parts, nor did it appear from the Scottish Law Commission commentary[172] on this model that there was any intention to eliminate it, nor, indeed, any hostility to it. The Lands Tribunal also found that such a model was not repugnant with ownership, and neither illegal, nor an unlawful monopoly, nor a breach of competition law.

In the past, having common areas conveyed to owners associations, which generally do not have any legal personality has been somewhat problematic. Where they have been set up, they usually operate in favour of trustees *ex officio* (eg the chairman, secretary and treasurer for the time being of the owners' association). It is, however, now possible to have an Owners' Association, set up by using the Development Management Scheme arrangements under Part 6 of Title Conditions (Scotland) Act 2003 (see para 9.11.7). This has a separate legal personality and can hold title to parts of the development, as well as having the power to contract in its own name.

8.28.4(iii) Developer conveys pro-indiviso shares along with each plot

The third main option, and one which was formerly extremely common, is to convey *pro-indiviso* shares – usually equal shares – of ownership in the common areas to each owner along with the conveyance of their unit. There are a couple of ways in which this has been done in the past: (a) by

171 LTS/TC/2014/27.
172 SLC Report on Real Burdens 2000 ScotLawCom 181.

reference to a detailed plan of the development, identifying all the areas that are to be communal and conveying shares in those areas in the Disposition with the plan attached, or by reference to the Deed of Conditions in which those parts are identified, and to which there is a plan attached or (b) by describing those common areas in the Deed of Conditions on an exclusion basis – in other words, by referring to every part of the development that is not to be conveyed individually to plot owners.

This second alternative in this option, which was the more popular of the two alternatives, was seen to give developers the flexibility that they often needed to make alterations to the precise location of the common parts, perhaps slightly alter the route of roads, or amend the configuration, if adjustments to the way in which the development was being built out were made. This approach was however resoundingly discredited in the Lands Tribunal decision in *PMP Plus Ltd v The Keeper of the Registers of Scotland*[173].

In that case, the original developer had purported over time to convey *pro-indiviso* shares in the external common parts in the development to each of the plot owners in the Dispositions in their favour. These common areas were identified by reference to whatever was going to be left at the end of the development once all the plots had been conveyed. However, at some point before the end of the development, the developer sold off a chunk of the same external common areas to PMP Plus for the purposes of building a health centre. Initially, because of the prior conveyances of *pro-indivsio* shares, the Keeper indicated that indemnity would be excluded in PMP Plus's title, but on appeal of this decision to the Lands Tribunal, it was decided that the conveyances of these prior *pro-indiviso* shares were invalid, due to the fact that the area of ground – the common areas – was not capable of being identified or mapped. Consequently, it was not possible validly to convey an uncertain area or a share in an uncertain area. This is due to the 'specificity' principle – which requires that land being conveyed must be specific, not uncertain – 'that which cannot be identified cannot be conveyed'.

Because it was such a common and popular method, it was a device employed in many developments, both residential and commercial, no doubt reinforced by the fact that the Keeper was happy to accept such deeds and produce Land Certificates reflecting the purported conveyances.

173 LTS/LR/2007/02.

Following on the decision in *PMP Plus*, of course the Keeper changed her policy, but only in relation to developments where the first conveyance of a unit takes place after August 2009[174]. For consistency, she continued to accept conveyances of such *pro-indiviso* shares in developments where such conveyances had already been accepted by her prior to August 2009. That policy does not necessarily make such conveyances any more valid, but it does represent equal treatment.

However, the advent of the 2012 Act, and its key requirement that there can be no registration without mapping has altered the Keeper's position. Now, if an application for registration seeks to include any rights of common ownership, the application must contain sufficient information to allow the relevant areas (the areas to be held in common) to be plotted on the cadastral map. The previous policy of continuing to include any common property rights where the development had begun prior to 3 August 2009 can no longer apply, if these areas cannot be plotted on the cadastral map.

The Keeper will not however reject a conveyance which purports to include unmappable common property rights. She recognises the difficulty in identifying these where they are based on prior vague descriptions of the *PMP Plus* type. Accordingly, the Keeper will accept such an application (assuming it is otherwise in order). The main property – eg house or other unit – will be mapped but the common areas will be omitted from the Title Sheet and won't be shown on the cadastral map. Where the common areas are described by reference to a Deed of Conditions which also contains other rights (such as pertinents) a note will be added to the Title Sheet indicating that the rights of common property have not been mapped and do not form part of the title. Further details on the Keeper's new approach is set out in Guidance[175].

Consequently, the only way to have such rights of common property included in the title Sheet is to sufficient information (such as a plan) with the application for registration to enable the areas to be mapped.

---

174 See Registers of Scotland Update 27 'Creation, Identification and Transfer of Rights in Common Areas of Developments. Available at: www.ros.gov.uk/__data/assets/pdf_file/0005/5936/update27.pdf. See also, the update following the case of *Lundin Homes Ltd v Keeper of the Registers of Scotland* at www.ros.gov.uk/__data/assets/pdf_file/0006/5937/Lundin-Homes-update.pdf.
175 See www.ros.gov.uk/__data/assets/pdf_file/0004/19777/General-Guidance-CM-mapping-common-areas.pdf.

Otherwise, if further information becomes available in the future that would enable mapping, the Title Sheet may be corrected by an application for rectification.

So, even if a right of common property has been included in a 1979 Act Title Sheet, due to the Keeper's earlier policy, it seems that it will be removed from the resultant 2012 Act Title Sheet. It appears that this will happen even if the *pro indiviso* right of common property is valid (ie the areas in question were properly identified). Unless a plan is available or the Keeper has already plotted these onto the cadastral map and the application is accompanied by a plan showing the areas, they will not be shown on the Title Sheet. In this case however, there will still be a perfectly good title to the areas, and if further information becomes available in the future to allow them to be mapped, the Title Sheet can be amended (through rectification) at that stage.

Is this disastrous? Well, not necessarily. The '*pro indiviso* share' model of ownership of common parts is not the only option (see eg 8.28.4(i) and (ii)), and there is no evidence that there is any effect on value of a property according to the way in which common parts are owned. It is, in truth, probably more of an inconvenience to developers, who thought that they had divested themselves of the whole title, but are in reality still in possession of title to common areas. This is not as problematic as it might appear. While the underlying issue in *PMP Plus* was that the developer 'took away' communal areas, and sold them off to a third party for a different purpose, that is, in the grand scheme of things, a rare occurrence.

It is too soon to tell how this will be resolved, but in the context of the drive to complete the Land Register, it means that there will be a considerable number of areas, in elderly developments, based on a developer's Sasine title, where a 'lace doily' of areas of land are not transferred onto the Land Register. Solicitors will, no doubt, take their usual pragmatic approach. As a land registration issue, it is currently kicked into the long grass.

8.28.4(iv) Conveying 'scheme property'

There is now a fourth option open to developers, which has the potential to be far more effective, and a lot less problematic, although it needs some forethought and a bit of specialist drafting.

Developers can choose to apply the Development Management Scheme (DMS) (see para 9.11.7) to their development, which, among other things, creates an Owners' Association. This is a body corporate, and so can own property in its own right. The DMS also permits the developer to define common areas, known as 'scheme property' in the DMS, which can be defined generally as the roads and footpaths, service media, amenity open space, landscaped open space and recreational areas, any play areas, cycle paths, etc. As this definition is not relied on for actually conveying scheme property, it does not fall foul of the *PMP Plus* rule. When the time comes for scheme property to be conveyed to the Owners' Association – and it can be conveyed in stages during the course of development, as and when common areas are completed – the disposition of the scheme property will include a plan showing the actual areas to be transferred.

8.28.4(v) Shared plots

Under sections 17 to 20 of the 2012 Act, it is now possible for a 'shared plot', eg common parts of a development, to be registered as a separate title, with its own Title Sheet. Any land that is owned in common by two or more people can now be allocated its own Title Number and Title Sheet. This may be a bit unnecessary and cumbersome for land that is owned by only a handful of people, (a mutual driveway perhaps) but for areas such as the common parts of a development, it will be easier to see which properties share ownership of these areas and in what proportions.

Not all mutual areas need to be shared plots, but the Keeper is likely to designate common areas in developments as such. This can be done even when there are several discontiguous areas, which often happens with external areas in developments. They can all be one shared plot. There will be a cross reference between the shared plot and the Title Sheets of the properties that hold the various shares: the sharing plots. No proprietors will need to be listed on the shared plot title. The share in the shared plot will transfer when the title to the sharing plot changes hands.

Making up a Title Sheet for a shared plot is not going to be easy, but over time, we may start to see these. There are transitional arrangements in the 2012 Act that cover situations where plots in developments have been conveyed both before and after the commencement of the 2012 Act, and for developments that were already completed.

8.28.4(vi) Transitional arrangements: Existing developments – completed

Where an area of land is owned in common and immediately before 8 December 2014, it is included in two or more existing Title Sheets, the Keeper may, if she thinks it appropriate, make up a 'shared plot Title Sheet' for that common area, in which case it will become a separate cadastral unit.

Where a shared plot Title Sheet is created in this way, the Keeper has to make all necessary consequential changes to the other Title Sheets for the individual plots affected, and to the cadastral map. However, the respective shares (ie the actual *quantum* share) of the proprietors of the shared plot only needs to be entered in the Title Sheet if they were already entered in the existing Title Sheets.

8.28.4(vii) Transitional arrangements: Existing developments – ongoing (developments begun before designated day)

The Keeper may create new Title Sheets for plots of land, where the plots are to be owned in common and are, immediately before 8 December 2014, included in two or more existing Title Sheets.

Where the respective shares (ie the actual quantum shares) of the proprietors were not entered in the existing Title Sheets, they need not be entered in the new Title Sheets.

8.28.5 Examining and Reporting

As the Deed of Conditions, if there is one, is likely to be the main document containing burdens and servitudes affecting the property, it is important that you read it, so that you can report on its terms to your client. For residential developments particularly it can be tempting to assume that it will contain the 'usual conditions' and that taking a photocopy to send to the purchaser is all that needs be done.

While the usual conditions may be familiar to the solicitor, the chances are that this is the first (and possibly only) time that the purchaser will see them. It can be a daunting prospect to read through and understand the significance of all the terms without some guidance. At the very least you should be pointing out provisions such as restrictions on alterations and extensions, restrictions on trade and the 'no pets rule', if there is one, as these things may be of great importance to your client.

In fact, there is a strong argument that, since you know the sort of conditions that that these deeds are likely to contain, you should be highlighting the prospect of such conditions at the initial stages of purchase, so that the purchaser does not find herself contractually bound to a purchase of a property that contains conditions that, while an 'industry norm', may be unpalatable to her lifestyle.

Commercial Deeds of Conditions tend to be far more bespoke affairs. For the commercial purchaser, you will be expected to read and report in some detail on the terms of the Deed, and flag up any conditions of which a commercial purchaser should be aware that might affect their business.

There are likely to be a lot of definitions at the start of the Deed, or possibly tucked away in a Schedule. While reading the document from the start is always a good idea, it can be counter productive to read all the definitions first until you know how the structure of the Deed itself operates. The meaning or effect of some definitions sometimes only becomes clear when you read it in the context of the operative clauses of the Deed. Commercial Deeds of Conditions will often contain complex management structures and service charge provisions, which your commercial purchaser client needs to know about from an administrative point of view, and clearly, use restrictions and the like may be of key importance to them.

8.28.6 Importing Pre-abolition Deeds of Conditions

Some Deeds of Conditions registered before 28 November 2004 dis-applied section 17 of the 1979 Act. Dis-application of section 17 meant that the burdens and servitudes contained in the pre-2004 Deed of Conditions would not be registered against the land affected at the time the Deed of Conditions was recorded or registered, but only when it, or parts of it, were conveyed in a deed and the terms of the Deed of Conditions were stated in that conveyance to apply to the land conveyed. Section 17 was repealed by the Title Conditions (Scotland) Act 2003. However, in some cases, these pre-November 2004 Deeds of Conditions will still apply to plots or units in the development that are conveyed after 28 November 2004. In that case, section 6 of the Title Conditions (Scotland) Act 2003 makes transitional arrangements to allow such Deeds of Conditions to cross the bridge between the old and new law. This is done by using words which will import the old deed of conditions into the title of the units being conveyed (see para 9.11.11). If this wording has not been used in the relevant circumstances, then the burdens in the Deed of Conditions will not be validly imposed on the unit concerned. It is not necessary to include this wording otherwise.

SITE ASSEMBLY ISSUES

8.29 When examining a title, you should always have in mind the type of property it is and, where appropriate, the type of property your client intends it to be after purchase, where that is different. If, for example, you are examining title for shop premises which your client plans to buy, you must check for prohibitions against the sale of alcohol, which could cause problems if your client intends, or may intend in the future, to have an off-sales section in the shop.

In rural locations, you need to be extra particular about access and drainage rights (amongst many other issues). When your client is buying land or property for development, there are some specific issues that are important to bear in mind, particularly when, as can often be the case, the site is being put together from several parcels of land or sites. By way of illustration of some of these issues, consider the following case study:

8.29.1 A Typical Site

Your client is Lightyear Development Company Ltd (LDCL), a company with considerable experience in putting together sites for development and onward sale or letting, which has been engaged in property development on a small scale for several years. Over the years, LDCL has acquired small-to-medium pieces of ground, sites and bits of property on a speculative basis, and land-banked these for future development potential when the circumstances are right. Having owned properties in the middle of Sardinia Terrace, in the market town of Kelvinforth, for several years, LDCL now has the opportunity to buy from the owner, Kelvinforth Investments Ltd (KIL), the block at the corner of Sardinia Terrace and Lombardy Street (see plan A on page 425), which is close to the main residential parts of town. LDCL has been in talks with the estates director of Prontomart plc, a national supermarket chain, with a view to building a supermarket on the cleared site (see plan B below), which LCDL would then let to Prontomart on a long lease.

Agents for a major pension fund have indicated to LCDL that their client is looking to expand their portfolio and would be interested in

PLAN A

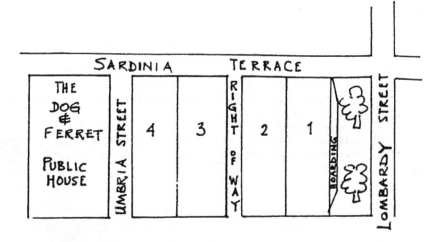

PLAN B

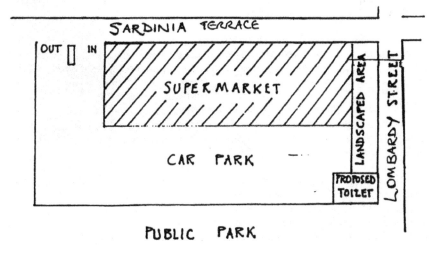

acquiring the developed and tenanted site as an investment, along with five other sites in Scotland currently being developed for Prontomart.

8.29.2 Title Considerations

While it is often preferable to wait until conclusion of missives before looking at the title, given the importance of title boundaries and conditions when assembling a development site, it is often more prudent to look at the title as early as possible, perhaps while the contract is being negotiated, because it is important for the developer to establish sooner rather than later whether the site is going to be suitable for development. Developing a site is a major investment in time and money for a developer, particularly as the acquisition will normally be subject to obtaining the necessary planning consent, which can take some time. The developer will want to know that his expenditure in that regard, which can be considerable, is not going to be wasted due to an insurmountable obstacle with the title to the land. This usually means that the missives will address some issues that the title examination throws up, which the developer might be expected to take a view on. The concluded missives will probably be conditional, or suspensive, on a number of conditions and other factors.

At an early stage you should identify the precise extent of the land required. This is usually assisted by obtaining a draft plan of the proposed development from the client or their surveyors. You need to ensure that there are no gaps in the title and that all the land you need is available, and not owned by someone else or unavailable in some other way, such as being the subject of an option in favour of some other party. Checking the title early on will identify whether the seller has title to all of the land required and whether there are any 'ransom strips' or rights in favour of others such as servitudes or rights of way.

In the Sardina Terrace site, it is clear from the Plan B proposals, produced by Prontmart's surveyor, that there are several issues:

  (a) Plan A shows a right of way which runs between Numbers 2 and 3 Sardinia Terrace, leading to the public park, and is regularly used by children from the nearby school. Note that rights of way and other third-party rights are often not apparent from the titles or plans and may only be apparent from a site visit.

(b) Umbria Street, between the pub and Number 4 Sardinia Terrace is a public road.

(c) A plot of ground with two large trees sits at the corner of Sardinia Terrace and Lombardy Street. These trees are the subject of a tree preservation order under section 160 of the Town and Country Planning (Scotland) Act 1997. They have become large and unwieldy and overhang Lombardy Street. The tree roots are intruding under No 1 Sardinia Terrace causing difficulties in the foundations.

(d) KIL does not have title to the land on which the pub on Umbria Street is situated, although an associated company, Kelvinforth Leisure Pursuits Ltd (KLPL) is the tenant. KLPL's employee, Desmond Moore, runs the pub and lives in the flat above.

(e) There is an advertising hoarding on the east gable of number 1 Sardinia Terrace, which is in regular use. It may be the subject of a lease or licence.

8.29.3 Boundaries

Clearly defined boundaries are of considerable importance and the site visit is of huge assistance here, once a preliminary title check has been made, to identify whether there are any problems. It is essential to have good quality plans based on the Ordnance Survey map to identify what is being acquired and to ascertain whether the boundary features themselves could pose any difficulties. For example, the site could be bounded by a river or a road, perhaps a wall that is listed, or a gable of an adjoining building with windows overlooking the development. A boundary feature may turn out to be onerous with significant maintenance obligations, for example, a canal bank or some other infrastructure, and this needs to be taken into account. Proximity to a river may give rise to considerations regarding flooding which could have significant impact on the planning considerations and construction costs.

A visual inspection during a site visit at this point can be extremely revealing. What looks like one thing on a two-dimensional plan can take on a completely different complexion once it is seen in reality, such as when a boundary over which some oversailing rights (for the boom of construction cranes to use adjoining airspace) are required turns out to be a vertical cliff. It is important to ascertain at an early stage in the process what if any oversailing rights will be needed, so that the relevant parties can be approached for consent. You should also make enquiries of the seller about any existing disputes with adjacent proprietors, whether in relation to boundaries or otherwise. Access and possibly oversailing rights will be needed over the public park next to the Sardinia Terrace site, since the site itself is quite tight and there are buildings on the other sides of the surrounding streets.

8.29.4 Site Visit

A site visit with your client and development team could be useful, when involved in a development. It enables physical issues that might not be clear from the title to be easily checked. It also gives you an opportunity, along with the development team, to look at issues of access to and from the site during construction and for the final development, and consider servicing arrangements, which might be affected by the topography of the land. A steep incline on the site will affect the route and locations for laying of drainage and water pipes, and might mean that different servitude rights are needed. It is also an ideal opportunity to get to know and benefit from the knowledge and perspective of the development team. A visual inspection of the Sardinia Terrace site discloses that locals are using the ground to the rear of the pub for car parking and as a site for car boot sales. You may need to investigate how long the parking area has been used. You also note that there is a small grocer's shop at the corner of Sardinia Terrace and Lombardy Street. These issues may well elicit objections to the planning proposals.

8.29.5 Access

A crucial part of any development is ensuring that there are adequate access rights. This can mean not just owning the land where points of access are taken, but also checking existing servitude rights and the sufficiency of them to allow the site to be accessed for all necessary purposes, both during the construction phase and for the final built out development. Even when a site abuts an adopted public road, it is still important to consider access carefully. The best position for forming a new entry point off the road and into the site may clash with the position on the site where the developer proposes to put new buildings. New rights might be needed or development proposals might have to be re-visited. For sites that are being acquired for residential development there are considerations of density of population and consequent traffic management issues, as well as increasing the burden on existing servitude rights, depending on how they are expressed. It is also important to check whether the site or any part of it is used as access by third parties, whose rights may need to be accommodated or re-negotiated. And remember that not all access rights will necessarily be set out in the title.

Access points to consider:

(i)   What are the current access arrangements: adopted public road or private access route?

(ii) What is the exact extent of adopted public road, pavement or verge? While a Property Enquiry Certificate may confirm that the road serving the property is adopted and maintained by the roads authority, it will not (usually) show the extent of the adoption. Although roads authorities take an expansive view of what constitutes the 'verge', it can sometimes be the case that little strips of land between the road and the title to the site exist in a no-man's land and are not included in the adopted extent. A plan should be obtained from the roads authority showing the exact extent of adoption.

(iii) Can the current access be used for the development or will new roads need to be constructed for which a Road Construction Consent will be required?

(iv) If the site is for residential development and roads to the adoptable standard are to be constructed, a road bond will be required[176].

(v)   Are the current entry points from the public road suitable for the development?

(vi) Where new access points off a public road are needed, does the site include sufficient ground for bell-mouth openings, visibility splays or deceleration lanes? If not, can land be acquired or servitudes obtained? Even in rural areas this can be an issue

176 Section 17 of the Roads (Scotland) Act 1984.

if lorries which require large turning circles are transporting large loads, such as turbines for wind farms, need to swing over adjoining land as they turn off the main road.

(vii)   Check that there are no other proposals, for example, roads authority plans for road widening or closure that might adversely impact on access to, or development proposals for, the site.

(viii)   If new access rights are required, who are the land owners to be approached either for renegotiating existing servitudes or obtaining new ones? There could be significant cost consequences, which might have an impact on the viability of the development. It is important to ensure that any new grants of access will be forthcoming and to clarify the cost.

(ix)   Are existing servitudes adequate for the proposed use of the development? For example, if the existing servitude right of access is for agricultural purposes, then it is unlikely to be sufficient for use as access to a retail park.

(x)   What, if any, third-party access rights are there across the site? These might be constituted as express grants but there are classes of servitude that can exist but not be evident from the title, as well as public rights of way.

(xi)   Is there sufficient access for service vehicles and delivery lorries? In a small site where there are already built up areas, this can be an important consideration. If the Prontomart supermarket is build on the Sardinia Terrace site, the architect will need to make sure that the access into and provision within the site is sufficient to accommodate the large articulated transporters that the supermarket chain uses to deliver supplies from its centralised distribution centres.

8.29.6 Ransom Strips

As described in the context of roads at para 8.19, so-called 'ransom strips' can occur in any title. Clearly, when assembling a title for development made up of various component parts of different titles and properties, there is greater scope for areas of ground, small or large, outwith the seller's title, to be necessary to complete the 'jigsaw' of the development site.

Some parties may seek to exploit ransom strips by holding back small areas of land when selling off sites, or may unintentionally find themselves in a position where they hold land that suddenly becomes crucial for a development proposal to come to fruition. The good news is that usually that the owner of the ransom strip wants to sell. The bad news is likely to be the cost, since such a piece of land will command a premium over the actual value of the land itself.

It seems likely that the site of the Dog and Ferret pub could be a ransom strip (or plot) for the Sardinia Terrace project. The pub is somewhat rundown and although it has a small hard core of loyal regulars, it is not a particularly profitable enterprise, and the lease to KLPL is due to expire in two years' time.

8.29.7 Services

Checking the arrangements for services to the site, such as water, drainage, electricity, gas, telecoms etc. is as important as checking the physical access arrangements.

Points to consider in relation to services include:

(i)   Check with the development team where service routes are intended and what additional rights they consider will be required.

(ii)   Are the existing services and associated servitude rights sufficient for the purposes of construction and eventual use of the development?

(iii)   Do any existing services need to be relocated or enlarged and, if so, are the existing rights sufficient? Is there adequate land available to do so? Modern servitudes for services will often incorporate 'lift and shift' provisions for relocating pipes and cables, but older servitude rights often don't specify these;

(iv)   Will third parties, such as adjoining land owners, need to be approached for servicing arrangements? Do you need to inspect titles to adjoining land in connection with services arrangements?

(v)   Do any service media serving adjoining property run through, or over, the site? A gas main that needs an unbuilt on a strip of land 20 metres wide across its route could effectively sterilise land for development purposes. Moving or diverting existing pipe and cable routes could be time-consuming and potentially prohibitively expensive.

8.29.8 Surveys and Reports

Any development will involve a number of professionals and specialists, who will produce surveys and reports on various aspects of the site and the proposals for development. While you are not expected to be expert in all the terminology or implications of these reports (unless of course that is your particular specialism), it is important that you obtain and read these reports, particularly the main surveyors' report and any environmental and conditional reports. Note of course that environmental issues in particular are an extremely specialised area. If there are environmental or contamination issues, then advice should be sought from persons specialised and experienced in these matters. On larger sites, and with most developers, Environmental Consultants will be instructed, retained or even employed in-house to cover these issues, but you should always check that these issues are being picked up.

However, there might be aspects that emerge from your title examination that should be reported in this context. Previous uses of the site your client is buying may contain clues that point to possible contamination. If the site was a former gas works or used for some industrial process for example, then this fact should spark a recommendation for an environmental survey if none has been carried out. Once the title is registered in the Land Register, of course, access to these older titles is less common and they might no longer be available[177]. A wealth of ancillary information is lost in this way.

It is also good practice, where appropriate, to obtain old maps of the area concerned which will often show up features of old uses and can also be invaluable in piecing together parcels of land that suffer from vague or archaic or historical descriptions.

Standard reports such as PECs, Coal Authority reports, British Geological Survey reports and utilities searches will all disclose information that may be relevant, and should be passed on to your client and/or his surveyor and advisers.

---

177 Although it is possible that these will be in the Archive Record of the Registers.

8.29.9 Existing Buildings and Features

Where the site includes existing buildings or other features that will need to be demolished or removed to allow the development to take place, this will also need to be addressed. Older buildings to be demolished may contain asbestos, which needs to be removed and disposed of in a carefully controlled and regulated manner. Consents for demolition will need to be obtained. If any of the buildings on the site are listed, then any alterations to them will require listed building consent in addition to other consents. The design of the site may need to accommodate protected structures that it is not possible to remove. Trees subject to Tree Preservation Orders can also pose an obstacle to development.

8.29.10 Planning and Other Consents

It may be that the site your client is buying already benefits from planning or other consents for its development. Invariably planning consents will relate to a number of physical features of a site and make provision for access, services, servicing, traffic management, parking, density, use and so on. The terms of the consents may require, for example, that the access to the site is to be widened to improve visibility or that additional entry points need to be created. These can impact on how much land the developer needs to acquire, as well as the other terms and conditions of the title. If additional land or rights are needed to comply with the terms of the planning permission, then this needs to be addressed early on. Indeed, you may need to make it a condition of the purchase of the site that any necessary additional land or rights are obtained. As well as inspecting the reports and surveys of your client's other advisers, they also need to see a copy of your Title Report, and elements of it should be composed with this in mind.

If the consents and other documentation produced are complex, then it will be necessary to consult planning and construction lawyers, if you do not have this expertise yourself. Otherwise you should make it clear in your letter of engagement that these aspects will not be covered by you, or your firm.

Clearly, the earlier that you can establish whether additional land/ areas will be required, the better. Therefore, ensure your Title Report is something that the architects/planning consultants (and indeed planning lawyers) have seen and are aware of in the context of their discussions with the planning officers as they prepare the planning application. You do not want to end up with a consent that cannot be implemented because additional land/access is required, or where payment will be required to a third party (who will by then be aware of the planning consent) to secure the land/access.

SERVITUDES

8.30 Servitudes such as rights of access, rights to lay pipes etc were unaffected by feudal abolition. Although it is now no longer possible to create a negative servitude (servitudes prohibiting certain action), negative servitudes were not extinguished on the appointed day. Instead they were converted into 'negative real burdens' for a transitional period of 10 years, and some of these may have been preserved by the registration of an appropriate notice before 28 November 2014. If no notice was registered, then these converted servitudes no longer affect the property. Servitudes are often couched with conditions that apply specifically to the exercise of the servitude. While they may look like real burdens, they are in fact 'servitude conditions' which survive with the servitude itself. Remember that servitudes can be validly created by the running of prescription for 20 years and can be extinguished in this way too. It is now possible for prescriptive servitudes to be included in the Title Sheet for a property. See also paras 8.19 and 8.21 for servitude rights that should be checked for, when examining title.

ADJUDICATION TITLES

8.31 An adjudication may be granted against a person who either: (a) does not pay a debt; or (b) contracts to sell property under missives and then refuses or delays to transfer the property. Adjudication titles are not very common.

In case (a): adjudication for debt – the title given to the creditor is a security title only, and the debtor may redeem within 'the legal', which is a ten-year period from the date of decree. The decree obtained is registered in the Register of Sasines or Land Register. Such a title should not be accepted by a purchaser until the legal has lapsed. Any title registered prior to expiry of the legal will exclude indemnity, and the charges section of the title sheet will disclose the security aspect of the decree, for the purposes of ranking in relation to other securities. To remove the exclusion of indemnity on expiry of the legal, the adjudger has to obtain and register a decree of declarator of expiry of the legal.

In case (b): adjudication in implement – the title is absolute and may be accepted by a purchaser or a lender in security. A decree of adjudication in implement is equivalent to a conveyance of lands, and the creditor (or 'adjudger') completes title by recording the decree in the Register of Sasines or registering it in the Land Register.

Section 79 of the Bankruptcy and Diligence etc (Scotland) Act 2007 will, once commenced, abolish adjudication for debt and replace it with a diligence called land attachment.

GRATUITOUS ALIENATION AND UNFAIR PREFERENCE

8.32 During the course of your examination of title, you have to be alert to the possibility that a transfer of the property may have taken place at a price under its true value or in favour of one creditor in preference to the general body of the transferor's creditors. While a person is free to convey their property at less than market value, as a gift, or to anyone they choose, the status of such transfers alters significantly if the person was insolvent at the time, or the transfer in question renders that person insolvent. This is a complex area of the law, and the following description is, of necessity, no more than a general summary of the main provisions.

8.32.1 Gratuitous Alienation

A gratuitous alienation is a transfer for no, or inadequate, consideration by an insolvent granter[178]. If a transfer of this type takes place and the transferor is subsequently sequestrated or grants a trust deed for the benefit of his creditors or, if a company, it is wound up or an administrator is appointed, then the insolvency practitioner (IP) or any creditor may challenge the transfer. A receiver may not challenge a gratuitous

---

178 Section 34 of the Bankruptcy (Scotland) Act 1985 (individuals) and section 242 of the Insolvency Act 1986 (companies).

alienation but the holder of the relevant floating charge would be entitled to challenge. Gratuitous alienation provisions can also apply where the debtor is deceased, and within 12 months, his estate is sequestrated or a judicial factor appointed.

Where the recipient is an associate of the debtor, the alienation must have taken place within the period of five years immediately preceding the date of sequestration, and in the case of any other type of recipient from the debtor, within two years prior to that date.

The term 'associate' has a wide meaning[179]. It includes the debtor's husband, wife or civil partner or a relative (brother, sister, aunt, uncle, nephew, niece, etc.) or the spouse or civil partner of a relative of the debtor or the debtor's spouse, or any person with whom the debtor is in partnership, and includes an employee and an employer. A director or other officer of a company is treated as being an employee of that company for these purposes. A company can be an associate of another company in certain circumstances[180].

Note that, in addition to the statutory challenge, there remain certain rights of challenge at common law. The onus of proof on the pursuer is higher, since fraud must be shown, therefore these are rarely used. However, the common law challenge is available for up to 20 years[181].

8.32.2 Challenge

A challenge to a gratuitous alienation may be made by action of reduction in the Court of Session or seeking other redress in the Sheriff Court. A challenge will not be successful if it can be shown that:

(i)   the debtor was solvent immediately after (or at any time after) the alienation was granted (ie that the debtor's assets were greater than his liabilities);

(ii)   the alienation was for 'adequate consideration'; or

(iii) it was a birthday or Christmas or other conventional present or a charitable gift which it was reasonable for the debtor to make.

Note that, the challenge is against the recipient, not the debtor.

179 See section 74 of Bankruptcy (Scotland) Act 1985.
180 Sections 74(5A)–(5C) and (6), above.
181 See *McBryde on Bankruptcy* (1995) 2nd edn, paras 12.11–12.57.

If the challenge is successful, the remedy is a decree of reduction of the alienation, such restoration of property to the debtor's estate as is appropriate, or 'other redress'. The courts will seek to reduce the alienation or restore the property in preference to other routes – see *Short's Trustee v Chung*[182].

8.32.3 Unfair Preference

An unfair preference is a transaction entered into by a debtor, which has the effect of creating a preference in favour of one creditor or creditors to the prejudice of the general body of creditors[183]. To qualify as an unfair preference under statute, the preference must have been created not earlier than six months before the date of insolvency. Some types of transaction, such as transactions in the ordinary course of business, are exempt from challenge[184] and may be pled as a defence by the recipient. An unfair preference can be challenged by creditors and insolvency practitioners (but not receivers).

As with gratuitous alienations, preferences may also be challenged at common law. Again, the transaction must be shown to be fraudulent in nature and is, therefore rarely used, despite the long prescriptive period.

A challenge to an unfair preference is either by way of action of reduction in the Court of Session or seeking other redress in the Sheriff Court.

8.32.4 The Position of a Third-party Acquirer

A third party who has acquired a property from or through a recipient of a gratuitous alienation or unfair preference, for value and in good faith is protected[185].

While it may be difficult to tell from the face of a title that it was given by way of unfair preference, it might be easier to spot a gratuitous alienation,

---

182 [1991] SLT 473 at 476 per Lord Sutherland.
183 Section 36 of the Bankruptcy (Scotland) Act 1985 (individuals) and section 243 of the Insolvency Act 1986 (companies).
184 Section 36(2) of the Bankruptcy (Scotland) Act 1985 and section 243(2) of the Insolvency Act 1986.
185 Sections 34(4) and 36(5) of the Bankruptcy (Scotland) Act 1985 and sections 242(4) and 243(5) of the Insolvency Act 1986.

as this may refer to a nil or nominal consideration, or consideration that appears to be clearly inadequate for the size or likely value of the property concerned. References to 'certain good (and onerous) causes and considerations' should be carefully considered in their context. If faced with a transfer of this nature in the title being offered, can a third-party purchaser be said to be 'in good faith' if they proceed with their purchase without further enquiry?

8.32.4(i) Is the transferor solvent?

Much of this is about identifying whether there is any risk to your client. If the transaction effecting the transfer took place more than five years ago and the granter has not been sequestrated or wound up etc, then it is outwith the statutory challenge period. If not, then you should raise a query with the seller's solicitor as to the solvency of the transferor. The search in the Personal Registers will disclose whether any insolvency proceedings have been applied against that party.

8.32.4(ii) Certificate or declaration of solvency

It is debatable whether there is anything that can be obtained that would provide complete protection from challenge. However, if you are acting for a transferee from an individual and the consideration is nil or clearly significantly less than full value, in order to ensure that in the future the transfer cannot be perceived as a gratuitous alienation, it might be possible to obtain either a declaration or affidavit from the granter, or (possibly) a certificate from their accountant confirming that as at any date after the transfer, the granter was absolutely solvent (a formal expression meaning that the assets of the granter were greater than their liabilities).

How willing accountants may be to give such a certificate is a moot point, but in family transactions there might be a greater chance that something of the sort would be forthcoming. It should not be assumed that there is a problem with solvency just because the accountant is unwilling to produce the certificate. The accountant can only comment on the basis of the information that has been given to him. If it transpires that information has been withheld from him, the value of the certificate would be questionable, although having made enquiry and having received some form of assurance can help to demonstrate good faith. Also useful would be a statement of the reasons why the transfer is being made. So for example a father who decides for reasons of tax efficiency, or for 'love, favour and affection' to transfer property to his daughter, could confirm that this was the reason why the transfer was being made.

It is much harder to obtain a declaration or certificate of this type retrospectively, but where you are acting for a purchaser from the transferee, enquiry should be made as to the circumstances of the transfer, and ask for confirmation that the granter was solvent when, and immediately (or at any time) after the property was transferred. It is a matter of judgement how far it will be necessary to pursue this issue. You can also consider audited accounts for business transferors as these show the financial position at a particular point in time. Although these are based on assumptions, they have at least been subject to audit. Also, a qualified statement in the accounts would be a sign of something to look into (ie where auditors state they are unable to certify).

8.32.4(iii) The insolvent transferor

If the search discloses that the transferor is in some form of insolvency, a sensible course of action is to ask the seller's solicitor to find out from the IP if he intends to challenge the transfer. On appointment, any IP will look into transfers effected in the past five years with a view to identifying any gratuitous alienation or unfair preference, and investigate the circumstances of any such transfer.

OCCUPANCY RIGHTS

8.33 The occupancy rights of spouses in the matrimonial home have been recognised as an overriding interest on the title to any property that qualifies as a matrimonial home since 1982, when the Matrimonial Homes (Family Protection) (Scotland) Act 1981 came into force. As the name suggests, the policy reason behind the Act was to protect spouses (predominantly wives) from domestic abuse and provide that, even if they did not own the marital home, they had rights to stay there that did not depend on the consent of their spouse, and in extreme circumstances could apply to the courts to exclude that spouse from the home. The Civil

Partnership (Scotland) 2004 extended similar rights to civil partners. These occupancy rights of the non-entitled spouse or civil partner are such that they would have priority over the rights of a purchaser or a heritable creditor. So it is necessary when purchasing from a single individual to ascertain his or her marital status and ensure that the rights of any spouse or civil partner are addressed.

This will normally involve either (i) incorporating the consent of the spouse or civil partner into the documentation, either within the disposition or standard security, or as a stand-alone form, or (ii) a renunciation of the occupancy rights by that spouse or civil partner. Where the seller is unmarried, the position is covered by obtaining (iii) a declaration from the seller to the effect that the property is not a matrimonial home in relation to which a spouse or civil partner of the seller has occupancy rights. For further details, see para 4.9.4. Occupancy rights of a non-entitled spouse or civil partner will extinguish after of period of two years of non-cohabitation and non-occupancy[186].

RAISING OBSERVATIONS ON TITLE

8.34 It would be a rare title indeed that did not throw up some question or requirement for clarification. During the course of your title examination, or once you have finished looking at the titles provided to you by the seller's solicitor, you may need some further information or need to see further documents. These are generally known as 'observations on title' or 'title requisitions'. They may include standard requests such as the request for search reports or updates of these, asking for information about something that is in the knowledge of the seller, such as when the last common repairs were carried out, and confirmation that there are no outstanding repairs bills; details of the identity of any managing agent or factor and so on. For residential properties, you will find the seller's position in the Property Questionnaire. For commercial properties, you might find the PSG Due Diligence Questionnaire of some assistance as a checklist of issues that might be relevant to your particular title, as well as an indication of what to ask for if they are.

This is also the time to be requesting clarification about any matters arising during the course of your title examination and which you were

---

186 Section 5 of and Schedule 1, para 3 to the Family Law (Scotland) Act 2006.

jotting down as you went along. It is good practice to raise all of these observations at the same time, where you can, as this will let the seller's solicitors know the general extent of your requirements. Although this is not always possible, there is nothing more frustrating for a seller's solicitor than a trickle of requirements, and in particular, key issues raised at the last minute. However, since there may be other matters you wish to raise that you haven't at that stage identified, or you might have supplementary observations to make when you see the seller's solicitors responses, it is sensible to make it clear that your list of queries is not exhaustive, by saying for example that these are preliminary queries and that you will let the seller's solicitor know if you have any others.

There will come a point, however, and this will depend on how the missives are worded, that the seller's solicitor may ask you to declare that you are satisfied as to title. Caution should be exercised before making such a declaration, or you may need to caveat it by saying that it is subject to seeing updated clear searches, for example.

REMEDIES FOR AN UNMARKETABLE TITLE

8.35 The purchaser is, of course, entitled to resile if presented with an unmarketable title, but we can presume that the purchaser and seller both want to complete the purchase if they can. Often a problem with a title can be remedied, and the seller should be given the chance to try to do so.

There are many ways of reaching a satisfactory position, enabling the transaction to proceed, and the following suggest some of the ways in which a problem can be rectified or resolved. Not all of these will be suitable solutions if the property is already registered in the Land Register, rather than still in the Sasine Register and vice versa.

8.35.1 Disposition *per incuriam*

If a disposition has a bad mistake in it, for example, if it conveys the top-floor flat right instead of the top-floor flat left, the error can be rectified by getting the original granter to grant this form of disposition. It simply narrates that *per incuriam* the earlier disposition conveyed the wrong flat, and then goes on to dispone the correct one. The use of the Latin tag hides the fact that it was done (literally) 'by mistake'. A disposition of this type cannot, however, be used to correct the error, once the title has been registered in the Land Register, although remedial conveyancing is still possible if the parties agree.

8.35.2 By use of the Requirements of Writing (Scotland) Act 1995, sections 4 and 5

Section 4 of Requirements of Writing (Scotland) Act 1995 sets up a presumption as to the granter's subscription or date or place of subscription by application to the court, where the deed has not been witnessed. This is likely only to be useful where the granter is unavailable whether through incapacity or death, untraceable or unwilling to assist, since it will usually be far more straightforward to simply have the granter acknowledge his signature to a witness. Section 5 of the 1995 Act sets out the provisions for dealing with alterations to deeds, both prior to and after execution. Careful use of the provisions of these sections may assist in resolving a number of defects of execution and mistakes in the deed.

8.35.3 By use of the Law Reform (Miscellaneous Provisions) (Scotland) Act 1985, section 8(1)(a)

This useful provision of law allows a disposition (or other defectively expressed deed) to be rectified by the court, if it does not reflect the common intention of the parties to the deed. This applies both to deeds in the Sasine Register and interests or rights in the Land Register.

8.35.4 Rectification of the Register

Inaccuracies and errors in the Land Register can be rectified by the Keeper in accordance with rectification provisions. Prior to 8 December, 2014, applications to rectify a 1979 Act title were competent under section 9 of the 1979 Act. However, any such application which had not been resolved by that date fell as at that date[187]. It is still possible to claim against the Keeper's indemnity under the 1979 Act if a person was entitled to claim prior to 8 December 2014, but had not done so, or had made a claim, but it had not yet been determined by that day.

---

187 Schedule 4, para 14 to the 2012 Act.

Rectification is also possible under the 2012 Act[188] but only if there is a manifest inaccuracy in the Title Sheet, and what needs to be done to correct that inaccuracy is also manifest. See also para 2.6.

8.35.5 Positive and Negative Prescription

The running of prescription can cure a number of defects, including absence of title itself (see para 8.10). The right to enforce a real burden in the event of a breach now prescribes after five years, regardless of any knowledge on the part of the benefited proprietor, although only to the extent of the breach and provided there has been no 'relevant claim' or 'relevant acknowledgement'[189] made which would interrupt prescription.

8.35.6 Title Indemnity Insurance

An indemnity policy can be taken out to cover a defect in title, which recompenses the purchaser if a claim arises from a third party. Title indemnity policies are available for all manner of risks including: absence of matrimonial affidavit, giving rise to a claim by a non-entitled spouse; an *a non domino* disposition, where there is a claim by the true owner within the prescriptive period (although see para 8.10.7 regarding issues with the prescriptive claimant process); failure to establish a link in title; lack of access rights; burdens imposed on the property and a possible claim by the benefited proprietor when they have been contravened without having been discharged; discrepancies in the description of land and incorrect detailing of plans.

A purchaser is not, however, obliged to accept an indemnity, as it does not render a title marketable. It is only an indemnity until prescription corrects the defect. Indemnity policies are usually taken out for a period that coincides with the relevant prescriptive period applicable. If considering this option, remember that arranging insurance is a regulated activity and you must comply with Law Society (or, exceptionally, the Financial Conduct Authority) requirements. As a general rule, most practitioners will not be individually authorised and you should check what authorisation

---

188 Sections 80 to 85.
189 As these expressions are defined in sections 9 and 10 of the Prescription and Limitation (Scotland) Act 1973.

status, if any, your firm has, and what internal compliance procedures you have to observe.

8.35.7 The *actio quanti minoris*

This remedy, which applies automatically in terms of the Contract (Scotland) Act 1997, unless specifically excluded by contract, involves a reduction of the price where there is something wrong in the title of the property.

8.35.8 *De minimis* non curat lex

('The law does not care about little things'.) If the defect is minor or trivial, then it may be possible to ignore it.

8.35.9 Variation or Discharge of Burdens and Title conditions

It is not necessary to tolerate unacceptable burdens in the title. There are a number of ways that these can be varied or discharged, and one of these options may prove appropriate in the circumstances. Note that in the case of a purchase it will be usual for the purchaser to require the seller to obtain the variation or discharge, particularly if this involves an application to the Lands Tribunal, when the burdened owner must make the application.

8.35.9(i) Applications for variation or discharge under section 90 of the Title Conditions (Scotland) Act 2003

This section contains the main powers of the Lands Tribunal and is the one under which most applications to the Tribunal for variation of discharge of title conditions tend to be made. An owner of burdened property or any other person against whom a title condition is enforceable can apply to the Tribunal for a discharge or variation of the condition. Notice must be served on the parties entitled to enforce the condition who will have 21 days to make representations to the Lands Tribunal in respect of the application.

When applications for variation or discharge of a real burden are made under sections 90 or 91 of the Title Conditions (Scotland) Act 2003, affected parties are entitled to make representation to the Tribunal during the notice period. This includes, not just the owner of the benefited property, but any person who has title to enforce the title condition, and any person against whom the title condition is enforceable. This may include tenants, non-entitled spouses, liferenters and heritable creditors in possession, as well as, in appropriate circumstances, the Owners' Association and the owner of any unit in a development where a Development Management Scheme applies.

The Lands Tribunal also has the power to determine the validity, applicability or enforceability of any real burden or rule under a Development Management Scheme, or how a burden or rule may be interpreted. Generally, Lands Tribunal orders come into effect on registration, but this does not apply to orders stating that a burden is invalid or unenforceable or as to interpretation. This is because contractual enforceability (as opposed to enforceability as a real burden that runs with the land) is unaffected by any order of the Lands Tribunal[190]. In practice, however, it seems that any application for determination is usually accompanied by an application for discharge.

8.35.9(ii) Applications for variation or discharge of community burdens

There are three procedures for varying or discharging community burdens. The first under section 91 of the Title Conditions (Scotland) Act 2003 provides that owners of 25% of the units in a community may apply to the Lands Tribunal for a variation or discharge of a community burden. Again, 21 days are to be given for representations to be made to the Lands Tribunal in respect of the application.

Section 33 of the 2003 Act provides for variation or discharge by a majority of owners (or such other percentage as may be expressly stated in the constitutive deed). Intimation requires to be made to other owners in the community who have a period of eight weeks to apply to the Lands Tribunal to have the burden preserved unvaried in respect of the minority dissenting owners.

Section 35 of the 2003 Act provides for variation and discharge by owners of affected units or by the owners of all adjacent units (within four metres of the affected unit). Intimation has to be sent to other owners in the community, either by notice, 'lampposting', or by local advertisement

190 Section 104(4) of the 2003 Act.

with an eight week period allowed for other owners to make application for preservation, unvaried, of the burden.

8.35.9(iii) Factors to which the Lands Tribunal are to have regard in determining applications

Whereas, prior to 28 November 2004, the criteria which the Land Tribunal could consider under the Conveyancing and Feudal Reform (Scotland) Act 1970 were somewhat limited, the Tribunal's powers were expanded significantly by the Title Conditions (Scotland) Act 2003. Section 100 sets out a list of factors for the Tribunal to take into account to a greater or lesser extent, and in whatever combination, as they see fit.

Very usefully, in an early Lands Tribunal case *Ord v Mashford*[191], the Lands Tribunal made a point of setting out the approach that they expected to take to each of the factors contained in section 100. In general terms, it seems that the main factors that the Tribunal look at are the balance between factor (b) namely the extent to which the condition confers a benefit on the benefited property (or the public) and factor (c), the extent to which the condition impedes the enjoyment of the burdened property. In addition, factor (a): any change in circumstances since the title condition was created, is also major consideration. Factors (a), (b) and (c) are very similar to the original grounds to be considered by the Lands Tribunal under section 1(3) of the Conveyancing and Feudal Reform (Scotland) Act 1970, which has been repealed. Since *Ord v Mashford*, the Lands Tribunal has refined its approach in this respect, and in *Franklin v Lawson*[192] it updates its approach to several of the factors.

The Section 100 factors are:

(a) any change in circumstances since the title condition was created (including, without prejudice to that generality, any change in the character of the benefited property, of the burdened property or of the neighbourhood of the properties);

The Tribunal indicated that in considering factor (a) 'it is unnecessary and inappropriate to approach change by seeking first to determine the extent

191 [2006] SLT (Lands Tr) 15 and LTS/LO/2004/16.
192 LTS/TC/2012/23.

of the neighbourhood. If change in a local area is relevant we can take it into account without the need to characterise it in any particular way'. This is a welcome simplification of the arrangements under the 1970 Act.

(b) the extent to which the condition: (i) confers benefit on the benefited property; or (ii) where there is no benefited property, confers benefit on the public;

Factor (b), which looks at the extent to which the condition either confers benefit on the benefited property; or, confers benefit on the public, can be difficult to assess. Put another way, it involves considering what the adverse impact would be on the benefited property if the development in question were allowed. In *Franklin v Lawson*, the impact was on the view from Mr Lawson's house and the Tribunal determined that the adverse impact would in fact be minor. Under the similar 1970 Act provision, it was used in the context of a balance of 'undue' burden against benefit, and little benefit was needed to persuade the Tribunal that an application under that section should be refused.

Now factor (b)(i) has a major role but has to be considered in the context of a typical benefited property, not the personal feelings of an individual in any case.

(c) the extent to which the condition impedes enjoyment of the burdened property;

Factor (c), is the direct counterpoint to factor (b) and invariably it is the balance between these two factors that will be crucial in the Tribunal's decision.

In *Ord v Mashford*, the Tribunal said it considered factor (c) to be relatively unimportant, given that it would be self-evident that enjoyment is impeded, hence the reason for the application in the first place. Practice has shown, however, that invariably factor (c) and the way in which it interacts with other factors, especially factor (b), now appears to be one of the factors most regularly considered. In *Franklin v Lawson*, the Tribunal said there was no doubt that the title restriction significantly impedes enjoyment of the burdened property. The term 'enjoyment' is used in a wide sense, encompassing all the uses an unburdened owner might seek to make of his or her property. In this case it would add value to their property by the extension and gain a significant benefit in terms of increased accommodation.

447

(d) if the condition is an obligation to do something, how (i) practicable; or (ii) costly, it is to comply with the condition;

The Tribunal didn't comment on this factor in *Ord v Mashford* as it was not relevant to that case. It does seem as though this will factor will always be entirely case specific.

(e) the length of time which has elapsed since the condition was created;

Again, in *Ord v Mashford*, the Tribunal considered this factor as usually unimportant, at least 'at first blush', since 'mere duration tells us little as to whether it can be regarded as out of date, obsolete or otherwise inappropriate.' But one possible effect of this provision is to direct attention to the need to have regard to the impact of gradual change in attitudes over time.

That would seem to be borne out by the fact that elsewhere in the Title Conditions (Scotland) Act 2003, old burdens are seen perhaps as more likely than not to be redundant – hence the 'sunset rule' provisions for burdens over 100 years old in Part 1 of the Act.

(f) the purpose of the title condition;

The Tribunal's original approach appeared to be to interpret factor (f) subjectively in its historical context. So rather than looking at what purpose the burden currently achieves, it would consider instead what was the intention of the original parties. This would mean that it would confine consideration of the benefit in terms of factor (b) to benefits that would pertain at the time of the original creation of the burden.

It now seems that the Tribunal will consider factor (b), even when the benefit concerned was not the original one in contemplation. That was specifically the case in *Franklin v Lawson*. The original purpose of the condition was probably to preserve amenity of the development and also at the time when the developer had a continuing role as superior, to generate income to the superior from applications for consent to alterations. Had that been the effect of factor (b), there would have been no allowing the issue in this case which was the protection of Mr Lawson's view – that would not have been the original intention of the condition.

(g) whether in relation to the burdened property there is the consent, or deemed consent, of a planning authority, or the consent of some other regulatory authority, for a use which the condition prevents;

In *Ord*, the Tribunal indicated that it sees this factor as a relatively neutral one. In contrast, in *Franklin*, it acknowledged that the grant of planning permission can be of significance where the general amenity of a scheme is in issue (although it was not the issue in *Franklin*).

(h) whether the owner of the burdened property is willing to pay compensation;

The Tribunal says in both *Ord* and *Franklin* that it is difficult to determine what weight can be given to this factor, but state that willingness to pay is hardly a factor in the merits of the application, merely that it could be a consideration if imposed that would determine discharge or not (ie if payment of compensation is a condition of discharge, payment would result in discharge, whereas failure to pay would result in no discharge).

(i) if the application is under section 90(1)(b)(ii) of the Act, the purpose for which the land is being acquired by the person proposing to register the conveyance; and

Factor (i) was not relevant in either *Franklin* or *Ord*. Section 90(1)(b)(ii) concerns applications concerning compulsory purchase where land is to be acquired by agreement under section 107 of the Act, and so will only be relevant in limited circumstances.

(j) any other factor which the Lands Tribunal consider to be material.

Both current and previous law provide for other factors to be taken into account. It remains the case, however, that personal interests of the parties are not relevant, the Tribunal is concerned with matters of heritable rights.

The Lands Tribunal has an overriding duty to act reasonably in considering any application. In respect of applications for variation of community burdens under sections 33 or 35, where a representation is made for preservation of the burden unvaried, the Lands Tribunal has to consider whether the variation or discharge in question is in the best interests of the owners of all the units in the community, or is unfairly prejudicial to one or more of those owners.

8.35.9(iv) Termination of burdens over 100 years old (the 'sunset rule')

Old burdens of over 100 years old (counting from the date of registration of the constitutive deed) may be extinguished by application to the Lands Tribunal for termination. This is designed to help to remove outdated amenity burdens, and does not apply to facility or service burdens, nor rights to work minerals, nor conservation or maritime burdens. The termination procedure also involves an intimation and notification procedure which is set out in ss 20 to 24 of the Title Conditions (Scotland) Act 2003.

8.35.9(v) Discharge by agreement

Traditional routes to extinction of real burdens continue to apply, so that parties may agree between themselves to extinguish burdens, whether neighbour burdens or community burdens, although in the latter case, unless the community is small, reaching agreement of all parties can be problematic. A Discharge of real burdens is often described as a 'Minute of Waiver'.

8.35.10 Acquiescence

Under section 16 of the Title Conditions (Scotland) Act 2003, where a real burden has been breached in a way that involves the incurring of material expenditure, and any benefit from the expenditure would be lost if the burden were to be enforced, acquiescence will apply, if the person entitled to enforce the breach consents to the breach, or is aware or (because of its nature) ought to be aware of the breach. They will be personally barred from objecting. If the party entitled to enforce the breach has not objected to the breach by the end of a reasonable period, not exceeding 12 weeks, from the date on which the activity constituting the breach is substantially completed, then the burden is extinguished to the extent of the breach. An important point to note concerning this provision, however, is that everyone who has an interest to enforce must not object to the breach for acquiescence to apply. If, for example, a tenant or a non-entitled spouse of a benefited owner objected, even if the owner did not, this would prevent the operation of this statutory acquiescence.

REPORTING ON TITLE

8.36 You will have to let your client know about the terms of the title they are buying. How much information you need to give them, and in what format, will depend on the type of property, the complexity of the title, and the type of client.

8.36.1 Reporting on Residential Property

If you are acting for a residential client purchasing a house, the chances are they do not expect to get, and probably would not welcome, a detailed Title Report in the form in which you would report to a commercial client. However, it is just as important that you ensure your client is made aware of the things about their property that they should, or need to, know and that you have ascertained from your title examination and inspection of searches and reports. The terms of the title to their house are just as important to a residential purchaser as the terms of a commercial purchase are to a commercial client. More so in some respects, particularly in relation to restrictions on use, access arrangements, boundary and other maintenance obligations. Depending on deadlines or timescales in the Missives, you may be sending them information, or having conversations or email exchanges with them from an early point in the transaction, to ensure that the extent of the property is correct, for example. Letting your client see a plan of the property is essential, and it may also be prudent to let the surveyor see the plan as well.

While purchasers of residential property do not usually need a formal Title Report for their record purposes, it is a good idea to send them copies of key items such as a Deed of Conditions for houses in an estate, provided of course that you provide them with a bit of an explanation. A single letter or e-mail summarising the important parts of their title that they will need to know for future reference, along with a plan, is a helpful reminder, both for you and your client.

8.36.2 Reporting on Commercial Property

The Report on Title is a fairly essential element of the purchase of commercial property, although again it is likely that, if there are issues arising during your examination of the title, you will have communicated with your client about them as you go along. Producing an interim draft Report at a key point in the transaction can be a useful way of drawing together the current state of play and summarising all of the issues that have been advised and discussed in phone calls and correspondence. If there are matters in the title or other aspects of your due diligence where remedial action or corrective steps are required, this draft Report will flag these. It can also identify reports or documents that you have still to examine, such as final searches or updated reports, and that might alter the terms of your final report.

8.36.3   Content and Style of Reporting

In any Report on Title, the essential thing to remember is that it should not look anything like your notes on title. The object of reporting on title is to give your client the key facts about the property, in a clear and readable format. They do not need to see details of the deeds in which some of the information is contained. For example, they need the Report to tell them that there is a use restriction preventing the property being used for industrial purposes, not that the use restriction is contained in a deed that was 'recorded in the Division of the General Register of Sasines for the County of Perth and registered in the Books of Council and Session on ... '

Consider whether you need to report to your client on *de minimis* issues or spent burdens. A lot of old title conditions were about regulating the use of properties in Victorian times and earlier, when there was little or no planning control. The fact that there is a prohibition against using the common yard as a dunghill, or that there is a prohibition against using the property as a candlemakers or a tannery, is irrelevant in modern times.

Use plans to identify both the extent of the property and issues that affect parts of the property, or burdens that affect only specific areas of it. If you are reporting on a site assembly, try to produce a composite plan showing how the title is made up and what conditions affect it. Attaching a series of copies of old and mutually inconsistent plans that make up the overall site are less helpful (although might be necessary for some elements of your Report) as it can be difficult for the client to piece together the different component parts from this motley collection, and this is one area where misunderstandings or lack of clarity can arise.

Finally, once you have put together your Report it is a good idea to insert an 'Executive Summary' at the start, highlighting the critical points that your client either needs to make a decision about, or at least that you need him to be consciously aware of. This is a particularly useful and helpful aspect of reporting for a client if the Report itself is lengthy and complicated, or if you are reporting on a number of properties.

EXAMINING TITLE ON BEHALF OF COMMERCIAL LENDERS

8.37 In commercial transactions involving funding, the lenders will instruct their own solicitors to act on their behalf, who will examine the title, unless arrangements have been made for the purchaser's solicitors to produce a Certificate of Title to the lender (see para 8.38). There are no real differences between examining title on behalf of a purchaser, and your examination of a title when acting for a lender in the taking of a standard security.

A good rule of thumb to bear in mind should the borrower default in the future, is that the lender will want to sell the property without any difficulties arising out of the title. This means you must be scrupulously thorough (as you would always be) in your examination of title and in raising observations on title and ensuring that any title problems are rectified. While the purchaser may, or may be expected to 'take a view' on certain title matters and accept them as they stand, lenders are less inclined to do this, and may simply be unprepared to compromise.

However, it is also the role of the lender's solicitors to advise their client and, where possible, a pragmatic approach should be taken. Remember that, when acting for a lender, you have a contractual obligation to adhere to their general 'standing instructions to solicitors' in the majority of cases. If a client lender decides to depart from the position as indicated by those instructions, for example if it agrees to lend despite there being some flaw with the title to the property, you must record the lender's instructions to that effect on your file, and to confirm these instructions in writing to them, or request written confirmation from them for record purposes. For the most part though, a lender is unlikely to accept something that might give it a problem with marketability in the future, as a future purchaser might not take a similar view, making the property difficult to sell, or resulting in a reduction in the price.

CERTIFYING TITLE

8.38 Reporting on title and certifying the title usually mean two different things, depending on whether the title is residential or commercial.

8.38.1 Residential Property

It is usual for the solicitor for a purchaser of residential property to also act for the lender to the purchaser, and to draw up the security documentation as well as the conveyance. The lender will expect that the purchaser's solicitor will certify to them that there is a good and marketable title to the property that is being given in security for the mortgage, and this will normally be done on the lender's form of certificate that comes with the loan instructions. You should ensure that you comply with any standard terms and conditions that the lender expects of the solicitor in this case. These may be contained in documents that accompany loan instructions; in particular, you must note and comply with any specific conditions that are applied to the particular borrower or the particular property, such as ensuring that building warrants and certification of completion are available for alterations to the property. Conditions with which you are expected to comply will also be included in the Council of Mortgage Lenders (CML) handbook, which contains not only general conditions but also specific requirements of particular lenders which may diverge from the standard position.

8.38.2 Commercial Property

In anything other than *de minimis* situations, the commercial property lawyer will not act for the borrower and the lender in the same transaction. Lenders will often instruct their own solicitors to examine the title that you have just examined for the purchaser. It is quite common for the purchaser's solicitor to be asked to produce a Certificate of that title for the benefit of the lender, based on the examination that they have already carried out for the purchaser.

Although some lenders (banks) have their own preferred style of certificate that they require solicitors to use, the industry standard style is the City of London Law Society Land Law Committee (CLLS) long form certificate of title. The Scottish equivalent produced in liaison with the CLLS is the PSG Certificate of Title, which adopts the same approach and format and is therefore particularly useful in cross-border transactions, where English solicitors will work from the CLLS Certificate and will expect the Scottish solicitors to work from a Scottish version of that document. It can, of course, be used on a standalone basis for Scottish transactions. Although principally for use in lending situations, it can be adapted for other purposes. The assumption is that the certificate will be granted by the solicitors acting for the purchaser/borrower, and it would require to be adapted if it were to be granted by the seller's solicitors in any given transaction.

The PSG Certificate is available on the website of the PSG[193] along with Guidance Notes and a Client questionnaire for use in conjunction with the Certificate. The current version at the time of writing is the seventh edition.

8.38.2(i) Basic structure of the certificate

The Certificate is intended to be comprehensive and strike a reasonable balance between the interests of those to whom it is addressed and the solicitors who give it. The solicitors who give the Certificate are described in the Notes as the 'certifier'.

There are essentially two distinct elements to the Certificate – the certification, contained in the front end and in Parts 1–5 of the Schedule, and the disclosures which follow each of the statements in each part of the Schedule and at the end of the main body of the certificate. This is a change from the previous edition of the Certificate where the disclosures were made in one part of the Schedule.

The certification sections provide the template which sets out the ideal position that the recipient of the Certificate is seeking to have certified. The disclosure sections are then used to provide further information on details of title, leases etc. and, most importantly, to make any qualifications necessary in relation to matters where there is any departure from the ideal position stated in the certification, in effect, proceeding by way of exception reporting.

---

193 See www.psglegal.co.uk/certificate_of_title.php.

The certification sections should be regarded as sacrosanct (subject to necessary drafting to tailor defined terms etc. to the particular circumstances) unless there are specific transactional requirements, on which both parties agree, to make amendments to the text. Clause 5 of the main body of the Certificate states that no changes have been made to the Certificate and would need to be disclosed against if amendments were agreed. The certification sections themselves should never be amended by way of making qualifications or disclosures, which properly belong in the disclosure sections. For example, if there is a title issue, the certification sections of the Certificate should still state that the title is valid and marketable, but the appropriate disclosure section should contain details of the defect or flaw or other issue affecting the title which qualifies the statement made in the certification. It is essential that this principle is followed if the Certificate is to be used properly.

On occasion, the certifier and recipient of the Certificate may agree that a particular transaction requires a different approach. It is crucial that any changes to the form of the Certificate are transparent (clause 5 of the main body of the certificate highlights that point).

8.38.2(ii) Content of the Certificate

As a general rule, the Certificate should summarise the effect of the title and other documents, instead of simply attaching copies of the relevant writs. It is intended to replace an investigation of title by the recipient's solicitors. If they have to read not only the Certificate, but also a bundle of documents attached to it, the point of the Certificate is, to some extent, lost. Having said that, there are occasionally circumstances when a document, or a part of a document, is so important and so complex that it cannot be summarised accurately. While such circumstances may be rare, where they do exist, it would be appropriate for the document, or an extract from it, to be annexed to the certificate.

In practice, each statement of certification in the front end certification part of the Certificate needs to be checked to decide whether the statement can be given without qualification. If it cannot, then the disclosure should be made in the appropriate Disclosure boxes so that it is quite clear what the granter of the Certificate is certifying, and it is also clear to the recipient of the Certificate the extent of the certification that can be relied on.

8.38.2(iii) Addressees of the Certificate

It is an important consideration to whom the Certificate is to be addressed, as the solicitor giving the Certificate will have a duty to that addressee, as though it were his own client. Multiple addressees should be resisted, as should the ability for the addressee to assign the benefit of the Certificate to other parties. Usually the granter of the Certificate will have in mind the nature of the addressee when he is drafting the Certificate. He does not want to suddenly find that he owes a duty to an assignee who may have a completely different set of requirements.

8.38.2(iv) Cap on liability for those giving the Certificate

The solicitors giving the Certificate may seek a limitation or 'cap' on liability where the same Certificate is addressed to more than one person, in order to prevent a double claim against the solicitors and to ensure that the solicitors' liability to all ultimate addressees does not exceed the liability to the original addressee of the Certificate. Any such limitation or cap must be a matter to be agreed by the solicitors and the addressees on a case-by-case basis.

Chapter 9

Conveying the Property: The Disposition and Other Deeds

INTRODUCTION

9.1 Having completed examination of title (or having examined enough of the title to know what is to be conveyed to the purchaser) it is time for the purchaser's solicitors to draft the conveyance. This is done by way of Disposition these days since, with the demise of the feudal system, the complications of feu contracts, feu dispositions, charters of novodamus and dispositions ad perpetuam remanentiam ('ad rem') are a thing of the past.

Once drafted, the disposition is sent to the seller's solicitor for revisal or approval. The seller's solicitor revises or approves the disposition and returns it to the purchaser's solicitor, who in turn has this document engrossed[1] and then sends the typed principal deed known as the 'engrossment', back to the seller's solicitor for signature by their clients. The draft disposition is also returned for comparison purposes. It is just as likely these days that this process will be done electronically, with the final version being sent to be printed out by the seller's solicitor, and the previous draft is compared using revision indicator tools.

A disposition needs to contain the following clauses:

(a) narrative clause: granter, grantee, any consents, and the consideration;

(b) dispositive clause: words of transference, destination of grantee, description (which can include postal address) of subjects, reference to burdens or title number;

(c) ancillary clauses: date of entry, and warrandice; and

(d) testing clause (see para 11.3.3).

---

1   An interesting term, which all lawyers understand, the origin of which is a little obscure. Suffice it to say that, in conveyancing terms, it means producing the final version of the document for signing, sometimes on better quality paper than the draft.

Drafting a disposition can be a very straightforward matter if your client is buying a property that is registered in the Land Register and no new rights or burdens are being created.

If the title to the property is still in the Sasine Register then a few more clauses are required, but the structure of a disposition follows a tried and tested format.

Things start to get a little more complicated when it is also necessary to impose new burdens and/or servitudes to implement the transaction, but help is at hand with a series of style dispositions that cater for these situations, available from the PSG website[2] (and see paras 9.11.4, 9.11.5 and 9.11.6).

There are specific considerations when the nature of the property means that the owner is selling it off in several parcels. This happens when a developer or builder buys land to build a number of houses or retail units or office buildings, and plans to sell each unit to individual purchasers. Very often, a standard form of disposition will be prepared by the seller's solicitor for use by the purchaser's solicitor, departing from the normal procedure, in which the disposition is drafted by the purchaser's solicitor. The imposition of new burdens and servitudes is handled differently, by using a deed that will be common to all of the units – a Deed of Conditions. Since the introduction of the Title Conditions (Scotland) Act 2003, new drafting options are open to the solicitor.

There is also a variety of circumstances when an additional clause or two may need to be incorporated into your disposition: special destinations; Lands Tribunal application time limits; or supersession clauses for example. These are all considered in detail in this chapter.

'VALID' DEED

9.2 If you are doing your job properly, and have examined the title thoroughly, using your experience and expertise (see Chapter 8), then, of course, it would be expected that the disposition that you are presenting for registration is 'valid'. However, the 2012 Act is very particular about 'valid' deeds, and includes a definition of what that should be:

---

2   See www.psglegal.co.uk/post_feudal_reform.php and www.psglegal.co.uk/residential.php.

'A deed on which an application under section 21[3] is based is "valid" for the purposes of this Act if, (a) by the registration applied for, a right would be acquired, varied or extinguished, or (b) the deed is certificatory of an acquisition, variation or extinction which has taken place'[4].

In other words, the deed has to actually and competently achieve what is intended – in the case of a disposition, to ensure that the disponee acquires right to the property. Essentially this means that the deed must be properly drawn and executed, and the granter of the deed must have both title and capacity to grant. Also, the deed must be capable of doing what it purports to do in each case. So a disposition must have dispositive effect, and a disposition intended to create real burdens must be properly constitutive in terms of section 4 of the Title Conditions (Scotland) Act 2003.

If the deed fails the validity requirements, the Keeper must reject it.

The following list of requirements for a valid and registrable deed must be present:

1   The granter of the deed has title and capacity to grant it.

2   The deed is a registrable deed and contains:

    (i)   Name and designation[5] of the granter that is correct and sufficient

    (ii)   Name and designation of the grantee that is correct and sufficient

    (iii)   Name and designation of any consenter that is correct and sufficient

    (iv)   References to any change of name

    (v)   Description of the property (sufficient for the Keeper to delineate it on the cadastral map)

    (vi)   Acceptable words of conveyance (eg dispone, convey, grant, assign, discharge).

3   The deed has been subscribed by the granter and witnessed. Any annexations or schedules and plans have been docquetted and signed (or subscribed if counterpart execution is being used).

---

3   Ie, an application for registration of any registrable deed.
4   Section 113(2) of the 2012 Act.
5   See section 113(1), above.

The deed must be self-proving in terms of the Requirements of Writing (Scotland) Act 1995.

4   The name and designation of the witness are included.

5   Where a plan is required:

    (i)   The plan meets the the Keeper's 'Deed Plan Criteria'

    (ii) Where the description of the property refers to a plan, it must be sufficient for the Keeper to delineate the property on the cadastral map

    (iii) Any reference to an approved Development Plan Approval must be correct

    (iv) The deed plan is attached and contains an appropriate docquet, and is signed by the granter (subscribed if the deed is executed in counterpart).

6   Where the application relates to a registered plot or plots, the deed must narrate the correct title number(s).

7   Deeds relating to seabed plots must contain boundary coordinates (see para 9.9.7).

8   Where the application is over part of a registered plot, the deed must contain a plan and/or full bounding description sufficient for Keeper to delineate it on cadastral map (unless DPA applies).

9   No part of the plot should compete with an existing registered title.

DISPOSITION OF REGISTERED PROPERTY WITH NO NEW CONDITIONS

9.3 If the title is already registered in the Land Register, your client is purchasing everything in the title, and no new rights or obligations need to be imposed. Provided you refer to the correct title number, the property, along with all its rights, pertinents and burdens will be effectively referred to and, on registration, conveyed in a very simple form of disposition. Such a disposition might look something like this:

I, JAMES BROWN, residing at as Forty Three Piemonte Place, Kelvinforth, Perthshire IN CONSIDERATION of the price of THREE HUNDRED AND FIFTY THOUSAND POUNDS (£350,000) Sterling paid to me by MICHAEL MONK, residing at 27 Lombardy Street, Kelvinforth, Perthshire HAVE SOLD and DO HEREBY DISPONE to and in favour of the said Michael Monk and his executors and assignees whomsoever heritably and irredeemably ALL and WHOLE the subjects known as Forty Three Piemonte Place, Kelvinforth registered in the Land Register of Scotland under Title Number PTH12345; WITH ENTRY as at 30 November 2015; and I grant warrandice: IN WITNESS WHEREOF

Or you might want to adopt the new style of disposition developed by the PSG and the Law Society, which provides a new simplified style for a variety of residential conveyancing situations:

In this disposition:

["Consenter" means [   ] residing at [   ]]

"Date of Entry" means [   ] 20[   ];

"Price" means [   ] POUNDS (£[   ]) Sterling;

"Property" means ALL and WHOLE the property known as [   ] being the subjects registered in the Land Register of Scotland under Title Number [   ];

"Purchaser" means [   ] [and [   ]], [both] residing at [   ];

"Seller" means [   ] [and [   ]], [both] residing at [   ].

2   Narrative

2.1 The Seller is the proprietor of the Property.

2.2 The Seller has sold the Property to the Purchaser for the Price.

2.3 The Seller acknowledges receipt of the Price.

3   Disposition

The Seller [, with the consent of the Consenter, the [spouse][civil partner] of the Seller, for the purposes of the [Matrimonial Homes (Family Protection) (Scotland) Act 1981 as amended,][Civil Partnership Act 2004,] DISPONES the Property to the Purchaser [equally between them].

4   Entry

The Property is sold WITH ENTRY and VACANT POSSESSION on the Date of Entry.

5   [Matrimonial Homes/Civil Partnership Declaration

[The Seller declares that the Property is neither a matrimonial home in relation to which a spouse of the Seller has occupancy rights, the expressions "matrimonial home" and "occupancy rights" having the meanings respectively ascribed to them by the Matrimonial Homes (Family Protection) (Scotland) Act 1981, as amended, nor a family home in relation to which a civil partner of the Seller has occupancy rights under the Civil Partnership Act 2004.]

6   Warrandice

The Seller grants warrandice: IN WITNESS WHEREOF this disposition [consisting of [   ] pages] is executed by [   ] [me] [us] at the place and on the date undernoted in the presence of the undernoted witness:

DISPOSITION OF PROPERTY ON FIRST REGISTRATION IN THE LAND REGISTER

9.4 A sale of any property or land for valuable consideration will induce a first registration in the Land Register. The form that the disposition takes is exactly the same as for previous dispositions in the Sasine Register, so you need to ensure that the description of the property adequately describes the property, for example by incorporating a description by reference to a previous descriptive writ; that all rights and pertinents are clearly identified and that the writs that are referred to for burdens affecting the property are clearly listed. Usually the approach is to take the terms of the disposition in favour of the seller and replicate its terms, substituting the seller's name and address for that of the previous disponer and inserting the purchaser's details as the disponee. The disposition could look something like this:

I, JAMES BROWN, residing at as Forty Three Piemonte Place, Kelvinforth, Perthshire IN CONSIDERATION of the price of THREE

HUNDRED AND FIFTY THOUSAND POUNDS (£350,000) Sterling paid to me by MICHAEL MONK, residing at 27 Lombardy Street, Kelvinforth, Perthshire HAVE SOLD and DO HEREBY DISPONE to and in favour of the said Michael Monk and his executors and assignees whomsoever heritably and irredeemably ALL and WHOLE the subjects known as Forty Three Piemonte Place, Kelvinforth in the County of Perth more particularly described in, disponed by and shown outlined in red and coloured pink on the plan annexed to Disposition by Lightyear Estates Limited in my favour recorded in the Division of the General Register of Sasines for the County of Perth on Eleventh May Nineteen Hundred and Ninety Six; Together with all rights of common property, the parts, privileges and pertinents thereof, including all servitude and other rights, all fittings and fixtures therein and thereon, and my whole right, title and interest present and future in the said subjects; BUT THE SUBJECTS HEREBY DISPONED are so disponed always with and under, in so far as still valid, subsisting and applicable thereto the burdens, servitudes and other conditions contained in: (One) Feu Disposition by Walter John McFarlane in favour of Caroline Rowan recorded in the said Division of the General Register of Sasines on Twenty Fifth September Nineteen Hundred and seventy eight; and (Two) Feu Disposition by Rowan Homes Limited (in liquidation) in favour of Lightyear Estates Limited recorded in the said Division of the General Register of Sasines on Eleventh May, Nineteen hundred and ninety four; WITH ENTRY and actual occupation [or vacant possession] as at 30 November 2015; And I grant warrandice: IN WITNESS WHEREOF

Again, there is a simplified PSG/Law Society style. The only differences from the style for a registered property are: a definition of 'Burden Writs'

'Burden Writs' means [*list all writs referred to for burdens in full*]

the incorporation of a conveyancing description of the property, in the definitions section:

'Property' means ALL and WHOLE the property known as [ ][*full conveyancing description of property from prior writs*] [being the subjects described in and disponed by [Disposition] by [   ] in favour of [   ] dated [   ] and recorded in the Division of the General Register of Sasines for the County of [   ] on

[   ]; [and shown [   ] on the Plan] TOGETHER WITH (One) the parts, privileges and pertinents; (Two) the Seller's whole right, title and interest present and future in and to the property disponed;

And the imposition of the burdens in a separate clause:

Burdens

The Property is disponed ALWAYS WITH AND UNDER so far as valid, and subsisting and applicable the burdens, servitudes, conditions and other encumbrances contained in the Burden Writs.

DISPOSITION WITH CONSENT OF SPOUSE AND TO JOINT DISPONEES

9.5 The examples in paras 9.3 and 9.4 give the two basic forms of disposition for use when conveying a property, but there are many additional clauses that may be incorporated or sub-forms used depending on the circumstances. In the two examples already given, which relate to the transfer of a residential property, the marital position of the disponer James Brown, should have been checked. He may be single and have given a declaration to that effect (see para 4.9.4) or if married or in a civil partnership, his spouse or civil partner may have already signed a form of consent or a renunciation. It is usually more convenient, however, to incorporate the consent of a spouse or civil partner in the disposition. All of the PSG/Law Society residential style Dispositions incorporate wording for either a declaration or the consent of the spouse (see para 9.3).

Where a husband and wife or both civil partners are purchasing a property jointly, both parties should be included in the disposition as disponees. There also needs to be a discussion with them as to how they want the title to be taken. For spouses and civil partners the implications of the options open to them need to be discussed carefully, particularly within the wider context of their testamentary intentions, so that the appropriate destination is used in the deed. For spouses who plan to leave their whole estate to the other, then the use of a survivorship destination in the disposition can be attractive, because it provides that automatically on the death of the first spouse, the whole title in the property will be vest in the survivor. No further action would be necessary to transfer the whole title to that surviving spouse. This can be extremely convenient.

However, it is essential that both parties are quite clear about this and agree, since it will override any provisions in the will of either party even if made subsequently. A survivorship destination has to be effectively discharged, or evacuated, by the parties who have put it in place, by another deed. Even that is not without its difficulties. Gretton and Reid's suggestion is to incorporate a renunciation within a disposition in which the destination is evacuated – a belt and braces approach that must surely work[6]. They provide a style clause at page 78 of that text, although you might want to replace 'hitherto' with 'until now'.

Such destinations also used to cause considerable problems, if the spouses split up. To address this particular problem, section 19 and Schedule 1 para 11 of the Family Law (Scotland) Act 2006 provide that unless the survivorship destination expressly provides otherwise, then on divorce or annulment of the marriage, or dissolution or annulment of the civil partnership, the survivorship destination will no longer apply, so that on the death of either party their share will instead form part of their estate. There may be many reasons why the couple prefer to deal with the property in a different way, and own half (or some other proportion) shares *pro indiviso* in the property. It is important never to assume that your client will take title in a particular way, and you must always take instructions on this point.

In the following example, Mrs Brown joins in the disposition as consenter for the purposes of the Matrimonial Homes (Family Protection) (Scotland) Act 1981, and two alternative options are shown for the way in which Mr and Mrs Monk will hold title:

I, JAMES BROWN, residing at 43 Piemonte Place, Kelvinforth, Perthshire IN CONSIDERATION of the price of THREE HUNDRED AND FIFTY THOUSAND POUNDS (£350,000) Sterling paid to me by MICHAEL MONK and MRS JESSICA LAPIN or MONK, spouses, both residing at 27 Lombardy Street, Kelvinforth, Perthshire HAVE SOLD and DO HEREBY with the consent and concurrence of MRS ELEANOR JARVIE BROWN, residing with me at 43 Piemonte Place, aforesaid, the spouse of me the said James Brown for the purposes of

6   *Conveyancing* (2005) pp 77 to 78.

the Matrimonial Homes (Family Protection) (Scotland) Act 1981 (as amended) DISPONE to and in favour of the said Michael Monk and Mrs Jessica Lapin or Monk equally between them [*option 1 survivorship*: and to the survivor of them and to their respective assignees and disponees and to the executors of the survivor] [*option 2 equal shares*: and to their respective executors and assignees] whomsoever heritably and irredeemably ALL and WHOLE the subjects known as Forty Three Piemonte Place, Kelvinforth in the County of Perth more particularly described in, disponed by and shown outlined in red and coloured pink on the plan annexed to Disposition by Lightyear Estates Limited in my favour recorded in the Division of the General Register of Sasines for the County of Perth on Eleventh May Nineteen Hundred and Ninety Six; Together with all servitude and other rights of servitude to the subjects, all rights of common property, the parts, privileges and pertinents thereof, all fittings and fixtures therein and thereon, and my whole right, title and interest present and future in the said subjects; BUT THE SUBJECTS HEREBY DISPONED are so disponed always with and under, in so far as still valid, subsisting and applicable thereto the burdens, servitudes and conditions contained in: (One) Feu Disposition by Walter John McFarlane in favour of Caroline Rowan recorded in the said Division of the General Register of Sasines on Twenty Fifth September Nineteen Hundred and seventy eight; and (Two) Feu Disposition by Rowan Homes Limited (in liquidation) in favour of Lightyear Estates Limited recorded in the said Division of the General Register of Sasines on Eleventh May, Nineteen hundred and ninety four; WITH ENTRY and actual vacant possession as at 30 November 2015; And I grant warrandice: IN WITNESS WHEREOF

Using the new style of Disposition the deed would look like this:

In this disposition:

'Burden Writs' means:

(One) Feu Disposition by Walter John McFarlane in favour of Caroline Rowan recorded in the Division of the General Register of Sasines for the County of Perth on 25 September 1978; and (Two) Feu Disposition by Rowan Homes Limited (in liquidation) in favour of Lightyear Estates Limited recorded in the said Division of the General Register of Sasines on 11 May, 1994;

'Consenter' means MRS ELEANOR JARVIE BROWN, residing with me at 43 Piemonte Place, Kelvinforth, Perthshire;

'Date of Entry' means 30 November 2015;

'Price' means THREE HUNDRED AND FIFTY THOUSAND POUNDS (£350,000) Sterling;

'Property' means ALL and WHOLE the property known as Forty Three Piemonte Place, Kelvinforth in the County of Perth more particularly described in, disponed by and shown outlined in red and coloured pink on the plan annexed to Disposition by Lightyear Estates Limited in favour of the Seller recorded in the Division of the General Register of Sasines for the County of Perth on Eleventh May Nineteen Hundred and Ninety Six; TOGETHER WITH (One) all servitude and other rights of servitude to the subjects, (Two) all rights of common property, (Three) the parts, privileges and pertinents; and (Four) the Seller's whole right, title and interest present and future in and to the property disponed;

'Purchaser' means MICHAEL MONK and MRS JESSICA LAPIN or MONK, spouses, both residing at 27 Lombardy Street, Kelvinforth, Perthshire;

'Seller means JAMES BROWN, residing at 43 Piemonte Place, Kelvinforth, Perthshire.

2   Narrative

2.1 The Seller is the proprietor of the Property.

2.2 The Seller has sold the Property to the Purchaser for the Price.

2.3 The Seller acknowledges receipt of the Price.

3   Disposition

The Seller, with the consent of the Consenter, the spouse of the Seller, for the purposes of the Matrimonial Homes (Family Protection) (Scotland) Act 1981 as amended, DISPONES the Property to the Purchaser equally between them.

4   Burdens

The Property is disponed ALWAYS WITH AND UNDER so far as valid, and subsisting and applicable the burdens, servitudes, conditions and other encumbrances contained in the Burden Writs.

5   Entry

The Property is sold WITH ENTRY and VACANT POSSESSION on the Date of Entry.

6   Warrandice

The Seller grants warrandice: IN WITNESS WHEREOF this disposition [consisting of [   ] pages][together with the Plan] is executed by [   ] [me] [us] at the place and on the date undernoted in the presence of the undernoted witness:

DESIGNING THE PARTIES TO THE DISPOSITION

9.6 The parties to the disposition: the granter (disponer) and the recipient of the title (disponee) need to be sufficiently identified, and in the case of the disponee, provision should be made regarding their successors in title as well (see eg para 9.5 regarding survivorship destinations.

9.6.1 Natural Persons

It is usual to identify people by their full name, and their current address. When a natural person is the disponee, it has been customary to provide that the title is granted to the disponee 'and his/her executors and assignees', but this is not strictly necessary[7] and the new style Dispositions omit these superfluous words.

Where title is taken in joint names, the destination will depend on the shares in which the title is to be held and whether or not a special destination is required.

Sometimes titles can be held in specific shares. These shares are usually referred to as *pro indiviso* shares. This means that each *pro indiviso* share holder owns a share of the whole property, indivisible from the others.

---

7   See style dispositions in Gretton and Reid *Conveyancing* 4th edn at paragraphs 11-04 and 11-05.

They can transfer their *pro indiviso* share independently of the others if they want although, in practice, this can be difficult if, for example, the *pro indiviso* shares are of the title to a house occupied by the parties. However, this is a typical way of dealing with shares in common parts of developments (but see para 8.28.4) but is also typical in family titles, such as where the title to a farm is held by the father and his three sons who operate the farming business. The actual amount of the share is usually expressed (having fully designed the parties in the narrative clause) as eg:

> 'to and in favour of (One) the said Eric Sweet to the extent of a one-half *pro indiviso* share; (Two) the said David Alexander Sweet to the extent of a one-sixth *pro indiviso* share; (Three) the said Preston Maxwell Monk Sweet to the extent of a one sixth *pro indiviso* share and (Four) the said Christopher Gavin Sweet to the extent of the remaining one sixth *pro indiviso* share.'[8]

9.6.2 Companies

A limited company incorporated under the Companies Acts should be designed by referring to the legal system in which it is incorporated, its registered office and its unique company number, and if it has changed its name since the date on which it acquired title then the changes should be narrated eg

> We, LIGHTYEAR DEVELOPMENT COMPANY LTD, (formerly known as Lightyear Estates Ltd, our name having changed conform to Certificate of Incorporation on Change of Name dated 12 August Two thousand and four) incorporated under the Companies Acts (Registered Number SC809908) and having our registered office at 65 Registration Row, Perth

Where the change of name takes place following on re-registration of a plc the reference is to 'Certificate of Incorporation on Re-Registration of a Public Company as a Private Company'.

When a company is the disponee it has been customary to convey the title to the company 'and its successors and assignees', but again, this is not strictly necessary.

---

8   You can also use decimals and percentages.

9.6.3 Partnerships

Although a partnership can take title in its own name, it is far more common that title will be held by the partners in trust for the firm. A partnership granting a disposition may be designed as:

> We, CAROLINE ROWAN, residing at Piemonte House, Kelvinforth, Perthshire and ERIC SWEET, residing at The Old Railway House, Florence Park, Kelvinforth, Perthshire, Partners of and (as such partners) Trustees for the firm of Rowan Retirement Homes of Piemonte House, Kelvinforth

The partnership as disponee will be designed in the same way in the narrative clause and the destination will run as:

> the said Caroline Rowan and Eric Sweet, the Partners of the firm of Rowan Retirement Homes as trustees for the said firm, and their successors in office as such trustees and the survivor of them as trustees

9.6.4 Executors

An executor can either be nominated in the will of the deceased (executor nominate) or, if there is no will or none of the executors nominate survived the deceased, then a family member identified through the rules applicable on intestacy can be appointed as executor dative. There may be more than one executor. The executor's entitlement to the estate of the deceased including heritable property is confirmed by the confirmation of the deceased's estate, obtained by submitting an inventory of all of the property in the deceased's estate to the Commissary department of the relevant Sheriff Court for the area, which will then (subject of course to payment of any inheritance tax and confirmation dues) issue the formal Confirmation. When transferring title belonging to the deceased, the executor will narrate the terms of the Confirmation:

> I, ERIC SWEET, residing at The Old Railway House, Florence Park, Kelvinforth, Perthshire, Executor nominate of the late MRS NORMA McNAUGHT MONK or SWEET who resided sometime at Lionheart Farm, Kinlochalmond, by Kelvinforth, and latterly at Rowan Retirement Home, Calabria Crescent, Kelvinforth conform to Confirmation issued by the Commissariot of Glasgow and Strathkelvin at Glasgow in my

favour on 10 March 2014 and as such Executor nominate now in right of the Property (defined term) [disponed] IN CONSIDERATION of the price of [ ] paid to me, as Executor foresaid...

9.6.5 Trustees

In dispositions granted by trustees, the trustees are named and the deed of trust or other document under which they are appointed is narrated:

WE, the RIGHT Honourable RICHARD BYRON CHILDS, Earl of Kinlochalmond and Dunvorlich, of Lochalmond House, Kinlochalmond by Kelvinforth Perthshire, THE RIGHT HONOURABLE ANN CHILDS, Countess of Kinlochalmond and Dunvorlich, of Lochalmond House aforesaid, and HENRY ROSE PINK of 65 Registration Row Perth the Trustees now acting under Deed of Trust by The Right Honourable Richard Glenalmond Childs, 4th Earl of Kinlochalmond and Dunvorlich dated 18 September 1982 and registered in the Books of Council and Session on 28 March 1988 (the 'Seller') heritable proprietors of the Property (defined term) [disponed]

When trustees acquire title, the dispositive clause may run along the following lines:

to and in favour of the said Richard Byron Childs, Ann Childs and Henry Rose Pink as trustees foresaid and their successors in office and the survivors and survivor of them as trustees and trustee foresaid

9.6.6 Limited Partnerships

The limited partner does not get involved in the day to day business of the limited partnership. Title is held in name of the General partner:

We, LIONHEART GENERAL PARTNER LIMITED, incorporated under the Companies Acts (Registered Number SC090909) and having our Registered Office at Lionheart Farm by Kinlochalmond Perthshire, as General Partner and Trustee of The Lionheart Limited Partnership, registered as a Limited Partnership under the Limited Partnership Act 1907 (Registration Number LP9999) and having its principal place of business at [ ]

When the limited partnership is taking title, the dispositive clause will generally say:

> to and in favour of the said Lionheart General Partner Limited as the General Partner of and as such, Trustee for Lionheart Limited Partnership

9.6.7 Limited Liability Partnerships

Limited Liability Partnerships refer to their incorporation under the Limited Liability Partnerships Act 2000 and provide their registered number:

> DUNVORLICH RENEWABLES LLP, incorporated in Scotland as a limited liability partnership under the Limited Liability Partnerships Act 2000, with Registered Number SO909090, and having its Registered Office at 204 St Kentigern Street Glasgow G2

9.6.8 Insolvency Practitioners

For dispositions granted by insolvency practitioners on behalf of insolvent companies the usual format is for the company to grant the disposition acting by the administrator, receiver or liquidator. Generally the disposition would not be granted by the administrator, receiver or liquidator itself as there is no vesting in the administrator, receiver or liquidator, who instead takes control of the Company. In a sequestration of an individual, however, the trustee becomes vest in the property of the bankrupt by virtue of the act and warrant.

In all cases of a disposition by an insolvency practitioner, they will want to exclude any personal liability on their part. The disposition should therefore contain words like:

> acting solely as agent(s) of the company and without any personal liability whatsoever and regardless of how it arises (whether directly or indirectly, express or implied)

In some dispositions you may see a more detailed narrative of the facts and circumstances of the appointment of the insolvency practitioner.

9.6.8(i) Administrator

We, ALMOND PET SUPPLIES LIMITED, (in administration) incorporated under the Companies Acts (Registered Number SC787878) and having our Registered Office at 8 Calabria Crescent, Kelvinforth, Perthsire (the 'Company'), acting through its joint administrators Findlay Alexander and Ernest Rascal, Chartered Accountants, both of Byron Childs, 27 Thistle Road, Perth appointed joint administrators of the Company to manage the affairs, business and property of the Company pursuant to an appointment by the directors of the Company on 12 August 2014, acting solely as agents of the Company and without any personal liability whatsoever or howsoever arising (whether directly or indirectly, express or implied)

9.6.8(ii) Receiver

WE, OFFSHORE HOLDINGS LIMITED (IN RECEIVERSHIP), incorporated in the British Virgin Islands (Company Number 121212) and having our Registered Office sometime at Plantain House Tortola, British Virgin Islands [and previously registered at Companies House as an overseas company (Company Number FC212121)] (the "Company"), acting through our Joint Receivers, Findlay Alexander and Ernest Rascal, Chartered Accountants, both of Byron Childs, 27 Thistle Road, Perth, (the "Joint Receivers") appointed by Instrument of Appointment by Scotland Bank plc in favour of the Joint Receivers dated [ ] pursuant to Bond and Floating Charge in favour of the Bank granted by the Company dated [ ]

9.6.8(iii) Liquidator

We, [ ] LIMITED (IN LIQUIDATION), incorporated under the Companies Acts (Registered Number [ ]) and having our registered office [previously] at [ ] [and now at [ ]] (the "Company") heritable proprietor of the Property (defined term) , acting through its Liquidator Ernest Rascal, Chartered Accountant, of Byron Childs, 27 Thistle Road, Perth, appointed by virtue of Interlocutor granted by the Court of Session at Edinburgh on 18 May 2013, subsequently being appointed Interim Liquidator on 9 June 2013 and then being appointed Permanent Liquidator on 28 July 2013, acting solely as agent of the Company and without any personal liability whatsoever or howsoever arising (whether directly or indirectly, express or implied) (the "Liquidator")

9.6.8(iv) Trustee in sequestration

I, Findlay Alexander, Chartered Accountant, of Byron Childs, 27 Thistle Road, Perth, the Permanent Trustee on the Sequestrated Estate of Xavier French residing at Almond Cottage, Florence Park, Kelvinforth, Perthshire duly confirmed conform to Act and Warrant by the Sheriff of the Sheriffdom of Tayside Central and Fife at Perth dated 11 February 2015, IN CONSIDERATION of the price of [ ] POUNDS (£[ ]) STERLING paid to me as Trustee [aforesaid] by

As the trustee in sequestration is vest in the property by virtue of the act and warrant, although a deduction of title clause is no longer required, the following wording would be appropriate, for those who still wish to incorporate one (and for the time being, at least, many still do):

Which subjects were last vested in the said Xavier French and from whom I acquired right as Trustee [foresaid] by the said Act and Warrant in my favour, [dated as aforesaid];

The examples given above can all be easily adapted for use in the modern style dispositions.

9.6.9 Heritable Creditor in Possession

The heritable creditor must comply with various statutory requirements before it can convey the property, and then it does so by virtue of the power of sale imported into the original standard security in its favour by Standard Condition 10[9]. It is customary to narrate the process in the disposition:

WE, SCOTLAND BANK plc incorporated under the Companies Acts and having our Registered Office at Alba House, Corries Road, Edinburgh WHEREAS in virtue of a power of sale contained in Standard Security [for £X] by Y residing formerly at [ ] and now at [ ] in our favour registered in the Land Register of Scotland under Title Number [ ], we advertised the Property (defined term) for sale and sold

---

9   Schedule 3, to the Conveyancing and Feudal Reform (Scotland) Act 1970.

the Property by private contract to [ ] residing at [ ] at the price of [£] being the best price that could reasonably be obtained and considering that the said [ ] has paid to us the said price of [£] therefore we HAVE SOLD and DO HEREBY DISPONE to the said....

This style can easily be adapted for use in the modern style disposition, moving the clause on exercise of the power of sale to the Narrative section.

9.6.10 Charities

The Charities and Trustee Investment (Scotland) Act 2005 requires that any body wishing to refer to itself as a charity, and that has a significant presence in Scotland, must be registered in the Scottish Charity Register. To be eligible to be entered in the Scottish Charity Register a body must meet the charity test set out in the 2005 Act: its purposes must consist only of one or more of the 'charitable purposes' specified in section 7(2) and the body must provide public benefit in Scotland or elsewhere.

Under the Charities References in Documents (Scotland) Regulations 2007, as amended, any body entered in the Scottish Charity Register must state legibly on all documents listed in the regulations (which includes all conveyances which provide for the creation, transfer, variation or extinction of an interest in land), and which are issued or signed on behalf of the charity after 31 March 2008:

(i)   its name as entered in the Scottish Charity Register;

(ii)   any other name by which it is commonly known;

(iii)   its registered number; and

(iv) where the name of the body does not include the word 'charity' or 'charitable', that it is a charity by using one of the terms referred to in the Charity and Trustee Investment (Scotland) Act 2005: ie charity; charitable body; registered charity; charity registered in Scotland; Scottish charity; or registered Scottish charity. The last two terms may only be used if the body is established under Scots law or is managed or controlled wholly or mainly in Scotland.

There does not appear to be a standardised form of words for designation of charities, but the wording will be competent provided it complies with the provisions of the 2007 Regulations. Examples of designations are:

THE UNIVERSITY COURT OF THE UNIVERSITY OF EDINBURGH, a charitable body registered in Scotland with registered number SC005336 and established under the Universities (Scotland) Acts and having our principal offices at Old College, South Bridge, Edinburgh, EH8 9YL

KELVINFORTH LEISURE PURSUITS LIMITED incorporated under the Companies Acts (Registered number SC876543) and a registered Scottish charity (Scottish Charity Number SC444444) and having its registered office at 999 Lally Street Glasgow G2 4XX

SCOTTISH SOCIETY FOR THE PREVENTION OF CRUELTY TO ANIMALS, a Company limited by Guarantee, Company Number SC201401, a registered Scottish Charity Number 006467 and having its registered office at Kingseat Road, Halbeath, Dunfermline, Fife, KY11 8RY

9.6.11 The Queen's and Lord Treasurer's Remembrancer (QLTR)

Where land falls to the Crown as *bona vacantia* or *ultimus haeres*, any subsequent conveyance of that land in Scotland is effected by way of disposition from the QLTR. This may also be the actual conveyance of land which has been identified for a possible a non domino transfer, but after following the prescriptive claimant procedures (see para 8.10.5), where the land is 'ownerless' and the Crown claims it, the correct procedure is to take title by way of disposition from the QLTR, rather than the a non domino route.

The current QLTR is Catherine Dyer. A disposition is granted by her in her capacity of QLTR, and the form of words for the relevant disposition will usually be provided by the QLTR's office. An example of the narrative of such a disposition, and the disclaimer of personal liability clause that such a disposition will contain, follows. The language is rather old fashioned, but not, of course, wrong:

9.6.11(i) Narrative

I, CATHERINE PATRICIA DYER, Queen's and Lord Treasurer's Remembrancer in Scotland, as Donee in Trust of the estate of

Kelvinalmond Land Holdings Limited which had fallen to Her Majesty Queen Elizabeth the Second as *bona vacantia* under a Deed of Gift of the said Estate in favour of one of my predecessors, Andrew Christie Normand, as Queen's and Lord Treasurer's Remembrancer foresaid and his successors in Office in Trust as therein mentioned given under the testimony of the Seal appointed by the Treaty of Union to be kept and used in Scotland in place of the Great Seal thereof on the First day of July in the year Two Thousand and Two and written and sealed under the testimony of the Seal above specified by the Keeper of the Registers of Scotland on the Nineteenth day of July in the year Two Thousand and Two and as Donee in Trust foresaid heritable proprietor of the subjects hereinafter disponed: In consideration of the price of...

9.6.11(ii) Disclaimer

And the said disponees by acceptation hereof bind themselves and their foresaids to pay and to free and relieve me and my foresaids of public burdens affecting the said subjects hereby disponed; And I, as Trustee foresaid grant simple warrandice and that without accepting or inferring any personal liability on myself, it being hereby declared that I the said Catherine Patricia Dyer as the Queen's and Lord Treasurer's Remembrancer in Scotland, as Donee in Trust, aforesaid contract solely as Trustee foresaid and shall incur no personal liability of whatsoever nature (whether directly or indirectly, express or implied) and howsoever arising:

DEDUCTION OF TITLE

9.7 Where the granter of the disposition does not have a recorded title, it is no longer necessary to include a clause of deduction of title[10] by which the documents that link the granter and his entitlement to dispone the property, with the person having the last recorded title are narrated (see para 8.14). However, in some situations, it can be a useful record of the links, which must of course still be in place for the disposition to be validly granted. In the spirit of historical interest, a statutory style of deduction of title clause was set out in the Conveyancing (Scotland) Act 1924, Schedule A, form 1:

10 Section 101 of the Land Registration etc (Scotland) Act 2012.

> Which lands and others (or subjects) were last vested [or are part of the lands and others (or subjects) last vested] in A.B. (designation of person last infeft), whose title thereto is recorded in (specify Register of Sasines and date of recording, or if the last infeftment has already been mentioned say in the said A.B. as aforesaid), and from whom I acquired right by (here specify shortly the writ or series of writs by which right was so acquired).

An example of a deduction of title clause in a Disposition by an Executor would look like this:

> Which subjects and others were last vested in the said Mrs Norma McNaught Monk or Sweet whose title thereto is recorded in the said Division of the Register of Sasines on Twenty ninth November Nineteen hundred and ninety and from whom I, as Executor foresaid, acquired right by the said Confirmation in my favour dated as aforesaid

And for Trustees might run along these lines:

> Which subjects were last vested in the said Richard Glenalmond Childs and me the said Henry Rose Pink as the then Trustees acting under the said Deed of Trust whose title thereto is recorded in the said Division of the General Register of Sasines on 2nd September 1989 and from whom we acquired right as Trustees foresaid by virtue of (One) Minute of Resignation by the said Richard Glenalmond Childs dated 11th and 27th both November and registered in the Books of Council and Session on 31st December all 1993; (Two) Deed of Assumption and Conveyance by me the said Henry Rose Pink in favour of myself and the said Richard Byron Childs and Ann Childs dated 14th, 24th and 29th all August and registered in the Books of Council and Session on 14th September all 1994.

Whether you continue to incorporate a deduction of title clause or not, it is likely that, once we become accustomed to its absence, its use will rapidly start to diminish.

CONSIDERATION

9.8 It is most common for the consideration for the conveyance of property to be a full monetary consideration. To ensure that there is no doubt, in case of a typographical error for example, it is usual to set out the price in both words and figures.

9.8.1 References to VAT

The sale, grant, assignation or surrender of a major interest in land for consideration is a supply of goods for the purposes of VAT. However, sales of a dwellings or a residential purpose building converted from a non-residential building or part of a building are zero-rated, therefore no VAT is payable on sale. Commercial buildings which are more than three years old are treated differently. Such buildings are exempt from VAT, which means that no VAT will be payable on sale, unless the owner of the building opts to tax the building. It is, therefore, necessary when purchasing commercial property to ascertain at the outset its VAT status (see 6.14.4). Since LBTT is payable on the grossed up consideration it is necessary to narrate in the Disposition of commercial property either that VAT is payable (in which case the consideration stated will be the total of the Price plus VAT at the current rate) or that none is payable (for whatever reason):

> IN CONSIDERATION of the price of [ ] POUNDS (£[ ]) STERLING [on which sum no Value Added Tax is payable][exclusive of Value Added Tax which will be payable in addition]

9.8.2 Non-monetary Consideration

The 'payment' made for property may not be in cash. There may be an exchange of property for shares in a company or the adoption of a debt. The usual way to narrate this is to say 'for certain good and onerous causes and considerations'

9.8.3 Gifts

Property may change hands with no payment being made at all: a transfer from one family member to another for example. In such cases the deed can refer to 'certain good causes and considerations' omitting the word 'onerous', or the consideration can be stated as 'Love favour and affection' as in:

> I, ALEXANDER RUPERT SWEET residing at Lionheart Farm, Kinlochalmond, by Kelvinforth IN CONSIDERATION of the love favour and affection which I bear towards my wife MRS NORMA McNAUGHT MONK or SWEET residing with me at Lionheart Farm, aforesaid DO HEREBY DISPONE to the said Mrs Norma McNaught Monk or Sweet …

DESCRIBING THE PROPERTY

9.9 A key element in successfully conveying property is to ensure that it is clearly identified. How this is best achieved will depend on the type of property that it is, and how its title is currently constituted.

9.9.1 Registered Title

Describing the property could not be simpler. Referring to the correct Title Number will ensure that the property and its pertinents are correctly and sufficiently identified.

9.9.2 Description by Reference

We have already considered descriptions by reference in the context of examination of title (see para 8.15). When conveying a property that has already been fully identified in a deed recorded in the Sasine Register, it can be competently described in the next transfer of the property (which includes a disposition that will induce first registration) by reference to that earlier descriptive writ[11]. These sections permit a particular description of property contained in a recorded deed to be inserted in subsequent writs by reference to that recorded deed. A statutory form of words is provided in Schedule D of the Conveyancing (Scotland) Act 1924, although it is fine provided the reference is in this form or 'as nearly as may be'. The form of words given in Schedule D is:

> All and whole the lands and others (or subjects) in the country of (or in the burgh of and county of as the case may) described in (refer to the conveyance, deed, or instrument in such terms as shall be sufficient to

11 See section 61 of the Conveyancing (Scotland) Act 1874 and section 8 of the Conveyancing (Scotland) Act 1924.

identify it, and specify the Register of Sasines in which it is recorded and date of recording, or where the conveyance, deed, or instrument referred to is recorded on the same date as the conveyance, deed, or instrument containing the reference substitute for the date of recording the words of even date with the recording of these presents)

Terms sufficient to identify the writ are: the names of the granter and grantee, or of the parties to the deed (no designations necessary) and if there are several granters or grantees or several parties acting in the same category, then it is enough to give the first named person followed by 'and others', eg

> being the subjects more particularly described in, disponed by and delineated in red and partly coloured green and partly coloured pink on the plan annexed and subscribed as relative to Feu Disposition by Richard Glenalmond Childs, 4th Earl of Kinlochalmond and Dunvorlich in favour of Alexander Rupert Sweet and others dated 4 April and recorded in the Division of the General Register of Sasines for the County of Perth on 4 July both 1964;

If any of the parties mentioned in the descriptive deed acted in a fiduciary capacity (eg trustees), it is unnecessary to list all the names and instead, reference can be made to that role, such as 'in favour of the Trustees of A.B.' This format for description by reference can be used when describing a larger area of which the property being conveyed forms a part. In other words you have particular description of the part, and then identify it further by reference to a recorded disposition in which the larger area was described (see para 9.9.4 below). Or if the property being conveyed forms part of only part of the lands described in the earlier deed, reference need only be made to that part, eg 'being the subjects more particularly described (In the First Place) in, and disponed by Disposition by....'. While this obviously helps identification purposes, from a technical point of view it does not matter if this distinction is made or not (ie it is just as valid to refer to the whole subjects described in the deed referred to for particular description, missing out '(In the First Place)').

9.9.3 Bounding Description

The first time a plot of land is conveyed as a separate entity, it needs to be clearly identified. While a taxative plan, such as one based on the

Ordnance Survey map, will often be sufficient to identify the location and extent of an area, a verbal description is often also required, particularly to establish the actual physical features of the boundary, eg the inner face of a wall, which a red line on a plan will not necessarily communicate.

The format of a full bounding description therefore will involve all, or a sufficient combination of, (i) a plan (now, of course, probably essential for first registrations), (ii) an area measurement (iii) boundaries identified by reference to (1) orientation (eg the points of the compass) (2) physical attributes (3) length and (4) direction. Areas and lengths should be expressed in metric measurements. It is recognised that there are limitations in scaling on maps. On a plan that uses a scale of 1:1250, one millimetre on the plan represents 1.25 metres on the ground, so the accuracy of the boundaries plotted on such plans is limited. Some leeway is afforded to take account of the limitations of scaling in maps, and the possibility of minor discrepancies in orientation or measurements, by use of the expressions 'on or towards' and 'or thereby'.

An example bounding description would be:

ALL and WHOLE that area of land extending to 1.12 hectares or thereby situated in Kinlochalmond in the County of Perth and bounded as follows: on or towards the northeast by the outer edge of the grass verge of the road leading from Kelvinforth to Kinlochalmond along which it extends in a southeasterly direction 51 metres or thereby; on or towards the southeast, again on or towards the northeast and again on or towards the southeast by the centre line of a stone wall separating the property hereby disponed from other property belonging to us known as Dunvorlich Cottage along which it extends 64.2 metres or thereby, 18 metres or thereby and 20.5 metres or thereby respectively; on or towards the southwest and on or towards the northwest by parts of the lands and estate of Kinlochalmond and Dunvorlich, following the outer face of a fence or wall to be erected by our said disponee as provided for in Part 2 of the Schedule annexed to this Disposition along which it extends 69 metres or thereby, and 84.7 metres or thereby respectively, all as the said area of land is shown delineated in red and coloured pink on the plan annexed and subscribed by us as relative to this Disposition.

9.9.4 Part and Portion/Conveyance of Part

When the property being conveyed by the disposition is being described for the first time, reference is made to the deed describing the larger area of which it formed a part. This might be a whole estate, or it might just be the title of the larger house and garden, a part of which is being sold off for a new house to be built, or a development which is being sold off in individual plots or units. Either way the approach is the same. Following the description of the part conveyed a reference is made to it being part and portion of the larger title. So the bounding description above (para 9.9.3) would continue:

> which area of land hereby disponed forms part and portion of ALL and WHOLE that area or piece of land lying in the said County extending to 151.61 acres or thereby described (In the Second Place) in, disponed by and delineated in red and coloured pink on the plan annexed and subscribed as relative to Feu Disposition by Richard Glenalmond Childs, 4th Earl of Kinlochalmond and Dunvorlich in favour of Alexander Rupert Sweet and others dated Fourth April and recorded in the Division of the General Register of Sasines for the County of Perth on Fourth July both Nineteen hundred and sixty four

Note that the reference to an imperial area measurement (acres) is permissible, because it is (i) the measurement specified in the deed referred to, which is historical and (ii) is not part of the particular bounding description of the actual area being conveyed.

A conveyance of part of property registered in the Land Register is a much simpler affair:

> I, ERIC SWEET, residing at The Old Railway House, Florence Park, Kelvinforth, Perthshire in consideration of the price of ONE HUNDRED THOUSAND POUNDS (£100,000) Sterling paid to me by SAMANTHA MIRREN DARLING, residing at 19 Lionheart Farm Cottages, Kinlochalmond HAVE SOLD and DO HEREBY DISPONE to the said Samantha Mirren Darling ALL and WHOLE that plot of ground at Lionheart Farm, Kinlochalmond in the County of Perth extending to 2.8 hectares or thereby Metric measure and shown delineated in red on the plan annexed and signed as relative to this Disposition; being part of the subjects registered in the Land

Register of Scotland under Title Number PTH41192 (insert any new title conditions; date of entry; warrandice)

9.9.5 Tenement Flat

There used to be a bit of a problem in providing an accurate description of a flat in a tenement building, whether residential or commercial. Traditionally, descriptions of floors in tenements have been quite short: 'the westmost first floor flat entering by the common passage and stair at 12 Sardinia Terrace, Kelvinforth' is sufficient to identify the location of the flat in question, and the common law dealt with horizontal separation and ownership of other parts of the tenement. This form of description of a tenement flat is still acceptable. While in modern multi-occupancy buildings it is possible to produce drawings showing floor layouts, for older properties, it used to be necessary to revert to verbal descriptions if the seller wanted clearly to identify the limits of the title – such as by way of reference to the point between the floors at which one floor starts and another floor ends. This problem has effectively disappeared with the statutory definitions of 'tenement' and a 'sector' of a tenement (eg a flat) and 'scheme property' of a tenement in the Tenements (Scotland) Act 2004, and these definitions will apply to any tenement to the extent that the title to the tenement does not make any provision. The definition in section 2[12] is quite technical, stating that the boundary between any two contiguous sectors (flats that are next to each other) is the median (mid point) of the structure that separates them (eg a floor or a wall). A sector (flat) extends in any direction to such a boundary. If the flat is not next to another flat at any of its boundaries, then it extends to and includes the *solum* or any other part of the tenement which is an outer surface of the tenement building; or it extends to the boundary that separates the flat from an adjoining, but separate, building.

If part of the boundary between two flats is some feature, for example a door or a window which wholly or mainly serves only one of the flats, then the entire thickness of that feature is part of that flat.

So far as ownership of 'common' parts of the tenement is concerned (as distinct from liability for maintenance) then, again in the absence of

---

12 Of the 2004 Act.

specific provision in the titles, the 2004 Act provides that a top flat will include the roof of the tenement over that flat, and where the roof of the tenement building slopes, will also include the airspace above the slope of the relevant part of the roof up to the level of the highest point of the roof. A ground floor (or basement where there is one) flat will include the *solum* under that flat, and will also include the airspace above the tenement building that is directly over the relevant part of the *solum* (except the portion of airspace that goes with the top flat where the roof is sloped). A close (or common stair) extends to and includes the roof over, and the *solum* under, the close.

For most normal purposes therefore there should not be any need to describe the boundaries of a tenement property, provided the parties do not, for some reason either need or want to depart from the provisions of the 2004 Act, which would be rare.

9.9.6 General Name

An early form of description by reference, describing property by a 'general name' is provided by section 13 of the Titles to Land Consolidation (Scotland) Act 1868. When several lands are brought together in one conveyance in favour of the same person, the conveyance could incorporate a clause declaring that the whole lands were to be known in future by a general name that is specified in the conveyance. Wording is provided in Schedule G[13]. Although still competent, this format is rarely (if ever) used in modern conveyancing, having been overtaken by the description by reference, and of course any transfer for value of such land will induce a first registration in the Land Register after which any description or conveyance will identify the lands by reference to a title number.

9.9.7 Plans

The system of registration of title in the Land Register is plan based, therefore it is important to have a good quality (as to clarity and accuracy) plan annexed to the title deeds. In a first registration, it is particularly important to ensure that the property is sufficiently identified for the

---

13 Of the 1868 Act

purposes of registration, to enable the Keeper to delineate the boundaries of the property on the cadastral map. The Sasine title may contain maps, plans or descriptions that adequately identify the property, and a Plans Report will establish if these are adequate for registration purposes, or whether it would be advisable to commission a plan of the property for annexation to the disposition.

The Keeper's 'Deed Plan Criteria' Guidance[14] is essential reading in order to ensure that your plan will be acceptable for registration..

Some general points to note:

- A scale (preferably a drawn or bar scale, to help the Keeper identify if there has been any distortion from photocopying) and the orientation of north must be shown.

- The Keeper produces title plans using three base Ordnance Survey mapping scales:

    (i)   1:1250 for urban properties;

    (ii) 1:2500 for rural properties, and

    (iii) 1:10,000 for mountain and moorland areas.

    Deed plans drawn for properties in these areas should therefore be adequate for the corresponding scale. However, sometimes the scale of the most appropriate map does not adequately show the necessary detail. In those cases, an inset plan at a larger scale may be used. For example, if a 1:1250 scale map doesn't provide enough detail, a plan at 1:500 can be used.

- Where the land is part of the seabed, there must be a description of the plot using OSGB36 coordinates (British National Grid (ESPG:27700) projected coordinate system) ideally presented in table format annexed to the deed, as well as a plan, and a location plan showing the land in relation to the coast of Scotland.

- 'Landranger' maps should not be used, as their scale is too small. Care should be taken with some map products (which are created using digital information). 'Raster' maps, for example, may not provide sufficient detail at the appropriate scale required for registration, and may be rejected (see the Deed Plan Criteria Guidance for an example of this).

---

14 See www.ros.gov.uk/__data/assets/pdf_file/0019/10783/General-Guidance-DPC.pdf

- The plan must not be stated to be 'demonstrative only and not taxative'.
- The plan must contain sufficient surrounding established detail such as fences, houses, road junctions and street names so that the position of the plot can be accurately fixed on the ordnance map.
- Where it is necessary for any measurement to be shown on the plan, metric units must be used to one decimal place.
- Coloured edging, tinting or shading, and other indicators such as hatching should be used to indicate the property and to differentiate features such as shared areas and any areas, less than the whole of the plot that are affected by encumbrances.
- Where no physical boundary exists, the line of the boundary must be accurately fixed to existing detail by metric measurements shown on the plan.
- Boundaries should be identified by description (eg centre line of wall, outer face or inner face of hedge, etc).
- Using Digital Data: While for most Land Register applications digital data is not required, the data on a traditional paper plan may be accompanied by digital data, particularly for applications that cover a large area of ground or contain complex plotting. The Keeper can accept digital plans containing GIS (Geographical Information System) and CAD (Computer-Aided Design) data in the majority of industry standard formats. The software name and version used to create it should be supplied.

Once a property is registered in the Land Register, no plan is required for conveyances or other dealings of the whole of the subjects in the Title Number. However, if the dealing relates to only a part of the registered interest, then as well as identifying the larger area by reference to the title number, a description or plan of the part, which is sufficient to enable the Keeper to identify the part on the existing title plan, is required. This applies to any dealing of part, not just transfers, for example if an owner is granting a standard security over only part of the property in the Title Number. For developments with Development Plan Approval of the internal layout, however, it is not necessary to provide a plan for an individual plot, as reference to the DPA number and Plot number will be sufficient to identify it.

If preparing a new plan for this purpose, then the guidelines set out above should be followed, and it should be clear from the new plan how the area relates to the larger subjects in the title, by showing sufficient detail of the adjoining property. However, it may be acceptable in these cases to use a copy of the Title plan with the relevant part carefully delineated, (if that can be done clearly) and with the addition of boundary measurements marked on the plan, although beware of the possibility of distortion in the copying process. The suitability of such a plan for registration purposes should be checked in advance by obtaining a Plans Report. If this option is to be used, copyright issues need to be addressed. An Ordnance Survey licence this will cover such copying, if your firm has one. A plan may not be necessary if the relevant portion subject to the dealing is sufficiently separately identified, such as already being tinted a different colour from the rest of the subjects in the Title number.

Any plan used must be taxative, that is to say it can be founded on. It was common in older deeds to refer to the plan being 'demonstrative only and not taxative', but a demonstrative plan will not be accepted by the Keeper, and this form of words can no longer be used.

9.9.8 Airspace

In some circumstances, the property being conveyed may consist of a portion of airspace that is going to be occupied in the future by some structure but, at the time of the conveyance, that structure has not yet been erected. Say a purchaser is acquiring several upper floors in a new building about to be constructed, or the building being acquired requires to be described on a separate title from a subterranean car park or storage facility beneath it. In such circumstances it is possible to describe the 'box of airspace' that will comprise the title, and this is typically done by reference to datum levels (Ordnance Datum). A datum level is a horizontal surface, for example sea level, which is taken as a reference point for identifying altitudes for maps, and is used in this context to determine the precise position of elevations, heights, or depths of the property or portion of airspace to be occupied by the property.

Mean sea level (MSL) is generally used. The level used by the Ordnance Survey is Ordnance Datum Newlyn which is based on the MSL at Newlyn in Cornwall between the years 1915 and 1921. With increasingly sophisticated technology, other measurement techniques may also start to be used. The datum level figures will be produced by the professional team involved in the construction project.

For example, in the description of a building which will exclude a self contained storage facility area being constructed beneath the building, and which will support the building structure, references to datum levels can be incorporated like this:

> ALL and WHOLE that area of ground and the building erected on it known as Unit 5A Lochalmond, Perth comprising five storeys including the ground floor storey, which area of ground is shown delineated in red on the Plan annexed and signed as relative to this disposition, which area of ground commences at Ordnance Datum level 24.500 MSL in respect of that area shown hatched black, and coloured pink on the Plan; at Ordnance Datum level 27.500 MSL in respect of that area shown cross hatched black and coloured green on the Plan and at Ordnance Datum level 29.100 MSL in respect of that area shown hatched black and coloured yellow on the Plan; but always excluding the Storage Facility Area beneath the area of ground

This technique is not without risk, as locations and levels may change during the construction process.

9.9.9 Pertinents

References to pertinents, or 'parts, privileges and pertinents' were often used as a bit of a conveyancing 'catch-all' and often without particular care or precision. The reference is generally understood to mean rights such as servitudes or common rights to things like common parts, for example the common passage and stair of tenements. There may be circumstances, however, where a general reference to parts and / or pertinents will be sufficient to transfer rights or parts that have been omitted from the description, but it will be a question of the particular circumstances of each case whether such rights or parts are effectively transferred. Where a servitude has been properly constituted in favour of a property, strictly speaking there is no need to refer to it specifically, but this is often done for clarity and certainty.

The relevance of a pertinents clause is less significant these days. It is normal conveyancing practice when conveying property to refer to rights such as servitudes specifically, and other pertinents that apply, and this is good practice when describing the property in a first registration, or when describing a split off from another title for the first time.

Section 3(1)(a) of the 1979 Act provided that the effect of registration was to vest in the person registered as entitled to the registered interest in land a real right in the interest and in any right, pertinent or servitude, express or implied, forming part of the interest.

Section 3 was repealed by the 2012 Act. Under section 6(1)(b) of the 2012 Act, the Keeper must include in the property section of the Title Sheet particulars of any incorporeal pertinents, such as rights of access or details of any burdened property. If pertinents that relate to the property exist but are not shown on the Title Sheet, for example a servitude acquired by prescription, it may be possible to add them by applying for rectification of the title sheet.

Various common rights as pertinents were a feature of descriptions of tenement properties, and when examining old tenement titles you will often see lists of parts referred to. Section 3 of the Tenements (Scotland) Act 2004 now sets out what the pertinents in a tenement property are, and provides that these will attach to each flat as a right of common property. These are equal rights except where the pertinent is a chimney stack, when the proportion will be according to the number of flues pertaining to a flat[15].

The parts attaching as pertinents are a close and a lift which provides access to more than one of the flats. If any flat is not accessed from such close or lift then it will not be a pertinent of that flat. Land that pertains to a tenement, other than the *solum* on which the tenement is built, will be a pertinent of the bottom flat closest to the land, but does not apply a path, outside stair or other way that also provides access to other flats.

Other parts that may attach as a pertinent to one or more flats may include a path, outside stair, fire escape, rhone, pipe, flue, conduit, cable, tank or chimney stack that wholly serves one flat or two or more flats. If serving more than one flat, it will attach to each of the flats served, as a pertinent, a right of common property in (and in the whole of) the part.

9.9.10 Common Property

As can be seen from para 9.9.9 above, pertinents in tenement flats are often held as common property by the owners of the flats in the tenement. But other land and property can also be held in common by specific reference

15 See section 3(5) of the 2004 Act.

in the title. Common property can be held by two or more owners, who will own the property in equal shares, unless some other configuration of shares in the property is specified. These shares are referred to as *pro indiviso* (undivided) shares, and the effect is that each of the owners owns an indivisible share of the whole of the property. This means that each co-owner has a say in what happens to the whole of the property, and if one owner wants to realise the property (eg by sale), but another does not, the matter can be forced, through an action for division and sale.

For style wording for *pro indiviso* shares, see para 9.6.1. When describing common property, reference should be made to a 'right of common property' and not merely a 'right in common' which, while it will probably be taken to mean a property right, is imprecise.

The 2012 Act introduced a new concept of 'shared plots' when a piece of land is owned in common by two or more persons[16]. If designated by the Keeper as a shared plot, a separate title sheet will be created for it. It is likely to be used in situations where owners of property also own some area, such as a mutual driveway, in common. Common parts of developments are also suitable for being designated on the Land Register in this way. The key thing to bear in mind is that the quantum share in the shared plot must be identified in the disposition: eg 'a one twenty-fifth *pro indiviso* right of common property in the common parts of the Development shown coloured green on the Plan'. It is not necessary to refer to the Title Number of the shared plot (the common area) in subsequent transfers of the sharing plot (the property)[17] as the Title Number of the shared plot appears on the Title Sheet of the sharing plot. However it is not wrong to do so if you wish. See para 8.28.4(v) for more detail on shared plots.

Common property should be distinguished from joint property, which is generally the way in which trustees and unincorporated associations hold title to property. In joint property there are no individual shares. Instead, the trustees all hold title jointly to the whole property. The removal, resignation or death of a trustee does not affect the title of the remaining trustees, which continues without the departed trustee, and without any conveyance being required, joint ownership being an incidence of the office of trustee.

---

16 See section 17 of the 2012 Act.
17 Section 17(4) of the 2012 Act.

EXISTING BURDENS AND SERVITUDES

9.10 It would be unusual (although by no means impossible) to find a title to property that is not affected by some form of title condition. Many of these may, of course, be of such antiquity that they are no longer relevant, and many burdens will have been extinguished by feudal abolition or under the transitional arrangements in the Title Conditions (Scotland) Act 2003[18]. Existing burdens and servitude 'run with the land' so will, or should, transfer when the property changes hands.

9.10.1 First Registration

As previously indicated, when conveying property in a sale or other transaction that induces a first registration, you should describe the property and the burdens that apply to it in the same way as though it was a transfer in the Sasine Register. So you must refer to all the relevant writs referred to for burdens, (see the style disposition at para 9.4) and, of course, if new burdens are also being created, these should be set out in full (see para 9.11).

9.10.2 Registered Property

Reference to the Title Number of a registered property transfers all rights, pertinents and burdens.

9.10.3 Servitudes in Conveyance of Part

If the title to the larger area is still in the Sasine Register, then you should specify the servitude and other rights that are to pass with the part being conveyed in clear terms.

Once property is registered in the Land Register, any servitudes form part of the title. Theoretically, therefore, it should not be necessary to refer to rights and pertinents when transferring part of a registered title, but in practice, it may not be entirely clear which rights should pass with the part being conveyed and whether some should not. Accordingly, it is good practice to specify in the conveyance of the part of the registered property the rights and servitudes to apply to that conveyed part.

18 See sections 49 and 80 of the 2003 Act.

In cases where the rights are narrated in a Deed of Conditions which is entered in the Title Sheet of the whole property, a reference in the dispositive clause of the conveyance to the deed of conditions, such as 'together with the rights specified in the deed of conditions...', will suffice.

> I, MICHAEL RUPERT MONK residing at [ ], in consideration of the price of Forty two Thousand Pounds (£42,000) Sterling paid to me by CHRISTOPHER GAVIN SWEET, residing at Lionheart Farm, Kinlochlmond, by Kelvinforth HAVE SOLD and DO HEREBY DISPONE to the said Christopher Gavin Sweet and his executors and assignees whomsoever ALL and WHOLE (describe the part conveyed in sufficient detail, and by reference to a plan, to enable the Keeper to identify it on the cadastral map) (the 'Property') being part of the subjects registered in the Land Register of Scotland under Title Number PTH45634 [All and Whole the subjects (First) registered under title number ( ) or All and Whole the subjects marked ( ) on the plan of title number ( )] Together with the rights specified in the Deed of Conditions by me dated [...] including a one twentieth *pro indiviso* right of common property in the common areas described in and shown coloured green on the plan of the Deed of Conditions; [but always with and under the following reservations, burdens and conditions viz.:- (insert additional burdens or conditions where appropriate)] [but declaring that the following rights (burdens, conditions) set out in title number(s) ( ) are not to apply to the Property]; with entry on (date of entry); and I grant warrandice: IN WITNESS WHEREOF

9.10.4 Division of Burdened Properties

Depending on the terms of the burden, on a division of a property that is a burdened property, each part of the property as divided will continue to be a burdened property, unless the burden cannot relate to a part or parts of the property once it is divided. So a use restriction affecting a property would continue to apply to each of the split off parts, but a facility burden relating to a wall located in one part of the property, but not the part conveyed, will no longer apply to the conveyed property[19].

---

19 Section 13 of the Title Conditions (Scotland) Act 2003.

9.10.5 Division of Benefited Properties

Before 28 November 2004, if a benefited property was divided, it was probable that each part became an independent benefited property (although the position was not always clear). The rules are now clarified for divisions of property made by a deed registered on or after that date. Section 14 of the Title Conditions (Scotland) Act 2003 provides as a default rule that the part conveyed will cease to be a benefited property – unless the break-off conveyance provides otherwise. The break-off conveyance can provide for both properties, or just the part being sold, to be benefited properties instead. It will also be possible to allocate different burdens from the larger title to the separate parts of the divided titles. Appropriate wording where the default position is not to apply is:

> [And we nominate [the Conveyed Property][the Conveyed Property and the Retained Property each] to be [a][the] benefited property in respect of [specify burden(s) by reference to the constitutive deed, where it is registered and the date of registration and identify the real burdens][And the Retained Property is to cease to be a benefited property in relation to the burdens specified]

No form of words is necessary if it is intended that on the sale of part of a property which is already a benefited property in an existing burden, the part conveyed will cease to be a benefited property. If both the part conveyed and the part retained are separately to constitute benefited properties, or if the part retained is to cease to be a benefited property, example wording would accordingly be:

> 'And we nominate the Conveyed Property to be a benefited property in respect of burden (Two) contained in Feu Disposition by Rowan Homes Ltd (in liquidation) in favour of Lightyear Development Company Ltd recorded in the Division of the General Register of Sasines for the County of Perth on 11 May, 2000;'

The rules regarding division of benefited properties apply in a different way to pre-emptions and other options, where only one property can be benefited. If the rule that the retained land is to be the benefited property is disapplied, the only alternative is that the conveyed property is to be the benefited property.

CREATING NEW BURDENS AND SERVITUDES

9.11 The rules relating to the creation of new real burdens are set out in the Title Conditions (Scotland) Act 2003. Many of the rules reflect the law that applied before the commencement of the 2003 Act, but several new rules were created and some of the previous rules were changed. It is important therefore, to be familiar with the provisions of this Act when drafting new real burdens. The rules relating to servitudes were not innovated on to anything like the same extent by the Title Conditions (Scotland) Act 2003, but a few changes and clarifications were set out in Part 7 of the Act.

9.11.1 Rules for Creation of Real Burdens

The system set up by the Title Conditions (Scotland) Act 2003 for creating real burdens provides the following rules:

9.11.1(i) Affirmative, negative and ancillary burdens

Section 2 divides burdens into three categories: affirmative, negative and ancillary burdens. Affirmative burdens are obligations to do something and can include a requirement to meet or contribute towards the cost of something, for example maintenance costs. Negative burdens consist of obligations to refrain from doing something. A prohibition against carrying out alterations or a use restriction prohibiting a particular use would fall into this category.

There had previously been some doubt about whether ancillary burdens, such as a right to enter a property in order to carry out repairs, ran with the land. The 2003 Act permits ancillary burdens which, in addition to a right to enter or make use of a property, can also include provision for management or administration, provided these burdens are for a purpose ancillary to an affirmative or negative burden that is imposed. An obligation to maintain common areas would support an ancillary burden that set out arrangements for management of the common areas, instructing repairs and recovering costs.

9.11.1(ii) Burdens must 'run with the land'

The mantra is that: a burden must burden a burdened property for the benefit of the benefited property. Only personal real burdens are excluded from this requirement. This was the law before 28 November 2004, but is now enshrined in sections 3(1), (2) and (3) of the 2003 Act. Known as the 'praedial rule', it always applied to real burdens but was often (and sometimes still is) overlooked, particularly in connection with the type of real burden which relates to commercial activity, for example a restriction on a type of trading. Often, there is no benefit to the benefited property in such a burden – the benefit is to the owner[20]. Section 3 provides that a real burden must relate in some way to the burdened property and that relationship may be direct or indirect, but must not merely be that the obligated person is the owner of the burdened property. So, unless it is a community burden, a real burden has to be for the benefit of the benefited property where there is one. A community burden may either be for the benefit of the whole of the community to which it relates or just some part of that community.

9.11.1(iii)   Content of real burdens

There are various rules peppered through the 2003 Act that relate to what a real burden may contain. A lot of prior case law in this respect continues to be relevant.

A real burden may not be contrary to public policy eg as an unreasonable restraint on trade[21]. This restates the pre-existing law. This is not to say that any burden which restricts trade is not permitted. Prohibition against use for business purposes may be considered quite reasonable in a residential development, although the case of *Snowie v Museum Hall* (see para 8.3) in 2010 appears to cast that contention in some doubt. Typical examples of an unreasonable restraint on trade are burdens which may be seen as being anti-competitive. Generally, these types of burdens are imposed for commercial reasons eg to prevent a business being set up in competition to an existing similar business nearby. Understandable, perhaps, but not enforceable as a real burden.

A burden may not be repugnant with ownership. Repugnancy with ownership would apply to burdens which attempt to impose unreasonable restrictions on freedom to use the property, such as prohibitions against selling or leasing.

---

20 But see the decision in *Hill of Rubislaw (Q Seven) Ltd v Rubislaw Quarry Aberdeen Ltd* [2014] CSIH 105 and the commentary on that case in para 8.25.16(i))
21 See section 3(6).

A burden cannot be created to secure payment of money, such as the 'clawback' type of burden previously popular, particularly in cases of land being sold for speculative development. Section 117 prohibits the creation of 'pecuniary real burdens', although, in fact, since 29 November 1970, the only competent method of taking a fixed security over heritable property in Scotland is by way of standard security (see para 10.2). There was some doubt as to whether pecuniary real burdens, by which a granter of a conveyance would reserve a right in security in respect of some existing obligation, were still permissible, although their use had been obsolete for many years. In contrast, however, it is permissible to provide in a burden for someone to pay for or contribute towards the cost of something, like maintenance of the property or common parts[22].

A burden must not have the effect of creating a monopoly[23]. Examples given are the provision that a certain person is to be the manager of a property or supplier of services to the property. This can be contrasted with the short-term monopoly that can apply when using a manager burden under section 63 of the 2003 Act which gives a period of exclusive right to appoint or be the manager of properties for up to five years.

Pre-emption rights are still allowed, but it is no longer competent to create rights of redemption or reversion, or other options to acquire the burdened property, as real burdens[24].

A burden which provides that someone other than the holder of a burden can waive compliance with it, or vary it is not competent. This again should be contrasted with the ability in community burdens to appoint a manager to do these things.

Personal real burdens, which are in favour not of another property, but of a person, such as Scottish Ministers or a local authority, are introduced by Part 3 of the 2003 Act, and there are various statutory instruments that nominate relevant bodies that are entitled to the benefit of such burdens. These burdens are each quite limited in their application and must be framed to relate to a particular purpose. Personal real burdens are created by statute and, as a concept, are not freely available for the ordinary benefited owner. Instead, they are of named types and the parties in whose favour such burdens can be created are also set out in statute.

22 See section 2(1)(a).
23 See section 3(7).
24 See section 3(5).

A **conservation burden**, for example, which can be created in favour of a conservation body or Scottish Ministers, must be for preservation or protection for the benefit of the public, of architectural or historical or other special characteristics of the land[25].

Economic development burdens, for the benefit of a local authority or Scottish Ministers, have to promote economic development.

Healthcare burdens in favour of an NHS Trust, or Scottish Ministers, have to relate to the provision of healthcare[26].

Maritime burdens relate to the sea bed or foreshore and benefit the Crown[27].

A **rural housing burden** is a type of pre-emption in favour of a rural housing body[28].

Manager burdens are also a type of personal real burden although not in the same category as those just described, and they also have a limited life span[29] (see para 9.11.6(iii) below).

Other types of personal real burdens can be created, for example section 68 of the Climate Change (Scotland) Act 2009 provides for a **climate change burden** which can be created in favour of a public body or trust, (essentially the same bodies that are conservation bodies) or Scottish Ministers for the purpose of reducing greenhouse gas emissions, by requiring that a property meets specified mitigation and adaptation standards in the event of development[30].

The terms of the burden must be set out in full in the constitutive deed[31]. The expression used is that it must appear in 'the four corners of the deed'[32], because an owner or a buyer of property must be able to ascertain from the face of the title what limitations or restrictions are placed on his use of that property. This is another restatement of the position as it has always been in law. Burdens which refer to extrinsic information or documentation such as a reference to statute eg 'only to be used for Class 1 Use under the Town and Country Planning Use Classes

25 See section 38.
26 See section 46.
27 See section 44.
28 See section 43.
29 See section 63.
30 For a critical discussion of its legislative form, see Sinclair, 'A new burden is born' (*Journal*, December 2009) and Leslie and Steven, 'Cool Drafting' (*Journal*, November 2010).
31 See section 4(2)(a).
32 Lord Guthrie in *Anderson v Dickie* [1914] SC 706.

Order' are ineffective. The only exception is in relation to payment of or contribution towards costs, where the amount is not specified in the deed, reference to some other document for the purposes of calculating the cost will be permitted, provided that the other documents referred to as the basis of calculation must be public documents or records[33]. Referring to the valuation roll, for example as a way of working out the proportion of liability for common repairs, would be permissible on this basis.

9.11.1(iv) Referring to 'real burden' or other named burdens

When drafting a real burden, you must use either the expression 'real burden'[34] or, if creating a type of burden which is 'a nameable type of real burden' then you can use that expression instead[35]. The nameable types of real burden in the 2003 Act are: affirmative burden, negative burden, ancillary burden, community burden, facility burden and service burden and also all the types of personal real burdens. There might be a danger, however, in naming the burden as a particular type of burden incorrectly (other than the personal real burdens) and so it is probably safest to stick with 'real burden' except in the case of community burdens, when using that expression had additional significance (see para 9.11.6(v) below). The commonly coined expression 'neighbour burden' is **not** one of the nameable types of burden, so should not be used in drafting.

9.11.1(v) The burden must be created by the owner of the burdened property

There is no change from the previous law[36], and section 123 of the 2003 Act clarifies that 'owner', for the purposes of creating real burdens, means a person who has right to the property whether or not that person has completed title.

9.11.1(vi) The constitutive deed

The Title Conditions (Scotland) Act 2003 provided a major change in the way in which real burdens can be created. Previously, only competent in

---

33 See section 5.
34 See section 4(2)(a).
35 See section 4(3).
36 See section 4(2)(b).

a conveyance of the burdened property or in a Deed of Conditions, now any deed may be used, provided of course it complies with the other rules relating to creation of real burdens. The main benefit of this in practice is that burdens can be created in stand-alone deeds – which have come to be known as Deeds of Real Burdens – without the need for a property to be conveyed. This can be useful for regulating or regularising title conditions between or among adjoining properties. It has become not uncommon to use Deeds of Real Burdens, even when there is property being conveyed, to impose burdens that are not community burdens, on the properties being conveyed and the property being retained, where these arrangements are complex. It is also competent now to impose burdens in a split-off disposition that affect the land that is retained. Formerly, it was not possible to impose real burdens in this way (despite frequent attempts to do so).

For styles of Deeds of Real Burden, and Dispositions imposing real burdens and servitudes, see the PSG website[37], and further details on their use in paras 9.11.4 and 9.11.5.

9.11.1(vii) *Identify the burdened and the benefited properties*

In non-feudal deeds imposing burdens before the appointed day, there was no legal requirement to identify the benefited property. Identification of the benefited property or any benefited party was therefore often omitted, making it difficult to work out who had a right to enforce the burden. Now a proper description of both the burdened and the benefited property is necessary[38], sufficient for the Keeper to identify both properties affected. For real burdens created since 28 November 2004, therefore, all enforcement rights must be express, and implied enforcement rights will not arise.

9.11.1(viii) *Dual registration*

Following on from the requirement to identify both the burdened and the benefited properties, the burdens must be registered in the title to both those properties (or recorded, if the title to one or both of the properties is

---

37 See www.psglegal.co.uk/post_feudal_reform.php.
38 See section 4(2)(c).

in the Sasine Register). In pre-28 November 2004 titles, invariably burdens do not appear on the title of the benefited property, and in many cases benefited proprietors may have no idea that they are entitled to enforce certain conditions. This requirement for dual registration has meant that we must now identify both the benefited and burdened property, and the owners of these properties, to effect registration against both titles. In the case of community burdens, which are often set up in a Deed of Conditions, the very fact of calling them 'community burdens' means that each property affected by the burdens is (or will be) both a benefited and a burdened property[39], and so registration of the Deed once is all that is required.

9.11.1(ix) Effect of registration

Formerly, parties could rely on the fact, where the benefited proprietor and the burdened proprietor were the original contracting parties, that even if there was no longer enforceability of the burden, such as where there is no interest to enforce, it might have been possible to enforce as a matter of contract. Section 61 disapplied that rule, so that now any such contractual link is extinguished on registration, and the burdens will only be enforceable as real burdens. Conversely, however, if the burden fails as a real burden, it may be enforceable as a matter of contract between the original parties.

It is possible to postpone the coming into effect of the burden by making appropriate provision in the deed, either for a future date when the conditions will come into effect, or by specifying some future event when the conditions will come into force such as, for example, the date of registration of a conveyance of particular units[40]. Careful thought should be given to the effect of postponement if this option is chosen.

9.11.1(x) Identify the burdened area on a plan

If the area to be affected by the burden is only part of the property being conveyed, then a plan, or description sufficient to allow the Keeper to delineate the boundaries of the lesser area affected by the burden should be either included in, or submitted with the application for registration.

---

39 See section 27.
40 See section 4(1)(a) and (b) of the 2003 Act.

9.11.2 Changes to Servitudes

A number of changes were made to the law of servitudes by the Title Conditions (Scotland) Act 2003[41], but the underlying law of the servitude has not otherwise changed. While the Act uses the expressions 'benefited property' and 'burdened property', the more traditional expressions 'dominant tenement' and 'servient tenement' are still applicable, although are less used nowadays.

9.11.2(i) New categories of servitude

Historically, a servitude had to be of a known and recognised type, many of the classes derived from Roman law. It was very rare for new categories of servitude to be added to the list. Section 76 permits, within reason, new types of servitude to be created provided they are created in writing, dual registered and not repugnant with ownership. Creating a servitude right of parking by express grant is now possible, it seems[42]. Servitudes created by other means, such as by prescription, are not affected, but will still need to fit into one of the categories of recognised servitudes. *Compugraphics International Ltd v Nikolic*[43] confirmed that the previously dubious 'servitude right of 'overhang' was recognised in Scots law as a servitude of projection, as well as, in that case, a servitude of support. A servitude of projection and also a servitude of support could, in *Compugraphics*, have been constituted by the maintenance in place of pipes, ductwork and associated support structures which protruded over, and were supported on metal stanchions concreted into, neighbouring land, for the prescriptive period, without any objection.

9.11.2(ii) Registration for written servitudes

A servitude that is contained in a written deed now needs to be registered to be effective. This does not affect unregistered deeds creating servitudes prior to 28 November 2004, however, and it will still be possible to obtain a right by prescription following on an unrecorded deed after 20 years. In addition, and reflecting the arrangements for real burdens, servitudes

---

41 See sections 75 to 81 of the 2003 Act.
42 In any event see *Moncrieff v Jamieson* [2007] UKHL 42; [2008] SC (HL) 1.
43 [2011] CSIH 34, [2011] SC 744.

need to be dual registered against the benefited property and the burdened property[44], with the exception of 'pipeline servitudes' (see para 9.11.2(v) below)

9.11.2(iii) *Registration of prescriptive servitudes*

It is now possible under 2012 Act rules (although there is nothing to this effect in the Act) to add a servitude, acquired by prescription to a Title Sheet of the relevant property. The Application Form contains a question (see para 14.11.2(vii)) that will allow the applicant to confirm that a servitude created in this way exists. Particularly if the servitude is one of access, you can include a plan showing the route, which will then be marked on the title plan. You must, of course, be satisfied that the servitude is unchallengeable, so affidavits and other supporting evidence, will be part of your due diligence exercise.

9.11.2(iv) *Same person can own the benefited and the burdened properties*

Section 75(2) disapplied the rule that the benefited and burdened properties must be in separate ownership at the time of registration of the servitude. If properties are in the same ownership at the time of registration of the servitude, it will remain inactive until the date when the two properties come into separate ownership. Thus, 'community' servitudes affecting a development can be effectively created in advance of conveying off plots or units – and will come into effect on registration of the conveyances of the plots or units.

9.11.2(v) *Pipeline servitudes*

The competence of a servitude to lead a pipe, cable or wire over or under land for any purpose is confirmed by section 77, and is deemed always to have been the case, so that previously created servitudes of this type are valid. Servitudes of this type do not need to be dual registered to be effectively created[45].

---

44 See section 75(1).
45 See section 75(3)(b).

This does not alter the position that to be a valid servitude, there must be both a burdened and benefited property. The difficulty with pipeline servitudes has always been in identifying a benefited property that will benefit from the pipe or cable that is subject to the servitude. Some ways of addressing this difficulty include: identifying a substation to which electricity cables will run or a waterworks or sewage works served by pipelines may be considered to be the benefited property. It may be that there is not an easily identifiable property in the ownership of the utility provider that can obviously be identified as benefiting from the servitude, and the longer the cable or pipe route, the more difficult it can be to identify the benefited property. While it is preferable to attempt to identify the benefited property, for example, the originating source of the water ie the waterworks or reservoir or the substation or power station, it seems, however, that a full conveyancing description of the benefited property is not necessary, and that something general will suffice.

In 2015, the Scottish Parliament issued a call for evidence on this issue, recognising that, particularly for major infrastructure projects, this uncertainty can cause problems. At the time of writing, the outcome of that investigation has not been published, but it is to be hoped that, having recognised the problem, some solution (perhaps in statutory form) will be forthcoming.

9.11.2(vi) Discharge of positive servitude

A positive servitude which has been registered, if discharged by deed, can only be discharged by deed registered against the title[46]. The position regarding extinction through non use for the prescriptive period, or by other legitimate methods, is not changed.

9.11.2(vii) Negative servitudes

It is no longer competent to create negative servitudes (eg servitudes *non aedificandi* (no building or not to build above a certain height) or *altius non tollendi* and *luminibus non officiendi* (not to obstruct prospect or light)). These types of provisions must now be created as negative burdens and dual registered.

---

46 See section 78.

Negative servitudes in existence on 28 November 2004 were automatically converted into negative burdens, ie obligations to refrain from doing something[47]. Known as converted servitudes, they were extinguished on 28 November 2014 unless they were preserved (as real burdens) by notice procedure and registered against the burdened property and the benefited property before that date.

9.11.2(viii) Conversion of certain burdens to positive servitudes

Any real burden that consists of a right to enter or use a property (unless it could be classified as an ancillary burden) ceased to exist on 28 November 2004 and became a positive servitude[48]. This happened automatically and no notice procedure is required. This does not affect burdens that were extinguished by feudal abolition.

9.11.3 The need for real burdens

The first thing to decide before you even get into the drafting issues is whether or not you need a real burden at all. Many real burdens of a certain vintage are all about control, either personal in the form of the superior, or social or public in the form of regulating the style and appearance of buildings. Much of what used to be covered by real burdens is now a matter of planning regulations. Indeed, there is a potential risk if your drafting is over-prescriptive in these matters, of having conflicting provisions. In developments for example, some developers still impose burdens about what the proprietors can and cannot do, according to what they want to happen in the development, in the same way they used to do when they were feudal superiors and had a continuing role in enforcement after completion.

A more realistic approach is to concentrate on what is necessary to ensure the smooth operation of the development. If everyone is required to maintain a uniform colour scheme, for example and all front doors must be blue – is there really going to be a material detriment to the value or enjoyment of everyone else's property if I paint my front door yellow?

The same considerations apply when drafting 'neighbour' burdens. Ensure that your client has a clear idea of what it is possible to achieve

---

47 See section 80.
48 See section 81.

with a burden, particularly in the light of having to establish not only title to enforce, but also interest to enforce. Some clients will still want the burden to be imposed, even if there is a possibility or likelihood that it will be difficult to enforce. In that case it is important that you have made it clear to your client what the realistic prospects of enforcement, in the event of a breach, are likely to be.

9.11.4 Creating real burdens and servitudes in a Disposition

While it no longer matters what form of deed you use as the vehicle for your real burdens (see para 9.11.1(vii) above), it is often still the case that the constitutive deed will be a disposition when the parties want to impose burdens on the property being sold for the benefit of property being retained by the seller. Sometimes it is appropriate to impose burdens on the property being retained too. The PSG has two styles of disposition for use in these circumstances[49]: a Disposition that imposes new real burdens and servitudes on the property being conveyed; and a Disposition that imposes new real burdens and servitudes on both the property being conveyed and the property being retained (Reciprocal). These styles can be freely used and can of course easily be adjusted to suit other circumstances.

The format of each disposition provides for the details of the new burdens and servitudes to be set out in a schedule at the end of the Disposition. The Keeper has confirmed that this approach will assist her in entering details of the burdens and servitudes on the title sheets for the benefited and burdened properties[50]. There are detailed guidance notes that accompany the PSG deeds, however, the following drafting suggestions are offered:

9.11.4(i) Using schedules

If you are only creating one or two new burdens or servitudes, a separate schedule may not be necessary. Experience has shown, however, that it is easy to get provisions confused in a format that uses continuous block of text, so do not feel that you cannot use the Schedule approach with

---

49 See www.psglegal.co.uk/post_feudal_reform.php.
50 See comment from the Registers of Scotland in the article 'Easing the Burdens' JLSS 18 April, 2011. See www.journalonline.co.uk/Magazine/56-4/1009611.aspx.

only a few provisions. This also makes the deed easier to revise during the transaction, and review when examining title in the future.

9.11.4(ii) Using definitions

Traditionally, conveyancers did not use defined terms in dispositions, (preferring references to 'the said' or 'as aforesaid') but as a drafting technique it often simplifies drafting and clarifies provisions, so it is now quite common to see defined terms in conveyances, either in the body of the deed, or in a schedule (or both as in the PSG style). It is particularly useful to use defined terms for the property being conveyed and the property being retained. In the PSG style, the definitions 'Conveyed Property' and 'Retained Property' are used, but alternative, more descriptive, terminology can be substituted. It is recommended, however, that you do not use the expressions 'benefited property' and burdened property' as your definitions in a grant of reciprocal burdens and servitudes, as your drafting will quickly become tangled and confused. The new PSG/Law Society styles of dispositions for residential property adopt this approach.

9.11.4(iii) Keep in mind the rules for creation

Even if the wording of the burden is 'standard' wording that has been used many times in the past, be critical about any style wording you find. It is an easy trap to fall into, since a lot of the time we are drafting new burdens that are the same burdens we always used to draft, so we fail to notice, because we are so used to them, that the burdens may not comply with the rules for creation. One of the most common failings is failure to adhere to the praedial rule – that the burden must burden the burdened property for the benefit of the benefited property. Both elements need to be in place. Too often, burdens burden the burdened property for the benefit of the owners of the benefited property, and it can sometimes be tricky to distinguish between the two. Distance between the two properties can be relevant too – although not an exact science, the further away the benefited property is from the burdened property, the weaker the praedial interest is likely to be, and the nature of the burden itself can often determine the extent to which interest to enforce will be able to be sustained[51].

---

51 See *Hill of Rubislaw (Q Seven) Ltd v Rubislaw Quarry Aberdeen Ltd* [2014] CSIH 105 on both points.

9.11.4(iv) Use clear and precise language

Remember that the burden or servitude you are drafting will (or probably will) be perpetual, and it is important therefore that you compose it in language that is as unambiguous and unequivocal as possible, so that future generations will be able to ascertain with ease the meaning and effect. It is crucial that, under no circumstances, should you take the wording about the nature of the burden that your client has thrown into an email to you, and transfer it straight into your drafting. Please. It is the responsibility of the solicitor, armed with knowledge of what is required to create a clear and enforceable burden, to use their skill to fashion wording that will do the job it is supposed to do. Also remember the rule of interpretation that burdens and servitudes will be interpreted *contra proferentum* (in other words in case of doubt or ambiguity the wording will be construed against the party in whose favour it was cast).

9.11.4(v) Check that your drafting does what it is supposed to do

Once you have drafted the burden or servitude, review it critically and in the context of what it is intended to achieve. It is particularly important to stress test provisions that involve some kind of calculation, in this way. Run a couple of examples to ensure that the right outcome will be achieved. It might even be appropriate to include a worked example, for illustrative purposes only, to make it clear what the effect of the provision is supposed to look like.

Example wording for a burden involving a calculation:

In each year, the total cost of carrying out landscaping maintenance will be arrived at by applying the formula:

$(10 \times OA) \times B$

Where OA (overall area) equals 52.83 and B equals the Unit Multiplier

By way of example, only, if the Unit Multiplier is £150 then the total cost of landscaping maintenance would be

$(10 \times 52.83) \times 150 = £79,245$

A definition of Unit Multiplier would be needed in this example.

9.11.5 Creating real burdens and servitudes in a stand-alone deed

It has always been possible to create servitudes in a freestanding deed, but only if that deed was a Disposition of the property to be burdened, or a Deed of Conditions. The Title Conditions (Scotland) Act 2003 does not change this, but permits any type of deed to be used. This is particularly useful when no property is being conveyed but burdens are required, and a deed of conditions would be too cumbersome or inappropriate to create the burdens required.

9.11.5(i) Deeds of Real Burdens

Two styles of Deed of Real Burdens are available from the PSG[52] to allow the creation of real burdens in this way. The Deed of Real Burdens (Unilateral) can be used where burdens are being imposed on one property in favour of the other, and the Deed of Real Burdens (Reciprocal) may be used where each property will have burdens imposed on it in favour of the other property.

In each case it is assumed that there will be only two properties involved, but deeds of real burdens can be used in transactions where there are multiple properties, and of course combined Deeds of Real Burdens and Servitudes can be created where required.

Creating real burdens in this way is otherwise no different from their creation in a Disposition. The same rules of creation apply, and dual registration is necessary.

9.11.5(ii) Deed of Personal Real Burdens

From time to time you may be required to draft a deed that imposes a personal real burden on land or property in favour of the relevant body entitled to the benefit of the personal real burden in question (see para 9.11.1(iii) above)

Again, there is a PSG style for this purpose, suitable for creating the six types of personal real burden introduced by Part 3 of the Act, ie conservation burdens, rural housing burdens, maritime burdens, economic development

---

52 See www.psglegal.co.uk/post_feudal_reform.php.

burdens, health care burdens, and climate change burdens. It is not suitable for the creation of manager burdens, which are also a type of personal real burden, to the extent that they operate in favour of persons, not property, but which are subject to their own set of requirements, and which are more properly created in Deeds of Conditions. The Deed of Personal Real Burdens could also be used for drafting other types of personal real burdens created in other legislation, such as climate change burdens.

When framing the terms of the Deed of Personal Real Burdens, the relevant section of the 2003 Act, and the relevant statutory instrument under which the entitled body is appointed, should be specified.

For the relevant sections of the 2003 Act see para 9.11.1(iii).

There are several Scottish SIs by which conservation bodies and rural housing bodies are entitled to the benefit of a personal real burden in their favour, and you will need to check for the correct SI (the one that refers to the body in whose favour the burden is being granted) to incorporate into the Deed. The main SI is the Title Conditions (Scotland) Act 2003 (Conservation Bodies) Order 2003, but there have been numerous additions to the list.

All personal real burdens, except for maritime burdens, require the consent of the relevant body in whose favour the burden is created to be obtained before the Deed of Personal Real Burdens is registered. While the 2003 Act does not require the consent to be incorporated into the deed creating the personal real burden, it is a simple and conclusive way of evidencing such consent to do so, and the style contains a suggested clause for this purpose.

The correct terminology (ie conservation, rural housing, maritime, etc) must be used, otherwise the personal real burden will be ineffective. When drafting the terms of the personal real burden, you should ensure that what it is intended to be creates as a personal real burden is permitted by the terms of the relevant section of the 2003 Act.

9.11.5(iii) Deed of Servitude

Creating a servitude in a stand-alone deed has always been competent and nothing in the 2003 Act changes that, except that of course deeds creating servitudes must be dual registered unless they relate to pipeline servitudes, and only positive servitudes may now be created. To complete the suite of documents creating real burdens and servitudes, the PSG styles also include a style Deed of Servitude drafted to incorporate the requirements of the 2003 Act and in a format that reminds the drafter to identify both the burdened and the benefited properties.

Invariably when drafting a servitude right, there will be corresponding servitude conditions that will also apply. It is important to distinguish between a condition that applies to the burdened property, and one that applies to the benefited property. Properly, servitude conditions regulate the use and terms of the servitude rights, and are for the benefit of the burdened property. If the conditions that are to be applied are for the benefit of the benefited property, such as an obligation on the owner of the burdened property to form a road or build a wall, then these should be created as real burdens burdening the burdened property for the benefit of the benefited property.

The importance of remembering this, when you are drafting a Deed of Servitude, is that when creating real burdens the expression 'real burden' or one of the equivalents must be used. Since this expression will not otherwise appear in a Deed of Servitude (which is designed to create only servitudes, for which no special expression is required) the absence of these words would render the real burdens in the deed ineffective (see para 9.11.1(iv)).

Where possible, the agreed basis for the way in which costs, such as maintenance and repair are to be shared in the particular circumstances should be specified as clearly as possible, to avoid any potential dispute in the future as to the proportion of costs due.

9.11.6 Creating Real Burdens and Servitudes in a Deed of Conditions

Probably the most recognisable document for creating real burdens and servitudes, the Deed of Conditions, is both familiar and daunting. Before the Title Conditions (Scotland) Act 2003, it was all we had if we wanted to create real burdens where there was no conveyance of the property concerned (although it was not without its issues). If parties wished to impose burdens on one property in favour of another, then a Deed of Conditions – something of a conveyancing sledgehammer in such cases – was the only alternative.

With the introduction of the concept of 'community burdens' in 2003 Act, the Deed of Conditions comes into its own. Often used for estates of houses or retail or office parks, the format lends itself to the situation where a number of properties are to be subject to the same conditions, and each proprietor is concerned to ensure that his neighbours also comply. Many examples of Deeds of Conditions have their origins in the feudal system, where the developer would be the feudal superior and would retain a high degree of control and enforcement rights, after the units were built, sold and occupied.

9.11.6(i) Problems with drafting

It is in that context of familiarity that some of the problems with modern day Deeds of Conditions can occur. In many cases, experienced developers still expect to apply the same kinds of control through title conditions as they did before feudal abolition. For the lawyer drafting the Deed, it is all too easy to use the same drafting that was used the last time – and that drafting probably dates back many years. If you compare a variety of residential deeds of conditions, drafted over a period of time, you are bound to find many similarities in the content. This is unsurprising – developments of houses usually need the same kind of regulation – preservation of amenity: no ball games; no trade or business; no breeding of dogs; no parking on the roads and so on.

Many of these conditions are perfectly fine, however, some of the conditions are concerned with 'control', such as not to change the appearance or colour scheme of the front elevation without consent. In feudal deeds the consent required would be that of the superior, but this does not translate itself well into a large community, where in reality only a handful of neighbouring owners have any real interest – in the actual sense, as well as probably in the legal sense of interest to enforce.

It is important in drafting terms, therefore, to move away from the feudal mentality and to help clients who might still have a lingering 'feudal hangover' to consider the purpose, effect and desirability of imposing real burdens, and not simply to replicate the same kinds of burdens and conditions that we were accustomed to drafting into pre-feudal abolition Deeds of Conditions. Developers are far less likely to have any continuing interest in the development once it is completed, compared with the ongoing involvement of superiors in the past. While some of that wording and those clauses are still perfectly fine for modern developments, it is important for the drafter and the client to be realistic about what it is possible to create as enforceable real burdens. By all means continue to draft for extensions and alterations and the like, but these should be framed in a way that recognises who should have enforcement rights.

There are a number of elements in a Deed of Conditions that are affected by the provisions of the 2003 Act. The PSG style Deed of Conditions, which can be used for any kind of development such as a retail park, housing development or industrial estate, provides a structure that addresses the principal issues that need to be taken into account to ensure that the Deed complies with the provisions of the 2003 Act, including the need to identify real burdens and servitudes separately, identifying relevant burdens as community burdens, providing for variation and discharge, and a suitable manager burden.

9.11.6(ii) Amenity

One of the principal purposes of burdens in a community is the preservation of the amenity of the community. The Deed should provide for reciprocal burdens that the owners of the units in the community are prepared to adhere to, and want to see imposed on their neighbours. These burdens will relate to such things as maintenance and use.

9.11.6(iii) Management

Inevitably, because of the numbers of units involved, issues of management need to be addressed in some form or another in Deeds of Conditions. Usually this involves the appointment of a manager or factor to be responsible for the organisation, and carrying out of repairs and maintenance of common parts, and for collecting shares of the costs from each of the owners. A majority of the owners in a development can appoint a manager and dismiss him, and set out what they want the manager to do[53].

A 'manager burden' created in accordance with section 63 has precedence over the power of the majority, for a maximum period of five years from the date of registration of the Deed of Conditions. A manager

---

53 See section 28.

burden allows the developer to be, or to appoint, a manager to act as the manager of related properties, such as the units in the development and, where it applies, gives a period of exclusivity of appointment for up to five years[54].

This means that the manager may not be dismissed by the owners until the expiry of the five-year period, although if the developer ceases to own one of the related properties before expiry of that period, (because he has sold all of the units in the development) the manager burden will cease to have effect.

The meaning of 'related properties' for this purpose is outlined in section 66, and is different from the way in which this expression is used in the context of implied enforcement rights. While that exclusivity of the power to appoint applies only for a period of up to five years, the same manager may well be approved to continue to act beyond the five-year period, by the owners, but of course is at risk of dismissal by them after that date. A manager burden can be used by the developer to exercise or retain some control over how the common parts of the development are run, in the early years of the development.

Complex management and administrative arrangements may also be needed, particularly in relation to service charge estimates, billing and accounting. Some form of decision making structure is also required, with arrangements for meetings, quorums, proxy voting and so on. Much of these arrangements have been provided for in the Development Management Scheme, a statutory model scheme of management provided by Part 6 of 2003 Act, and it is worth considering incorporating some or all of these rules either as they are drafted or amended to suit the particular circumstances of the development, into your Deed of Conditions or on a standalone basis (see para 9.11.7 below).

9.11.6(iv) Commencement

You need to think quite carefully about whether you want to postpone the effect of the terms a Deed of Conditions. If nothing is said in the Deed, then on registration in the relevant Property Register, the whole land

---

54 In the case of sheltered housing, the period of exclusivity of appointment is three years. In the
    case of manager burdens relating to right to buy housing, the period is 30 years.

affected by the Deed of Conditions will be burdened with the provisions in the deed. It is possible to postpone the creation of the burdens by making express provision in the deed for creation to take place on some other date, either a fixed date or the date of registration of some other deed, like the Dispositions of each individual plot[55].

In the past this was seen as a useful mechanism if the developer wanted to retain the flexibility to make changes to the layout of the development in the future. It is difficult to see, nowadays, how such changes could be made, given the requirement for a deed constituting community burdens (which these are going to be) to specify the community that is affected, and with greater certainty of the extent of the development being required at an early stage in the process, it seems that there is little to be gained from postponement of the effect of community burdens. If you do decide to postpone the date of effect of the burdens, however, then clearly it is important to remember to trigger their creation in the Disposition of each plot. Recommended wording to incorporate into each disposition is:

> but always with and under the real burdens contained in the Deed of Conditions by [ ] dated [ ] and registered in the Land Register for Scotland under Title Number [ ]

If there is no wording in the Dispositions applying the conditions in the Deed of Conditions, when the date of effect has been postponed, then the plots will not be burdened by the conditions, and there is a risk that not all maintenance and other costs can be recovered.

9.11.6(v) *Identify the community*

For burdens to qualify as community burdens, the 'community' must be identified[56]. More often than not, this will be the whole development, and using the words 'community burden' has the effect of making the units which are subject to those burdens both benefited and burdened, setting up the reciprocal arrangement typical of communities. This is further support for the notion that communities should get on with it themselves without external interference, once they are set up, by providing that each owner

---

55 See section 4(1).
56 See section 4(4).

has (subject to establishing interest to enforce) enforcement rights against the others.

When identifying the property to which the community burdens will apply, care must be taken to ensure that parts of the development held in separate ownership but not part of one of the units are not inadvertently included as a burdened or a benefited property. For example, the development may consist of a number of units conveyed to individuals, and extensive common parts retained in the ownership of the developer or held by a management company. It would not be the intention for the owner of the common parts either to have burdens that affect the units imposed on them, or to be entitled to enforce those burdens against the units. In such a case, the community burdens should be imposed on the units in the development rather than the whole development. Separate burdens, for example restricting the use of the common parts to open space, should be imposed on the common parts for the benefit of the units.

9.11.6(vi)   Common parts – identification

We have already considered the effect of the case of *PMP Plus v the Keeper of the Registers of Scotland* on identification of common parts of a development, in relation to examination of title (see para 8.28.4). Instances where developers sell off large parts of the common amenity areas to other commercial interests will be rare. The view had been expressed[57] that, while the conveyance from the developer may be void, future transfers by plot or unit owners to a purchaser may operate as an *a non domino* title which will be perfected through prescription. There is less support for this view these days. Under 2012 Act rules, it is unlikely that such shares will be transferred to updated title sheets.

In drafting new Deeds of Conditions, we have to be mindful of the *PMP Plus* decision and define elements of the development, such as common parts, in a better way. Using a plan to define them is one option, but it is not without risk, particularly for larger developments where, for perfectly good reasons, the developer might need to depart, even slightly, from the original layout meaning the initial delineation is no longer correct.

---

57 Gretton and Reid *Conveyancing* (2008) pp 145–146.

Another possibility is to identify certain community rights, such as access over roads and liability for external boundaries, in an over-arching Deed, followed by later Deeds over smaller areas, confining liability for common areas for example to those in the immediate vicinity. Again this option is not entirely satisfactory, particularly if a park or play area in one section is intended to be used by everyone. The individual circumstances of each development need to be considered with care, and an appropriate structure devised.

9.11.6(vii) Common parts – ownership

Much of the concern expressed about the *PMP Plus* case stems from the fact that ownership of the common parts needed to be transferred to the individual owners. But, of course, that is not the only alternative. There does not appear to be any objection to the alternative approach of having the common parts owned by the developer, or some third party, (although the case of *Marriot v Greenbelt Group Limited*[58], demonstrates that failure to adequately identify the benefited property[59] can prove fatal to the burden. In that case, a burden was imposed on the proprietors in a development, to contribute towards the cost of maintenance of open ground in the development, owned by Greenbelt. The definition of the open ground referred to its definition in a planning consent, as amended or modified. The Lands Tribunal held (quite correctly – see para 8.25.16(ii)) that the benefited/burdened property had not been adequately identified for the purposes of section 4(2)(c) of the Title Conditions (Scotland) Act 2003) provided the burdened properties have some interest in the common parts. Section 3 of the 2003 Act says that a real burden must relate in some way to the burdened property and that that relationship may be direct or indirect. This could be interpreted as meaning that, provided that the owners of the units have freedom to use the common parts for leisure and recreation for example, and use the roads for access and egress, there is a sufficient connection and praedial interest for the burden to be validly constituted, without the necessity for the common parts to be owned by the individuals responsible. This view would appear to be supported

---

58 LTS/TC/2014/27.
59 As required by section 4(2)(c)(ii) of the 2003 Act.

by comments in the Lands Tribunal case of *Greenbelt Property Ltd v Riggens*[60] and also by comments made by the Lands Tribunal in *Marriott*.

The Development Management Scheme (see para 9.11.7) has the potential to be of considerable assistance in the setting up of provisions to regulate developments.

9.11.6(viii) Servitude rights

As well as real burdens, a Deed of Conditions will typically contain a number of servitudes. The sensible use of servitudes in a Deed of Conditions can help to resolve some of the difficulties that we might encounter with real burdens affecting common parts. For example, it is of course perfectly valid and acceptable to grant servitude rights of access over access roads to be constructed within the development, meaning there would then be no requirement to convey the property. It is also perfectly valid for such servitudes to have, as a servitude condition, an obligation to contribute towards the cost of maintenance.

As well as access, a typical Deed of Conditions will contain servitude rights over other units for the purposes of maintenance, repair, cleaning and similar purposes. There may need to be construction servitudes for access for construction traffic or for oversailing, and also rights reserved and granted for laying, maintaining and renewing service media. Style wording for these types of servitude is contained in the PSG Deed of Conditions.[61]

9.11.6(ix) Plans and site visits

Before starting to draft a Deed of Conditions, it is essential to have a reasonably detailed plan showing what the developer proposes for the site. This will identify issues relating to access, emergency access, what is to happen in communal external areas, areas that are to be exclusive or shared among only some of the owners, parking and access to parking spaces, boundaries, service strips, amenities such as play areas, recreational areas. Although not always possible, it can help to conduct a site visit – not

---

60 [2010] GWD 28-586.
61 For further exploration of the use of servitude in development titles see 'Servitudes, Developers and Flexible Rights' by Professor Roddy Paisley JLSS, February 2011. Available at: www. journalonline.co.uk/Magazine/56-2/1009301.aspx.

necessarily when the development is a muddy field (although if you act for an active developer, it can be a good idea to keep a pair of wellies in the boot of your car just in case) – but once some of the infrastructure is in and foundations have been laid. Actually visiting the site may flag up issues on the ground that are not obvious from a two-dimensional plan, in just the same way as a site visit can be of immense value when examining title. Access issues, land contours that may require height restrictions to be imposed or issues that may affect privacy or amenity can be identified.

9.11.7 Creating Real Burdens and Servitudes Using the Development Management Scheme

The Development Management Scheme has a number of extremely attractive elements that can help to provide a structure for the maintenance of a development. Practitioners who advise developers on a regular (or even infrequent) basis would benefit from becoming closely acquainted with the rules of the scheme, and the way in which it can operate and be adapted for use in any development.

9.11.7(i) A statutory scheme for management

The Development Management Scheme (DMS) is provided for in Part 6 of the 2003 Act[62]. It consists of a set of rules, similar to real burdens, which can be applied to land intended to be developed with a number of units that will be subject to the same provisions, as you would do in a Deed of Conditions. However, in contrast to the rules for management of tenements in the Tenement Management Scheme attached to the Tenements (Scotland) Act 2004, which automatically apply to tenements in default, the DMS is an optional scheme that you can choose to apply to your development or not, and with the ability to vary or omit some of the rules.

The rules provide a structure for management of shared facilities, and set out arrangements for a number of administrative matters, such as appointment and duties of a manager; convening meetings, and procedures at such meetings (eg constituting a quorum and voting arrangements);

---

62 The full details of the DMS are contained in Schedule 1 to the Title Conditions (Scotland) Act 2003 (Development Management Scheme) Order 2009 (SI 2009/729).

instructing emergency work; and financial matters including fixing a budget and applying service charge.

These rules function like real burdens and, in particular, community burdens and specific provisions of the 2003 Act apply to these rules as they do to real burdens. With the exception of the rules that relate to constituting and naming an Owners' Association, the rules in the DMS can be varied as you wish, added to or omitted, so that it is possible to tailor the DMS to the requirements of any development.

9.11.7(ii) Form of deed of application of DMS

The DMS can be applied to the title by a deed of application. There is no fixed form required for such a deed and the DMS rules could either be used on their own, with some words of application attached, or, as is envisaged in the PSG Deed of Conditions, incorporated as a schedule into the Deed, with a clause of application of the DMS in the body of the Deed. Any variations to the DMS can be drafted in the Deed of Conditions or by amendment to the Schedule. Alternatively, the DMS rules themselves could be incorporated in the body of the Deed, with the addition of amenity burdens dealing with use and maintenance.

9.11.7(iii) Owners' Association

Application of the DMS to a development will set up an Owners' Association for the land, which will be a body corporate, and thus able to own land in its own name, enter into contracts and conduct other juristic acts of an entity with legal personality, which previous owners' associations were not able to do without incorporating or setting up some form of trust arrangement. All owners of units in the development will automatically be members of the Owners' Association, and the Owners' Association must have a manager to deal with the day-to-day management of the shared facilities.

With separate legal personality meaning that that the Owners' Association can take title to land, it is clearly an ideal vehicle for taking title to common parts of the development, either during the course of the development or at the end, and there is no reason why the common parts could not be conveyed to the Owners' Association in several parcels so there would appear to be no impediment to different sections of, for example, common parts being conveyed at different times. This raises interesting possibilities.

9.11.7(iv) Enforcement of DMS rules

Under the rules of the DMS, the manager manages the development for the benefit of the members, and has the power (so far as it is reasonable to do so) to enforce the provisions of the DMS and of any regulations which have taken effect and any obligation owed by any person to the association (Rule 8). Accordingly, the members (owners) themselves do not have enforcement rights in respect of the rules, although provision can easily be made for this if wanted[63]. One advantage of enforcement through the manager is that he does not need to show interest to enforce. This is another aspect of the DMS that may make it more attractive than the traditional Deed of Conditions route, given the uncertainty that surrounds interest to enforce.

TRUST CLAUSES

9.12 Trust clauses go in and out of popularity according to the vicissitudes of the decisions of the courts. The purpose of the trust clause is to offer some protection to the purchaser from the seller's insolvency occurring in the period between settlement or completion (when the price has been paid and the disposition delivered) and perfecting a real right to the property by registering that disposition in the Land Register. A real right of ownership only passes when the purchaser effects such registration. Until then, the real right remains with the seller. The purchaser is exposed to the risk of the seller's sequestration or liquidation between settlement and registration. As the real right in the property remains with the seller, it continues to form part of the seller's estate in the sequestration/liquidation, and will be available to the seller's creditors. Floating charges are an exception as shown by the earlier House of Lords' decision in *Sharp v Thomson*[64]: the purchaser is safe even if the company goes into receivership on crystallisation of a floating charge in the 'gap' period.

---

63 Article 10 of the Title Conditions (Scotland) Act 2003 (Development Management Scheme) Order 2009.
64 [1997] SC (HL) 66.

Following the decision of the House of Lords in *Burnett's Trustee v Grainger*[65], which confirmed that in cases of insolvency of any legal person (other than in the floating charge exception referred to above) there is still a race to the register and trust clauses reappeared.

Opinion is divided on their use and effectiveness, and even whether it is appropriate for the seller to be holding the property in trust for the purchaser at all. Some firms have taken the view neither to ask for a trust clause in dispositions in favour of their clients nor to give trust clauses in dispositions by their clients. Academic opinion appears to be firmly against them, the consensus apparently being that 'they have never really worked', and there is no clear trust purpose. It is also felt that recent changes to bankruptcy legislation which impose a 28-day moratorium on a trustee in sequestration, during which they cannot complete title, render the clause unnecessary[66] (although note there is no such moratorium in corporate insolvency) and that the use of such clauses should be discontinued.

It is always incumbent on the purchaser's solicitor to submit the purchaser's disposition for registration as soon as possible after settlement/ completion. If you **do** decide to seek a trust clause the following style may be of assistance:

> The Seller declares that he/she/it/they hold[s] the Property in trust for the Purchaser absolutely until the earlier of 14 days from the date of entry, and the date of registration in the Land Register of Scotland of the Purchaser's interest in the Property, but for the sole purpose of holding title to the Property. From the Date of Entry the Seller *qua* trustee under the trust will not be under any duty to maintain or preserve the Property nor to insure the Property against fire or other insurable risks.

Some seller's solicitors will also include provision that the purchaser will indemnify the seller in respect of anything that imposes any liability on them in the period as a result of the trust.

SUPERSESSION

9.13 The former rule that delivery of the disposition superseded the missives was considered to be a 'Bad Rule' and generated elaborate

---

65 [2004] SC (HL) 19 and see KGC Reid and GL Gretton *Conveyancing* (2004) pp 79–85.
66 See section 17 of BAD Act 2007; see also para 8.18.5.

provisions in missives that were never entirely satisfactory in their effect. The SLC 'Report on Three Bad Rules in Contract Law'[67] resulted in the Contract (Scotland) Act 1997 which flipped the rule over, so that as a result of section 2, any unimplemented terms of the contract will not be superseded on delivery of a deed in implement of a contract.

The practical effect of this is that, instead of having to provide in missives and in dispositions for the contract to survive delivery of the disposition for a period of time, it is now necessary to provide for expiry of the missives after a period – usually two years – from the date of delivery of the disposition, or according to circumstances if there are particular elements of the contract that require to remain in force for a longer time.

This is normally now dealt with in the missives and, strictly speaking, there is no longer any need to make provision in the disposition – since delivery of it no longer supersedes the contract, which was really the point of 'non-supersession' clauses. The contract will normally provide for the provisions of the missives to cease to be enforceable after the specified period except in so far as they are founded on in any court proceedings which have commenced within the period stated (see paras 6.10.25 and 6.14.31). If, however, the missives are silent but the parties want to put a cap on the period then there is no reason why this could not be put into the disposition[68] along similar lines:

> And the Missives [either a defined term or (constituted by letters between [ ] and [ ] dated [ ] and [ ]) will cease to be enforceable after a period of [two] years from the Date of Entry except insofar as they are founded on in court proceedings which have commenced within the said period;

IMPORTING DEEDS OF CONDITIONS

9.14 The now repealed section 17 of the Land Registration (Scotland) Act 1979 provided that burdens set out in a deed of conditions would become real obligations burdening the land on recording or registration of that deed. It was possible to disapply section 17, so that the burdens would only have effect on a conveyance of plots of (or other units in) that land

---

67 Scot Law Com No 152.
68 See section 2(2) of the Contract (Scotland) Act 1997.

and reference was made in the disposition to application of the terms of the deed of conditions. A number of pre-28 November 2004 deeds of conditions disapplied section 17.

Accordingly, the Title Conditions (Scotland) Act 2003, in repealing section 17 had to make provision to allow such deeds of conditions which applied to units or plots conveyed after 28 November 2004 to be capable of being imported into the title of the unit or plot, essentially to correct the old and new law. Section 6 of the 2003 Act makes provision for importing the old deed of conditions into the title of the units being conveyed. Wording is given in Schedule 1 of the 2003 Act:

> There are imported the terms of the title conditions specified in Deed of Conditions by [ ] dated [ ] and [recorded in the Division of the General Register of Sasines for the County of [ ] on [ ]] [registered in the Land Register of Scotland under Title Number [ ] on [ ]];

There is no need to use this import wording in pre-2004 Deeds of Conditions where section 17 had not been disapplied nor, of course, is it required in relation to titles where Deeds of Conditions have been registered after the appointed day.

COMMUNITY INTEREST IN LAND DECLARATION

9.15 If the property is subject to an entry in the Register of Community Interests in Land (RCIL) (see para 7.9) by which a community body has registered an interest, the property cannot be sold other than to that community. Section 40 of the Land Reform (Scotland) Act 2003 sets out certain circumstances in which a property can be sold regardless of an entry in the RCIL, including where the sale is in implement of missives that were concluded on a date before the entry appeared on the RCIL.

Where one of the section 40 exemptions applies, the disposition must contain a declaration to that effect. The PSG wording for this declaration is:

> [The Seller declares that the transfer effected by this disposition is excluded from the operation of section 40(1) of the Land Reform (Scotland) Act 2003 by virtue of para [insert appropriate para number] of section 40(4) of that Act][*If, but only if, the exempting paragraph is (a), (e) or (h) insert the following*: The Seller further declares that the

transfer effected by this disposition does not form part of a scheme or arrangement and is not one of a series of transfers mentioned in section 43(1) of the said Act];

Part of the difficulty here is one of timing. There may be no entry in the RCIL when you draft the disposition, but if one appears just before completion, a declaration is required. Obviously if the property is in an area which is excluded land for the purposes of the community right to buy provisions in Part 2 of the Land Reform (Scotland) Act 2003, no wording will be necessary, since it is not possible to acquire excluded land by way of the community right to buy. Excluded land is defined in the Community Right to Buy (Definition of Excluded Land) Order 2009[69]. Plans are available online, which delineate the excluded areas so it is easy to check. In the future, however, once the provisions of the Community Empowerment (Scotland) Act 2015 come into force, the right to buy will apply to all of Scotland, so the concept of 'excluded land' will cease to be relevant.

If there is a possibility that an entry could appear in the RCIL at the last minute (and the owner of the land should be well aware of this possibility since the preparations of a community body leading up to registration will be well known), then it would be worth inserting the necessary declaration into the disposition anyway, to avoid the deed being rejected by the Keeper. A declaration that turns out to be unnecessary will not invalidate a disposition.

If you have incorporated a declaration on a 'just in case' basis but it turns out not to be necessary, because no interest is registered in the RCIL, you should point this out in your application for registration, to avoid any confusion. The PSG suggests the following wording for a covering letter to the Keeper:

The Property disponed in favour of the Applicant does not lie within 'excluded' land as defined in regulations made under Part 2 of the Land Reform (Scotland) Act 2003. Accordingly, we have included in the disposition a declaration, under section 40/43 of the Land Reform (Scotland) Act 2003, to allow registration of the disposition in the event of an entry, affecting the Property, being made in the Register

---

69 SSI 2009/207.

of Community of Community Interests in Land ('RCIL') in the period between conclusion of missives for the sale of the Property, and registration of the Applicant's title.

We understand that a declaration of this type will neither invalidate a deed, nor an application for registration, in the event that the declaration is not ultimately required. No such entry in the RCIL has been made as at today's date. If this remains the case [(and we have no reason to believe otherwise)] as at the date of registration of the Applicant's title, please disregard the declaration.

APPLICATION TO THE LANDS TRIBUNAL

9.16 There is in theory no reason why a burdened owner could not now apply to the Lands Tribunal for discharge of a burden as soon as it has been created (although it is not known how the Lands Tribunal would regard such an application). Section 92 of the Title Conditions (Scotland) Act 2003 allows the parties to impose a moratorium on applications to the Lands Tribunal to vary the terms of the burdens or servitudes, for up to a maximum period of five years, and if the parties agree, the following clause preventing applications to the Lands Tribunal can be included. It is now fairly common to insert this clause as a matter of course in deeds that create new burdens and servitudes:

No application may be made to the Lands Tribunal for Scotland under section 90(1)(a)(i) of the Title Conditions (Scotland) Act 2003 in respect of the [real burdens set out in [Part [ ] of the Schedule] [and] [the servitudes set out in Part [ ] of the Schedule] for a period of [five years] after the registration of this disposition in the Land Register of Scotland;

ENTRY

9.17 Entry is generally expressed either as 'entry and actual occupation' or 'entry and vacant possession'. It is customary to insert the date on which the purchaser is entitled to take entry to the property into the disposition. The clause may also refer to 'vacant possession', although this is not appropriate if the property is leased and is being bought for investment purposes. Traditional wording also distinguished the date of entry from the date of execution of the deed, but this wording is often now omitted:

WITH ENTRY and actual occupation as at 14 March 2012 [notwithstanding the date hereof];

WARRANDICE

9.18 Warrandice in the context of transfer of heritable property is a guarantee from the granter that the title is good. A disposition of heritable property will usually contain a clause of absolute warrandice. If the deed omits a clause of warrandice, then it is implied; the type of warrandice implied will depend on the nature of the transaction. Accordingly, if the granter intends to grant no warrandice, then the deed must say 'And I/we grant no warrandice'.

If the granter of the title knows that there is a problem with an aspect of the title, then that aspect can be excluded from the warrandice.

9.18.1 Absolute Warrandice

A grant of absolute warrandice protects the purchaser from the past and future acts and deeds of the disponer, and from the acts of third parties and is a guarantee from the granter that the title is good, and not subject to unusual conditions of title that are unknown to the disponee. It is expressed by the words 'And I/we grant warrandice'.

9.18.2 Fact and Deed Warrandice

This is a guarantee against both the future acts or deeds and the past acts or deeds of the granter. In effect it is an undertaking by the disponer that he has not done anything in the past, and will do nothing in the future to prejudice the title granted in the disposition. This type of warrandice is usually given by granters acting in some representative capacity, such as executors or trustees, in which case generally they will also bind the trust or the executry estate in absolute warrandice. It is expressed by the words 'And I/we grant warrandice from my/our own facts and deeds only'.

9.18.3 Simple Warrandice

Where the property is being transferred for no consideration such as a gift simple warrandice is implied in such deeds unless other provision is made. It offers protection from the future voluntary acts or deeds of the granter but not past ones, or third party acts. It is expressed by the words 'And I/ we grant simple warrandice'.

Some examples of warrandice clauses used in particular cases are:

And I grant warrandice, but declaring that warrandice is excluded to the extent that the Keeper has excluded warranty in respect of that strip of ground shown shaded in pink on the attached plan.

And we the said [ ] and [ ] grant warrandice from our own facts and deeds only and bind the Trust Estate under our charge in absolute warrandice:

And I the said [ ] as Trustee foresaid grant no warrandice but in so far as I have power to do so bind the Sequestrated Estate under my charge in absolute warrandice

And we grant warrandice, but excepting from warrandice the Lease between [ ] and [ ] dated [ ] and registered in the Land Register of Scotland under Title Number [ ]

9.18.4 Warrandice in Insolvency Transactions

It used to be reasonably usual market practice for the insolvent company to grant some form of warrandice. These days, however, Insolvency Practitioners are far more cautious about incorporating such warrandice into any conveyance of property. The records of the company may be unclear or in disarray and the IP may not be able to ascertain that the company did not in the past grant any deeds that might conflict with what is being granted in the transaction.

There might in any event be little value in a grant of warrandice by an insolvent company, whose assets may already be fully secured to, or distributed among, its creditors. Although it is possible that the company might one day recommence trading, it is equally possible that it will be wound up. An IP is also going to be very wary about committing the company to the possibility of a future claim on warrandice, the value of which is entirely unknown, and which potentially could impact on the position of the other creditors, not to mention the IP's own expenses.

In particular, if the disposition is following on an asset sale or other transfer arrangement, it may be the case that it has already been agreed that no warrandice or title guarantee will be given. If that is the case then a purchaser would not be entitled to insist on any warrandice in the disposition, and so this should be checked.

It is now the invariable practice of IPs to insist that nothing in the contract or in the conveyance in any way implies or expresses personal liability upon them. Indeed, most also now insist, not only on no grant of warrandice, but also that the exclusion of personal liability is also incorporated into the disposition. In some drafting you may see both fact and deed warrandice and an exclusion of personal liability, and there is clearly an inconsistency between the two statements.

When acting for a purchaser from an insolvent company therefore, you should expect that neither the IP nor the insolvent company will grant any warrandice, and personal liability of the IP will also be excluded.

If the purchaser insists on having a grant of warrandice from the IP, then this might have to be explored in individual circumstances. Fact and deed warrandice does impose personal liability on the IP, however minor that may be. Solicitors acting for IPs in these circumstances **must** get specific instructions from the IP before agreeing to such a proposal[70].

The absence of warrandice from either the company or the IP should not pose any problems with the Keeper's warranty when it comes to registering the title, provided the title is good. The Keeper will exclude warranty where there is a defect in the title, but the absence of warrandice is not a defect (although there are circumstances where a seller does exclude warrandice because of a defect). When faced with an absence of warrandice, the Keeper will enquire into the circumstances, and the Keeper recognises that a sale by an IP will invariably omit or qualify warrandice for reasons that are nothing to do with the title.

---

70 For commentary on the issues surrounding warrandice and insolvency practitioners, see
   Kenneth Ross and Colin Gilchrist: 'To grant or not to grant?' 19 April 2010. Available at: www.
   journalonline.co.uk/Magazine/55-4/1007936.aspx.

CONTRACTS OF EXCAMBION

9.19 Circumstances may arise where the parties wish to exchange areas of land and, while this can be done by way of separate dispositions, there is also a form of deed – the Contract of Excambion, whereby the whole exchange can be narrated in one deed. In the days before stamp duty land tax (SDLT) and land and buildings transaction tax (LBTT) there used to be a benefit to using an excambion, if the values of the properties were the same, there was only a nominal payment of stamp duty. However, under the SDLT rules, replicated in the LBTT rules, the tax (if any is due) is calculated on each of the transfers, and as a result, the popularity of the Contract of Excambion has waned. They were never particularly easy documents to draft anyway, incorporating, as they do, all the elements of two dispositions, with all the descriptive, part and portion and burdens clauses having to be incorporated, there was huge scope for a very confusing document to result.

VOLUNTARY REGISTRATION

9.20 Voluntary registration will become more common in the push to complete the Land Register (see para 2.5.3). However, a key point to note is that no disposition is required. Voluntary registration is simply a move from one Register to another: there is no actual transfer (conveyance) of the property.

Chapter 10

Security

SECURED LENDING

10.1 Most purchasers of heritable property will need to borrow funds to finance the purchase. This applies equally to residential and commercial property. When a bank, building society or other lending institution makes money available for the purchase or financing of heritable property, it will require, among other things, to be granted a fixed charge over the title to the property. That fixed charge will be registered against the borrower's title to the property and gives the creditor a certain amount of control over the voluntary sale of the property, effectively preventing the borrower from selling the property and making off with the sale proceeds without repaying the loan. It also provides the lender with powers and remedies in the event the borrower defaults on the loan. While the lending criteria may be different depending on the type of property, the document by which such lending is protected is the same – the 'Standard Security'.

THE LEGISLATIVE BASIS FOR STANDARD SECURITIES

10.2 Since November 1970, the Standard Security is the only form of document by which a fixed charge over heritable property in Scotland may be created. You may, in the course of examination of title, come across earlier forms of heritable security such as the bond and disposition in security, or the *ex facie* absolute disposition, but none of these documents can now be used for creating a fixed charge over property.

Standard securities were introduced by the Conveyancing and Feudal Reform (Scotland) Act 1970 which also covered other aspects of property law reform, including the procedure for variation and discharge of land obligations by the constitution of a Lands Tribunal for Scotland – the precursor to the provisions in Part 9 of the Title Conditions (Scotland) Act 2003, and the reduction of the period of prescriptive possession from 20 years to 10 years.

The 1970 Act contains a number of forms and styles of the documents and procedures which it introduces, including the Standard Security and forms for Assignation of a standard security, a Deed of Restriction, a Discharge, and a Deed of Variation of a standard security.

The 1970 Act also introduced a codified set of conditions which automatically apply to the provisions of any standard security, without the need to mention it in the document. These Standard Conditions, contained in Schedule 3 to the 1970 Act, relate to practical matters aimed at preserving the value of the property, such as maintenance and repair, alterations and letting of properties, as well as enforcement such as calling-up and notices of default. Most, but not all of them can be varied to suit the lender's specific requirements.

The enforcement rights of heritable creditors in the event of default by the borrower are also set out in the 1970 Act.[1]

THE STANDARD SECURITY AND OTHER FORMS

10.3 The 1970 Act provides a collection of styles for use in connection with secured lending.

10.3.1 Standard Security

The 1970 Act provides that a Standard Security may be in one of two forms. Styles of Form A and Form B are given in Schedule 2 of the Act. These statutory forms give some uniformity to securities, while providing flexibility to cater for the many different lending criteria.

Form A is used where both the personal obligation of the debtor as well as the details of the mortgage and the grant of security over the property are all contained in one document. This form is the one that is most widely used by lenders in residential mortgages.

Form B just contains the grant security over the property and the personal obligation and sometimes also the details of the mortgage do not appear on the face of the security, but are contained in a separate unregistered document. This method is mostly used in commercial loans where the lending arrangements are often complex and lengthy (see para 10.3.2).

---

1   Sections 19 to 29.

A simple form of Form A security using the style in Schedule 2 to the 1970 Act:

WE, FREDERICK ROWAN, residing at Piemonte House, Kelvinforth Perthshire and MISS FLEUR LAPIN MONK residing at 27 Lombardy Street, Kelvinforth, Perthshire (the 'Borrower') hereby undertake to pay [*this is the personal obligation part*] to SCOTLAND BANK PLC incorporated under the Companies Acts and having its registered office at Alba House, Corries Road, Edinburgh and its successors and assignees (the 'Bank') on demand the sum of TWO HUNDRED THOUSAND Pounds Sterling (£200,000) with interest from [date to be inserted] at 3.95 per centum per annum payable monthly on the First day of each month commencing on [date to be inserted] and all sums of principal, interest and charges now due and that may become due to the Bank in any manner of way by us whether solely or jointly with any other person or persons, corporation, firm or other body and whether as principal or surety; And any account or certificate signed by the Treasurer and General Manager, or other person so authorised by the Bank shall ascertain, specify and constitute the sums or balances of principal, interest and charges due and that may become due as aforesaid; For which sums we the said Frederick Rowan and Miss Fleur Lapin Monk GRANT a Standard Security in favour of the Bank [*this is the standard security part*] over ALL and WHOLE the subjects known as Flat 12 Florence Park, Kelvinforth, registered in the Land Register of Scotland under Title Number PTH2803; The Standard Conditions [*see para 10.04 below*] specified in Sch 3 to the Conveyancing and Feudal Reform (Scotland) Act 1970, as amended, and any lawful variation thereof operative for the time being shall apply and we agree that Standard Condition 5(a) shall be varied to the effect that the sum for which the security subjects shall be insured in terms of said Condition 5(a) shall be reinstatement value and not market value [*this variation is always made in practice*]; And we grant warrandice; And we consent to registration of these presents and of the said account or certificate aforementioned for execution; IN WITNESS WHEREOF

Note that it is sufficient to describe the security subjects so as to identify them so that a postal address or other common law description would be sufficient[2]. For property registered in the Land Register the Title Number

---

2   Schedule 12, para 30(23) to the Abolition of Feudal Tenure (Scotland) Act 2000.

should also be included and, for property in the Sasine Register, a Sasine description eg by reference to a descriptive writ should be used.

A Form B security is made up as above, but omitting the personal obligation, the amount of the loan, the rate of interest and repayment details, and the consent to registration for execution, which are contained in a separate unregistered minute of agreement. In commercial loans this document may also carry heavy variations of the standard conditions and trading conditions.

The majority of lenders – banks, building societies and funding institutions will have their preferred style or format of standard security, and this will be provided to the lender's solicitors as part of their instructions. Most of these documents are now produced electronically and a number of lenders provide their solicitors with electronic versions of their branded documents in their preferred style and format.

Usually, lenders try to resist revisals to their house style. It is rare for any amendments to be made to residential standard securities, which are usually pretty straightforward affairs. For commercial securities, permitted revisals will depend on individual circumstances.

If any collateral security is given to the lender, such as a life assurance policy, an assignation of that additional security must be drawn up, signed by the borrower and intimated to the life assurance company. Forms of assignation and intimation will also be provided by the lender with their instructions.

After a standard security has been granted and registered, it is possible to assign it to another creditor[3] to make amendments to the extent of the property it secures, or the amount of the debt to which it relates[4] vary its terms as between debtor and creditor[5] or to discharge it completely when the loan has been repaid, or the obligations it secures have been satisfied[6]. See paras 10.3.3 to 10.3.6 below.

10.3.2 Personal Obligation – Personal Bond

As we have seen the security must contain two components – the obligation to pay or perform, and the grant of the security over the property. When

---

3 Section 14 of the 1970 Act.
4 Section 15 of the 1970 Act.
5 Section 16 of the 1970 Act.
6 Section 17 of the 1970 Act.

a Form B style of security is used, the personal obligation is contained in a separate document, the simplest form of which is the personal bond. Instead of the undertaking to pay, the Form B standard security will say:

> 'We...hereby IN SECURITY of all sums due and that may become due to Scotland Bank plc...and its successors and assignees (the 'Bank') in terms of Personal Bond granted by us the said [...] in favour of the Bank dated [......]'

The Personal Bond will contain more or less the first section of the wording in the style Form A security, with reference to rates and payment, or may relate to all sums that may be due at any time or from time to time and so can be used in a flexible way. The personal obligation of the debtor can relate to any obligation due, or to become due at a point in the future, to repay money or pay money, or to do something or perform some act, (an *ad factum praestandum* security). This type of security obligation is sometimes used to secure performance of development obligations. Where the personal obligation is located in a separate deed in this way, it can be referred to in several standard securities, which need not be granted at the same time as the personal bond.

Most commercial lenders will usually look for an 'all sums' security. This provides that the Borrower will pay all sums which are due to the lender in any manner of way, including interest, charges, costs etc, and thus can relate to several different loans. Some 'all sums' obligations may relate to a specific loan or facility arrangement between the borrower and the lender – for a particular project or development.

There is also a distinction that can be made between 'direct' and 'indirect' securities, and they appear in both residential and commercial loans. A direct security is one which is granted by the borrower over property that he owns, in security of his own debts and obligations. An indirect security is one where the borrower grants the personal obligation to pay or perform in respect of the debt or obligation, but someone else grants the security over property owned by that third party. Situations where this might arise are where an individual is prepared to give security over his house in security of borrowings by his business which he runs through a company, or a close relative may provide a property in security of the indebtedness of a family member. Clearly the circumstances in which such securities are taken must be considered with care, since the third party granting the security is placing their property at the risk of performance of the obligation to pay or perform of another party, and they may have little or no control over how that person manages their affairs.

Before an indirect security is granted, it is important to ensure that the third party has received independent legal advice. There are many cases of indirect security arrangements over matrimonial homes where the lender's security was reduced because the parties to the security were not given proper advice as to the effect of the document they were signing (see para 10.5.3).

10.3.3 Assignation

A standard security can be assigned by the lender[7] and there are two styles of assignation. These are contained in Schedule 4 to the 1970 Act and may be in Form A (a separate document) or Form B (endorsed on the standard security). Unless provided for in ancillary documentation, the borrower's consent is not required to an assignation, nor does it require to be intimated, although it must be registered in the Register of Sasines or Land Register to be effective. This procedure can be used by lenders to raise finance, by selling their portfolio of loans to another lender.

Assigning a standard security is not without its pitfalls, however. Special care needs to be taken when assigning a Form B type standard security, where the personal obligation is contained in a separate deed, as the obligation in respect of the debt also has to be assigned. Otherwise the new lender would have security over the property, but no obligation from the debtor to make any payment to it. A document known as a bond of corroboration of the obligations of the debtor may be required in addition to the assignation in these circumstances. This will, in effect, confirm or corroborate the personal obligations of the borrower in favour of the new lender. It is always open to the lender to discharge the existing security, and for a new one to be constituted in favour of the new lender, but one of the advantages of assigning the existing security is that the priority or ranking of the original security is preserved. If there are other securities over the property that are registered after the original security, they would gain a prior ranking status if the original security is discharged (see para 10.6.6).

---

7   Section 14 of the 1970 Act.

It would be unusual, but not impossible, for a standard security to be assigned by the borrower to a new borrower, but it is not an attractive option, given that the assignation does not discharge the original borrower.

10.3.4 Variation

Variation may be appropriate where any alteration of the standard security is required which is not a change of lender, when assignation might be suitable, or a change to the amount or area, when a deed of restriction would be appropriate. Variation of the security in the style of Form E in Schedule 4 of the 1970 Act would deal for example with changing the debtor (eg transferring title to the property and the corresponding security from joint names to just one of the parties) or to correct an error in the original standard security, or to alter some of the original lending criteria.

10.3.5 Deed of Restriction

The Deed of Restriction (also sometimes called a Deed of Disburdenment) operates to restrict the terms of the standard security by removing part of the security subjects from its ambit, and can also operate as a partial discharge of the standard security. Again there are statutory forms in Schedule 4 to the 1970 Act – either Form C which disburdens the property described in it from the security, or Form D, which incorporates a partial discharge as well. A full description of the subjects being disburdened, ideally (and usually) with a plan, should be incorporated in the deed of restriction. Such deeds are typical in transactions that deal with the sale of plots in a development, where the developer granted a standard security over the whole site. On the occasion of each plot sale, in addition to granting a disposition of the plot, the same description and plan are used for the deed of restriction, which is signed by the creditor and delivered to the purchaser at or around settlement, to be registered along with title to the plot in favour of the purchaser.

A style of Deed of Restriction is available with the PSG/Law Society Residential styles[8].

8   See www.psglegal.co.uk/residential.php.

10.3.6 Discharge

Form F of Schedule 4 to the 1970 Act contains the style to use for a document that discharges the standard security in its entirety.

All deeds assigning, varying, restricting or discharging a standard security must be recorded or registered in the appropriate Property Register. If the title to the property is still in the Sasine Register and all that it happening is that the security is being discharged, the discharge will not induce a first registration, so the discharge should be recorded in the Sasine Register too. The grant of a standard security on its own does not currently induce a first registration in the Land Register either although this will cease on 1 April 2016, when the Sasine Regiser will close to standard securities.

There is a style discharge of standard security included in the PSG/ Law Society residential styles.

THE STANDARD CONDITIONS

10.4 There are a number of typical conditions that all or most lenders would want to apply to the basis on which they are lending money on a property, and that the borrower should be obliged to do – maintain and insure the property for example, or comply with any statutory notices that are served on the property. Section 11 of the 1970 Act provides that a number of conditions and obligations that are 'standard' in any lending situation should be incorporated automatically into every grant of a standard security. These conditions, known as the 'Standard Conditions' are listed in Schedule 3 to the Act and are intended to make sure that the borrowers do not imperil the security of the lenders by allowing the value to deteriorate, and if they do, the lenders are entitled to several remedies.

10.4.1 The Standard Conditions

The standard conditions are either variable (V), non-variable (NV), or partially non-variable (PNV). Variable conditions may be, and in practice often are, varied by the lenders either within the standard security itself or by a longer, separate deed of variations, which will usually be registered in the Books of Council and Session. Most large lenders tend to favour the latter method, and print the variations and give a print to the borrowers.

The standard conditions are summarised as follows, and their appropriate status is marked:

(1) *Maintenance and repair:* The borrower is to keep the property in good and sufficient repair throughout the loan period, in order that the lender's security is not endangered. He must allow the lender to enter the property and inspect the state of repair on seven days' notice being given (V).

(2) *Completion of buildings and prohibition of alterations*: The borrower is to complete buildings but make alterations, extensions, or demolish the property only with the lenders' authority, in accordance with any statutory consents or licences and exhibit evidence of these. Obviously, carrying out alterations, or failing adequately to maintain the property could have an adverse effect on the value of the security subjects (V).

(3) *Observance of conditions in title and general compliance with law*: The borrower is to observe any condition or perform any obligation that applies to the property, including paying rates (or Council Tax) and taxes, and comply with any requirements of law imposed by statute. This would include complying with any statutory repair notices (V).

(4) *Planning notices etc*: The borrower is to deal with planning and other notices, and provide the lender with copies of any received, and if appropriate and the lender wishes to object to a planning notice, the borrower is to object or join with the lender in objecting to the notice: eg proposals for an unsuitable use of neighbouring property that might damage the value or amenity of the security subjects (V).

(5) *Insurance*: The borrower is to insure (or permit the lender to insure) the property for 'market value' and the proceeds of any claim are to be dealt with as directed by the creditor. 'Market value' is almost universally replaced in standard conditions by 'reinstatement value' (see eg the style in para 10.3.1), especially in older buildings built with traditional materials and craftsmanship, where the cost of replacing on a like for like basis will be in excess of the market value. The borrower must pay the insurance premiums, and also let the lender know in the event of

any claim. For commercial properties that are let to occupational tenants, the leases will usually provide that the landlord must insure on specific terms and the tenants will make payment of the premium. It may be necessary to vary this Standard Condition to ensure that it is compatible with the insurance provisions in the leases (V).

(6) *Restriction on letting*: The borrower is not to let the property without the lender's consent. In practice for residential property, this means that the lenders must approve the terms of the letting, and ensure that the requisite notices are served to prevent the tenant obtaining security of tenure, which would affect the lender's security. For commercial properties which are, or are going to be, the subject of occupational leases, a suitable variation of this standard condition is required (V).

(7) *General power of creditor to perform on failure of debtor*: If the borrower does not fulfil any of the duties imposed by the standard conditions, the lender may do so itself, at the borrower's expense, and is entitled, on giving notice, to enter the property for this purpose (V).

(8) *Calling up*: A lender is entitled to enforce the security by the calling up procedure set out in section 19 of the 1970 Act, if the lender wishes to require repayment of the loan, where the borrower is in arrears and unable to pay, for example. See para 10.7. The lender may exercise the remedies provided in standard condition 10 (V).

(9) *Default:* A borrower will be in default: (a) where a calling-up notice in respect of the security has been served and has not been complied with; (b) where there has been a failure to comply with any other requirement arising out of the security; or (c) where the proprietor of the security subjects has become insolvent (V).

(10) *Rights of creditor on default:* This Standard Condition sets out the remedies given to the lender if the borrower is in default:

(10)(1) The lender will be entitled to exercise any other remedies arising from the contract to which the standard security relates, and also exercise the remedies given in the following paragraphs in accordance with the operative provisions of CFR(S)A 1970, in particular sections 19 to 25 and any other relevant enactment (V).

(10)(2)   Sell the property (see para 8.18.3) (NV).

(10)(3)   Enter into possession of the property and receive or recover rents (V).

(10)(4)   Let the property (V).

(10)(5)   Grant leases of the property, and manage and maintain it (V).

(10)(6)   Repair, reconstruct, alter and improve the property (V).

(10)(7)   Foreclosure. This is a remedy carried forward from the Conveyancing (Scotland) Act 1924, which enables the lender, after an unsuccessful attempt to sell the property, to petition the court to convert a security title into an absolute one. It is probably rarely appropriate, as the 1970 Act gives lenders ample powers anyway, and is in reality rarely used. The Standard Condition relating to sale and foreclosure (Standard Condition 10) may not be varied either directly or indirectly. Any other variation of the Standard Conditions which may purport to vary this non-variable Condition will not be effective. (NV)]

(11)   *Exercise of right of redemption:* The borrower is entitled redeem the loan on giving notice of intention to the lender. This provision was intended to prevent borrowers from being locked into loans on a long term basis. This does not affect any contractual provisions that may have been applied to a mortgage requiring payment of an early redemption penalty. This provision is non-variable (in other words, the debtor must always be entitled to a right to redeem the loan), but the lender may dispense with a formal notice, or choose to vary or dispense with any period of notice to which he is entitled (NV). In 2014, the Scottish Government published a consultation on proposals to exempt certain heritable securities from this 20-year rule[9], since this could be a restriction on some shared equity and equity release schemes.

---

9   See www.gov.scot/Publications/2014/10/3328.

(12) *Debtor liable for expenses:* The borrower is liable for the expenses of the preparation and execution of the standard security, any discharge or partial discharge or restriction of the security, registration dues, and any costs incurred by the creditor in enforcing the security. The borrower is, however, not liable for the expenses of the assignation of the standard security to a third party (V).

10.4.2 Variation of Standard Conditions

Any changes can be made to the variable Standard Conditions, and are often done so according to circumstances, and the type of loan facility being made available. If the property consists of a development in the course of construction, a borrower may wish to have the provisions relating to completion of buildings and the prohibition against alterations (Standard Condition 2) tailored to suit the actual circumstances. For investment properties, which are subject to occupational leases, the borrower may want the standard conditions relating to letting and the insurance of the subjects varied. A Standard Condition can also be excluded in its entirety, provided it is not Non Variable.

10.4.3 Additional Conditions

Entirely new conditions can also be imported into a standard security over and above the Standard Conditions. A number of lenders incorporate considerable additional conditions in their house style standard securities, either in the body of the deed itself, or, by way of a separate 'Deed of Variation of Standard Conditions' which is then referred to within each standard security. Conditions relating to specialist types of property, such as industrial or agricultural property or licensed premises can also be built in.

ACTING FOR THE RESIDENTIAL LENDER

10.5 Most loans for the purchase of residential property are either made by banks, building societies or former building societies that have become banks. Other bodies may be lenders, such as local authorities, particularly in the purchase of public sector housing. Broadly speaking, however, the procedure is the same whoever the lender may be.

10.5.1 Acting for both Purchaser and Lender

Lenders (or most of them) are now represented by a central body known as the Council of Mortgage Lenders (CML), the mortgage lenders' representative body, which produces a Handbook detailing the practices of various lenders, and issuing standard forms (see para 10.5.2).

Generally, lenders will permit solicitors acting for the borrower in the purchase of a house, to act on the lender's behalf as well, provided the solicitors are on their approved list or panel, if they have one. This practice, which is permitted under the Law Society Practice Rules by way of an exception to the conflict of interest provisions, means a substantial saving on duplication of work, and thus a saving of costs payable by the borrowers.

Law Society guidelines permit the solicitor to act for both borrower and lender, despite the apparent conflict of interest[10]. In terms of Rule B2.1.4, the terms of the loan must have been agreed between the parties before the solicitor has been instructed by the lender and the granting of the security must only be to give effect to such agreement. It should always be borne in mind however, that if a genuine conflict of interest does emerge, the solicitors must immediately stop acting for both parties. You must always remember that the lender is also a client. Solicitors must not reveal information to one client and not the other, eg information as to prices paid for the property. This was clearly established in *Mortgage Express v Bowerman & Partners*[11]. If solicitors find themselves in possession of information that is clearly detrimental to one of the parties, they are under a duty to reveal it to the other party, for whom they also act. If they feel unable to do so, they should then withdraw from acting.

In residential lending, the borrower will receive an offer of loan which will set out the basic terms and conditions on which the loan will be made and there are usually also extensive standard terms and conditions which the borrower is required to acknowledge. The borrower's solicitor will

---

10 See www.lawscot.org.uk/rules-and-guidance/section-b/rule-b2-conflict-of-interest/guidance/b21-conflict-of-interest-generally/.
11 [1996] 2 All ER 808.

receive a copy of the offer of loan, and should take time to explain the meaning and implications of the loan to his clients and encourage them to read the material and raise any questions they might have. There can be a bewildering amount of paperwork generated at this time and the solicitor should make sure that his client understands the key elements of the mortgage he is taking, and particularly the details of any lock-in arrangements or early redemption penalties, and whether or not a fixed or capped rate mortgage is 'portable' (ie if the property is sold during the period of the fixed rate, but the borrower takes out a new mortgage with the same lender over his new property, that the fixed rate can be transferred to the new mortgage with no redemption penalties).

The following conveyancing steps should be taken by the solicitor acting for both purchaser and lender:

- Receive and carefully peruse the lender's instructions, noting any specific conditions that have to be complied with;

- Check provisions of CML handbook for particular lender (see para 10.5.2);

- After examining title (see Chapter 8), they draft a standard security and any other papers required by the lenders.

- Have the standard security and other papers signed by the borrowers.

- If title is taken in the name of one spouse or civil partner only, obtain consent by the non-entitled spouse/civil partner (Note that this can be incorporated into the standard security or in a separate deed. See para 4.9.4 for Matrimonial Homes and Civil Partnership documentation generally. In the same way that a seller's solicitor must obtain the necessary document for satisfying the purchaser's solicitors, so too must the borrower's solicitor ensure that the lender's position is protected against the occupancy rights of a non entitled spouse or civil partner.

- For single borrowers, obtain Matrimonial Homes or Civil Partnership declarations as appropriate relative to the granting of the standard security.

- Send the report on title to the lenders, with the firm's opinion that the title is in order, and request the loan funds. This should be done in good time for settlement, allowing sufficient time for funds to be organised and remitted to the solicitor's bank account. Loan instructions will often specify the amount of notice that the lender requires for draw down of funds. It can be as much as 10 working days.

- The standard security with a completed and signed registration application form should accompany the disposition to the Land Register.

- Intimate any assignation of a life assurance policy to the assurance company in duplicate to validate the transfer, and on return one receipted copy is put with the assignation document

- Check any insurance requirements. The lenders may insure the property against fire and other damage but may require that the borrower arranges this. If the latter, make sure that the borrower has arranged for insurance cover from the date of entry, if not before.

10.5.2 CML Handbook

The Council of Mortgage Lenders is the trade association for the residential mortgage lending industry, whose members, which include banks, building societies and other mortgage lenders, are responsible for around 94% of residential mortgage lending in the UK. The CML provides support, and acts as a representative voice for its members and residential lending, as well as providing research, statistics, training and information.

One of the key resources produced by the CML is the Lenders' Handbook. This provides detailed instructions for solicitors acting on behalf of lenders in residential transactions, and has separate handbooks for Scotland, England and Wales, Northern Ireland and the Isle of Man. Your instructions from an individual lender will indicate if you are being instructed in accordance with the CML Handbook. If you are, the general provisions in part 1 and any lender specific requirements in part 2 must be followed. In addition you may receive further instructions applicable to the individual loan.

Part 1 is the main set of instructions that apply to all mortgages by CML lenders. Part 2 contains specific requirements of each lender who is a member, overlaid onto the provisions of Part 1. Many lenders requirements will be the same as the Part 1 provisions, in which case no changes will be made, but where they have different or additional requirements these will be specified.

Accordingly the CML Handbook should be your first port of call whenever you receive instructions from a lender in a residential transaction. It may even be a good idea to check for a lender's specific requirements as soon as you know who will be providing finance to your client, in case of any specific variations which might affect your clients purchase or which might have to be incorporated into the missives. Your duty to the lender when acting on its behalf will include compliance with its CML handbook requirements.

The CML Handbook is available online[12]. First select the appropriate country from the drop-down menu, then select the appropriate lender from the further drop-down selection. You can choose to see Part 1 only (the main conditions) Parts 1 and 2 (the main provisions overlaid with the particular lender's requirements) or Part 2 only (specific requirements only)

The handbook contains general instructions as to the standard of care expected of the conveyancer, and requirements to comply with Accounts Rules, anti-money laundering regulations and professional guidance and codes as well as the basis on which communications between the solicitor and lender should be conducted. It also provides instructions regarding the valuation of the property and, in the case of new properties, whether a re-inspection is required before draw-down of funds. All of the due diligence elements are covered, such as title examination, reports and enquiries, title conditions and servitudes, adoption of roads and sewers, insurance, Matrimonial Homes (Family Protection) (Scotland) Act 1981 or Civil Partnership Act 2004 rights and planning and building regulations issues. Also covered are home warranty schemes for new build homes, or, in their absence, the requirement for a Professional Consultants' Certificate (see para 6.12.3(xiii)).

The Handbook also reminds you to explain the terms of the standard security and any other documentation to the borrower, and that your fees and outlays are payable by the borrower too.

---

12 See www.cml.org.uk/cml/handbook.

Types of mortgages: A short word about residential mortgages. The 5th edition of this book provided details of some typical types of residential mortgages available and the different repayment methods. It was about that time that problems with terminal payments on endowment policies linked to mortgages was becoming a common theme, and given the borrowing difficulties encountered by purchasers during the recession, the mortgage market, never an uncomplicated place, has become increasingly elaborate. Residential purchasers seeking mortgage advice should consult specialist mortgage advisers with access to detailed product information, to ensure that they obtain the best mortgage product most suitable to their requirements.

10.5.3 Acting for Spouses

When conveyancers are asked to act for a married couple in a conveyancing transaction, they may do so, since acting for related parties is exempted from the general rule of conflict of interest, laid down by the Law Society of Scotland Practice Rules 2011. There is a temptation to treat a married couple as one unit, but it should be remembered that husband and wife have separate interests, and the solicitor must ensure that both partners signing the standard security understand its terms and effect.

Difficulties can, and frequently do, arise in situations where a wife is asked to sign a standard security over the marital home in support of the husband's business, (or vice versa, of course). These are referred to by George Gretton as 'cautionary wives'. It is essential to ensure that the spouse receives independent legal advice as to the nature and effect of the obligation, as the various cases over the years have illustrated (see *Barclays Bank v O'Brien*[13], *Smith v Bank of Scotland*[14], *The Royal Bank of Scotland v Etridge (No 2)*[15], and *Clydesdale Bank plc v Black*[16].

The House of Lords' decision in *The Royal Bank of Scotland plc v Etridge (No 2)* set an extremely high threshold for the 'core minimum requirements' necessary for solicitors acting in cases where one party in the relationship, usually the wife, acts as guarantor of the other party's

13 [1994] 1 AC 180.
14 [1997] SC (HL) 111.
15 [2001] 3 WLR 1021.
16 [2002] SC 555).

business debts. Given that it was a House of Lords' decision, for a short period it seemed as though its requirements would apply in Scotland, but two Court of Session cases (*Clydesdale Bank plc v Black* decided in the Inner House in 2002 and the Outer House decision in *Thomson v The Royal Bank of Scotland plc* 28 October 2003 (unreported)) made it clear that the 'core minimum requirements' set out in the *Etridge (No 2)* case do not apply to the substantive law of Scotland, where the position is governed by the principles that were applied to Scots law by the House of Lords in *Smith v Bank of Scotland*.

Accordingly the approach required in Scotland may be summarised as follows:

- Lenders looking to take security from a third party for the indebtedness of a borrower must take 'reasonable steps' to advise the third party about the risks of the transaction, and should act in good faith throughout the proposed transaction.

- Good faith will be shown by warning the third party of the consequences of entering into the obligation, and by advising them to take independent legal advice.

- The duty applies whenever the third party is in a 'non-business relationship' with the person with the principal obligation to repay the debt (eg a marriage).

- If the lender does not take reasonable steps, the courts could set aside the obligations undertaken by the third party, but this is always subject to the proviso that the third party can demonstrate that they entered into the arrangement as a consequence of undue influence, misrepresentation or other coercion from the debtor.

- The lender has to have been put on notice that the third party may have entered into the transaction because of the undue influence of the borrower.

Undue influence may be identified by reference to the four elements in the definition in *Gray v Binny*[17], namely:

- the existence of a relationship between the parties which creates a dominant or ascendant influence;

17 7R 332 at p 347.

- the fact that confidence and trust arose from that relationship;

- the fact that a material and gratuitous benefit was given, to the prejudice of the granter (ie the third party); and

- that the granter had entered into the transaction without the benefit of independent advice or assistance.

If all four elements exist, then the lender should be put on notice, although whether there was in fact undue influence will depend on the individual facts and circumstances.

Although the decision in *Etridge* does not apply to Scotland, many lenders operating both north and south of the border, for consistency, will apply the core minimum requirements set out in Etridge.

The Law Society of England and Wales provided a style letter for its members to send when acting for the wife in an inter-spouse guarantee transaction, and a similar style was also adopted by the Law Society of Scotland. The style letter does not appear to be held currently on the Law Society website, but a copy of it is replicated in GL Gretton and K Reid *Conveyancing* (2003) at pp 80 to 82.

Guidance on the Law Society Practice Rules states:

'Another area of difficulty in relation to loans is where the jointly owned home is to be put up as security for a business loan to only one of the owners. There is a clear conflict of interest between the owners and you should not act for both of them. Not only must you make it clear that you are not acting for the owner who is not getting the benefit of the loan, when sending the standard security for signature by that person you must accompany it with a letter in terms of rule B2.1.7 ....'[18]

An article in the JLSS March 1999 by Alistair Sim[19] is still sound guidance in these situations and includes a detailed checklist.

---

18 Rule B2.1.7.states '2.1.7 When you are acting on behalf of a party or prospective party to a transaction of any kind you shall not issue any deed, writ, missive or other document requiring the signature of an unrepresented party to that party without informing that party in writing that: (a) such signature may have certain legal consequences, and (b) he should seek independent legal advice before signature'.

19 See 'Conflict of Interest between Borrower and Spouse'. Available at: www.journalonline.co.uk/Magazine/44-3/1001124.aspx.

10.5.4 Acting for both Seller and Seller's Lender

When property is sold and there is an existing security created by the seller, the seller's solicitors usually act for the lenders in attending to its discharge. There is rarely any conflict in doing so, and this is common in residential transactions and often adopted in commercial transactions. In conveyancing terms, the following steps should be taken:

- Inform the seller's lenders of the proposed sale and obtain the titles, if held by the lender.

- Draft a form of discharge and send the draft to the purchaser's solicitors for revisal.

- Request details of the sum required to repay the loan as at the date of entry (the redemption figure).

- On return of the draft discharge, have the principal discharge prepared and send to the seller's lender for execution.

- The seller's lender will (usually, although there are some exceptions) return the signed discharge to the seller's solicitors to be held as 'undelivered' pending repayment of the loan. In some circumstances, the purchaser's solicitors or the purchaser's lender's solicitors need to be able to hold the discharge as undelivered before the purchaser's lender will release funds for the purchaser. As far as possible this should be facilitated.

- At settlement of the sale, the seller's solicitors deliver the discharge together with a signed application form. These are sent to the Land Register by the purchaser's solicitors, and once the Keeper is satisfied with the discharge, the old standard security will simply be removed from the title sheet, and the new disposition and standard security will be registered.

- In cases where the discharge is not available at settlement, the usual practice in residential transactions is for the seller's solicitor to give an undertaking to deliver it. The practice has also developed recently for the seller's solicitor to forward the discharge to the Registers himself – the end result being the same that the Title Sheet is cleared of the outstanding security.

ACTING FOR THE COMMERCIAL LENDER

10.6 There are different consideration for the solicitor acting for a commercial lender, not least in the matter of separate representation.

10.6.1 Separate Representation

It has been standard practice for many years now for borrowers and lenders in commercial transactions to be separately represented by different solicitors, due to the increased risk in acting for both, and the potential for conflict of interest to arise at various stages throughout the transaction. The Law Society originally issued its guidance on this subject in 1994, and this remains the position. It is accepted that there will be occasions where the lender may wish to instruct the same solicitors to act for both parties where the amount of the loan is regarded as '*de minimis*'. That is currently accepted as meaning less than £250,000. Funds required to redeem the standard security being discharged must be remitted to lenders after completion.

In commercial lending circumstances, most lenders will have a panel of solicitors that they have approved to act on their behalf, and will also produce standing instructions to panel solicitors, to which the solicitors acting for them will be expected to adhere whenever an instruction is given. In addition there may be transaction specific instructions that will be issued to the solicitor at the time. There is no commercial equivalent to the CML handbook, although it may a useful resource to check for a particular lender's policy on certain standard conveyancing procedures, such as when a PEC would be regarded as out of date.

10.6.2 Conflict of Interest in Commercial Security Transactions

Anyone acting for a commercial lender in Scotland should also be familiar with the Law Society guidance on this area[20], which is available on the Law Society website and is summarised below. The Professional Practice Team at the Law Society is always willing to provide advice or guidance in this type of transaction, as well as in other cases of doubt or uncertainty on professional matters.

20 Law Society Practice Rule B2.1.

The Law Society provides a definition of 'commercial security transaction':

'A commercial security transaction relates to the secured lending to a customer of a bank or other lending institution where the purpose of the loan is clearly for the customer's business purposes.'

While the key element is clearly a loan for business purposes, it is incumbent on the solicitor, when receiving instructions to act for a lender and a borrower in any type of transaction, (but particularly a commercial security transaction), to exercise the necessary judgment in the context of the Conflict of Interest Rules about acting for both parties. Some thought is required in this connection, and it is necessary to anticipate as far as possible, given the circumstances of the instruction, what type of conflict situation might arise. The Law Society provides some examples:

10.6.2(i) Disclosure of all relevant circumstances

Either the solicitor may know more of the borrower's position than has been communicated to the lender or vice versa; or there may have been a reluctance by the borrower or lender fully to disclose their respective positions because of dual representation. These circumstances may affect the extent to which impartial 'best advice' can be given.

10.6.2(ii) Ongoing negotiations

Negotiations between the borrower and lender may have only reached the 'Outline Terms' stage. Further detailed consideration or negotiation of covenants, undertakings or events of default may be required. In such negotiations the borrower and lender may have different negotiating strengths, so there may be competing pressures on the solicitor as to whose interests are to be promoted.

10.6.2(iii) Defects in title/Due diligence package

A borrower may be prepared to 'live with' a minor defect in title or some lack of planning or building consent whereas a lender may take an entirely different stance.

10.6.2(iv) Security by companies

Apart from the complexities and time restraints for registration of security, companies may well be subject to negative or restrictive covenants or powers affecting the security on which the borrower, but not necessarily the lender, may be prepared to take a commercial view. In these circumstances separate advice may be required.

10.6.2(v) Competing creditors' ranking agreements

The circumstances as to the inter-relationship/enforcement of security between lenders may merit separate advice. A solicitor may be involved in preparing a ranking agreement and negotiating its terms on points which have a bearing on the borrower's position.

10.6.2(vi) Security over commercial property

The permitted use, associated licences/quotas and specific standard conditions may merit separate advice. Particular risks arise on the transfer of a licence where the lender's interests may conflict with the borrower's commercial ambitions.

10.6.2(vii) Leased property as security

The circumstances in which a lender requires protection in the event of irritancy may merit separate advice. Invariably the borrower is trying to strike the best deal during his occupation while the lender needs protection in the event of the borrower's failure through insolvency or otherwise.

10.6.2(viii) Enforcement of security

The solicitor acting for both borrower and lender may be placed in difficulty in the event of subsequent enforcement of a security. For whom does the solicitor act in such circumstances? Do both clients know and understand their respective positions?

10.6.2(ix) Powerful clients

A major business client may bring subtle or even open pressure on a solicitor to follow a particular course, or to turn a blind eye to a matter which could prejudice a lender's position, eg discrepancies between a valuation and purchase price.

10.6.2(x) 'All sums due' securities

Solicitors should advise fully joint obligants (eg husbands and wives) of the nature of an 'all sums due' security. In particular it should be drawn to their attention that additional loans, for example in respect of one obligant's business, may give rise to further secured borrowings without the other obligant requiring to sign the documentation. In such circumstances there is also a conflict of interest between the joint obligants.

10.6.3 Facility Documentation

We have seen that in residential lending, the borrower will receive an offer of loan with basic terms and conditions of the loan and this is also sent to the borrower's solicitor. The terms and conditions of a commercial loan can be far more intricate, and often negotiating the terms of the loan facility takes some considerable time and may require specialist legal input before being finalised.

The facility documentation will contain a number of conditions, some of which, known as 'conditions precedent' have to be implemented by the borrower before any funds can be drawn down. These can include obtaining planning permission, a satisfactory examination of title, signing the standard security, obtaining a parent company guarantee and so on. There will be other 'conditions subsequent' which the borrower will have to implement at some later stage, after some or all of the funds have been drawn, for example in funding for a development there will be key milestones to be met for building out the development. Other consents or licences may be needed for the property. Failure to comply with facility conditions may be made an 'event of default' in terms of the facility agreement, entitling the lender to apply some penalty or call up the loan. The underlying forms and structure of commercial lending is beyond the scope of this book, but there are some key aspects of commercial secured lending that need to be borne in mind, which the following paragraphs introduce.

10.6.4 Registration of Charges

If you take nothing else from this chapter, please remember the importance, when a standard security is granted by a company, of registering the details of that security, or 'charge', in the Company's Register of Charges, within the 21-day period allowed by statute. This **must** be done for a security to be effective, and for the rights of the creditor under the security to be exercisable against the borrower. The consequences of failing timeously to register a charge are too dreadful to contemplate. Without registration in the Register of Charges, the lender's rights to enforce the standard security are not protected. Failure to register would render the charge void as against a liquidator and any competing creditors. While registration after the 21-day period may be technically possible, the charge remains void against a liquidator or administrator appointed under proceedings which were started between the date of execution of the charge and the date of registration, and anyone who acquired an interest in the charged property in that period.

Invariably, it is the responsibility of the lender's solicitor to register the charge, and steps should be followed to ensure that this is done expeditiously (see para 10.6.4(iii) below). If the Company is registered in Scotland, the relevant Register is in Edinburgh. If the Company is registered in England or Wales, the Registrar is based in Cardiff. The 21-day period begins on the day after the date of creation of the charge.

10.6.4(i) Date of creation

The date of creation of the charge for the purposes of registration in the Register of Charges depends upon the nature of the charge. Note that this need not necessarily be tied to the date of completion and action may be required before the transaction settles, for certain types of charge:

- Standard Security: date of creation of a Standard Security is the date of recording in the Sasine Register[21] or registration in the Land Register

---

21 Only possible until 31 March 2016.

557

- Floating Charge: date of creation is the date of execution

- Ranking Agreement, incorporating an alteration of a Floating Charge: date of creation of the charge is the last date of execution, regardless of the date of subsequent recording or registration in the Property Register.

10.6.4(ii) Forms

There is a selection of 'Companies House' standard forms that must be used when notifying the charge to the Registrar of Companies, and these vary according to the country in which the company is registered. These forms can be accessed and downloaded from the Companies House website. Some firms of solicitors subscribe to specialist software applications that provide forms of many types, including company forms, which can be completed on-screen and saved to a master file, then printed for signing and submission to the Registrar of Companies.

For registering a charge created by a company registered in Scotland, the appropriate form is MG01s, and it should be accompanied by a certified copy of the charge and submitted to the Edinburgh office. For companies registered in England, a certified copy of the charge requires to be submitted with forms MG01 and MG09, which are submitted to Cardiff.

There is a charge of £13 (at the time of writing) for registering each charge which must be prepaid to the Registrar, ie accompany the forms and copy charge.

The restriction or discharge of a standard security may also need to be registered in the Company's Register. Deeds of Restriction and Discharges can be registered by way of Memorandum of partial or full satisfaction of the charge. The Company forms for this are MG02 and MG04 for English companies and MG02s and MG03s for Scottish Companies. There is not the same urgency for registering the discharge of the charge created by a standard security in the Companies Register, since the relevant property register will disclose the discharge, and sometimes this is overlooked or not done, without any adverse effect from the conveyancing point of view.

10.6.4(iii) Procedure and reminder system

There are, as they say, no prizes for getting it wrong, and never more so in the registration of a charge. It is essential to set up a system of reminders and diary entries to ensure that any charge for which you are responsible is registered on time, and so that the all important Certificate of Registration of a Charge is issued. In some firms, a particular partner may take responsibility for signing the forms and checking the timings.

- Remember to take a photocopy of the executed standard security as this is required to accompany the MG01s or MG01/MG09 forms (Company Form).

- Prepare the form. The information you need to complete includes the Company name in full and company number, a description of the charge, the amount secured (or 'all sums due'), short particulars of the property charged (usually put in the ALL and WHOLE description from the standard security), and in the case of a floating charge, details of any restrictions or ranking arrangements that it contains. The other key piece of information (which you have to wait for if the charge is a standard security) is the date of creation.

- Under 2012 Act rules, the Keeper will no longer confirm the date of registration of a charge. There has been some confusion in the early months about which date on the acknowledgement form is the date of registration. The date in the acknowledgement form that appears as 'date of application' is the date that should be inserted in the MG01s form as the date of creation of the charge.

- If the charge you are registering is a floating charge or ranking agreement the 21 days start to run from the date of execution, and so that date is inserted in the Company Form, which is then signed and submitted to the Registrar along with a certified copy of the charge and a cheque for the filing fee.

- For a standard security, as soon as you have the e-mail acknowledgement, complete the Company Form, have it signed and submitted to the Register along with a certified copy of the charge and a cheque for the filing fee.

- Certifying a copy involves writing onto the copy document the words 'Certified a true copy of [description of the document]' with the date of certification and the signature of the solicitors. Some firms have an embossed stamp for this purpose.

- Once the Company Form and copy charge has been sent, diarise to check with the Registrar that they have received it – your 21-day clock is still ticking. If there is some major flaw with the submission, the Registrar may have to return the form for correction and this might mean that you run out of time (see 'Informal corrections' below).

- Once you are satisfied that the charge will be registered in time, you can relax until the next time.

- When the Certificate of Registration of the Charge is received from the Registrar, make sure that you retain the principal Certificate carefully. There is no longer any requirement to send a copy to the Registers. Breathe.

10.6.4(iv) Informal corrections

The Registrar of Companies has the power under section 1075 of the Companies Act 2006 to informally correct a document delivered to the Registrar which appears to be incomplete or internally inconsistent, before registering it. The power only applies to documents for the registration of mortgages and charges, and the power is designed to help companies (and their advisers) meet the statutory time limit for the delivery of particulars of charges for registration. Informal Correction Guidance published by the Registrar[22] contains a full list of the documents to which the power applies, and exceptions to the exercise of the power are contained in that Guidance.

Anyone who wishes to take advantage of the power must first agree to be contacted and to give the Registrar whatever instructions are needed to correct the document. The Registrar must be satisfied that the person giving instructions is authorised to do so. For solicitors, this means identifying a senior solicitor, and submitting their details to the Registrar, and obtaining an authorisation code.

Then, if any registration of charge forms submitted by anyone in the firm require to be corrected and can benefit from the informal correction

---

22 See www.gov.uk/government/publications/avoid-missing-deadlines-for-mortgage-filings-informal-correction/informal-correction-guidance-notes.

arrangements, the Registrar can contact the authorised person, who can instruct the Registrar to make the correction. Once the Registrar has corrected the document, it will be treated as having been delivered when the correction was made, so any correction procedure must still be finalised within the 21-day period.

10.6.5 Floating Charges

A standard security is often characterised as a 'fixed charge'. It applies to the heritable property to which it relates on registration, and unless specifically varied, continues to do so until discharged. So the property over which the creditor would be able to enforce rights is fixed and known from the start.

10.6.5(i) Effect of a floating charge

By contrast, a 'floating charge' does not identify specific property to which it attaches, instead it 'floats' over the assets of the company named in the charge, usually in general terms, eg 'the whole of the property, assets and rights (including uncalled capital) which are or may from time to time be comprised in the property and undertaking of the company'. A key aspect of the floating charge is that for as long as it continues to 'float' and does not 'crystallise', the company can intromit with, trade and sell the assets concerned (subject to any other fixed charge that may exist) without any discharge from or consent of the holder of the floating charge, unless restricted from doing so by the wording of the floating charge.

Scottish floating charges differ from their English counterparts, in that they derive their legal basis entirely from statute, however, the document can be in any form, so long as it is clear that it is 'for the purpose of securing any debt or other obligation (including a cautionary obligation) incurred or to be incurred by, or binding upon, the company or any other person, to create in favour of the creditor in the debt or obligation a (floating charge) over all or any part of the property (including uncalled capital) which may from time to time be comprised in its property and undertaking'[23].

23 See section 462 of the Companies Act 1985.

10.6.5(ii) Registration of floating charges

Floating charges must also be registered in the Companies Register. Unlike standard securities, they are not (currently) registered in any other register, and consequently registration in the Companies Register is required to make their existence public to those having dealings with the company, such as creditors and prospective creditors.

A floating charge continues to float over whatever property and assets it encompasses that are owned by the company from time to time, until it is caused to attach to those assets – known as 'crystallisation'. That will happen if the company goes into liquidation, or if a receiver (if it is a floating charge created prior to 15 September 2003) or an administrator (for floating charges after 15 September 2003) is appointed (see paras 8.18.8 and 8.18.9). It is then crystallised as a fixed charge over the assets and property of the company at the time of crystallisation. Where a company that has granted a floating charge sells property, the purchaser's solicitors should ask to see a letter of non-crystallisation from the floating charge holder (see paras 8.18.10(v) and 11.7.9).

10.6.5(iii) The prospective Register of Floating Charges

The statutory basis of floating charges in Scotland is prospectively changed by the provisions of the Part 2 of the Bankruptcy and Diligence etc (Scotland) Act 2007. While not yet in force, and with no date for coming into force yet appointed, sections 37 to 49 of the Bankruptcy and Diligence (Scotland) Act 2007 set out a structure for floating charges in Scotland for the future. As well as changing the law relating to floating charges in Scotland it will consolidate the existing law and prospectively repeals the relevant sections of the Companies Act 1985.

Part 2 of the 2007 Act proposes the setting up of a new Register of Floating Charges, to be kept by the Keeper of the Registers of Scotland – not by the Registrar of Companies – and once the relevant provisions are in force, a floating charge will be created by registration in this new Register. As company law currently stands, security rights granted by companies have to be registered in the Companies Register. This includes fixed charges, which means that a standard security has to be registered twice: first in the Land (or Sasine) Register and then in the Companies

Register. This has often struck practitioners as unnecessary duplication. Since publication to a company's creditors and those planning to have dealing with the company is the object of the exercise in registration, it would be administratively burdensome if the introduction of the Register of Floating Charges were to mean that double registration would be required for floating charges as well.

However, section 893 of the Companies Act 2006 allows orders to be made dispensing with double registration. An order can be made which will provide that a charge granted by a company which is registered in a 'special register' will not have to be separately registered in the Companies Register. Whoever keeps that special register will send details of the charge to the Registrar of Companies direct who will put the information in the Companies Register. 'Special registers' include the Land Register, the Sasine Register, the Patents Register, the Shipping Register and so on.

The prospective Register of Floating Charges will be a special register as well, and once it is activated (by section 893 order), a floating charge will only have to be registered once, in the new Register of Floating Charges. It is anticipated that there will also be a section 893 order made, at some point in the future, in relation to the Land Register, so that standard securities granted by companies will no longer have to be double registered either.

10.6.6 Ranking Agreements and Arrangements

It is possible to have more than one standard security over the same property. But not everyone can be first in the queue for repayment in the event of a sale of the property. Instead, multiple securities will rank in relation to each other, in accordance with the rules of priority, which will determine the order in which they are entitled to payment in the event of enforcement of these securities.

10.6.6(i) Priority of ranking

A security can rank prior to another. In other words the creditor under the prior security will have first call on the sale proceeds of the property.

A security can rank **postponed** to another. In other words the entitlement of the creditor under the postponed security, to the sale proceeds of the property, will be subject to the rights of the prior security holder.

Securities can rank *pari passu*. In other words the securities rank equally.

The ranking implied by law without the need for a separate document is first past the post ie the order in which the securities were recorded or registered in the relevant Property Register. If they are received on the same day by the Keeper, they will rank equally. Note that a fixed security has priority over a floating charge, regardless of their respective dates (see para 10.6.5) unless there is wording in the Floating Charge to the contrary, which there invariably is (see para 10.6.6(iii)).

10.6.6(ii) Section 13 Intimation

There is a statutory cut-off point for prior ranking however. Section 13 of the 1970 Act provides that where the creditor under a standard security receives notice of the creation of a subsequent security over the same property, then the preference in ranking of that prior creditor is restricted at that point to security for its present advances, and any future advances which it is already contractually obliged to make, and interest and expenses on those advances. In other words, the security of a secured lender who receives a section 13 notice will only have priority ranking for any further advances it makes, if it is already committed to make them.

10.6.6(iii) Ranking of floating charges

A Ranking Agreement, which is a document entered into among all of the creditors and the borrower, setting out the priority arrangements among them, will usually be needed where there is also a floating charge granted by the company, because a fixed charge has priority over a floating charge, regardless of the respective dates of registration of the securities[24]. However, floating charges will invariably contain what is called a 'negative pledge' by which the borrower is prohibited from creating any subsequent fixed security. Most creditors of fixed securities will want to rank prior to the floating charge or to restrict the entitlement of the floating charge holder, and therefore the respective ranking of fixed and floating charges where there is more than one creditor will need to be agreed between

---

24 See section 464 of the Companies Act 1985 (prospectively repealed by section 46 of the Bankruptcy and Diligence (Scotland) Act 2007, not yet in force).

the creditors and the borrower, and the agreement set out in a Ranking Agreement.

A Ranking Agreement can be recorded in the Sasine Register or registered in the Land Register. If it alters the provisions of a floating charge, it requires to be registered in the Register of Charges at the Companies Office within 21 days of the last date of execution of the Ranking Agreement (see para 10.6.4).

Once the provisions of Part 2 of the Bankruptcy and Diligence (Scotland) Act 2007 come into force ranking of floating charges and fixed securities will change and they will then rank according to date of creation.

10.6.7 Overseas Companies

As we have seen (para 8.18.10(ii)) when transacting with an overseas company, it is necessary to obtain an opinion from a firm of solicitors in the jurisdiction in which the company is incorporated, to confirm that the company has the powers and capacity to enter into the transaction, and this applies equally when the borrower is an overseas company, to ensure that it can validly grant a valid and enforceable security. Such an opinion should confirm a number of things, including that the company is validly incorporated, validly exists and is in good standing, and has the necessary powers both to purchase or acquire property and to grant the security. It should also cover such matters as execution and any procedural formalities which require to be followed, as well as confirming the directors and secretary of the company.

10.6.7(i) Registration requirements

In addition to any UK registration requirements, the firm providing the opinion should also be asked to confirm whether there are any local registration requirements which require to be followed for the security to be valid.

Currently, overseas companies may register with the Registrar of Companies in the UK.

Since 1 October 2009, the position relating to registration of changes created by overseas companies has been governed by the Overseas Companies (Execution of Documents and Registration of Charges)

Regulations 2009, which provided that the requirement to register a charge created by an overseas company (including standard securities and floating charges) only arose if that company has actually registered with the Registrar of Companies. In terms of the Overseas Companies Regulations 2009, an overseas company had to submit registration details to the Registrar.

However, overseas companies ceased to be subject to the scheme for registration of company changes from 1 October 2011, so there is now no need to be concerned with registration issues where overseas companies are involved.

ENFORCEMENT AND REPOSSESSION

10.7 The rights of heritable creditors to enforce their security in the event of default by the borrower, and the safety measures to protect debtors, that have been introduced over the years, since the establishment of the current regime by the 1970 Act, mean that the law in this area is becoming increasingly elaborate, and a whole book would be required to do justice to the topic (in which respect see DJ Cusine and R Rennie *Standard Securities*). Baldly put, if the debtor is in default and the lender requires to enforce its security, it is arguably not a job for a conveyancer, but is a matter that the conveyancer's litigation colleagues will attend to. Having said that, the conveyancer should have a high level of knowledge, at the very least, of the remedies that are available to the lender, not least because, when acting for a client purchasing from a heritable creditor in possession, they need to know that the relevant statutory formalities have been complied with. The decision of the Supreme Court, in 2010, in the case of *Royal Bank of Scotland plc v Wilson*[25] rather upset most conventional wisdom regarding routes to sale for the heritable creditor. Also the restrictions placed on heritable creditors' remedies by the Mortgage Rights (Scotland) Act 2001 and Home Owner and Debtor Protection (Scotland) Act 2010, among others, mean that this is increasingly becoming an area of law where the uninitiated should not tread, and instead is becoming a legislative and judicially-determined labyrinth that demands a careful and informed approach.

25 [2010] SLT 1227.

10.7.1 1970 Act Remedies

The provisions relating to enforcement of standard securities are contained in sections 19 to 29 of the 1970 Act with Schedules 6 and 7 providing statutory styles of notices. These sections have been amended by the Mortgage Rights (Scotland) Act 2001.

Scots Law on enforcement previously had a reputation for being relatively creditor-friendly. The 1970 Act set out enforcement procedures which could be challenged only in fairly limited circumstances.

The 1970 Act provided three methods of enforcement (or so we thought):

- Service of Calling-up Notices
- Service of Notices of Default
- Immediate court action – section 24 Action

Royal Bank of Scotland plc v Wilson tells us that the position is not so simple, and that for a heritable creditor to be in a position to sell the security subjects, the calling up procedure must always be followed.

10.7.2 Calling-up Notice

A calling-up notice requires the owner of the property to pay to the creditor the whole sum secured by the standard security within two months of the date on which the calling-up notice is served on him. This period of notice may be dispensed with or shortened in certain circumstances. Generally, calling-up notices are served in circumstances where the creditor wants the debt secured by its standard security to be discharged in full. It is always competent for the creditor to serve a calling-up notice unless either:

- the creditor has agreed to restrict its ability to serve calling-up notices under a particular standard security (which in practice is very unlikely to happen); or
- where the creditor has received notice from the debtor's trustee in sequestration that the trustee intends to sell the security subjects[26].

Calling-up notices must be in the form set out in the 1970 Act, Schedule 6 Form A, and must be served in accordance with section 19 of the Act, ie on the person with the last recorded or registered title to the property.

---

26 See section 39(4)(b) of the Bankruptcy (Scotland) Act 1985.

Generally there is an obligation on the creditor to serve a copy of the calling-up notice on any other person against whom it wishes to preserve a right of recourse in respect of the debt, which will cover service on guarantors and joint and several debtors.

After service of the calling-up notice, the borrower has two months in which to pay the sums demanded. If the owner of the property does not comply with the calling-up notice, the creditor may exercise any of the remedies available to it in terms of Standard Condition 10, subject now to the provisions of the Home Owner and Debtor Protection (Scotland) Act 2010 in respect of residential properties (see para 10.7.7).

10.7.3 Notice of Default

A notice of default can be served in circumstances where there has been a breach of the terms of the standard security and the breach is remediable. The notice of default requires the debtor or the owner (as appropriate) to remedy the default specified in the notice within one month of the date on which the Notice is served. This period of notice may be dispensed with in certain circumstances.

Notices of default are typically used where a debtor has fallen into arrears or has failed to maintain the security subjects and the creditor simply wants to have the default remedied. Notices of default must be in the form set out in Schedule 6 Form A to the 1970 Act and must be served in accordance with section 21 of the Act. The decision in *Royal Bank of Scotland plc v Wilson* now means that it cannot be used as an alternative to the calling up procedure, where the creditor wished to have the whole debt repaid.

10.7.4 Section 24 Court Action

Prior to the decision in *Royal Bank of Scotland plc v Wilson* a practice had evolved of heritable creditors going straight for a section 24 court application and decree, to entitle them to enter into possession, bolstered by the Inner House decision in 1999 in the case of *Bank of Scotland v Millward*[27] that the calling up notice was, in effect, optional. The practice had been followed, despite wording in the 1970 Act stating that where a creditor in a standard security intends to exercise its power of sale, that

27 [1999] SLT 901.

creditor '**shall** serve a notice calling up the security'. That wording had generally been regarded as a permissive and not a mandatory provision. The Supreme Court decision, which clearly overrules *Millward*, is that this interpretation of the legislation is wrong.

Section 24 procedure is therefore only now to be used after calling up or default procedure, and **must** be used after calling up procedure for residential properties as a consequence of the provisions of the Home Owner and Debtor Protection (Scotland) Act 2010 (see para 10.7.7).

10.7.5 Effect of the Mortgage Rights (Scotland) Act 2001

The Mortgage Rights (Scotland) Act 2001 allows the debtor (and certain other persons) to apply to the court for an order suspending the enforcement process, once enforcement steps have been initiated, (and before they have been completed) and provides that the court will have the power to make orders suspending the lender's rights 'for such periods' and 'subject to such conditions' as the court thinks appropriate. The provisions of the 2001 Act do not significantly change the initial enforcement procedures, other than amending the form of the notices, and making it necessary to serve notices on the occupier of the property (who may or may not be the debtor), but can impact considerably on the process after that.

Mortgage rights applications to the court can be made by the borrower, or the granter of the standard security if the security subjects (in whole or in part) are that person's sole or main residence; by the non-entitled spouse or civil partner of the debtor or proprietor where the security subjects (in whole or in part) are a matrimonial home or family home and the sole or main residence of the non-entitled spouse or civil partner, or by a co-habitee (for longer than six months) of the debtor or proprietor, where the security subjects (in whole or in part) are the sole or main residence of that co-habitee, and it is also the sole or main residence of a child of the co-habitee and the debtor or proprietor.

10.7.6 Requirement for Notices under Section 11 of the Homelessness (Scotland) Act 2003

Since 1 April 2009, heritable creditors who take steps to call up any security where all or part of the security subjects is used for residential purposes must give notice of the service of the calling-up notice to the relevant local authority in the form required in terms of The Notice to Local Authorities (Scotland) Regulations 2008 issued under the Homelessness (Scotland) Act 2003. This provision also affects residential landlords who seek to recover possession of property which they have let.

Note that some courts insist that the Notice must be in precisely the terms of the statutory style: in other words presented as a notice, and not converted to letter form. Whether that is a correct interpretation of the regulations or not, it would be prudent to conform exactly to the statutory style.

10.7.7 Home Owner and Debtor Protection (Scotland) Act 2010

The Home Owner and Debtor Protection (Scotland) Act 2010 makes changes to procedures for enforcement of standard securities over residential properties, and provided new forms of Calling up notice and Notice of Default for both residential and commercial properties. For residential repossessions[28], unless the debtor voluntarily surrenders the property, Calling up Notices must now be followed by an action for possession under section 24 of the 1970 Act. The Act also imposes new obligations on creditors in securities over residential properties to go through certain pre-action procedures with a debtor before they can raise an action. This involves providing the debtor with prescribed information, including the terms of the standard security and the amount due under it including arrears and any additional charges, as soon as the debtor is in default. Lenders must now take reasonable efforts to agree proposals for future payments with the debtor, and must provide him with information including contact details on sources of advice and help with managing debt, and contact details for the local authority housing department.

Finally, it should be pointed out that, prior to conclusion of a contract to sell the security subjects, following on enforcement action having been taken, the debtor has the right to redeem the standard security without purging the default specified in the Notice of Default. A debtor,

---

28 See *Westfoot Investments Ltd v European Property Holdings Inc* [2015] SCEDIN 58 which held that the requirements do not apply to companies who own residential property (see para 8.18.3).

or proprietor as the case may be, in a standard security can redeem the security on giving two months' notice of his intention to do so. The procedure and forms to be used to exercise this entitlement are set down in Standard Condition 11 and Schedule 5 to the 1970 Act.

The provisions of the 2001 Act and the 2010 Act only apply to property used for residential purposes (but see para 8.18.3) so it could be said that Scots Law remains relatively creditor-friendly in relation to enforcement of standard securities over commercial premises.

CERTIFICATES OF TITLE

10.8 We have already touched on Certificates of Title in the context of acting for the purchaser of the commercial property, and being asked to certify the title to the lender (see para 8.38.2). In these circumstances, even though the lender's solicitors are excused from examining the title and other due diligence items, and reporting on their terms to the lender, there is still usually a requirement on the lender's solicitors to review and consider the provisions of the Certificate and advise the lender as to the acceptability of it, for the purposes of agreeing to lend.

The current version of the CLLS and PSG Certificates is the 7th edition. Solicitors acting for commercial lenders should make themselves familiar with the appropriate version of the Certificate in common use.

Guidance on how to use the 7th edition Certificate of Title is provided on the PSG website[29], and this is summarised at para 8.38.2). The lender's solicitor is looking for the Certificate to be as clear as possible, and limited to matters which are material to the interests of the lender in the context of the loan and the value of the property. The disclosures in the Certificate should enable the lender to assess the extent of risk attached to the property being offered as security, and it should be clear to the lender's solicitors in reviewing the Certificate what those risks might be. Accordingly, the lender's solicitor is entitled to expect that the Certificate will contain a fair summary of the effect of the title and other documents, but that copies of titles should not be attached, as this would defeat the object of the exercise. Only if the title contains documents that are so complex that their terms cannot be accurately summarised would it be acceptable

29 See www.psglegal.co.uk/certificate_of_title.php.

for the document, or an excerpt from it, to be attached to the Certificate. Even complex documents, if they are in terms usual and acceptable for the type of property, may not need to be attached, unless there is reason why the lender must know the detail of them, and the purchaser's certification could be expressed along the lines of 'containing no unusual or unduly onerous conditions' or 'in terms usual for documents of this type relating to properties of the nature of the security subjects' or similar wording.

There is a balance to be achieved between the purchaser's solicitor and the lender's solicitor in these situations: the purchaser's solicitors must accept that they need to make sensible disclosures, based on commercial considerations that might have a bearing on the value or viability of the property from the lender's point of view, but should resist the temptation to produce pages and pages of disclosures on every point arising out of the title, some of which may relate to minor matters. Professional skill and judgement is required in deciding on what must appear in the Certificate, and what can be left out or modified.

On the other hand, the solicitors for the lender ought to accept that there will be limits to what the purchaser's solicitor is able to certify, and this will usually not include an assessment of the risks that might arise from any problems or issues that the Certificate discloses. The function of the Certificate is to provide specific information about the property, to allow the lender, with the help of its own professional advisers, to decide whether the property is one which can be accepted for the transaction in question.

That is not to say that the lender or its solicitors or other advisers are not entitled to ask for further information or clarification, to enable a proper assessment to be made of any risks disclosed by the Certificate.

Chapter 11

Settlement and the Final Steps

HEADING FOR COMPLETION

11.1 Commercial lawyers refer to 'completion', while residential conveyancers speak of 'settlement'. We mean the same thing, and much of the procedure is the same too, although commercial property lawyers probably see fewer keys.

Once title has been examined and any unsatisfactory points resolved, all reports and searches have been examined and are clear, the disposition, the standard security and any other documents required have been drafted, revised and approved, there are two essential things to set up to achieve settlement: signing and money. All of the conveyancing documents need to be properly executed, and arrangements made for the transfer of funds from the purchaser to the seller, either via their solicitors, or sometimes (in commercial purchases) directly between the parties or their respective banks.

The actual logistics of settlement of the transaction can become complicated, particularly in commercial deals. Usually residential settlements involve two or three documents (discharge, disposition, standard security) and the same solicitor organises requisitioning the loan monies and pays the price, although they can become more complex. Because of separate representation of the parties, however, sometimes even 'simple' commercial property completions can become rather tortuous. There are usually several parties involved, all of whom are separately represented: the purchaser, the seller, the purchaser's lender, the previous lender, perhaps the proposed occupier; sometimes other parties such as the local authority can be involved in the conveyancing process too.

It is good practice to clearly establish the completion requirements of each party as early as possible, and work out how these are going to be achieved. Issues normally revolve around payment of funds and release of the key documents, and the tension that exists because of the respective requirements of the parties. The purchaser needs to have the disposition to register his real right, but must release the purchase price, while the seller will not deliver the disposition without payment; the lender will only release the loan funds if they are assured that they can perfect their security, which often means having possession or control of both the disposition in favour of the borrower and the signed standard security. The previous lender may only be willing to release the discharge in exchange for repayment of the outstanding loan, funds for which are coming from payment of the purchase price.

The time-honoured way to resolve the apparent stalemate that these entrenched requirements creates, is for the respective solicitors to agree and undertake to hold documentation and sometimes also funds as 'undelivered'. The end recipient of the deeds (and funds) receives the deeds and/or funds but must not intromit with them in any way – so for example, the purchaser must not submit the disposition to the Land Register until the seller has received the funds. Usually when there are loan funds required to finance the purchase of commercial property, the lender's solicitors will require to be in possession of all of the documents, holding them as undelivered, so that, as soon as the funds arrive with the seller, the documents immediately become 'delivered' and the lender has immediate possession and can proceed to have them registered. The alternative would be for all of the solicitors to assemble in the same place for a completion meeting and wait for the funds to be transferred from one bank to another before handing over the documents. For those solicitors still using cheques, frequently the cheque will be sent to the seller's solicitor and simultaneously the seller's solicitor will send the settlement items to the purchaser's solicitor, in both cases to be held as undelivered until each confirms to the other that the items have been received. This is common and convenient in residential completions. Settlement cheques are virtually unheard of in commercial completions, particularly when there are often back-to-back telegraphic transfers of funds required on the same day, because, although a solicitor's cheque is guaranteed funds, it is not cleared funds. The sums of money involved are greater, therefore interest per day is much greater. It is also a more secure method of transfer of funds.

One of the key documents in any conveyancing transaction is the Discharge of the security granted by the seller. Here, however, there is a bifurcation in conveyancing practice. Residential conveyancers are happy to accept an undertaking from the seller's solicitors to deliver the executed discharge after settlement. Such an undertaking is still 'classic' for the purposes of the Master policy insurance (see para 11.4.1). However, invariably in a commercial transaction, completion cannot take place without the executed discharge being available, to be held as undelivered and then treated as delivered at completion. Some lenders have been known to refuse to release the executed discharge, even to their own solicitors, until the loan is repaid; although these rather self-defeating instances are comparatively rare, there is recent evidence to suggest that they are becoming more common.

Under the payment regime for land and buildings transaction tax (LBTT), it is up to the purchaser's solicitor to account for the tax to Revenue Scotland. Under the previous stamp duty land tax regime (which ceased to apply to Scotland on 1 April 2015) it was not uncommon in commercial transactions for the lender's solicitors to deal with arrangements for payment of the tax, and submission of the deeds, to ensure that the standard security in favour of their client is put on the register as swiftly as possible. In residential transactions, where the solicitor almost always acts for both borrower and lender, there would not usually be any issue. Now, however, payment of LBTT involves a more intimate relationship between the purchaser's solicitor and Revenue Scotland. Submission of the LBTT return must take place no later than completion, so that the purchaser's solicitors can confirm the LBTT payment arrangements on the registration application form (see paras 11.8 and 14.11.2(iv)).

A checklist of completion items and requirements is a vital tool in anything other than the most straightforward completion. This can be circulated around the other solicitors to make sure that everyone's requirements have been covered, and that everyone knows the settlement items for which they are responsible. The PSG Completion checklist (see para 11.9) is a reasonably comprehensive starting point for most transactions, and is available to download from the PSG website[1].

EXECUTION

11.2 The option of electronic execution of conveyancing documents, such as dispositions, has moved closer with the introduction of electronic

1 See www.psglegal.co.uk/completion_checklist.php.

documents, electronic conveyancing and electronic registration under Part 10 of the Land Registration etc (Scotland) Act 2012, although it is still only possible within the ARTL system (see para 14.12), and, until 'ARTL 2' is developed, the limitations of the ARTL system continue to mean that electronic registration is not a realistic option for anything other than the most straightforward of conveyancing transactions dealing with the whole of a registered title.

Specification of the required standard of electronic or digital signature is now set out in the Electronic Documents (Scotland) Regulations 2014[2]. To a certain extent, the terms 'electronic' and 'digital' are interchangeable (or at least in ordinary language, we tend to mean the same thing), although the Law Society distinguishes between the two terms in its guidance on the use of Smartcards (which have been issued to Scottish solicitors during 2015)[3]. For an electronic document required by section 1(2) of the Requirements of Writing (Scotland) Act 1995 to be valid, the electronic signature of a granter incorporated into (or logically associated with) that document must be an advanced electronic signature (section 9B), and for such an electronic document to be presumed authenticated by a granter under section 9C of the 1995 Act, the electronic signature must be an 'advanced electronic signature' and be certified by a 'qualified certificate'.

A qualified certificate contains certain verification information, must meet certain other requirements, and be provided by a certification-service-provider who must also fulfil prescribed requirements. Advanced electronic signatures and the requirements for qualified certificates and certification service providers issuing qualified certificates are set out in the Electronic Signatures Regulations 2002. In layman's terms what this means is that the type of electronic signature required for electronic conveyancing must be of a very high standard of security and authenticity, independently verified by an authorised verification body. It is secure and reliable and is linked to the document in which it is incorporated in such a way that any subsequent change in the document after 'signing' can be detected.

As the application of electronic conveyancing for documents such as dispositions and standard securities that are to be registered is still

2   SSI 2014/83.
3   See www.lawscot.org.uk/members/smartcard/using-your-smartcard/smartcard-practical-advice-guide/.

only possible using ARTL, for the purposes of this chapter, we confine our comments largely to 'wet' signatures of traditional documents to give them effect. The equivalent provisions relating to authentication of electronic documents are contained in regulation 9 of the Land Register of Scotland (Automated Registration) etc. Regulations 2014[4], which amends the Electronic Documents (Scotland) Regulations 2014.

The 1995 Act is the key piece of legislation when it comes to the formalities required for execution of documents in Scotland. Not always an easy Act to read, it is nonetheless vital for the conveyancer to be familiar with its provisions and effect. It has been extensively amended by Part 10 of the 2012 Act to cover electronic writing and signing. Note that the 1995 Act is subject to any statutory provision to the contrary. For the purposes of the conveyancer, it starts as relatively straightforward: writing is required – both for the constitution of a contract or unilateral obligation for the creation, transfer, variation or extinction of a real right in interest in land (eg missives), and for the creation, transfer, variation or extinction of a real right in land, (otherwise than by operation of a court decree, enactment or rule of law) (eg a disposition etc) (sections 1(2)(a) and (b) of the 1995 Act).

Rules for execution of these (and other) documents are also set out in the 1995 Act. There are two parts to this: validity and probativity. For formal **validity**, all that is required is the subscription of the granter (section 2). So far so good. But a document that has merely been signed, while valid, is not self-proving (ie probative or self-evidencing), and this is where witnessing comes in. If the granter's signature is witnessed – only a single witness is necessary – this bestows an evidential presumption that the document was signed by the granter (section 3). To be recorded in the Sasine Register or registered in the Land Register, a document needs to be self-proving (section 6) ie witnessed, although it should be mentioned that section 4 of the 1995 Act provides an alternative route to probativity for a document that has been merely signed, but not witnessed, by making application to the court. This may be appropriate in cases where the granter's signature cannot now be witnessed, such as where he is now deceased or incapax, so that it is likely to be of use in proving wills for example, rather than a

4   SSI 2014/347.

realistic alternative for conveyancing transactions. A granter can always acknowledge his signature, in the presence of a witness, some time after he has signed, and execution by the witness at that stage will confer the self-proving presumption. Any collateral agreements need to be self-proving to be registered in the Books of Council and Session.

New sections 9B and 9C of the 1995 Act set out the requirements for validity, and presumption of authentication of electronically signed documents.

At the risk of being overly simplistic, perhaps the easiest way to understand the provisions of sections 9B and 9C is to compare them to sections 2 and 3. Sections 2 and 9B deal with validity, and sections 3 and 9C set up a legal presumption of probativity (self-proving status). In the electronic environment, subscription (validity) and witnessing (probativity) are replaced by authentication – by incorporating an electronic signature into (or logically associating it with) the electronic document (validity), and satisfaction of the conditions for authentication for electronic documents (probativity).

The types of documents to which section 9B relates, are electronic equivalents of the traditional documents listed in section 1(2) of the 1995 Act, as amended by the 2012 Act. Wills and other testamentary documents are currently excluded from the electronic execution provisions.

Where it becomes a bit more difficult to sustain the comparison between the requirements for traditional versus electronic signatures is that, in the digital situation, both validity and probativity can be achieved by a single act (application of the electronic signature) as opposed to two acts (subscription by the granter and witnessing by a separate witness). It is the type of electronic signature used that will satisfy the conditions for setting up the legal presumption of authentication.

So, to digitally sign an electronic document, the granter must incorporate the electronic signature of the granter into the document. The electronic signature must be created by the person by whom it purports to be created, and satisfy the requirements prescribed in the regulations. However, as outlined above, not just any old electronic signature will do. For the presumption as to authentication to apply, that electronic signature must be an advanced electronic signature certified by a qualified certificate. Not many of our clients will have one of these.

SUBSCRIPTION AND SIGNING: SPECIAL CASES

11.3 Schedule 2 to the 1995 Act sets out the methods by which certain classes of person may sign, with, in some cases, adjustment to the witnessing arrangements. These, and some other common execution arrangements, are itemised below.

11.3.1 Subscription

A granter should subscribe at the end of the last page of the deed. If there is more than one granter, it is sufficient that at least one of them signs on the last page of the deed and the others can sign on an additional page (ie a blank sheet of paper). There must always be part of the deed on the first signing page – even if it is one word.

If there are any annexations to the deed – such as schedules or plans, then (for deeds relating to land) each of those annexations must also be signed (but do not need any witnesses' signatures). For this reason, it is usual in Scottish deeds for any Schedule to be a single annexation of Parts, so that only one signature on the last page of the whole Schedule is required. Compare this with the practice in England where deeds can contain many individual Schedules, as there is not the same execution requirement. Note, however, that each plan, drawing or other representation that is attached to a deed relating to land and which describes or shows any part of the land, must be individually signed[5]. Invariably, in property transactions in practice, all schedules and other annexations are signed. If you are presented with an executed deed, however, where not all of the annexations have been signed, that is the test – does the annexation 'describe or show all or any part of the land to which the document relates'. It should also be noted that section 8(2)(c) of the 1995 Act specifies that such annexations need to be 'signed', not subscribed. Compare this with the wording of the Legal Writings (Counterparts and Delivery (Scotland) Act 2015 (see para 11.4.2) which requires 'subscription'.

An annexation should be referred to in the document (eg 'the real burdens set out in the Schedule annexed and signed as relative to this disposition') and identified on its face as being that annexation. No prescribed way of doing this is set out in the 1995 Act but, in practice, (and

---

5   Section 8 of the 1995 Act.

it is good practice that should be followed) identification of any annexation is done by putting wording at the top of the first page of the annexation (eg 'This is the Schedule referred to in the foregoing Deed of Real Burdens between Lightyear Development Company Ltd and Kelvinforth Leisure Pursuits Ltd [dated [ ]]'). The interpretation of the 'face' of the document means that the Keeper will reject any plan (or other annexation) where a label has been stuck onto the annexation and the signature is put on the label.

For plans and other representations that need to be signed on each page, the wording is endorsed onto it in some convenient place. If, for example, an A1 size plan is attached to a deed, it will often be folded in such a way that the bottom right-hand corner of the plan is uppermost. For convenience, the wording (eg 'This is the Plan 1 referred to in the foregoing Disposition by Eric Sweet in favour of David Alexander Sweet and Preston Maxwell Monk Sweet') can be written on this uppermost section.

11.3.2 Witnesses

A witness has to see the granter sign the document, and sign after him, or be present when the granter acknowledges his signature, and the witness must then sign. Signature and witnessing must be one continuous process. A witness has to be over the age of 16 and not be mentally incapax, blind, or unable to write. The witness must know the granter whose signature he is witnessing. It is sufficient that at the time of witnessing he has 'credible information' as to the granter's identity. The witness should not be a granter of, or other party to the deed.

11.3.3 Testing Clauses

The details of the execution of the deed are added after signature. There are broadly two ways of doing this: the first, and arguably more popular with conveyancers, is the testing clause, which is a narration of the date and place of signing, and the authority of the signatory if necessary, plus details of the witness typed into the document after signature. To ensure that there is enough room for a testing clause to be typed on to the deed afterwards, a space on the engrossment is 'ruled off', usually by drawing a diagonal pencil line after the words 'IN WITNESS WHEREOF' and adding the words 'please leave blank' in pencil. Underneath the diagonal pencil line, further pencil lines are marked with the initials of the party or the words 'witness' next to it and the signatories are instructed to sign along these pencil lines.

Any alteration to the deed before signature must be declared in the testing clause to be effective.

The alternative method is for a signing block or docquet to be typed onto the deed before execution; the details of place and time can be written in at the time of signing. Signing blocks are becoming more prevalent and often appear on pre-printed security documentation already. See the example that follows. Testing clauses are still used a lot by conveyancers, though, so some examples are also given below, and there are some signing situations for which it is difficult adequately to cater with a signing block. Section 10 of the 1995 Act tantalisingly offered the possibility of a prescribed form of testing clause, through regulations, but this has never materialised. Appendix B to the Scottish Law Commission's Report on Requirements of Writing[6] contains some model forms of testing clauses, which are a hybrid form of signing block, but these particular styles have never really been adopted for general use. A signing block looks like this:

IN WITNESS WHEREOF these presents (or 'this disposition etc.') consisting of this [and the [ ]] preceding pages are [together with] [the Schedule] [and the plan(s)] annexed] executed as follows:

SUBSCRIBED for and on behalf of LIGHTYEAR DEVELOPMENT COMPANY LIMITED at [ ] on the [ ] day of [ ] 2014 by

_____ Authorised Signatory

_____ (Full Name) signing by virtue of Power of Attorney by Lightyear Development Company Limited in his favour dated [ ] 2014

before this witness (or 'in the presence of')

_____ Witness

_____ Full Name

_____ Address

---

6   Scot Law Com 112.

11.3.4 Individuals

Individual natural persons who are granters, or who are signing as, or on behalf of, a granter, sign in accordance with the principal provisions of the 1995 Act, ie they subscribe the deed, and their signature should be witnessed at the same time as signing, by a single witness who also signs the deed. This applies for all individuals, so will include persons signing as executor, administrator, trustee etc. Where more than one granter signs at the same time, then only one witness to all of their signatures is necessary. Where a person grants a document in more than one capacity (eg as an individual and as an executor) that person only needs to sign the deed once. An example testing clause:

> IN WITNESS WHEREOF this disposition consisting of this and the three preceding pages are executed by me the said Eric Sweet, as an individual and as Executor nominate of the said Mrs Norma McNaught Monk or Sweet, at Kelvinforth on Tenth April Two thousand and fifteen, in the presence of Wendy Robertson, Trainee Solicitor of 42 Piemonte Place, Kelvinforth.

11.3.5 Partnerships

Schedule 2, para 2 to the 1995 Act provides that where the granter of a document is a partnership, it is signed on its behalf by one of the partners, or by a person authorised to sign the document on behalf of the partnership. The signatory can either use their own name or the firm name. This deals with validity. For probativity, a witness will also be required. An important point to note, however, is that, invariably, title to heritable property is held, not in the firm's name (although this is competent) but in the names of the individual partners as trustees for the firm. Accordingly, where the document relates to heritable property, execution should be in accordance with trust law, ie either all of the trustees or a quorum, should sign the deed. There is a view that a quorum, or a majority of trustees is sufficient, but the law is uncertain on this point[7]. An example testing clause (incorporating how to refer to the firm name if signed):

---

7   See Gretton & Reid: *Conveyancing* 4th edn, para 25–19.

IN WITNESS WHEREOF this disposition consisting of this and the preceding two pages are, together with the Plan annexed, signed by the said Caroline Rowan and the Eric Sweet as partners of and trustees for the said firm of Rowan Retirement Homes, the firm name being adhibited by the said Caroline Rowan, one of its partners, all at Kelvinforth on First November Two thousand and fourteen, in the presence of Samantha Mirren Darling of 7 Lionheart Farm Cottages, Kinlochalmond, Perthshire.

11.3.6 Limited Partnerships

There is no specific reference in the 1995 Act to execution by a Limited Partnership. Usual practice is for documents to be executed by the general partner, although the partnership agreement for the Limited Partnership may make specific provision regarding execution of documents, so this should always be checked. A limited partner has no power to bind the partnership and should not sign the deed. A witness is required for the deed to be self-proving.

11.3.7 Limited Liability Partnerships (LLPs)

For self-proving execution by an LLP either the signature of one member with a witness, or the signatures of two members without a witness is required[8]. An example testing clause:

> IN WITNESS WHEREOF this disposition consisting of this and the preceding page are subscribed for and on behalf of the said Dunvorlich Renewables LLP, acting by Stuart James, a Member for and on behalf of the said Dunvorlich Renewables LLP, at Glasgow on Twenty Ninth October Two Thousand and fifteen, in the presence of Alan John Gaunt of 204 St Kentigern Street, Glasgow.

11.3.8 Companies

Section 78 of the Companies Act 2006 provides that Scottish companies executing a deed in accordance with the 1995 Act will have effect as if executed by a company affixing its common seal. Companies signing

---

8   Schedule 2, para 3A to the 1995 Act.

deeds have a variety of signing options[9]. For self-proving status, a deed requires subscription by either:

- one director and one witness;
- the secretary and one witness;
- one authorised signatory and a witness;
- two directors;
- a director and the secretary; or
- two authorised signatories.

As a matter of practice, the Companies Search obtained for a seller should include details of the current directors and secretary. If, however, the company execution is by authorised signatory(ies) then confirmation of the basis of authority should be exhibited to the purchaser's solicitors. Example testing clauses:

Signatory and witness:

> **IN WITNESS WHEREOF** this standard security consisting of this and the seven preceding pages are signed for and on behalf of the said Lightyear Development Company Limited by Richard Byron Childs, one of its Directors, at Perth on the Fifth day of April Two Thousand and Fourteen in the presence of Celia Bloomsbury of 65 Registration Row, Perth PH12 5TJ.

Director and Secretary:

> **IN WITNESS WHEREOF** this disposition consisting of this and the seven preceding pages are signed for and on behalf of the said Lightyear Development Company Limited by Richard Byron Childs, a Director of the said Lightyear Development Company Limited and Rory Redknapp, Secretary of the said Lightyear Development Company Limited at Perth on the Fifth day of April Two Thousand and Fourteen.

As a matter of style, you can use defined terms such as 'the Company' or 'Lightyear'.

Where the company is the borrower, the lenders will often require to see a Board Minute or Officer's Certificate from the company, containing

---

9   Schedule 2, para 3 to the 1995 Act.

details of the resolution by the Board of directors that authorises the taking of the loan, the granting of the security, and naming or nominating the directors or other authorised signatories of the company who will sign the standard security. Many banks will produce their preferred style of Board Minute, which the company (or its solicitor) types and completes with the details of the relevant meeting of the directors of the company. This does not need to be a formally constituted occasion, and a normal meeting of the directors or a sufficient quorum of them will be adequate.

'BOARD MINUTE

of

Lightyear Development Company Limited

(Registered in Scotland, Registered Number 809908)

MINUTES of MEETING of the BOARD of DIRECTORS of

LIGHTYEAR DEVELOPMENT COMPANY LTD (the 'Company')

held at 65 Registration Row, Perth

on 16 July 2015 at 11am.

PRESENT: Richard Byron Childs (Chairman)

Rhuaridh John Darling (Director)

Rory Redknapp, Secretary

1. Quorum

The chairman confirmed that notice of the meeting had been given to the Directors and the Secretary, and noted that a quorum was present and accordingly it was competent to proceed to the business of the meeting.

2. Standard Security

There was then produced to the meeting a draft of the proposed Standard Security to be granted by the Company in favour of Scotland Bank plc relative to the proposed development at Sardinia Terrace, Kelvinforth.

After careful consideration, the Directors resolved that it was in the best interests of the company to grant the Standard Security

The terms of the Standard Security were approved and it was resolved that Richard Byron Childs be and was duly authorised to execute the Standard Security on behalf of the Company.

3. Further business

There being no further business, the meeting was closed.'

11.3.9 Local Authorities

For valid execution by a local authority, Schedule 2, para 4 to the 1995 Act provides that, unless an enactment expressly provides otherwise, signature on its behalf by the proper officer of the local authority is required. The local authority will have a scheme of delegation or a scheme of appointments of proper officers, and lenders will often ask to see a certified copy of the scheme.

To be probative, then either the document must also be signed by a witness, or in addition to the signature of the proper officer, the document is sealed with the common seal of the authority.

11.3.10 Other Bodies Corporate

Schedule 2, para 5 to the 1995 Act applies to any body corporate other than a company incorporated under the Companies Acts, or a local authority, which includes industrial and provident societies, universities, building societies, and companies incorporated by Royal Charter. Again, unless there is other provision in another enactment where a granter of a document is a body corporate, the document is validly signed by the body if it is signed on its behalf by either:

- a member of the governing board of the body or (if there is no governing body) a member of the body;
- the secretary of the body by whatever name he is called; or
- an authorised signatory of the body.

For the document to be self-proving the signature must either be witnessed or the common seal of the body must also be applied, in addition to the signature.

11.3.11 Overseas Companies

The rules relating to 'Other bodies corporate' apply to execution of documents by overseas companies. Regulation 5 of the Overseas Companies (Execution of Documents and Registration of Charges) Regulations 2009 modifies section 48 of the Companies Act 2006 so that it provides: 'For the purposes of any enactment (a) providing for a document to be executed by a company by affixing its common seal, or (b) referring (in whatever terms) to a document so executed, a document signed or subscribed by or on behalf of an overseas company in accordance with the provisions of the Requirements of Writing (Scotland) Act 1995 has effect as if so executed.' Note that English companies are not overseas companies.

11.3.12 Ministers of the Crown and other Office Holders

Where a granter of a document is a Minister or an office holder then, unless another enactment provides otherwise, the document is subscribed by the Minister or office holder if it is signed:

- by him personally; or

- where an enactment or rule of law permits a document by a Minister to be signed by an officer of his, or by another Minister, by that officer or other Minister; or

- where an enactment or rule of law permits a document by an office holder to be signed by an officer of his, by that officer; or

- by any other person authorised to sign the document on his behalf.

A witness is required to achieve self-proving status. In terms of the Ministers of the Crown Act 1975, it is presumed that such a signature is, in fact, authorised. In practice, each UK ministry sets out its signing procedure in the incorporating statutory instrument. For example, Article 3(2) of the Secretary for State for Business, Innovations and Skills Order 2009, SI 2009/2748 provided that a document will be executed by adhibiting the corporate seal or by being signed by an authorised person.

11.3.13 Scottish Ministers

In terms of section 59(4) of the Scotland Act 1998, deeds executed on or after 1 July 1999 by the Scottish Ministers are validly executed if signed by any member of the Scottish Executive (now known as 'the Scottish Government') or under the Scottish Ministers' delegated authority.

COUNTERPART EXECUTION

11.4 Until 2015, it was not competent, under Scots law, to execute a document in counterpart (ie in more than one version of the original document) although there was a view, not, however, generally held, that execution in counterpart was competent, based on such authorities as the seventeenth century case of *Smith v Duke of Gordon*[10]. The Scottish Law Commission, as part of its ongoing major review of the law of contract in Scotland, decided to consider counterpart, which has resulted in the Legal Writings (Counterparts and Delivery) (Scotland) Act 2015.

11.4.1 The Case for Counterpart Execution

Counterpart execution is already used extensively in England and Wales, where it is seen as an extremely efficient way of allowing multi-party and sometimes, multi-jurisdictional, transactions to complete by way of simultaneous remote all-party signings. The inability to do this under Scots law could often result in a protracted and time-consuming signing process, creating inconvenience and delay, particularly in commercial transactions.

The Legal Writings (Counterparts and Delivery) (Scotland) Act 2015 is a very short Act – only seven sections and no Schedules – and yet its impact on conveyancing, commerce, contracting, transacting and doing business in Scotland has the potential to be enormous.

The Act deals with two issues, as the title suggests:

- execution of documents in counterpart (that is in two or more duplicate, interchangeable parts); and

- delivery of traditional documents by electronic means.

10 [1701] Mor 1698 7.

The provisions relating to counterparts set out the legal permissibility of counterpart execution, how counterparts will be made up, when a document executed in counterpart will become effective; delivery arrangements, and management of the counterpart elements.

11.4.2 The Mechanics of Counterpart Execution

Counterpart execution enables a single document to be signed by the various parties to it in several parts. For execution in counterpart you need a document in two or more duplicate, interchangeable, parts.

No single part is subscribed by both or all parties, but each party must sign either (i) as many copies of the document as there are parties or (ii) one complete copy of the document. Whichever of (i) or (ii) is chosen will depend on the option chosen for delivery.

On such execution, the counterparts are treated as a single document, which is made up of:

- both or all of the counterparts in their entirety, or
- the whole of one of the counterparts, together with the page or pages on which the other counterparts have been subscribed.

The language of the 2015 Act is 'subscription', not 'signing'. This is particularly relevant in the context of annexations that have to be executed. Since this applies to documents that relate to land, there is every likelihood that they will also require to be registered. Guidance from the Registers of Scotland[11] specifies that any annexations to a document that has been executed in counterpart and is then submitted for registration must be 'subscribed', ie signed at the bottom.

11.4.3 Delivery of Counterparts

A counterpart document becomes effective on delivery. However, if the parties have agreed that a document is to be held as undelivered, pending their authority that it may be delivered, or pending the satisfaction of certain conditions, the document is not to be treated as delivered (for effectiveness) until authority is given, or the conditions are satisfied.

11 See www.ros.gov.uk/services/registration/legal-updates/legal-writings-act-2015.

Delivery means delivery in accordance with the existing law, and although this is not spelt out in the 2015 Act, this means actual physical delivery, unless the provisions later in the 2015 Act regarding electronic delivery of traditional documents are relied on. Delivery and effectiveness will generally be the point at which the parties intend to be bound by the terms of the document.

There are two options for achieving effective delivery of a counterpart document (subject always to any other step needed by an enactment or other rule of law).

11.4.3(i) Multiple delivery option

The first option is that each counterpart is to be delivered to the party or parties who did not subscribe the counterpart. This will mean that if there are, say, five parties to a deed, each party must sign five copies of the deed. They then retain one copy for themselves and deliver a signed copy to each of the other four parties. They will each receive a signed copy of the deed from each of the other four signatories. The end result is that each party (or more probably, their respective solicitors) will end up in possession of five versions of the same deed, each version signed by one of the parties only. Together these five signed versions make up the single document.

11.4.3(ii) Single delivery option

The alternative option is that a party or parties to the document can nominate one person to take delivery of one or more of the signed counterparts. In that case, each party only needs to sign one copy of the deed. Each party sends their signed copy to a central point for collation.

11.4.3(iii) Nominated person

A nominated person can be one of the parties, or the agent of one of the parties. It seems that in a transaction there could be more than one nominated person, ie each of whom would take delivery of some, but not all, of the signed counterparts.

The agent route is probably preferable, since there could be an issue with one of the parties themselves taking delivery of the counterparts – since a person cannot 'deliver' their own version to themselves.

Actual arrangements for receipt, management and intimation of receipt of and satisfaction of any delivery conditions to the signatories or their solicitors, is left to the parties themselves to decide. The reality is likely to be that, how these matters are to be handled, and whether there is to be delivery to each of the signatories of a copy of each of the other signed version or collation by one or more nominated persons, will be agreed early on in the transaction, where it is clear that counterpart execution will be used, or at the point in the transaction where it becomes obvious that counterpart execution is going to be the preferred route.

The only duty of the nominated person, in terms of the Act, however, is to 'hold and preserve' the delivered counterparts for the benefit of the parties, although the parties can agree otherwise. The effectiveness of the document is not affected if the nominated person does not comply with these requirements provided, of course, that the legal requirements for effective counterpart execution are achieved. Early practice in this respect appears to be that the nominated person will expressly contract out of this duty.

11.4.3(iv) Traditional and electronic execution

Counterpart documents can be traditional or electronic, and executed appropriately, ie by wet or electronic signature, whichever is suitable. There is no reason why different copies of a counterpart document could not be produced in a mixture of traditional and electronic formats and signed by wet or electronic signature as appropriate to the document format. It would be competent for there to be a mixture of formats within one single final counterpart deed.

In reality, however, it seems unlikely that electronic execution of a document in counterpart will be used, since the main benefit of counterpart execution is to allow several parties who are remote from each other to sign a document simultaneously, or at around the same time, without having to wait for a single traditional document to be sent round all the parties, in the traditional 'round robin' signing procedure.

11.4.3(v) Counterparts clause?

There is to be no legal requirement for a counterpart document to contain some wording that authorises its execution in counterpart. This will provide flexibility to the parties to execute traditionally or in counterpart, whichever method is more expedient. It is, however, probably prudent for some reference to the possibility that the deed might be signed in counterpart to be included, particularly if the deed has to be registered, to provide evidence on the face of the deed that the parties contemplated counterpart execution. In England and Wales, it is usual for a counterparts clause to be included in the deed.

11.4.3(vi) Registration of counterpart documents

There is nothing in the 2015 Act about registering counterpart documents. While the Land Registration etc (Scotland) Act 2012 specifically excludes electronic documents from being recorded or registered in the Property Registers, or in the Books of Council and Session, unless authorised by regulations, which currently only apply to ARTL documents[12], there is no bar to a traditional document that has been executed in counterpart being registered. While it might look a bit peculiar, and there are arguments concerning the order in which parties execute, the dates of execution and so on, the Registers of Scotland are geared up to accept such documents (see para 11.4.2).

11.4.3(vii) Differences between Scottish and English counterpart execution

For those who are familiar with execution in counterpart in England and Wales, there are some key differences to bear in mind:

Scotland	England
Statutory basis for counterpart execution (Legal Writings (Counterparts and Delivery) (Scotland) Act 2015.	No statutory basis – counterpart execution based on custom and practice.
No formal validity for execution of separate single-signing page only.	Single-signing page, printed, signed and returned accepted as sufficient for delivery of executed counterpart for certain types of document.
No standard procedural format or Law Society guidance.	Law Society of E&W protocols.

---

12 Land Register of Scotland (Automated Registration) etc Regulations 2014, SSI 2014/34.

Scotland	England
'Counterparts clause' not legally required under Scots law (although useful for setting out basis for execution and delivery of document).	'Counterparts clause' generally used in any document which is being executed in counterpart.
Electronic execution (ie by a suitable digital signature) of an electronic counterpart is permissible (enabled by Part 10 of the LRetc(S)A 2012).	No authority for electronic execution of legal documents in electronic format.
Electronic delivery of part only of a traditional document (including at least the signing page) is authorised by statute.	Electronic delivery of part only of a traditional document (including at least the signing page) relies on custom and practice.

ADVANCE NOTICES

11.5 The introduction of Advance Notices represented a major transformation for conveyancing practice in Scotland, and one that many in the profession would regard as long overdue. It is often said that Advance Notices 'replace' letters of obligation but, of course, the letter of obligation was not a component of the previous land registration regime. It was a necessary evil which was developed by solicitors in Scotland, because of the shortcomings in the Sasine and land registration systems.

There are still circumstances in which a letter of undertaking will have to be given. The advance notice procedure does not, for example, cover the situation where a discharge of a standard security is not available at settlement, (assuming that you are prepared to give or accept such an undertaking) or all the other things that we undertake on behalf of clients to produce but they should eliminate most, if not all, of the instances of underwriting that the register will be clear.

11.5.1 What are Advance Notices?

Advance Notices are introduced by sections 56–64 of the Land Registration etc (Scotland) Act 2012. The Advance Notice concept is similar to, but not exactly the same as, the priority period which currently exists for registration of documents in the Land Registry of England and Wales. In England and Wales it is tied in with a register search.

An application is made to the Keeper for an Advance Notice in respect of a deed that it is intended to be granted. For a fee of £10, an Advance Notice application can be submitted, eg when your client has agreed to sell a piece of his land, and will be granting a disposition in favour of the purchaser. This application is submitted in advance of the completion date and once it is registered, it provides a period of protection of 35 days (beginning with the day after the Advance Notice is registered) in which any competing disposition, or another Advance Notice, would not have priority.

So, if some other person attempted to submit a disposition for registration in respect of the property in question, the existence of the earlier Advance Notice would prevent the bogus disposition from prevailing, provided the purchaser submits his disposition within the 35-day period of protection given by the Advance Notice.

However, if the purchaser doesn't submit his disposition within the 35-day period, the earlier registered disposition will take effect on expiry of the 35-day period. Advance Notices will apply to other types of deeds such as a standard security or deed of servitude, and will also apply to titles that are in the Register of Sasines, on first registration. Not all deeds are eligible for an Advance Notice – there has to be a granter and a grantee so unilateral deeds are not included, at least not at the moment.

11.5.2 Effect of Advance Notices

As all dispositions, whether for valuable consideration or not, will induce a first registration, if the title is still in the Sasine Register, Advance Notices can be recorded in the Sasine Register in those cases. For a title that is already in the Land Register, the Advance Notice will be registered in the Application Record of the Land Register.

Registering an Advance Notice will give a period of protection of 35 days. If for any reason your transaction is delayed, it is possible to apply for another Advance Notice giving you another 35-day period of protection. However, this is not an extension of the first Advance Notice period: it is a separate period of protection. So, if someone submits a competing disposition during the first period, it will be on the register, and the second priority period will not protect against it. Of course, you will be able to see that it is has been registered and deal accordingly.

One innovative effect of an Advance Notice is that if an inhibition is registered against the granter during the protected period, if the protected deed is registered, it will not be affected by the inhibition.

Advance Notices will not protect against the insolvency of the granter of the deed, however.

Advance Notices do not affect potential liability for costs under the Tenements (Scotland) Act 2004 or the Title Conditions (Scotland) Act 2003. This appears to mean that if a notice of potential liability for costs is registered during a protected period, it will still apply to the property.

11.5.3 Conveyancing Procedures for Advance Notices

Conveyancing practices have been adjusted to incorporate the advance notice procedure into conveyancing practice.

Offers now contain standard wording dealing with Advance Notices (see paras 6.10.18 and 6.14.14). Since it is only the person who may validly grant the deed to be protected and who intends to grant that deed, in a purchase, it is the seller who has to make the application for the Advance Notice. However, a person who has the consent of the person who may validly grant the intended deed can also make an Advance Notice application. This will apply in situations where, for example, a purchaser wishes to obtain an Advance Notice to protect the standard security he will be granting to his lender.

The Advance Notice protection starts very quickly. The Keeper's aim is to enter the Advance Notice on the application record on the day of receipt of the submission, meaning the protected period starts the following day.

There are differing views on what is the optimum time in the transaction to submit the Advance Notice application.

Clearly, you want it to subsist until your application to register your deed has actually entered the application record, so it needs to extend beyond the settlement date, and potentially for up to 14 days after – or whatever reasonable period of time is appropriate. In reality, it may be a lot closer to settlement before the Advance Notice application is lodged, to make sure that the maximum period of protection is available after settlement.

The approach taken in commercial transactions, as reflected in the PSG Offers to Sell, is for submission not earlier than say five working days before completion or settlement. This allows for as much of the protected period as possible to cover the period after settlement, in case of delays or rejection of the application in the first instance. The approach for residential transactions is for submission up to 10 working days before settlement.

It is, however, a balancing act and the parties should not think this is a rigidly fixed provision. It would seem to make sense that the more time after settlement you have, if your application is rejected for some reason, there is a better chance that you might be able to deal with whatever was wrong and get the application submitted again, still within the protected period of your notice.

The form of Advance Notice should be adjusted with the purchaser, since it is the purchaser who gains the protection after all. The Advance Notice will only protect that particular deed granted by that seller to that purchaser, so the purchaser's solicitors want to be sure that the purchaser's details are correct. This should be borne in mind in the case of nominees, because if the person taking title changes at the last minute, the Advance Notice won't protect a deed in favour of that party. The system for creating an Advance Notice Application form did not originally allow for drafts to be saved, so the PSG provided forms of draft Advance Notice application forms in Word format. However, the Keeper was prevailed upon to adjust the online system to accommodate saving drafts; this functionality is now available.

Once the Advance Notice application has been submitted, the seller's solicitor can instruct a Legal Report, or Legal Continuation Report which will disclose the Advance Notice, (which will appear in any searches of the application record from the day after it was entered ie on the day the protected period starts) giving the purchaser comfort that it has protection from any competing deeds that subsequently appear on the Register. With Advance Notice protection in place, no letter of obligation undertaking to clear the records of any deed, decree or diligence is necessary. The main thing is to ensure that there are no gaps; that you can see when the protected period starts (the day after the date of registration) and there are no deeds registered in the period between the date of the last search and the start of the protected period that need to be dealt with.

For Advance Notices relating to the standard security that the purchaser intends to grant, or for any other deeds – perhaps the purchaser is planning on a back to back sub-sale, consent of the seller is deemed by the standard wording in offers, so that the purchaser can go ahead and make the application for protection of any deed it intends to grant direct. This would also apply to dispositions to be granted by the purchaser in a back to back sub-sale.

If there is a back-to-back sub-sale, but the purchaser doesn't want the seller to know about it, then care would need to be taken in relation to applying for an Advance Notice for that deed. It will show up in a Legal Report, which the seller will see. Either some very careful timing is required, to make the application after the Legal Report is obtained but before completion, or no Advance Notice application can be made. Arguably, however, if the purchaser's Disposition is still protected, then any prior competing deed would be removed, but a subsequent or simultaneous deed granted by the purchaser would not.

11.5.4 Applying for Advance Notices

Applications for an Advance Notice are created electronically, within the Registers of Scotland e-services portal, for which solicitors must register. In the online form, you provide details which include the name of the granter, the name of the grantee, the type of deed it is, and details of the property, including the Title Number if it is registered or a conveyancing description if it is not.

There are drop-down options, from which you select whether the transaction type is a first registration, dealing of whole, transfer of part etc. Not all Advance Notice applications can be submitted electronically, however – some have to be printed out, signed and submitted in hard copy.

The Advance Notice system will accept five types of application:

11.5.4(i) A first registration

This is where the Advance Notice is in respect of the grant of a deed that will take the property out of the Sasine Register. However, the Advance Notice has to be recorded in the Sasine Register, as the title to the property is not yet in the Land Register – that will only happen when the intended deed is actually presented for registration. As the Advance Notice has to be recorded in the Sasine Register, and because every writ to be registered in the Sasine Register has to be impressed with a stamp or seal, you must print out the Advance Notice form and submit it in paper form.

11.5.4(ii) An intended deed that applies to the Whole of a Registered Interest.

This type of application can be submitted electronically. Note that if the deed being granted relates to property part of which is a Sasine title and part of which is in the Land Register, then two Advance Notice applications will be required for the same deed – one for each Register.

11.5.4(iii) An intended deed that applies to Part only of a Registered Interest

If the transaction is a transfer of part, then you will have to provide a plan to identify the part. The standard of that plan is going to have to be sufficiently high so that it can be shown immediately on the cadastral map. If you have a suitable electronic plan file this can be uploaded to the system, otherwise you will have to submit the application in hard copy with a copy of the plan. However, if the part being transferred is a plot in a development which has Development Plan Approval, which identifies the individual plots, then no plan is required and all you need to do is provide the Development Plan Approval number and plot number.

11.5.4(iv) Discharge of an Advance Notice on the Land Register

This will only be necessary if the Advance Notice needs to be removed from the application record during the currency of the 35-day period. Perhaps a sale has fallen through at the last minute and there is another purchaser available who wants to complete – and therefore have an Advance Notice registered for their deed – within the original protected period. In some cases there may be a last-minute decision for the title to be taken in favour of a nominee. Strictly speaking, if it is the same transaction, there would be no need to discharge the first Advance Notice, since the seller is not now going to grant the disposition in favour of the original party. If the purchaser insists on a second Advance Notice for its nominee, it is not really a fight worth having, since the cost (£10) is so modest.

If the Advance Notice has to be discharged, then the consent of the person in whose favour the deed was to be granted must be obtained. Again, this is built in to the standard missives wording.

Normally, however, a notice will just be allowed to expire, or the intended deed will have been registered within the relevant protected period. The Keeper must remove details of Advance Notices from the application record of the Land Register once they have expired.

11.5.4(v) Discharge of an Advance Notice that is recorded in the Sasine Register.

Advance notices recorded in the Sasine Register will not be automatically removed. It is possible to submit an application for a discharge of such a notice but, since it will be obvious from the dates that it has expired this seems an unnecessary thing to do as a matter of course.

11.5.5 Signing the Advance Notice Form Declaration

Unless you can submit the Advance Notice application electronically, the hard copy form must be signed, usually by a partner, or by a person specifically authorised by the firm to sign applications.

The application form contains a declaration that certifies the correctness of the information, and also that the applicant is one who can apply for an advance notice in terms of the legislation:

'Applicant Statement and Declarations

I/We hereby certify that the person to whom the intended deed would be granted consents to this application to discharge the advance notice relating to that deed in accordance with section 63(3)(a) of the Land Registration etc. (Scotland) Act 2012.

I/We certify that the information supplied on this Form is complete and correct to the best of my/our knowledge and belief.'

11.5.6 Acceptance of Advance Notice application

When you submit an online Advance Notice application, the Keeper will acknowledge submission with an automated email confirming that submission was successful. For paper submissions, there is no equivalent acknowledgement. The Advance Notice is then entered in the application record and a notification emails including a link to a pdf of the Advance Notice is issued overnight to the e-mail addresses specified on the Advance Notice. The Advance Notice will confirm the period of protection that it covers.

GIVING UNDERTAKINGS AND LETTERS OF OBLIGATION

11.6 With the introduction of the Advance Notice procedure, in the vast majority of transaction the traditional 'letter of obligation' has become a thing of the past. There are, however, still circumstances where a letter of obligation is appropriate, either because an Advance Notice is not available for the transaction type or in some cases where it has not been possible to obtain Advance Notice protection in time for completion or settlement[13].

The issue is that there is a time lag between the date to which the Searchers can certify the records in the Property Registers, and the date on which the purchaser (or other grantee) obtains a real right to their interest in the property, through registration. In that gap period, the purchaser is vulnerable, because a competing title may be registered or the granter may become insolvent, or a standard security over the property could be granted without the purchaser's knowledge. Before the advent of Advance Notices, that gap period was traditionally covered by a solicitors' undertaking, which was covered by the Professional Indemnity Insurance for solicitors – the Master Policy. This covers any undertaking given by a solicitor in the normal course of his business, but the 'letter of obligation' – as such property undertakings were known – had a special treatment under the Master Policy: if the letter of obligation was 'classic' which meant not only that the letter should be in a particular form but, more importantly, that certain steps and checks had been carried out by the seller's solicitor before giving it, then if any claim arose out of the firm

---

13 For the background to the use of letters of obligation, and a comparison with the Advance Notice system, see Ann Stewart 'A New Era in Conveyancing: Advance Notices and the Land Registration etc (Scotland) Act 2012' in *Essays in Conveyancing and Property Law in Honour of Professor Robert Rennie*. Available at: www.openbookpublishers.com/product/343/essays-in-conveyancing-and-property-law-in-honour-of-professor-robert-rennie.

having to honour the undertaking, this would be met by the Master Policy (subject to limits of cover etc). No excess would apply and there would be no adverse impact on the level of that firm's Master Policy premium.

11.6.1 Classic Undertakings

When a letter of obligation was granted in a variety of situations it would qualify as 'classic' when given in appropriate circumstances, defined in the Master Policy as any situation involving 'the disposal for onerous consideration of any interest in property of any description or the granting of security over any such property by a client of that solicitor'. This included undertakings given in lender/borrower transactions as well as sale/purchase transactions. It also included transactions involving leases.

The undertakings that were usually included in a letter of obligation were to provide clear property and personal searches, and executed/recorded discharges. To qualify as 'classic' certain risk management controls had to be observed:

- a search must have been carried out 'immediately prior to settlement' (which in practice meant dated not more than three days prior to settlement, although the CML Handbook specifies three **working** days). In Sasine cases, this would include a search in the Computerised Presentment Book, and the search must be clear;
- the granter of the letter of obligation had to have control of sufficient funds to pay the loan (and know the identity and whereabouts of the party entitled to the redemption money) before giving an undertaking to deliver a discharge of a standard security;
- the granter of the letter of obligation must have made proper enquiry of the client regarding any outstanding security or other matter which might adversely affect the search; and
- the granter of the letter of obligation had to be unaware of any other security or matter which might adversely affect the search.

The period that the letter of obligation covered was not indefinite, for obvious reasons. The 'gap' that the letter of obligation covered for clear records had to be no more than 14 days from settlement. This was the maximum period covered by the Master Policy.

11.6.2 Giving Undertakings

There are still, however, occasions when a 'letter of obligation' style undertaking will be required. While these are much less frequent than before, it has been confirmed by Marsh, the Master Policy insurers, at least for the policy year commencing 1 November 2015, that cover for 'classic' letters of obligation will still be available on the same beneficial terms. It should be noted that even if those beneficial terms cease to apply, a solicitor may still give a 'letter of obligation'-style undertaking, when it is given in the ordinary course of business. It will, however, be subject to the same restrictions as any other type of undertaking given by solicitors, covered by the Master Policy, ie subject to the application of a double excess (double deductible) if a claim is made and met, and will be taken into account for any discount or loading to Master Policy premiums for the firm in question.

11.6.2(i) Standard security over a Sasine title

Until April 2016, it will continue to be possible to record a standard security over a Sasine title, without any requirement for the title to move to the Land Register. Advance Notices are not available for deeds that are not destined for the Land Register and so it will continue to be appropriate for a letter of obligation to be given. A suitable style undertaking is available on the PSG website[14].

11.6.2(ii) Lease of less than 20 years

Only leases of over 20 years' duration are registrable. Since the lease cannot be registered in the land Register, no advance notice protection is available. A style letter of undertaking is also available on the PSG website.

11.6.2(iii) Where an Advance Notice is not available in time

There are occasionally situations where there is a delay in obtaining the Advance Notice protection. These were common in the early days of the 2012 Act regime, but they are less common now.

---

14 Style undertakings are available on the PSG website at: www.psglegal.co.uk/letters_of_ obligation_undertaking.php.

However, there may still be the odd time when it is not possible to get the Advance Notice protection in time eg delays at the Registers, rejection of the application due to error, or if settlement is sprung on you at short notice. In those circumstances, it is permissible to give a hybrid form of letter of obligation to cover the period from completion or settlement, until the date that the Advance Notice protection kicks in.

This particular undertaking proceeds on the basis that the Advance Notice has been applied for (the application must be for a deed that the granter intends to grant, so it must be made before settlement takes place) but is not in place in time for settlement, and so the firm's undertaking covers the period between the settlement date (or the latest date of the legal report) and the date the Advance Notice protection starts, or 14 days, whichever is the shorter period. In reality, since Advance Notices are activated very quickly, the period of exposure should be no more than a day or two.

FUNDS AND SETTLEMENT

11.7 Making sure that funds are available for settlement or completion and attending to apportionments and allocation of other costs, such as rates and common charges are key elements of the completion stages in a property transaction.

11.7.1 Funds

The purchaser's solicitor must ensure that the necessary financial arrangements are in place in good time for completion. If there are any payments that are made in respect of the property that require to be apportioned between the seller and the purchaser as at the date of entry, then the seller's solicitors prepare a 'State for Settlement', or Completion Statement which will show the purchase price and the plus or minus effect on it of any apportionments. A Completion Statement is usual in commercial investment properties where the rents received from the tenants are apportioned. Usually, since the seller will have received the current quarter's rent already, the proportion of these to which the purchaser is entitled will be reflected as a deduction from the price. The draft completion statement is sent to the purchaser's solicitors to approve:

'[STATE FOR SETTLEMENT][COMPLETION STATEMENT]

in connection with the Sale of 104 to 110 Lombardy Street, Kelvinforth

Sellers: Dunvorlich Investments Ltd Per Gaunt Mitchell LLP,
Solicitors, Glasgow

Purchasers: Lightyear Investments Ltd Per O'Neill Middleton,
Solicitors, Perth

Date of Entry: 9 January 2015

Purchase Price	£1,950,000
Less	
Portions of rents due to Purchasers as per Schedule:	51,523
	£1,898,477

SCHEDULE OF APPORTIONMENTS

104 Lombardy Street, Kelvinforth

Rent £120,000 pa from 9 Jan 2015 to 27 Feb 2015 (50 days) (£328.76 per day)	£16,438.00

106 Lombardy Street, Kelvinforth

Rent £89,750 pa from 9 Jan 2015 to 27 February 2015 (50 days) (£245.89 per day)	£12,294.50

108 Lombardy Street, Kelvinforth

Rent £64,930 pa from 9 Jan 2015 to 27 February 2015 (50 days) (£177.89 per day)	£8,894.50

110 Lombardy Street, Kelvinforth

Rent £101,440 pa from 9 Jan 2015 to 27 Feb 2015 (50 days) (£277.92 per day)	£13,896.00'

Where funding for the purchase is coming from a bank or building society, the purchaser's solicitor must ensure that sufficient notice is given so that funds are in the solicitor's clients account in time for settlement. When also acting for the lender in residential transactions, the loan instructions should be checked at the start to note any period of notice that the lender requires for draw down of funds. When separate solicitors are acting for the lender, bank account details for where funds are to be sent should be given to them in good time.

Where funds are coming from the client, any cheque must be given to the solicitors in plenty of time for it to be cleared through the banking system. This is crucial. A solicitor's cheque from their clients' account is treated as guaranteed funds. If, therefore, a solicitor issues a cheque, it is incumbent on them to ensure that they have funds to meet it, as the solicitors may not stop the cheque once issued, other than in the most exceptional circumstances. So, if the solicitor issued a cheque and then the cheque from his client was not honoured, the risk rests with the solicitors, and any attempt to shift the problem to the sellers may amount to professional misconduct. The following statement by the Law Society[15] made the position clear:

> 'A solicitor acting for a purchaser in a conveyancing transaction has a duty to ensure either that he has cleared funds in his clients' account for the settlement of such a conveyancing transaction or that any cheque which he has received for his client will be met by the paying bank. There is a principle that a cheque drawn by the solicitor acting for a purchaser on his client bank account and handed over in settlement in a conveyancing transaction to the solicitor acting for the seller should not be stopped except in exceptional circumstances.
>
> Such exceptional circumstances would arise in the event of circumstances amounting to breach of contract on the part of the seller, as for example when the purchasers are unable to receive vacant possession or if the subjects have been destroyed (and these circumstances are contrary to the terms of the missives) or in the event of a postal settlement where the disposition which is delivered contains a defect in execution.'

In this unfortunate event, the purchasers' solicitors would be well advised to inform the Law Society before they stop their cheque.

15 1981 JLSS 357.

It is, however, far more common these days for funds to be transmitted by way of BACS or CHAPS transfer. Cleared funds must be in the client's account before this can be instructed. If receiving funds by way of cheque from a client, the cheque must be banked several days in advance of completion to clear in time.

11.7.2   Council Tax and Rates

Apportionment of council tax, for residential properties and non-domestic rates, for commercial properties are dealt with by the relevant local authority. A notification of the change of ownership is prepared by the seller's solicitors, approved by the purchaser's solicitors and sent to the local authority at settlement.

11.7.3   Notice of Change of Landlord

In investment purchases of commercial property, the occupational tenants may be oblivious to the fact that the identity of their landlord is about to change. There is no need or requirement to involve the tenants in the sale, but once ownership changes hands, there is an administrative and management requirement to ensure that future rents and other payments are made to the new owner, or its managing agents, and for future interactions between landlord and tenants, the tenants should know who to contact or send intimations to for the future.

Accordingly, the seller's solicitor and the purchaser's solicitor will adjust draft notifications of the change of landlords to be sent to the tenants at completion. Either the seller's solicitor or the purchaser's solicitor can deal with this. Each party has an interest in ensuring that the new arrangements are put in place. The following style notification (which forms a Part of the Schedule to the PSG Offer to Sell Investment Property) is suitable for this purpose:

'To: [Insert name of Tenants]

Dear Sirs

[ ] ('Property')

On behalf of our clients, [ ], [incorporated under the Companies Acts (Registered Number [ ]) and having their registered office at [ ] we intimate to you ('**Tenants**') that, as from [ ] 20[ ], our clients have sold their interest as your landlords in the Property to [ ], [incorporated under the Companies Acts (Registered Number [ ]) and having their registered office at [ ]] ('**Purchaser**').

Future rent demands will be issued to you by or on behalf of the Purchaser and future communications concerning any matter arising from the letting should be addressed to the Purchaser or their managing agents, namely [ ].

[We also intimate that we have received a retrocession from [ ], [as agent and trustee], of their right, title and interest to the rent and other sums receivable in terms of the assignation of rents granted by [ ] in their favour dated [ ] and created on [ ] (a copy of which accompanies this letter).]

This letter is enclosed in duplicate. Kindly post the duplicate, with the docquet on it duly signed, [using the accompanying pre-paid addressed envelope] to [ ], the solicitors acting for the Purchaser.

Yours faithfully'

These notices are usually sent in duplicate, with a receipt docquet endorsed on the duplicate for the tenant to sign in acknowledgement, and return.

11.7.4 Common Charges

Where a flat in a tenement building is sold, any property manager or factor (if there is one) should be asked by the seller's agents to apportion the common charges for maintenance of the building between the parties. This can be done when the property manager or factor is informed of the change of ownership by the sellers' solicitors. In modern practice it is usual for the property manager or factor to ask an incoming owner for a deposit to meet future charges. This deposit is set against these charges. Purchasers' solicitors should ask to see the latest common charges receipt.

Practice seems to vary geographically in relation to factors. It is common in Glasgow, for example, for residential tenement buildings to have a factor appointed to deal with common repairs and routine matters. Such arrangements are less common for Edinburgh tenements however. It is more typical for commercial properties in multiple ownership or occupation to have a property manager, who will deal with matters or repair and maintenance and collect the costs from the owners or occupiers through a service charge arrangement.

Over the years the activities of some factors have received a poor press, with complaints of poor service and high costs. This has resulted in the Property Factors (Scotland) Act 2011.

The 2011 Act is designed to protect homeowners who contract with property factors by establishing a public register of property factors in Scotland and making it a criminal offence for a property factor to operate without being registered. A mandatory code of conduct is to be introduced setting out minimum standards of practice and training required of registered property factors[16]. A Homeowner Housing Panel was established to deal with disputes between homeowners and property factors.

11.7.5 Interest

When settlement takes place properly on the agreed date of entry, the question of interest does not arise – that is to say when the full purchase price is paid by the purchaser and the property is made available with the disposition, the titles and the keys. Where, however, one party or the other cannot meet their obligation, the question of interest arises and this will generally be regulated by the provisions of the missives – see paras 6.10.14 and 6.14.3. If there is any delay that results in an interest payment being required then the parties will need to agree the amount of the additional payment due at settlement/completion. It will usually fall to the seller's solicitor to do the calculation, and agree this with the purchaser's solicitor. It is sensible to work out the daily amount, so that it is clear what sum will be due on any particular day. See para 12.4.4 for further detail.

11.7.6 Bridging Loans

If the date of entry arrives and the purchaser's funds are not yet available, it may be possible for the purchasers to ask their bank for a bridging loan to avoid being in default on the date of entry. However, if the purchasers have not yet sold their house or do not have an approved offer of mortgage,

---

16 A consultation on the proposed code was published in August 2015. See www.gov.scot/ Publications/2015/08/6563.

the bank may not be willing to provide 'open-ended bridging' (see para 12.4.3). For this reason it is essential to ensure that availability of funds is certain.

11.7.7 Settlement/Completion

If funds are available in good time, and settlement is being dealt with by way of cheque, then settlement can usually be effected by post – ie the purchaser's solicitor send the cheque by post or DX/Legal Post the night before the date of entry. The settlement documents are similarly sent to the purchaser's solicitors overnight. On the day of settlement, a phone call should confirm receipt by each solicitor of the respective items, and the seller's solicitor then authorises release of the keys. Alternatively, settlement in person can be arranged, in which case the tradition is that the purchaser's solicitor goes to the seller's solicitor. More often than not, however, settlements nowadays are carried out by post overnight or by courier on the day.

To get round the difficulty of the cheque or the disposition reaching the other solicitor before the other part is received, and being misused, the sender of the cheque or disposition will usually present it on the basis that it is held as undelivered until the corresponding settlement items are received. The Law Society guidelines[17] on settlement cheques or funds sent electronically being held as undelivered is as follows:

> **'Cheques and Electronic Funds to be Held as Undelivered**
>
> Where postal settlement of a transaction is envisaged, good practice is to agree in advance the arrangements for the sending of and intromission with funds and other settlement items.
>
> It is recognised that in a postal settlement it is appropriate for the buyer's solicitor to send a cheque to be held as undelivered either pending fulfilment of conditions in the missives or pending confirmation that the solicitor is in funds and the cheque can be encashed. This practice avoids alternative courses of action such as bridging or effecting

---

17 Law Society of Scotland Rules and Guidance, Division C: Conveyancing, Guidance, Cheques and Electronic Funds to be Held as Undelivered. See www.lawscot.org.uk/rules-and-guidance/section-f-guidance-relating-to-particular-types-of-work/division-c-conveyancing/guidance/cheques-and-electronic-funds-to-be-held-as-undelivered.

settlement in person, all of which can be viewed as adding expense, though agents should consider the alternative of electronic transfer of funds (which may have certain advantages and disadvantages on which see below). Assuming trust between practitioners, arrangements which rely on mutual acceptance of an undertaking not to cash the cheque or intromit with funds sent electronically can be made. This is analogous to the customary sending of the settlement cheque to be held as undelivered pending dispatch of a duly executed disposition, etc.

It is also important to bear in mind that the question of conditional delivery of a cheque is dealt with in s. 21 of the Bills of Exchange Act 1882.

Where loan papers are issued late in a transaction, there may be consequent urgency to deal with remaining practicalities before settlement. In these circumstances it is acceptable for a purchasing agent to seek to impose unilaterally a condition making delivery and encashment of a settlement cheque conditional upon the purchasing agent authorising that. Where this happens the selling agent is not entitled to cash the cheque in breach of such condition provided that it was sent subject to the words "to be held as undelivered". The Professional Practice Committee and the Council confirm that where money or deeds are sent to be held as undelivered pending purification of a condition, they should be so held if the condition is not purified. Settlement will not take place until they can be treated as delivered, with consequent penalty interest if provided for in the missives. The matter is one of practice between agents rather than of law.

When sending funds by electronic transfer, it is good practice to agree in advance that those funds will be held as undelivered pending fulfilment of certain conditions.

In the case of either cheque settlement or settlement by electronic transfer, if the buyer's solicitor does not receive the titles, keys etc. in return for a client's account cheque or electronic settlement which has been sent to be held as undelivered he can either demand the return of a cheque or electronic settlement or stop the cheque (in extreme circumstances). A seller's solicitor can also protect the seller by attaching conditions to deeds etc sent by post, including a condition about interest on the price if settlement has been delayed.

Traditionally, when a selling solicitor received and banked another solicitor's client account cheque, he could write his own client account cheques to redeem his client's loan or settle his client's purchase on the same day. Problems are encountered very occasionally if the solicitor receiving the cheque banks at the same branch of the same bank as the solicitor sending the cheque although that is rare.

Since the introduction of the cheque clearing process known as 2-4-6 there is a risk that the cheque sent out will be presented for payment at the sender's bank before the cheque paid in has cleared. The Professional Practice department at the Society has received a number of telephone calls from solicitors affected in this way.

These problems may be surmounted by either:

(1) clients arranging short term bridging loans, or

(2) solicitors arranging a temporary facility with their own bank that would allow the bank to transfer sufficient funds into the client bank account to meet the presentation of an outgoing cheque where the incoming cheque has still to clear. Any interest payable could be charged to the client although that would have to be specified in the relevant Terms of Business.

If neither of these options is adopted, a third option namely

(3) settlement by electronic transfer is suggested to avoid the possibility of a shortfall in the client account that may in turn lead to a failure to comply with Rule B6 (the Accounts etc rules).

If a selling solicitor is also purchasing for his client on the same day and wishes the sale to be settled by electronic transfer the selling solicitor should put a clause in the missives requiring the sale to be settled electronically. That will be subject to agreement by the buyer, but it must be in the missives or it cannot be insisted upon.

Subject to these considerations, the Professional Practice Committee remains of the view that settlement by cheque between solicitors is in both clients' interests as the cheque can be sent in advance to be held as undelivered pending delivery of relevant items and/or confirmation that the sender is in funds, and the disposition can be sent in advance subject to the seller's conditions.

LENDERS and CLIENTS

The Committee agreed however that so far as settlement with the client and the lender are concerned the seller's agent should ascertain in advance whether the seller would prefer to meet the cost of an electronic transfer of funds or opt for the issue of a cheque in relation to (a) redemption of the loan (if the method is not prescribed by the lender) and (b) remit of the free proceeds of sale to the seller. Such instructions will of course be subject to the solicitor ensuring that there are sufficient cleared funds to meet whatever method of payment is adopted.

ENGLAND and WALES

If a client is purchasing a property in England or Wales out of the proceeds of sale of a property in Scotland, it is important to ascertain the requirements for settling the purchase at the earliest possible stage. Purchase and sale transactions routinely settle by electronic transfer in England and Wales and the client's English or Welsh Solicitor will assume that he will receive funds by electronic transfer. If there will not be sufficient time for a cheque to clear before funds are required in England or Wales, the selling solicitor should explain that to the client and conclude the bargain for the sale on the basis that settlement will by electronic transfer or advise the client that he will need to arrange temporary bridging facilities to await cleared funds. Failure to address these issues at an early stage is likely to lead to a dissatisfied client and a possible complaint to the Scottish Legal Complaints Commission.'

Current practice is that, invariably, the solicitors will have agreed either by phone or e-mail that items and funds are to be held as undelivered in this reciprocal way.

It is common for bank-to-bank transfers of funds, and the norm in commercial transactions. A CHAPS (Clearing House Automated Payment System, or telegraphic transfer) payment is arranged from the account of the purchaser's solicitor to the account of the seller's solicitor. Again, this obviously necessitates the purchaser's solicitors having cleared funds in their clients' account, since the removal of funds from one account to the other takes place that day – no period of clearing is required. Bank-to-bank transfers do not happen instantaneously, however, and waiting for funds to arrive can be a stressful part of the completion day for all concerned, as the process sometimes takes several hours.

Careful planning is required and the instruction should be given to the bank as early as possible.

When the settlement items change hands, this amounts to delivery of the disposition in its technical sense. Before the disposition is registered, the fact of delivery can be an important issue for the purchaser, particularly if insolvency of the seller intervenes.

11.7.8 VAT

The rules on whether VAT is payable on the purchase of commercial property are complex but the basic rule is that no VAT is payable unless:

- the property is less than three years old;
- the type of commercial property falls within one of a number of special categories (a common example being where the property comprises parking facilities); or
- the seller of the property has opted to tax the property for VAT.

In any of these situations, VAT will be payable on the price of the property at the standard rate which is currently 20%. However, if the sale of the property constitutes a Transfer of a Going Concern (TOGC), the purchase will fall outwith the scope of VAT as the transfer of a business (namely, the letting of the property), resulting in no liability to VAT on the price (see para 6.14.4). If VAT is payable on the price (only in commercial transactions as VAT is not payable on residential purchases) then the seller should produce a VAT receipt for the purchaser, to allow it to offset the VAT in its VAT return. The seller's solicitor should ask his client for this in good time for completion.

11.7.9 Letter of Non-crystallisation

When purchasing from a company that has granted a floating charge, the seller's solicitors should deliver a letter of non-crystallisation from the floating charge holder dated not more than one or two days prior to the date of settlement/completion. See paras 8.18.10(v) and 10.6.5.

LAND AND BUILDINGS TRANSACTION TAX

11.8 Since 1 April 2015, purchases of property above a certain price level have attracted a tax known as Land and Buildings Transaction

Tax (LBTT), which replaced its precursor, Stamp Duty Land Tax (SDLT) in Scotland. This was introduced under the Land and Buildings Transaction Tax (Scotland) Act 2013. SDLT still applies to property transactions in England and Wales, and will, in some exceptional circumstances (where the contract for sale has been concluded prior to 1 May 2012 (the date of Royal Assent of the Scotland Act 2012)) continue to apply in Scotland. LBTT operates in a similar way to SDLT, although there are a number of differences in the fine detail. The principal significant difference, however, is the way in which the tax is charged: instead of the 'slab tax' approach of SDLT (where the highest applicable rate of tax is charged on all of the price), LBTT is charged on a 'progressive' basis, ie charged only on the proportion of the price within, and at the different rates set for, the relevant band or bands. The theory is that the amount of tax paid is accordingly more closely related to the value or price of the property. This approach subsequently appealed to the UK Government, as they altered the charging regime for SDLT on residential properties in December 2014, to adopt this progressive approach. Rates for SDLT and LBTT on residential properties are different, however, and there are also different rates of LBTT for commercial properties.

The main elements of the basis of charge are:

- LBTT is payable on a land transaction where a chargeable interest is acquired, although some land transactions are exempt from charge;

- the charge is based on a percentage of the chargeable consideration;

- the liability to pay the charge falls on the buyer (which definition includes tenants, assignees etc); and

- a land transaction return (which is made on an online submission form to Revenue Scotland – see para 11.8.6)must be made within 30 days of the effective date and 'arrangements satisfactory' (see para 11.8.7) for payment of the tax due must be in place.

This is the technical stuff:

11.8.1 Land Transaction

A land transaction is any acquisition of a chargeable interest ie:

- a real right or other interest in or over land in Scotland (not including land below mean low water mark); or

- the benefit of an obligation, restriction or condition affecting the value of any such right or interest,

other than an exempt interest, which is: any security interest (ie a standard security) and certain exempt interests in relation to alternative property finance arrangements This means that the purchase of land or the taking of a lease of land will be a land transaction. A land transaction is an exempt transaction if there is no chargeable consideration for the transaction. Most leases of residential property and licences to occupy are exempt transactions, as are transactions where the purchaser is a government entity including Scottish Ministers, the Scottish Parliamentary Corporate Body, a Minister of the Crown, the Corporate Officer of the House of Lords, and the Corporate Officer of the House of Commons[18].

11.8.2 Chargeable Consideration

Chargeable consideration amounts to any consideration given in money or money's worth given directly or indirectly by the buyer, or on the buyer's behalf, and includes any VAT actually paid. In other words: the price or a premium paid by a tenant or assignee. A just and reasonable apportionment must be made of any consideration that does not relate only to the land transaction (eg apportionment to fittings). If non-monetary consideration is paid, it is valued at market value as at the effective date of the transaction.

11.8.3 Definition of Buyer

The 2013 Act refers to 'buyer'. The buyer is the person who acquires the subject matter of the transaction and has given consideration for, or is a party to, the transaction. The seller is the person who disposes of the subject matter of the transaction. The subject matter of the transaction is the chargeable interest acquired or disposed of. The expressions translate into lease transactions so that the 'buyer' will also be the tenant under a new lease; the assignee of a lease; and the landlord in a renunciation.

18 Schedule 1 to the Land and Buildings Transaction Tax (Scotland) Act 2013).

11.8.4 Effective Date

Where a contract is entered into which will be completed by a conveyance of the property, the contract itself is not the land transaction which is taxable. The effective date is determined by the following rules:

If a transaction is completed without having been previously substantially performed, then the contract and the completion are treated as a single transaction and the effective date of the transaction is the date of completion. However, if the contract is substantially performed without being completed, (eg if the purchaser were allowed to take entry to the property, before the disposition is delivered) the contract is treated as if it were the transaction provided for in the contract. The effective date of the transaction is when the contract is substantially performed. However, where the contract is subsequently completed by a conveyance, both the contract and the transaction effected on completion are notifiable transactions, and LBTT is chargeable on the completion to the extent (if any) that the amount of tax chargeable on it is greater than the amount of tax chargeable on the contract. In most cases there will be no additional tax, as the consideration will not have changed.

A contract is substantially performed if:

- the buyer or a person connected with the buyer takes possession of the whole, or substantially the whole, of the subject matter of the contract; or

- a substantial amount of the consideration is paid or provided, or

- there is an assignation, sub-sale or other transaction (relating to the whole or part of the subject-matter of the contract) as a result of which someone other than the original buyer becomes entitled to call for a conveyance (ie in effect, a sub-sale)[19]. This is different to the position under SDLT, although there are provisions for limited sub-sale relief under LBTT where development is to take place[20].

---

19 Section 14(1)(c) of the 2013 Act. There is some controversy over the interpretation of section 14(1)(c).
20 See Revenue Scotland guidance on sub-sale development relief at www.revenue.scot/land-buildings-transaction-tax/guidance/lbtt-legislation-guidance/exemptions-reliefs/lbtt3010/lbtt3044.

11.8.5 Practical Effects

It is important to be familiar with the concepts of LBTT – especially 'effective date' and 'substantial performance' as these will trigger not just liability on the part of your client but also the requirement for action on your part. Actually, the subtleties of 'substantial performance' tend to come into play more in lease transactions, but might, from time to time, be an issue in sale/purchase transactions. The usual situation, however, will be that settlement or completion will trigger the requirement to make an LBTT return and pay any tax that is due.

As the liability to pay any LBTT that is due falls on the purchaser, it is up to the purchaser's solicitor to ensure that they have sufficient funds at settlement to meet the tax, since it is not possible to register the disposition in favour of the purchaser, without confirming to the Keeper, that an LBTT return has been made to Revenue Scotland.

11.8.6 LBTT Submission

The LBTT application form must be submitted to Revenue Scotland no later than 30 days after the effective date of the transaction. The due date is known as the 'filing date' and there are penalties for late filing.

Although a paper form of LBTT return is available, in practice, Revenue Scotland is keen to encourage online submission unless the person making the submission does not have access to the internet, or there is a prolonged system outage. Online submission is available by registering to use the Revenue Scotland online portal. For those who have made SDLT submissions (whether paper or online), the good news is that the LBTT submission is a much simpler affair. Objectively, the LBTT form is much easier to complete and the online portal is comparatively easy to use, allowing the saving of drafts and the ability to download a PDF of the finished form, and save it to the relevant matter file.

It is the legal responsibility of the buyer in any transaction to ensure that the LBTT return is correct and complete. Section 36(1) of the 2013 Act requires the purchaser to sign a Declaration to that effect.

That is obviously not possible when the buyer's solicitor is submitting electronically; however, section 36(2) of the 2013 Act permits submission by the agent provided that:

(i)   the buyer (or each of them) has authorised the agent to complete the land transaction return on its behalf;

(ii)   the buyer (or each of them) makes a declaration that, with the exception of the effective date, the information provided in the return is to the best of his knowledge correct and complete, and

(iii)   the land transaction return includes a declaration by the agent that the effective date provided in the return is to the best of his knowledge correct.

Accordingly, although you can be authorised by your client to submit the LBTT return on its behalf, you require written authorisation to that effect. This can be achieved either by having the client sign the declaration in the return, or for the client to make a separate declaration. In either case, this should be obtained and placed on the file before submission.

Returns completed on the Revenue Scotland Online portal can be printed off in advance of submission for signature or approval by the client. If you are unable to complete the effective date at that time, you should advise the client that you will insert the effective date, once it is known, on their behalf in the final version that is submitted to Revenue Scotland.

From a practical point of view this means either:

● printing off the form and sending it to the client by post, or

● sending it electronically by attaching a PDF of the form to an e-mail,

then:

● either having the client sign it and return it to you by post or email (by a PDF of the signed version); or

● having the client sign a letter of authority which can also be sent either by post or e-mail.

Whichever approach is used, a PDF of the forms should be saved to the client matter file. It is particularly important to ensure that you have a copy of the signed client approval copy or approval letter stored on the file.

When the effective date is inserted and the actual online submission made, the final version of the form should be printed and also saved to the matter. In other words, the matter should have copies not only of the client-approved version, but also of the final submitted version.

As soon as online submission is made, you should receive an acknowledgement from Revenue Scotland. This is evidence that the submission has been made and can be exhibited to eg the lenders' solicitors as evidence that the LBTT return has been submitted. Payment must follow (see para 11.8.7 below), so there is no need to provide undertakings to complete the LBTT process, as submission by the agent commits them to payment.

There have been a few instances where payment has not followed online submission in time. Revenue Scotland have made it clear that persistent offenders will run the risk of not being able to rely on the 'arrangements satisfactory' procedures, although there is no suggestion that they would be withdrawn wholesale. On the whole, the process appears to be working well.

11.8.7 Payment and 'Arrangements Satisfactory'

The buyer is responsible for paying any tax due at the same time as the LBTT return for the notifiable transaction is made to Revenue Scotland, regardless of whether the return is made on paper or online. In this last respect the arrangements differ from those under SDLT, which permitted a grace period of 30 days from the date of online submission within which to make payment of the tax. Under LBTT, making the submission and paying the tax must be done virtually simultaneously.

However, any tax due is treated as paid if arrangements satisfactory to Revenue Scotland are made for payment of tax at the same time as the LBTT return is made to them[21].

Depending on circumstances, payment can be made by cheque, credit card, debit card, BACS or CHAPS or Direct Debit.

When an online submission is made, a unique nine character Transaction Reference (which starts with 'RS') will be displayed on the screen. This reference must be quoted when making payments in relation to the transaction or when contacting Revenue Scotland about the transaction. The nine-digit transaction reference number is not relevant for paper returns, as they must be accompanied by a cheque in payment of the amount of LBTT that is due.

21 See section 40(4) of the 2013 Act.

11.8.7(i) Payment by cheque – paper returns only

For LBTT returns completed and submitted by paper, Revenue Scotland will only accept payment by cheque, and a separate cheque is required for each return. Cheques should be made payable to Revenue Scotland and the amount must exactly match the rounded amount on the tax return. However the LBTT form and the cheque should be sent to the Registers of Scotland at either their Edinburgh or Glasgow office

11.8.7(ii) Online submission

For LBTT returns made online, Revenue Scotland will accept payment by direct debit, BACS/CHAPS, cheque, credit card or debit card.

Cheques should be made payable to Revenue Scotland and the unique nine character transaction reference number must be written on the reverse of the cheque. Cheques must be received by the third working day after submission, and sent to Registers of Scotland at either their Edinburgh or Glasgow office.

BACS or CHAPS payments and 'Faster Payments' should be made to the Revenue Scotland bank account[22] and must quote the unique nine-character transaction reference as the payment reference. When giving instructions to your cashroom to make payment be sure to let them know that the transaction reference number must be quoted.

A separate payment must be made for each transaction and the latest 'payment date' must be a banking day.

If the return is submitted before the effective date, the 'payment date' must be no later than the fifth working day after the effective date.

If the return is submitted on or after the effective date, the 'payment date' must be no later than the fifth working day after the submission date, or the last working day which is, or precedes, the thirtieth calendar day after the effective date, if this is earlier. If you want to make payment of LBTT by direct debit, you will have to contact Revenue Scotland to set up these arrangements. The majority of solicitors use BACS or CHAPS, as these payment methods are within their control, whereas direct debit passes control of debiting your account to Revenue Scotland, and therefore has considerable risk management considerations.

---

22 Guidance on how to pay LBTT, and Revenue Scotland bank account details are available at
   https://www.revenue.scot/land-buildings-transaction-tax/guidance/how-to/pay-lbtt.

In both cases (paper or online submission), payment of registration dues to Registers of Scotland must be paid separately.

CHECKLIST

11.9 The PSG Completion Checklist is reproduced here with kind permission of the PSG. It has been compiled for use with any property transaction and you will need to tailor the checklist for each individual transaction.

The missives will contain details of all the documents to be delivered at settlement. Ensure that all documents that the seller has undertaken to deliver are included in the list.

The responsibility for producing most of the documents will fall on the seller although the purchaser's solicitors will be responsible for producing the SAF or Application Form for registering the disposition and any new standard security and for the LBTT forms.

While the checklist attempts to cover most eventualities, it does not purport to be appropriate or sufficient for any particular transaction, which will need to be carefully considered on a case by case basis.

COMPLETION CHECKLIST for: [Name of Property]			
	PROPERTY DOCUMENTS	*RESPONSIBILITY*	*COMMENTS*
	Disposition/Assignation (with landlord's consent)/ Lease (the 'Deed')		
	Application form for registering Deed and SAF if necessary for registration of any new burdens/servitudes against benefited property, cheques for recording/ registration dues (including fee for dual registration if necessary)		
	LBTT Return and payment of any LBTT due.		

COMPLETION CHECKLIST *for: [Name of Property]*			
	PROPERTY DOCUMENTS	RESPONSIBILITY	COMMENTS
	Particulars of signing for Deed [and evidence of authorised signatories power to sign document or any other authority needed eg Power of Attorney ('signing authority')]		
	Title deeds/Land Certificate		
	[Discharge/Deed of Restriction of existing standard security, particulars of signing and any signing authority required]		
	Charges search & company file search showing where relevant directors and/or company secretary who have signed Deed are duly appointed		
	Legal continuation report including personal searches and searches in community interests and agricultural tenant's interests sections of the RCIL if appropriate]		
	[Any other searches due in terms of missives eg Plans Report, Property Enquiry Certificates, coal mining search, search in the register of insolvencies]		
	Original planning and building control documents		
	CDM Health & Safety File		
	[Maintenance agreements/ operating manuals]		
	Energy Performance Certificate		

COMPLETION CHECKLIST for: [Name of Property]			
	PROPERTY DOCUMENTS	RESPONSIBILITY	COMMENTS
	[Collateral warranties, particulars of signing and any signing authority required]		
	Letters of non-crystallisation of any floating charges		
	Notice of change of ownership to the rating authority		
	Signatories certificate		
	Capital Allowances Election (s.198 Capital Allowances Act 2001) for fixed plant and machinery.		
	LEASE DOCUMENTS (delete if no occupational leases)		
	Principal or extract leases and lease documents (including any subleases and sublease documents)		
	Notifications of change of ownership to tenants		
	[Back letters due to be granted by purchasers to existing tenants]		
	[Assignation of any guarantees, signing particulars and any signing authority required]		
	[Assignation of any rent deposits, signing particulars and any signing authority required]		
	[Assignation of any service contracts, signing particulars and any signing authority required]		

COMPLETION CHECKLIST for: [Name of Property]			
	PROPERTY DOCUMENTS	*RESPONSIBILITY*	*COMMENTS*
	FINANCE DOCUMENTS		
	Completion Statement		
	[VAT invoice]		
	[Insert details of any TOGC documents which remain outstanding]		
	Account details where purchase monies to be sent		
	SECURITY DOCUMENTS (delete if no security being granted)		
	New standard security, particulars of signing and any signing authority required application form and any registration dues		
	[Retrocession of any assignation of rents, signing particulars and any signing authority required]		
	[Assignation of rent, signing particulars and any signing authority required]		
	[Intimations of assignation of rent]		
	[Board minute authorising granting of standard security]		
	[Ranking Agreement, particulars of signing and any signing authority required]		
	Undertaking(s) to submit LBTT Return and any LBTT payable, and deal with any requisitions raised by Revenue Scotland		

COMPLETION CHECKLIST for: [Name of Property]			
	PROPERTY DOCUMENTS	*RESPONSIBILITY*	*COMMENTS*
	OTHER		
	[Insert here any other documents or things to be handed over at settlement in terms of the missives]		
	Keys		

Chapter 12

The Collapsing Contract

'Contract: an agreement that is binding on the weaker party' —
Frederick Sawyer

THE THREE 'Rs'

12.1 Contracts are, in effect, private legislative acts. As we have already seen in Chapter 6, once a contract is agreed, the law requires it to be observed by the parties. The courts are traditionally very reluctant to depart from this principle unless there are very exceptional and compelling reasons to do otherwise.

You need to understand the legal position of the other party's failure in order to understand the remedies available, so let's be clear about the 'three Rs' in contract law:

12.1.1 Repudiation

This means to indicate clearly, by words or acts, that the repudiator will not perform the obligation, but having no right to withhold or refuse performance. A repudiation is a wrongful rejection or renunciation of the contract. It does not end the contract but gives the other party an option to accept the repudiation, rescind and claim damages for the breach.

12.1.2 Recission

From the verb: to rescind, this means the 'un-making' of a contract, bringing it to an end, at least so far as concerns the future performance of primary obligations, in response to a repudiation or material breach by the other party. Recission puts the parties back to the position that they were in before the contract was made.

12.1.3 Resile

To resile means to withdraw from a contract lawfully, in the exercise of a right to do so, but not in response to a repudiation or breach. For example a party may be unable to 'purify' (fulfil) a suspensive condition, entitling the other to resile. The parties effectively 'call it quits'.

There is a lot of confusion between resiling and rescinding and sometimes they are, incorrectly, used interchangeably. However, the difference is this: if you look at Condition 2.4 of the PSG Offer to Sell Investment Property (see para 6.14.3) you will see that the seller is entitled to *rescind* the contract if the purchaser has effectively repudiated the contract by not paying on time. A damages claim would normally follow recission. In Condition 7.3 of the Offer (see para 6.14.11) however, the purchaser is entitled to *resile* from the contract, should the seller's title disclose any aspect that is materially prejudicial to the purchaser. There is no obligation in the contract or at common law to make good any losses of the seller.

Should you find yourself in a collapsing contract situation, there are remedies available to your client but which one to use will be largely dictated by the circumstances.

WHAT IS THE CONTRACTUAL POSITION?

12.2 First, review the missives. The Scottish Standard Clauses, the PSG Offers to Sell and almost all other standard and bespoke missives will contain a detailed clause, setting out what is to happen if settlement does not proceed as planned.

It is important to note that both the Scottish Standard Clauses and the PSG Offers to Sell contain an 'entire agreement' clause. This is important to the interpretation of the contract, as it will operate to exclude any extraneous evidence as to the parties' intention in reaching the agreement. The courts will only intervene in cases of misrepresentation or if the contract is unclear as to what is meant. Thus in *Houldsworth v Gordon Cumming*[1], a plan used by the parties during negotiations was found to be admissible by the House of Lords to define what the missives meant by 'the estate of Dallas', when this description did not feature in the title deeds.

---

1   [1910] SC (HL) 49.

It is usual, and it is the position in Clause 18 of the Scottish Standard Clauses (see para 6.10.19), that the parties agree that the price has to be paid in exchange for a signed disposition in favour of the purchaser, good and marketable title, vacant possession and the other items agreed to be deliverable on the Date of Settlement. Clauses 12 and 13 set out what is to happen in the event of a breach by either party (see paras 6.10.13 and 6.10.14).

If the seller is unable to settle on the date of entry, there is no obligation on the purchaser either to take entry or pay interest[2]. If, however, the purchaser wishes to take entry, they have the option to consign the price on deposit with a bank[3] (although it would not be possible to consign the price if the purchase is being funded by a lender: the lender will usually only release funds on condition that its standard security is being presented for registration immediately). When the money is on deposit neither party has control over it, without the consent of the other.

WHEN ARE YOU DUE TO PERFORM?

12.3 There are three dates that you need to be aware of:

(1) The Date of Entry is referred to in the Scottish Standard Clauses as a necessary definition in the covering offer which will incorporate the clauses. The covering offer must refer to a specific date and may provide '… or such other date as may be mutually agreed in writing'.

(2) The 'due date' is defined as the later of:
- the Date of Entry; or
- the date on which payment of the price was due having regard to the circumstances of the case, including any entitlement to withhold payment owing to the non-performance by the seller.

(3) The Date of Settlement means the date on which settlement is actually effected whether that is the Date of Entry or not.

These could all be the same day, but sometimes they are not. So the date of entry is when settlement should take place, the due date is when the

---

2 *Bowie v Semple's Executors* [1978] SLT (Sh Ct) 9.
3 *Prestwick Cinema Co v Gardiner* [1951] SC 98.

liability to pay interest or damages arises and the date of settlement is the end point, when the price plus any interest or damages is paid.

In the PSG offers to Sell, 'Date of Settlement' is replaced with 'Completion', and the expression 'due date' is not used.

REMEDIES

12.4 There are a number of options that may be open to the parties, when matters start to go awry.

12.4.1 Non-performance by the Seller

Before you take any action, you should ascertain whether there has been any non-performance by the seller that would entitle non-payment by the purchaser. This would mean that the due date for payment is, in fact, after the date of entry.

In practice, non-performance by the seller is likely to manifest itself long before settlement: in standard missives, the seller is obliged to produce a number of items on which the purchaser has to satisfy itself within the agreed timescale, failing which the purchaser can resile. Once the seller has produced these satisfactorily, there should be no reason why the seller should not be in a position to settle.

It would not be unknown for the seller's solicitor, for whatever reason, to exhibit the disclosed documents too close to the agreed date of entry for the purchaser's solicitor to satisfy themselves within the timescale set out in standard missives. In that case the purchaser's solicitor would be entitled to claim that there was non-performance on the date of entry, and that consequently the due date would be once the appropriate period (eg 10 working days) has elapsed. Communication between solicitors is the key here, and often a mutually acceptable position can be agreed.

12.4.2 Renegotiate the Missives

You may have noted from the definition of the Date of Entry, the door is not closed on re-arranging the date, provided the other party agrees. The next option, if a default looks likely is, therefore, to explain to the other party's solicitor the reason for the anticipated delay and seek to amend the date of entry in the missives. The solicitor would need to take clients' instructions. Some parties will take a generous view and try to accommodate your client's request as a matter of goodwill and not wishing to stray into the default minefield, others may insist on sticking to the letter of the contract, as they are entitled to do, often because they have to co-ordinate with an onward transaction.

Remember that when acting in a residential transaction, you are dealing with real people in what, for some, can be a very stressful situation. A house move has to be meticulously planned well in advance and your purchasing client will care little for the legal niceties when they are sitting in the street in front of their new home, surrounded by all their furniture and belongings. Similarly, a client purchasing commercial property may need immediate entry to start or continue trading. Many sellers are also purchasers and vice versa. Problems at completion may also have a knock-on impact on other transactions or arrangements with removals or fitting out, for example.

Neither party will want long-drawn out litigation, but will look to you to provide a practical remedy. Delays are possibly slightly less stressful for the commercial purchaser, unless the property is being acquired for owner occupation and they have to be out of their existing premises by a deadline. But although it may be more expensive than they planned, putting office furniture into storage or leaving it in a removal van overnight does not have the same personal impact on a business and their employees, who still have homes to go to.

12.4.3 Bridging Finance

The next practical solution, should a rescheduling not be available, is for the purchaser to ask his bank for a 'bridging loan', that is to say, a short-term loan, usually given on the basis of the probability of the borrower receiving funds on a certain future date. The purchaser can say to his bank: 'My building society loan is coming through next week and I'll repay you then'. It should be emphasised that bridging loans are expensive and should only be taken on a short-term basis. The bank may ask for a hefty 'arrangement fee' for arranging the loan which may make these loans unattractive, except in an emergency.

Banks are not, however, so keen on lending against a payment on an uncertain future date; for example, if the purchaser is still selling his own house and has not found a buyer yet, his bank may not be willing to provide open-ended bridging finance. Banks like their loans to be short term and repayment to be certain, unless they make a specified arrangement as in a 'personal loan'. This provides for regular payments to account, and the banks charge more handsomely for a personal loan.

At the time of writing, interest base rates have been at an historically low level of 0.5% for a number of years. Banks are risk averse and an arrangement fee could be as high as £1,000 for bridging finance. Your client might consider other options, maybe an inter-family loan or an inter-group loan[4]. We would never advocate that a party breaches a contract intentionally, but it might be the case that default interest would be cheaper than bridging, especially for less than two weeks' delay. Some sellers may be prepared to delay and collect default interest. This sort of situation needs to be managed carefully, and tempers can become a bit frayed in these circumstances. Again, we cannot over-emphasise that communication between the solicitors is crucial.

12.4.4 Damages or Penalty

If none of these practical remedies can be agreed, and the payment price is still not forthcoming, the purchaser will be in default on the date of entry. Both the Scottish Standard Clauses and the PSG Offer to Sell make provision for what is to happen in the event of default by the purchaser and in the Scottish Standard Clause, the default of the seller, too). See commentary in respect of these clauses at paras 6.10.13, 6.10.14 and 6.14.3. Provisions of this type in contracts have to be carefully drafted to ensure that they are not perceived as a penalty clause, which would be unenforceable, as opposed to a liquidated damages clause which usually would not.

Parties can agree in the contract the basis on which damages will be calculated in the event of a breach. Often, to avoid disputes in quantifying the amount of the actual loss, such a clause sets out in advance what the defaulting party must pay. These are known as liquidated damages clauses, and are generally regarded as enforceable, if the damages are

---

4   In cases of wilful breach, the court will be less inclined to treat a harsh commercial remedy as unconscionable. See *Forrest & Barr v Henderson, Coulbourn & Co* [1869] 8 M 187 per Lord Neaves at p 202.

proportionate to the loss. Such clauses assume that the aggrieved party will suffer loss because of the breach, and this type of provision provides a basis for calculating what the parties agree will be paid as damages for that loss. If, however, the purpose of the provision is to punish the defaulting party for his failure to perform, or frighten him into performing, then it is likely it will be seen by the court to be a penalty provision in the strict sense and will be unenforceable.

Whether a clause is enforceable as a liquidated damages clause or unenforceable as a penalty clause will depend on the facts and circumstances, at the time of entering into the contract, not when the breach occurred, and also on what was intended by the parties. What the clause is called in the contract is not necessarily a material factor, since if the effect of a provision is to penalise, then the fact that the contract describes it as a liquidated damages provision will be irrelevant.

The principles underlying the law relating to penalty interest clauses had not been considered by the UK Supreme Court or by the House of Lords until the UK Supreme Court heard two appeals in 2015.

In *Cavendish Square Holding BV v Talal El Makdessi and Parking Eye Limited v Beavis*[5], Lords Neuburger and Sumption state in the leading judgment that the test is whether the provision in doubt is a secondary obligation which imposes a detriment on the defaulting party:

'... out of all proportion to any legitimate interest of the innocent party in the enforcement of the primary obligation.'

Their Lordships go on to say:

'The innocent party can have no proper interest in simply punishing the defaulter. His interest is in performance or in some appropriate alternative to performance.'

The court held that where a straightforward damages clause is used, in which interest will rarely extend beyond compensation for the breach, the following tests, formulated by Lord Dunedin in *Dunlop Pneumatic Tyre Co Ltd v New Garage and Motor Co Ltd*[6] out of earlier case law, would be sufficient to determine its validity:

---

5   [2015] UKSC 67.
6   [1915] AC 79.

- If the amount of the sum specified is 'extravagant and unconscionable' compared with the largest amount of loss that could conceivably be proved to have followed from the breach, then it will be held to be a penalty.

- If the breach is simply not paying a sum of money, and the amount specified in the provision is greater than the amount which was due to be paid, then it will be a penalty.

- There is a presumption that it is a penalty when there is provision for a single sum to be payable as compensation on the occurrence of different events, some of which may be serious but others trivial.

- The sum specified must be a genuine pre-estimate of damage, even where the consequences of the breach would have made accurate pre-estimation impossible.

For more complex negotiated contracts, the legitimate interest test may permit greater contractual freedom, where courts will look at the commercial justification for the penalty rather than simply considering recoverable loss.

12.4.5 Enforcing the Missives

The position of a seller in default is governed by the common law. The purchaser will either seek a decree of implement, requiring the seller to deliver a disposition in their favour in exchange for the price, or alternatively, if that is not possible, treat the seller as being in material breach of contract, rescind the missives and seek damages to make good their losses (see para 6.10.13).

It is more usual, if there is going to be a party in default, that it will be the purchaser. All standard offers contain provisions covering what is to happen in that event. The heads of claim for wasted expenditure are covered in some detail in both the Scottish Standard Clauses and the PSG Offer to Sell (see paras 6.10.14 and 6.14.3). There is a danger from the seller's perspective that, unless these heads are comprehensively set out, the courts at common law may not allow a claim under a particular head to succeed. In *Tiffney v Bachurzewski*[7], it was held that the equitable principles governing

---

7 [1984] SC 108.

restitution of the seller will be narrower than the usual contractual provision and unforeseen expenses not within the contemplation of the parties (in this case, bridging finance) will be disallowed.

If the purchaser has repudiated the contract, there are two options open to the seller:

- accept the repudiation, rescind and claim damages for losses sustained under the heads of damages; or

- keep the missives alive and raise an action for specific implement (an order to implement the contract by paying the price against delivery of the disposition)[8].

It should be remembered that, if settlement or completion finally takes place after a delay, searches and reports will need to be updated by the seller's solicitor, and other checks re-made.

INSOLVENCY OF THE SELLER

12.5 Only a few words now need be said about the risk to a purchaser, having paid the money in settlement to a seller who subsequently becomes insolvent. The disposition in favour of the purchaser will have been delivered before any appointment, or registration of a competing title in favour of the insolvency practitioner, and therefore (because it is incumbent on the purchaser's solicitor to ensure that the disposition in favour of the purchaser is presented for registration as swiftly as possible after settlement) will have reached the Land Register first. There were some horror stories in the cases of *Sharp v Thomson*[9] and *Burnett's Trustee v Grainger*[10].

AVOIDING CONTRACT DISPUTES

12.6 Without wishing to sound trite, when you reflect on this chapter, consider that the risks of a contract dispute can sometimes be minimised or avoided by the simple expedients of:

---

8   There is conflicting case law on whether merely a decree for payment of the purchase price is competent. The Sheriff Principal's judgment in *AMA (New Town) Ltd v McKenna* [2011] ScotSC 11 said not, but the Inner House held the opposite in *AMA (New Town) v Law* [2013] CSIH 61. See commentary on these cases in Gretton and Reid *Conveyancing* (2013) at pp 124–131.
9   [1997] SC (HL) 66.
10 [2004] SC (HL) 19.

(a)   managing your client's expectations and inserting a suitable contractual clause in missives to cover delays;

(b)   ensuring that the purchaser has made satisfactory financial arrangements;

(c)   choosing a sensible and realistic date of entry; and

(d)   keeping the transaction running on schedule until settlement.

Chapter 13

Tidying Up and Feeing

'Do not plan for ventures before finishing what's at hand.' — *Euripides*

So the transaction has settled satisfactorily and the clients are happy. You can give yourself a well-earned pat on the back, but not yet plan for ventures. There is still work to do.

FEES AND BILLING

13.1 Both sets of solicitors should attend to their fee. Your firm is a business and has been laying out expense for weeks, sometimes months, on behalf of the client. Now is the time to recover.

The purchaser's solicitor should have sent the purchaser a settlement/completion statement before the date of completion, showing the funds required and including his own fee and any outlays. The fee note should be ready in anticipation of the funds coming in for settlement. If this is not done, experience dictates that it sometimes becomes harder to recover from a client who has moved on to other interests (and is himself planning for ventures!). Having to instigate debt recovery procedure against what was once a happy client is never a pleasant task, far less being desirable for business development.

The seller's solicitor has to attend to the distribution of the sale proceeds. Usually there is a bank loan to be redeemed and a cheque or bank transfer for the amount stated in the redemption statement should be sent immediately. If there is any doubt about an extra day's interest, then it may be sensible to hold some money back which you can repay to the clients later, if it is not needed. It is always better to be sending an unexpected reimbursement than an unexpected demand!

Estate agents and surveyors often have an understanding with the seller that they will be paid by the seller's solicitor from the proceeds of sale. In fact, this will often be stated in the estate agent's terms of engagement. So you must ensure you have received their final account in advance and pay this immediately too.

An organised solicitor will have arranged to deduct their fee from the proceeds of sale. The ideal position is that the fee note is ready before settlement, and to achieve this, there must be a high degree of administrative organisation. All final outlays should be recovered. Check back to the letter of engagement as to what was proposed for the fee, even if you think you remember. All-time entries must be up-to-date across the firm, so that the fee is reflective of the work carried out (unless it is a fixed fee with no additional work).

The vital job of the seller's solicitor is to transmit the net free proceeds of sale to the client as soon as they have cleared, unless they are required for purchasing another property in a back-to-back transaction. However good the conveyancing has been and however clearly it was set out in the initial letter of engagement all those weeks ago, experience has shown the seller will not understand why there is a delay in remitting the money to them unless it has been recently and explicitly explained to them.

FILE CLOSING

13.2 Once everyone has been paid, and all documentation received (see paras 13.3 and 13.4), it is time to close the file. Check with the cashroom whether there are any balances held on the ledger, particularly if, as suggested above, you retained a small positive balance to cover any unforeseen expenses. Now that all accounts have been settled, you should return any remaining balances.

All filing should be up-to-date, including all e-mails, letters, scribbled notes and (where you are using a paper file) sorted into chronological order. Many draft documents can be securely disposed of. Once principal contract documents have been agreed, drafts are of no help in interpreting the contract where there is an 'entire agreement' clause (which is typically the case). That said, it can sometimes be useful to see how certain elements of a document evolved during a transaction, in case of ambiguity or uncertainty later, even if they do not have any evidential status. The file should then be closed by being sealed and archived if a paper file, or electronically archived if an electronic file. Original signed documents should be retained in a sealed and archived 'papers' file.

The Law Society requires that client files are held for at least ten years, so it is useful to date stamp the file with the date for review in ten years' time.

TITLES, LAND CERTIFICATE AND TITLE SHEETS

13.3 The purchaser's solicitor must attend to the registration of the title. That means sending the documents to be registered to the Keeper with the requisite forms and cheques (unless paying by direct debit). Where the application is a first registration, all relevant titles that are required to make up the information on the Title Sheet are sent to the Keeper with the application. The Keeper will acknowledge the application and assign a Title Number (if a first registration) and an application number to the application with a priority date. If used, ARTL will provide an electronic acknowledgement of applications on submission. See Chapter 14 for registration procedures.

Some titles will remain and are no longer of much use. Some titles contain historical information that may be of interest to the client. These can be returned to the client, securely disposed of, or retained as part of a title package held on behalf of the client. Documentation such as planning permission, building control documents etc are usually held with the titles rather than in the file, so that they are not destroyed unwittingly.

Assuming that all has gone well with the registration process, then a pdf of the Title Sheet will eventually be produced in certain types of transactions. The landing page on which this pdf is located is only available for 50 days, and so the pdf itself should either be saved electronically to the matter file, or printed and saved on the paper file.

WHERE A LETTER OF OBLIGATION HAS BEEN GIVEN

13.4 Prior to the introduction of Advance Notices, letters of obligation were routinely given by sellers' solicitors. There will still be a number of these waiting for completion of a 1979 Act application and production of a Land Certificate from the Keeper. If you have already closed the file you will need to re-open it to deal with the finalisation and return of the letter of obligation, marked as implemented.

The first thing that the purchaser's solicitor should arrange to be done is a comparison between the disposition (and other titles) that was submitted to the Keeper, with the terms of the resulting Land Certificate or Title Sheet. There can occasionally be omissions in the Land Certificate or Title Sheet, and in that case, the Land Certificate should be returned for correction immediately or the error on the Title Sheet brought to the Keeper's attention. The Keeper should not require a rectification application for minor typos or other clerical errors. For an example of a Land Certificate that wasn't checked – and the consequences which followed – see *Willemse v French*.[1]

If the Land Certificate or Title Sheet is in accordance with your submissions and you are now satisfied that your client has received a good and marketable title, then for 1979 Act titles, the final thing the purchaser's solicitor should do is to retrieve the seller's solicitor's letter of obligation from the file, score through it and mark it as 'implemented' – the seller's solicitors are now released from their obligation and the letter of obligation, duly marked as implemented, should be returned to them. There is no equivalent requirement for a 2012 Act Title Sheet unless a hybrid form of letter of obligation was given, because Advance Notice protection wasn't available.

Now you can plan for ventures.

---

1 [2001] CSOH 51.

Chapter 14

Registration of Title

COMPLETING THE CONVEYANCING PROCESS

14.1 As soon as settlement (or completion) has taken place, the purchaser's title needs to be registered. If there is a lender, that lender's standard security must also be registered. On taking delivery of the deeds, any testing clause is added, or the signing docquet checked and any missing information as to date and place of signing, or witness details added in. It is perfectly permissible to do this after the event, (just as, of course, it is correct to add the testing clause later). If Land and Buildings Transaction Tax (LBTT) is due, then the LBTT return must be made and the tax paid within the parameters of 'arrangements satisfactory' (see para 11.8.7) to allow the submitting solicitor to tick the appropriate boxes on the application form (see para 14.11.2(iv)).

The Application for Registration form is completed, signed and submitted to the register along with the deed. A separate application form is required for each deed submitted. Since 8 December 2014, all deeds transferring property, whether for valuable consideration or not, induce first registration in the Land Register. Recording in the Sasine Register, for which the relevant form is a Sasine Application Form (SAF) is now applicable only to other types of deeds affecting a Sasine title. From 1 April 2016, it will no longer be possible to record a standard security in the Sasine Register and, in the fullness of time, the Sasine Register will be closed to other types of deeds.

Registration dues must be pre-paid. Either a cheque for the correct amount of dues should accompany the application, or alternatively, solicitors can set up a dedicated account through which payment of registration dues can be made. A Variable Direct Debit account will be drawn from by the Keeper whenever that firm of solicitors makes an application for registration. Careful checks and protocols must be in place at the solicitor's firm to ensure that funds from the clients account are deposited into the direct debit account to meet the liability for registration dues as they arise. Solicitors should not send the application for registration without checking that they have sufficient funds to meet the registration dues. Every firm of solicitors is given a FAS number by the Registers. This number (eg FAS4040) must appear on every application form for registration or recording of a deed. It identifies the firm for billing purposes. Firms with variable direct debit accounts are given an additional FAS number for that account, which must be put in the form when payment is to be debited from that account.

Before the application is submitted, the deeds and forms should be carefully checked to avoid the application being rejected by the Keeper. Under the 2012 Act rules, the Keeper no longer permits post-submission requisitions. Therefore, it is particularly important to have a system of pre-submission checks to ensure that your application is not rejected for some minor omission. Make sure that all check boxes in the Application Form are completed and that the form is signed (usually by a partner of the firm, or by someone authorised to sign the form by the firm). A copy of the Keeper's Application for Registration Checklist is reproduced at the end of this chapter under Crown Copyright rules. The following paragraphs provide some more detail to help ensure that the registration process is as trouble-free for you as possible. You can also consult the regularly updated Guidance from the Keeper.

WHY REGISTER TITLE?

14.2 The missives and the disposition give the purchaser personal, contractual, rights in relation to the property, but it is the effect of registering that disposition that creates a real right in the property. Personal rights are rights against persons, such as the obligations contained in a contract, whereas real rights consist of rights in things, and ownership of property is one of the principal real rights. Obtaining a real right in something means that it is protected from challenge 'against all mortals' as the saying goes[1]. Registration of a person's title to property is the essential last stage of the conveyancing process and may be characterised as the method by which the personal right – in the disposition – is converted into the real right – the registered title.

---

1 But includes any natural or legal person!

Security over property is another of the real rights in property and this is relevant in relation to the rights of a heritable creditor under the standard security.

The recording of a deed in the Register of Sasines confers a real right to the property, although this does not in itself guarantee valid title to a property. In the Land Register, the act of registration gives a real right of ownership on the person entered on the Title Sheet as proprietor, and the Keeper's indemnity (see para 2.4.16) for titles registered before 4 December 2014, and Keeper's warranty, for titles registered from 8 December 2014 onwards, provide a form of state guarantee of title.

RECORDING IN THE SASINE REGISTER

14.3 Since 8 December 2014, a conveyance of property, the title to which is recorded in the Sasine Register will result in the title moving out of that Register and into the Land Register. Under the 1979 Act, not all types of transaction induced a first registration in the Land Register. In particular, a gratuitous transfer, such as a conveyance for 'love, favour and affection' over an unregistered interest did not require to be registered in the Land Register. The 2012 Act anticipates that, eventually, all deeds will have to be registered in the Land Register, and the Sasine Register will be closed to all new deeds.

For now, it continues to be competent to record certain deeds in the Sasine Register, where the title to the property is still in that Register. The Sasine Register is a register of deeds, so all that is required when submitting a deed for recording in the Sasine Register is:

- the deed itself;
- a completed and signed SAF form; and
- a cheque for the correct amount of the recording dues, or where the firm has a Variable Direct Debit account, the special FAS number for that account should be put on the SAF form.

Once the recording process has been completed, the actual deed is returned to you with a recording stamp on the first page of the deed giving the recording County, the folio and fiche number (which denotes where a facsimile of the deed has been stored in the records of the Registers) and the date of recording.

643

PRE APPLICATION ENQUIRIES

14.4 During the course of a transaction, there may be issues that arise, where it is unclear to the solicitor how the Keeper might react to, and deal with those matters. Under the 1979 Act regime, the Keeper would entertain 'Pre-Registration Enquiries' from the solicitor, by which the solicitor could submit a query in writing to the Keeper and ask for a statement from her of how she would deal with the matter when the application for registration was submitted. The response from Pre-Registration Enquiries might suggest a course of action that must be followed for the application to be acceptable to the Keeper.

The Pre-Registration Enquiry service was discontinued under the 2012 Act. This fact, coupled with the 'one shot rule' (meaning that if the application is not correct in all respects, it will be rejected) (see para 2.4.15) has resulted in a climate of uncertainty throughout the profession. The Registers 'helpline' has not proved to be an equivalent service. The Registers' position is now that it is up to the solicitors themselves to judge these matters. This is understandable, indeed, is as it should be, where the matter is a legal one. But where the issue is one of registration practice or policy, it is less apparent to the profession how certain aspects of an application will be handled. To be fair to both the profession and the Registers, the first year of implementation of the new regime has been a steep learning curve on both sides. Many of the staff at the Registers are as helpful as they can be, and the Customer Services team is regularly contacted on matters that would formerly have been pre-registration issues.

The alternative is for the solicitor to make the best possible evaluation of how registration issues are likely to be treated, make provision in the application accordingly, and submit it. If the application is rejected, then the Keeper should indicate the reason for rejection and steps that can be taken to correct matters. This is not a satisfactory state of affairs either for applicants or for the Registers but, as with so many other aspects of registration practice and policy at this stage, matters are evolving. Some indication of how certain aspects of an application will be treated by the Keeper can be obtained from the Registers' 'Legal Manual'[2]. While this

---

2   See: https://rosdev.atlassian.net/wiki/display/2ARM/Home.

is not as comprehensive as its 1979 Act predecessor, nevertheless, it can provide some insight into the likely approach once the application is submitted.

A recently introduced 'Application Checking Service'[3] may provide some relief in applications for first registration. For a fee of £50, the Registers' staff will carry out some basic checks on the deed being submitted and the application form, ie:

(a)   the deed induces first registration;

(b)   the deed is signed;

(c)   the application form is signed;

(d)   the information in the deed matches information in the application form;

(e)   the extent deed has been submitted;

(f)   the deed for registration is ex facie valid and the execution is self-evidencing;

(g)   whether or not the subjects fall within a research area and, if not, the burdens writs not on the keeper's common deeds index have been submitted;

(h)   the burdens question has been answered in line with the information contained in the deed;

(i)   the servitudes question has been answered in line with information contained in the deed; and

(j)   the fee is correct.

On one view, these are checks that the solicitor should be carrying out anyway, and it might be a little difficult to justify re-charging this fee to your client, when it covers things that should be a part of 'doing the job properly'. These basic checks appear, however, to consist of issues that form the main reasons for rejection of applications (see para 14.5). At the time of going to print, there is no feel for how much take-up there is likely to be of this service. At the very least, each of the items on this list should form part of your own internal pre-submission checks.

Once an application has actually been submitted, any enquiries should be directed to the relevant team at the Registers.

---

3   See: www.ros.gov.uk/services/application-checking-service.

MAIN REASONS FOR REJECTION

14.5 A key aspect of the 2012 Act is that applications should be right first time, and that 'bad' applications should simply be rejected. This is characterised as the 'one-shot rule'. To be clear, however, this does not mean that you only have once chance to get it right. If the application is faulty in any way, it will be rejected, but you then have the opportunity to correct it and re-submit. The difference between this, and the requisitions approach that operated under the previous regime, is that any amendments or corrections are made away from the Register. The practice of putting an application in 'standover' while the changes were dealt with, or any issue was resolved, has ceased. Once the amended application is resubmitted, it will be given a new date of registration.

Most of the common reasons for rejection of an application for registration are wholly avoidable – unsigned forms, cheques not included, deed not signed or witnessed etc. A 'rejection checklist' is now provided with rejected applications[4] and there is a dedicated helpline to help you understand why the application has been rejected, and how to avoid it in future. It is strongly recommended that you put in place your own pre-submission procedures – the Registers' Application for Registration Checklist which appears at para 14.18 is a good starting point – to ensure as far as possible that your applications are sticky, not bouncy.

The 2012 Act introduces some additional criteria that must apply for a deed to be accepted for registration, in addition to the usual conveyancing requirements.

14.5.1 Registrable Deed

The deed must be a 'registrable deed', which means that registration must be authorised (either expressly or by implication) by the 2012 Act or another enactment[5]. It is interesting to observe that, until the 2012 Act, no enactment specifically authorised a disposition as a registrable deed. Neither is a deed of servitude expressly authorised, although it is fairly clear that it is authorised by implication[6]. The Keeper has produced a

---

4   See www.ros.gov.uk/services/submit-an-application.
5   Section 49(1).
6   Part 7 of the Title Conditions (Scotland) Act 2003.

comprehensive list of the deeds that she considers are 'registrable'[7]. All of the most common deeds that conveyancers use appear in this list. If you wish to register a deed that does not appear on the list, you must provide the Registers with details of the enactment under which it is authorised. If the deed is not on the list, or is not authorised by an enactment, then it cannot be registered.

14.5.2 Documents and Plans

The application must be accompanied by all documents and information that are necessary to complete the Title Sheet and map the property onto the cadastral map. This includes the deed to be registered, of course. For first registrations any deeds that describe the property and/or show its extent, as well as deeds containing rights, burdens and servitudes must be included with the application. You do not need to submit a prescriptive progress of writs. A suitable plan should be included, where appropriate. The plan should include the route of any prescriptive servitude, where this can be shown. If only part of the land is affected by a burden, or other encumbrance, the extent affected should also be shown. These need not be shown on the deed plan (unless being created in the deed)[8].

14.5.3 Souvenir Plots

The property concerned must not be a souvenir plot. This was also true for applications for registration under the 1979 Act. A souvenir plot is a plot of land 'of inconsiderable size and of no practical utility'.

14.5.4 Completed Application Form

An application form must be submitted for each deed to be registered. Every form must be signed and dated, and all relevant questions in the form must be answered. Using the online application form available through the Registers' e-services means that, once the application type has been selected, it will only present questions that are relevant to that application type.

---

7   See www.ros.gov.uk/__data/assets/pdf_file/0014/11372/General-Guidance-Registrable-Deeds.
    pdf.
8   Sections 23(1)(d), 25(1)(c) and 28(1)(b) of the 2012 Act.

14.5.5 Fee

The correct fee must be paid, either by cheque accompanying the form or through the direct debit arrangements. The online form will calculate the correct amount of registration dues, based on the consideration, or deed type.

14.5.6 LBTT

If the transaction is a notifiable transaction for LBTT purposes, then a land transaction return must have been completed and 'arrangements satisfactory' (see para 11.8.7) for payment of the LBTT due must be in place.

14.5.7 Valid Deed

The deed to be registered must be valid (see para 14.6.2). This is a key component of the conditions for registration of all deeds set out in the 2012 Act. To be frank, this is a key component of competently carried out conveyancing.

14.5.8 No *ex facie* Defect

There must be no defect on the face of the deed. Any such defect will result in rejection. Granters and grantees should be named and properly designed. The deed must contain acceptable words of conveyance, or other grant. The property must be sufficiently described, either by reference to the correct Title Number, if registered, or a suitable conveyancing description and plan. The deed must be subscribed by the granter and witnessed, with the name and designation of the witness included, and any plan and other annexations must be docqueted and signed.

14.5.9 Mapping Requirements

The plot must be capable of being mapped onto the cadastral map, and its boundaries must not conflict with any other registered plot. This means that the property must be sufficiently described, eg by a full bounding description, and/or accurately delineated on a plan that meets

648

the Keeper's deed plan criteria, to a suitable scale, with that scale clearly shown on the plan and a north point. If the plot is subject to Development Plan Approval, references to that DPA must be given. For seabed plots, suitable boundary coordinates must be provided, using the projected coordinate system: OSGB 1936 | British National Grid (EPSG:27700) providing the coordinates of the plot, preferably in the form of a table, which will be incorporated into the property description of the Title Sheet.

GENERAL APPLICATION CONDITIONS AND CONDITIONS OF REGISTRATION

14.6 The Keeper must accept an application for registration, if the applicant satisfies the Keeper that, at the date of application, the conditions for acceptance of an application for registration have been met.

All applications must comply with the General Application Conditions (set out in section 22 of 2012 Act) (see para 2.4.10(i)), and any particular Conditions of Registration that relate to the type of application ie first registration, automatic plot registration, registration of a registered plot, and voluntary registration[9] (see para 2.4.10(ii)).

If on the date of application the relevant conditions are not met, the Keeper must reject the application.

14.6.1 General Application Conditions

The General Application Conditions relate to the application itself, whereas the Particular Conditions of Registration relate to the deed or plot being registered.

The General Application Conditions are:

- that the application contains all that will enable the Keeper to comply with here Part 1 duties (see para 2.4.10(i))
- the application must be in the prescribed form;
- the registration fee must be paid at the time of the application, or confirmation that satisfactory arrangements have been made for payment;

---

9   The Particular Conditions of Registration are set out in sections 23, 25, 26 and 28 respectively of the 2012 Act.

- the application must not relate to a souvenir plot;
- the application must not fall to be rejected by section 6 of the Requirements of Writing (Scotland) Act 1995, which makes self-proving status (eg the deed must be subscribed and witnessed) a requirement for registration in the Land Register; and
- the application must not fall to be rejected by virtue of a prohibition in any other enactment (eg the prohibition on registration under the Land and Buildings Transaction Tax (Scotland) Act 2013, without LBTT having been paid)[10].

14.6.2 Particular Conditions of Registration

There are particular Conditions of Registration set out in sections 23, 25, 26 and 28 of the 2012 Act. They are applicable specifically to the deed or plot being registered. Different conditions apply depending on the type of application submitted:

- section 23 relates to transfers of unregistered plots (i.e. first registrations);
- section 25 relates to deeds that trigger registration of the underlying plot of land (automatic plot registration);
- section 26 applies to deeds relating to registered plots (dealings of whole and transfers of part); and
- section 28 relates to applications for voluntary registration.

As with the General Application Conditions, the particular Conditions of Registration are applicable as at the date of application. If the deed being registered fails to meet any of the registration conditions when the Keeper receives it, the Keeper must reject the application.

One of the main conditions of registration, applicable to all deeds being registered, is that the deed must be **valid**:

> 'A deed on which an application under section 21 is based is "valid" for the purposes of (this) Act if (a) by the registration applied for, a right would be acquired, varied or extinguished, or (b) the deed is certificatory of an acquisition, variation or extinction which has taken place.'

---

10 Section 43 of the Land and Buildings Transaction Tax (Scotland) Act 2013.

Essentially, the person granting the deed must have title and capacity to do so. Either the granter of a disposition must be the last registered owner or there must be sufficient links in title from the last registered owner to the granter to establish their entitlement to make the grant.

The deed must contain the necessary operative provisions to achieve what is intended. For example, a disposition must clearly convey, transfer or dispone property. A disposition intended to create real burdens must be properly constitutive in terms of section 4 of the Title Conditions (Scotland) Act 2003. A deed of variation of a lease or the extinguishing of a survivorship destination must effectively do so. A discharge must effectively extinguish the security or right that it purports to discharge. A notice of title must clearly set out the basis of a person's right to the property or right concerned. The present tense should be used, eg (I dispone/I grant).

If the deed fails the validity requirements, the Keeper must reject it.

For first registrations, the plot must be sufficiently described to enable the Keeper to delineate it on the cadastral map. Any encumbrances affecting only part of a plot must also be sufficiently described, or shown on a plan, for mapping purposes.

For applications relating to a registered plot, the deed must narrate the title number of each Title Sheet to which it relates. Note, however, that where the deed narrates the title number of a sharing plot Title Sheet (ie one of the plots of ground, the owners of which hold the shared plot in common), the title number of the shared plot Title Sheet (ie a Title Sheet relating to ground held in common) does not need to be narrated[11].

14.6.3 Deeds to Accompany an Application for Registration

According to the 2012 Act, the application must be such that the Keeper is able to comply with her duties under Part 1 of the 2012 Act. Part 1 sets out the information that must be entered in the relevant sections of the Title Sheet. For example, the property section must contain a description of the plot together with any pertinents; the proprietorship section must contain the name and designation of the proprietor; and the burdens section must contain details of any encumbrances. The onus is on the applicant to provide the Keeper with all the documents and information necessary to

---

11 Section 17(4) of the 2012 Act.

comply with these duties. If any material information is omitted from the application, it will be rejected.

When submitting an application over an unregistered plot, the applicant is asked to identify deeds in which burdens are contained. This gives you an opportunity to highlight any burdens that you consider to be extinguished, if appropriate (see para 14.11.2(ix)). The Keeper will rely on the information provided and will not search for other deeds that may affect the plot. However, if the plot is in an area where the Keeper has already carried out preparatory work (a 'research area' – see para 2.5.4(iii)) and has identified other deeds that contain burdens, the Keeper will continue to disclose these burdens in the Title Sheet notwithstanding that the applicant has not included them. Most research areas are residential in nature and will typically consist of a development of a number of plots that have common prior titles and similar burdens.

If the applicant refers to a deed for burdens but does not submit it with the application, the Keeper could reject the application in terms of section 22(1)(a). If, however, the applicant knows that the Keeper has already examined a deed containing burdens, the applicant can note this on the inventory contained within the application form. The Keeper will not reject the application provided sufficient information is available to enable her to complete her duties under section 9 of the 2012 Act.

Where automatic plot registration applies (eg on the grant of a lease, a sub-lease or an assignation of an unregistered lease) the Keeper must also register the owner's plot of land to the extent of the deed being registered. This means that the tenant, sub-tenant or assignee has to provide the Keeper with the all of the documents and information required to enable the Keeper to make up a Title Sheet for the plot of land as well. Failure to do so is likely to result in rejection of the application to register the deed.

14.6.4 How the Keeper deals with Applications

Remember that the onus is on the applicant to satisfy the Keeper that the application complies with the General Application Conditions and the particular Conditions of Registration. The applicant has to certify on the application form that the application meets with the relevant conditions (see para 14.11.3). In all cases, this includes a condition that the deed is valid, which will include certification that the granter has title and capacity to grant the deed. The Keeper will rely on this certification when registering the application.

The Keeper's staff will no longer carry out any investigation of the title[12], and instead rely on the certification given in the application form.

From a practical point of view, this means that a lot of the supporting documentation that would previously have accompanied an application for registration under the 1979 Act, no longer needs to be submitted. Accordingly, you do not have to submit links in title, or produce the prescriptive progress of titles. The application form certifies that valid links in title exist and that there has been an examination of the title.

The provisions establishing the duty of care and offence provisions[13] apply to, and are specifically referred to in the application form. This means that both applicants and granters (and their solicitors) are under a duty to take reasonable care to ensure that the Keeper does not inadvertently make the Land Register inaccurate. Section 112 provides that it is an offence to knowingly or recklessly make a materially false or misleading statement in relation to an application for registration.

The Keeper's checks on receipt of an application will be limited to ensuring that the application is in order and that there are no obvious defects on the face of the deed to be registered. In practice, this is turning out to be a fairly rigorous check. It includes ensuring that the parties are properly identified and designed, that appropriate operative words are used, and that the deed has been properly signed and witnessed.

14.6.5 Limited Scope for Requisitions

The 2012 Act provides only very limited scope for the Keeper to make requisitions.

The Keeper may consent to a substitution or amendment to the application (by making a requisition) in certain circumstances. The application and registration conditions must still have been met as at the date of application, so consent to making a requisition can only be given where the application already meets the conditions of acceptance.

---

12 Although there have been instances in some applications, where some investigation that goes beyond mere checking, is being done.
13 Sections 111 and 112 of the 2012 Act.

Requisitions will, therefore, be restricted to matters that are evidential as to the state of affairs at the date of application.

Registers' Guidance has provided the following as examples of situations where consent to a substitution or amendment may be given:

- where the reinforcement of certain information or evidence that has been provided is desirable;

- where evidence is submitted in support of a request to extend warranty but further evidence is required;

- where evidence is submitted in support of a prescriptive claimant application under section 43 but further evidence is required;

- where a search in the Register of Inhibitions discloses a potential adverse entry, the Keeper may require confirmation that the name match disclosed is not that of the party in question; and

- where a supporting deed or document has been submitted in error, it may be possible to substitute it for the correct one. For example, where a deed has been referred to for burdens, but the wrong one has been submitted because more than one deed between those parties was recorded on the same day.

Examples where consent to a substitution or amendment will not be given are:

- where the deed to be registered has not been submitted;

- where the deed to be registered contains an error that strikes at its validity, eg parties are not named and designed; The deed not signed by the granter, or not signed by the witness; the witness is not named and designed; there are no acceptable operative words; the deed plan is not docqueted; or where the plan or description of the plot is such that the Keeper cannot delineate it on the cadastral map;

- where the plan or description of an encumbrance affecting part of the plot is not sufficient for the Keeper to delineate it on the cadastral map;

- where a deed is referred to for burdens but is not submitted, and is not marked on the application form as a deed that the Keeper has already examined; and

- where the plot to be registered, or any part of it, competes with an existing registered title.

In the limited circumstances in which requisitions will be allowed under the 2012 Act, the period for meeting a requisition is 42 days. If you know that it will not be possible to meet that deadline for a particular requisition, then your only option will be to withdraw the application.

Failure to comply with a requisition will not necessarily result in rejection, since the conditions for application must already have been met. It is more likely to mean that there may be a limitation or exclusion from warranty, or that certain matters will not appear on the Title Sheet.

FIRST REGISTRATION

14.7 Any transfer of unregistered property will induce first registration in the Land Register. Deeds which induce first registration are set out in section 48(1) of the 2012 Act:

- a disposition;
- a lease (where the lease is for more than 20 years and regardless of whether it is for valuable consideration or not (a lease with a duration of less than 20 years will induce first registration if it contains a provision allowing the landlord to extend its term to exceed 20 years); and
- an assignation of a lease;

No deed of these types will be accepted for recording in the Sasine Register, nor will any other deed that relates to a registered plot of land or a registered lease.

Under the 1979 Act regime, the Keeper's staff would examine title on the first occasion when the title to the property moved from the Sasine Register to the Land Register. Under the 2012 Act, however, they will no longer examine the title. The application for registration of the disposition must be accompanied by all the title deeds that are relevant to allow a Title Sheet to be made up. This will include:

- the descriptive writ and any deed outside the prescriptive progress which contains a plan that identifies the property;

- any break off writs that are relevant to allow identification of the property being registered;
- all writs referred to for burdens, so far as extant; and
- any other deeds relevant to the application, such as the discharge of the seller's standard security. Standard securities granted by the purchaser will also be submitted at this time.

While it is no longer necessary to include a prescriptive progress of writs, nor copies of any links in title, you must examine these, to ensure the validity of the deed being submitted.

The Application for Registration Form is completed, selecting the option 'Deed over an unregistered plot' as the application type. A list of the deeds and documents that accompany the application is incorporated in the Form (at the end of Part A). This replaces the separate Form 4 that was used for 1979 Act applications under the previous regime. All the relevant information from the title deeds is extracted and put into a new Title Sheet that is created by the Keeper for that property, divided into four sections: the property (A) section; the proprietorship (B) section, the securities (C) section and the burdens (D) section. The property is also given a unique Title Number, and its extent is delineated on the cadastral map (using the Ordnance Survey Map as a base). The Title Plan also forms part of the Title Sheet. Where the property to be registered is a tenement flat or other property the Keeper will identify it by the 'steading method' (see paras 8.27 and 9.9.5).

All Title Sheets for properties in the Land Register reside in the Keeper's mainframe computer, but the applicant will receive an e-mail giving access to a PDF copy of that Title Sheet, following completion of the registration process. Where the application for registration was submitted before 4 December 2014, registration will be completed under 1979 Act rules. At the end of that process, the Keeper will issue a Land Certificate, containing details of the Title Sheet as at the date of issue. The Title Sheet replaces the bundle of title deeds recorded in the Sasine Register. The PDF copy (or Land Certificate, if applicable) is a record of the information registered in the Title Sheet for the property as at the date of its issue, so it should be borne in mind that it simply represents a snapshot in time of what the Title Sheet contained.

The PDF copy of the Title Sheet is not covered by the Keeper's warranty. A person who suffers loss as a consequence of any error is entitled to be compensated by the Keeper[14]. However, the Keeper will not have any liability under this provision where:

- the loss could have been avoided if the person making the claim had taken certain measures which it would have been reasonable for that person to take, or
- the loss is too remote, or
- the loss does not relate to the property[15].

For this reason, a number of law firms have taken the view that, for the purposes of examining title and reporting on it or certifying it, the PDF should not be relied on. An extract of the Title Sheet should be obtained instead.

The Title Sheet and corresponding Land Certificate (if applicable) will not show up overriding interests under the 1979 Act. Overriding interests do not feature under the 2012 Act. Any exclusion of the Keeper's indemnity (under the 1979 Act) or limitation or exclusion of the Keeper's warranty (under the 2012 Act) will appear as a prominent note on the Title Sheet. This will, of course, be reflected in the Land Certificate or PDF, whichever is applicable.

For commercial property that is subject to leases, the Keeper can be asked to note short particulars of these in the Property section too. These are usually put into a schedule or table under the property description.

The Application for Registration Form is completed for all application types. Following submission, the Keeper sends an e-mail acknowledging receipt of the application, which should be retained for record purposes. The Keeper's e-mail will provide the allocated Title Number, and an application number to be quoted when making any enquiries to the Registers about the progress of the application.

Application for registration of an accompanying Standard Security is made on a separate Application for Registration Form. Since this application follows the registration of the disposition, it is treated as a dealing with a registered interest, the disposition having triggered registration of the whole title. For first registrations, where submission of the disposition and the standard security are usually simultaneous, the Keeper accepts that the Title Number has yet to be allocated and will deal with that during

14 Section 106(1)(b) of the 2012 Act.
15 Section 106(2) of the 2012 Act.

the registration process. Under the 1979 Act, every standard security has a separate Charge Certificate. The actual security document itself will be attached to the Charge Certificate, as well as appearing in the Charges section of the Land Certificate. Under the 2012 Act, the standard security will appear as an entry in the Securities section of the Title Sheet.

VOLUNTARY REGISTRATION

14.8 Voluntary registration of a Sasine title was always possible under the 1979 Act, although the Keeper had a discretion to decline to accept a voluntary registration application. That discretion continued under the 2012, but it will be removed on 1 April 2016[16]. The Keeper now positively encourages voluntary registration because of the requirement to complete the Land Register within 10 years.

Voluntary registration involves an application to move a Sasine title into the Land Register, where no transfer of the title is involved. This would often be appropriate in developments where the title to the land is still in the Sasine Register, but was now to be developed and sold off in individual plots.

An application for voluntary registration is similar in many respects to an application for first registration, except that there is no deed transferring the property. The application should be accompanied by the same sorts of deeds as under a first registration, to enable the Keeper to make up a full Title Sheet. Often the quality of plans or the property description in the titles will not be sufficiently accurate or detailed to enable the land to be plotted on the cadastral map. In that case, a new plan will be needed, to accurately delineate the land which is to be registered.

REGISTERED TITLE

14.9 Once the title to a property has been registered in the Land Register, the subsequent conveyancing procedures become a lot simpler. The disposition of a registered interest is shorter. The Keeper can update the Title Sheet showing the registered proprietor and the new lender's details, much more quickly than in a first registration.

---

16 Article 2 of the Registers of Scotland (Voluntary Registration, Amendment of Fees, etc) Order 2015.

Application for registration of the Disposition is made using the Application for Registration Form, selecting the option 'Deed over the whole of a registered plot' as the application type. Any deeds that accompany the application should be listed in the Inventory section of the form. This is a much shorter list than for a first registration, obviously, and should include all deeds relevant to the application being submitted. You should not submit any prior Land Certificate or Charge Certificate with any applications for registration in a registered interest. The Keeper neither wants nor needs these, and will destroy them if they are submitted.

DUAL REGISTRATION

14.10 If new burdens or servitudes are being created in the deeds being presented, then they must be dual registered ie registered against both the benefited property and the burdened property. This might mean an additional set of application forms from the seller or granter of the deed, to register the burdens or servitudes against his property as well, if title to that property is recorded in the Sasine Register. Where both the burdened and the benefited property are registered in the Land Register, the Keeper will allow you to put both title numbers onto a single application form. The application will be rejected where there is a dual registration requirement, but the application fails to identify both properties.

COMPLETING THE REGISTRATION FORM

14.11 Solicitors can register to use Registers of Scotland's e-services, which include access to eforms such as the Application for Registration Form. It is a dynamic form that provides a variety of drop-down options for selection. Depending on the application type selected, it will only present the relevant questions for that application type. It should be noted, however that, depending on the deed type, not all questions will be relevant eg a discharge of a standard security. The vast majority of registration applications are now made using this service, although it is also possible to use the PDF versions of the form instead. Although the eform and interactive PDF versions are completed electronically, the completed form must be printed off and signed before being submitted in hard copy with the accompanying documents.

Invariably, applications for registration will be made by the applicant's solicitor. It is possible for a non-legally qualified person to submit an application for registration, but such application must be accompanied by a completed Identification Form and proof of identity. This is to protect against fraud.

The questions in the Application Form for applications under the 2012 Act are quite different to those under the previous 1979 Act regime. Previously, during the conveyancing process, the purchaser's solicitor would pass a draft of the application form to the seller's solicitor for confirmation that the answers to the questions on their form were correct. This was because a number of the questions related to matters of which the seller would have knowledge. Now, the questions on the form are more concerned with matters of title and search results, of which the purchaser's solicitor will have knowledge from their examination of title and reports. It is no longer necessary (nor, in fact, appropriate) to send the draft application form to the other side for approval. The only exception to this, is where the transaction triggers automatic plot registration (eg where the underlying Sasine title of the landlord under a lease has to be registered in the Land Register, so that the lease or an assignation can also be registered properly (see para 2.5.2)). In those cases, two Title Sheets are registered, one for the landlord's heritable title and one for the tenant's leasehold rights. Since the majority of the questions in the Application Form for the lease concern the heritable title, it would be appropriate for the landlord's solicitors to check that they are correct and accurate, even though the application form in this case is submitted by the tenant's solicitor, since it is the application for registration of the lease or assignation.

The Keeper has produced detailed Guidance[17] on how to complete the Application Form. A lot of the questions are self-explanatory, but it is not always entirely clear how to complete the form in certain circumstances. The Keeper has updated this Guidance in the initial months following the designated day. Further updates may be issued from time to time on the Registers website, or in articles in the Journal.

The Application Form consists of: Part A, for details about the application, deed type, the parties, the agents, the price or other

17 See www.ros.gov.uk/about-us/2012-act/general-guidance/application-forms.

consideration and the property; and Part B, in which information concerning the title and the outcome of searches and reports is confirmed. There is also a section at the end of Part B, for 'Further Information'. This section is a valuable tool, where you can add some explanatory information about aspects of the application or the deed that may be slightly unusual. Do not assume that the Keeper's staff will appreciate all the nuances of your transaction. Use this space to clarify the situation, wherever there is something even marginally out of the ordinary. For example, the deed to be registered will contain a date of entry 'or such other date as may be mutually agreed'. Although there is a space on the form for you to insert the date of entry, if that date is different from the date in the deed, the Keeper's policy is to put the date in the deed on the Title Sheet, because there is a discrepancy between the deed and the form. If settlement was delayed by a few days, causing the actual date of entry to be different from that in the deed, use the Further Information box to explain the discrepancy.

There is also an Additional Information section that can be used, in cases where there are multiple granters or applicants, or multiple properties, for example.

If you are in any doubt at all, use these Further Information and Additional Information sections to explain what is going on. It could mean the difference between acceptance or rejection, or an accurate or inaccurate Title Sheet.

14.11.1 Part A – Basic Information

Part A of the Application Form requires to be completed with basic information about the application type, agents, payment and price details, the property, the applicants and the granters. Once your firm has registered with e-services, the forma will be pre-populated with the submitting agent's details and FAS number.

This part also provides for notification details to be inserted – up to four e-mail addresses can be provided. The Keeper will acknowledge submitted applications by e-mail, so the applicant's solicitor should ensure that their email addresses are accurately completed. It may also be appropriate for the granter's solicitor's email address to be included in this part.

14.11.1(i) Application type

There are five options to choose from:

- Deed over an unregistered plot. This option should be selected for first registrations.
- Automatic plot registration – select this option where the deed to be registered affects a title that is still in the Sasine Register, and is a type of deed, such as a lease, where that underlying title has to move to the Land Register, for the deed to be given effect[18].
- Deed over the whole of a registered plot.
- Deed over part of a registered plot – for example for a disposition of a plot in a registered residential development.
- Voluntary registration.

14.11.1(ii) Payment details

The price being paid, as shown in the disposition, or any non-monetary consideration, such as 'love, favour and affection' should be inserted in this section.

This section also requires the agent's FAS number to be inserted, for payment of registration dues. Depending on the transaction type, the form will calculate the amount of the registration dues automatically. For dual registration of burdens in the Land Register, the form will automatically include the additional £60 for the dual registration fee, provided that both title numbers for the burdened and the benefited properties are included in the form.

For a deed transferring part of a registered title, the Title Number for the part being conveyed will, of course, only be allocated after the application is submitted. For the correct registration fee to be calculated, the parent title number has to be entered in the form twice.

14.11.1(iii) Deed type

The deed to be registered must be a registrable deed. The form contains a drop-down list of all of the deeds that the Keeper has identified as being registrable deeds, and the appropriate selection should be made.

---

18 Section 24 of the 2012 Act.

14.11.1(iv) The property

Only a short description of the property to which the deed being registered relates is required on the form; that is an identifiable postal address with postcode, for example, rather than a full conveyancing description.

If the property is a plot in a development for which Development Plan Approval has been obtained (see para 6.12.3(iii)), then the DPA number and Plot number should be inserted.

For multiple properties, the Additional Information sections should be completed.

14.11.1(v) Applicants and granters

Full details should be given, including the name and address of the applicant (eg purchaser or lender) who is applying for registration. If the granter is acting in some fiduciary capacity eg as executor, then the form contains options for these to be inserted. If the application is for voluntary registration, the name of the owner of the land should be given.

A non-natural person, such as a company, or building society, must be fully designed. The designation of non-natural persons must include details of the legal system under which the person is incorporated eg 'incorporated under the Companies Acts'; the Company number eg SC123456; and any other identifier peculiar to that person, whether or not a number[19]. Examples of non-natural person designations are given in the Application Form Guidance.

14.11.2 Part B – Title and Search Information

This Part of the Form deals with matters of title and the outcome of searches and reports. The responses in this Part will be relied on by the Keeper, when updating or creating the Title Sheet for the property, underpinned by the certification to be given at the end of the form (see para 14.11.3).

14.11.2(i) Plans

Having an accurate plan of the property has always been important in land registration, but under the 2012 Act, it is essential, since there can

---

19 Section 113(1) of the 2012 Act.

be no registration without mapping, and there can be no overlaps on the cadastral map[20].

The Plans Report (see para 7.7) is now an essential element of most, if not all conveyancing transactions. The first question in Part B of the Application Form elicits information about the delineation of the property on the cadastral map. The question doesn't apply if the application relates to the whole of a registered plot of land, although that does not necessarily mean that you don't need a Plans Report, when dealing with a registered title (see para 7.7.1).

None of these questions are mandatory (other than the last section), but if a Plans Report has been obtained, the information will assist the Keeper in identifying whether the plot of ground is already delineated as a cadastral unit, and whether it is the subject of an area that is delineated on the cadastral map because of an Advance Notice application.

In the case of a flat within a tenement, the whole tenement steading (ie the block of flats plus any common ground applicable) will usually be allocated a single cadastral unit number. Each flat within the tenement will have a separate Title Number, but they will all be shown as lying within the same cadastral unit.

Where the application is for a first registration, then a cadastral unit will not yet have been created (unless it is an unregistered flat in a tenement where the tenement steading is registered, because one or other flats in that tenement have been registered).

The final part of this question is relevant for first registration or the first registration of part. Any plot to be registered has to be identified sufficiently so that it can be delineated on the cadastral map. This means that either a sufficient plan, or a sufficient bounding description, must be included in the disposition. A disposition that does not sufficiently identify the land in question, to enable it to be mapped, will be rejected.

14.11.2(ii) Common areas

Under the 2012 Act, areas that are owned in common can be given their own Title Sheet as a 'shared plot' (see paras 2.4.7, 8.28.4(v) and 9.9.10). This question seeks to elicit whether any part of what is being conveyed is owned

20 Section 12(2) of the 2012 Act.

in common, and, if it is, whether that common area is already registered. Where there is a shared plot title, the Title Number of the shared plot (ie the common area) must be given. The Keeper's Guidance on this question states that you should ensure that the deed narrates the Title Number of the shared plot. However, this should not be necessary, as section 17(4) of the 2012 Act provides that any reference in a document to a sharing plot is to be taken to include a reference to the share in the shared plot, unless specifically otherwise provided. Put another way, if you refer to the Title Number of the sharing plot that carries the share in the shared plot with it.

14.11.2(iii) *Register of inhibitions*

If the granter of the deed has been inhibited, then effect cannot be given to the deed in the Register if that inhibition applies before the granting of the deed or prior to an unconditional obligation to convey the property (conclusion of missives).

Most deeds are capable of being affected by an inhibition, unless it is not a voluntary act of the granter, such as Compulsory Purchase Order. So the default response to the question: 'Is the validity of the deed to which this application relates capable of being affected by an entry in the Register of Inhibitions' should be 'Yes'.

The next part of the question asks whether a search of the RoI has been carried out. This will invariably have been the case, but, if not, the Keeper's staff will check the RoI themselves. The date to which this search is certified should be entered. The search will disclose whether or not there is an inhibition. Usually the response to the next part of the question will be 'No', and all will be well. But if there is any entry disclosed in the search, details must be provided. An inhibition will mean that the application cannot proceed until steps are taken to resolve it, either by way of discharge, or partial discharge releasing the property in question from the ambit of the inhibition. If not, the Title Sheet will be marked with the fact that an inhibition affects the deed, which is likely to affect its validity.

14.11.2(iv) *Land and Buildings Transaction Tax (LBTT)*

LBTT replaced Stamp Duty Land Tax (SDLT) in Scotland in April 2015. LBTT is similar to SDLT in many ways. One crucial difference is that there is no formal piece of paper that denotes payment of LBTT. Under the SDLT regime, an SDLT5 form of receipt is issued by HMRC to confirm payment. The SDLT5 was submitted to the Keeper to demonstrate that the SDLT had been paid and the deed could be registered.

No evidence of payment of LBTT needs to be submitted with the application form, but you must indicate on the form if the transaction is notifiable[21]. If it is, you need to confirm that a Land Transaction Return has been made, and that arrangements satisfactory (see para 11.8.7) to Revenue Scotland are in place for payment of the LBTT. If you do not tick the 'Yes' box, where there is LBTT to be paid, then the Keeper will reject the application. The Keeper has a duty[22] to reject an application for registration of a deed relating to a notifiable transaction unless a Land Transaction Return has been made, and any LBTT payable in respect of the transaction has been paid. LBTT is, however, to be treated as paid, if satisfactory payment arrangements are in place.

14.11.2(v) Title examination

Probably the most controversial question in the form is the requirement to confirm whether there has been any limitation or restriction on the examination of title. This question caused a great deal of concern to solicitors when the content of the Application Form was revealed, and there remains some confusion within the profession about how best to answer it. A practice has emerged for some solicitors to answer this question by saying 'usual restrictions'. While this response has apparently been acceptable to the Keeper, it is unclear what it is intended to mean.

The purpose of the question is quite simply to determine whether or not an examination of title, according to the usual standard of care of a solicitor for the type of transaction in question, has been carried out. Arguably, this question ought to be unnecessary. If the submitting solicitor is signing the certificate on the form – which he has to, if the application is to be accepted – then the solicitor must have examined the title to be able to confirm, as the certificate requires, that the deed being submitted is valid.

---

21 Under section 30 of the Land and Buildings Transaction Tax (Scotland) Act 2013.
22 Under section 43 of the 2013 Act.

However, as it is not possible to qualify the certificate in the form, this question provides the opportunity to explain any limitation or restriction on the examination of title.

In the majority of cases, a full or appropriate title investigation will have been conducted. This aspect of the Application Form will impact where you are instructed to carry out only a limited or sample examination of title. In a portfolio acquisition, for example, it is sometimes the case that instructions are given to review only a selection of the titles, not all of them. Another example is in a family transfer by way of gift. Often your client does not want any title examination carried out and, instead, instructs you just to draft the conveyance.

Clearer Guidance on this particular question would be welcome, to give more certainty to the profession, of the effect, particularly on Keeper's Warranty, of a disclosure in this section of the form. At the moment the Guidance says that where there has been a restriction or limitation on the examination of title, this may result in the application being rejected, or the deed being registered, but with the Keeper's warranty being excluded or limited. We do not know in what particular circumstances an application will be rejected (other than, obviously, saying that there had been no title examination at all), or what will cause limitation or exclusion of warranty where the title examination question is an issue. The Guidance states that the examination of title must be suitable for the application.

Balanced with this concern of course, has to be an acknowledgment by the certifying solicitor that the application must meet the General Application Conditions and the Particular Conditions of Registration. Although this question will apply to all types of application for registration, not just first registration, clearly it is more significant if there has been a limitation on examination of the title when it is moving from the Sasine Register to the Land Register. When you are dealing with a first registration, you are likely to be conducting a full examination of the titles, to make sure that your client's title in the Land Register accurately reflects the Sasine version that precedes it.

For family transfer situations, like those mentioned above, where the granter's title is in the Sasine Register, it now may be a case of advising your client that **some** scrutiny of the titles will be required, because the conveyance (even if for no consideration) will trigger first registration. This scrutiny will ensure that the application for registration contains all the relevant components to enable the Keeper to accept it for registration, and that the deed of transfer is valid. At the very least, this will require you to look at the granter's title and, if it is within the prescriptive period, check the prescriptive progress. You will have to do this anyway, to be able to draft the disposition. While you will need to check the titles to identify writs that create burdens, it is not necessary for you to examine those burdens in detail, although attention might need to be given in case a pre-emption right exists, for example. This might result in the Title Sheet containing burdens that are actually extinguished, although even with a full examination of the title conditions, it is not always possible to say with certainty whether or not a burden is still enforceable anyway. For further advice on this particular aspect, see para 14.11.2(ix).

For sample title examinations in multiple acquisitions, it would be useful to have some clarity about the extent to which a limitation on title examination would mean rejection, or whether the titles would be registered, but may attract exclusion of warranty only. In certain circumstances, a limitation or exclusion of warranty might be acceptable to the party acquiring the portfolio, perhaps with a title insurance wrapper instead. However, this is something that needs to be clear at the instruction stage, not when the application is being made.

Clearer guidance will be difficult to formulate, since each case will depend on the circumstances. Therefore, it is vital to explain to your client what the consequences of a limited or restricted title examination would be. No examination of title at all must surely mean rejection, which defeats the object of the exercise. Instructions of this kind are invariably based on cost. It will be necessary to find the most cost effective way of checking the title to meet the validity requirements, while at the same time addressing as far as possible the client's wishes.

Usually the intention behind this sort of instruction is that the purchaser does not want or need a detailed title examination and a report. But they will expect a conveyance of the property, and will want it to be a valid and effective one. To be able to draft this, you need to look at the titles, Land Certificate or Title Sheet. You need to be able to identify the owner, and check that this is the same as the granter, and to be able to provide a description of the property or refer to the Title Number. In the case of a first registration, you should identify and list the burden writs. You must check any links in title. In the case of a granter whose title is recorded within the prescriptive period, check that a prescriptive progress of writs, linking one granter to the next, exists. If you carry out these minimum steps, then arguably you have done enough to be satisfied that the deed is valid. If you must indicate that there has been some limitation or restriction on your examination, then use the Further Information box in the form that will appear if you select 'Yes' to explain what you have examined and the reason why the examination has been limited or restricted. The more information that you give in this box, the easier it will be for the Keeper to evaluate the position and make an informed judgement on a suitable level of warranty.

If the portfolio of properties contains a mix of Sasine titles, and registered titles, then your focus should be on including the Sasine titles in the sample that you actually check. Those titles are where a lack of examination will certainly result in rejection.

14.11.2(vi) Certification in relation to links in title

Links in title no longer have to be submitted with an application for registration. The Keeper will not examine any title documents. Instead the applicant must certify that the appropriate links are in place. This is directly connected with the requirement for the deed to be valid, so your title examination must have included checking all links between the last registered proprietor and the granter, so that, if you have to answer 'No' to the question 'Is the granter the last recorded/registered proprietor', signing the certificate to the form means that you have carried out satisfactory checks.

If your response is 'No' because the disposition is *a non domino*, no links will exist. The form requires you to confirm if the disposition is *a non domino* – by reference to prescriptive claimants[23]. The 2012 Act has other requirements with which the applicant must comply for an *a non domino* disposition to be accepted for registration (see para 8.10).

One point to note is that for applications for registration of a deed granted by a person who is not yet, but is about to become, the owner, eg the purchaser's standard security, the Application Form must specify the deed by which the applicant will take title. There is a space for this in the declaration section of the form, and you should enter the disposition in the purchaser's favour.

---

23 Section 43(1) of the 2012 Act.

14.11.2(vii) Servitudes

It is now possible to enter the existence of a servitude acquired by prescription, rather than by express grant, on to the Title Sheet. The certifying applicant must be satisfied that the servitude has been validly constituted in this way, and must submit a plan, where appropriate, showing the servitude, such as the route of a right of access, or a sufficiently detailed description, so that it can be shown on the cadastral map.

Although this question will only appear in forms dealing with first registration, if an applicant wants a prescriptive servitude to be shown on the Title Sheet of a title that is already registered, details can be provided in the 'Further information' section of the form. See also para 9.11.2(iii) on prescriptive servitudes.

14.11.2(viii) Heritable securities

This question only applies in first registration applications. The search you obtain when dealing with a Sasine title should disclose any heritable securities affecting the land and details of the date to which the search has been obtained. If any securities have been disclosed, details should be inserted in the form. In this section, as elsewhere in the form, there is the facility to select deed details from the Inventory of Deeds within the Application Form.

14.11.2(ix) Burdens

This question also relates to first registration and seeks details of pre-existing burdens affecting the land to be registered. As the writs relating to burdens will need to be included in the Inventory of Deeds within the Application Form, it is a simple matter of selecting the deed numbers concerned from the Inventory list, once you have created it in the form. Simply select the appropriate deeds for burdens by ticking the relevant boxes next to them.

You must make sure that any burdens writs that are included in the Inventory of Deeds are submitted with the application for registration. Failure to do so could result in rejection. In some cases (where the property lies in a 'research area' (see para 2.5.4(iii))) the Keeper has already examined deeds that are common to all of the properties in that area, Failure to include those deeds in that case will not mean rejection. The Keeper will enter those burdens in the Title Sheet unless it is expressly stated on the Application Form that those burdens no longer apply. Where it is clear to the Keeper that certain deeds referred to for burdens in a research area title are physically remote from it, or contained only obsolete burdens, these will not be included in the new Title Sheet.

If there are spent or extinguished burdens in any of these deeds, you have the opportunity to deal with these in this part of the form, if you choose to do so. The field that is presented in this part of the form can, however only accommodate 5,000 characters, so if there is a lot of text, you may have to continue this information in the 'Further information' box at the end of the form.

There are several ways to deal with this. You could list the particular burdens according to deed and burden 'number' in this box. For example, you could state 'Omit from the Title Sheet: Deed number 4, burdens (Second), (Fourth) and (Fifth) (extinguished feudal burdens)'. Alternatively you could physically mark up the burden writ itself, perhaps with a coloured highlighter, to show the burdens that should be omitted, and in the box say 'please omit burdens shown highlighted yellow in deeds numbers 4, 6 and 7'. You don't necessarily have to say why you think the burdens should be omitted, but it would be a helpful addition if you did. For example: 'burden now extinguished under section 49 of the Title Conditions (Scotland) Act 2003'. The Keeper will not disclose the burden, if she is satisfied that it no longer exists, so this additional information will be of assistance to the Keeper in reaching a view.

Some concern has been expressed, that failure to identify extinguished burdens could be in breach of the duty of care, in that the appearance on the Title Sheet of a burden that has been extinguished is an 'inaccuracy'. The view of the writer is that the correct approach to take is that if it is beyond doubt that a burden is extinguished, then ask for it to be removed. This will tidy up the Title Sheet. Otherwise, if it is less than obvious whether a burden continues to be enforceable (eg implied enforcement rights under section 52 or 53 of the Title Conditions (Scotland) Act 2003 might apply), then it should not be necessary to go to extreme lengths to try to get to the bottom of whether or not they are still applicable (often extensive investigations in these cases are inconclusive (see para 8.25.5)). Your client may neither want, nor be prepared to pay for this work, particularly if the burden gives them no cause for concern. If in doubt, leave the burden alone.

If there is nothing in the Application Form, but there are burdens in the title which are clearly extinguished or obsolete, then the Keeper may omit these from the Title Sheet without prompting. This is particularly likely in the case of references to feuduty or ground annuals, feudal irritancy clauses, and prohibitions on subinfeudation, for example.

This particular question has been amended since the Application Forms originally appeared. In the first edition, the question included the words 'e.g. a long lease, long sub-lease, public right of way, path order, tree preservation order or any other encumbrance the inclusion of which in the register is permitted or required, expressly or impliedly, by an enactment'. This reflects the wording in section 9 of the 2012 Act, although title conditions are also encumbrances. This led, not surprisingly, to many solicitors assuming that the information required in this part of the form was not about burdens, but rather about these other types of encumbrances. Guidance on 'Encumbrances and Off-Register Rights' provides some clarification of the Keeper's requirements[24]. In particular, it should be noted that Tree Preservation Orders affecting the property should be included in the list. Although these may be of such a vintage that they don't show up in a 40-year search, if still applicable they should have been disclosed in a Property Enquiry Certificate, so a copy should be obtained for submission with the application.

'Over-riding interests' are no longer a feature of land registration under the 2012 Act. However, certain types of these 'off-register rights' continue to be relevant, namely public rights of way, core paths, and servitudes that have not been created by express grant (eg by prescription).

If the property is affected by a public right of way, this should be mentioned in the 'Further Information' section. Where it is along a defined route, a plan of that route should be submitted with the application. The route could be shown on the plan of the property accompanying registration, if it is suitable. If the route is not capable of being defined, then this should be stated on the form, and a sufficient description should be given.

---

24 See www.ros.gov.uk/__data/assets/pdf_file/0015/11391/General_Guidance_Encumbrances_orr.pdf.

If the property is affected by core paths, then an order (under section 22 of the Land Reform (Scotland) Act 2003) will have been issued, showing the route of the path. In these cases, a copy of the path order and plan should be submitted along with the application.

See para 14.11.2(vii) for prescriptive servitudes.

14.11.2(x) Extension of warranty

Generally, a title registered under the 2012 Act will benefit from Keeper's warranty. Certain things are excluded from this warranty as a matter of default. These are listed in section 73(2) of the 2012 Act (see para 2.6.2(ii)). So the Keeper's warranty does not, as a matter of practice, extend to warranting, for example, that the property is not affected by a public right of way, or that the owner has right to the minerals under the land.

An applicant does, however, have the opportunity to request an extension of warranty to matters excluded under section 73(2), if they can provide satisfactory evidence that an excluded category can be included in the warranty. So, for example, if the applicant can demonstrate title to the minerals under the land (according to the Keeper's requirements (see para 8.25.12) then reference to section 73(2)(f) should be inserted in the form, and the relevant items of evidence included with the application. For most of the exclusion, a request for extension of warranty will require to prove a negative, eg evidence that there are no rights of way, or no core paths, where confirmation from Scotways, or the relevant local authority would be required.

However, if warranty has previously been excluded, or limited in any way, it might be possible, at some later date, to apply to have the warranty varied – essentially upgraded back to full warranty – if the reason for the exclusion or the limitation has been resolved. This can be applied for at any time, and there does not need to be an application for registration. Application is made using the 'Application to Vary Warranty' form, which is available in PDF format on the Registers of Scotland website. Evidence supporting the application should also be submitted. A likely situation where this will be appropriate will be where the original disposition was *a non domino*, warranty was excluded, and it can be proved that the period of prescriptive possession has now run.

14.11.2(xi) Supplementary information – land use

A non-mandatory section of the form invites you to indicate the primary use of the property, whether residential, commercial (land with existing commercial premises on it), land only (eg a house plot, building site or piece of garden ground), agricultural, forestry or other.

This information is purely for statistical purposes and does not affect the application.

14.11.3 Declaration and Certification

Since the Keeper's staff no longer conduct any title examination, they will instead rely on the certification made in the Declaration section of the Application Form by the applicant and the applicant's presenting agent at the time of submission.

The certification contained in the Application Form will depend on the application type, but is broadly that the application complies with the General Application Conditions and any relevant particular Conditions of Registration. So, for an application for a deed over a registered plot, the applicant and the applicant's solicitor must certify: '(I/We)...certify that this application complies with the general application conditions in section 22, and the particular applicable conditions mentioned in section 21(2)'.

This certification is underpinned by the duty of care provisions in section 111 of the 2012 Act, which means that applicants and granters, and their solicitors have a duty to take reasonable care to ensure that the Keeper does not inadvertently make the Land Register inaccurate. The Keeper is entitled to compensation for any loss incurred as a result of a breach of that duty. If the Keeper has to pay compensation for a breach of her warranty as a result of having to rectify a manifest inaccuracy in the Register, there is clearly the potential for this to be offset by her entitlement to be compensated if the duty of care is breached (see para 2.4.17(i)).

The onus is therefore on the applicant (and the applicant's solicitor), not only to satisfy the Keeper that at the date of application the conditions for acceptance of an application for registration have been met, but also to conduct an investigation of title that is sufficiently rigorous to ensure that no inaccuracy appears on the Register.

There is no option but to agree to, and sign the Declaration. The form cannot be completed without it.

ARTL

14.12 The System of Automated Registration of Title to Land (ARTL) at the Land Register has been operating since August 2007. Although the ARTL system has been used for sales of property where the title is already registered, the vast majority of transactions in ARTL are remortgages and discharges of standard securities. It has, it is fair to say, fairly limited application in all but the most 'plain vanilla' transaction types. There is talk of 'ARTL2' being developed at some point in the future. There is a comprehensive text available dealing with ARTL and wider Scottish conveyancing technology issues[25], which we would commend to the budding ARTL practitioner. Robert Rennie has opined on the use of mandates in the ARTL system for the Law Society. These opinions are on the Law Society's website.

Once your firm has registered to use the system, the ARTL team from the Registers will help you through the process, come and visit your offices to set up the ARTL system, and provide training for all users. There are also online training demonstration modules in the ARTL section of the Registers of Scotland website. Further details and copy forms of mandate that must be obtained from clients before using the ARTL system are located on the Law Society's website[26] and see para 14.12.2).

There are a number of procedures required for a firm to be able to use ARTL, including appointments, registration, obtaining of digital signatures, and obtaining of smartcards to be able to submit forms and smartcard readers to connect to PCs.

14.12.1 Local Registration Authority and Practice Administrator

Each firm needs to appoint an individual to be the 'local registration authority' (LRA), responsible for administering ARTL within the firm. The Law Society recommends the LRA should be a solicitor.

A practice administrator (who can be the same person as the LRA) should also be appointed. The practice administrator is responsible for compliance with the ARTL terms and conditions and for the actions of all members of staff who are given access to the system. Both the practice

---

25 Robert Rennie and Stewart Brymer *Conveyancing in the Electronic Age* (2008) W Green.
26 See www.lawscot.org.uk/rules-and-guidance/section-b/rule-b8-miscellaneous-client-protection-requirements/advice-and-information/b82-artl-mandates/.

administrator and the LRA have to ensure the users comply with internal procedures and are responsible for preserving usernames, passwords, PIN numbers and the like in connection with digital execution of documents.

The Law Society recommends that the firm should apply the same criteria allowing people access to digital signatures to complete application forms for registration as they do in allowing individuals to sign Application Forms etc. Digital signatures of actual documents will be a different matter.

14.12.2   Digital Signatures and Mandates

To be able to digitally execute any document on behalf of a client, it will be necessary to obtain a mandate from the client authorising an individual in the solicitor's firm to do so. The mandates have to be submitted electronically to the Keeper along with ARTL application.

Standard wording for the style of mandates appear in PDF format on the Law Society' website. There are two forms – Mandate A is for use in general cases, and Mandate B is for use in unrepresented borrower cases (eg in remortgages). Firms using the ARTL system should create their own styles of these mandates and obtain the client's signature at a reasonably early point in the transaction.

Protocols will need to be put in place within the firm as to who may have authority to execute a digital signature in implement of a mandate. This is likely to be partners or senior solicitors.

14.12.3   Digital Signatures and Execution of Application Forms

A digital signature will be required to execute the Application Form with which an application for registration through ARTL is made. This does not require the express authority of the client. It is likely that more individuals within a firm will be enabled to digitally sign Applications Forms, than are authorised to digitally execute deeds.

14.12.4   Digital Signatures – Smartcards and Smartcard Readers

The Keeper provides ARTL users with digital smartcards which contain encrypted signatures. The smartcards are provided free of charge.

However, the law firm will need to purchase smartcard readers to read and verify the user's credentials. These are small gadgets which plug into the individual's computer. The Law Society has a preferred supplier of these readers which are modestly priced. Ultimately, all ARTL users should have a smartcard reader and smartcard with encrypted signature.

The Law Society now issues all solicitors in Scotland with a smartcard which combines a digital signature with an identity card and will contain details of the solicitor's practising certificate. Each smartcard is issued with a card reader. These cards are not to be confused with Registers' smartcards, which have been issued specifically in relation to ARTL.

14.12.5 IT Matters

The Registers of Scotland must obtain information about a firm's IT compatibility with ARTL, as part of the initial application for ARTL registration. A firm's IT staff will require to be involved throughout the registration and implementation period and for ongoing IT support.

14.12.6 Letters of Engagement

Registration dues are discounted when transactions are submitted through ARTL. Accordingly, if a firm of solicitors is ARTL-enabled and able to deal with a transaction through that system, then it is recommended that reference to ARTL is incorporated within the firm's letter of engagement. It may be appropriate to quote two sets of registration dues depending on whether or not ARTL can be used. It needs to be borne in mind that, even if the solicitors are ARTL-enabled, the solicitor on the other side of the transaction also has to be ARTL-enabled for the system to be used. So it may not be possible for a solicitor to offer this procedure, and the reduction in recording dues to the client, if the solicitor on the other side of the transaction is unable to transact in this way.

14.12.7 Risk Management

Every firm of solicitors that registers to use ARTL will need to consider the risk management issues for their firm, and ensure that the necessary procedures and protocols are put in place and incorporated within the firm's guidelines., This applies particularly in relation to the implementation of mandates, the submission of digitally executed documents, and confirmation of completion of an ARTL transaction. Events which trigger the requirement to pay registration dues mean sums will be debited from the Variable Direct Debit account that the firm must set up with the Keeper on registering to use ARTL.

THE TITLE SHEET

14.13 On completion of the registration process, a link to a PDF of the Title Sheet is e-mailed to the applicant's solicitors, and any other persons whose email addresses appear on the Application Form. Depending on the complexity of the title, it can take many months for a first registration to be completed, and in the past has been known sometimes to take several years. The deeds sent with the original application are also returned.

For registration applications submitted before 4 December 2014, a Land Certificate (and Charge Certificate, where applicable) will be issued. At the time of writing, the Keeper expects to meet the target of completing all applications made under the 1979 Act by the end of 2015.

The purchaser's solicitors should check the PDF of the Title Sheet or the Land Certificate when it is received, to ensure that that there is no unexpected exclusion of indemnity contained in the Land Certificate or unexpected exclusion or limitation of warranty in the Title Sheet, and that it contains no mistakes. If any mistakes are found in the Land Certificate it should be returned to the Keeper for correction. In the case of mistakes in the PDF of the Title Sheet, these should be referred back to the Registers for amendment. Practice is still unsettled at the time of writing, but in the case of some 'errors' in the Title Sheet, the Keeper asks for an Application for Rectification of an 'inaccuracy' to be submitted. Logically, if there has been an error in translating some aspect of the application onto the Title Sheet, this should be a simple matter of correction, not 'rectification'. If the Title Sheet is correct according to the information submitted, but the position changes, resulting in an inaccuracy, rectification would be the appropriate course of action in those circumstances.

In the case of 1979 Act applications, the purchaser's solicitors can discharge the letter of obligation that will have been given, once they are satisfied with the resulting Land Certificate (usually by writing the word 'implemented' on it and dating and initialling it) and return it to the sellers' solicitors. A letter of obligation will only rarely be required in 2012 Act applications.

A Land Certificate, when sent in hard copy, has a bright yellow cover (making it easy to find in even the untidiest of workspaces). The PDF of the Title Sheet, in contrast, arrives electronically, and should be saved and stored in the electronic matter file, or printed and added to a paper file if appropriate. In both cases, the contents are very similar and include:

(1)   **The Title Number** and a short description of the property (eg the postal address)

(2)   **Statement of indemnity under the 1979 Act**: A Land Certificate will contain the following statement 'Subject to any specific qualification ... a person who suffers loss as a result of any of the events specified in section 12(1) of the [1979] Act shall be entitled to be indemnified in respect of that loss by the Keeper of the Registers of Scotland in terms of that Act.'

The PDF of the 2012 Act Title Sheet does not benefit from Keeper's Warranty, and so is silent, unless there is a limitation or exclusion of warranty to disclose.

(3)   **Section A – the property section.** A description of the property and a coloured plan based on the Ordnance Survey scale 1:1,250 for densely populated urban areas; 1:2,500 for less densely populated urban areas and farms; or 1:10,000 for hill farms, mountains and moorland.

(4)   **Section B – the proprietorship section.** The name and designation of the proprietor, the date of registration (ie when the real right was created), the price and the date of entry.

(5)   **Section C – the charges or securities section.** Details of fixed securities affecting the property, whether previously existing or created by the proprietor. A separate charge certificate is issued for applications under the 1979 Act only.

(6)   **Section D – the burdens section.** A verbatim note of all land obligations affecting the property, in so far as still relevant and existing. The Keeper discards what she considers all irrelevant information: such as narrative and ancillary clauses; descriptions etc.

The PDF of the Title Sheet, or Land Certificate completely takes the place of the title deeds. If a Land Certificate or the PDF is lost, an extract of the Title Sheet can be obtained from the Keeper. An extract is to be accepted for all purposes as sufficient evidence of the contents of the original Title Sheet[27]. You can, in theory at least, tear up all the title deeds – but before you do so remember: (1) it is better to keep them until at least the first sale, just in case there has been a mistake that has been overlooked; (2) they belong to the owner of the property who might want to keep them; (3) often, the original titles are invaluable in clarifying some aspect of the title that is less clear from information that has been incorporated into the Title Sheet, such as the extent of burdens; and (4) the deeds may have historical interest and may be worth preserving for that purpose. The writer remembers examining the title to a property in Edinburgh's Ann Street some years ago. The original Feu Charter, granted by Sir Henry Raeburn (after whose wife Ann, the Street is named) would probably be worth quite a tidy sum these days, and definitely not one to throw into the shredder.

If the purchaser sells the property in the course of registration, there can be a difficulty, as the titles are all in the Keeper's possession for the purposes of the first registration application. The Keeper can be requested to return the title deeds, but this only delays the registration. Alternatively, the Keeper can be asked to supply photocopies of the title deeds, but this is an expensive and time-consuming procedure. The Keeper suggests that, if there is any likelihood of the property being sold before registration is complete, the applicants' solicitors should take photocopies of the deeds presented before sending them. This is not totally satisfactory either particularly as the purchaser's solicitors are entitled to expect to examine the principal titles. It is the practice of some solicitors to keep copies of all deeds presented anyway.

APPLICATION FOR REGISTRATION OF A TRANSFER OF PART OF REGISTERED HOLDING

14.14 This procedure is similar to that for a registered title (see para 14.9), except that the disposition needs to contain a description of the part of the registered title being transferred. The application type option 'Deed

---

27 Section 105 of the 2012 Act.

over part of a registered plot' should be selected when applying to register a dealing in part only of a registered title. This is perhaps most commonly seen in house plot sales, where the developer's title to the development is registered in the Land Register and allocated a Title Number. Each time a house or other unit is sold off, the 'parent title' reduces. Equally if a title is being split into two, for example where the garden of a large house is being sold to build another separate home, the same procedure applies.

The disposition should contain a proper conveyancing description for the plot of land being split off the larger, registered, property (see para 9.9.4). However, if the development is one where Development Plan Approval has been obtained, it is possible to describe the plot by reference to the DPA number and plot number. A plan may not be necessary if the DPA has already identified all of the plots.

APPLICATION FOR RECTIFICATION OF THE REGISTER

14.15 Where it appears to any party that there is an inaccuracy in the Register, the Keeper may be requested to rectify this, using the Notification of Inaccuracy Form. An inaccuracy will include any incorrect or erroneous entry in, or omission from the Register or an error on the cadastral map. Under the 2012 Act, for an inaccuracy to be rectified, it must be 'manifest' and what is required to rectify the inaccuracy must also be manifest. See para 2.7 for details of the rectification and compensation provisions under the 1979 Act and the 2012 Act.

RECTIFICATION OF BOUNDARIES

14.16 When there is a discrepancy in a common boundary between two properties as shown in their respective titles, under section 19 of the 1979 Act, it used to be possible for the parties concerned to enter into an agreement and register this against their respective titles. This was a short cut in conveyancing procedure when otherwise a contract of excambion (see para 9.19) or two dispositions would be required, and was a useful little device in these circumstances. However, the Scottish Law Commission in their Report on Land Registration[28] opined that,

---

28 See paras 5.31 and 5.32 of Scot Law Com No 222.

due apparently to 'obscurity' section 19 should be repealed without replacement. And so it has come to pass.

The 2012 Act introduces a new boundary realignment provision, although it is thought that it is not likely to be used very often. Section 66 introduces the concept of 'shifting boundaries', which may be relevant in rural settings. Where the boundary between adjacent plots of land is a river or other water course, the actual boundary line can alter over time, due to the effect of alluvion – where sediment, or deposits of land change the character of the river bank. In times of flood, large deposits can attach to the bank, altering the position of the river boundary. The owners of adjoining land can, if they choose to do so, enter into an agreement to fix the line of the boundary between their lands, so that regardless of the effects of alluvion, the boundary (and the respective Title Sheets) will remain constant. The Registers have chosen to call this a 'Shifting Boundary Agreement' (although it seems more appropriate to characterise it as a 'fixed boundary agreement').

LONG LEASES

14.17 The transfer of an interest which is held under a long lease is also a registerable event. A long lease is defined in the Land Tenure Reform (Scotland) Act 1974, as being a lease of over 20 years' duration. In practice, many commercial leases, particularly ground leases, were for a long period, sometimes hundreds of years (although the maximum period for a long lease is now up to 175 years[29]. One reason for that is that only by registering a lease may a security over that lease be created. The Land Tenure Reform (Scotland) Act 1974 also prohibited the creation of leases of residential property for a period exceeding 20 years[30]. This is, therefore, a matter principally for commercial leases, although a pre-1974 residential long lease may still be registered, if it hasn't been already. Similarly, an assignation of a registered long lease, a sublease, a sub-sublease, or a standard security over any part of the property contained in the registered lease, may be registered. In passing, it is worth noting that the trend over recent years has been for much shorter periods in commercial leases, so that fewer require to be registered.

---

29 Section 67 of the Abolition of Feudal Tenure (Scotland) Act 2000.
30 See section 12.

If an unregistered long lease has less than 20 years to run, but its length was originally over 20 years, it may still be registered. Thus (writing in 2015) a lease for a 25-year period, granted say in 1996, may still be registered although it has only a life of a further six years. The registration of a long leasehold interest proceeds in similar fashion to the registration of a right of ownership.

APPLICATION FOR REGISTRATION CHECKLIST

14.18 Version 01 dated 04/09/14 of the Application for Registration Checklist produced by the Registers of Scotland is reproduced below under Crown Copyright rules):

What do I need to include with an application for registration?

For all applications you will need to include:

- a completed application form that relates to the deed or plot of land to be registered;
- the deed to be registered, eg disposition, standard security, discharge or long lease;
- the appropriate fee or satisfactory arrangements for payment; and
- [an SDLT certificate, if appropriate].

What else do I need to include?

For transfers of unregistered plots or certain other deeds you will need to include:

- a plan and/or full bounding description identifying the extent of the plot, if applicable;
- deeds containing rights (including, if there is a burdened property, the particulars of that property in so far as known);
- the deeds in which servitude rights are constituted;
- a plan or full description of extent of any servitude right constituted by prescription over the plot;
- a plan or full description of any lesser area within the plot in respect of which a registrable encumbrance (burden?) is constituted;

- any outstanding heritable securities over the plot or lease;
- deeds containing burdens, including long leases, long sub-leases, public rights of way, path orders, tree preservation orders, and any other encumbrances the inclusion of which is authorised by enactment;
- the last recorded disposition or conveyance in favour of the owner of the plot (if current deed is not a disposition or notice of title);
- any deeds affecting the lease, if applicable;
- any other material information, eg where there has been a limitation or restriction on the examination of title, or where the applicant does not know with any certainty who the current landlord is in relation to an automatic plot registration.

For deeds relating to registered plots you will need to include:

- the deed to be registered, narrating each title number (this is extra information, rather than just the general information in the first paragraph) to which the deed relates;
- a plan and/or full bounding description identifying the extent of the plot, where over part of a registered plot;
- any other material information eg where a registered proprietor has died and the survivorship destination has operated to give the survivor proprietor the legal right to grant the deed, or where new information has come to light, such as a house name.

Index